BILLY MARTIN

BILLY MARTIN

Baseball's Flawed Genius

BILL PENNINGTON

Houghton Mifflin Harcourt

BOSTON   NEW YORK

2015

For information about permission to reproduce selections from this book,
write to Permissions, Houghton Mifflin Harcourt Publishing Company,
215 Park Avenue South, New York, New York 10003.

www.hmhco.com

Library of Congress Cataloging-in-Publication Data
Pennington, Bill, date. author.
Billy Martin : baseball's flawed genius / Bill Pennington.
pages cm
ISBN 978-0-544-02209-6 (hardback) — ISBN 978-0-544-02294-2 (ebook)
1. Martin, Billy, 1928–1989. 2. New York Yankees (Baseball team) — History.
3. Baseball managers — New York (State) — New York — Biography.
4. Baseball players — New York (State) — New York — Biography. I. Title.
GV865.M35P46 2015
796.357092 — dc23
[B]
2014039677

Book design by Patrick Barry

PRINTED IN THE UNITED STATES OF AMERICA
DOC 10 9 8 7 6 5 4 3 2 1

To Joyce, Anne D., Elise, and Jack:
the best of patience, support, wisdom, and inspiration

INTRODUCTION

THE MULTICOLORED CHRISTMAS LIGHTS in the trees at the foot of the driveway dotted the crest of the ridge that is Potter Hill Road. You could see them from a distance of several hundred yards as you approached from beneath the rise — little bulbs of red, blue, and green piercing the snowy darkness.

At 5:45 p.m. on Christmas night 1989, as Billy Martin's pickup truck turned toward home, the ornamental lights waved a holiday greeting, bobbing from the branches of evergreens that framed the path to his farm in upstate New York.

It was a peaceful country setting, calm and serene, but earlier a gusting wind had left a glaze on a road that had been plowed but was never completely cleared of snow. Billy's pickup truck approached a sharp bend 100 feet before the driveway to his 150-acre property.

It took no more than five seconds, but this is when and where Billy Martin died. With an ill-timed turn of the steering wheel, Billy's Ford truck slid off the road into a ditch, then lurched forward until it crashed into a five-foot-wide culvert and bridge that spanned the trench. The truck came to a halt at the foot of Billy's driveway, the Christmas lights that he had hung in the trees reflecting on the vehicle's crumpled blue hood. Slumped inside, Billy had fractured his neck when he slammed headfirst into the windshield.

Twenty-four hours after the accident, on December 26, 1989, I drove to the scene. I stood at the end of the driveway and bent over to pick up a piece of headlight glass gleaming in the snow. It was quiet, a kind of rural quiet, and the hush and bitter cold accentuated the isolation of the landscape.

Inconceivably, Billy Martin, the big-city, bright-lights manager cheered by millions in his time, which included five loud stints as a central character in George Steinbrenner's 1970s and 1980s mix of follies and championships, had died in the still of a lonely, pastoral road.

"Billy would probably be alive today if he was wearing a seat belt," Ken Billo, an officer in the local sheriff's office, told me at the crash scene.

Perhaps that's true, but if there was anyone who went through life without a seat belt on, it was Billy Martin.

And yet, standing next to the nondescript, barren piece of country road just north of Binghamton, New York, I found it hard to believe that this was where it had all ended, the last act of a tumultuous life.

After all the firings, the suspensions, the fistfights, the dirt-throwing incidents with umpires, the hobnobbing with celebrities, the funny beer commercials and television appearances, the media wars and all the back-biting warfare in clubhouses and executive suites, it was natural to believe Billy was indestructible. He had wiggled his way out of countless bar fights, close games, and back-alley tight spots. Then a slick country road sneaked up and claimed him.

As a Yankees beat writer from 1985 to 1989, I had traveled all over the country with Billy. I had been threatened by him, almost beaten up by him. I had also been charmed by him, benefited from his natural graciousness, and enjoyed being in his charismatic presence for countless hours on the baseball trail. It was my job to be at his side day after day, year after year, in hotel lobbies, team buses, and chartered jets, in ballpark offices before and after games and into the wee hours of the morning as Billy — and the Yankees beat — was transported into a thousand bars, lounges, and saloons around the continent. In that time, I discovered that Billy was without question one of the most magnetic, entertaining, sensitive, humane, brilliant, generous, insecure, paranoid, dangerous, irrational, and unhinged people I had ever met.

In the more than twenty-five years since his death, I always pondered writing a book about Billy principally because I saw the fascination in people's eyes when I told them stories about him. Across the decades, at cocktail parties or any gathering when I would be asked to tell tales from my more than thirty years as a sportswriter, I could always depend on Billy Martin to entertain and intrigue. No other single figure would draw people in, or get as many laughs, or leave listeners puzzled and curious. He was someone they could visualize instantly, a character they knew as genuine and yet flawed, with a common-man vulnerability that set him apart. Billy's emotions, ever so apparent, would seem to make him an open book, but his actions left a different impression, one both undefined and hauntingly mercurial.

At the same time, it was the lack of orchestration or affectation in his life that gave him a deeper appeal. Billy was beloved because he represented a traditional American dream: freedom.

He lived independent from rules. He bucked the system. He lived the life he wanted to live, despite the many personal costs. People admired him because he did what they wished they had the courage to do.

He told his boss to shove it. Often.

Unafraid of failure, he repeatedly faltered, then resurrected himself to succeed again.

He never backed down, even when to do so would have been an act of self-preservation and career conservation.

He was the hero, the antihero, and the alter ego — or some combination of all three — for several generations of American sports fans, as both a player and a manager.

Born in a broken home surrounded by a shantytown, he was raised with fists clenched, ever ready to mete out punishment aimed at resolving the societal inequities he saw in his hardscrabble life. Rescued by sports, he found a mentor in Casey Stengel, who made him a professional athlete and eventually a Yankee, where he found success as a scrappy, beloved, and clutch player. For the next four decades, no one in baseball ever ignored him, least of all his legion of fans. He was not the kind of guy you could, or should, turn away from.

This was true right up to the last seconds of his life. Just before making the final turn in the road near his farm, just before the concluding twist in a life of many curves, Billy's truck rumbled past the Hickling farm on Potter Hill Road. There was a beep of a horn and a wave.

"He always waved or stopped to talk to you," Colleen Hickling said later. Then she added something that could have summed up Billy's sixty-one-year life: "Billy wasn't going to ignore you; he would always try to catch your eye."

At that he succeeded. He spent forty years catching people's eye and came in close contact with practically every prominent figure in the history of twentieth-century baseball. He played for baseball royalty in the game's Golden Age. He was the *other* second baseman in New York in the 1950s — opposite the Dodgers' Jackie Robinson, who went head-to-head against Billy nearly every fall in the World Series. He managed more than thirty Hall of Famers and revived a browbeaten, demoralized Yankees franchise in the late 1970s. He made memorable television commercials and movie appearances, gambled with Lucille Ball, played pool with Jackie Gleason, golfed with Jack Nicholson, and lived on the back page of the New York tabloid newspapers. He could talk for hours about Civil War history and Robert E. Lee's battlefield strategies just as easily as he could explain the history of bunt coverage schemes dating to the 1800s. He never refused autograph seekers, would sit for hours in hotel lobbies talking with children, and slipped clubhouse boys and valets $100 bills like they were nickels. His smile, natural and unforced, could disarm any audience, from the field at Yankee Stadium to the couch on Johnny Carson's *Tonight Show*.

At the same time, he could get in a growling snit with a complete stranger because of the way the man ordered a drink. He started arguments on bus rides just to see who would argue back. He sensed insult in nominal things, like whether someone called him "buddy," which he did not like for some reason. Clasping the rail of a bar, his fingers would tense into a fist when someone made that mistake.

Especially late in his life, he routinely ignited alcohol-laden brawls, a confirmation of an immaturity, or a substance dependency, he could never entirely regulate.

Altogether, they were the paradoxes of a complicated but compassionate life. Billy, for example, loved people; that's why he always drank in public. He despised phoniness and wanted to be with regular folk, relishing his role as the endearing underdog, a man of the people who always had a joke and an open bar tab. And yet, something about Billy's rough-and-tumble roots left scars that always made him feel he was being judged by those same people — and never quite measuring up. He saw slights everywhere.

As his dear friend Mickey Mantle said, "Billy is the only guy in the world who can hear someone give him the finger."

Unfortunately, since Billy's death, all the contradictions and complexities of his personality and life — all the considerable good, the notable bad, and the eternally puzzling — have been simplistically molded into a crude caricature. He was the guy who was frequently hired and fired, almost fought with Reggie Jackson in a dugout, and drank a lot. Many raised on ESPN know Billy only as the guy who kicked dirt on umpires. All of those things happened. But separately or altogether, it is a wholly incomplete depiction.

It also overlooks a remarkable record of achievement beginning with five World Series championships as a player when he was considered the unofficial captain of the Yankees. In that period, the only time the Yankees did not play in the World Series was when Billy was in the military. As a dugout manager he may have had no peer. The Hall of Fame manager Tony La Russa told me in 2013, "Without reservation I would call Billy the most brilliant field manager I ever saw. He was unmatched. None of us felt up to him."

The Elias Sports Bureau, one of the most respected analytical entities in American athletics, spent years in the latter part of the twentieth century devising a formula to measure the effectiveness of baseball managers. The model assessed each team's record in a given season going back to 1903. The rubric took into account the team's performance in the previous season and the succeeding season and all kinds of personnel factors. In the end, the Elias calculators assigned a number of projected wins — an expected record — for each team in each season. The managers of those teams were then assigned a negative or positive number depending on whether the team had exceeded or underachieved based on the projected/expected record.

At the time, among those who had managed at least 1,000 Major League games, Billy was the top-scoring manager, averaging 7.45 more wins per season than expected in a sixteen-year career. The next-best manager averaged 6.38 wins. As the Elias analysts wrote, *"Billy Martin happens to be the best manager in the history of Major League baseball"* (the italics are theirs).

That, naturally, could start an argument in many a barroom, something Billy would have surely enjoyed — and stoked, most likely with a wink of his eye.

As Billy once said, "I believe if God had ever managed, he would have been very aggressive, the way I manage. Of course, God would never have been wrong and then had to face all the consequences."

The consequences were many, and not just in Billy's professional life. In his heart of hearts, Billy longed for a family and a white-picket-fence existence, something he achieved at various stages in his four marriages. But as his son, Billy Jr., said to me as he flipped through a family album that contained picture after picture of father and son playing in the backyard or relaxing in front of the living room television, "Whenever everything was going good, whenever things were too calm, that's when he had this uncontrollable need to shake things up. He had to create some excitement. It was his tragic flaw."

Creating excitement was what made him Billy Martin, even if it was often his undoing.

Not that he lived unhappily. Billy had as much fun as anyone in an adult life that stretched from 1947 to 1989. He laughed, partied, caroused, sang, danced, and drank — often with no consideration for the next day. During the more than two years of research for this book, when I told interview subjects that I was doing a book on Billy, almost everyone I contacted immediately started smiling or laughed over the phone. The mere memory of Billy amused them. A very few scowled, snorted, or refused to discuss him. But even those who ended up criticizing him harshly usually began by saying something like, "There was never a boring minute around Billy."

Earl Weaver, his most bitter managerial rival, said, "There were plenty of times I wanted to wring Billy's neck. And I know he felt the same way about me. But deep down I believed he was a good guy just trying to get everything he could out of every situation. But we didn't live at a time when you sat around waiting for those things to happen. You fought tooth and nail for everything you could get."

Significantly, Billy was a man of his times — all of them, because, as his son said, Billy liked change. But it is also true that Billy was a creation of a bygone era. American sports will never see someone like him again. In the age of several round-the-clock ESPN channels, the ceaseless chatter of sports talk radio, and omnipresent smartphone cameras, Billy could not exist. At least not as an employed baseball manager. A prying news cycle and the need for instant analysis would not grasp the nuances of Billy's genius, and it certainly would not tolerate his precarious excesses. His popular legend would not have had time to grow organically as it did from 1950 until his death. His grass-roots appeal might never have the space it needed to flourish.

Which is all the more reason to remember him.

The ditch that Billy's pickup truck slid into on Christmas Day 1989 has been filled in to make the turn at the top of Potter Hill Road safer. It remains a lonely, secluded spot that is hard to find. And yet, it is still a destination for those unwilling to forget Billy Martin.

Bob and Rhoda Lerman, who now own the house and farm where

Billy lived, said people regularly leave mementos of Billy at the foot of their driveway, which is a 130-yard drive from the property's house. There will be commemorative coffee cups with photos of Billy and the 1977 championship Yankees team, a T-shirt from the halcyon Billy Ball days in Oakland, or a ticket stub from Billy Martin Day in 1986 when his number was retired at Yankee Stadium.

"We left the house one day and found two guys sitting by the end of the driveway having a beer for Billy," Bob Lerman said when I visited him in 2014. "Sometimes it will be a husband and wife who say they just wanted to see where it all ended for Billy. One time, it was three fans all wearing Billy's number 1 Yankee jersey.

"I've gone down the driveway and found people standing there weeping."

Lerman has lived in the house since 1998, which he agreed to buy before he knew of its famed former owner. A native New Yorker, he knows the fable and folklore of Billy's life. Nonetheless, he remains awed by the renown of his quiet country corner in upstate New York.

"How long ago did he die?" Lerman asked. "It's like twenty-five years, right? But they still come. They do not forget.

"I guess that's it. They want to make sure Billy is not forgotten."

"BLESS ME, FATHER, for I have sinned," Billy Martin said.

He was in second grade.

Billy did this every Friday in 1936, entering the confessional of St. Ambrose Church to sit before the same priest, Father Dennis Moore. Like most second-graders, Billy did not actually have that many wrong deeds to tell Father Moore about. To what could he possibly confess?

Failing to honor his mother and father? Billy did not talk back to his parents. For one, he did not know his father, who left his mother when Billy was an infant. And he did not dare cross his mother, who ruled her household with an iron fist — a representation that was more than figurative. Jenny Martin knew how to throw a punch. Everyone in the family had seen with their own eyes her prowess in a fistfight, with women, and men.

Would little Billy confess to stealing?

In the gritty, crowded, downtrodden streets of West Berkeley where Billy lived, there was almost nothing to steal. California in the Great Depression was indeed a Garden of Eden, "a paradise to live in or see," as Woody Guthrie sang in a ballad of the era, but no one would ever sing the praises of Billy's neighborhood. He lived in one of the hundreds of tiny homes crammed against the East Bay docks across from burgeoning San Francisco. The tightly spaced West Berkeley houses were scruffy, set back just ten feet from busy, unkempt streets. They were homes without lawns and with tattered backyard fences. Factories and fish-canning plants towered over the neighborhood and seeded the sky with a smoky haze. The smell of the processed seafood filled the streets.

Two miles east of the water, the verdant hills of greater Berkeley climbed, a setting dotted with two-story middle-class homes and princely estates belonging to the administrators, professors, and staff from the nearby University of California at Berkeley. The roads in those shady hills were lined with flourishing fruit trees, graceful sequoias, and ponderosa pines. These were homes spread across spacious lots, leaving room for front and back yards and a driveway for the family car. There was a steady breeze off the water, and except when it was foggy, their view was San Francisco and the shimmering distant harbor — so long as they did not look down at the roughly square mile of West Berkeley dreariness below them.

No, Billy Martin didn't steal. Only if you count some of the cooked crabs kitchen workers left to cool behind Spenger's Fish Grotto, the roomy seafood restaurant near the docks. But that truly was not stealing. The Spenger's workers, who had walked the few blocks from their West Berkeley homes, left the crabs out on purpose, knowing it was a furtive way to help feed the neighborhood.

What else could Billy confess to? Cursing? Taking the Lord's name in vain?

His mother, who, unlike her five children, did not go to confession, had that commandment cornered, splicing profanities into virtually every sentence.

"Swearing was like breathing to my mother," said Billy's sister Pat Irvine. "She didn't leave room for anybody else to swear. And if one of us swore, we'd get the back of her hand across our face anyway.

"So we did not swear."

What else for Billy to confess then?

There was nothing of note, and in the dark of the confessional, Billy would instead strike up a conversation with Father Moore. He was never shy, always at ease with adults even as an eight-year-old. He had a crooked mouth and bad teeth, but he flashed his smile easily, and Father Moore, like others in the neighborhood, enjoyed being around the little boy who lived at 1632 7th Street, next to the house his grandmother moved to near the turn of the century. Billy most often regaled the priest with tales of the games he played at Kenney Park, just ten blocks away. There was basketball, swimming, diving, football, boxing, table tennis, and, of course, Billy's favorite, baseball. Father Moore, seated deep in a quiet corner of St. Ambrose's white concrete cathedral, heard about them all.

And when Billy was done talking about sports, the priest would ask about school and Billy's friends. And only then would Billy talk about being embarrassed to wear the same clothes to school when some classmates clearly had a closetful of choices. He talked about being ridiculed for his overly large nose and jug ears, knowing that other kids called him "Pinocchio" behind his back. They made fun of his dungarees, which were frequently marked with grass stains and dirt — the evidence of his nonstop play at Kenney Park. But he wore them every day anyway. They were the only pants he had that fit.

While there was always food on the table at home, Billy said he knew his stepfather, Jack Downey, had to work two or three jobs to produce enough money for a household of six and he worried for him. There never seemed to be enough money to go around in a neighborhood where few of the adults had gone to school past eighth grade.

His mother had no car and had to walk everywhere, and Billy said he wanted a car. In fact, he wanted a big car someday, like the ones he had seen in the Berkeley hills. The kids from the crowded, flat, and uninspiring streets of West Berkeley called the well-dressed people they saw striding up and around the hills "the Goats," a term still uttered in West Berkeley today and still delivered with a familiar disdain.

Billy wanted a car like the Goats had. And he wanted their clothes. And he wanted the money to go to the movies every day of the week if he chose. And he wanted his own bedroom, even if he did not mind sleeping with his aging grandmother, who had helped raise him since birth.

But as Father Moore related in a newspaper interview nearly twenty years later, "Life had already made Billy most vulnerable." And that unnerved the priest.

"There was an insecurity, a lot of the kids from West Berkeley had it," Moore said of Billy. "It's the worry that you might some day have nothing. It was the idea, a constant fear, that it could all be taken away at any moment."

But Father Moore also said that little Billy Martin had a plan. He knew the only way to get all the things he wanted was to work his way out of grimy West Berkeley. And at eight years old, Billy already knew that his way out was going to be baseball.

The greatest baseball team in the world in 1936 was the New York Yankees, the team of Lou Gehrig, Joe DiMaggio, Tony Lazzeri, and Red Ruffing. Beginning in 1936, the Yankees won six of the next eight World Series and were runners-up in a seventh. It was a team that was a continent and seemingly a civilization away from 7th Street's foundationless, roughhewn houses, but Billy told anyone who would listen that he was going to be a New York Yankee.

"He told me he would play professional baseball in New York," Father Moore said.

Billy told his best friend, Ruben de Alba, the same thing.

"We'd be walking down the street and Billy would say, 'I'm going to play for the Yankees someday,'" de Alba said seventy-six years later as he sat in a Bay Area assisted living facility. "I'd say, 'Yeah, sure, Billy.' I kind of laughed it off. You know, like, 'Yeah, sure, whatever you say, Billy.'

"But he wasn't kidding. He would turn to me and say, 'Listen, you wait and see. I'm going to come back here and remind you of this when I'm playing for the Yankees.'"

Father Moore, meanwhile, had less time for the wild dreams of the second-grader in his confessional. The priest eventually decided that while Billy's aspirations were admirable, they were also driven in part by jealousy. Was not one of the commandments "Thou shalt not covet thy neighbor's house" (or field)?

Father Moore ordered Billy to clean the church pews as penance. And Billy did. Father Moore then said he would see Billy at Sunday Mass. And Billy would be there. He even woke his cousins who lived in the neighborhood to accompany him.

"I'd be asleep and Billy would be tapping on my bedroom window telling me and my brother, Nick, to get up and go to church," remembered Mario DeGennaro, whose mother was the sister of Billy's mother. "My house was just a couple of blocks away and he'd come get me, badgering me until I went with him.

"It was easier to get up and go than to argue with him because Billy, like his mother, knew how to argue."

DeGennaro, now in his eighties, has lived his entire life in the Berkeley area, where for many years younger locals would ask him to explain the Billy Martin he knew.

"There were a lot of things people completely missed about him," said DeGennaro, whom Billy always called "Cousin Mario." "The one thing that always surprises people is how religious Billy was, even as an adult. I know he did a lot of crazy and wild things, but even in his final days, he was a guy who would quietly go to church. You could find him sitting there thinking to himself.

"When we were kids, me and my brother, we would start talking or horsing around in the church pew. But Billy would jab us hard in the ribs with an elbow and say, 'Shut up. Don't do that here. Show respect.'

"Billy was one of the guys in our neighborhood — he fought and scrapped and wanted to get somewhere like the rest of us. But he always had this other side, too. Like in church. He sat there and behaved."

After church, the DeGennaro boys — Nick was two years younger than Billy, and Mario the same age — would walk back from St. Ambrose's — which was halfway to the Berkeley hills. They returned to the densely packed streets near their homes, near the intersection of 7th and Virginia streets.

"On so many of those walks Billy would be talking about baseball," Nick DeGennaro said. "And he'd say to Mario and me, 'I'm going to play for the Yankees.' And we heard it so much we wouldn't even look at him after a while. We would just say, 'Yeah, sure, Billy. We know.'

"But we didn't believe him. Not then at least."

2

BACK IN 1928, IN mid-May, Jenny Martin wanted to have her baby. It was time. There was one problem. The doctor would not come to her house until it was wired for electricity.

Jenny's mother arranged for the electrical circuitry, and Jenny's son was born in the upstairs bedroom of the house and circumcised on the kitchen table of the first floor. He was named after his father, Alfred Manuel Martin, a truck driver for the City of Berkeley. But whenever Jenny's mother, whose name was Raphaella but whom everyone called "Nonna," held the baby in those first days of Billy's life, she repeatedly cooed to him, "*Bello*," Italian for "beautiful."

"Bello" soon became "Billy" to the rest of the family. It was all anyone ever called the little boy with the bony facial features forevermore, although his half sisters and half brother still to this day refer to him as "Bill." In the West Berkeley streets, he was "Billy" to everyone. On the first day of seventh grade, when a teacher took a roll call of the class, she asked for an "Alfred Martin." Billy looked around the classroom, wondering who the new kid with his surname might be.

"I think that's you," the teacher said. "Alfred Manuel Martin."

Billy told the teacher she was wrong.

"You better go home and ask," the teacher answered.

That night Jenny told Billy the story of his name.

In Jenny's world, names were frequently subject to change. Her own mother did not use her given name. Jenny, meanwhile, had been born Juvan Salvini. Her father, Nicholas Salvini, had emigrated to San Francisco, where his brother lived, from Italy in 1879. An arranged marriage soon united him with Raphaella, who began having the first of her ten children.

The Salvinis moved from San Francisco to the less prosperous shores of Berkeley at or about 1906, the year of San Francisco's devastating earthquake. Different parts of the family disagree on whether the move was before the earthquake or spurred by it, but one thing was certain: after the earthquake, many of their relatives — and other Italian, Portuguese, eastern European, and Mexican immigrants — made their way across the bay and settled in the flat, farmable land directly next to the shore.

It was also a handy locale for those in the fishing trade, like Nicholas Salvini.

Juvan Salvini, born in 1901, never liked her name although her mother, who never learned to speak English, did not understand why. Like many children of immigrants, Juvan wanted to seem more American than European. Strong-willed and determined even as a child, the ten-year-old Juvan announced she was to be called "Jenny." And so she was for the rest of her eighty-eight years.

Jenny did not get her way in all matters. When she was seventeen, she was ordered to marry Donato Pisani, ten years her senior. They had one son, Frank, whom Jenny for some reason — no one remembers why — called "Tudo." What's in a name?

But Jenny and Donato divorced after three years, and Donato headed back to Italy. In the many at-home interviews Jenny gave to reporters during Billy's fame as a manager — she traveled to New York only once, on Billy Martin Day in 1986 — she said Donato was not a faithful husband and that he died a few years after their divorce.

With Donato in her past, Jenny did a little wild living, running with a tough-talking, motorcycle-riding crowd that hung out in nearby Oakland or on the miles-long, wide boulevard that intersects West Berkeley, San Pablo Avenue. Jenny was at home in any group that existed just beyond the bounds of the law since her sister Theresa ran a small brothel and speakeasy a few miles away in the town of Emeryville.

Years later in his autobiography, *Number One*, Billy called it a cathouse as he recalled sitting on a sofa with his mother in Aunt Theresa's place of business when he was seven or eight years old, drinking a soda as men came and went. Years later, it occurred to him that it was a whorehouse.

"I just knew that it was a place that the men would buy me a Coke and pat me on the head," Billy said years later. "What a naive kid. What did I know?"

Jenny met Al Martin in Oakland on another summer evening as her mother baby-sat Tudo on 7th Street. Martin was a Hawaiian of Portuguese descent who sang, danced, and played guitar in local clubs. Though Jenny was only four feet eleven inches tall — she claimed she was five feet and could fly into a rage if someone insisted she was shorter — she was outgoing and at ease around men, who were drawn to her. She was shapely and had what people then called "a nice figure."

As an adult, Billy recalled walking in the West Berkeley streets as an eleven-year-old with his mother at his side. Men whistled. Billy turned and glared. His mother grabbed him by the neck.

"Do you know why they're whistling at me?" she asked. "Because I have the best-looking ass in town and don't you forget it."

Al Martin, a tall man with a long, thin nose who sported the kind of pencil-thin mustache favored by movie stars in the 1920s, had a long list of girlfriends, but he was soon married to Jenny and then, on May 16, 1928, had a son with her, although the family does not believe Al was in Nonna's 7th Street house when his namesake was born. There are different versions told of the first few months of Billy's life, but everyone agrees that Al Martin left Jenny before Billy knew he existed.

The most established family history, now related by Jenny's surviving children — Pat Irvine, her sister, Joan, and her brother, Jack Downey — is decidedly Jenny's side of the story and not Al Martin's. As told by Jenny, Billy's dad liked to stay out late in the clubs where Jenny was convinced he was cavorting with other women. Billy himself for decades would tell the story of his mother finding Al Martin with another woman, and afterward going home and throwing all of Al's clothes in a suitcase, which she threw out onto the street.

For good measure, and Billy used to smile when he told this part of the story, Jenny then went out to the curb and broke the windshield and the windows of the new car she and Al had just bought.

Billy's face would become a weird mix of glee, pride, and sadness that acknowledged a certain fatalist understanding of life as she — and perhaps he — saw it: "She knew he would take the car. But she didn't want him to have it without a cost. Even if it cost her too."

Seeking vengeance with forethought but without much concern for the consequences was Jenny's way. It would, it seems, become an inherited trait. But there was a tangible, lifelong consequence: she would never again see Alfred Manuel Martin Sr., her first love. Her sisters would later recall a period of melancholy, but Jenny rebounded in typical saucy fashion.

Every one of her children, and grandchildren, remembers how Jenny, even into her eighties, always referred to Al Martin. He was forevermore "the jackass."

"She never used his name," Pat Irvine said.

What's in a name?

But Jenny's story is not the only story of what happened to the Martin marriage. While Al Martin returned to Hawaii when Billy was an infant and all but remained out of his son's life, he did occasionally return to the Oakland area and he would tell a different story to those who asked about his breakup with Jenny. And many years later, he kept in touch with Billy's daughter, Kelly Ann, who had reached out to her grandfather and developed a close relationship.

Al's story was that Jenny was working the streets as a common hooker, something she learned from working at her sister's brothel. Al would find her walking the streets and drag her home, Kelly Ann told Billy biographer David Falkner in the early 1990s. Al would go to work, or go out at night, and Jenny would return to the streets, pocketing extra cash, until Al would pick her up again and bring her back home.

This went on for weeks or months until one night, after Al had brought Jenny home from the streets, she picked up a knife and held it to the neck of their infant son. She threatened to kill Alfred Jr. — Billy — if Al did not leave and never come back. Al Martin left without another word.

Billy's siblings and cousins from the neighborhood scoff at Al Martin's version of things. They also vehemently deny that Jenny ever turned tricks.

Yes, they say, Jenny worked at Theresa's speakeasy and whorehouse, but she worked downstairs serving drinks, not upstairs with the three or four girls that Theresa employed.

"She cleaned up and helped out," Pat Irvine said of her mother. "It's ridiculous to say she did more than that. She knew where to draw the line and so did Theresa. Most of us stayed away from that house."

Before Billy's first birthday, Jenny met another dashing man who wooed her with his singing voice. This latest interest was an Irish tenor by way of Toronto.

Again, there are slightly different accounts of how Jenny met her third and last husband. One thing is certain: Jack Downey was working one of the ferryboats that regularly crossed the bay since there were no bridges spanning that body of water at the time. In interviews, Jenny alternately said Jack was a cook or a singing waiter on the boat and that he had sung professionally in Chicago.

His name was John, but everyone called him "Jack."

The children of the Downey marriage said they were told by their mother that she met their father on the ferry, and that he sang to her and a romance developed from there.

Jack Downey, who was no more than five foot five and weighed about 120 pounds, was a quiet man who rarely if ever entered into debate with Jenny. She would get riled about something, inserting F-bombs between syllables at a pace of two or three a sentence, and Jack would just laugh at her.

"That's a good one," he'd say. "I haven't heard that one before. Hey, why don't you take it easy? That's enough of that."

But he would let her dominate the conversation, taking a back seat to the dynamo that was Jenny. The only time Jack seemed emboldened was when he sang.

Still, as tranquil and good-natured as he was, it's hard to imagine what Downey thought of the situation he encountered on his first visit to the home where Jenny lived in early 1929. She had one son from her first marriage, who was now a young teen, and she had an infant from her second husband. She lived with her mother, a warm but unsophisticated woman from the Old Country, and from the previous century, who did not speak English and did not plan to learn it.

The household had almost no income; Jenny's sisters and brothers brought groceries over to the house regularly, as did the priests from St. Ambrose's. One sister, on a visit bearing supplies, recalled sitting in her mother's kitchen and asking where Billy, Jenny's baby boy, was.

"Out back," Jenny said. The sister walked through the back door and saw Billy sitting in a tuft of unmown grass drinking milk out of a beer bottle with a nipple attached.

But into this world Jack Downey married, reciting his wedding vows on November 5, 1929, seven days after the stock market crashed.

And soon thereafter, the Salvini-Pisani-Martin fraternity found out something else about diminutive Jack Downey: he was a hard worker.

One of the truths about jobs in America is that many of them tend to sound like, or even depict, the nature of the work involved — accountants count, lawyers deal with the law, teachers teach.

So what does a lumper do? A lumper lifts lumps of things and loads them into a truck or a hold of a ship. That was one of Jack Downey's early jobs down at the docks of his new neighborhood in Berkeley.

"They didn't want to give my dad the lumper's job," Billy Martin, who always referred to Jack Downey as his dad, said. "They looked at this 120-pound guy and said, 'How are you going to lift 75-pound bags of stuff into a truck?' And my dad said, 'Where are the bags?'

"They pointed to a big pile and he went over and hoisted one onto his shoulders and flung it into the truck. Then he grabbed about four more. They gave him the job."

A lumper's pay wasn't enough, though. So Downey was a simple laborer at a local prune warehouse, where he shoveled the fruit into a vat. He also did some heavy lifting at a cider factory, working alongside his stepson Tudo and a crew of other young men.

As his family grew — Joanie, Pat, and Jack Jr. joined his two stepsons — he developed another side job as a carpenter and handyman in the neighborhood. He bought an aging Model T engine, outfitted it to work as a saw, then went down to the waterfront to collect stray driftwood. He cut the wood behind his house and sold it as firewood. The Downeys had moved into the house at 1632 7th Street, next to Nonna's house, and Downey repaired the fixtures and rebuilt the exterior and interior. It was a two-story house, a rarity then along 7th Street. Today, it still stands out for its height.

"We never missed a meal," said Pat Irvine. "We always had clothes, not many, but what we needed. And it was all because of Jack. And he raised Bill. He didn't correct him in front of my mother; that was her job. She disciplined Bill when she had to.

"But Jack did everything else he could for Bill."

Billy fondly remembered Downey.

"My dad was a great guy — quiet and small but the kind of guy who would come over your house and help you with some project even if you didn't ask for the help," Billy said. "He didn't have a lot of money but he would slip a kid who needed a few bucks the money. He'd ask the kid to come help him haul some wood from the docks and then he would overpay him.

"He would go to local pickup games and help pay for a couple of new baseball gloves or a bat. They were small things but I saw him do it a thousand times in a thousand different ways."

Everyone agreed that Jenny had the most influence on Billy as a child. She filled him with the defiance and burning determination, the willingness to try anything, and the combativeness. But Jack Downey had an understated role and a low-key bond with Billy, whom he introduced to people as his son, not his stepson. (None of the Downeys used terms like *stepbrother* or *stepchild*— then or now.)

Billy watched Jenny impose her will with a boundless fury and by railing against a thousand real or imagined enemies or obstacles, but he also watched Jack Downey pass through life fruitfully and happily without confrontation, opening doors with gestures of benevolence and goodwill.

"His mom was the fire but his dad was the compassion," de Alba said. "And Billy had a ton of both."

It was a sentiment affirmed by many who knew Billy well. With Billy, there were always the dual, or dueling, personalities. He was his mother's son. He was, as Jack Downey told everyone in the East Bay area, his son.

Jenny, who was not one for admitting mistakes, talked late into her eighties about her biggest regret in life. She wished she had arranged for Jack Downey to adopt Billy when they were first married. Then all the fame that was to come in the 1950s and beyond would have been bestowed on Billy Downey — a fitting tribute, she thought.

3

IN A MARTIN FAMILY scrapbook, there is a picture of Billy at age three. He is standing alongside his house and smiling broadly. He is wearing a light-colored sweater pulled over a shirt buttoned to his neck and thick, dungaree-like pants that stop a couple of inches short of his black shoes. The front of his pants is soiled and dirty with large stains across both thighs, and there's a smudge on his sweater, too.

"We had clothes but not enough of them and you sometimes looked a little ragged," said Mario DeGennaro, who was born two months after Billy. "If somebody had to go to a wedding, or later in life, if you had a date, you would go around the neighborhood borrowing things. Billy might have a nice dress shirt and my other cousin might have nice dress pants. Somebody else would loan you some new shoes. Eventually you'd have a presentable outfit.

"For those of us living below San Pablo Avenue toward the docks, the parents were always in and out of work. Nobody had any education; I don't think my mother or father went past sixth grade. It was a tough place, but people got by and there wasn't a lot of bitching."

The Downey house was big for the neighborhood but usually full.

"There were people everywhere — kids, grandkids, aunts, uncles — they all came to be near my grandmother," Pat Irvine said. "They made a lot of noise, but Billy liked the hubbub I think. He was a happy-go-lucky kid."

Ruben de Alba said Billy was popular and moved easily among West Berkeley's various factions.

"Billy didn't know or care about ethnic makeup," said de Alba. "He was Italian and Portuguese with an Irish stepfather. Who was he to say anything to anybody about their background? He was well liked by the teachers, the coaches, other kids. He didn't give anyone any trouble. Later, as we all got older, there was more turmoil.

"But when we were younger, we were always running from our little houses to someplace we could play and staying there as long as we could."

The one place where they all ran was James Kenney Park, a rectangular stretch of grass and blacktop about two blocks from Billy's home. It had basketball courts and some playground equipment at one end, but its primary feature was wedged against the corner formed by 7th and Delaware streets. It was a tall, chain-link-fence baseball backstop that loomed over a Major League–size baseball diamond. And beyond the diamond there was room for a vast outfield in Kenney Park, one big enough to contain 380-foot fly balls.

The dirt of the infield was manicured by Berkeley city workers who also cut the grass, which was more lush and green than any of the stubby lawns in the neighborhood. High fences near the backstop kept foul balls in the park. The pitching mound and batter's boxes were made of real red clay.

It was an oasis of refinement in West Berkeley's crude jumble of frayed houses, boarded-up businesses, and smelly factories.

In the late 1930s and during the World War II years, it was the place for boys from miles around to come play baseball, the unquestioned national pastime in America during the middle of the twentieth century. And to Billy Martin, it became a second home and, with Northern California's generally temperate climate, a place to play year-round.

"Oh, my God, it's like he never left the park," said Pat Irvine. "He'd eat breakfast and disappear to the park. I don't know what he did for lunch but he didn't come home. Then my mother would send me to get him for dinner. She'd say, 'Tell him he has to come eat and then he can go back to the park after that.'

"And that's what he would do. Eat for twenty minutes and then run back to the park. Baseball, baseball, baseball — you never saw someone so in love with baseball."

If being born in West Berkeley meant you were disadvantaged, there was an overriding benefit: it put you close to Kenney Park. And if you were a youngster who loved baseball, it only got better each fall and winter when the many Major Leaguers who hailed from the area would come home and make Kenney Park their off-season training ground.

Augie Galan, an outfielder for the Chicago Cubs and a lifetime .287 hitter, came to the park most often. His family owned a laundry six blocks away, near San Pablo Avenue. But he was accompanied by, among others, Bill Rigney, an All-Star for the New York Giants who was raised just up the road in Alameda; Les Scarsella of the Cincinnati Reds, who lived in San Francisco; and Ernie Lombardi, the future Hall of Fame catcher who had also been a star for his hometown Oakland Oaks of the Pacific Coast League. There were other noted players who came to Kenney Park, too, guys in their late teens and early twenties who had been signed to minor league contracts and were eager to play with the established stars. One of the local kids invited to play because he was a good pitcher — and eventually would play some minor league baseball — was Billy's older half brother, Tudo.

And though Billy was eight to ten years younger than the other players, he went to these workouts, which evolved into regular weekend games.

"The other players would get on Tudo for bringing his kid brother," Mario DeGennaro said. "Billy didn't care. He didn't play but he watched everything and waited."

Billy was more than a mascot at the games. Throughout life, Billy was not intimidated by fame or celebrity. The kid from the downtrodden neighborhood that should have made him feel like an eternal outsider instead somehow found it easy to make connections with the renowned, illustrious, or legendary. He made them feel at ease with his undaunted response to their notoriety.

Years later, when Billy was acquired by the Yankees in October 1949, he stunned his new teammates the following spring by making friends with Joe DiMaggio on his very first day in the team's clubhouse. Few people approached the famously aloof DiMaggio without invitation, let alone a raw, skinny rookie. Billy sauntered up and introduced himself, talking about their similar Italian Bay Area backgrounds.

And at the end of Billy's first day with the Yankees, the other Yankees were floored when the distant, never gregarious DiMaggio ambled over to Martin's locker and said, "Hey, Dago, want to have dinner tonight?"

For Billy, this kind of unceremonious approach to fame became a way of life.

"Billy thought he could relate to anyone," said Lew Figone, whose mother was a good friend of Billy's mother in the 1930s. Figone rose to a place of prominence in the East Bay business community as an adult, but he remained a lifelong friend, business partner, and confidant of Billy's.

"Billy knew some people had a lot of money or better looks or more smarts, but he still thought he could talk and learn from them. He wasn't afraid of anyone."

This attitude was apparently ingrained by 1940, because Billy was not intimidated by the Galans, Lombardis, or Rigneys who showed up at Kenney Park. He thrust himself into the scene, asking questions, helping with equipment, warming up the outfielders and infielders before games. If a game got started and he wasn't part of it, he would watch and offer a kind of play-by-play commentary from the bleachers. Except Billy's version of commentary included an occasional jibe or joke. He knew how to get the players snickering.

The players took a liking to the little runt who was always watching.

"I loved being there and helped out, but I also figured that eventually someone would not show up or get hurt and they would need an extra player — and that would be me," Billy wrote years later. "And I did get to play."

Galan, who was a good friend of Tudo's from Berkeley High School, took a personal interest in tutoring a young Billy Martin. He taught Billy how to change his grip on the bat if he wanted to pull a ball or punch it to right or center field. He showed him the footwork necessary to bunt for base hits. He strengthened Billy's throwing, adjusting his motion.

Billy always came back for more. Rube de Alba remembers a workout when Galan was hitting hard ground balls to Billy. One grounder took a bad hop — or Billy misplayed it since he did not have especially soft or nimble hands as a youngster — and it struck him squarely between the eyes.

"Billy had a big mouse just over his nose and it kept swelling," de Alba said, telling the story sixty years later. "We told Billy to get off the field. He just kept telling Augie to hit him another one. And he did not come off the field until we were all done."

Galan appreciated the perseverance and rewarded Billy with more of his attention.

"Augie almost lived at our house," Pat Irvine said. "He would be there talking baseball to Bill all the time."

And if Augie wasn't at his house on 7th Street, Billy would go to the nearby Galan house and wait outside until Augie was ready to leave for Kenney Park. He would carry his gear and listen for the next piece of advice.

As Galan, who died in 1993, would relate years later, "The thing with Billy was that I never had to tell him anything twice."

And for every piece of instruction, Billy had a question for Augie. Why does the second baseman take the cutoff throw from right field instead of the first baseman? Why does the shortstop cover third base on a steal attempt if it's a bunt situation? Why do the corner infielders play in when a team is trying to induce a double-play ball?

Galan had answers, and if he didn't, he brought Billy to Rigney, the Major League infielder, who could offer expertise on the inner workings of tactics within the baseball diamond. Rigney, who would play several seasons for Giants manager Leo Durocher and take over for Durocher in 1956, had an established pedigree when it came to baseball strategy. He soon noticed that Augie Galan's young friend Billy Martin was more than just curious about the thought that went into a seemingly simple game of baseball. Strategy was a way to make you better as a player and, in the end, make the players into a better team.

"Billy picked the brains of Rigney and Augie — all those guys — for years," Rube de Alba said.

Because, even at twelve or thirteen years of age, Billy knew there was the game, and then there was the game within the game.

"He wasn't like the other kids," Rigney said in an interview thirty years later when he was an executive with the Oakland Athletics — and before Billy managed there. "He loved to play baseball but he was serious about it. He wasn't just passing the time or showing off for his friends or for the girls watching."

The games were his schoolwork, the diamond his classroom, and a dugout filled with Major Leaguers his laboratory staffed by the game's certified scientists. Billy knew what he was doing. He was an apprentice in the trade of baseball. It was an art and it was a skill, but to Billy it was always more of an intellectual passion and a measure of tenacity.

There was the physical component to baseball, and Billy had above-average athletic ability. But that wouldn't get him to the Major Leagues and he knew it. He would have to do more.

Galan was the first to tell him how. Because he had been there, and not just as a flatlander who lived on the wrong side of San Pablo Avenue.

When he was eleven, Augie Galan broke his right arm in a pickup game of baseball on his way home from school. Since he was supposed to have gone straight from school to the family laundry that day, Galan hid the injury from his parents. It was a small fracture near his elbow, but since it was not set by a doctor, it healed wrong and left Galan with a deformity that inhibited his ability to throw properly for the rest of his life.

Galan learned to speed up his release when throwing the baseball in the outfield, adapting his throwing motion to make up for the deformity. He also studied opponents, learning their tendencies and memorizing how they ran the bases and where they liked to hit the ball. This made Galan a more capable left fielder, despite a weak throwing arm by Major League standards. He committed just 32 errors in 841 games in the outfield of Major League games, and though he would occasionally suffer from a sore throwing arm — an ailment that eventually ended his Major League career — he also played sixteen years in the majors with some distinction.

While Billy had no physical abnormalities, Galan knew his feisty, popular young charge was neither especially big nor strong. He was quick enough, crafty, and adept at almost any sport — basketball, football, swimming, and diving.

"Oh, I can still see Bill at the city pool on the high diving board doing flips and twirls," said his sister Joan Holland. "The whole pool would stop when he climbed the ladder, waiting to see what he would do next. He was a good athlete."

Undoubtedly he was, as he would prove when he got to high school. But cocktail parties in America are full of guys who were good athletes but not Major Leaguers. As a youngster, Billy was a talented athlete, but by most measures not exceptional. Galan saw himself in Billy, and on those walks back and forth to Kenney Park he preached a recurring message: Billy's talent wouldn't be enough; he would have to do more than everyone else with a passionate resolve unequaled by any of his peers. Galan explained something else — there was an enduring, tangible power in being the overlooked underdog because it allowed you to sneak up on people.

"I was a hustler on the field," Galan said years later. "And I sat a young Billy down and told him that he had to be relentless about hustling for everything. I tried to insert that into him — just never give up, bear down all the time. Never, ever stop until the game is over."

Galan and the other big leaguers also took Billy and his friends Rube de Alba and Howard Noble to movies at the showpiece Rivoli Theatre on San Pablo Avenue. The West Berkeley kids with the hand-me-down clothes started to feel like something else — part of a baseball fraternity. The Major Leagues did not seem so far away when a real Major Leaguer was paying for your popcorn at the Rivoli.

When the Brooklyn Dodgers star Cookie Lavagetto, raised in Oakland, started coming around to Kenney Park, Galan immediately assigned Billy, now fifteen years old, to learn at Lavagetto's side.

It was the start of a long, fruitful relationship, one that would last five decades.

A few years later, when Martin debuted with the Oakland Oaks and Lavagetto was winding down his playing career with the same team, he was asked by a reporter for the *Oakland Tribune* if he knew Martin.

"Billy? Sure, he's the kid from Kenney Park we used to let tag along," Lavagetto said. "He's been learning from us for years and we taught him well. But yeah, that's the same kid. We got kind of a bang out of him. You'll see."

Then Lavagetto said something others in baseball would say for years to come. Different people used different words, or it was paraphrased in other terms, but whatever the language and whatever the town in Billy's rolling-stone baseball existence, the appraisal was unchanged.

"You won't ever meet anyone like him," Lavagetto said.

4

BILLY MARTIN AS AN adult had a lot of sayings, things he repeated from year to year, job to job. It is not an uncommon habit for leaders, and especially baseball managers born before 1940, who were the raconteurs of the game. Before television transformed how fans followed the game, a standard news vehicle was the pregame chat with the baseball manager. In this setting, baseball managers made proclamations, and scribbling newspaper reporters took their notes upstairs to the press box to build entire stories around what they had been told.

Billy played this game and had a few oft-spoken canons: Games are won by the mistakes you force the opposition to make; the shortstop and second baseman, not the catcher, run the on-field defense; a fastball should never be the first pitch to a hitter without power; a third-base coach isn't doing his job if no one gets thrown out at home; batting averages are overrated; put your best outfielder in left field at Yankee Stadium, not center field. And, finally, to recall his most bizarre saying in his near-boundless catalog of tenets: "I would play Adolf Hitler and Benito Mussolini if they could help me win. I don't have to like them."

Billy said this often over the years and never with any indication that he realized it might be considered offensive. He was making a point: he wanted to win at all costs, and he did not play favorites based on personality or good comportment. Whenever someone would suggest that he was prejudiced toward one player or another — or had ulterior motives as a manager based on his prejudices — Billy would rally to defend himself with his patented Hitler saying.

As this choice of words demonstrably illustrates, Billy would often overdo it when trying to defend himself — both verbally and, as the world eventually learned, physically as well.

Which leads to another one of his frequent sayings: "I never started a fight in my life."

For most people who knew and traveled with Billy, the statement rang true. He often threw the first punch but he did not start the disagreement.

But for an adolescent in a tough West Berkeley neighborhood, fighting was part of the routine of life. Billy's childhood friends and family say he did not often instigate fights. It is, looking back, a matter of perspective and understanding the times. In the twenty-first century, there is little appreciation of what America in the 1940s was like, or what the country's foremost sporting passions were at the time. Baseball might have been king, but boxing was almost as celebrated and nearly as closely followed. The newspapers covered championship fights like presidential elections, and the heavyweight champion of the world was as recognizable as any world leader.

Billy and his West Berkeley chums — sports fans all — had been schooled in boxing at the local YMCA by the time they were eight. And they had all been in a ring during organized youth league bouts, including ones run by the St. Ambrose Christian Youth Organization. The Sunday morning Bible reading in church might have been about turning the other cheek. The Sunday afternoon tutelage in the church gym was about how to deliver a crushing left hook.

"I'm telling you Billy didn't fight any more than anybody else," Mario DeGennaro said. "He was just better at it. And sometimes when you're better at it people come gunning for you.

"We all got into regular scraps and fistfights. But for Billy, his nose was just a constant source of agitation. Kids called him 'The Horn' and 'Pinocchio.' And pretty soon he developed a quick trigger. He didn't take it. He would come punch you, and like I said, he was good at it."

Jenny Martin had told her son early and often, "Don't take shit from anybody." Some Martin biographers have made this into the mantra for Billy's life. It seems an easy fit. But anyone who knew Billy Martin for more than a month came to understand that nothing about him was ever that simple. Billy did, in fact, take all kinds of shit from all kinds of people in his life. He could be diplomatic and behave politically — if not politically correctly — and he was calculating. He sized up people and tried to appeal to their best interests when it was in his best interests. He was cunning and a strategist, and not just during baseball games.

Billy did not navigate his existence wildly swinging his fists at a thousand imagined slights. Yes, there were many moments like that, dozens of them that have been documented — and there were certainly many that have not been documented (more on that later). But in most settings, Billy was in control and overly polite because Billy, eager to be seen as someone other than a kid from the wrong side of the tracks, valued politeness. Unless you were one of his players, for whom he had a different set of rules, the easiest way to earn Billy's respect was to be polite to him and around him.

Still, if there is an origin of what would become the celebrated, almost mythic code of Battlin' Billy Martin — a figure carved in American sports history — it begins in adolescence, and by most accounts, it begins with Billy not being the one to start the fights.

He was, however, good at finishing them.

"We had to walk through Kenney Park to get to junior high school," Nick DeGennaro, Mario's brother, said. "There would be older kids sitting on benches in the park. Sometimes they'd ignore you. Sometimes they wouldn't. And you know, Billy had that big nose and kind of big ears.

"They'd say, 'Nice elephant ears, Dumbo.' And I saw Billy keep walking many, many times. But then there would be the day when he would put his books down and walk over and say something back. If the kid wanted to fight, Billy knew what to do. He had practiced for that too."

At the Kenney Park community center clubhouse, Dick Foster, a former professional prizefighter, worked with all the kids. He was a paid employee, part of the city's recreational services department. Foster had been a middleweight of local renown with a ring record of 34-11-4. Most of his fights had been at the Dreamland Auditorium in San Francisco or the Oakland civic auditorium, where fight cards were held regularly and much promoted. From 1934 to 1939, Foster was busy in the ring, taking on rising stars and journeymen alike, many with the most colorful names: Midnight Bell, Wild Bill Sutton, Cowboy Jack Potter, Sailor Jack Riley, and Young Corbett III (twice).

Foster won his first four fights in 1934 by knockout, but in the succeeding years it wasn't always so easy for him. In a losing bout on March 16, 1938, Foster was knocked down seven times. Proving just how different the times were, the fight was not stopped. Athletes did not get concussions in the late 1930s; those were reserved for auto accident victims.

It was at this time that Foster was working at Kenney Park, and one of his star pupils was the feisty little Billy Martin.

"Dick Foster worked a lot with Billy, and nobody could make that speed bag patter back and forth like Billy," said Jack Setzer, one of Billy's classmates. "Billy had fast hands and he was coachable. Dick Foster taught him technique — how to fire punches from the inside without looping his arm. He taught him how to use his feet to deliver a harder punch. It was all boxing technique, the leverage, the shoulder and elbow movements, and how to rotate the wrist and fist."

And when the kids would spar, everyone recalled that Billy, who was already renowned for his fearlessness, just dominated everyone. His cousin Mario DeGennaro recalls squaring off with Billy.

"He could fire five or six punches in a machine-gun-like tempo," Mario said. "And they weren't jabs. They were hard punches to your nose or side of the head. He would hit you and knock you down. He had what all the boxing trainers called 'heavy hands.' He hit really hard."

Foster sponsored and encouraged Billy in the amateur boxing circles for a year or so, taking him around the Oakland area for informal bouts. Billy's friends don't recall him losing. But there was one significant problem.

Jenny Downey did not want Billy in the boxing ring.

"After a while, my mother just wouldn't let him go anymore," Pat Irvine said. "I'd hear her yelling, 'No more boxing. You're staying home.' And that was that."

Nick DeGennaro said Billy sneaked out and sparred locally anyway, but by the time he was fourteen, he had stopped. That didn't stop Foster from coming to the Downey home in the mid-1940s hoping to convince Jenny to let Billy turn pro as a boxer. Jenny was unmoved. She didn't let Billy play football either.

The unofficial fisticuffs continued nonetheless, in part because there was also a new tension in West Berkeley. The outbreak of World War II thinned the male populace between eighteen and thirty-five. San Francisco and Oakland were major transfer points for troops heading to the Pacific Theater. To equip the convoys heading west, small war munitions factories sprang up, many of them in the Richmond area north of Berkeley. The nearby shipyards were also brimming with work. The new workers manning the factories came from around California, Mexico, and the Deep South, and the new faces changed a West Berkeley social dynamic that had largely remained the same for three decades.

In Billy's recounting of the period, new families meant new kids who did not know him. And that naturally led to more fighting.

"I awoke every morning knowing that there was a good chance I was going to have to get into a fight with somebody," Billy said.

His cousins and friends explained.

"A tough place just became tougher," said Nick DeGennaro. "It didn't matter what it was. Take your schoolbooks, for example. I don't know when but it became not cool to carry schoolbooks through the park but that happened. Being smart or being a kid who studied would get you made fun of. So if you were carrying schoolbooks, somebody would say something. And they'd maybe come up and knock your books out of your hands.

"Well, what are you going to do?"

Mario DeGennaro answered the question: "You had two choices: fight or run. And you didn't want to run. Not unless you were never going to come back."

The fastest way to and from their homes on or near 7th Street to Burbank Junior High School was through Kenney Park, and that's where many of the older kids would be hanging out.

"Seeing if they could get someone into a fight was like their entertainment for the day," Setzer said.

Some of Billy's friends would just take the long route and walk around the park. No one who watched Billy Martin play Major League baseball in the 1950s or manage on national television in subsequent decades would be surprised to learn which route he took to school. Billy Martin may not have started fights and he may have been a happy-go-lucky little kid and he may have been devoutly religious and he may have been the quiet one in the family home compared to his mother, but there was never any backing down when it came to Billy Martin of 1632 7th Street.

Everybody in West Berkeley knew that, except the new kids in town. And they soon learned.

As Billy and his friends emerged from puberty, they became more curious about what might be found outside West Berkeley. It wasn't only a search for girls who weren't the local girls they had known since kindergarten; it was an adventure. Even on foot or by bike, the crowded communities of Albany and Richmond to the north were easily reachable. And, of course, the hills near Cal-Berkeley were enticing for a host of reasons, including vast, unguarded fruit orchards.

A group of four wandering West Berkeley teens on one weekend became a group of twelve West Berkeley teens after the original four returned with pockets full of pears and tales of girls in tight, fancy cashmere sweaters. By the next weekend, it was twenty teens out exploring the

World War II–era communities not hemmed in by the bay and San Pablo Avenue.

"I think we did it just to bug the rich Goats," Mario DeGennaro said. "And it worked."

They started to call themselves the "West Berkeley Boys," whom some considered a gang and others a roving group of friends. Billy, who was prone to portraying life in us-against-them militaristic metaphors, wrote that the group was called "the Prussian Army" and that it could sometimes be a hundred strong.

"A hundred kids?" Rube de Alba said, his voice rising in disbelief when the number was repeated to him. "No, it wasn't a hundred kids. Maybe twenty."

But de Alba and others, including school administrators who warily watched the changing West Berkeley communal dynamic, agreed on one thing: Billy was a leader.

"Kids listened to him and he motivated them," Nick DeGennaro said. "He had an air of confidence and we followed. Things could get pretty tense if it looked like there was going to be a fight with some guys from another town, but Billy wouldn't flinch. He was like a field general even then."

Billy developed a reputation in West Berkeley as a person to watch, and to watch out for.

"In our world, you got respect for not backing down no matter what," de Alba said. "And we didn't lose many of those battles. Although I've always said that writers who come around asking about Billy make too much of this. There were no knives, guns, pipes, or whatever. It was just fists and lots of wrestling and swearing."

Pat Irvine always thought it was "just boys who were bored."

"It was what the teenage boys of West Berkeley did back then to amuse themselves," Irvine said, waving her hand as if describing a prank like ringing a doorbell and running away. "But it wasn't a gang. It was mischief. I mean, did anyone get arrested? I know Bill didn't. My mother would have beat the hell out of him — or out of the cop who brought him in."

Laughing, Pat Irvine added, "I wouldn't have wanted to be that cop trying to drag Bill into our house."

Irvine stood in the dining room of her home in the foothills above her old neighborhood.

"Those boys were doing all this during World War II," she said. "You know, you have to understand the times."

The West Berkeley Boys were too young to enlist, too old to be content with the thirty square blocks of their childhood, and too ornery after years of hardscrabble existence to kowtow to their more privileged neighbors. If they couldn't go to war to battle for prized territory in the Pacific islands or Europe, they would fight for turf beyond San Pablo Avenue.

"Things changed when they got to high school," Pat Irvine said. "It was another way to get out of the neighborhood. Bill, in his own way, thrived there. Of course, I guess it was always his own way."

And his own way included a code of behavior, not one suited to many but one that summed up what he learned as an adolescent — and how he lived his life forevermore.

In 1971, Billy gave an interview to the *Sports Illustrated* writer Ron Fimrite, who graduated from West Berkeley's Burbank Junior High School three years after Billy. Said Billy to Fimrite, "I never push first, but if you push me, I'll push back harder. The day I start a fight is the day I lose one."

5

THE CURRENT BERKELEY HIGH is an eight-building campus of more than 500,000 square feet. The Berkeley High that Billy Martin entered in 1942 was far smaller but still an imposing four-story structure built in 1904 that was the pride of the city, a beacon of secondary education and an attraction for families looking for a respected school district. Berkeley High looked like a fortress from the outside, but within its walls, large windows provided ample ambient light and warmth.

Into this sunny atmosphere Billy stepped and immediately felt dim and despondent. At Berkeley High, Billy came face-to-face with a culture from which he had largely been shielded. He had navigated West Berkeley's racial and ethnic divides by ignoring them, or circumventing them when necessary. At Kenney Park and at the park's indoor community center building black faces were rare, but he had played with the offspring of various ethnicities. His closest friends were the sons of Puerto Ricans, Cubans, Germans, Italians, and Irishmen.

But at Berkeley High, for the first time, Billy was given a lesson in how class in America worked. It was not what he had expected to be taught. He knew he would be relegated to the vocational classes while the sons and daughters of the Goats from the hills took the college preparatory classes. But the segregation at Berkeley High, which had 3,500 students, was more palpable than that.

"The Goats ran the school," Billy said. "They were on the student council, got the good grades, and went to college. They were the social mainstream and we weren't."

Adding to his unease, Billy Martin at fourteen was far from a polished presence.

"We were all a little jagged and out of sorts then," Mario DeGennaro said. "And Billy? Well, Billy was small, maybe 115 pounds. His teeth weren't straight and he had a Roman nose as people used to say back then to be nice. What they meant was that he had a very big nose. He was respected in West Berkeley among the guys, and the girls, too, but at that big, vast high school, it was like, 'Who's this little runt? And what's he wearing?'"

Billy's hand-me-down clothes shouted West Berkeley poor and excluded him from the popular clubs and cliques within the school. Worse, and this was becoming increasingly important to Billy, his faded, unstylish wardrobe did not compare favorably with the meticulous and trendy clothes of the sons and daughters of Cal-Berkeley professors and administrators. That made him an undesirable suitor for most of the girls at Berkeley High.

The Goats had expensive jeans — and several pairs — and wore leather navy flight jackets. Billy and his friends had one pair of discounted jeans and wore cheap navy pea coats. Billy wrote that he had one pair of jeans that he ironed so often they developed a sheen that glistened, which was not the look he was going for.

The West Berkeley boys — in this setting and in every sense, it was said with a lowercase *b* — were not scorned. One has to be noticed to be scorned.

"No one gave a shit about us," Howard Noble, another longtime friend of Billy's, said. "We were meaningless."

The West Berkeley boys — called "shop boys" — were even shunted to a detached wing at the school, the industrial arts annex. The rules of engagement were changing. This was not an environment where you could just fight your way out.

But even at Berkeley High there was one place where there was at least an attempt at equality. And that was in athletics. The Goats did not always like it, but they had to play with the flatlanders. They needed them for their teams. And a 115-pound Billy Martin proved that right away.

Billy's first entrée to high school sports was on the junior varsity basketball team. His backcourt mate was Ruben de Alba.

"Billy wasn't all that skilled at basketball," de Alba said, recalling the winter of 1942–43. "I mean, he could dribble and shoot OK, but what really set him apart was that he played with such determined force. We won games because he would wear people out.

"Diving for balls, fighting for rebounds, just running up and down the court and pounding the ball toward the basket. He was unstoppable and tenacious on defense — just the kind of kid you never want to play against."

Billy and de Alba, who had an indomitable spirit as well, were a persistent duo, especially as they grew and put on a few pounds. By their junior year they were varsity starters, and by his senior year Billy was an all-county guard.

A 1945 story in the *Berkeley Gazette* praises the aggressiveness of the "quick Billy Martin" who drove the Emeryville team to distraction with "steals and rapid moves to the basket." The newspaper then used a word, *sparkplug,* that would appear in sentences with Billy Martin's name for several decades to come.

"Bill was kind of the heart that drove the team," Billy's sister Pat Irvine said. "People would come to the games just to see what that Martin kid was going to do this time. He was always finding some way to win even if it was agitating some kid on the other team until the kid started making mistakes or fouling too much."

Billy was five foot nine by his senior year, about an inch from his adult height, and more than big enough to be effective on the basketball court in an era when the average height of an American male was five foot seven and one-half inches. But as good a player as Billy was, that was not the complete story of his high school basketball career. There were off-the-court issues.

"With his style of play, he rubbed opponents the wrong way and they would challenge him," de Alba said. "They would say, 'I'll get you after the game.' And, of course, Billy wasn't going to hide."

Billy's friends recall a couple of postgame donnybrooks when Billy pummeled a few foes, which twice led to his suspension from the team.

While there is obviously room for interpretation about who instigated what — as there was for the rest of his life — Billy's take on things was clear. He was just doing whatever he could to win, which sometimes meant getting under an opponent's skin. And if that meant he had to stand up for himself afterward, well, so be it. It's all part of the contract, and that went for sports or life because it is important to remember the times. Did Jimmy Cagney's characters ever back down? Did John Wayne, that young actor from California who was just beginning his career?

While Billy first made his name at Berkeley High playing basketball, it was still just a diversion. Billy's real love was baseball, and he made the Berkeley High varsity baseball team as a freshman, the only one to do so. He played sparingly that first year as a third baseman, then moved to second base as a sophomore and hit .320. Eventually, he became the team's shortstop and its most vocal leader. His coach, Elgin Erickson, was a soft-spoken teacher who watched Billy warily, but he also cut him loose on the field.

"Billy knew what everybody on the diamond should be doing and he had no problem telling us all about it with regularity," de Alba said. "Not after the fact, but before a play. Billy would walk in from shortstop, point at us, and say, 'Hey, if they bunt, here's what you do, and here's what you do, and here's what you do. If they steal, then let's do this.' He was thinking ahead of every play even then. He was a coach on the field."

Billy was voted an all-county player in baseball during his senior year when he hit .450. He did not hit with much power, but he was handy with the bat, slashing singles through the infield and line drives into the outfield that he fearlessly turned into doubles. He played with the same edginess he had brought to the basketball team. If an opposing player slid into him too hard, a common tactic in all levels of baseball in the 1940s, Billy doled out his own retribution. The next runner coming into the base would get tagged in the face.

"The Kenney Park baseball games were pretty rough—those guys took no crap from anybody," Howard Noble said. "So Billy was schooled in an attitude of how to play the game and he took that to his high school games."

Billy willed his high school team to victories and, to no one's surprise, clashed with umpires. Rube de Alba, who played second base, was his accomplice in the quarrels with umpires. A primitive cartoon drawing in the 1945 Berkeley High yearbook shows Billy with a long beak for a nose, arguing face-to-face with an umpire. The umpire is saying, "Out—I sez he's out." Billy, who is wagging a baseball bat behind his back and wearing a baseball uniform, is answering, "Shaddap yez tramp, he was safe!"

The umpire is holding his hat behind his back. De Alba has surreptitiously put a large firecracker in the umpire's hat and is in the process of lighting it. Under the cartoon there is a caption: "Never a dull moment with Martin and de Alba around."

Billy has a presence elsewhere in the yearbook. His hands are clamped to a large sanding machine in a woodworking class, and he is among a group of students surrounding a drill in another shop class.

In Billy's recollection, he did not take only shop, vocational, or technical arts classes. He insisted he took several years of history and got As for grades. And as an adult, Billy would sometimes lead long discussions of Civil War history, debating Robert E. Lee's battle choices at Gettysburg — he did not support the aggressiveness of Pickett's ill-fated charge, for example. At those moments, it was clear Billy still resented his place on the wrong end of the Berkeley High academic ladder.

His friends at the time, however, noticed that his studies were not his number-one, or his number-two, interest.

His principal preoccupation was baseball. But there was a prominent secondary fixation. Billy liked the company of young women, and he pursued their affection with the same unremitting passion he brought to athletics.

His dress was still not first-rate, but his sports celebrity in the school clothed him in a notoriety that worked for him in many circles of the sports-mad Berkeley High culture. He had also grown into his body a little, which made him appear less angular and rawboned. He had an engaging sense of humor, charisma, and boundless self-assurance (publicly at least), and he could be charming in almost any setting if he wanted to be.

But mostly, Billy would not let up if he had his eyes on a female classmate, or someone from an adjoining town who came to see a show at the sparkling Rivoli Theatre on San Pablo Avenue. He was rejected often — he was still a flatlander from West Berkeley and that disqualified him in many quarters — but that did not dissuade him much. Billy was a player, a Don Juan as they said in the 1940s, and dating and loving was another game he had figured out how to play better than most.

"He knew a lot of girls," his cousin Mario said. "Geez, all of us would hang around him just to be around all the girls he knew. There were plenty of girls that would tell him to go to hell, but it sure seemed like an awful lot were intrigued by him — just kind of drawn to him."

Billy's sister Pat Irvine was three years behind Billy in school, but she had many older friends at Berkeley High, and classmates who asked her to fix them up with Billy.

"They kind of liked his bad-boy image," Irvine said. "I'd say, 'He's my brother and I love him but he'll only go out with you for a while. He'll love you and leave you.' But so many would go out with him anyway.

"They'd come around later and say, 'You were right.' And I'd be like, 'He's seventeen, what do you expect?'"

In his autobiography, Billy wrote that when he first made love to a girl he was naive and scared. "I didn't know where to put my peter; I thought the place was higher up," Billy wrote. "I was trying to put it in her belly button. After we finally did it, I felt so bad that I had sinned that I cried."

Pat Irvine read that passage when Billy's book came out in 1980.

"What a bunch of baloney — next time I saw him I said, 'You might have felt bad but you certainly got over it,'" Pat said, smirking. "Where did he get these things he told to writers?"

But Billy insisted that he went to Father Moore after his first sexual encounter and confessed to adultery because he "had relations with a woman who was not my wife."

Finally, something for Billy to actually confess to.

Father Moore set him straight. And sent him off after a penance of five Our Fathers and five Hail Marys.

As Billy's high school career entered its final stages, he had much to look forward to. World War II had ended, eliminating the battlefield anxiety that had dogged his older classmates. Soldiers were coming back to Berkeley and jobs were aplenty. The economy was booming. Billy was one of the best high school baseball players in the East Bay area, and he was connected to the big leaguers from the region because of his Kenney Park ties. Billy felt sure he was on the cusp of greatness.

There was a plethora of minor league teams in California at the time, and then there was the Pacific Coast League with teams from San Diego to Vancouver. The Pacific Coast League was officially a Class AAA minor league, a notch below the vaunted Major Leagues, but no one on the West Coast treated it that way. Some local ballplayers might dream of playing in New York, Detroit, or St. Louis, but most aspired to play for the Oaks, or even better, the classy San Francisco Seals across the bay (Joe DiMaggio's former team). The salaries were high in the PCL and the crowds were sizable.

Billy still longed to wear the Yankees uniform but he was not impractical. He knew he could use a steppingstone to his New York dream, and the Oaks, the best baseball team in the East Bay, were a big step up.

The Oakland Oaks had been sending scouts to Berkeley High games in 1945 and 1946, but the understanding was that they were there to look at Berkeley's talented center fielder, Bill "Babe" Van Heuitt, who would eventually play professional minor league baseball. Still, the Oaks scouts could not help but notice the heart of the team, the doughty, unconquerable shortstop, Billy Martin.

He was viewed as a likely second baseman or third baseman, a pepperpot infielder in an era when home runs were sparse in comparison to today's baseball. The scouts reported that the Martin kid would be versatile. They said he would be a "sparkplug." The Oaks had Billy on their radar. They were looking forward to seeing how he played in the postseason playoff games and the one or two high school all-star games that showcased the players from the area. They would wait for his high school graduation.

Then Berkeley played Hayward High School, whose top player was Pete Hernandez. Hernandez and Billy were jawing at each other early in the game and the tension mounted. When the game ended, Billy claimed Hernandez ran at him and missed with a wild punch, and Billy knocked him cold with three punches to the face. Billy was pulled off Hernandez. Then lots of other fights started on the field, some involving fans. Billy said he ran to the locker room.

But Mario DeGennaro and his brother, Nick, were at the game, and their recollections don't match Billy's. And as for nearly all the fights in Billy's lifetime dossier, there is no film or video to document the truth. The DeGennaros do not recall fights all over the field. Mario, in particular, remembers that Billy had warned him there was going to be a fight with Hernandez.

"Everyone kind of knew it and came to the game to see it," Mario said. "And it was a real good fight. I remember them trading punches for a while. The Hayward kid was a pretty good fighter, too."

But the brothers agree that Billy won in the end.

"Dick Foster would have been proud," said Nick. "Billy just cut him down, punch by punch, like a big tree."

As is usually the case, what seemed like a premeditated fight had a predictable consequence. The Berkeley principal called Billy to his office and suspended him from the team for the rest of the year.

During an interview in 1971, twenty-five years later, Billy recounted the conversation with shock and sorrow in his voice.

"The principal said I wasn't fit to represent the school," Billy said. "He said I should learn to turn the other cheek. I told him that in my neighborhood I wouldn't be alive if I turned the other cheek. He kicked me off the team as a disgrace to the school. The school was still going to be there, the buildings would be the same, but what about the boy, a boy baseball was everything to? If I'd been a different kind of kid, I might be a criminal today."

Decades later, Billy called it the "most unfair thing that could have happened."

Billy was certain his suspension from the Berkeley High team would affect his pro baseball prospects. He worried that he would be unable to impress scouts in the coming all-star games. He questioned, not for the last time, whether a reputation for trouble would complicate the gilded path he had begun to see laid out before him.

But as he would find out so many times in succeeding years, baseball does not fear the feisty. Or fisticuffs. Certainly not in the 1940s and not so much seventy years later either. The suspension was noted by pro teams. It was discussed. But it did not cause them to remove Billy from their list of potential recruits.

Martin graduated from Berkeley High. His picture is in the senior yearbook, *Olla Podrida*. Each of his family members vividly recalls attending the graduation ceremonies in June of 1946. But the rest of Billy's high school records are mysteriously missing and have been absent for decades. There is no high school transcript for Alfred Manuel Martin within the files of the Berkeley school district, and there is no explanation for how it disappeared when it had been under lock and key along with the transcripts of thousands of others. In fact, other than short, bite-size newspaper stories detailing his basketball and baseball exploits in the *Berkeley Gazette,* a few yearbook and family pictures, and Billy's unremarkable birth certificate on file with Alameda County, there is not a wealth of documented evidence of Billy's first eighteen years of life.

Lew Figone, Billy's friend, keeps his company's one-story offices lined with memorabilia and trinkets from Billy Martin's life.

"He gave me all this stuff," Figone said. "He said, 'Lew, I don't know what to do with this but somebody should be keeping it.' Some of it I have saved myself since we were kids."

On one wall in a large conference room in Figone's office, Billy is posing with eight other West Berkeley kids.

"The St. Ambrose CYO basketball team," Figone said, pointing at the picture. "They had a little party at the end of the season and took this picture. Cupcakes and soda. That's maybe ninth grade."

Billy is kneeling on the floor in the first row wearing a faded white shirt and over it the oddest, dark, patterned V-neck sweater. The sweater is a little too large for Billy's shoulders, but more noticeable is the sweater design: uneven horizontal lines, almost Nordic in style. But across the chest are recurring primitive drawings of birds, like something you would see on a hieroglyphic wall. The horizontal lines and birds clash and the wool is threadbare. It is the kind of sweater you would not forget once you saw it.

Billy is smiling wanly in the picture, barely showing his irregular set of teeth (corrected with cosmetic dental surgery years later). His hair is mussed, the camera has caught his thick, bony nose in not the most favorable light, and his ears look too big for his head.

"Billy didn't have it easy," Figone said. "But it made him more determined. Life was hard, Billy got harder."

As upset as Billy was about his suspension from the baseball team, he did get a tryout with the Brooklyn Dodgers. The Dodgers were apparently not overly impressed. They said they might call but never did. Eight months earlier, the Dodgers had signed another middle infielder from California who would play many games as Billy's rival, Jackie Robinson.

Billy returned to Berkeley and began working in a slaughterhouse. He rode the bus or borrowed a ride to other towns to play in games at other well-known fields, mostly to ask around about other pro tryouts. He was for several weeks a baseball player without a team: have glove, will travel.

Among those who ran into Billy during this time was an old Kenney Park friend, Red Adams, the trainer of the Oakland Oaks who was a long-time comrade of Augie Galan's. Adams, who liked Billy and had been watching him play for Berkeley High, convinced Oaks manager Casey Stengel to give Billy a tryout.

In 1965, Stengel described the day to a reporter from United Press International:

"I had this college shortstop I was looking at in a workout. He was neat as a pin. Did everything according to the book. Wore his pants just so, put his cap on straight and looked like something out of Spalding's guide.

"I made up my mind to sign him for $4,000 when the club trainer, Red Adams, came along and said I was signing the wrong guy. Told me he had a much better looking prospect. 'Show him to me,' I said.

"Well, he brings this kid out and you never saw such a sight in your life. It was Martin here and you oughta see him. Uniform all dirty, one pants leg rolled up and the other falling down. Never saw anything like it before in my life."

Stengel worked Billy out himself. He hit about twenty routine grounders that Billy fielded cleanly. Then Casey started hitting them harder and farther from Billy — about another sixty ground balls.

"I caught them and threw back at him with a smirk," Billy said. "I was looking at him like, 'Is that all you got? I can do this all day.'"

Casey turned to Red and said, "That ragamuffin. I've hit him so many grounders I think he's trying to wear me out. He's not going to back off, is he?"

Stengel was suitably impressed, even if he sent Billy home without a contract. Billy was back in the slaughterhouse the next day. But within weeks an infielder with the Oaks' lowest-level minor league team in Idaho Falls, Idaho (yes, the Pacific Coast League had its own minors), was injured. An Oaks scout, Jimmy Hull, who had been watching Billy in high school, persuaded Stengel and Oaks owner Brick Laws to offer Billy a contract for $200 a month.

But the Oaks were well aware of the high school suspension and, like everyone else, knew that West Berkeley was a tough place. Laws proposed that the contract include a clause stating that it could be nullified if Billy got into fights or was guilty of other transgressions. The first of many attempts to write a "misbehavior" section into a Billy Martin baseball contract failed as Billy refused to sign it. Billy was desperate to get out of the slaughterhouse, but even a desperate Billy Martin was always a defiant Billy Martin — and it did not matter if that attitude might cost him everything. He would not back down.

The Oaks needed an infielder for Idaho Falls the next day. Laws gave in, setting a precedent repeated by baseball front-office executives of one kind or another for years to come.

In that moment, Billy's long-held dream had come true. The kid from the crowded, tumultuous house at 1632 7th Street, who had camped out for years at Kenney Park waiting for the older guys to let him play, was a professional baseball player.

When he signed his contract at a table in the corporate offices of the Oaks, Billy held a pen as Brick Laws steadied the contract with his left hand. A newspaper photographer captured the scene of a smiling eighteen-year-old Billy Martin.

In the photo, Billy is wearing a faded white shirt and over it an odd, dark, patterned V-neck sweater, the very same sweater from the picture of his ninth-grade St. Ambrose CYO basketball team.

Billy would be leaving his West Berkeley neighborhood the next day. But it was as plain as the clothes on his back that the neighborhood would be going with him. And he would never forget it.

6

―

BILLY LOVED TO TELL the story of how he got from West Berkeley to Idaho Falls. He told it with a smile.

After signing the contract, Brick Laws asked Billy if he had a suit to wear during his trip to his new job.

"Nope, my family took my only suit and used it to dress my uncle in his casket last year," Billy said.

What about a suitcase?

"No, my brother took it on a trip and ended up selling it to pay for his train ticket back home," Billy answered.

The story goes that Laws took pity on Billy and gave him $300 to buy a suit, some neckties and slacks, and a suitcase. And that's how Billy got to the train station the next day.

Pat Irvine rolled her eyes when the story was recounted to her.

"He had a suitcase," she bellowed. "Don't be ridiculous."

And a suit? Pat Irvine paused. She was not so sure.

His cousin Mario DeGennaro does indeed remember Billy's suit being used to make an uncle look presentable in death.

"Deaths in the family often meant a raid to your closet," Mario said. "Deaths were bad for your wardrobe."

But Mario also believes Billy probably had a suitcase but perhaps saw the advantage in not admitting to it. Billy was plenty street-smart at eighteen; he could have recognized an easy way to get an extra $300 out of Laws, the wealthy movie theater magnate who had bought the Oaks in 1943.

Whatever the circumstances, everyone agrees that Billy showed up at the train station the next day wearing at least a sports coat, carrying a suitcase, and sporting a wide grin.

His childhood friend and former high school teammate Billy Castell said several people came to the train station to see Billy off.

"But we were not awed," Castell said. "This was the day we expected."

The train was bound for Salt Lake City where Billy would meet his new team, the Idaho Falls Russets of the Class C Pioneer League. Though he had not played third base since his freshman year of high school, that was his new position, and he struggled with the throw from the far corner of the left side of the infield. His arm was strong enough, but erratic.

He booted the very first ground ball hit his way, one of 16 errors he made in just 32 games at Idaho Falls, but he did bat a respectable .254 in 114 at-bats with 7 doubles. Moreover, he kept his nose clean. There were no reports back to Brick Laws about a brawling Billy Martin. From the beginning, he did things that got the attention of his manager, Eddie Leishman, who had been a player, coach, or manager in the minors since 1930.

"Billy read the field, read the other players, read the umpires, read the situation, and anticipated better than any eighteen-year-old I had ever seen," said Leishman, who had played ten years in the minor league system of the New York Yankees during the 1930s. "Some players wait for the game to come to them; not Billy."

Even at eighteen, Billy only waited for the moment to do something to alter the course of the game.

The average age of the Idaho Falls team was twenty-three. Billy was the only teen on the roster but played as if he were older. One teammate, right-handed pitcher John Conant, recalled a game he was pitching when his wily new third baseman seemed to steal two big outs at a big moment.

"It was a one-run game and we were playing the Twin Falls Cowboys, a Yankee farm team that used to beat us like a drum," Conant said, telling the story nearly seventy years later. "The Cowboys had runners on first and second base with one out. The batter ripped a screaming one-hopper down the third-base line.

"It was foul; I'm sure it was foul, but Billy snagged it in his glove, stepped back and touched third base, then flipped the ball to second base for the double play all in one motion. Then he dashed right off the field. We all just followed him and ran off the field, too. It happened so fast I think the umpires were stunned. Billy had kind of made the call for them — end of inning, you know? What were they going to do? Call us back?"

Billy's sheer and absolute conviction that it was a fair ball and a double play had led everyone on the field to the same conclusion — not the last time that conviction sealed a verdict, in Billy's life or any other.

Years later, Billy would resurrect his end-of-inning ploy with a twist, having his infielders run off the field after a routine force-out when, in fact, there were only two outs. The idea was to fake any other runners still on base into thinking the inning was over. The infielder who had caught the ball for the force-out would always absent-mindedly linger somewhere on the diamond with the ball in his glove. Everyone else would head for the dugout. When a base runner — seeing nearly everyone leaving the field — stepped off the base thinking the inning was indeed over, at that moment Billy's infielder with the ball would tag him for the third out. Then the inning was over.

As Billy would say, it always worked, "except when the stupid umps would get fooled too and not be looking as we were making the tag."

The Idaho Falls Russets finished with a 53-76 record, good for second-to-last place. Billy enjoyed the life of a professional athlete that summer, especially the playing baseball every day part. A city kid through and through, he did complain of the remoteness of eastern Idaho, though the isolation had one benefit that Billy thought significant: it allowed him to save several hundred dollars of his salary.

And Billy wanted that money in his pocket for something important. As soon as he returned to West Berkeley in the fall, he had the first of several operations to reduce the size of his nose.

"I remember picking him up at the hospital after that operation," said Lew Figone. "But truthfully, cosmetic surgery was so bad back then, they only cut his nose down a little bit. It wasn't that obvious a change. It would be two or three operations later before his nose got noticeably smaller.

"I drove him home from those too."

Billy was sent to the Phoenix Senators of the Arizona-Texas League in the spring of 1947. It was a higher level of minor league ball, although Billy bristled at the assignment. He had been in the Oaks' preseason training camp practicing alongside five former Major Leaguers, including Vince DiMaggio, Joe's brother, who had played ten seasons in the National League.

Billy, nineteen, felt he measured up to the veterans and should remain with the Oaks. In an era when it was not uncommon for future Baseball Hall of Famers to play three or four years of minor league baseball (there were only sixteen teams in the Major Leagues), Billy's assignment to Phoenix was hardly an insult.

But Billy did not take it that way.

"You sure blew one," he told Stengel.

"Prove me wrong," Stengel responded, who was just beginning to understand how to motivate his young charge.

"You wait and see," Billy said.

The remote, sun-baked, and grubby 1947 Arizona-Texas League was an unlikely incubator for the professional career of someone who, in just a few years, would shine beneath the bright lights of New York's Golden Age of baseball. But it was the irregular, hard-to-explain Arizona-Texas League where Billy went from a minor leaguer with dreams of being a Major Leaguer to a bona fide big-league prospect.

The Arizona-Texas League was actually a U.S.-Mexican league, in which the best team was from Juarez, Mexico, across the border from El Paso. The Juarez team was made up of hardened, grizzled veterans in their late twenties or early thirties. It was one of only four or five teams playing in the league, in a round-robin schedule that bred familiarity, and contempt, among the teams.

Games were played on dried-out fields where the infield clay — if it was clay — cracked and split under a midday sun that would often elevate temperatures into triple digits. The Phoenix players were housed in barracks beyond the right-field wall, a sultry garrison cooled only by a rare breeze. The team played almost every day, and when it did not, there was a workout. Transportation between games was by bus, or worse, station wagon behind which the baseball equipment was dragged in trailers.

The circumstances and regional/national rivalries made ballplayers ornery, a tension stoked by sold-out ballparks full of half-drunk fans swilling beer and tequila as they enjoyed one of the few entertainment vehicles in the frontierlike atmosphere. It was like a scene from an old Western, except the games replaced the gunfighters' pistol duel in the middle of town.

Fights in Arizona-Texas games were almost as common as the seventh-inning stretch, and while Billy did not lead the circuit in fisticuffs, unlike in Idaho Falls, he did not shy away from one or two when it seemed unavoidable.

It was a punishing environment designed to separate those who liked baseball from those who planned to make it a vocation. It is not known what Billy thought of all this, but this much is documented: in his first game for the Phoenix Senators he had 6 hits, and the next day he had 4 more hits and drove in 5 runs. Within two weeks, the Phoenix newspaper had run a feature story on the Senators' new third baseman. He started the season as the eighth hitter and quickly moved up to the third spot.

At mid-season, Billy was still hitting over .400, and he had become a vocal, assertive team leader despite giving away four or five years to most of the other players.

Akry Biggs was the team's manager who played second base until a game just past mid-season when a Yankees farm product named Clint Courtney, a catcher who had been released from the U.S. Army two months earlier and had already earned a reputation for spikes-high slides, slammed into Biggs at second and cut him. Biggs, like many other players in the league, did not need to be coaxed into a fight. With the baseball in his right hand, he punched Courtney in the face.

The fracas that followed was not eventful except for the fact that Biggs came out of it with his right hand swollen, painful, and broken.

Phoenix needed a second baseman. Though he had never been a regular second baseman, Billy was the only one on the roster with middle-infield experience. He took over for Akry Biggs and played more than one thousand games at the position for the next fourteen baseball seasons.

The day after Biggs was injured, Courtney spiked another Phoenix player at third base, which obviously didn't go over well with the Senators. The first player sprinting across the diamond from his second-base position to jump Courtney was Billy. They would tussle a couple more times that year, and again in the Major Leagues, in 1952. And in 1953.

Those two fights were hardly big news in the league. One brawl between Billy's Senators and the Globe-Miami Browns spilled into the stands and was not quelled until police threw tear gas on the diamond. Then, once everyone's eyes had cleared, the teams resumed play.

But throughout the summer of 1947, Billy was doing more than establishing his willingness to defend teammates and stand up for himself. He was having one of the best seasons of any minor leaguer — or Major Leaguer — in America.

There were some issues as he acclimated at second base, but the shorter throw wasn't one of them. And at the plate, he exhibited impressive batsmanship. With 230 hits in 586 at-bats in 1947, he hit .392, with 48 doubles, 12 triples, and 9 home runs. His slugging percentage was .561.

Billy was thriving, having the kind of season that he knew was the ultimate comeback to Stengel's end-of-spring-training retort: "Prove me wrong."

He was also shaping pieces of a persona, one cultivated without nuance but in bold strokes. In 1947, for example, he chose jersey number 1, something he tried to wear at every baseball stop thereafter. He adopted second base as his home on the diamond and was fittingly territorial about it. He played every inning of every game, not wanting others in *his* spot. And he did not favor trespassers on his dominion either. Opposing players encroaching into the second-base area were treated like marauding invaders and dealt with punitively. Meanwhile, he found comfort in the inconvenience of the Arizona-Texas League logistics, strangely at ease in the conditions that were wearisome to the other players trying to survive the heat and enervating circumstances of the Arizona, Texas, and Mexico summers.

Billy was named the league's Most Valuable Player in 1947 — a triumph everyone in baseball had to notice on some level. The Oakland Oaks surely did as they called Billy up for the final fifteen games of their season. Billy won two games with doubles that drove in runs. When the team returned home, Billy was immediately popular with the fans in Oaks Park, a square-shaped old bandbox of a ballpark in Emeryville about three miles from Billy's boyhood home. People in the stands knew him, or knew of him, and he played to the crowd when they applauded his at-bats — tipping his cap and smiling warmly at them. Unpolished, ungainly Billy — his nose still protruding over his lips — loved being applauded. Popularity was, and always would be, like a drug that soothed Billy's misgivings about the world around him.

But Billy did not play that often on a veteran team closing out a solid year. And in all that time off the field Billy took to sitting next to Stengel during games.

"He was glued to Casey," said Dario Lodigiani, the Oaks second baseman who was with the team after stints in the Major Leagues with the Chicago White Sox and Philadelphia Athletics. "I don't think it was to get in Casey's good graces because neither of them was like that. I think Billy was trying to learn what was going on inside Casey's head as the game was going on. Both of them had real active brains. Billy was a nonstop stream of questions for the old man."

Knee to knee and shoulder to shoulder in the Oaks' dugout, nineteen-year-old Billy and fifty-seven-year-old Casey spent the final month of September in tandem, the early stages of an eventful, ten-year dance together. Billy stayed in touch throughout the winter, visiting Casey periodically at his Oakland home, and when they were reunited in uniform during spring training of 1948, they picked up where they had left off the preceding season.

The Casey-Billy relationship has often been described as one akin to father and son. While that might seem simplistic or theatrical, like a novelist's convenient leap, it also had the advantage of being authentic and discerning. To Billy, Casey was a father figure the likes of which Billy had never had. Jack Downey instilled values in Billy, of work and perseverance, but he was not a sportsman. Stengel, meanwhile, was a man who lived for baseball as Billy did. He had an aggressive and irascible temperament, but he also had a cunning, measured, and analytical side. Stengel's worn, creased face was called clownish by some, but others saw in his countenance an expression of knowing worldliness. For Casey Stengel, born in the previous century and a professional baseball player before World War I, had seen many things beyond the East Bay and San Francisco. Stengel was not a man to be taken lightly, and Billy certainly did not. He knew Stengel, for instance, had done what Billy hoped to do — play professional baseball in New York, and for nine seasons. Stengel was clever like an old sage, using humor and a fractured sense of the English language to disguise his intellect and deflect his inner thoughts when it served his purposes. People who underestimated him usually regretted it.

Years later in the 1940s, for example, when Casey began managing the Yankees, many of his stars were breaking curfew, knowing that their manager, their elder by thirty-plus years, was not going to stay up to the wee hours to catch them. Casey devised a different strategy. When he went to bed on the road, he tipped the hotel elevator operator, gave him a new baseball, and told him to ask for the autographs of each player who came in after midnight. The hotel operator left the evidence for Casey at the front desk in the morning.

Casey was wily, fearless, and daring and in Oakland in 1947, not too old or too afraid to punch someone in the nose if he thought he deserved it.

Still a teen, Billy looked at Casey and probably saw a reflection of himself. So he inched forward for a closer look until he was at Casey's side at all times.

In Billy, Stengel no doubt saw the son he never had. This probably did not happen immediately, since it was only a year earlier that he had described Billy as "that ragamuffin." But Casey was nonetheless drawn to Billy, seeing some of himself in the charming if raffish youngster. The marriage of Casey and the former Edna Lawson, which would last fifty-one years, produced no children. And Casey had no nieces or nephews in his family either. Slowly, Casey warmed to Billy, alternatively scolding him and throwing his arm around him as a parent would. To his face he called him "Kid," and to others Billy was "that kid."

Around the Oakland Oaks, Billy was soon dubbed "Casey's boy," a term that stuck.

Stengel believed in players like Billy, whose effect on baseball games could not be summed up in statistics or completely grasped by watching him swing a bat or field ground balls in practice. Casey looked at Billy and saw not just his raw resolve but his knowing faith that the game was played at various levels that few recognized, be they physical, mental, or spiritual. He saw in Billy the zeal to know and master it all and to let baseball take over his life until it took him everywhere he ever wanted to go.

Because that is how Casey saw his life. Baseball had done much for him already, and somehow, at fifty-seven, it was as if he was just getting started again. As Stengel would later say, summing up any number of memorable moments, "There comes a time in a man's life, and I've had plenty of them."

As with most Casey-isms, it sounded like a joke, but it was not.

Charles Dillon Stengel was born on July 30, 1890, in Kansas City, hence his nickname as a ballplayer (derived from K.C.). After high school he began driving a cab for pay for his tuition at Western Dental College. An outfielder who batted and threw left-handed, he augmented his income by playing a summer of minor league professional baseball for the teams in Kankakee, Illinois, of the Northern Association and Maysville, Kentucky, in the Blue Grass League.

In his autobiography, Stengel wrote of Maysville, "I was full of fire and vinegar and practiced my sliding into third, second or first base on my way to and from the dugout between innings. There was a lunatic asylum behind center field and the people out there used to applaud my slide more than home runs. They must have recognized a kindred soul."

By the summer of 1911, Casey had moved on to the team in Aurora, Illinois, and he was struggling with his dental studies in part because he could not afford left-handed dental instruments. By chance, a Brooklyn Dodgers scout spotted Casey in Aurora. Three hundred dollars later Stengel was a Brooklyn farmhand, and one year later he was playing in Brooklyn. He had four hits in his first home game, and the Brooklyn fans took a liking to the plucky Stengel, who smiled at fans in the stands and carried on conversations with them as he roamed the outfield. He was daring and boisterous, swaggering his way around the bases and calling attention to himself whenever he could. When the veterans on other teams told him to tone down his act, Stengel told them to shove it and tried to think of something more ostentatious he could do to get under their skin.

He got away with his theatrics because he was a solid player, twice batting over .300 for the Dodgers, and he hit .364 during their 1916 loss to the Boston Red Sox in the World Series. When Ebbets Field opened in 1913, Stengel hit the first home run in the ballpark. Traded to Pittsburgh because of a contract dispute, he continued to play well, although World War I and the U.S. Navy intervened briefly. Returning to Brooklyn for a Sunday game in 1919, Casey struck out twice and misplayed a fly ball. The fans of his old team were jeering him mercilessly. On his way to the bench at the end of the sixth inning, he saw a teammate holding a small sparrow he had captured in the bullpen. Casey put the bird under his cap and held it there. As he approached home plate during the top of the seventh — without television commercial breaks, one inning in 1919 followed another inning very quickly — the Brooklyn fans booed. Casey tipped his cap and out flew the sparrow. If they were going to give him the bird, he could give them one, too. Brooklyn's baseball fans cheered Casey anew.

By 1922, Stengel was with the New York Giants, whose crusty manager, John McGraw, loved the hard-driving style of his new outfielder. Stengel was now thirty-one years old and a bit worn out from eleven years on the road. Baseball players in the early part of the twentieth century were a hard-drinking, brawling lot — the best hotels would often refuse to lodge them, treating them like circus performers. Casey was at home in a bar like any other player and wondering how many years he had left. McGraw platooned the left-handed-hitting Casey with another outfielder, the right-handed Bill Cunningham, and while Casey did not like his part-time status, he saw the benefits. Casey hit .368 in 1922 facing right-handed pitchers and Cunningham batted .328 facing the lefties. The wisdom of the system stuck with Casey for decades.

Casey also watched McGraw carefully, mesmerized by his tactics and psychological approach to running a team. No two players were treated the same. Some players were upbraided for mistakes in front of the rest of the team while others were talked to privately. Some players were given cash bonuses for getting hit with a pitch or executing a squeeze bunt; others were rewarded for good play with more playing time. McGraw was devilish, taunting and berating umpires, and he loved trick plays.

McGraw noticed that Stengel was studying him and invited him for dinner at his home in Westchester County. The two would talk baseball all night.

Stengel was also a good reclamation project, especially in the 1922 World Series when he hit .400 in the Giants' victory over the New York Yankees, a performance that added to Casey's reputation in New York for World Series heroics.

In 1923, the year majestic, regal Yankee Stadium opened across the Harlem River from the Giants' dull, unimaginative Polo Grounds, the Giants and Yankees again met in the World Series. In six games contested in two venues about a mile apart, Casey, who hit .339 in the regular season for the Giants, tormented Babe Ruth's ascendant New York Yankees throughout the World Series.

In the first game, coming to the plate with two outs in the top of the ninth inning with the score tied, he hit a drive into the vast left-center-field gap of the Yankees' new Bronx ballpark. Casey scurried around the bases before the ball could be returned to home plate even though he nearly lost a shoe rounding second base and tripped over third base. But Casey's inside-the-park homer dash was the first World Series home run in Yankee Stadium, and it won the game for the Giants, 5–4.

The Giants also won the third game, 1–0, on Stengel's home run in the seventh inning. The Yankees players had been making fun of Casey during at-bats ever since his stumbling circuit around the bases in the series opener. But when Casey's drive crested the Yankee Stadium right-field wall, they watched silently as Casey, who was jogging slowly around the bases, turned to the Yankees' dugout and thumbed his nose.

The home run and nose-thumbing were the Giants' last gasp as they lost the series in six games. But Casey Stengel, who hit .417 in the series and .393 in three World Series, had made his place in New York postseason baseball history — a fact he no doubt later impressed on Billy. The legend of World Series heroes in New York never dies.

Dealt to the Boston Braves after the 1923 season, Casey retired in 1925 at the age of thirty-four when the Braves asked him to instead manage the team's minor league team in Worcester, Massachusetts.

Eight years and one minor league championship later, Brooklyn named him manager. After three losing seasons, he was fired and returned to

Boston to manage an even worse team, the Braves, who played in a cold, windy park beside the Charles River.

Stengel's Braves had losing seasons five times in six years. There was little talent on the roster, so he did what he could to help the cause by entertaining the baseball writers and fans with various antics. When storm clouds and rain greeted the beginning of one game, Casey brought the lineup cards to the umpires holding an umbrella in one hand and a lantern in the other. But eventually Boston fired him, too.

As Casey said years later, "I became a major league manager in several cities and was discharged. We call it discharged because there is no question I had to leave."

He resurfaced in Milwaukee for the 1944 season, where his team won the American Association, and then he worked one year for the Yankees' AA minor league affiliate in Kansas City, where he caught the notice of Yankees owner Del Webb. The Yankees wanted Casey to stay, but he wanted something bigger than AA ball, and being back in Kansas City did not thrill his wife after so many years in cosmopolitan New York and Boston. The Yankees said they understood when he left and surreptitiously decided to keep an eye on his next team.

Casey landed in the Pacific Coast League in 1946, which was a good choice for the high quality of play. The bad news was that Casey agreed to manage the Oaks, who had not won the PCL title since 1927. It seemed a long way from the majors. Most people in baseball figured Casey Stengel's Major League managing career was over anyway.

The unpolished Oaks were mocked in their own market, ridiculed in comparison to the more professional, moneyed San Francisco Seals across the bay. Their park was tattered and lifeless from years of losing, rows of plain wooden bleachers where the fans would lounge, seemingly more interested in sunbathing than in the game on the field.

In 1945, the Oaks had been a 90-93 team, but in 1946 Casey led the team to a 111-72 record. A second consecutive winning season in 1947 rejuvenated the franchise and brought crowds back to the Emeryville park. Casey's roster was full of castoffs but they were a hard-nosed crew that battled, scraped, and defied the regal San Francisco Seals, defeating them in head-to-head matchups more often than not. The perennially underdog citizens of Oakland treasured the opportunity to beat San Francisco at anything and embraced Casey's upstart Oaks.

By 1948, three years into his plan, Casey Stengel finally had molded the team in his image: older but wiser and holding on for one last sprint for the brass ring. There was a former Major Leaguer at every position and only five players remaining from the roster Stengel inherited in 1946.

And many of the new players were something else — Kenney Park regulars from before World War II. Billy knew them all, which made it easier in the Oaks' 1948 preseason workouts, which were memorable because of Billy's cheeky presence.

Stengel, for all his clowning, was a stern taskmaster about baseball fundamentals, and none of his players talked back to him when the subject was the rudiments and techniques of the game. Casey's word ruled. He talked and players listened. No one else had a speaking part.

Until, that is, Billy came along. Early in 1948, Casey was watching Billy turning double plays at second and stopped the drill. He thought Billy was wasting too much motion. He wanted his second baseman to turn the double play with as few moving parts as possible, and he demonstrated how.

"Forget the Fancy Dan stuff," Stengel said.

Billy considered what Casey was saying.

"My way is just as good because I have faster feet and hands," he said.

"Kid, you ain't on the floor jitterbugging," Casey answered.

"Don't knock it just because you can't do it," Billy fired back.

The other players awaited an explosion from their manager. At the very least they thought Billy would be sent to another field, or to the clubhouse.

Instead Stengel turned and walked away, hiding a smile with his hand. It was the kind of thing the twenty-year-old Casey Stengel, the ex-cabdriver, might have said in 1910. All these years later, Casey could do no more than laugh.

The Oaks were stacked with talent that year. The U.S. Supreme Court at the time was renowned as "Nine Old Men." And as the Oaks broke camp, it was what the Oakland sportswriters called Stengel's seasoned lineup: "Casey's Nine Old Men."

Billy turned twenty in May and saw the field rarely, but in time, injuries and other infirmities to the aging lineup earned him playing time all over the infield. The sportswriters started to amend their description of the team. They were the Eight Old Men and the Kid.

It was by far the highest level of baseball Billy had ever played, but he blended in, playing good defense even if he hit under .200 in his first 75 at-bats. Stengel made sure his young charge was not thrown into the mix before he was ready. He wanted Billy to watch the veterans play, and he did not care if Billy seethed on the bench game after game.

Casey had Billy sit with him while he pointed out various nuances he saw on the field, including how some infielders were tipping which kind of pitches were about to be thrown by moving left or right on the diamond too soon. Billy watched and listened as Casey predicted every pitch — breaking ball, fastball, changeup — all by watching the shortstop and second baseman.

It's common for middle infielders to change their position on the diamond on most every pitch, but the stealthy infielder does not move until the pitcher is in his wind-up so the batter cannot read his movements and accurately guess what kind of pitch is coming.

But Stengel was ever vigilant, waiting to spot a slip-up of technique so he could use it to his advantage. Billy learned the value of seeing the whole field. Every game was an evolving mosaic, with one seemingly indiscriminate piece having the ability to affect another more crucial part of the game. It was one of the many tricks of the trade he learned at the side of his mentor.

Finally, in the second month of the season, Casey inserted Billy into the starting lineup. But Billy was unhappy because he was batting eighth, just ahead of the pitcher.

"The groundskeeper is probably hitting higher than me," Billy snapped at Casey. "I hit .392 last year."

"Get a bat, Dago, and shut up," Casey said.

As Billy walked to the on-deck circle, Stengel suppressed a giggle. "That fresh punk," he said. "I love him."

7

BILLY DROVE A 1934 Chevrolet to Oaks Park for games. His cousin Mario, who would soon begin a sixty-four-year career in the auto parts industry, helped him find the car for next to nothing at auction. It came cheap because it was missing a fender and the driver's side had been bashed in. Only the passenger-side doors worked, so everyone getting in the car entered on that side and slid across the bench seats.

There was a VIP/players' parking lot next to Oaks Park, and it was filled with the swell cars driven by the ex–Major Leaguers on the roster. There were Cadillacs, Buicks, and spiffy Oldsmobiles. When Billy rolled in with his '34 Chevy missing a fender, the other players asked him to park it at the far end of the lot. They didn't want Billy's wreck to sully the aura of prosperity and professionalism that the rest of the cars connoted to fans and passersby.

Billy heard his teammates' requests. Then he started arriving at the ballpark first.

"Bill would park that junk heap of a car in the first spot closest to the entrance," his sister Pat said. "They either had to park near him or park their cars at the other end, which was a longer walk and out of the way, too.

"They just gave up and parked next to Bill's car. He thought that was a riot. The owner, Brick Laws, even said something to him. So Bill told Laws, 'If you don't like my car, you can buy me a new one.'"

The Oaks got off to a fast start in 1948, Stengel's veterans capturing the rest of the league by surprise. Stengel was working the home crowds from the third-base coaching box, encouraging their rowdy nature to make Oaks Park an undesirable stop for visiting teams. Even a few dozen noisy, boisterous fans could impact the game in the close confines of a park that sat about twelve thousand and often peddled discounted beer for 25 cents a cup.

While Casey was cheering on the fans' raucous inclination, he had also chosen Billy for a key role: bench jockey.

It's a lost art, and now considered beneath players making $15 million a year or more, but taunting and badgering the other team verbally from the dugout was once an accepted and prized part of baseball from high school through the Major Leagues. Casey was adept at it in his playing days, and he encouraged it in his players. Billy, who throughout life had a high-pitched, piercing voice when he yelled, knew how to get inside opposing players' heads, and he could definitely be heard.

"There was something about his voice," said his longtime friend and Oaks teammate Mel Duezabou. "You could hear it wherever you were on the field. When he was in the infield, he'd yell something to the catcher or the left fielder and you'd hear it clear as day. When he was in the dugout, he could yell across to the other dugout, to the second-base umpire, or the center fielder and he would be heard.

"And you know Billy, he wasn't always yelling sweet nothings to them."

Stengel noticed that Billy's provocative nature did not just unnerve the other team; it kept the Oaks in games. They would laugh at something Billy said and watch the game more closely to see what happened next. The other team would often respond with a dare or a taunt that would challenge and motivate the Oaks to raise their game. The level of intensity would get ratcheted up, with everyone leaning forward on the dugout bench following every pitch — just what Casey wanted — and it all might have started with Billy making fun of the way someone ran to first base.

This was good baseball, Casey thought, and it helped create a bond on the team, which was important because the Oaks traveled a lot. The PCL stretched from Washington State to Southern California, and though the teams flew on planes when they could, the journeys still dragged with every team playing about 180 games a year, many more than the 154 the Major League teams were playing at the time. But these long trips proved important to Billy culturally as they inculcated in him the ways of top professional athletes. Billy, though streetwise, had little sophistication in the interactions of the middle class, let alone people with money to spare in their pockets. He did not know how to behave, or how to make that money open doors for him.

But by watching the Nine Old Men, most of whom had been Major Leaguers, he saw that a dollar tip to a waitress on her arrival at the table brought better service, good advice on what to order, a larger piece of pie for dessert, and maybe the waitress's phone number too. Billy had never seen the 25 cents he customarily left for a tip accomplish that. He saw that the big leaguers knew how to barter the commodities that they had — tickets, autographs, and small talk about life in the Major Leagues — for things they wanted, which was dinner reservations at top restaurants, a better hotel room (or suite), or a cab in the rain at a busy train station. The younger players learned that these same commodities, and their status as professional ballplayers who might someday be famous, differentiated them from a crowd at a hectic nightclub and could turn the heads of pretty young women on the road. It was a perk of the ballplayer fraternity.

The length of the Oaks' trips also made roommate combinations a central consideration of the manager. Stengel initially had Billy room with Duezabou, a lifetime .300 hitter in the minors. The goal was for Duezabou to teach Billy some batting techniques. Instead, Stengel observed that both Billy and Duezabou kept late nights — and not in the hotel either but in bars. Billy was also making up for whatever shyness or inadequacies he felt around women as a teen. He soon had a black book filled with women's names and numbers, divided by PCL stops: Portland, Sacramento, Hollywood.

Stengel, no stranger to bars himself, did not mind his players having a good time and would, in fact, disdain players who did not drink as "milk drinkers who can't be trusted." But Billy worried him in the summer of 1948 because Billy the player wasn't getting any better.

Stengel hatched a new plan. One day, the thirty-five-year-old Lavagetto, fresh from a turn as a World Series star for the Brooklyn Dodgers, approached Duezabou and announced that he was Billy's new roommate.

Lavagetto was supposed to do more than rein in Billy's wildest habits. He was to educate him in the highest levels of professional baseball. Lavagetto had a willing pupil, and like many of Billy's mentors, he came to admire his student and learned what made him tick. Lavagetto discovered that keeping Billy out of the bars wasn't too hard if Billy was distracted with baseball talk. Lavagetto invited questions, and Billy asked for a detailed description of every Major League ballpark. Billy had Lavagetto go over dozens of pitchers he had faced in the big leagues. Billy inquired about the Major League umpires and how to deal with them. He did the same for the baseball writers. Lavagetto was Billy's baseball oracle.

Recognizing Billy's craving for knowing all the intricacies of the game, Lavagetto, who was in the midst of his sixteenth year of professional baseball, started working with his young roommate before games. He wanted to improve his footwork in the infield, and he had teammate Lodigiani, who was thirty-two, help as well.

"Billy was still pretty raw," Lodigiani said. "Casey was right to try to change the way he turned the double play. We worked for hours on doing it more efficiently."

That included teaching Billy to stop winding up to make the throw from second to first base. Power wasn't as important as getting the ball on its way quickly — before an oncoming runner could prevent the relay. The tutoring did not stop when the ballplayers left the field. Instead of barhopping, Lavagetto would put a pillow in front of a full-length mirror in a hotel room and have Billy practice his double-play pivot by hopping over it time and again.

Lavagetto also related how pitiless Major Leaguers could be. Middle infielders know that advancing base runners are trying to knock them down or into the outfield, and during the 1940s such collisions were common and permitted without penalty. It was all part of the game. The infielder's only defense was the ball, and Lavagetto told Billy that if a base runner did not slide to get out of the way, Billy should aim his double-play pivot throw right at the runner's forehead. It would induce a slide in a hurry and it might be a good relay as well.

Billy bragged of doing just what Cookie taught him throughout the 1950s, and he taught his infielders the same thing for three decades thereafter.

The ingenious Lavagetto had all kinds of theories on making a player better.

"He'd make me sit in a restaurant and stare at a wall without blinking my eyes," Billy wrote in his autobiography. "I'd practice that for hours. Try it sometime. It isn't easy. He had me do that because he felt that when you were up at the plate, the ball would go by so fast that if you accidentally blinked, that fraction of a second would be enough of a distraction to make you miss the ball."

Lavagetto's influence started to take effect as the 1948 season continued. Billy started hitting, which was timely because mid-season injuries to Lodigiani and another starter meant Billy was in the lineup for 132 of the Oaks' 188 games that season. Billy was more popular than ever at Oaks Park, both among the regular fans and especially in the VIP section of the seats where a pretty young woman from Berkeley was sitting for every game. She was Lois Elaine Berndt, and she got her prized seats from Billy, whom she had known since she was in ninth grade.

Lois, four years younger than Billy, had been his friend for years. They had also dated on and off in the mid-1940s and had remained in constant contact since Lois was best friends with the girlfriend and eventual wife of Billy's good friend Howard Noble. Lois was from a neighborhood north of San Pablo Avenue, though she did not live far enough up the hill to be called a Goat — or at least Billy never thought so. After Billy's relationship with longtime high school girlfriend Bobbi Pitter ended — a victim of the long summer in the Arizona-Texas League — Lois became Billy's permanent guest at Oaks games. He would leave tickets for her and his family, which would sometimes be awkward because Billy's sisters and his mother rarely approved of any of Billy's girlfriends and that included Lois.

"We always thought she was kind of stuck-up," Pat Irvine said. "She was never warm to us. She wouldn't really talk to my mom and it was hard not to talk to my mom."

Lois, asked sixty years later to recall her first interactions with Billy's family, sighed.

"I'm not getting into that," she said. "Let's just say we were on opposite sides with Billy in the middle. I had one view of him. They had another view."

Lois recalled that Billy was very attentive to her.

"He was always the gentleman — opening doors, holding your chair for you, putting his coat around you if you were cold or it was raining," Lois said. "You know, he has this reputation for being rough and a fighter. He wasn't like that. Get him off the field and away from baseball and he was quiet and sensitive."

Then, in a considerable understatement, one that eventually may have served as a summation of her time with Billy, Lois said, "Of course, getting Billy away from baseball was never easy."

But Lois, like many others, saw two sides to Billy. He was affectionate and wanted to go to out-of-the-way places where no one knew him.

"We would take long walks all the time," she said. "We would talk about what we wanted to do with our lives. Billy especially had a lot of dreams."

Billy wanted to see the world, metaphorically he wanted to set it on fire, but Billy also dreamed of coming back to Berkeley to live without the sizzle.

"There were always two Billys," Lois said.

And two dreams.

Deep into September 1948, the Oaks hung tough with the San Fran-cisco Seals. It was a taut, two-team race. Stengel kept the troops loose with his brand of John McGraw–inspired inducements. A victory meant a free case of beer in the clubhouse afterward. Getting hit by a pitch with men on base, a successful squeeze bunt, or an opportune hit-and-run would all be recognized with some reward — gift certificates from local businesses or tickets to a movie house.

Billy and others noticed that Stengel's leadership style was more than glad-handing.

When a fight broke out in Portland one night — fighting was common in the PCL as it was in most American professional sports at the time — Billy charged from the dugout to join the fray. He had been in the middle of two fights of his own that season already, one that involved his future boss with the Yankees, Al Rosen, but this time he was sprinting to help a teammate. Approaching the diamond, Billy saw that a half-step behind him, dashing from the dugout at a gallop, was his fifty-eight-year-old manager.

And when both reached the scrum, Casey wasn't there to be a peace-maker. He dove into the pile and started punching and grappling with the other team. When things calmed down, Casey's ill-fitting wool uniform was torn, and he had scratches on his arms and bruises across his jowls.

"Something like that really affects a team," Billy said years later, de-scribing Casey's willingness to mix it up. "I saw how the guys reacted. We all said, 'He really does have our back.' That is loyalty. I wanted to be like that."

The 1948 season came down to the final day, Sunday, September 26. The Oaks swept a double-header to clinch the pennant before a sold-out home crowd, some of whom slept overnight along the right-field foul line to reserve their seats the next day.

The Oaks finished with a 111-74 record, the best finish by any Stengel team, including his championship Yankees. A film crew caught the cel-ebration on the field afterward, including an interview with Stengel as he stood next to Billy.

"I owe it to all these players," Casey said. He hugged Billy with one arm and continued, "The Nine Old Men, they said. And how about this fresh kid here?"

A celebration was held in downtown Oakland five days later, the players parading through the streets sitting in the back of convertible cars. Stengel was in the car he won as the league's Manager of the Year. Billy, who hit .277 with 42 runs batted in and 28 doubles, did not drive his 1934 vehicle with the missing fender in the parade. He instead had a new black 1948 Chevy convertible, a gift of Oaks owner Brick Laws.

During the 1948 season, the New York Giants had offered Laws $50,000 to sign Billy. Casey talked Laws out of it. For one, he had a pennant to win with the Oaks. And besides, Casey wondered if he might get another chance to manage in the Major Leagues again. And if he did, he planned to take Billy with him.

Ten days after the Oakland parade, at a packed news conference at the swanky 21 Club in midtown Manhattan, the Yankees named their new manager for 1949: Charles Dillon Stengel. The news shocked the eastern baseball establishment. In the Major League circuit at the time, where the westernmost team was in St. Louis, Stengel had dropped off the Earth and was never expected back.

Now he was leading the Yankees, the gold standard of all American professional franchises?

"This is a big job, fellows, and I barely have had time to study it," Casey told the newspaper writers and another new media constituency that the *New York Times* described as a "television operator."

The Yankees' new owners, Dan Topping and Del Webb, flanked Stengel.

"He's been here before," Webb said. "He knows what it takes to win in Yankee Stadium."

Casey Stengel smiled.

It was October 12, 1948, exactly twenty-five years to the day since Casey had lifted a pitch into the right-field seats at Yankee Stadium to win a 1923 World Series game, then circled the bases while thumbing his nose at the Yankees' dugout.

8

WHEN THE 1949 SEASON commenced, Billy was in a funk, dispirited and feeling deserted. He had spent the winter waiting for the Yankees, or their new skipper, to call.

"Billy was devastated that Casey had left," said his cousin Nick DeGennaro. "You know, Billy was a vulnerable guy. He was easily hurt. I didn't hear him criticize Casey but out of nowhere sometimes he'd ask, 'You think maybe he's waiting for somebody to get hurt? You think maybe then he'll call?'

"And I would say, 'Maybe, Billy.'"

Billy spent time with Lois in Berkeley — and other women in other towns because Billy's roving eye was now well developed and he had an inclination to give in to it. He also hung out with his old buddies, driving his new car around to bars and parties throughout the East Bay. But his longtime friends were getting jobs or getting married. They were transitioning to the rest of their lives.

Mario DeGennaro, born two months after Billy, recalls driving everywhere with his cousin that winter in the new Chevy. Looking back, it was Mario's view that those months were the beginning of the end of Billy's time as one of the West Berkeley Boys. And one of the last times the West Berkeley Boys were as they once had been.

"He was waiting to move on," Mario said. "We *were* moving on."

Mario remembers sitting in the new Chevrolet with Billy that winter, waiting at a red light on San Pablo Avenue in Albany, one town north of Berkeley and one notch up the socioeconomic ladder. Mario looked to his right and saw a Help Wanted sign in the window of an auto parts store. He opened the passenger-side door of the Chevy, got out, and told Billy he was going in to apply for the job.

"Billy said, 'Get back in, we're going up the road to meet some girls,'" Mario said in 2012, sitting in his living room in Brentwood, fifty miles east of Berkeley. "I said, 'No, you go have a good time. I'll find my way home.'

"He was confused. He said, 'Why are you doing this now?' And I just said to him, 'It's time. You go ahead. I've got to get a job.'"

Mario got the job on the spot and started that day, the dawn of a career that eventually saw him own several prosperous auto parts stores in the area.

"I didn't see much of him after that, not for a couple of years," Mario said. "Here and there but not like before. I know he went back to the Oaks. I was too busy to go to the games."

The new Oaks manager was Charlie or Chuck Dressen, a former player who was fired as a Yankees coach when Stengel was hired. Dressen was Stengel's opposite in style and philosophy — meticulous, fastidious, and militaristic when it came to preparation and rules. There would be no free cases of beer in Dressen's clubhouse after victories, only more analysis of what had worked and what had not worked.

In upbringing and background, Dressen was not unlike Stengel. He had been a scrappy player in the National League who knew and liked old-school baseball. Billy did not like Dressen when he met him; he found him arrogant.

But in time Billy saw that his new manager had a strategic outlook on baseball that Billy had never fully considered. Dressen believed all games were won by the team making the fewest mistakes. And he was convinced that a zealous, aggressive style of play — stealing, hit-and-run, taking the extra base — would force the other team into the pivotal game-losing mistakes and errors. A team won games, Dressen preached, by putting pressure on the other team. The idea was to make them crack first.

Dressen could do something else that fascinated Billy. He could steal any opposing catcher's signs. Dressen was pretty good at stealing the third-base coach's signs, too. This kind of baseball skullduggery left Billy spellbound. The notion that there was another layer of the game that existed in full view and yet was slyly duplicitous at the same time appealed to him. And, of course, it reinforced what he had learned at Kenney Park — there was always another way to beat the other team if you looked for every advantage. Billy, following his lifelong pattern of learning from his baseball elders, wanted to know what Dressen saw and when he saw it. Dressen, not accustomed to having a player that interested in an obscure talent, happily schooled Billy in everything he knew, which mostly hinged on discerning patterns of movements and becoming a master at reading body language.

Billy, the everyday second baseman, played 172 games that year and sat next to Dressen in the dugout during games, picking his brain.

The Oaks would not win the PCL pennant in 1949 but Billy would flourish. He hit .286 with 12 homers and 92 RBIs and had a whopping 623 at-bats, which might have been his most impressive stat because it proved the bony West Berkeley boy was durable.

Back in New York, Stengel was being enshrined as a genius, shepherding the Yankees through a difficult, injury-plagued season that ended with Joe DiMaggio recovering from pneumonia in time to lead the Yankees to consecutive victories over the Boston Red Sox on the last days of the regular season, completing a come-from-behind chase for the American League pennant. The Yankees then won the World Series against the Brooklyn Dodgers.

Billy had not communicated directly with Stengel, but the wily manager was communicating with his protégé indirectly. He had noticed Billy's stellar play in Oakland during the 1949 campaign, and throughout the end of that season Stengel talked up Billy in the New York press, which most of the writers found odd since the Yankees' infield was set with established players. The shortstop, Phil Rizzuto, was only thirty-one. Jerry Coleman and Bobby Brown, each twenty-four, were at second and third base respectively. All three were having solid seasons. Puzzled, some in the New York press even went off on their own and decided that perhaps this "Coast star," as they liked to call Billy, would be converted to the outfield when he was lured to New York as everyone was now expecting.

On October 13, 1949, a promotional blimp that used to circle Oaks Park with local advertising messages instead flashed a news bulletin: OAKS PLAYERS JACKIE JENSEN AND BILLY MARTIN SOLD TO NY YANKEES.

The crowd began to cheer, and the players on the field paused to look up at the blimp. After the game, an Associated Press photographer had Billy and Jackie Jensen pose at the dugout railing because the New York papers wanted a shot of the two newest Yankees.

Jensen was a six-foot, two-hundred-pound former All-American football star at Cal-Berkeley with blond hair, blue eyes, a barrel chest, and muscular forearms. He was a perfect specimen of post–World War II America and, by the measure of Billy's old neighborhood vocabulary, 100 percent a Goat. Billy stood next to Jensen. In the picture, Billy's nose still looks too big for his face and his ears protrude. His uniform is baggy, the sleeves hanging to the elbows, and his belt is cinched tight around a narrow waist that looks like it was still being fed by mustard sandwiches. The photograph captures, in real terms, one of Billy's last moments as a West Berkeley boy.

He wrapped an affectionate arm around Jensen's shoulder and offered a thin smile.

As much as Billy had realized a childhood dream, having willed his way from ramshackle 7th Street to the most famous sports team in the world, he was far from satisfied. The New York newspaper accounts the next day mostly focused on Jensen and called Billy "a utility infielder." Billy also soon learned that he was taking a pay cut to go to the Yankees, his salary dropping from $9,000 to $7,500. Jensen, meanwhile, was seen as a possible heir to DiMaggio in center field (in 1949, Mickey Mantle was a wild-armed shortstop in Class D ball). Jensen had signed a three-year contract worth $80,000.

The day after Billy was sold to the Yankees, the *New York Times* did use that word again — *sparkplug* — in describing "the sprightly 21-year-old from the Coast." They also identified him as Alfred M. Martin, another thing that annoyed Billy to no end. No one called him "Alfred." At least not to his face.

Billy, who had never been east of Texas, joined the Yankees the next spring, although not before another brief visit to a San Francisco hospital.

"Another nose operation," said Lew Figone. "But at least this one worked. It was finally smaller."

Billy's family does not recall any prominent sendoff when Billy left in February for what the Yankees were calling an instructional league — a pre–spring training camp in Phoenix.

Billy's friend Billy Castell recalls being in the house at 1632 7th Street just before Billy departed.

"His mom gave him a pep talk like only she could," Castell said. "You know, practically all four-letter words. She said, 'Now listen, don't you let any of those fucking New York big shots give you any fucking bullshit. You know how to fucking play baseball just as fucking good as they do.'

"Billy just looked at her and when she turned away he looked at me and smiled. But I think he heard her."

Phoenix was an intermediate stop in many ways. It was also a some-

what secretive gathering — in 1950 you could have forty-three professional baseball players and ten coaches work out for two weeks in Arizona
and have no one know it in the New York offices of the commissioner of
baseball. There was no local TV news let alone smartphones and Internet
service. The Yankees surreptitiously ordered some of their best young
prospects, rookies, and young players to Phoenix. By 1951, Commissioner Happy Chandler had found out about this "league" and decided it
breached the rules prohibiting spring training from starting earlier than
early March. It was henceforth prohibited.

But in 1950, before anyone caught on, the cream of the Yankees' young
crop stepped off trains in Phoenix, including a shy eighteen-year-old
Oklahoman named Mickey Mantle. Yogi Berra, though he had already
logged more than a thousand Major League at-bats, came from St. Louis.
Syd Thrift, a lanky first baseman from Virginia who would never make
the Major Leagues but would become a pioneering general manager for
the Pittsburgh Pirates in the 1980s and a not-so-successful one for the
Yankees in 1989, was there. Whitey Herzog, an outfielder who later spent
many a postseason matching managerial wits with Billy, was there from
Illinois. A smiling Whitey Ford, whose nickname then and forevermore
was "Slick," stepped off a plane he had boarded near his home on Long
Island.

The instructional league was not a league at all except that the congregation occasionally played scrimmage games in the afternoon. The intent
of the gathering was mostly to inculcate in the young players the Yankee
Way as preached by Casey Stengel and his lieutenants, principally Frank
Crosetti, who had played seventeen consecutive seasons as a Yankees infielder beginning in 1932.

Billy had two advantages in Phoenix. He already knew the Yankee Way
because it was the unique baseball proselytization of Casey Stengel, with
which Billy was quite familiar. His second advantage was that he felt confident he could get away with most anything because he was "Casey's boy."

"I remember that we had a curfew and we were supposed to stay away
from the dog track in Phoenix," said Berra, whose lifelong friendship with
Billy began in 1950 at Phoenix. "So the first few nights we were good and
stayed in but it was boring. By the fourth night, Billy and I just decided to
go to the dog track.

"I said, 'What if the old man finds out?' And Billy said, 'Case? He won't care. He's probably there right now himself.' So we went to the dog track that night and almost every night after that."

There was a popular bar at the dog track. The Phoenix-based Yankees, even if they were the youngest ones in the system, were celebrities. Billy thought to himself that he could get used to this kind of status.

Thrift was Billy's roommate in Phoenix.

"Billy had a gleaming smile and a twinkle in his eye," Thrift said. "Women loved that look he would give them. It was a look that said, 'Hey, we're having fun over here. Why don't you come join us?' And they did most of the time.

"But he was all business once the baseball part started the next day. And the thing I remember most about that camp was that he was cocky from the moment he walked into the clubhouse. He was telling everyone how he was going to take Jerry Coleman's starting job."

Coleman, the Yankees' second baseman, had just won the American League Rookie of the Year award.

Many years later, Thrift said he learned something about Billy that he did not know in 1950.

"In the 1970s, I reminded him of how brash and boastful he was when we were roomies way back when," Thrift said. "And you know what he said to me? He said, 'Syd, I was scared shitless. I just wasn't going to show it.'"

Though less verbose, Ford was nearly as self-assured, and he and Billy became immediate pals. Like a little bug drawn to the incandescence of a neon light in the darkness, the shy Mantle saddled up next to Whitey and Billy, captivated by their worldliness and street smarts. Mantle was so raw and discomfited that the simplest of logistics could confound him. The first day of practice he had missed the players' bus to the ballpark. Stengel had to swing by in his car and rescue him.

The Phoenix tutelage did not last long. The defending World Series champions surreptitiously convened a camp to hone the next generation of champions, but then the newest Yankees were spirited to the epicenter of elite baseball in March 1950: Miller Huggins Field, the Yankees' official spring training home in St. Petersburg, Florida.

If Billy was shaking inside as he entered his first truly big-league clubhouse, he did not show it. Writers in spring training then and now devote much of their early attention to new faces on the team, especially if they are new Major Leaguers. And once they had done breathless stories on the Samson-like Jensen, they wandered over to the angular, intriguing Alfred M. Martin.

He welcomed them with a declaration he wanted to get off his chest before the first of their questions.

As Milton Gross, a popular writer from the *New York Post,* wrote, "The new kid from the Coast wanted us to know something. 'The name is Billy Martin,' he said. 'And don't you forget it.'"

9

BILLY HAD NEVER BEEN in a baseball camp like the one at Miller Huggins Field, the ballpark named for the Yankees manager who had won three World Series and six American League pennants in the 1920s. Yes, there was Stengel's usual instruction-based process, a series of stations with each one stressing a different baseball fundamental: bunting, sliding, baserunning, relay throws, and fielding by position. But here future Hall of Famers awaited him at virtually every station.

The peerless DiMaggio glided around the diamond in the baserunning drill. Tony Lazzeri, the five-time world champ and now a coach, ran the outfield/infield relay station. Bill Dickey was tutoring the catchers, including Berra, and Stengel took the outfielders. Phil Rizzuto was the infield leader. Johnny Mize, thirty-eight years old and sweating in the Florida heat, was flawlessly picking grounders off the Bermuda grass near first base, showing everyone why he was nicknamed "The Big Cat."

That's seven players who would eventually have plaques in Cooperstown, and that grouping does not include two other future Hall of Famers who would join the team in less than a year: Ford, a 1950 mid-season call-up, and Mantle, who debuted at the big-league spring training camp in 1951.

Billy knew he was among baseball royalty. These were players whose names he had read in newspapers at the drugstore at the corner of 9th Street and University Avenue. He had watched them in newsreels at the Rivoli Theatre on San Pablo Avenue. Now they were standing next to him.

"It could be an intimidating environment," said Coleman, who remained in baseball into his late eighties as a radio analyst for the San Diego Padres (and was inducted into the broadcasting wing of the Baseball Hall of Fame). "It was an atmosphere of high achievers. And Casey Stengel ran a tight ship between the lines. Off the field, it was different, but when Casey was on the field, he was all work and no play."

Billy noticed the change in his mentor immediately. The clowning jester who had entertained fans from the third-base box at Oaks Park was stern at Miller Huggins Field. He was no longer a baseball lifer having a good time. He was a bona fide baseball genius, having won with the Yankees the Major League Manager of the Year award in 1949, and a fawning New York press corps hung on his every word.

Billy kept his place in this setting, at least for a while. He accepted jersey number 12, because the veteran George "Snuffy" Stirnweiss had already claimed number 1. He performed all the drills as instructed and kept his mouth shut.

Rizzuto, the 1948 American League Most Valuable Player, did not know what to make of the new young second baseman from California in those earliest days, but he was certain something was bugging Billy.

"You know how Billy gets that look when he's frustrated?" Rizzuto said years later after he had become one of Billy's closest friends. "He had that look all day when he first got there. I remember thinking, 'Holy cow, this kid is going to explode. Something is bothering him.'

"I could always see when something was getting under his skin and that's a good thing to know when you're around him."

At the 1950 spring training camp, what was irking Billy was the adulation being heaped on Coleman. Frank Crosetti, who had played his entire seventeen-year career for the Yankees, was schooling the middle infielders on the fine art of playing shortstop and second base.

Billy valued Crosetti's guidance and had regard for him for a variety of reasons. He was from the same North Beach San Francisco neighborhood that had produced the DiMaggio brothers, Lazzeri, and the current backup Yankees catcher, Charlie Silvera, who was becoming one of Billy's good friends on the team. Crosetti, known as "The Crow," had been an All-Star and a steady mainstay up the middle on four successive Yankees championship teams from 1936 to 1939. He was Billy's kind of player, renowned for the hidden-ball trick and for shoving an umpire during an argument in the middle of the 1942 World Series.

But Crosetti was enamored with the fielding stylings of Coleman, whom he had praised for a week on the practice diamond. Coleman was smooth and elegant, and Crosetti wanted all the Yankees infielders to turn the double play that way. As Casey Stengel already knew, Billy had a thing about being told how to turn the double play. Plus, he had since received hundreds of hours of additional instruction on the pivot at second base from Cookie Lavagetto. And he planned on taking Coleman's job anyway.

On the fifth day of Crosetti trying to get Billy to emulate Coleman, Billy erupted.

"That's not how I learned to turn the double play; I've got a better way," Billy said loudly in that strident, high-pitched voice that carried across every baseball diamond whether it was Kenney Park or Comiskey Park.

As usual, everyone heard him now, especially the Yankees veterans.

"No one talked back to the Crow," Rizzuto said. "I was shocked."

Before anyone could say anything else, Billy took a baseball from Crosetti and demonstrated his way of turning the double play. Crosetti disagreed and told Billy why. Billy countered with the whys and hows taught him by Lavagetto. It was near heresy to be quoting a former Brooklyn Dodger infielder in a Yankees camp, but Crosetti let the debate go on for a while.

"The Crow saw that Billy had thought about this and practiced it — he wasn't just starting an argument," Rizzuto said. "The old Crow did not agree, but he let Billy be. And meanwhile, Stengel was in the outfield listening — he always saw everything — but he never said a word.

"We just moved on and Billy kept doing it his way."

The Yankees' third baseman, Bobby Brown, who was attending medical school in the off-season, recalled the conversation more philosophically.

"It was a baseball theory squabble," Brown, who was standing a few feet away, said. "We hadn't seen that before. But we were learning a lot of things about Billy that first year."

By all accounts, Crosetti did not take it personally. Instead, he instructed Billy in all the little things on the field that mattered — hitting behind runners to move them over a base, bunting, hit-and-runs, and purposeful sacrifice flies. Crosetti in his day had what baseball men of the era called "a clever bat." Billy liked the sound of that. He wanted to learn how to have a clever bat. Throughout the spring of 1950, like other old-timers before him, Crosetti was happy to oblige his inquisitive — if argumentative — young charge.

"It was hard not to like and help Billy," Brown, who became a cardiologist and eventually the American League president, said. "He had an aggressive personality, and at first I think some guys were put off by him.

But in time we saw that he was just so determined to get better. People wondered what made him tick."

To the astonishment of everyone, the player who seemed most curious about Billy was DiMaggio, who befriended few teammates.

"Yeah, Joe loved hanging around with Billy," Rizzuto said. "It was the most weird thing. Here was Joe all reserved, quiet, and perfectly groomed and Billy who was loud and noisy."

Said Brown, "I think DiMaggio was intrigued by Billy. Like Casey was, like a lot of us were."

As the 1950 regular season began, Billy still did not have a regular position on the field. It was Coleman at second base, Rizzuto at shortstop, and the platoon of Brown and the right-handed-hitting Billy Johnson at third base. But Billy went to New York with the big club that spring anyway, an almost magical accomplishment.

In his autobiography, Billy wrote that he saw Yankee Stadium for the first time from the train that took the team from Florida back to New York. He had seen the stadium on the television at a West Berkeley barber shop — he did not have a TV at home — and he had listened to many Yankees World Series games on the radio. But stepping from the train, he was now walking inside the imposing concrete edifice that loomed over River Avenue, the most famous stadium in the world. As other players unpacked at their lockers, Billy quickly scurried onto the field.

"I stood there for the longest while, staring into the grandstands and the bleachers and the dugouts, noticing how beautifully the grass was cut," he wrote.

He then made his way to the dugouts, thinking that these were the same dugouts where Lou Gehrig and Babe Ruth had waited to hit.

"I reached down and touched the steps where they used to walk up and down," Billy wrote. "I was just so happy to be a Yankee."

The acclimation to his new environs was made infinitely easier because of his friendship with DiMaggio. The Yankee Clipper squired Billy around Manhattan, showing him how a Yankees celebrity could own the town. DiMaggio brought Billy to the best tailors and restaurants. Both kinds of establishments were happy to have representatives of the regal, revered Yankees and would not charge them a dime if they posed for a picture that would be put in a prominent place on the wall for all to see. DiMaggio introduced Billy to the scores of women who flocked to

DiMaggio's side, a benefit Billy much appreciated and did not soon tire of. Because DiMaggio preferred blondes, Billy did, too.

"They were the original odd couple," Berra said decades later. "Behind their backs we called them the big dago and the little dago."

And Billy kept his youthful irrepressibility. DiMaggio may have refined him some but he did not change him. An oft-told 1950 story had the always-dapper DiMaggio arriving in the clubhouse before one game in a pressed white shirt and light gray suit.

Billy ran over to greet him holding a fountain pen and a baseball he said he wanted autographed for someone back in California. But as Billy thrust the pen at the Yankee Clipper, it squirted ink all over DiMaggio's white shirt and suit.

The clubhouse went silent. DiMaggio was aghast. Billy waited a bit, then confessed that it was a gag. He had bought disappearing ink at a novelty store.

"I still thought Joe might slug him," Rizzuto said. "Joe was steamed. Billy kept saying, 'It will disappear, Joe. Really, it will.' But it was a tense few minutes until it did.

"Then ten minutes later, Joe was joking around with Billy again. Billy just had a way with Joe. Nobody else on the team would have dreamed of pulling any kind of prank on Joe."

Charlie Silvera, a catcher, was another Bay Area product who knew Billy from informal workouts at Oaks Park. He became a major Yankees prospect, more valued as a youngster than Berra had been. (People always underestimated Yogi.) Silvera lived with Billy during the 1950 season and became Billy's lifelong friend, coaching for him in Minnesota, Detroit, and Texas.

Silvera now sees 1950 from a different perspective. Billy may have been DiMaggio's buddy, but that did not earn him much playing time and that, Silvera said, vexed Billy.

"What I remember about 1950 was how hard we worked to try and get ourselves into the lineup," Silvera said more than sixty years later. "Yeah, Billy went out with Joe a little but not like he did with Mickey later when he was an established starter. In 1950, we were at the end of the roster in every way. We were desperate to do something impressive."

Like many other Yankees, Billy, Silvera, and outfielder Hank Bauer lived at the Concourse Plaza, a hotel four blocks west of Yankee Stadium's outfield walls. The Concourse Plaza was an ornate, twelve-story redbrick hotel with three vast ballrooms that hosted the speeches of presidential candidates as well as countless weddings and bar mitzvahs. It stood on a hill at the corner of the Grand Concourse and 161st Street at a time when that part of the Bronx was a moneyed place of refuge for corporate titans eager to escape Manhattan's gritty bustle.

Not only did the Yankees stay at the Concourse; so did visiting baseball teams, and the New York football Giants, too.

Billy walked into the decorative, sumptuous lobby of the Concourse Plaza a week before opening day in 1950, turned to Silvera, and said incredulously, "We're living here?"

But the Concourse Plaza did more than awe the newest Yankees; it was within easy walking distance of Yankee Stadium. Bauer had a starting job, but Billy and Silvera quickly developed a routine that they kept throughout the early months of the season. They woke early and went to the stadium for early batting practice. The clubhouses sometimes would not even be open, so a coach left a bucket of balls in the dugout.

Billy and Silvera took turns pitching to each other until the bucket was empty. Then they would run around the field and retrieve the balls and hit and pitch again until the regulars showed up for their batting practice. The Yankees played no more than fifteen of their seventy-seven home games at night in the early 1950s, so Billy and Silvera could get in at least two hours of practice before yielding the field.

The Yankees opened the 1950 season at Boston's Fenway Park. Eager to avenge their 1949 collapse, the Red Sox jumped out to a 9–0 lead through five innings. The Yankees scored four runs in the sixth, and in the eighth, with two runners on, Stengel sent Billy to the plate as a pinch hitter for his first Major League at-bat.

Before the game, reporters asked Billy what he thought of Fenway Park, which even then was steeped in baseball history.

"It's a ballpark and if it's a ballpark I can hit in it," Billy answered.

And what of the big wall in left field?

"It's close," Billy said.

Now in the eighth, Billy faced Boston's crafty left-hander Mel Parnell, who had won 25 games in 1949. The Pulitzer Prize–winning columnist Arthur Daley described the scene for the *New York Times*: "Up to the plate stepped Billy Martin, the cocky 21-year-old kid from the Coast, for his major league debut at bat. Billy was so awed and terrified that he spilled a double off the left field wall."

A run scored and the Yankees' rally continued until they had batted around. Billy's second Major League at-bat came with the bases loaded. He singled to center field for two more runs. It was the first time in Major League history that a player had two hits in one inning of his inaugural game. The Yankees won, 15–10; the *New York Daily News* referred to Billy's hits as "lightning bolts from an effervescent rookie."

Billy did not play for another two weeks. Later in life he joked, "I guess if I had gotten three hits I would have sat for three weeks."

As much as it was apparent to everyone that Billy was Casey's pet, the players had learned from the previous season that Stengel was not sentimental when it came to making out his lineup. He wanted to win and he could be as cold and unemotional as an auditor when it came to apportioning playing time.

"He benched anyone anytime, sometimes without rhyme or reason," Coleman said. "He had his plan but we weren't always apprised of it and we didn't always understand it. We just did it."

Billy sat at Casey's knee just as he had at Oaks Park, and he pestered him about playing time. Casey's response was that Billy could contribute in other ways. Knowing how skilled Billy was in the art of bench jockeying, he encouraged his rookie to stand on the top step of the dugout and get the attention of the opposition. He did not have to tell him twice.

"And when Billy did get on the field in 1950, he made sure people heard him," Coleman said. "Phil Rizzuto was kind of a quiet guy out there. So was Bobby Brown. Joe Collins didn't talk much at first. Billy took charge, yelling commands, encouraging everyone."

Added Brown, "And that voice of his — I'm sure they heard him fifteen rows into the stands."

Perhaps they did, and it seemed they liked what they heard. Billy became a player that the home crowd noticed. Always in motion, always jabbering at someone, he was entertaining and people cheered for him. Billy's Yankee Stadium fan base, which would stay loyal to him with unwavering devotion for thirty-eight more years, got its start in the spring of 1950.

But playing sparingly was no way for a twenty-one-year-old to develop. Plus the Yankees' roster had not only Coleman but his predecessor at second base, the aging Snuffy Stirnweiss. Carrying three second base-men was also costly to the team. After the day game on May 15, Stengel called Billy into his office to inform him that they were sending him to the Yankees' minor league team in Kansas City.

"Give us a few weeks and we'll sell Stirnweiss and bring you back," Stengel said.

It was a day before Billy's twenty-second birthday. Surprised and embarrassed, he wept in the manager's office. Casey, who hated seeing Billy distraught, consoled him and conceded that he did not completely agree with the decision, which ultimately was made by general manager George Weiss, whose decisions were often made with a different motivation. Weiss received a bonus annually from Yankees ownership if he kept the payroll below a certain number. Casey and Billy talked for a while until finally Casey suggested that if Billy really did not like Weiss's decision making he ought to go tell him so. It was not good advice. It was the kind of thing that a twenty-one-year-old Casey Stengel would have done, and it's also the reason that despite his .284 lifetime batting average Stengel was traded four times in a fourteen-year playing career.

But Billy didn't need much of a push, especially from his mentor. He confronted Weiss, something not in vogue in 1950. Curt Flood's reserve clause suit to end what amounted to slavery in professional team sports was nineteen years away. Few players, let alone rookies, angrily spoke up to top executives (if they spoke to them at all). Weiss was cool and reserved and expected the same demeanor from his Yankees. He tolerated Stengel's eccentricities but demanded that the manager have a certain standard of comportment in his presence.

"You'll be sorry for this," Billy shouted at Weiss.

Whatever relationship the two had at the moment only took a turn for the worse. And it never got better.

Billy went to Class AAA Kansas City, and upset as he was, he did not show it on the field, compiling a .466 slugging percentage with 6 doubles, 2 triples, and 4 homers in 29 games.

Stirnweiss was traded to the St. Louis Browns exactly a month after Billy's demotion, and Billy was recalled from Kansas City the next day. A week later, he drove in the winning run with a single. But playing time was still sparse. On the road, he roomed with Rizzuto, who liked to be in bed by ten at the latest.

"We talked baseball until we fell asleep," Rizzuto said.

Rizzuto noticed something else about his new roommate.

"He kept a Bible in his suitcase," Rizzuto said. "I'm not saying he read it every night. But he did read it. And in the middle of a train or bus ride somewhere, guys would be carrying on or arguing about something and out of nowhere Billy would quote a Bible passage that applied to the argument or whatever.

"Guys would stop and look at him, like, 'Did Billy just say that?'"

Sitting out of the lineup annoyed Billy, but it did afford him an inside view of what made the Yankees the most successful sports franchise of the twentieth century. It was a twenty-five-man unit, and each player was held to a standard passed on through generations and motivated by the most primitive of incentives: money.

With the average player's salary around $13,000 and the check per player for winning the World Series at about $5,700, the Yankees cared deeply about winning in the regular season and the postseason for what it meant to their bankbooks. If a Yankee did not make a throw to the right base and it cost the Yankees a run, and in the end, a game — even during a random game in July — that Yankee heard about it from another Yankee.

When a young Berra did not run out a pop-up and it fell for a single when it could have been a double had Berra been running hard — and when a subsequent single would have scored Berra with the tying run in what became a Yankees loss — Berra was upbraided in the dugout immediately afterward by several veteran Yankees.

"Don't fuck with our money," the burly, intimidating Yankees outfielder Charlie Keller growled at Berra.

There were other protocols. Yankees were not supposed to publicly complain about playing time because Yankees supported whoever was trying to win the game that day. Reserves kept their mouths shut and stayed ready. Even personal habits were scrutinized and evaluated based on how they might impact the team.

Yankees who arrived late for batting practice or did not partake in the daily fielding practice — Major League teams took team-wide infield and outfield practice before every game until the mid-1980s — were rebuked.

There would be an admonishing query: "Where were you?"

"In all my time with the Yankees I never heard one guy say, 'Have fun,'" infielder Gil McDougald said. "It was the opposite — 'Get serious, we have to win this game.' Nobody thought failure was fun. After the game, we had fun. First, you had to win the game."

It was all about the paycheck, and it was a deadly serious pact that twenty-five Yankees made to each other. Devotion to the team always came first. Wives and girlfriends were not supposed to get in the way of anything related to what happened on the field. Even staying out late would be noticed and commented on if the other players thought it was affecting a player's on-the-field performance. It was no room full of saints and early risers, but there was a code: Never let it cost the team on the field. As the Yankees veteran pitcher Eddie Lopat said, "It doesn't matter if my infielders are beer drinkers, whiskey drinkers, or tea drinkers as long as they turn the double play. And if they don't, I hate them equally."

Billy observed and learned the all-important Yankee etiquette from his seat on the bench in 1950, and he absorbed the efficiency of its ways. The Yankee Way was more complex than he had probably perceived, but it appealed to Billy because of its elemental purpose. Everything a Yankee did was in the service of winning.

Billy went to the plate only 39 times in 34 games in 1950, hitting .250 with 1 home run and 8 RBIs.

His roommate, Rizzuto, had the best year of his career and was voted the league's Most Valuable Player after he batted .324 in 734 plate appearances with 7 home runs and 66 RBIs. Rizzuto turned 123 double plays and had just 14 errors in 1,351.2 innings in the field.

"Years later, the Yankees' brass talked about Billy being a bad influence on guys with the club," Rizzuto said. "All I know is the year he roomed with me I won the MVP. A couple years later, he roomed with Yogi and Yogi won the MVP. In 1956, he was rooming with Mickey, and Mickey won the MVP. Some bad influence."

The Yankees swept the Philadelphia Phillies in the World Series that October, but Billy never got on the field in any of the four games. Coleman was the series MVP. Billy was happy for his buddy Whitey Ford, who won the clinching game of the series, but he felt odd in the champagne-soaked clubhouse afterward. He always wanted to be a part of the biggest games. The $5,738 winning players' check was a salve for his hurt, though, and Billy headed home to Berkeley. Stengel went with him; he was managing a barnstorming team of all-stars in the Bay Area that month and had asked Billy to play for him.

Billy was playing for Casey again "on the Coast." So much had changed and so much had not changed.

10

THE ALL-STAR TEAM CASEY was parading around Northern California had the usual Bay Area baseball talent, some Oakland Oaks and San Francisco Seals players, Silvera, Ernie Lombardi, and Billy. On October 20, 1950, thirteen days after the World Series ended, Billy played in a late-afternoon game for Casey's all-stars at Oaks Park. He scurried from the park after the game, quickly grabbing his things and dashing for his car. That wasn't Billy's postgame style. He usually liked to sit and have a few beers and talk about the game. About the only thing that made Billy ditch a clubhouse in that kind of a hurry was a woman.

And on this Friday evening, there was a woman waiting for Billy. It was eighteen-year-old Lois Berndt, dressed in a wedding gown at St. Ambrose Church. Billy arrived fifteen minutes late and hastily changed into his rented black tuxedo in a vestibule behind the altar. Somehow his dress shoes had not made the trip to the church.

Billy came out for the wedding wearing his baseball shoes. Years later, Lois called it an omen. But the wedding went on, and all of Billy's West Berkeley friends were there. Billy eventually borrowed a friend's brown dress shoes, though they clashed with his black tux.

Billy said that he got married because his buddy Howard Noble had married his girlfriend, who was Lois's best friend. He also called Lois "a doll, a real pretty girl."

"Lois kept telling me how depressed she was with me away from home playing ball, and all that same old baloney you always hear," Billy wrote in 1980.

Billy's sister Pat said Billy was not dragged to the altar. In fact, as she would do with each of his four wives, Pat tried to talk him out of the marriage and failed.

"I said, 'Bill, this isn't the right girl,'" said Pat, who conceded she never liked Lois, whom she had known since they were in junior high school together. "I said, 'She just wants to get married.' But he wouldn't listen. I think he was lonely. He wanted something to hold on to. Bill was like that."

All of Billy's closest friends from the 1940s to the 1960s, whether they knew him in West Berkeley or west of Minneapolis twenty years later, agreed that Billy always yearned for a traditional family life of the kind that existed in a Norman Rockwell painting. Ever the romantic, he had a vision for his life that came to him, some said, in the dark of the Rivoli Theatre as he watched Hollywood's depiction of small-town, stable family life in the 1940s. One can imagine young Billy falling in love with the quiet country qualities portrayed in *The Yearling* — he was the ultimate sentimentalist — or being wooed by the homey contented life from *It's a Wonderful Life.*

And then Billy left the theater and walked onto chaotic, grimy San Pablo Avenue and headed back to the tumult of his 7th Street home. But he could dream.

Lois Berndt would eventually marry one of Billy's classmates, Sam Curtain, and she remained in the Berkeley area for most of her life. In a 2012 interview, Lois said that she and Billy married "because it seemed like the natural thing to do after all the years of going out. And Billy, in his heart, wanted a home life."

Billy's Berkeley friends and family stressed that the biggest attraction for connecting with Lois was the foundation she offered because Lois came from a close, traditional family where the dinner table wasn't constantly punctuated by four-letter-word arguments. It was Billy's dream to have the same kind of family life, something he brought up in newspaper interviews for the next three decades. And at various times Billy lived his dream. Being a family man was important to him. He had multiple suburban homes in his life, charming residences that seemed to be right out of TV's *Father Knows Best.* But the first of those homes was within the home of Lois Berndt's parents, where the Martin honeymooners lived in November 1950. Billy had respect for Lois's father and lived by his rules in the Berndt household. But he did not stay long.

A family member of another sort, Uncle Sam, intervened to call him away. The Korean War had begun on June 25, and by December, President Harry Truman called for an emergency increase in the number of men drafted into the armed forces. Billy became one of the more than 1.5 million conscripted during the next three years, and he was not happy when he left Berkeley for basic training at Fort Ord near Monterey Bay in Northern California. Fort Ord was considered one of the best places to be stationed in the country — the beach was nearby and the weather was wonderful — but Billy was miserable.

Eight months earlier he had finally started playing for the Yankees, and now he was playing soldier instead? It was more than he could bear, and he immediately asked for a discharge by the start of spring training in 1951. His first requests for a discharge were denied, but with the help of a commanding officer who was a baseball fan — and a former Oaks fan — he was instructed in the various hardship discharges available and how best to be granted one.

Billy told the army that his stepfather was ill and had recently lost his job, which made Billy the sole means of support for his mother, father, and siblings, as well as his wife.

According to some of Billy's family and friends, the hardship claim was mostly a sham. Jack Downey had voluntarily reduced his workload, perhaps at Billy's urging. Billy was indeed now subsidizing the household with a biweekly check of $80, but it was by choice so he could get back to the Yankees. For a while it looked like Billy's pleas were going to be ignored. Finally, in March there came word that Billy's hardship ploy had worked and the paperwork, which might take a month, was being processed.

Word of Billy's imminent discharge made its way to New York and, of course, to Berkeley where the *Berkeley Gazette* ran a story about Billy's "hardship." When he returned to the Berndts' house on a weekend leave from Fort Ord, he was not as welcome in the neighborhood as he had been a few months earlier. Many young men from Berkeley had been drafted, to serve not at Fort Ord but in the ferocity of war throughout the Korean peninsula. Billy's hardship discharge, arriving at a time when his able-bodied brothers, Tudo and Jackie, were still living in the area, did not sit well with the locals, a group highly suspicious of the powerful or the privileged pulling strings to get their way. It came off as something a Goat would do, and there was no greater insult west of San Pablo Avenue.

"There was resentment," said Rube de Alba, whose older brother was sent to Korea. "Some people were cold to Billy. They talked about it behind his back and he knew it."

Billy was perhaps Berkeley's most famous resident at the time. The *Berkeley Gazette* published several letters to the editor that were critical of Billy's discharge. It made Billy uncomfortable in a way he had never felt in the familiar streets of West Berkeley.

In mid-April, with his hardship paperwork completed, Billy was happy to get out of California and back to New York, and he hoped his absence would help the army deferment issue dissipate.

On April 27 against the Boston Red Sox, Billy made his first appearance for the Yankees in 1951 when he ran onto the field to pinch run for Johnny Mize. He was, for the first time with the Yankees, wearing jersey number 1. But Billy's presence in Yankees pinstripes instead of a wartime uniform was noted in the newspapers, in part because he was not the only young Yankee deferred from the armed services.

Mickey Mantle was in a feud with his local draft board over his claim that he had a degenerative bone condition, osteomyelitis, that made him unfit for duty. The condition sounded believable until people turned on their televisions and saw Mantle galloping across the Yankee Stadium outfield as fast as a deer and as strong as a horse.

Mantle had already supplanted Jackie Jensen as the heir apparent to DiMaggio, who had announced on March 2 that 1951 would be his last season. For now Mantle was toiling in right field, beating out routine ground balls with a stunning burst of speed from the left-handed batter's box, and clouting long home runs to all fields.

"He has more speed than any slugger and more slug than any speedster," said Stengel. "This kid ain't logical. He's too good."

Everyone agreed that Mantle's talent for baseball was out of this world, and off the field, he was the most unworldly rookie any Yankees veteran had ever seen. Embarrassed by the sharp twang in his voice, Mantle talked softly — if at all — and he avoided eye contact. The baseball writers terrified him, and he hid from them whenever he could.

Mantle longed to be at ease around the veteran players, but he instead sidestepped them and retreated to his rented room at the Concourse Plaza. The Yankees' dependable outfielder Hank Bauer, who had moved to an apartment over the Stage Deli with Charlie Silvera, coaxed Mantle into a few visits to midtown Manhattan. Bauer helped Mantle buy a couple of sport jackets and showed him around a bit. They stopped at a few bars where Mickey, who was engaged to marry his high school sweetheart, discovered that New York women introduce themselves to ballplayers.

Still, Mantle had many lonely hours after games at the Concourse Plaza. Until, that is, Billy, now a second-year player who acted as if he had been in the big leagues for ten years, started taking Mantle to dinner after games.

"Billy liked people and I think it bothered him that Mickey was so un-comfortable," Bobby Brown said. "It was not a combination that surprised me. Joe DiMaggio was starting to recede at that point. Billy gravitated to Mickey."

Though Billy was about to turn twenty-three and Mickey was nineteen, the two had a connection and were soon acting like fraternity brothers away from home for the first time. Water pistol fights in the hallways of Yankee Stadium, food fights in the clubhouse, and whoopie cushions on the seats in the dining car on the team train — it was all in a day's fun for the M & M boys, a designation given to them in 1951 (ten years before it was resurrected to describe the more famous Yankees home-run-hitting pair of Mantle and Roger Maris). Early in the season, they acquired a new device, the instant camera later known as a Polaroid. It produced some-thing once thought to be impossible: a photograph thirty or forty seconds after it was taken. Billy and Mickey thought it was endlessly hysterical to use the instant camera to take pictures of teammates on the toilet. Their goal was to catch everyone on the team, except DiMaggio and Stengel, in this setting. And they apparently succeeded, posting the photos in the training room when no one was looking.

Gil McDougald, a skilled rookie that year who sometimes was called the "third M" on the team, recalled that "Mickey and Billy would do all these things and start giggling until they had tears in their eyes."

"They really were the best of friends," McDougald said. "Some of the older guys wanted to wring their necks at times, but they were like two little kids. People would just smirk and say, 'There they go again.'"

There was a kinship between the two that others saw as almost sibling-like.

"They brought out the best in each other," Bobby Richardson said, al-though that was the opposite of what some people, like their future wives, would say. "Billy had a facility with people that Mickey benefited from, and Mickey had a good-natured acceptance of people and situations that softened Billy."

Tony Kubek, another Yankees infielder who came to the team late in Billy's Yankees career but who stayed in touch with both men throughout their lives, said their connection was unshakable.

"When you were with them, they talked to each other like no one else was even there," Kubek said. "They went off in their own world. The bond never wavered."

The bond was also a source of never-ending mischief. One night in Boston Mickey and Billy arrived at the team's hotel fifteen minutes after Stengel's midnight curfew. Before entering, they gazed through the revolving front door, and across the lobby they saw Casey telling stories to entertain a bevy of writers.

They went around to a back entrance used by the hotel kitchen staff. It was one of their favorite maneuvers. But this time the back door was locked. There was a transom high above the door.

"Billy said that if I boosted him up, he'd crawl through the transom and open the door for me," Mantle said. "So I stood on a garbage can and he climbed on my shoulders and then he scooted through the transom.

"After a minute I hear him shouting through the door, 'Hey, Mick, this door is chained shut. I can't open it. I'll see you tomorrow.' And he went to our room."

Mantle, who was wearing a new, expensive sharkskin suit, piled three garbage cans on top of each other and, bracing himself with the extension of a fire escape, tried to get through the transom as well.

"I fell a few times and ripped some holes in my new suit," he said. "I knocked over the garbage cans and had lettuce hanging off me and rotten tomatoes stuck to the sleeves. I was a mess but I eventually got through the transom.

"When I got to the room, Billy was asleep. When we got up the next morning, Billy said, 'Why does this room smell like garbage?' I think the cleaning bill for my suit was almost as much as the curfew fine might have been."

For a while that summer, Lois had come to live with Billy at the Concourse Plaza, but even with the Yankees at home she was often left waiting. Mickey and Billy had a habit of making lengthy detours from Yankee Stadium to the Concourse Plaza, four blocks away. There was always another adventure to pursue. On the road, teammates got used to hearing the frat-boy duo of the Yankees giggling in hotel hallways at 2:00 a.m. or later.

Stengel considered splitting them up on the road, forcing them to room with other players.

"What good would that do?" Billy said. "It would just keep two other guys up late."

But there was a problem, at least in 1951. Mantle's debut with the team was not going as promised. He had holes in his swing, and big-league pitchers always find them in a new slugger by the end of May. Baseball history is replete with guys who hit 15 home runs in April and May of their rookie season and only 50 more homers for the rest of their careers. Only the good ones who adjust survive. American League pitchers in 1951 adjusted, but by mid-July, Mantle had not and was sent down to AAA Kansas City.

That gave Lois her husband back for a while, but it would have been a happier experience had Billy been playing more than sparingly. McDougald, who was platooning with Coleman at second base and also playing at third, was having a season that would win him the 1951 American League Rookie of the Year award. Billy played only occasionally. By all accounts, he continued to adhere to the Yankee Way. He did not complain. He worked on his fundamentals, continuing to perfect his double-play pivot — his way. And he had not dropped his friendship with DiMaggio, who was struggling through a variety of injuries and certain he had made the right decision to retire at the end of the year.

DiMaggio also had begun dating Marilyn Monroe, and Billy had dinner with Joe and Marilyn on a few occasions.

"She was polite," Billy said. "And she was much more beautiful in person than she was in the movies."

Billy gave Monroe credit for DiMaggio's late surge that season.

"He was happy again once he was going out with Marilyn Monroe," he said.

Mantle was back in New York by late August. Lois headed back to Berkeley. A New York summer in the days before air conditioning was not as inviting as it once sounded for a Northern California girl, especially with her husband on the road half the time. Billy ended up playing in 51 games during the 1951 regular season with 58 at-bats. He hit .259 with only 2 RBIs, or 6 fewer than he had in 1950.

The season was certainly a setback statistically, but there wasn't a lot of available playing time in an infield crowded by the precocious McDougald. There were other gains for Billy. He was a genuine Yankee — no more trips to the minors. And he had taken over jersey number 1, which he considered essential. Single-digit Yankees had done all right so far: Ruth, Gehrig, DiMaggio, Berra, and Dickey. Mantle in 1951 was wearing number 6.

Billy was also getting seasoning, learning the quirks of playing in the then seven American League ballparks and intensely studying the league's pitchers at a time when a batter had to acquire a dossier on just thirty opposing starting pitchers and about fifteen relief pitchers. Starters finished most games, and the ten- or twelve-man pitching staff was decades away.

Billy did his work and kept his eyes open. He was a popular player even if his teammates had to put up with his high jinks with the Polaroid and the occasional presence of an overly ostentatious blonde on his arm. And in the 1951 World Series against the New York Giants, he presaged his knack for making big plays on baseball's biggest stage.

Late in the second game of that series, the Giants, who were only two days removed from Bobby Thomson's "Shot Heard 'Round the World," trailed the Yankees 2–1. But the Giants had been threatening in several previous innings and seemed on the verge of catching up to the Yankees' starter, Eddie Lopat. In this tense setting, Bobby Brown singled and Billy pinch ran for him. Billy went to second base on a force-out, and pitcher Eddie Lopat smacked a single to center field, where Willie Mays charged and threw home. The Giants' catcher, Ray Noble, fielded the ball ahead of Billy's arrival. But as Noble went to make the tag, Billy eluded it with a classic left-legged hook slide — just as he had been schooled to do by DiMaggio, who may have been the most artful player sliding into a base in the history of the game. The insurance run let the Yankees comfortably close out the game, especially after the Giants' Monte Irvin led off the final inning with a single.

Giants manager Leo Durocher noticed Billy's contribution.

"Good slide by Martin; that's a big run," he told reporters afterward.

Durocher, who once had a fistfight with Casey Stengel under the stands at Ebbets Field, paused.

"Ol' Casey has all the answers," Durocher said. "Found the right player there."

Mantle blew out his right knee — most likely a tear of the anterior cruciate ligament — in the same game. It was a scene from a Greek tragedy. Mantle, extracted from the Oklahoma mine country like a precious gem, was running at full speed after a soft Willie Mays fly ball to right-center field. DiMaggio, a player so graceful his play seemed more like divine art than athletics, was limping on a bad heel toward the ball as well. But Mantle had been told by Stengel to cover for the aging DiMaggio, who was playing one of the last games of his career. Mantle was supposed to try to get to anything he could.

The ball was descending equidistant between the two outfielders, and at the last instant DiMaggio appeared to Mantle's right and called for the ball. Mantle knew his place.

As he later said, "No rookie could just crash into the Yankee Clipper in the middle of a sold-out Yankee Stadium during the World Series."

But as Mantle tried to stop from colliding with DiMaggio, the spikes of his right shoe also landed and stuck into a rubber drain covering. The foot came to a stop but the rest of his leg and body kept going. Mantle's knee shredded, and he went to the grass in a helpless heap as DiMaggio caught the ball next to him.

Second baseman Jerry Coleman, who served in the Marines in World War II, said he wondered if Mantle had been shot.

"That's how he went down, like a soldier in battle," Coleman said. "Just crumpled."

As Mantle curled into a fetal position and remained there for several minutes, some fans in the stands later said they thought the rookie might have had a heart attack.

As Mantle was carried off in a stretcher, his knee ballooned and he was hospitalized. But it would be at least twenty-five years before surgeons developed any techniques for repairing the ACL. Mantle would simply play with a gimpy knee for the rest of his career.

Five days later, the Yankees won the series in six games. Billy returned to Lois's parents' home — for exactly four days. Then he was off to Hawaii and Japan with a team of Yankees and West Coast stars, including DiMaggio, who toured Japan to play a series of exhibition games. Billy would be in Japan for more than a month.

Billy made it home to Berkeley for Thanksgiving. There was an uneasiness in the neighborhood. The month-long Battle of Heartbreak Ridge in an area of North Korea known as the Punchbowl had claimed more than three thousand lives, many of them from the First Cavalry Division, which had a large representation of young men from the Bay Area.

Not long after, West Berkeley learned of the death of Rube de Alba's older brother, a leader and popular figure west of San Pablo Avenue. The funeral brought together all the West Berkeley Boys. Billy was a pallbearer. Many of Billy's old friends were in uniform. His conceived hardship deferral never came up but it did not have to. A few weeks later, Rube, Billy, and some other friends went out drinking. Some teasing between Rube and Billy led to more serious taunts and then insults. The two old friends started slugging it out. In a nasty exchange, Rube got the worst of it.

They got together a few days later and both apologized.

"We stayed friends for life," de Alba said. "But we were never the same. That was it. Blame the war, the deferment, or my brother's death. I don't know for sure. But something had changed forever."

11

THE UNITED STATES ARMED services had been a thorn in Billy's side the previous year, but in 1952 the government did Billy a favor. It called Jerry Coleman back into the Marines.

Stengel announced that he would shift McDougald to third base and make Billy his regular second baseman.

"He's ready," Stengel told the writers. "I learned him everything I know."

Billy was more than ready. He was desperate. He had burned some bridges back home. He did not fit into post–World War II America in the same way as others his age as he was neither a veteran nor a family man like most of his friends and cousins. He was a professional baseball player, but so far all he had to show for it was a Pacific Coast League championship and the underwhelming total of 24 Major League hits—19 of them singles.

Joe DiMaggio, whose acceptance helped lend Billy credibility for two seasons, was no longer there to throw an arm around Billy in the clubhouse, call him "Dago," and take him to dinner with Marilyn Monroe. Billy was way past being a rookie but not accomplished enough to be called an established player either. He did not own a home or a car. He had been feted in the New York press for his potential, but they, too, were done writing about Billy Martin's future. They wanted results. And in the off-season, George Weiss had tried to trade Billy to several teams.

Billy knew he would either make it in New York now or be in Cincinnati, Pittsburgh, or Washington by the next baseball season, a banishment that could destine him to obscurity. There are no noted "fireplug" players on losing teams playing before meager crowds.

Filled with a sense of urgency, Billy was impressive as spring training opened.

Stengel regaled the reporters after the early workouts with how in harmony Rizzuto and Billy looked.

"Martin is turning the double play as quickly as anyone now," Casey said. And everyone agreed. He wasn't ballet-like as Jerry Coleman was, but he had become just as quick when it came to catching the throw and relaying it to first base. He was also wielding a hot bat. But one morning, an awkward slide snapped two bones in his ankle and Billy was sidelined for about two months. He was crestfallen. He had finally made the starting lineup and yet he was still watching from the dugout.

In May, Billy returned to the lineup during a 5–3 Yankees victory against the first-place Cleveland Indians. To that point, the Yankees were slumping by their standards, losing as much as they were winning and mired in fourth place. After one defeat, Stengel had harshly called his team "soft." DiMaggio was gone. Coleman and Brown were in the military. The Yankees lacked leaders.

"Billy never asked permission to take charge," Yogi Berra said years later, describing the Yankees of the early and mid-1950s. "It was just what he did."

On May 24, during Red Sox batting practice before that day's game, Boston's rookie Jimmy Piersall, whom the local papers called a "sharp-tongued bench jockey from Connecticut," started taunting the Yankees as they warmed up near the visitors' dugout. The slumbering Yankees trailed the third-place Red Sox by two games in the standings. Billy told Piersall to shut up.

Piersall answered by telling Billy that he only listened to "guys who actually played." That got everyone's attention. There was some more back-and-forth until Piersall called Billy "a dago busher." A busher was an unqualified amateur, short for "bush league," which meant something or someone unworthy of the Major Leagues. Billy dropped his glove to the ground and challenged Piersall to meet him under the Fenway Park grandstand.

Piersall disappeared into the Red Sox' dugout and Billy into the Yankees' dugout as both raced to their respective clubhouses. At Fenway Park, then and now, the doors to both clubhouses empty directly into a concourse used by fans walking to their seats. It was in this concrete common area behind home plate that Piersall and Billy met and started throwing punches.

Several players from both teams were there to watch, but no one thought to break it up. Billy quickly landed two right hands to Piersall's face that knocked the Red Sox player to his knees. When Piersall got up, Billy hit him again, and the two began wrestling as Billy landed more punches. Billy's cheek was cut, but Piersall was semiconscious with blood from his nose and mouth spilling onto his ripped jersey when finally Yankees coach Bill Dickey and Boston pitcher Ellis Kinder stepped in and separated the brawlers.

"What do you think now, big shot?" Billy screamed at Piersall as more players arrived at the scene.

Stengel grinned broadly when news of the fight reached his office twenty-five yards away.

"It should wake up the other tigers," he told reporters. "It's about time they realize they gotta fight harder this year. I just hope that some of the kid's fire spreads to some of the others."

Two weeks later in Cleveland, with their thirteenth victory in their last eighteen games, the Yankees trounced the Indians 11–0 to climb into first place. Billy had hit .360 since his fight with Piersall. The Yankees had won twenty of the twenty-seven games since Billy returned from his broken ankle.

Piersall would eventually be hospitalized with a mental disorder, which Billy later said made him feel ashamed.

"I didn't know he was sick like that," Billy said. "Maybe we deserve each other. Sometimes I think I'm ready for the guys with the white coats myself."

Piersall and Billy would eventually become lifelong friends. When Piersall was out of baseball in the mid-1970s, Billy got him a job in the front office of the Oakland A's. Later that same decade, when Billy was managing in Texas, he arranged for Piersall to become a team broadcaster. Piersall parlayed his Texas radio experience into a long-term job as a television announcer for the Chicago White Sox.

"I love Billy Martin," Piersall told the *New York Post* in 1980. "He helped me when I was down."

Of the 1952 fight, Piersall said, "It was just one of those things that happened in baseball back then. Neither of us held a grudge."

As spring became summer in 1952, the Yankees kept winning. Not only was Billy the everyday second baseman, but Stengel had installed Mantle as the team's center fielder after Jackie Jensen was traded in May. The Yankees won fourteen of their first seventeen games with Mantle in center field.

Billy and Mickey were fixtures in the lineup and nearly inseparable off it in 1952. They rented adjoining apartments at the Concourse Plaza where their wives had joined them. Lois had come to New York determined to be a companion to Billy for more than a few weeks a year.

Lois knew Billy was immature about the concept of matrimony — more in love with the notion of a wife to come home to than he was actually interested in the wife and the coming-home part. But seventeen months into her marriage, Lois was not giving up yet.

Now in the Bronx, on hot nights, the Mantles and Martins would leave open the door that connected their rooms to encourage a cool cross-ventilation in the days before air conditioning. The apartments were not roomy and hardly plush. They had a telephone, but a television cost $10 a month. Lois and Billy, because of Billy's larger salary, rented a TV and the Mantles would come over to watch it, although either Mickey or Merlyn Mantle would have to sit on the floor because the apartment was furnished with only one two-person couch and one chair.

When they did retire for the night and if they closed all the doors, Billy and Mickey liked to sneak out on the ledge of their adjoining balconies and try to catch the other couple in bed. They did this on the road when they knew a teammate was having a one-night stand or had arranged for an "import," as road girlfriends or steady paramours were called.

It was a childish prank and it sometimes put the two in danger — they crawled around a hotel ledge fifteen stories above the streets in Detroit one night — but Billy and Mickey were nothing if not childish.

That spring of 1952, the Martins and Mantles hung out together in the South Bronx or they dined in Manhattan on occasion, but whenever the four were together, it was Billy and Mickey entertaining each other as if their wives were not there.

"They were their own party," Lois said. "They didn't need anyone else."

By the time Lois joined Billy in New York, she had arrived with news: she was pregnant. It was not necessarily by design; Lois worried about all the time Billy spent away from home. And she was not naive about what Billy and Mickey might be doing on the road. For a short time, Lois had companionship and support from the other Yankees wives, a close-knit group. Merlyn Mantle was pregnant, too. Lois found the days when the Yankees were playing at home tolerable, but when the team was on the road, she felt an enduring loneliness. It was no different for Merlyn Mantle. Then Mantle's father, Mutt, who had shaped Mickey's life and career, died in May, and Mickey receded farther from his wife.

By the summer, Lois and Merlyn Mantle went home.

"Merlyn and I both felt neglected," Lois told journalist Maury Allen in 1982. "And when we told the boys we were leaving, they didn't exactly put up a fuss. I remember that we just left. That was that."

Billy and Mickey were not highly introspective at that juncture of their lives. If Billy saw the significance in Lois's return to California, no one close to him recalls him speaking of it at the time.

"Being a baseball wife is not easy," said Charlie Silvera. "I think Billy just thought she was going home to see her parents and get out of a hot New York summer."

Besides, from his perspective, he had a lot on his hands. He was playing full-time for the best-known sports team on the planet. And being on the field all the time exposed Billy on a regular basis to a kind of testosterone-laced challenge that was routine to Major League Baseball at the time. Rough play was customary and expected. In June 1952, the *New York Times* published accounts of eight fights during Major League baseball games. That was in one month.

Many of the ballplayers in 1952 were World War II veterans who weren't averse to fighting with their enemies, or their comrades if tempers got hot in a ball game, a card game, or a barroom. In his autobiography, Billy matter-of-factly described two scenes from the 1950s that serve as a window into a ballplayer's life at that time, and how routine a fistfight was in their lives. In the first story, five Yankees started conversing in the team's hotel lobby with five women who had just left a hotel function. A minute or two later, five guys arrived who had been the women's dates for the night, and they weren't too pleased that five Yankees appeared to be trying to steal their girls. One of the guys wanted to fight the Yankees.

Billy, Mickey Mantle, and Charlie Silvera were part of the group, and so was Hank Bauer, an ex-Marine who had earned two Bronze Stars and two Purple Hearts in World War II. Also present was Ralph Houk, the future Yankees manager but now a backup catcher who as an army major had been awarded a Bronze Star and a Silver Star for his bravery in the Battle of the Bulge.

Bauer and Houk calmly went about discussing who was going to take on the guy who wanted to fight. It was like a business meeting, with Houk saying he probably wouldn't play the next day so it didn't matter if his knuckles hurt, and Bauer countering that he hadn't been in a good fight for a while. In the end, it didn't matter who stepped forward; the guy annoyed by the Yankees' flirting was knocked down three times. The Yankees went to bed.

The second story Billy told was more head-spinning. Several Yankees got into an argument with several bar patrons after one of the Yankees said something to a woman whose boyfriend wasn't too pleased. (This happened often.) As the dispute escalated, four or five bouncers arrived, and one of them pulled a gun on the Yankees. Houk quickly grabbed a whiskey bottle, broke it on the bar, and put the broken bottle up to the neck of the bouncer holding the gun. As Billy wrote, "Ralph said: 'I'm not afraid of guns. You put that gun away or I'll cut your throat.' The bouncer said: 'O.K.' And using him as a hostage, we all walked backward out of the bar with the bottle to his throat. Did you ever see eight guys get into a cab? We all jumped in one cab and got the hell out of there."

It was in this context that Billy was involved in the first of his many celebrated on-field fisticuffs on July 12, 1952. In recent games, the bespectacled St. Louis Browns catcher Clint Courtney, who had briefly been a Yankee and with whom Billy had tussled in the Arizona-Texas League, had several times slid into Yankees infielders with his spikes aimed above the ankles. Rizzuto had nimbly avoided Courtney once, as had Billy and Gil McDougald. But the Yankees infielders had discussed retaliation.

In the eighth inning, with a Ladies' Day crowd of 22,327 at Yankee Stadium looking on, Courtney attempted a delayed steal of second base. When Billy took the high throw from Berra, he gave the crowd an example of the ungentlemanly ways that 1950s ballplayers handled internal squabbles. He tagged Courtney right in the kisser with a hard smack of ball and glove. Billy paused over the dazed Courtney, then jogged off the field, but Courtney soon rose and ran after him.

As the *New York Times* wrote the next day, "Billy heard Courtney's approach, wheeled quickly to meet it, and on the theory that the best defense is a speedy offense, promptly met Courtney with two perfectly aimed righthanders to the jaw."

The thirty-two words in that sentence more or less describe most of the public, and not so public, fights Billy would get into in the next thirty-five years. Some would call this tactic a sucker punch. And it is likely that on more than a few occasions, as hostilities in a barroom were brewing but had not yet reached a flash point, Billy would just haul off and clock someone. Some people argue, shove, threaten, and then fight. Billy, especially when he was younger, would occasionally just skip the intermediate steps and proceed right to the punching stage during a difference of opinion, which no doubt surprised many a combatant.

But in many cases, Billy saw a genuine unavoidable threat coming and decided to act first. The 1952 Courtney fight was a classic example.

Courtney was a worthy opponent, though, and he squared off with Billy as each player threw haymakers and the benches emptied. Billy and Courtney swung and wrestled, bowling over two umpires who tried to stop them. The fight went on for a couple of minutes with dozens of players involved. Pictures of the scuffle appeared in newspapers across the country the next day.

"That's the fight that got me labeled a brawler," Billy later said. "And I didn't start that fight."

It is true that Courtney was ejected from the game and fined $100 by the league while Billy finished the game and was not fined.

It's also true that Billy had to be dragged off Courtney, flailing and thrashing like a madman. It is how most of Billy's fights or near-fights ended. From Clint Courtney to his dustup with Reggie Jackson in a Boston dugout twenty-five years later, the final scenes are always the same: Billy, wild-eyed and out of control, trying to get at someone to continue the fight.

Most of the rest of the season the Yankees were holding the American League lead with Billy contributing in quieter, less newsworthy ways. He was also increasingly ducking the chance to fight. In late August, the *New York Post* described a batting practice session in Cleveland: "The Indians bench jockeys were on Martin. 'Hit it with your nose, Pinocchio,' they shouted. 'How did that pitch get past your nose?' they shouted again. Billy the Kid ignored them."

Billy was also playing spectacularly in the field and seemed to have a knack for being in the right place when the Yankees most needed a game-changing play. In a victory at Cleveland in August, Billy made the pivotal play when a line drive ricocheted off the glove of first baseman Joe Collins, and Billy dashed into shallow right field to dive and snag the ball before it fell to the grass. He then scrambled to his knees and threw to first base to double an Indians runner off the base and end a Cleveland threat.

The Yankees took the American League lead over the Indians on September 12 when Billy had a home run and a triple in a win in Chicago. Soon after, the Yankees tore up Billy's contract and signed him to a new one through 1953 worth $10,000 annually. On the next-to-last day of the season, the Yankees clinched the pennant when Billy singled with the bases loaded in the eleventh inning of a tied game against the Philadelphia Athletics.

Pictures from the jubilant Yankees' locker room showed Stengel between Mantle and Billy, the manager hugging each with one arm.

"What did I tell you about these two fresh kids?" Stengel said.

Billy batted .267 for the season with 33 RBIs and 3 home runs. More important to the pitching-rich Yankees, he had helped turn 92 double plays and made just 9 errors in 107 games and 576 fielding chances.

Mantle in his first full season hit .311 with 23 home runs and 87 RBIs and made 12 errors in 374 fielding chances.

The World Series was against the Brooklyn Dodgers, who had never won the championship. The Dodgers had been losing to the Yankees since Casey Stengel patrolled right field in Brooklyn. The Dodgers were led by their All-Star second baseman, Jackie Robinson, the National League MVP a few years earlier. Not surprisingly, Robinson received most of the attention in the newspapers before the series.

The Dodgers won the first game of the series, but in the second game, Billy broke open a tied game with an RBI single. In the sixth inning, he added a three-run home run, giving him four RBIs in the game, which was just one short of the record set by Yankees Tony Lazzeri and Bill Dickey in 1936.

The teams split the next four games. There was, however, one remarkable game-changing sequence between former manager and former player in the fourth game. The Dodgers manager was Billy's mentor from the 1949 Oakland Oaks, Charlie Dressen, who had taught Billy many of his sign-stealing secrets. In the top of the fifth inning with the Yankees ahead 1–0, the Dodgers had runners at second and third with one out and pitcher Joe Black at the plate.

Dressen, as he had been in Oakland, was also the Dodgers' third-base coach. From his position at second base, Billy watched closely as Dressen flashed a flurry of signals at Black. Dressen's tempo and movements in the coach's box quickened, which Dressen — watching opposing managers — had always said was a tip-off that some kind of play was on. Sizing up the situation, Billy suspected a suicide squeeze and got Yogi Berra's attention behind the plate. He made a fist, turned his hand upside down, and waved it slightly — the sign for a pitchout. Berra crouched and made the same signal to Yankees pitcher Allie Reynolds.

The pitch was appropriately wide of the plate, and Black could not reach it with his bat as he attempted to bunt. Berra then easily tagged out the Dodgers' Andy Pafko, who had dashed toward home plate on the pitch. The suicide squeeze had failed. The Dodgers never scored in the game, losing 2–0.

"Tell me another player who would have seen that?" Stengel asked reporters afterward. "That's why he's my winner."

The back-and-forth between the evenly matched teams continued throughout that first week of October, dominating the headlines in the New York tabloids, which barely made room for news from Australia that Great Britain had exploded its first atomic bomb. The drama culminated with a taut seventh game at Ebbets Field, which the Yankees led 4–2 in the seventh inning when the Dodgers loaded the bases with two outs.

What followed next was the crucial moment of the series. To some, it was a pivotal moment of 1950s baseball.

Robinson was the batter, and he worked the count to 3-2. The runners took off on the next pitch, but Robinson undercut a fastball that he skied high in the air just to the first-base side of the pitching mound. It was a sunny but windy day and the ball was wavering in the air, drifting back toward home plate and away from the Yankees infielders.

By the time Robinson's pop-up had reached its peak above the diamond and began its descent, one Brooklyn runner had crossed the plate, a second was steps away, and a third was on his way home. Yankees relief pitcher Bob Kuzava moved out of the way, as pitchers are instructed to do. Berra, rising from his crouch behind the plate, stepped toward the pop-up, but he would be too late and it wasn't a catcher's responsibility anyway. Berra was calling for first baseman Joe Collins to make the catch.

Robinson was a right-handed pull hitter with power, which meant that McDougald at third base, Rizzuto at shortstop, and Billy at second base were playing deep and toward left field. It was Collins's ball, but he froze at his position, later saying he had lost the pop-up in the sun.

As the ball dropped through the fading light of a crisp October afternoon, no one was charging toward the ball.

Describing the scene after the game, Casey Stengel said, "My feller at first base is asleep and my feller behind the plate, I don't know what he's doing. I'm watching, but I can't swallow because my heart is in my throat."

The World Series in the 1950s was like a second baseball season unto itself with a vast, nationwide audience. In the twenty-first century, with media of all kinds splintering the nation's attention, it's hard to comprehend how one series of baseball games could collectively engross an entire country. But the World Series in the middle of the last century had that kind of pull, luring in dedicated, hard-core baseball fans and casual fans drawn to the only meeting of the National and American League champions each year. Even non–baseball fans could not ignore the national pastime's singular, featured event. Long before the Super Bowl, televised Olympic Games, and the NCAA tournament's March Madness, there was the World Series in America, an annual rite of the fall as important as Halloween.

And within this ritual, there was no drama like a seventh World Series game, which brought American office workers, factory workers, outdoor laborers, and schoolchildren to a stop for the day. With the contest played in the afternoon, people propped up radios on desks, in cars and trucks, and in factories to follow the action. At schools, offices, and living rooms across the country where people were playing hooky from other obligations, televisions were tuned to the game.

In this setting, with blue-collar Brooklyn once again trying to upset the stately, regal Yankees, Robinson's seventh-inning, seventh-game pop-up came off like staged theater, a cliffhanger at the end of a seven-act play. One little five-ounce baseball hung in the air, a moment of terror for the usually self-assured Yankees fans and a moment of blessed hope for beleaguered Dodgers fans. As the ball plunged back toward the diamond, the fans at Ebbets Field and baseball fans everywhere rose from their seats.

The ball might have landed no more than twenty-five feet from home plate, and yet it could have changed the outcome more than any titanic home run. It could have liberated a downtrodden but proud baseball borough, and it could have cast doubt and disquiet throughout a storied franchise still not 100 percent sure who would save the day with Joe DiMaggio gone.

It all depended on whether someone — anyone — got to the ball before it met the ground.

Suddenly, from the right side of the diamond, with his chin jutting forward, his arms outstretched, and his legs churning beneath him in a full sprint, Billy Martin raced past the motionless Yankees Kuzava and Collins. The wind was blowing the ball toward home plate, and Billy's hat flew off as he sped past the pitching rubber. An instant later, Billy lunged, his hands about two feet from the Ebbets Field infield grass. He extended his glove, where the ball nestled, and he closed his other hand around the floppy leather to keep it there.

Three outs. No runs.

Billy's momentum carried him toward the Yankees' third-base-line dugout, and still in a full sprint, he tossed the ball behind him onto the diamond without looking back. It was a sort of ho-hum reaction, as if to say, "The inning is over, let's get in the dugout." Billy was a few strides from the dugout when he realized his cap was still on the field, so he circled back to retrieve it. At this point, he was surrounded by other teammates coming off the field.

"I didn't think it was that big a deal until everyone started slapping me on the back," he said.

"It was the greatest clutch catch I had ever seen," Mantle said. "Everyone froze. Except Billy."

The Yankees won the game, 4–2, capturing their fourth consecutive World Series. Stengel crowed afterward.

"People wondered why I wanted that kid from Berkeley," he said. "Look at that Robinson pop fly, that's why. It isn't even his ball but that 140-pound fresh kid on second comes tearin' in after the ball. If that kid doesn't make the catch we blow the World Series right there."

Billy was a Yankees World Series hero. For days afterward, he was praised for a diversity of contributions. Recalling the Dodgers' botched suicide squeeze from the fourth game, McDougald called Billy's subterfuge "our $70,000 steal," which was the difference between the winner's share of the World Series money pool and the loser's share, or about $1,800 per player. His four RBIs in Game 2, with the Yankees already down in the series, were considered the early spark the Yankees needed after a long, tiresome pennant chase. A picture of his lunging grab of Robinson's pop-up was voted the best sports photo of 1952. The film of the catch was replayed in thousands of movie houses across America, as an announcer described the streaking infielder in the middle of the screen as "the Yankees' firebrand second baseman."

Baseball fans around the country and Americans not terribly interested in baseball knew Billy Martin's name now. He was the Yankee who had made that World Series catch of Jackie Robinson's wind-blown pop-up — the one who came flying in from nowhere, lost his cap, and held the ball.

Within a week, Billy was back living at Lois's parents' house, but requests for him to appear at various athletic and civic functions came rolling in from around the country. He traveled up and down the West Coast and sometimes back to the East Coast for dinners and other appearances.

If Billy was smiling for newspaper photographers on a regular basis that fall, it was a different scene at home, where there was a palpable tension. Lois would not give birth to the couple's daughter, named Kelly Ann, until December 20, but she and Billy were moving in different directions long before that.

At that point, Billy was going to baseball banquets about four nights a week, and he did not spend much time with Lois at the end of her pregnancy. He was at the hospital when Kelly Ann was born, but when Lois brought their daughter home, Billy later said, "I could see that she hated even to see me. She hated everything about me."

Billy's sisters had told him that Lois had been hanging around other men while Billy was back in New York, but as Billy wrote, "Looking back, it really didn't matter. We never should have gotten married in the first place."

Still, about six weeks after Kelly Ann's birth, Billy said he was shocked when he was served with divorce papers while taking a nap at Lois's parents' home.

He returned to the house at 1632 7th Street, where his mother had raised him after his father had left her and her infant son. Billy stayed in a cramped second-floor bedroom and waited for the 1953 season to begin.

12

THE YANKEES WON ELEVEN of their first fourteen games to open the 1953 season. Behind Mantle, Billy, and Whitey Ford, who had returned from his military obligation, the Yankees had the fresh blood to vault the team out of the Joe DiMaggio era and into another generation of Yankees championship teams. The trio also portrayed a different image from that of the Yankees of the previous decades. While those teams featured reserved, refined, soft-spoken tacticians, the 1953 Yankees were light-hearted, boisterous, and flamboyant.

The New York papers had already depicted in jovial detail the extra-curricular spring training exploits of Mantle, Ford, and Billy — missed team flights because of late-night excursions to distant bars that led to $500 cab rides the next morning, a steady stream of pranks played on one another and teammates, and largely harmless, if drunken, misbehavior on train junkets.

Stengel rolled his eyes — when they weren't averted. His Yankees were in first place and pulling away from the rest of the field.

But on May 6, bad news interrupted the party for Billy. His grandmother, Nonna, in whose bedroom he had slept until he was of high school age, had died. He flew home to Berkeley. The trip also became the first chance for Billy since he left for spring training to see his daughter, Kelly Ann. It also gave him a chance to make a plea for reconciliation with Lois.

Billy was inconsolable about the breakdown of his marriage and challenging the divorce. He begged Lois to take him back. Lois was adamant; the relationship was over.

"You can't stay in love with a newspaper clipping," she said. "Too much baseball. Too little married life."

Billy said the divorce was a complete surprise. Lois disputed that. "No one gets a divorce and is not aware," she said. Her lawyer continued to pursue the divorce, sending correspondence to Billy in Berkeley and in New York.

He refused to open the letters. Distraught and feeling guilty, Billy was also devoutly Catholic, and in 1953, divorce defied church doctrine.

"He was pretty broken up about Lois," said his cousin Nick DeGennaro. "It was sad but anybody would have seen it coming. Billy was running around everywhere and Lois was alone at home. Billy just didn't see it."

Billy liked being married; he just did not know how to be married.

"To him, the divorce was a failure," said DeGennaro. "And Billy never handled failure very well. He wasn't a good loser."

Back in New York, the Yankees continued to win, and Billy was having a stellar year at the plate for a middle infielder. In one stretch from late May to mid-June, the Yankees won eighteen consecutive games. But Stengel and other Yankees noticed that their fiery second baseman seemed precariously on edge — even for him.

In a game at St. Louis, Billy was a central figure in a second brawl involving catcher Clint Courtney. Half a dozen Yankees converged on Courtney after he drew blood with a high slide into Rizzuto. Whitey Ford stomped Courtney's eyeglasses into pieces as they lay in the infield dirt. Four Yankees were fined, including Billy. But the league report on the fracas especially noted that it took several minutes and multiple umpires to subdue Billy, who continued to fight on the field even after some semblance of order had been restored.

Billy told Mantle that he felt like he was on the verge of a nervous breakdown. And his teammates noticed something else: Billy seemed to be withering away in front of their eyes. Gus Mauch, the team trainer, approached waiters at team hotels on the road and asked if they had noticed anything about Billy's eating habits (the players got breakfast, lunch, or dinner for free as part of the hotel meal plan).

The waiters told Mauch that Billy would order his food, but then not eat much of it. Mauch and other players bodily lifted Billy onto a scale in the locker room one day in Philadelphia. Billy, who normally played at about 165 pounds, weighed 132.

In 1957, for a lengthy story for the *Saturday Evening Post,* which was a publication of major import during the 1950s, writer Al Stump conducted several extensive interviews with Billy across two weeks. The tone and message of the story were that Major League Baseball was a pressure-filled existence and not all fun and games — even for the dynastic Yankees.

Stump's case in point was Billy, who described to the magazine what he was going through in 1953.

Billy said that doctors had discovered he had high blood pressure, insomnia, and a nervous stomach that made it hard for him to eat comfortably. Billy was prescribed sleeping pills, which he said made him drowsy during the day so he took "greenies" during games to be more alert. The use of amphetamine tablets — also known as speed and common along the frontlines during wartime combat situations — was widespread in baseball during the 1950s and 1960s. But Billy had taken the routine to an extreme.

"I was on them almost all season — two a day," Billy told Stump. "I took over 300 goof balls. Then more pills to get back to sleep, which didn't work many nights. I'd be walking the floor until daylight. I was a wreck.

"Everything seemed to be going wrong."

Things got worse in 1953 when a Chicago newspaper wrote about the divorce proceedings and reported — inaccurately — that Billy was not sending money to Lois and Kelly Ann. The newspaper wrote that mother and child were back in California without food and basic services because of Billy's neglect.

The next day, as Billy was coming off the field at Chicago's Comiskey Park, a fan threw a baby bottle on the field and yelled, "Go home and feed your baby, you no-good bum." Other fans in other cities heckled him about being a deadbeat dad.

News of the divorce and the situation with Kelly Ann, though never substantiated, spread nationally. When in New York, Billy regularly attended Mass at St. Patrick's Cathedral on Fifth Avenue. He went to church throughout his life, but in 1953, he was frequently seen quietly sitting in a pew, praying for guidance about his unsettled personal life. Leaving St. Patrick's one day, another parishioner approached him on the long staircase outside the cathedral.

"If you're a member of this parish," the man said to Billy, "then I quit."

The taunting about abandoning his family continued for several weeks until Stengel, irked by the displays wherever the Yankees went, used his power with the press to defend Billy.

"The Yankees send those checks back to Mrs. Martin themselves," Casey said. "So I know what he's paying and it's plenty. There is no disputing that this is the truth."

Through all this, Billy was having his best season as a Yankee. In fact, it would be the best season statistically in his eleven-year career.

"He was always very confident, but at that point he had seen a lot of baseball and he knew exactly how to work the pitchers into the counts he wanted," said Charlie Silvera. "He wasn't a .300 hitter but he seemed like a .350 hitter when the game was on the line."

By July, Billy had replaced Rizzuto, then thirty-five years old, as the Yankees' leadoff hitter. He had become an adept bunter, he was a good batsman in hit-and-run situations, and he knew the value of a well-placed ground ball that moved a base runner from second to third. He also found other ways to unnerve opponents and motivate — or entertain — his teammates.

In a July game against St. Louis, opposing shortstop Billy Hunter slid into second base safely on a stolen base attempt, just eluding a tag by Billy, who then pretended to toss the baseball to Whitey Ford on the mound as Hunter, who was bent over, knocked the dust and dirt from his uniform pants.

Billy kept the ball in his glove and lingered near second base as Ford turned his attention to the next batter. When Hunter stepped off second base to take his lead, Billy leaped toward him and tagged him out. It was the hidden-ball trick, something Billy did often and taught to generations of Yankees infielders.

That summer, Ty Cobb was asked by a San Francisco reporter which current players he liked to watch play.

"If I were managing a ball club," Cobb answered, "I certainly would do everything within my power to get a player like Billy Martin. Sure, there are better hitters and better fielders, but for fight, spirit and whatever it takes to win a game, Martin is something special."

In the 1953 season, Billy, Mickey, and Whitey acquired a nickname: "the Three Musketeers." And they earned it. But one of the Musketeers was usually painted as the ringleader and took most of the blame if something went awry.

"I don't know why, but Billy always got labeled the instigator, which wasn't true at all," Ford said. "Mickey just had that innocent, country-boy look and I was quiet about a lot of things in public. But Billy didn't care about appearances and he had that mischievous grin, so people just thought he was stirring us up all the time. It wasn't really the case. We got into plenty of trouble on our own."

Whitey Ford, like Silvera, Hank Bauer, and other Yankees from the 1950s, insisted that Billy was not a heavy drinker in this period of his life.

"We used to make fun of him for nursing a drink for an hour," Ford said. "I'd catch him dumping Scotches we bought for him in potted plants. I'd say, 'Where's your drink?' And he'd say, 'I drank it.' And I'd say, 'Then, where's the ice? You drank the ice, too?'

"He stayed out late with us, but he wasn't the one keeping us out late. But he would always be the one getting blamed for us drinking too much and staying out too late. It got to be a joke between us. We'd tease him that he was leading us astray. We'd say, 'We should go home but let's have another drink because Billy is a bad influence.' Billy would get pissed at us because he knew that's exactly what people would say."

"I'm no playboy drinker," Billy told the *New York Times* columnist Arthur Daley in 1953. "Sure, I go places. I'm single and I can't sit in a hotel room talking to the floor lamps."

The Three Musketeers were busy off the field, often mentioned in gossip columns for hanging out in Manhattan or Chicago with Frank Sinatra and Dean Martin, but they were still producing on the field. By late August, the Yankees had a nine-game lead over the second-place Chicago White Sox.

The dichotomy of Billy's season continued at every level. He was playing his best baseball, but Billy could not escape a pervasive melancholy. He was still contesting his divorce and made periodic calls back to Berkeley to ask his sister Pat what Lois was doing.

"She's moved on without you, Bill," Pat told him. "And you should move on without her."

"I'm still a mess," Billy told his sister.

To the *Saturday Evening Post,* he said, "Mothers and fathers of kids think you get ahead on ability and opportunity. They don't know about the outside pressure. The guys who are playing ball up here are the people who can adjust to the nuthouse they have to live in. Some of us can. Some can't. I've never been able to get a good, steady grip on myself in this racket."

Twenty-five years old, he missed just two games and led the team in plate appearances and at-bats. He had career highs in home runs (15) and RBIs (75) and batted .257, which eventually was his career average. In 812 fielding chances, he made 14 errors. By comparison, McDougald had 23 errors in 525 chances at third base and Rizzuto made 24 errors on

647 chances at shortstop. With the help of his infielders, Billy turned 126 double plays. He also managed to get hit by a pitch 6 times, which led the team. And he led the team in sacrifices.

The Yankees won 99 of the 151 games they played that year, a winning percentage that would be equivalent to a 106-win season in the Major Leagues' current 162-game schedule.

In his autobiography, Billy makes no mention of his 1953 regular-season totals. He was focused, he said, on the Yankees winning a fifth consecutive World Series.

On September 30, the day that California governor Earl Warren was chosen to become the new chief justice of the United States Supreme Court — and just days after Senator John F. Kennedy married Jacqueline Bouvier — the World Series between the Yankees and Dodgers opened at Yankee Stadium.

Cy Young, who had thrown the first pitch in the inaugural World Series fifty years earlier, was invited to throw out the ceremonial first pitch of the 1953 baseball postseason. Young, born two years after the Civil War ended and the winner of 511 Major League games, reared back on his right leg and fired a crisp strike to Yogi Berra.

In the bottom of the first inning, with the Yankees ahead 1–0, Billy came to the plate against Brooklyn's Carl Erskine, a 20-game winner in 1953. The bases were loaded with two outs.

In the original Yankee Stadium the left-field foul pole was just 301 feet from home plate, but the wall in straightaway center field was 461 feet away. The center-field wall was so far away, the Yankees placed three large, chest-high stone monuments to Lou Gehrig, Babe Ruth, and Miller Huggins on the warning track just to the left of the 461-foot sign and left them in play — if anyone could hit a ball that far.

Billy was making his twenty-seventh World Series plate appearance, having played in each of the two previous Fall Classics. It was a bright and sunny Wednesday afternoon, and the red, white, and blue bunting that came out only for World Series games was draped across each of Yankee Stadium's three decks, which were filled with a sellout crowd of 69,374.

When Billy lofted Erskine's curve ball toward left-center field, Jackie Robinson, who had switched to left field for the Dodgers, was the first to race for it. Brooklyn's center fielder, Duke Snider, soon gave pursuit as well.

The ball sailed over both outfielders, bounding twenty feet to the left of the monument to Gehrig. Mantle, Bauer, and Gene Woodling charged home. Billy went into third base standing up with a triple and three RBIs. In the fourth inning, he bunted and ended up on third when both the pitcher and right fielder made bad throws. Billy added an eighth-inning single — his third hit — in a 9–5 Yankees victory.

In the second game, the Dodgers had a 2–1 lead when Billy led off the seventh inning with a long home run over the left-field fence against Brooklyn's Preacher Roe. It was his second hit of the game. Mantle won the game an inning later with a two-run homer.

Brooklyn won the third game, 3–2, on a late home run by Roy Campanella, and then the Dodgers evened the series with a 7–3 home victory. Billy had a single and a walk in Game 3 and a triple early in Game 4, which ended when Billy, who had singled in the ninth, was thrown out at home trying to score on Mantle's hit to right field.

Billy also tried the hidden-ball trick in the second inning with Brooklyn's Junior Gilliam at second base. But Charlie Dressen, Billy's old Oakland Oaks manager, suspected what Billy was up to and called time out from the third-base coaching box to warn Gilliam.

Between the fourth and fifth games of the series, the New York newspapers were filled with stories about eight-year-old Johnny Durkin of the Bronx, who had recently been stricken with polio. A playground baseball fixture, Durkin had recently been confined to his bed when he lost the use of his left leg.

His father, Lawrence, knowing that Billy was Johnny's favorite player, made a plea to the Yankees for something to cheer his disconsolate son. Martin posed for a photo autographing a baseball for Johnny Durkin, then autographed the photo, too. Both were sent to the boy at Willard Parker Hospital in the Bronx.

"Johnny forgot completely about the fact that he couldn't move one leg when he saw that picture and the baseball," Lawrence Durkin told the *New York Daily News*. "He couldn't believe Billy Martin would find time during the big World Series to send him a ball and a picture."

The Yankees rolled over the Dodgers 11–7 in Game 5 with Billy getting two hits, including a two-run home run. The series returned to Yankee Stadium for the sixth game with the home team hoping to end the series. A nervous struggle ensued. Billy had a ground-rule double in the fifth but did not score. He hit a line drive that bounced at the feet of Gilliam at second in the first inning that was scored as an error, a controversial decision at the time — and later. Bauer scored on the play.

The Yankees had a 3–1 lead in the ninth until Carl Furillo hit a two-run homer into the right-field stands to tie the game. In the Yankees' half of the ninth inning, Bauer walked and Mantle beat out a weak grounder to third base for a single. With one out and runners at first and second base, Billy left the on-deck circle and started walking purposefully toward the plate. The day had begun with sunny skies but clouds had moved in, and Billy was blowing on his hands in the late-afternoon chill of an October day as he readied for his at-bat.

"Nobody ever said anything to Billy in those situations," Yogi Berra said. "You wouldn't interrupt him. You didn't have to talk to Billy. He knew what to do."

Watching from the dugout, Charlie Silvera examined his former Concourse Plaza roommate and noticed how much had changed since Billy was a raw 1950 rookie.

"When he came up to the bigs, Billy could be fidgety in the batter's box," Silvera said. "I remember looking at him that day and seeing that he just stepped into the batter's box without any messing around — no dirt kicking, no tapping his spikes. He stood upright. No nonsense."

Bauer gazed into home from second base.

"Billy was born for that moment," Bauer said years later. "I wasn't sure he'd get a hit but I was sure he'd hit it hard somewhere."

The Dodgers' Clem Labine had pitched two scoreless innings in relief. Billy took Labine's first pitch for a ball, then fouled off a fastball. Labine offered a sinker to Billy, who smacked it past the pitcher's mound. The ball bounced once in front of second base and didn't bounce again until the outfield grass just behind second base.

Bauer roared around third base and beat the throw to home without sliding. A small gaggle of Yankees hugged him and about twenty Yankees, led by Stengel, sprinted toward first base where Billy was mobbed. The newsreel of the game shows a smiling Billy being hugged by Stengel and Dan Topping in the clubhouse. Seemingly every Yankee came by to tousle his hair. Rizzuto came over and, holding Billy's chin in his right hand, kissed Billy on the cheek.

Stengel, meanwhile, was holding up his right hand with his fingers and thumb spread wide. No team had ever won five consecutive World Series, and Stengel was making sure everyone could count the five extended digits of his hand. It was the Yankees' sixteenth championship in the last thirty years.

Billy had 12 hits in 24 at-bats with 8 RBIs, 2 home runs, 2 triples, and a double. Billy's 12 hits set a record for a six-game World Series and tied the record for hits in any World Series (several writers commented that he would have broken the record had his hot shot at Gilliam in the final game been scored properly). His .500 batting average was the highest in any series that had gone more than four games, and his 8 RBIs were the most in a six-game series. Billy's slugging percentage in the series was .958, which was .328 more than any other batter on either team. He was voted the Most Valuable Player of the series in a landslide.

"That Martin must be the best .250 hitter in the world," said Labine.

"Martin's the best on the club," said Dressen, the Dodgers manager. "He just kills you."

During the series, Billy had been writing a short diary for United Press International.

After the final game of the World Series, under the byline Billy Martin, the series MVP began his diary with this sentence: "The ball I hit in the ninth inning went out into center field, they tell me, but I'll always believe it rolled into the Promised Land."

He later wrote:

It seemed to me as if it was happening to somebody else, not me . . . it's the way you think about it as a kid but then it's real, and if what I am saying now isn't making too much sense you'll have to excuse me. I'm still so excited that I can't keep my thoughts from colliding with one another. All I know is that when I came up to face Clem Labine in the ninth I thought to myself how nice it would be if I could come through with just one last RBI this year.

Billy wrote that he ran to first base, not feeling his feet touch the ground. He briefly mentions the celebration, and then Billy being Billy, he couldn't help but mildly complain that his one-hopper at Gilliam should have been scored a hit. But he rallied nicely, thanking his teammates and Casey. In farewell, he wrote, "Now I'm just going someplace quiet and relax for a long time. Any minute I expect someone to jab me in the ribs and say: 'Hey, Martin, wake up! You're dreaming.'"

13

THE DREAM SOON BECAME something akin to a nightmare, at least for someone as restless, ambitious, and baseball-centric as Billy. For most of the next two years, Billy did not play another Major League game.

Billy's latest problems were actually a holdover, and they stemmed from an evident reality: it is hard to be a celebrated World Series hero and a hardship case at the same time.

At this juncture in his life, Billy could have used the advice of a sage public relations executive. Instead, his life remained as it usually was — an open book. That included the financial ledgers of his new fame as Billy made no effort to hide the many monetary benefits of his dazzling World Series performance. At home, he was given a baby-blue 1954 Cadillac convertible by a local car dealer, who took a picture of Billy standing next to the car and displayed it in all the Bay Area newspapers.

As part of the winning team, he got his World Series share of the gate receipts: $8,280.68, a payout that drew headlines in an era when hefty compensation for professional athletes was news, not commonplace.

Billy also accompanied other American Leaguers on a ten-day barnstorming tour. When he returned home and reporters asked what he was paid for the trip, he told them, "About $5,000."

Less known, except in the neighborhood, was what Billy did with the other car he received in 1953 — a Pontiac for winning the World Series MVP award. He donated that to Father Dennis Moore at St. Ambrose Church. He also told his sister Joanie that he would pay for her college tuition.

For a while, Billy had no reason to suspect that his hardship deferment from the army would soon be challenged. And besides, he was distracted; he was leaving with other Yankees for a series of exhibition games in Japan. He took with him his childhood friend Bill Castell.

"The Japanese people treated Billy like a visiting god," Castell said in 2012, sitting in his California home. "I remember riding in a parade with him, propped up in the back of a big convertible sipping a drink called a grasshopper. These women, like Geisha girls I guess, kept running up to the car and giving us grasshoppers.

"We sat there waving to the crowd, and every once in a while Billy would look over at me and say, 'How about this? Not bad for a couple of nobodies from West Berkeley.'"

Castell also recalls the decorative Japanese dolls and other mementos and souvenirs that Billy mailed home to his mother. Jenny bragged about the gifts to her neighbors, showing them to anyone who came to her house.

At about this time, according to a *Berkeley Gazette* story, the local draft board began reviewing Billy's hardship case because, as an official told the newspaper, "now he is in the money." Asked about it when he got back from Japan, Billy answered, "I haven't heard anything about that. I haven't received any notice. But I'm here if they want to come and get me."

And come and get him they did. But not without months of governmental paper pushing to reclassify his draft status. So for about a week, Billy went to rest at his mother's house, moving back into the second-floor bedroom. Bored, he called Mickey. Then he called his cousin Nick.

"Billy says to me, 'Want to drive to Oklahoma with me?'" Nick DeGennaro said. "And that's how I went to Mickey Mantle's house — a trip I'll never forget."

The baby-blue Cadillac rolled toward Oklahoma with stops along the way in Reno and Las Vegas. Not long after they crossed the Oklahoma state line from New Mexico, Billy and DeGennaro stopped for gas next to a tiny roadside diner.

"I remember Billy standing there getting gas with a little cigar in his mouth," DeGennaro said. "The kid pumping the gas goes, 'You look like Billy Martin.' And Billy laughed and said, 'I better since I am him.'

"The kid was all excited and got an autograph. We decided to go inside the diner for dinner. Well, the kid had apparently run around and told everyone in town that Billy was there, and the diner started to fill up with locals who wanted to meet him. We were sitting at the counter and people were slapping him on the back and asking him about the World Series. There was almost a line for autographs, and girls were sitting on his lap and having their picture taken with him.

"After a while, a couple of these good ol' boys at the other end of the counter were getting fed up with all the attention Billy was getting. They started saying things to each other and doing it loud enough for us to hear, stuff like, 'He ain't very big — except for those ears.' They were making fun of his clothes and calling him a skinny shit. They were kind of heckling Billy. Another one said something like, 'Some big-league brawler, I'm sure I could take him.'

"Billy said, 'Let's get out of here.'"

DeGennaro said they paid their bill — Billy left his usual big tip — and started for the door. But somebody else stopped Billy to talk.

"We were standing there with our backs to the counter and there was a mirror on the wall we were facing. One of the guys who had been making comments gets up and starts toward us. I could see him in the mirror. He raised his arm real quick like he was going to grab Billy from behind, and all at once Billy wheeled around and just decked the guy. He hit him square on the jaw so fast the guy just went down in a heap. He's lying on the floor of the diner.

"Everybody kind of froze and we walked out the door."

But some of the male patrons from the diner eventually followed Billy and his cousin.

"We got in the Cadillac and they're yelling things at us standing in the dirt parking lot but no one is coming near Billy," DeGennaro said. "They're standing back and just yelling. Billy just laughed at them. He said, 'Go fuck yourself,' and we roared off. One of the guys picked up a rock and threw it.

"Billy turned to me and said, 'See what I have to put up with?' I'll tell you what, I understood his new life a lot better."

The welcome in Mickey's hometown of Commerce near the Kansas and Missouri borders was considerably warmer. No one from the Yankees had ever come to Mickey's birthplace. The arrival of the 1953 World Series MVP was cause enough for a weeklong celebration in Commerce.

"We went from one party or bar to another," DeGennaro recalled. "It was like Mardi Gras."

Said Mickey about the visit, "Everybody loved Billy — even the wife of one of my best friends."

The boys went hunting and fishing, and Billy started buying and borrowing the Western-style clothing everyone else in Oklahoma was wearing.

"He bought cowboy boots and a hat," DeGennaro said. "He really threw himself into that."

Throughout his early and later life, Billy spent hours reading historical fiction about the Old West. He loved Louis L'Amour's frontier-story novels and could quote from dozens of them, especially one appropriately enough called *The First Fast Draw.*/

DeGennaro recalled that they hunted during the day and by midafternoon they were drinking.

"All I saw of the two of them that winter was their backs going out the door," Merlyn Mantle wrote in *A Hero All His Life,* the book she authored for the family after Mickey's death. "If they did all the hunting and fishing they claimed they were doing, the fish and quail population of Oklahoma and Missouri took a fearful beating."

It is during this period that Mickey began telling a story about one of his hunting excursions with Billy. When Mickey was paid to speak at baseball-related dinner engagements from the 1960s to the 1980s, he often told the story and it always brought down the house with a sustained, uproarious laugh. It perfectly captured the two men, impish and always playing off each other. And it certainly sounded like Billy. The story may be apocryphal, and some say it dates to vaudeville comedians, but none of that ever mattered to audiences across America who drank it in when the great Mickey Mantle told it.

Mickey would stand at the microphone and in his syrupy drawl start to talk about how Billy in the 1950s wanted to hunt on private land where no other hunters, or strangers, would interfere or bother him.

"So I told Billy I knew a guy who had a big ranch where the hunting was terrific but we would have to drive about three hours to get there," Mickey would say to start the story.

And everyone would smile, drawn in by the notion that they were going to get an inside look at what it was like to be young, a world champion, and a Yankee at play.

"So we get to the ranch and I park my pickup truck," Mickey would continue. "And I said to Billy, 'Let me go inside and say hi to the guy and ask his permission to hunt on his land. It's just a courtesy.'"

As Mickey told the story, he talked to the rancher who was happy to have Mickey and Billy hunt on his land, but the rancher asked a favor. One of his aging mules had gone blind and was lame but the rancher didn't have the heart to shoot him.

"Would you shoot that mule for me before you go out to hunt?" the rancher asked Mickey.

Mickey agreed to put the mule down, but as he walked out the door, it occurred to him that the situation might present yet another opportunity to pull a prank on his good friend. Suppressing a grin, Mickey stormed from the rancher's house. As he approached his truck he said, "That no-good bastard won't let us hunt on his land. We drove all the way down here for nothing."

Mickey reached for his shotgun in the back of the pickup and started marching toward the rancher's barn. As Mickey told the rest of the story:

> I said, "Come on, I'll show him."
>
> Billy grabbed his gun and ran after me. "What are you gonna do, Mick?"
>
> When I got to the barn, I said, "That bastard." Then I aimed my shotgun at the blind mule and pulled the trigger — bam!
>
> And then, right behind me, I heard two more shots — bam, bam! I turned around and Billy has shot two of the rancher's cows. He says, "That bastard, should we shoot more?"

For all the hunting and carousing Mickey and Billy were doing, Billy later wrote that he also soaked up the benefits of the quiet, rustic culture. Merlyn Mantle cooked for him — he developed an appetite for quail — and Billy gained about twenty pounds during his Oklahoma vacation. The lifelong city slicker said he felt at peace in the country environment.

On January 15, 1954, the day after Joe DiMaggio married Marilyn Monroe at San Francisco City Hall, Billy's hardship deferral was withdrawn by the Selective Service Board No. 47 in Berkeley. Billy was reclassified 1-A, which meant the army could draft him at any time, and if that happened, he would be obligated to report for duty in about two weeks. Billy had already served nearly six months in 1950, but the requirement was two years of service.

Billy's induction notice arrived at the Yankees' spring training complex in early March. Stengel was crestfallen.

"Miss him?" Stengel said, responding to a question. "Certainly I'm going to miss him. Why, the kid's been terrific. Sure, he told off the owners. He also let George Weiss have it, and he had me seeing red. But he made us like it because he proved he could do everything we thought he couldn't do on that ball field. They haven't recovered yet from what he did to them in Brooklyn last October. I think he would have had his greatest year this season."

Billy left spring training telling reporters, "The Yanks will do all right. Please say so long to the Dodgers for me. They're on their own now."

It wasn't the best time to be entering the military if you were a professional athlete. Congress had launched an investigation into whether athletes were receiving preferential treatment and cushy assignments that amounted to nothing more than playing on a stateside army baseball, basketball, or football team.

Billy arrived at California's Fort Ord in his Cadillac, which irked his superiors. The base's chief officer, General Robert McClure, promptly announced that Billy would not be allowed to play for the Fort Ord baseball team.

"Martin's too hot," McClure declared. "You might say he's radioactive."

Billy was making $215 a month. Per a court order issued as part of his still-unresolved divorce proceedings, he had to pay $150 a month in matrimonial and child support to Lois and Kelly Ann. Billy was at Fort Ord less than a month before he was sent to Fort Carson just south of Colorado Springs, Colorado. He was part of the Fourth Infantry Division. At first, Billy was mostly ordered to do kitchen duty, which he said he did not mind because the cooks were Italians with whom he connected — and they gave him extra food when he left duty each day.

Eventually, he was assigned to a patrol unit, which required long treks up Colorado's mountains. The cooks snuck beers into his knapsack for the road.

By the spring, the Fort Carson commander had another assignment for Billy — player/coach of the camp baseball team. So much for worrying about cozy assignments.

"I had never really thought about managing," Billy told the *New York Post*'s Maury Allen in the late 1970s. "I was still young in 1954. I knew I would play again after I got out and I didn't really consider anything past playing. I found that I enjoyed it. It was something that opened my eyes."

Billy was the ultimate players' manager, loaning his Cadillac to anyone who wanted it for a date or to drive into town. The Fort Carson squad had a 25-4 record and won the league championship with Billy mostly playing center field and pitching.

The camp commander did something afterward that few of Billy's future superiors would do — he awarded his manager a good conduct medal. Billy was also promoted to corporal.

It was a strangely quiet year in the young life of Billy Martin. Sequestered in central Colorado, he was removed from fundamental cultural developments. The world was vaulting out of the World War II era in multiple ways. The French incursion into Vietnam ended in defeat and withdrawal, the first domino in a succession of events whose consequences would reach into the 1970s. Roger Bannister broke the four-minute barrier in the mile. Boeing introduced the 707 jetliner. Elvis Presley made his debut on *The Ed Sullivan Show.*

But the news that Billy followed most closely came in daily updates from the American League pennant race where the Cleveland Indians were running away with the title. For the rest of his life, Stengel would note that the only year the Yankees did not win the pennant in the early to mid-1950s was when Billy was not on the team. There was no hiding the Yankees' deficiencies in the middle of the infield where Billy's replacement, Jerry Coleman, batted just .217 and Rizzuto .195. Berra and Mantle had strong years at the plate, but to most observers, the Yankees looked out of sync. Stengel would always insist it was because he had lost his field general.

The New York Giants swept the Indians in the World Series, which history has remembered primarily for Willie Mays's over-the-shoulder catch in Game 1. Billy was hiking up another mountain that day, and he spent most of the week sleeping in a pup tent in freezing temperatures at ten thousand feet.

Three days after the World Series ended, when Billy was back at Fort Carson, he read that Marilyn Monroe had sued his old friend Joe DiMaggio for divorce. Monroe cited conflicting career demands. Billy was still contesting his divorce from Lois.

When the Yankees' 1955 season began, Coleman had been sacked as the starter at second base and Rizzuto, now thirty-seven, was expected to be replaced by Billy Hunter, the former Browns and Orioles shortstop (and one-time hidden-ball-trick victim of Billy). McDougald had taken over at second base, but the Yankees were also looking at a nineteen-year-old second baseman from South Carolina, Bobby Richardson.

The Yankees trailed the Chicago White Sox for most of the season until late August, when Stengel suddenly announced that Billy would be granted a temporary leave from the army because of accrued time.

"Just in time to get us to the pennant," Stengel crowed, who added that he planned to play Billy at shortstop.

On September 2, batting third and playing shortstop, Billy was in the Yankees' lineup for the first time since the final game of the 1953 World Series.

Before the game, Billy addressed the team in a players-only meeting. He talked about how his absence from the Yankees had been a blow to his finances.

"I had to sell my Cadillac and my father's car back home to get by this year," Billy said in a voice that was stern and lecturing. "I'm broke. Broke, you hear me? I'm broke and we're playing like we're trying to lose. We have to get into this World Series. We have to!"

In the game that followed, Billy stroked a single and a double in a 4–2 win over the Washington Senators. The *New York Times* ran a picture of that day's winning pitcher, Whitey Ford, flanked by Billy and Mickey, who hit a long home run. The Three Musketeers were reunited.

On September 23, in what was their fifteenth victory in their last twenty games, the Yankees clinched the pennant, defeating the Red Sox 3–2 when Billy, back at second base with Rizzuto at shortstop, drove in the winning run with a single in front of Boston center fielder Jimmy Piersall.

Billy played in just twenty games during the 1955 regular season (his teammates nonetheless voted him a full share of the team's World Series earnings, an amazing endorsement). He had 21 hits in 70 at-bats, the only season he hit .300 in his career. Entering the World Series against Brooklyn (who else?), the Yankees were seen as favorites, but mostly because they had beaten the Dodgers four times in the previous eight years and had not lost a World Series since 1942. Besides, Brooklyn was not happy about the Yankees having Billy back.

Interviewed the day before the series was to start, Jackie Robinson told writer Louis Effrat, "Billy is not brash or a dead-end kid or any of the other things people like to say about him. That's his image. What he really is, is a smart player, cool and calculating. A player like that gets to be a pain in the neck to some people, but it has nothing to do with the man. He has always played up to the fullest all the times I've played with him."

The Yankees won the first game behind Whitey Ford in a game that featured two controversial attempts to steal home. Jackie Robinson was called safe when it appeared he might be out. Billy, who also had a triple and a single in the game, was called out trying to steal home when it appeared he might be safe. The Yankees won the second game, 4–2, with Billy cleverly using his baseball acumen to significantly aid his team's cause.

In the fourth inning of a game the Dodgers led 1–0, Billy tied the game with an RBI single to left field. But it's what he did next that mattered most. The next batter, Ed Robinson, was hit by a pitch, which advanced Billy to second base and loaded the bases. With pitcher Tommy Byrne at the plate, Billy had a clear view of Brooklyn catcher Roy Campanella's signals. Knowing Billy's proclivity for stealing signals, every Yankees batter watched Billy closely if he was at second base.

After two pitches, Billy deciphered Campanella's signal pattern and removed his cap, the signal to Byrne that he could forecast the pitches for him. The Yankees had a preset code in this instance; if Billy raised his right leg before the pitch, it was a fastball, if he raised his left leg, it was a curve. The 2-2 pitch was a fastball — as Billy had predicted — and Byrne laced it to center field for a two-run single. The Yankees never trailed in the game again.

Brooklyn won the next two games to tie the series. Billy was having another good World Series, but the evenly matched teams traded victories, setting up a tense Game 7 at Yankee Stadium.

The Dodgers had a 2–0 lead in the sixth inning when Billy led off with a walk and McDougald singled. The left-handed-hitting Yogi Berra, normally a pull hitter, went the other way, slicing a drive toward the left-field corner where Brooklyn's Sandy Amoros ran it down just inside fair territory. Inexplicably, Amoros was not playing Berra to pull the ball. McDougald was doubled off first base on the play and the Yankees never seriously threatened again.

For the rest of his life, Billy could be riled to agitation if someone brought up Amoros's play.

"There is no way Amoros should even be there," Billy said. "Brooklyn had a good pitching staff and maybe we don't win but that game should have been tied in the sixth inning."

In the Yankees' locker room after the loss, Billy pounded his fists on his locker until his knuckles bled. In tears, he hid out in the trainer's room so reporters wouldn't see him. One media member waited an hour for Billy to emerge, a lawyer from Brooklyn who dabbled in broadcasting named Howard Cosell.

Cosell complimented Billy on his play during the series — Billy had batted .320 with 4 RBIs.

"I'm disgusted that I let down Casey," Billy told Cosell. "A man like that shouldn't have to lose a World Series."

Billy returned to Fort Carson three days later. He was discharged with an honor guard farewell in tribute. Outside the base, in uniform, Billy smiled for photographers. Pinned to his breast was his good conduct medal. That was a picture worth saving.

The next day he was back in Berkeley. In late October, he met Lois at a lawyer's office on San Pablo Avenue where together they signed divorce papers formally ending their five-year marriage.

His cousin Nick drove Billy the few blocks to his mother's house because Billy did not have a car. His bedroom on the second floor awaited. By all accounts, Billy did indeed rest for a while.

14

SINCE 1947, BILLY HAD approached every season with some measure of hope, uncertainty, or desperation. The stakes, it seemed, were always high, presaging another life-changing development. His career was usually hanging in the balance, or he had new personal responsibilities, like marriage or fatherhood.

But in 1956, things were different. For one, the Yankees were no longer defending world champions. It was Brooklyn's time on the stage. The Yankees were still *the* Yankees, but writers felt little sizzle in their presence.

Calm and free of any controversy for the first time in years, Billy fit right in. With Rizzuto one year away from a forced retirement, Billy was nearly the elder statesman of the infield. He was healthy and had gained weight, a model of sinewy fitness: fifteen-inch collar, thirty-one-inch waist, with thick forearms and shoulders.

Billy the Kid, as he was incessantly called in print, turned twenty-eight on May 16. In a 4–1 victory over the Cleveland Indians that day, Billy hit a home run; Mantle hit two. The win put the Yankees in first place, where they stayed for the rest of the season. There were no formidable American League challengers, and the Yankees cruised. The only issue Stengel was having in 1956 was finding a replacement for Rizzuto. The Yankees' brass knew that the double-play combination of the future was Tony Kubek at shortstop and Bobby Richardson at second base, but they were still raw minor leaguers. For now there was a revolving door of Yankees shortstops, including Rizzuto. It was not the Yankee Way but it was working in 1956.

There was no rocking the boat on a Yankees team that was destroying the rest of the American League. Mantle was having a year that would cement him as the player of the decade. He won the Triple Crown, leading the league in home runs (52), RBIs (130), and batting average (.353). Billy would end up hitting .264 with 9 home runs and 49 RBIs. He made the

All-Star team for the only time in his career. Whitey won 19 games with just 6 losses and a league-leading ERA of 2.47.

The Three Musketeers were in the prime of their careers, and they had hardly slowed down off the field. They had never needed any schooling in how to be big league in that category. Whitey Ford remembered that when he was called up as a rookie, he met the team at its hotel in Boston in time for breakfast. Billy greeted him with that DiMaggio staple: blondes.

"Billy takes me into the lobby and standing there waiting for us are two of the most beautiful blondes I have ever seen in my life," Ford wrote. "A couple of knockouts. Now, here we are, two rookies, one just up from the minor leagues that day and we're parading through the lobby of the Kenmore Hotel with these gorgeous blondes. And the older guys like Allie Reynolds and Bobby Brown are standing there glaring at us because it looks like the girls have just come with us from our rooms. I haven't even checked into my room, but it was a nice impression we made."

Asked more than sixty years later if he recalled the scene Ford described, Brown answered, "No, not something I would have cared to recall. But yes, those guys knew how to live it up."

Some of Billy's childhood friends were old enough in 1956, or financially stable enough, to make trips to New York to stay with their old pal. They came back to the Bay Area with stories that seemed incomprehensible to those still living in the dingy neighborhood along the Berkeley docks.

Jack Setzer, an original member of the West Berkeley Boys, recalled going to dinner with Billy and heavyweight champion Rocky Marciano. They went to a nightclub where Frank Sinatra was singing. Setzer was stunned when he and Billy were seated near the stage and thunderstruck when Sinatra introduced Billy to the crowd and later joined them for a drink. The next night, while having dinner at the 21 Club, Setzer realized he was sitting one table away from Grace Kelly and Monaco's Prince Rainier, who had been married that April. From the 21 Club Billy and Setzer went to the Stork Club for drinks with Sid Caesar, Carl Reiner, and Doris Day.

"Billy not only knew all these people, he talked to them like they had grown up with him in Berkeley," Setzer said. "There was no barrier. You were a big deal if you were a pro baseball player in New York in the 1950s."

Billy did not lack for female companionship on any of these occasions, though anything resembling a steady girlfriend was rare, especially since the Yankees were on the road half the time. The lasting relationships were within the Three Musketeers, although Whitey, the New York native, had a house and a wife on Long Island and did not participate in the Manhattan nightlife with the same nonstop fervor that Billy and Mickey did. (Merlyn Mantle was chiefly preoccupied with her two young sons, including one named Billy, born in 1955.)

It was during 1956 that sportswriters began to hear rumors that the Yankees management was worried about Billy's influence on Mickey, the face of the franchise if not Major League Baseball. In this tandem, it was always Billy leading Mickey astray and never the other way around. The drinking and carousing were never a mutually arrived-at choice. Mickey was always cast as the simple country boy corrupted by Billy, the cunning street kid. It may have been true, although Mickey did not change a bit when Billy eventually became his ex-teammate.

So the truth is probably more nuanced. The 1950s were marinated in alcohol. If the decade had a logo, it might show a lot of things — the birth of rock-and-roll, the growth of television, the expanded role of the automobile in an increasingly suburban society — but the best shape for a 1950s logo would be the outline of a martini glass. The term *drinking responsibly* is a modern notion. In the 1950s, the opposite was admired. Men had to drink often enough and long enough that they could learn to "handle it," which was the ultimate compliment.

On job interviews for many white-collar positions, potential employees would be taken to lunch and observed. If they drank little or not at all, they probably wouldn't get the job. If they drank and got tipsy, they wouldn't get the job. If they drank and could handle it — at lunch, mind you — they were right for the job.

And that was just in the workplace. After hours, even in mainstream America, it was cocktails for everyone — Scotch, gin, vodka, and bourbon flowing. Beer was treated like a nectar of life, as harmless as Kool-Aid. People drank to excess and drove their cars without a thought. It was almost impossible to get arrested for drunk driving. If you flipped your car or drove it into a pond, the cops or the tow truck driver just drove you home. As social mores go, it is certainly nothing to venerate, and as a lifestyle it had significant health consequences, not to mention the damage it did to careers and family lives. But it was, in fact, a way of life.

In this context, it is hard to discern who was influencing whom. Or how much of it was just the times. Some have said that Billy brought out the worst instincts in Mickey, which is undeniably possible. But it is easy to notice that most of the stories that the 1950s Yankees players reconstruct and tell usually involve a group of at least four or five Yankees out on the town — Bauer, Berra, and others like Charlie Silvera or pitcher Bob Grim. Billy, Mickey, and Whitey on the road might have been the most roguish, intent on pushing the party to its utter limits, but drinking and staying out late were ingrained habits of ballplayers who did not have to report for work until 11:00 a.m. the next day.

Billy and Mickey drank a lot — dangerously so — and the Yankees were a hard-drinking crew. So were the other fifteen Major League teams. From the beginning, baseball was a traveling, athletic-themed entertainment, and like many a circus, it bred some hard-living routines. There was free booze in every clubhouse in the country, and every stadium had a press room lounge where the drinks were complimentary. Players, coaches, reporters, and managers congregated in these press room bars after games, sometimes for hours. It was a tradition that dated to the 1920s, one that did not die out until the end of the twentieth century.

The trains on which the players traveled had multiple bar cars. The planes gave away free booze. So yes, the 1950s Yankees got drunk often. Billy, like the leader he was, was right there with them. The whole bunch of them were Mad Men before twenty-first-century television writers created *Mad Men*.

But Yankees general manager George Weiss was different. Raised in Connecticut, the land of steady habits, he was a short, stout, and jowly man who had been the manager of his high school baseball team and was educated at Yale University. As a young man in the 1920s, he made his name in baseball as the owner and chief publicity agent of a minor league team in New Haven, where he befriended Casey Stengel who was passing through. Weiss then led the Baltimore Orioles when they were a top minor league team.

In 1932, Yankees owner Jacob Ruppert hired Weiss to build a Yankees minor league system, which collected and developed top players for years thereafter. With an imprimatur of proven success, Weiss advanced through the ranks and remained with the Yankees until 1960. He was named baseball's Executive of the Year ten times.

Billy believed to his death that Weiss, who died in 1972, had held a grudge against him because of Billy's impetuous outburst in 1950 when Weiss ordered him to the minors.

"Four of us would be out somewhere and get in a little trouble," Billy said. "But I would be the one called into Weiss's office afterward."

There is documentation backing up Billy's claim, beginning with the multiple stories about private detectives that Weiss hired to tail Billy. He also had detectives following Mickey and Whitey, but their transgressions rarely came up. Weiss respected Stengel, enough to rehire him when Weiss took over the New York Mets in 1961, but he never warmed to Casey's boy. The sportswriters who covered the team in the 1950s frequently wrote that Weiss, a quiet, decorous man often seen in three-piece suits, had repeatedly expressed his opinion that Billy sullied the dignified image Weiss wanted the Yankees to project. The more the writers called Billy "brash" or "brassy," the more it offended Weiss, who, when asked what his hobbies were in a newspaper interview, answered that he liked to play golf and putter around his country house in Greenwich, Connecticut.

"Weiss liked that Billy helped the Yankees win," John Drebinger of the *New York Times* wrote in 1958. "He did not like how Billy helped the Yankees win."

And in 1956, with Richardson waiting in the wings, Weiss surely did not believe the Yankees would stop winning if Billy were on another team. So throughout the 1956 season, Weiss, no stranger to strategic marketing, started floating the idea in the New York press that Billy was an unwelcome influence on the greatest player in baseball.

It was a calculated campaign because Weiss knew that trading Billy would be met with a backlash in the New York press and with the Yankees' fan base. Billy was exceedingly popular with reporters and columnists. He knew the writers and hung out with them on the road and at that way station of Manhattan athletic culture, Toots Shor's, the saloon with a landmark oversize circular bar at 51 West 51st Street. Yankees fans were also drawn to Billy's hustle, fiery demeanor, and reliability in pressure situations. He was an Everyman hero even then.

So as early as 1956, Weiss did what he could to lay the groundwork for his opinion that Billy must eventually go. It was for the good of the franchise and its franchise player.

In the meantime, the 1956 Yankees juggernaut chugged on with an air of invincibility.

During a game at Fenway Park that year, third baseman Andy Carey was at the plate when Stengel called time out and summoned Billy from the on-deck circle.

"Go tell him to pick out a good pitch and hit a home run," Casey said.

"What did you say?" Billy asked.

"I said to tell that son of a bitch to swing at a good pitch and hit a home run," Casey repeated.

Billy trotted to the plate and relayed the instructions. Boston catcher Sammy White turned and said, "You guys have got to be kidding."

On the next pitch Carey slammed a high drive over the Green Monster in left field. As Carey rounded the bases, White looked over at Billy. "I've never seen anything like that in my life," he said.

Replied Billy, "When the old man tells us to do something, we do it."

The other memorable incident involving Billy in 1956 was a tussle with a portly little pitcher with the Kansas City Athletics named Tommy Lasorda.

Lasorda had been pitching inside to a couple of Yankees batters, and when he nearly hit Hank Bauer in the head, Billy jumped to the top step of the dugout and screamed at Lasorda, "I'm going to get you later."

Lasorda stalked off the mound in the direction of the Yankees' dugout.

"I said to him, 'You don't have to wait, banana nose, come out now,'" Lasorda barked. "And, of course, Billy being Billy, he did."

There was a scuffle involving several Yankees and Athletics, but no punches were thrown.

"The next day, Billy comes over to me before the game and says, 'You know, you've got balls. Two tough dagos like us shouldn't be fighting,'" Lasorda said. "And we shook hands and went out for a drink that night. And from that moment forward we were the best of friends."

Lasorda was out of the Major Leagues by the next season, but his path crossed Billy's numerous times thereafter, conspicuously when they managed against each other in the 1977 World Series.

The Yankees won the 1956 American League pennant by nine games. For his 1956 performance, Mantle won the first of his three MVP awards.

Billy had another strong year at the plate, but there was a sense that he might have lost a step in the field from his two years off in the army. Maybe it was the weight he had gained, although he was still lean and gangly. Maybe he had lost some incorporeal edge because he was no longer popping two greenies a day. Or maybe it was injuries. Billy missed 28 games with a swollen knee and a troublesome back. Whatever it was, it was subtle. The Yankees' infield was still the glue that protected the pitching staff, and it had led to 97 victories and a pennant. But some people, like George Weiss, thought they saw a difference defensively in Billy. The mid-1950s was no time to crunch numbers so it was hard to prove, but modern baseball researchers have a statistic they call the "range factor." It is a player's putouts and assists divided by innings played. Billy's range factor at second base in 1953 was 5.35. It dropped to 4.77 in 1956. If he played 140 games, that would equate to about 81 fewer putouts and assists. Billy's total fielding chances in 1956 dropped to 978.1 from 1,288.1 in 1953. Since Billy also played in 28 fewer games in '56 than he did '53, the number would be expected to drop, but the number of fielding chances per game nonetheless dropped by a significant .56 per game, which would equate to about 80 fewer fielding chances in a 140-game season.

It seemed that Billy's twenty-eight-year-old legs were getting to fewer balls than his twenty-five-year-old legs had. There was some talk of moving him to third base in 1957.

None of this was part of the conversation in October 1956 as baseball fans turned to yet another World Series pitting the Yankees against the Dodgers. While there was a "here we go again" familiarity to the matchup, it would turn out to be the last all–New York World Series for forty-four years, until the Mets and Yankees met in 2000. It may have gone unannounced, but it was an end of a baseball era, one populated by players who became legends in the game.

Nineteen players who were eventually voted into the Baseball Hall of Fame played or managed in 1950s all–New York World Series games: DiMaggio, Rizzuto, Ford, Mantle, Berra, Stengel, Campanella, Robinson, Durocher, Mays, Duke Snider, Pee Wee Reese, Sandy Koufax, Don Drysdale, Enos Slaughter, Monte Irvin, Johnny Mize, Walter Alston, and Dick Williams.

The series opened on the same day that the world was marveling at an engineering wonder: the first telephone cable laid across the floor of the Atlantic Ocean, stretching from Newfoundland to Scotland. The Dodgers won the first two games of the 1956 World Series at home, but in Game 3 at Yankee Stadium, the Yankees won behind Ford and Billy's second home run of the series. In Game 4, Billy broke open a tied game with an RBI single in the fourth inning. In that game, Billy also faked Jackie

Robinson into running toward second base when Robinson should have tagged up on a fly ball—a deception that likely cost Brooklyn a run. It began when the Dodgers' Sandy Amoros lifted a foul ball to deep left field, which Robinson did not pick up initially. Seeing Robinson's indecision, Billy went through the motions of fielding a ground ball. Fearing he would be doubled up on the bases, Robinson broke for second. By the time Robinson realized Billy was deking him into a mistake, it was too late to tag up. Robinson would likely have scored on a single later in the inning.

In Game 5, Stengel went with a last-minute hunch and decided to pitch Don Larsen, a journeyman starter known throughout baseball for his heavy drinking. Only two years earlier, Larsen had led the American League with 21 losses for Baltimore. He showed up for Game 5 hung-over, then went out and pitched the greatest game in World Series history. As Dick Young, the famed *New York Daily News* columnist, said that day, "The imperfect man pitched a perfect game." (Amazingly, Young donated that line to his colleague Joe Trimble, who was stricken with writer's block trying to sum up the weight of Larsen's accomplishment.) In a famous photograph of Larsen delivering his last pitch of the game, Billy is in the background just over Larsen's shoulder.

Billy later wrote that he was happy for Larsen but added, "But to be honest, I wasn't all that excited or thrilled about his pitching a perfect game. I was just glad that we won. Otherwise we would have gone to Brooklyn down three games to two."

It was a good thought because the Dodgers won Game 6, 1–0. On the Yankees' bus back to Yankee Stadium after the game, Billy sat next to Casey Stengel. Slaughter had misplayed a fly ball in left field for the only Dodgers run. Billy told Casey to get the forty-year-old Slaughter out of the lineup. Billy wanted him to play twenty-seven-year-old Elston Howard. And he wanted twenty-five-year-old Bill "Moose" Skowron to replace the thirty-three-year-old Joe Collins at first base.

"If you don't go with the youth, we're going to lose this thing," Billy told Casey.

Stengel listened. Howard had a double and a home run in Game 7 and played flawlessly in left field. With the Yankees ahead 5–0, Billy led off the seventh inning with a single and was standing on third base three batters later when Skowron drilled a grand slam to right field. The Yankees broke the Brooklyn fans' hearts again, romping to a 9–0 victory for their seventeenth championship since 1923. It was their fifth World Series title of the decade.

In the newsreel footage of the final out, Billy is in the middle of the celebratory pack jumping up and down, his head bobbing above the throng as if he were attached to a pogo stick. It had been three years since his 1953 World Series fame, but he was back on top of the baseball world again.

Billy batted .296 in the series with 2 home runs and 3 RBIs. When he struck out in the eighth inning of Game 7, it was the 99th at-bat, and the last, of an illustrious World Series career.

With 33 hits in five World Series dating to 1951, Billy had batted .333 with 19 RBIs and 5 home runs in 28 games. His slugging percentage was .566. By way of comparison, Mantle, considered one of the best postseason power hitters ever, had a career World Series slugging percentage of .535. In 252 innings at second base, Billy made 1 error.

Billy would play another 537 games in the Major Leagues and stride to the plate another 1,983 times. But he never again played in the World Series spotlight that brought out his best. In the center of the diamond during the final baseball act of the 1956 baseball season, he had indeed made it to Yankee Stadium and the October cheers were for him. A baseball star on the best-known sports team in the world, he had lived the fantasy he invented as a kid at Kenney Park.

What he did not know is that the biggest piece of his childhood dream was over.

15

BILLY DID NOT GO back to Berkeley during the winter of 1956–57. Nor did he go to Japan. Or to Commerce. He lived in the Hotel St. Moritz overlooking Central Park South. The St. Moritz was a thirty-six-story, thousand-room gathering spot of East Side Manhattan high society. Designed so that most rooms had windows facing Central Park, the hotel featured cooling breezes and a sense of airiness much prized in bustling midtown. The façade of the building, now a Ritz-Carlton hotel, was made of brown sandstone, and the lobby floors and walls were built of Rosso Levanto marble from Italy. The hotel had an opulent dinner-dancing nightclub on the thirty-first floor, a tearoom, and a rooftop garden where an orchestra played during lunch and dinner.

Alfred Manuel "Billy" Martin of 1632 7th Street, West Berkeley, was seen often walking through the sumptuous St. Moritz with a wide smile on his face. Bellmen loved him (and his big-tipping ways). Entertainers loved that he was not awed by their fame. The playwrights who used the tearoom as a writing salon were enamored of his easygoing manner, especially since they knew it also hid a forbidding intensity. He reminded them of a complicated, fascinating character they wished they had invented with pen and paper. Musicians meandered through the St. Moritz, and Billy, who kept the same night-owl hours as they did, knew them all. Essayists and authors frequented the St. Moritz, too, and Billy, who could talk to anyone, would engage them in conversation. His was not an academically trained mind, but it was nimble and perspicacious — at least before too many drinks — which is why in the mid-1950s many a magazine and newspaper writer found time to compose a probing, intellectual treatise on the Yankees' gifted but enigmatic second baseman.

All of this mattered not at all to Billy, who was simply enjoying himself. In the 1950s and for decades thereafter, people would psychoanalyze Billy, or suggest he would benefit from psychoanalysis. Billy always had his own brand of therapy. And it was having fun.

One of Billy's frequent pals that winter was comedian Jackie Gleason, whose show *The Honeymooners* had started filming in New York in 1955. Gleason loved to drink and gamble, in that order, a combination that often led to an inebriated Gleason daring bar patrons to challenges that involved some kind of athletic performance. Billy, often standing not far away, was always game — much to the delight of many a saloon gathering.

When Billy and Gleason got tired of the standard barroom dares — balancing shot glasses on a forehead while jumping up and down or vaulting from the floor to the seat of a barstool without spilling a beer — they moved farther afield. One regular stop: the city's many bowling alleys. Gleason and Billy had several high-stakes matches at bowling alleys, almost all of which Billy won. It took a while for Gleason to realize that bowling was a blue-collar sport, and West Berkeley Billy, not surprisingly, had plenty of experience at it. He was an excellent bowler who routinely rolled games in the 225 range. So after Gleason got tired of losing at bowling, they gambled at dart boards around the city. And after losing at that, Gleason finally took Billy to pool halls. This is where Gleason had the edge, although Billy could be unnerving with an acerbic tongue and sharp, jabbing wit. The duo also went to the racetrack together, sometimes accompanied by another Gleason pal, Desi Arnaz, who often brought his wife, Lucille Ball.

Billy's hobnobbing with television's top-rated male and female stars was great fodder for New York's more than ten daily newspapers, which happily ran pictures of Billy with his famous friends. The Yankees' George Weiss saw the images. Billy was also often seen in the company of an assortment of pretty young women, his arm around a rotating cavalcade of Broadway dancers and chorus girls. Billy was single, that was his business, but the Yankees' front office was already fast-forwarding to the approaching 1957 season. What effect would Billy's newly magnified Manhattan nightclub lifestyle have on Mantle, the married man with children who was supposed to be an All-American hero? The Yankees had been worried about Billy's influence before. Now they feared the worst.

Weiss summoned Billy to his office as the 1957 season approached to warn him.

"It was the same old bullshit," Billy said. "Mr. Weiss said, 'You better not stay out late once, you better not make one false move, because if you do, you've had it.'"

Bobby Richardson was in the 1957 spring training camp. He did not see any of the turmoil he read about years later and was completely unaware Billy was on a short leash.

"Billy was the unquestioned leader of the team and everyone listened to him, including Mickey and Casey," Richardson said.

Sports Illustrated put Billy on its cover, and the story included this sentence: "Billy is the bee which stings the Yankee rump, the battery which fires the Yankee engine, the fellow who makes the Yankees go."

By May, the Yankees had won nearly two-thirds of their games. Billy, Mickey, and Whitey had not changed their ways, but they had not gotten into any off-the-field trouble either. The team was scheduled for consecutive days off on May 15 and 16. The latter was Billy's birthday, and Berra's birthday was May 12. Several Yankees thought it would be fun to take the two Yankees out on the town. A week in advance a dinner was arranged at Danny's Hideaway, a large, famed restaurant on East 45th Street, which was then known as Steak Row. The dinner was planned for the fifteenth because the players figured they could stay out late knowing there was no game the next day. It was a big group. Former teammates Bob Cerv and Irv Noren, in town with the Kansas City Athletics, were invited, as was pitcher Johnny Kucks and Berra, Ford, Bauer, and Mantle and their wives. When a rainout from earlier in the year was unexpectedly scheduled for the sixteenth, the dinner went on as scheduled because the wives had already arranged for babysitters.

Danny's Hideaway was packed and the service was a bit slow. The Yankees and their guests did not mind. They passed the time drinking. None in that group needed encouragement. After dinner, the party, minus Cerv and Noren, moved to the Waldorf Astoria, where Johnny Ray was singing. The Waldorf baked a birthday cake. After Ray's show, the group climbed into three cabs and were driven the ten blocks to the Copacabana at 10 East 60th Street. They got there twenty minutes before the 2:00 a.m. show of Sammy Davis Jr.

This was Billy's neighborhood, just a few blocks from the St. Moritz. The Copa, known as "the hottest club north of Havana," was an incongruous fit for a neighborhood so close to posh Fifth Avenue. But it had a fantasy atmosphere. Descending into the Copa's basement location was like flying south to the Caribbean, with tropical plants, pink gardenias, and a Latin-style décor. Seeing the Yankees early that morning, the Copa manager quickly set up a new table right next to the stage, a large, semicircular banquette. The party was in full swing.

Even though the next hour or so was the subject of dozens of newspaper stories (there were newspaper reporters in the room at the time), and even though the events of the next hour led to a court case with testimony taken from several witnesses, including the Yankees, it has never been established exactly what happened next. There is one central established fact: Edwin Jones, forty, a delicatessen owner who lived at 600 West 188th Street in northern Manhattan and one of nineteen members of a bowling club out for a night on the town, ended up unconscious in the cloakroom with a broken nose and bruises on his ribs, scalp, and chin.

The other established fact: George Weiss blamed Billy for it. Billy was there and it occurred on his birthday.

Jones's bowling party, which had been drinking heavily as well, was seated near the Yankees' table. At some point, words were exchanged between the two groups. The Yankees said that one of the bowlers had called Davis "a little sambo." Davis interrupted his show to protest the insult. Bauer, other Yankees said, told the bowlers to shut up. Jones in particular jawed back at Bauer and wanted to fight.

Billy always maintained that at this juncture Jones's brother, Leonard, approached him and asked to talk in private. They went to an anteroom and the brother told Billy that he would calm down Edwin if Billy calmed Bauer. Billy agreed, and as they left the room he heard a commotion toward the back of the nightclub, near the cloakroom and kitchen. He ran over to see Jones knocked out cold.

Mickey came running over shouting Billy's name — "Billy, Billy, Billy!" — because Billy had been missing for a few minutes as he talked with Leonard Jones.

"I said: 'Mick, I'm over here.' But when the reporters came snooping around, everyone had heard Mickey call my name and as a result some of the people evidently thought I hit the guy," Billy said.

Every Yankee denied hitting the man. As Berra said, "Nobody did nothing to nobody."

Bauer, the most likely suspect then and now, said he went to the back of the room with Edwin Jones. He said he wanted to throw a punch but couldn't because Berra and Kucks rushed up behind him and held his arms. Bauer also said the bouncers told him they would take care of things.

The combination of newsy elements — famous Yankees, Sammy Davis

Jr., a nightclub of note and esteem, and a punched-out patron — made front-page headlines in the afternoon papers.

IT WASN'T A NO-HITTER, screamed the bold text of the *Journal-American*.

The Yankees' clubhouse was mobbed with reporters before the May 16 game. Yankees owner Dan Topping summoned the Copa Six — as they were already being called in media reports — into his office and fined each of them $1,000 (which he rescinded after they won the pennant). At the time, he was livid.

"I warned you sons of bitches," Topping screamed.

Afterward, Bauer asked Mantle when they had been warned.

"You wasn't at that party," Mantle answered.

Stengel benched Berra, Ford, and Billy for that day's game and dropped Bauer to eighth in the order. Mantle still hit third. Stengel said he was mad at Mickey too but he had a pennant to win.

The New York tabloids piled on the coverage: WHICH YANKEE SLUGGER DOLED OUT THE BIG HIT?

Another headline read: INSIDE BAD BOY BILLY'S BIRTHDAY BRAWL.

Weiss issued a statement: "The Yankees have made a preliminary examination of the facts surrounding Billy Martin's birthday party, which was attended by certain players, all with their wives with the exception of Martin." Weiss then said that the team was going to let the courts settle any culpability.

After the game, Billy told Mickey that he was returning to his hotel so he could start packing. "I'm gone, pard," he said.

"But you didn't do anything," Mickey said.

"Doesn't matter," Billy answered.

The next day, an item in the *Washington Post* said that Senators manager Charlie Dressen was weighing a trade offer from the Yankees — Martin and infielder Andy Carey for Washington third baseman Eddie Yost and either pitcher Camilo Pascual or Pete Ramos.

Edwin Jones pressed charges against Bauer, who was charged with felonious assault. Asked by his lawyer if he hit Edwin Jones, Bauer, who was hitting .203 at the time, said, "Hit him? I haven't hit anybody all year." Among the other Yankees who testified was Mantle, who took the stand and removed gum from his mouth.

"I was so drunk I didn't know who threw the first punch," Mickey said. "A body came flying out and landed at my feet. At first I thought it was Billy, so I picked him up. But when I saw it wasn't, I dropped him back down. It looked like Roy Rogers rode through the Copa on Trigger and Trigger kicked the guy in the face."

The jurors laughed heartily. A little while later, they absolved Bauer of guilt. It did not help that Edwin Jones's memory of the night was sketchy and unconvincing. And no one else came forward who said they saw Jones being hit. Billy testified, denying he hit anyone. That night.

Jones, who lived to be eighty-two, died in 1985. His son, Edwin Jr., became a bar owner in Meriden, Connecticut. In 2011, he told his local newspaper that his father told him that Bauer jumped him in the bathroom.

The elder Jones remained a Yankees fan to his death.

"He loved the Yankees, even Bauer," Ed Jr. said. "He wouldn't talk about the Copa fight. If he did, he'd say, 'What happened, happened.'"

If the Yankees' Copa Six went on with their lives unscathed, Billy felt certain he was going to be the enduring victim. But as the June 15 trading deadline approached, Billy was still a Yankee.

However, with each succeeding day, he was playing less and less. Richardson was being installed as the everyday second baseman — and playing well.

On Monday, June 3, the Yankees had an off day. Whitey Ford arranged to rent a boat and invited Mickey, Billy, and pitcher Bob Grim to spend the day deep-sea fishing off Long Island. Ozzie Sweet, often called "the Babe Ruth of sports photographers," had an assignment to take pictures of Mantle for a story being prepared by *Sports Illustrated*. Sweet accompanied the four Yankees and offered to bring the beer and a bucket of fried chicken.

At one juncture in the journey Sweet captured the four in the back of the boat with Mickey and Billy sitting in chairs bolted to the deck. Grim and Ford are perched on the port railing. Grim has stripped down to a sleeveless undershirt and is looking toward the bow. Mickey, who was dressed in a golf shirt and plain gray pants rolled up at the cuffs, and Billy, who wore a print shirt with short sleeves and brown pants, are half turned away from the photographer. Only Ford, in a white T-shirt and beige khakis, is looking at the camera. Seeing it all, the man they called "Slick" is smiling broadly. No one is speaking. No one is making eye contact.

Billy and Mickey are holding bottles of Coca-Cola, which may be what Whitey is smiling about. It was a setup. Sweet later said the four drank only beer that day.

But that's not what makes the scene one of the most memorable sports photos of the 1950s. It is a picture of an era, a portrait in time. The four are gathered in repose, idle and calm even as they are surrounded by furious ocean waves. It's a scene of young men in the prime of their lives, separated from their other world but together and at ease in their own. It's a photo of friendship with Billy positioned in the middle. He is something he rarely seemed to be: motionless.

Years later, Sweet commented on the picture.

"Those guys were great friends," he said.

In the photo, Billy has removed his right foot from one of his loafers and propped that foot on his chair. His left foot is half in and half out of the other loafer, which he has raised in the air, leaving it dangling from his toes. It is the other shoe waiting to drop.

Eight days later in Chicago, after Yankees pitcher Art Ditmar nearly hit White Sox hitter Larry Doby, a nasty brawl ensued. It took thirty minutes to restore order. Four suspensions, including one to Billy, were handed out. That was Tuesday, June 11. The trading deadline was Saturday, when the Yankees would be in Kansas City, where George Weiss had established the Yankees' first farm system team in 1932. Kansas City was like a second hometown to Weiss, and he would be on the trip with the team.

On Friday, June 14, Billy played third base and in the sixth inning lined a single to left field that scored two runs and put the Yankees up 6–0. In the ninth inning, Billy grounded out to second base.

Billy was not in the lineup for the next night's game. He hid out in the bullpen, hoping that if they couldn't find him, maybe they couldn't trade him. But by the seventh inning, only an hour before the trading deadline, Stengel sent for Billy, telling him to come to the visitors' clubhouse.

Casey had first set eyes on Billy as an unkempt, skinny infielder with a torn and soiled uniform. Since then, they had been on five championship teams, including the 1948 Oakland Oaks. Billy was and always had been Casey's boy.

When Billy reached the visitors' clubhouse, Casey said, "You're gone."

It was later learned that Casey had protected Billy from the Senators trade and two other trades. But Weiss was not to be dissuaded this time. Not with this player in these circumstances. Not when he wanted to send a message to the rest of the team. Besides, Kubek was already in New York, ready to play shortstop. For the Yankees' youth movement in the middle infield to be complete, Richardson had to take over at second base.

Casey, his eyes welling with tears, told Billy that the Kansas City owner, Arnold Johnson, was coming to the clubhouse in a few minutes.

"I'm going to tell him what a great person and player you are," Casey said.

Billy interrupted.

"Don't you say shit, Casey," he said. "When I needed you to protect me, you let me down. So don't say shit."

Johnson walked in seconds later.

"Mr. Johnson, don't listen to him," Billy said, near tears. "I'll play my best for you. That's what you want, right?"

Johnson nodded uncomfortably.

"OK, thank you," Billy said, and walked toward the showers.

Despite a 9–2 Yankees win, Richardson recalled the scene in the clubhouse afterward as gloomy.

"Billy was the most popular guy on that team," Richardson said. "People had heard the trade rumors but it never seemed real until it was official.

"Whitey and Mickey were crying in the locker room. Other players, too. I remember that I showered quickly and quietly, dressed, and boarded the bus that would take us back to our hotel in downtown Kansas City. The entire team was on the bus except Casey and Billy."

Richardson, who was twenty-one years old, said the wait on the bus was nearly an hour. Finally, Stengel emerged from the ballpark alone. He sat in the first-row seat reserved for the manager.

"I was wondering if we would see Billy at all," Richardson said. "Then he came out and got on the bus. He walked by Casey and came up the aisle. The seat next to me was empty and he sat down next to me. He said, 'OK, kid, it's all yours now.'

"I'll never forget it. He told me I was going to be a great player. He said I was good enough and to just take my time and to listen to Casey. We talked a little baseball but not for too long. Then we sat there in silence for a while. When we got to the hotel, everybody got off the bus and walked into the lobby. Billy walked off down the sidewalk by himself."

Two weeks later, in an interview with the *New York Times,* Billy recalled the night he was traded: "I can't explain how I felt. I heard Casey say, 'You're gone,' and yet I was sort of numb, unable to think, hear or feel. He told me how much I had meant to the ball club and to him. At least that's what I think I heard."

More than twenty years later, Billy was more succinct: "My heart was broken."

16

BILLY DID NOT WANDER the streets of Kansas City alone for long. He was joined by Whitey and Mickey, and the three alternately laughed and cried and lamented and celebrated on through the night. It was a late night even by their standards. Billy never did go to sleep.

The next day, wearing his new Athletics uniform for the first time, Billy met with reporters.

"I will miss the Yankees but I play hard all the time," he said. "It doesn't matter what uniform I'm wearing."

It was the right thing to say. It also proved to be anything but the truth.

In his first Kansas City at-bat, he singled off the wall in left field. He led off the eighth inning with a home run that tied the game. In several books about Billy published in the 1980s and 1990s, it was written that Ford pitched in the game the day after the trade, and that he signaled to Billy that he was going to throw a slow curve so Billy could hit a home run. It is an oft-told story to this day. Billy would tell it himself. But in the Internet age of websites like Retrosheet, it takes only seconds to check box scores of any game on any day in baseball history. It was Johnny Kucks on the mound for the Yankees that day, not Ford.

Two months later, Ford did give up a home run to Billy at Yankee Stadium. Perhaps that was when one friend tipped off another. History has apparently made those two months disappear for the sake of a better story.

In that first game as an Athletic, Billy's game-tying home run only delayed the inevitable when the Yankees scored three runs in the tenth inning to win the game. Billy visited with his ex-teammates in the hallway outside the visitors' clubhouse after the game. There were teary hugs and handshakes.

Then the Yankees got on their bus, heading to the airport for a flight back to New York. The Athletics, who were already thirteen games out of first place, were heading to play the only team they were ahead of in the American League, perennial doormat Washington.

One person Billy did not hug or greet after his first game as an Athletic was Casey Stengel. Billy would not talk to Stengel again for nearly seven years, an estrangement that disheartened both men. It was a rift driven by Billy, who not only avoided Casey when the two were at the same ballparks but generally did not talk about Casey to reporters either.

Casey stewed in silence, still praising his former protégé when his name came up. Casey also sent missives to Billy asking for a reunion or at least a phone conversation. Billy ignored the invitations.

Years later, Billy explained his frame of mind, as if it needed to be explained.

"I couldn't bring myself to be the same way with him — to act like nothing happened," Billy said. "I thought we had a pact, like two members of the same family. I thought he would protect me forever. And I could not forgive him. At least not for many years."

When Billy finally made an effort to reconcile with Stengel in 1964, he conceded Casey was not to blame for the falling-out. But he did not apologize for his reaction to the trade from the Yankees. The hurt ran too deep.

"I wasn't the same for quite a stretch there," he said. "Loyalty is everything to me and I felt betrayed. I was bitter that I had given the Yankees everything I had and they had cut me loose. And being mad at Casey was part of that."

Billy hit .360 during his first 10 games with the Athletics. It did not matter. The Athletics lost 9 of those games. For the season, his batting average with Kansas City was .257, up from the .241 he batted in the 43 games before the trade. He finished the season with 10 home runs and 39 RBIs.

But for Billy, to whom winning was everything, Kansas City was baseball's Alcatraz. Kansas City was a prison where the punishment was irrelevance. The Athletics would end up losing 94 games and finish 38.5 games behind the first-place Yankees.

Billy lived at the Berkeley Hotel in Kansas City, considered the finest hotel in the Midwest. It was the hotel of choice of airline pilots and their crews, then called stewardesses. And Trans World Airlines, known as TWA and considered the gold standard of U.S.-based airlines, was based in Kansas City. Many flight crews lived downtown, too.

Billy, not surprisingly, did not sulk in his room. He met a lot of stewardesses. With all the nonstop losing the only thing he looked forward to was his off-the-field adventures. But the Berkeley Hotel was not the St. Moritz. Jackie Gleason was not waiting for him in the lobby.

"He had nights when he was up and fun-loving," said Lou Skizas, a teammate in Kansas City who also played briefly with the Yankees in 1956. "But he had a lot of nights when he was blue and down-and-out. He would get in a funk and talk about how he wasn't the same guy without the Yankees."

His old team might not have been the same either.

The Yankees lost the 1957 World Series in seven games to Milwaukee. Richardson barely played in the series, giving way to Jerry Coleman at second base. Coleman played well, but several New York writers noted that the Yankees lacked their customary October edge.

YANKEES MISSING THEIR FIERY LEADER? a *New York Post* headline asked after the series. In the story the writer wondered if the Yankees had become too nice without "Battlin' Billy."

At the time, the Yankees' one-time fiery leader was selling cars in Kansas City, a job he got through a teammate. Billy was also looking at real estate in Kansas City and would eventually buy an apartment complex that grew in value rather handsomely as Kansas City blossomed as a model midwestern city in the middle of the twentieth century.

Billy spent the winter mostly in Kansas City, though he did make a two-week visit to Berkeley, spending time with Kelly Ann and with his mother.

His sister Pat recalled that after the trade to Kansas City she thought she saw an increase in how much Billy was drinking.

"It wasn't like he was drunk a lot," Pat Irvine said. "But a drink was more important to him. And boy, my mother got on him about that. All her life, she screamed at him about alcohol — 'Stop drinking so much,' she would yell. Bill was usually all fun and games. For a while there, he wasn't the same."

In November 1957 Billy was part of a thirteen-player trade that sent him to the Detroit Tigers, the beginning of a long, nomadic slog around the Major Leagues. In the next five years, he was traded or released six times.

Wherever he went, he was the "ex-Yankee star," and wherever he went, he was expected to provide the spark that some demoralized team needed.

In his first days as a Tiger, the Detroit manager, Jack Tighe, said of Billy, "He is the key to our future. It's as simple as that."

The Tigers got off to a decent start but slumped badly in May. They were a flawed team with Harvey Kuenn driving in just 54 runs in the middle of the lineup. The Detroit pitching was also suspect. Billy rubbed many of his new teammates the wrong way. In 1957, *Sports Illustrated* might have called Billy "the bee which stings the Yankee rump," but in Detroit he was seen as a pain in the ass. His needling and demanding ways only irritated the Tigers, a no-nonsense, unobtrusive team that reflected the blue-collar city they represented. Billy made too much noise. And he did not have the mercurial but nonetheless domineering Casey Stengel in the dugout to back him up.

These were also not players raised in the Yankee Way, nor did they want to be. Billy yelled at Tigers players who he believed were not focused enough. He tried the intimidation that the Yankees veterans had used on him, getting in guys' faces in the dugout — "Don't fuck with my money." He barked orders on the field in his high-pitched voice. None of it went over well. It did not help that among the Tigers' biggest problems was Billy, whom the Tigers had decided to turn into a shortstop, something Billy had never been for more than a few games. It was a failed experiment. Billy did not have the range of a Major League shortstop, and now, at thirty, he had other limitations, too. He made 20 errors in 1958, the most in any season of his eleven-year career. The Detroit fans, who had berated him for years as a hated Yankee, were not any happier to see him. They booed his errors mercilessly.

Billy batted .255 with 7 home runs and 42 RBIs for the Tigers, who quietly, almost sleepily, finished in fifth place, 15 games behind the Yankees, who then redeemed themselves in the 1958 World Series with a rematch victory over Milwaukee.

Nearly one year to the day after he was traded to Detroit, the Tigers sent Billy to Cleveland. The Indians said they would make him their everyday second baseman.

"The fireplug, ex-Yankee star could give the moribund Indians some sorely needed leadership," wrote the Cleveland *Plain Dealer* after the trade.

The Indians did challenge the Yankees, jumping to an early lead in the standings, and on May 16, Billy's birthday, Cleveland was in New York for a three-game series with the Yankees. Billy announced that he was going out to dinner with his Indians teammates to celebrate.

"And my old Copa gang isn't invited," he said, adding with a smile, "Well, maybe Mickey and Whitey."

But Billy's 1959 season was star-crossed. And he was breaking down. When a star player becomes a journeyman, it does not happen overnight. The easy assessment of Billy's playing career after 1957 is that he was brokenhearted and never approached the game with the same spirit and resolve. The presumption is that the Yankees lifted him just as he lifted them. Without the Yankees uniform, he was a desultory player with average skills.

But the decline from unofficial captain of the game's best team to a bit player on mediocre teams was in fact slow and piecemeal. In early 1959, Billy was batting nearly .280 and playing a steady second base when he charged a ground ball near the pitcher's mound, scooped it from the turf, and threw underhanded to first base for the out. Even the most graceful and athletic infielders make the play somewhat off-balance with their momentum carrying them forward. The across-his-body throwing motion can send a player tumbling to the grass.

Billy had made the play countless times, including the little somersault forward. But this time, when he fell, he did not roll and bounce with the elasticity he once had. This time, he separated his right shoulder. When he came back four weeks later, he discovered he could not throw with the same force he once had.

"I tried whipping the ball as hard as I could but the ball had nothing on it," Billy said. "I said to myself, 'You've got to be kidding.'"

Today, an MRI might have diagnosed the problem, and advanced physical therapy or arthroscopic surgery would fix Billy's ailing shoulder. In 1959, Billy simply had a weak throwing arm for the rest of his career.

Although just thirty-one years old, Billy was also having trouble with his knees, especially the left one that took much of the pounding from sliding base runners at second base. In 1959, Billy's left knee started giving out on him periodically. He would run to his left and stumble to stay upright.

He was also warring with his manager, Joe Gordon, the Yankees Hall of Fame second baseman from 1938 to 1950. Gordon did not like the way Billy turned the double play either (here we go again). Billy made just one error at second base in 1959 but it cost the Indians a game, and afterward Gordon criticized Billy, saying Billy did not field the Yankee Way — certainly not as Gordon had done in his time in New York.

Incensed, Billy had someone in the Indians' public relations department look up Gordon's Yankees fielding records. Then Billy passed the statistics around to the Cleveland writers: Gordon committed 188 errors in seven Yankees seasons. Billy committed 42 errors in his seven Yankees seasons.

Gordon was none too pleased with Billy's research.

Still, on the Fourth of July, the Indians were in first place with a four-game lead over the Yankees (if just two games over the Chicago White Sox).

On August 5 in Washington, in the first game of a double-header, Billy singled home the tying and winning runs for the Indians. He led off the second game, and the third pitch from Washington pitcher Tex Clevenger, a fastball that sailed up and in, crashed into Billy's face next to his left ear.

Batting helmets were not yet mandatory and Billy was not wearing one. The pitch knocked Billy to the ground. Blood began pouring from his nose and ears.

Cleveland catcher Russ Nixon was one of the first players to reach Billy.

"I never saw a man look so dead," Nixon told the Associated Press. "He didn't even flutter or move. Then his face swelled up like a beehive in minutes. By the time they brought out the stretcher, Billy was moving a little and moaning. But he couldn't talk. His face was crushed."

With a fractured jaw and broken cheekbone, he was brought to Georgetown University Hospital, his season over. There would be surgeries to fix the broken bones. A few days later, Clevenger visited the hospital, and news photographers took pictures of Billy's grossly swollen and stitched face as Clevenger sat on the edge of his hospital bed with a wan smile.

When the news photographers left, Clevenger and Billy both wept. Clevenger had been a dependable pitcher to that point, with a career record of 23-21. Though just twenty-nine years old, he started only eleven more Major League games and retired.

Billy recovered at home in Cleveland and his face healed without any obvious disfigurement. He watched as the Indians played .500 ball throughout September and fell five games short of the AL pennant. The

Yankees slumped to third place, and the first questions about whether Casey Stengel had been in the dugout for too long began to surface in the press.

On December 15, the Indians traded Billy to the Cincinnati Reds along with a top minor league prospect and pitcher Cal McLish, a 19-game winner whose full name was Calvin Coolidge Julius Caesar Tuskahoma McLish. The Indians received in return the Reds' All-Star second baseman, Johnny Temple. Gabe Paul, the Reds' general manager and Billy's future boss with the 1970s Yankees, pushed to include Billy in the trade.

It had taken a little more than two years, but Billy's gradual descent from All-Star to journeyman was complete, and the evidence was in the Cincinnati newspapers the next day when no story made much of the Reds' new second baseman, the former Yankees World Series hero. Most writers wondered about McLish's prospective contribution (and the origin of his full name). When the Cincinnati writers got around to discussing Billy, they did not use the usual words — *firebrand, fiery, sparkplug.* One used this phrase: "The stormy Martin . . ."

Billy, now thirty-one, had batted more than a thousand times as an ex-Yankee. Ten years earlier, the Yankees had bought his contract, and shortly thereafter, he made his American League debut with a double off the wall in Fenway Park. Now he would be making his debut in the National League with a bum shoulder, a balky knee, and the psychological scars of a beaning that was probably an inch from being fatal.

By the time he put on the Reds uniform, it would be a new decade. John F. Kennedy would be the Democratic candidate for president, black college students were staging sit-in protests at North Carolina luncheonettes, and Fidel Castro was entrenched in Cuba.

The 1950s, the cheery, self-indulgent decade that shaped Billy as an adult and established many of the tenets, values, and habits by which he lived the rest of his life, were ending. Billy might not have known it at the time, but he would be sad to see the 1950s go. It was a decade when he made an almost unimaginable ascent, going from a minor leaguer in a browbeaten West Coast city to a national sporting figure whose face graced the covers of prominent magazines. The 1950s in America were a time of limitless hope and optimism, an attitude inculcated in Billy since he had lived a rags-to-riches American dream worthy of a screenplay.

Most of all, the 1950s made Billy a Yankee to his core. And that would never change.

17

THE NIGHT BEFORE BILLY was traded from the Yankees in 1957, Cyril Winkler, a successful cattleman from Alliance, Nebraska, and a Yankees fan, drove to Kansas City to see the team play. His twenty-two-year-old daughter, Gretchen, who had moved to Kansas City when she joined TWA as a stewardess two years earlier, accompanied him and his wife in box seats near the field. Seated next to them were four sailors, who were drinking beer at a one-every-half-inning pace.

"I remember the sailors got feeling pretty good and they were yelling at Billy — nothing nasty, just teasing him and trying to get him to acknowledge them," Gretchen said, recounting the scene in 2013. "And Billy just kept smiling at them and waving his glove. He was kind of playing with them.

"I remember my mother saying, 'Oh, that Billy Martin is the cutest thing.' She liked the way he carried himself. And I remember reading the next day that Billy was traded to the Kansas City Athletics."

Gretchen did not know Billy at the time. And she had no plans for that to change. Less than a month later, she was working on a flight from Kansas City to San Francisco on the Fourth of July. A passenger in a middle seat had a complaint, which she handled. The passenger in the adjoining window seat caught her eye.

"You look like Billy Martin the ballplayer," Gretchen said.

Billy, beaming, replied, "That's because I am Billy Martin."

Gretchen snickered.

"I answered rather dismissively, 'Sure you are,'" Gretchen said. "And I went back to the front of the plane. I just ignored him. I knew the Athletics were in Chicago and flew together as a team. It couldn't be Billy Martin.

"My friend in the crew said, 'Did you see who we have on board? It's Billy Martin.' I said, 'It can't be him, the team is in Chicago.' And she said, 'He hurt his arm last night, didn't you see the sling on his arm? I think he's going home for a while.'"

Gretchen Winkler, pretty and curvaceous, had attended the University of Nebraska for two years before she decided to enter the TWA stewardess training program in Kansas City in 1955. She had met some Athletics ballplayers in her time but generally avoided them. As she said more than fifty years later, she had never been in love.

"I was still playing hard to get," she said.

She was embarrassed and mortified that she had snubbed Billy and spent the rest of the flight evading eye contact. But Billy talked to Gretchen's crewmates and got her name and the name of the San Francisco hotel where the crew was staying that night. He called the hotel and invited all the women to his mother's house in Berkeley for dinner.

"We had plans so we couldn't go," Gretchen said. "One of the other girls called to tell him that and apparently gave him my home phone number because we all lived pretty much together. So when I got home a few days later, he had left messages with my three roommates, asking me to call him."

But Gretchen did not return Billy's call.

"That wasn't my style," she said. "I didn't know him. But he kept calling. And calling. We had a rule in the house that no girl could flirt with any man calling for someone else, but one morning a couple weeks later the other girls said, 'Are you going to date Billy Martin or not? Because if you're not going to call him back, we are.'

"So I called him. He wanted me to go to the second game of a doubleheader and then out to dinner. And that's what I did. I brought one of my roommates and we ended up double-dating with Ralph Terry, the Yankees pitcher who was traded to Kansas City with him."

A half-century has not dimmed Gretchen's recollection of the evening.

"My mother was right, he was the cutest thing," she said. "So charismatic and so charming. He just had me laughing and talking all night. As I told everyone for years and years later, I had never met anyone like him."

Gretchen and Billy dated throughout 1957 and into 1958 when Billy was in Detroit. In the *Detroit Free Press,* there was a mention in a gossip column revealing that "the stunning stewardess on Billy Martin's arm is named Gretchen Winkler, one of TWA's most fetching." Once the schedule-makers at TWA got wind of the romance, they started looking more closely at the Detroit Tigers' schedule.

"I think those men in scheduling were fascinated with our relationship — they thought it was neat," Gretchen said. "So they'd call me and say, 'Listen, Winkler, you're scheduled to go to Chicago next week but the Tigers are playing in New York. Do you want to go there instead?' And, of course, I jumped at the chance.

"I saw a lot of ball games in 1958 and 1959 and I saw a lot of Billy."

They were engaged mid-season in 1959 and planned an October 7 wedding at Las Vegas's Desert Inn. The groom would be eight years older than the bride.

"He made you love him," Gretchen said. "He looked you right in the eye and commanded your attention. When Billy was talking to me, I was the only person that mattered in the room."

The night before the wedding, Bobby Darin, whose single "Mack the Knife" was the number-one best-selling song of 1959, serenaded the wedding party in a private performance.

After a honeymoon in Europe, the couple returned to the Bay Area because Billy was opening a new restaurant in the town of El Cerrito, four miles north of Berkeley on that umbilical cord of the East Bay, San Pablo Avenue. His longtime friend Lewis Figone was the primary investor, with a few other partners. Billy and Gretchen, who involved herself in everything her husband did, including his finances — she saw their marriage as a partnership, whether it was business or social — recalled that they did not have to put up any money. It was his name that had the financial clout.

Billy Martin's Cerro Square had a yellow and green façade — the future colors of the Oakland A's — and was in a shopping plaza near the commuter train station. Newspaper advertisements in 1959 invited customers to come sit in its "rocking chair lounge."

The menu was Italian with lots of seafood. Mickey Mantle and Dodgers hurler Don Drysdale attended the grand opening, which got the restaurant's publicity in every Bay Area newspaper and television news station.

Nick DeGennaro went to work there as a bartender and recalled that on opening night the place was so busy they needed eight bartenders to keep up with the crowd. Throughout the winter of 1959–60, the restaurant was busy — "at least four bartenders," said Nick — and Billy was a constant presence.

He and Gretchen had rented an apartment in Oakland where they would live until the Cincinnati Reds opened their spring training camp in Tampa.

"Billy was very good working the room and talking to the guests,"

Gretchen said. "For a while, everybody came and the place had a kind of buzz. We would be there all the time. Billy loved to dance and he was a fabulous dancer, good enough that he once appeared on Arthur Murray's dance TV show."

When a band would play at the restaurant on weekends, Billy would also sing.

Was Billy a good singer?

Gretchen laughed. "I used to tell him he needed to practice," she said.

One night, Gretchen and Billy were sitting in a booth facing the front door when a tall man walked through the door.

"I gasped and my mouth flew open," Gretchen said. "I turned to Billy and said, 'That has to be your father.' And it was.

"I can't say I ever saw Billy speechless or at a loss for words but he was at that moment. They sat down and talked. It was awkward. That night was the quietest that I ever saw Billy. His dad, who looked like him except taller, sat with us for quite a while and he did most of the talking. He was talking about how he wasn't proud about not being around when Billy was growing up but he said that Billy's mom wouldn't let him near Billy.

"Billy was cordial and so was his father and it was nice that they got to reconnect, but you could also see that it wasn't going to go too far. Billy was a little out of sorts. I don't think I ever saw his father again after that night."

During that winter, Billy brought Gretchen to the house on 7th Street often. He wanted his mother to teach Gretchen some of her recipes.

"He'd leave me there with her while she was supposed to be teaching me how to make baked ravioli or whatever," Gretchen said. "But you could see she didn't really want me to learn. She would leave ingredients out and when I went to the restroom she did three steps while I was gone and then wouldn't tell me what they were.

"She probably wanted to make sure her recipes kept Billy coming back, which is understandable, I guess. But she wasn't welcoming in any other way either. She was a troublesome little woman."

In the spring of 1960, Billy left for spring training. The restaurant prospered for about six months, but the crowds slowly dwindled without the presence of its star attraction. Eighteen months after it opened, Billy Martin's Cerro Square closed.

"To own a restaurant you have to be there all the time," Figone said. "None of us could do that."

Figone smiled, picking up a black-and-white photo from the grand opening that showed Billy and Mickey Mantle in chef hats working behind the grill.

"We had a lot of fun there while it lasted," he said.

As Billy began his tenth Major League season, his face had healed from Clevenger's fastball. It did not mean there were no scars. From the beginning of the training, Billy noticed he was shying away from inside pitches, which was far from an uncommon reaction after being hit in the head by a pitch.

He decided he needed to be hit again to overcome his fears. So he put on a helmet and four Reds jackets and wrapped towels around his neck. He stood at the plate while batting practice pitchers deliberately hurled balls at or near his chest and arms. It did not matter. He did not overcome the fear of being hit, especially in a game situation with a big-league pitcher. It took almost two years for the anxiety to dissipate. Then it was too late.

But Billy was the Reds' regular second baseman. He would have to sort out his problems at the plate while playing, though it would not be easy. A lifelong American Leaguer, Billy was greeted suspiciously during his first days as a National League player. But he defused any budding tension effortlessly. It was his gift in any crowd, in any decade of his life.

"He invited everyone out for dinner the first night and paid for the whole thing," said Lee Walls, a Reds teammate in 1960 who would become a coach for Billy in several of his managerial stops. "He learned the names of everybody's wife and kids. He did favors for people and played with their kids every day."

Almost all children loved Billy because he could talk like Donald Duck. It got a shy kid to smile every time.

"He was the nice guy he always was," Walls said. "If you were nice and polite to him, he would give you the shirt off his back."

In that spring training, Walls, like others after him, was also witness to what it was like to be Battlin' Billy Martin.

"We went to a bar in Tampa in the early afternoon after a workout and there was one lonely guy sitting there nursing a drink at the other end of the bar," Walls said. "The bartender recognized Billy and bought us both a drink. The guy at the end of the bar said, 'Hey, Fred, I've been coming here for twenty years and you never bought me a drink just for walking in.'

"So Billy laughs and buys the guy a drink. The guy got up, walked over, and threw the drink in Billy's face. In an instant, the guy was lying on the floor."

Walls was a fearsome, baldheaded giant who resembled the muscular guy on Mr. Clean bottles (without the smile). He had seen plenty of guys in bar fights. He had not seen anything like the five-foot-ten Billy Martin.

"Billy hit him with one short, crushing right hand and the guy just collapsed," Walls said. "The man knew how to throw a punch. But you know, Billy was disgusted. We drank fast, Billy left a nice tip, and we left."

On the field, Billy struggled at the plate. Teams continued to pitch him inside, close enough that Billy hit the dirt repeatedly. Darrell Johnson, a scout for the St. Louis Cardinals who had been friendly with Billy when the two played for the Yankees in 1957, saw Billy just before the Reds were heading to Chicago for a series with the Cubs. Johnson told Billy that the entire league had the same scouting report: Knock him down, then throw outside.

The next day, three pitches buzzed by Billy's hands and shoulders. After the game, he told Cincinnati reporters that he was going to retaliate if he kept getting pitched inside.

It was August 4 in Wrigley Field, one day before the one-year anniversary of Billy's beaning by Tex Clevenger, when the Cubs' six-foot-two Jim Brewer, a left-handed rookie, threw a pitch that sailed toward Billy's head until he deflected it with his left arm. The umpire said the pitch struck Billy's bat as well and called it a strike.

Billy was doubly incensed — with the location of the pitch and with the umpire's call. He decided he would use a frequent tactic of hitters who were upset at the pitcher — he would make Brewer "skip rope." This is when a batter swings at a pitch and pretends to lose control of the bat, flinging it along the ground at the pitcher's mound. The pitcher usually has no trouble getting out of the way but the batter sends a message: I can throw things at you, too.

On the next pitch Billy did just that, except his aim was off and the bat skittered harmlessly to the right of the mound, halfway between the mound and first base. Billy walked onto the diamond after his bat. In his version of the sequence to follow, Billy said he saw Brewer coming at him from the left as he got close to his bat. Brewer had a clenched left fist and Billy was sure a punch was coming.

Brewer's version was that he yelled at Billy, "You want to fight?" And he said that Billy answered, "No, kid, relax, I'm just getting my bat."

Unlike the fight at the Copa, thousands were watching, so what is indisputably known is that just as Billy was reaching his bat Brewer was converging on him. Billy suddenly wheeled to his left and smacked Brewer with a perfect right hand to the jaw. Billy also said — that day and forevermore — that he never hit Brewer again. As in almost every baseball fight, there was a pileup of players.

"At one point, Brewer kicked our Cal McLish in the ribs and Cal went nuts," said Lee Walls. "He just started whacking Brewer with punches to the face — three, four, five. He did some damage."

Brewer was taken to Wesley Memorial Hospital with a fractured orbital bone near his eye.

"I'm sorry if he's hurt; I'm sorry that happened, but he threw at my head," Billy said in the locker room. "I was in the hospital for weeks last year. Nobody is going to throw at my head again."

When Billy was suspended for five games and fined $500 the next day, he thought no more about it. Brewer, released from the hospital, said the suspension surprised him.

But Brewer ended up needing two surgeries to repair his fracture and an infection that invaded the area. When the Reds returned to Wrigley Field on August 22, Billy was served court papers: Brewer and the Cubs were suing him for nearly $2 million.

Deadpanned Billy, referring to the Wrigley chewing gum heir who owned the Cubs, "Ask Mr. Wrigley how he would like it, cash or a check?"

It did not seem so funny when the game began and fans in the right-field bleachers held up signs that read: KILL MARTIN. Chicago police escorted Billy to and from Wrigley Field for the next two days.

Still, Billy did not take the suit seriously. He maintained he had hit Brewer on the chin once. He knew McLish had done the real damage. The suit went through two trials — the Reds testified that McLish probably caused the fracture.

"Cal told us he did it," Gretchen Martin said.

In the end, Billy, as the aggressor, was ordered to pay Brewer $22,000 for his suffering and legal fees, which was more than a year's salary. But the last harm was that Billy was linked to another brawl, and the trials kept it in the newspapers for more than a year.

Billy batted .246 for the Reds with 3 home runs and a paltry 16 RBIs in 317 at-bats. In the 1960 World Series, which Billy did not attend, the Yankees lost in seven games to Pittsburgh.

The defeat would result in the firing of Casey Stengel, the runaway managerial genius of the 1950s. Said Casey, "I was fired for turning 70 years old. It is a mistake I will never make again."

The country was moving on, emphatically putting the 1950s in the rearview mirror. John Kennedy had been elected president in November, Clark Gable died a few days later, and the first birth control pill went on the market right after Thanksgiving.

On December 3, the Reds dealt Billy to the Milwaukee Braves, where his old Oakland Oaks manager Charlie Dressen was now in charge. The Reds got just less than $20,000 for Billy, the minimum allowed under waivers. Reds general manager Bill DeWitt said he tried to acquire a player for Billy. "No one made me an offer," DeWitt said.

Before the 1961 season began, a Milwaukee reporter asked Billy if he had ever gotten over being traded by the Yankees.

"I think so," Billy answered. "Although I admit I felt a little like a little kid whose father told him not to come in the house any more. I can still play though."

During spring training with the Braves, it was clear there was no starting spot for Billy. Even Dressen could not find much use for Billy once the 1961 season began.

Billy had six hitless at-bats with the Braves before they sent him to the Minnesota Twins for a minor leaguer. Cookie Lavagetto was the Twins' manager.

Happy to be back in the American League, Billy was installed as the Twins' starting second baseman and went on a tear at the plate. Seven days after the trade, he won a game with a late two-run home run. A couple of days later, Billy drove in four runs. The Twins were in their first year of existence — the Washington Senators franchise had moved to the Twin Cities — and during his first month as a Twin, Billy hit over .300. It was his last gasp as a player. Billy went into a slump that dogged his season. His batting average sank to .220, and he had to rally late just to get his 1961 season average to .246.

"Deep down, I think Billy knew his time was ending," Gretchen said.

Years later, Billy said of the season, "It's like dying because playing was something I had been wanting to do since I was a child. You never, ever admit to yourself that one of these days you're going to have to quit."

Lavagetto had been fired during the 1961 season, but Billy knew and liked the new Twins manager, Sam Mele, a former Red Sox outfielder. Certain that Mele would give him a fair shake, Billy went to the Twins' 1962 spring training camp in the then-sleepy inland Florida city of Orlando.

Late in spring training, Billy was getting ready to leave the clubhouse at aging Tinker Field when Mele approached and asked Billy to sit down so they could talk.

Throughout his career, Billy was renowned for being the last man out of the clubhouse — a player who never wanted to leave. It was true on this day, too. Billy and Mele were alone in the room.

Mele had broken into professional baseball in 1946, the same year as Billy. He had played for ten years, including for six teams in his final four seasons. He had never wanted to stop playing either.

Mele put his arm around Billy.

"I told him that he had had a great career," Mele said. "But I said that Twins owner Calvin Griffith and I both thought it was time for him to give it up."

Billy started to cry. So did Mele.

"He started pleading with me but I knew what I had to do," Mele said. "I told him that every good thing has to come to an end. It's the saddest thing. We just sat there crying."

Billy the Kid, the one who cajoled his way into sandlot games at Kenney Park, the one who lit up Oaks Park with his vivacity and forced his way into the lineup of a Yankees dynasty, was thirty-two years old.

18

BILLY TURNED DOWN A three-year contract worth $100,000 to play baseball in Japan and instead accepted an offer to be a Twins scout. The job paid just $10,000 a year, but Billy was tired of life as a traveling publicity stunt and weary of living off accomplishments from another era. He was understandably vulnerable, and he also worried that if an American baseball man left the finite inner circle of Major League Baseball, he might never be let back in.

Never lacking in energy, Billy threw himself into his new assignment with the Twins. Unwilling to be an unseen, unnoticed scout, Billy took it upon himself to be the Twins' de facto ambassador to the community. He became a promoter and troubleshooter and hung close to owner Calvin Griffith and his brother Sherry Robertson. Curbing some of his contentious ways, he learned that an office was not a clubhouse or a ball field, and in this new phase of his life, he needed to acquire a sense of diplomacy. It was a workplace that years later would be called a "cubicle world." These barriers were not the outfield fences Billy was accustomed to — you could not just power your best shot over them. Billy kept within the confines and played nice.

He did hit the road on occasion and he came up with players for the Twins, helping to establish a pipeline for young players, especially from the Caribbean and Latin American countries. It was talent that proved fruitful for the Twins — and Billy — in subsequent years. Billy, to no one's surprise, had an eye for skilled players. He begged the Twins to sign a young high school pitcher from Scottsdale, Arizona, he had scouted even though the pitcher, James Alvin Palmer, wanted the princely sum of $50,000 as a bonus. Billy himself had negotiated the deal and the Twins would have first dibs. Billy insisted it would be worth it. But Griffith balked.

Jim Palmer, inducted into the Hall of Fame in 1990, signed with the Orioles instead and ended up in six World Series.

To augment his salary, Billy took a second job as a sales rep at the local Grain Belt Brewery. Billy became known in countless bars across Minnesota, where he bought drinks and talked up the Grain Belt brews and the Twins with equal fervor.

In his three years as a scout, Billy was never in trouble. There were no dustups with coworkers, bosses, or customers. He may have been working for a brewery, but his drinking habits were considered moderate. Billy had rehabilitated his reputation, at least in Minnesota. After the 1964 season, the Twins announced that Billy would be Mele's new third-base coach. It was the owner's idea.

Before Billy got to spring training, on December 4, 1964, Gretchen gave birth to a seven-pound, thirteen-ounce baby boy, Billy Joseph. Billy told everyone that he was most pleased that his son had inherited his mother's nose and ears and not his. The *Minneapolis Tribune* ran a picture of the proud parents in the hospital with Billy holding a pen and a contract. The story said the Twins had signed Billy Joe — as he would be called until he was nearly forty — to a $100,000 contract with a $1 million signing bonus. There was a stipulation in the contract: "Player to receive $1 million with the understanding that all consultation concerning the fine arts of baseball shall be with his mother rather than his father."

Billy Joe, Gretchen's only child, would have a respectable high school baseball career but never play professional baseball. But at the side of his father, he would be a close witness to some of the defining, and most memorable, scenes in the last few decades of twentieth-century baseball history.

There was one other significant development in Billy's life in December 1964. Attending baseball's annual winter meetings in Nashville, Billy was walking across a hotel lobby when he spotted Casey Stengel, who was then the New York Mets' manager, holding court with some writers.

Billy approached and announced, "Don't listen to this senile old man."

Stengel looked up and immediately launched into stories from the 1950s.

"Now this fresh kid here," Casey said, "he just about single-handedly beat those Brooklyn Jackie Robinsons in 1953. He broke the heart of a whole borough."

Billy had decided to let bygones be bygones.

"I missed him," he later said.

The two retired to the hotel bar. Casey had some advice and suggestions about coaching third base. The two remained close until Casey's death in 1975.

When the Twins' 1965 spring training camp opened, the writers covering the team knew things were going to be different as soon as they saw the players wearing rubber suits over their baseball pants. The rubber suits — with sneakers — were Billy's idea of a safe way to practice sliding in the outfield grass that Billy had wet with a sprinkler. The next day, the clinic was in how to bunt. The next day it was about the hit-and-run. Then the double steal. Then stealing home.

"He had every player, even the slow ones, out there doing the stealing-home drills," said Mele. "It wasn't that they were all going to steal home, but he wanted them thinking about going home on a wild pitch or an infield ground ball. It was about putting pressure on the other team. And it worked."

In the Twins' regular-season-opening victory over the Yankees, the Twins, who had stolen just 46 bases in 162 games the previous year (an average of 0.28 per game), stole 2 bases. They executed the hit-and-run twice. The 1965 Twins charged and never looked back.

"The opposing teams started rushing throws and you could see the infielders getting tense," Mele recalled decades later. "That was all Billy."

Billy had a way of keeping the dugout alive, too. As usual, he was stealing signs and trying to outguess the opposing manager. He got some of the players in on the guile, trying to get them to steal signs — anything to keep the bench involved in the game within the game.

"The guy impressed everyone because of the things he saw," Tony Oliva, a star outfielder on the team and now an executive with the Twins, said. "We all listened to him."

Oliva, born and raised in Cuba, may have listened more than most. The Spanish-speaking players all gravitated to Billy, notably Zoilo Versalles, the Cuban-born shortstop. Versalles, a regular in the Twins' infield since 1961, was gifted but moody and he clashed with Mele and many of the coaches. The Twins had tried throughout the winter of 1964–65 to trade him.

But Billy, who had learned enough Spanish to communicate in a rudimentary way, took Versalles under his wing. He taught him to bunt more effectively and encouraged him to use his speed. Versalles ended up leading the league in runs — a statistic Billy valued above all else — and he drove in 77 runs, too. He had 45 doubles and 12 triples to go with 19 home runs. Amazingly, a player the Twins had been desperate to unload only months earlier became the 1965 American League Most Valuable Player.

Billy got much of the credit in the local press for the Twins' improvement from an 87-win team in 1964 to a 100-win team a year later. Mele said he did not mind.

"Billy was responsible for a lot of new energy," he said.

Billy did not get along with everyone on that Twins team. He warred with the other coaches, particularly his former Yankees teammate Johnny Sain, the pitching coach.

"It's always Billy against the world," pitcher Jim Kaat, an 18-game winner in 1965 for the Twins who would become a Yankees broadcaster, said. "It's almost as if he needs adversaries in his life."

The Twins won the pennant by seven games over second-place Chicago. The aging, disintegrating Yankees were twenty-five games out. For Billy, the lone disappointment of the season was the Twins' seven-game defeat by the Dodgers in the World Series. It was a minor setback in what had been a long period of contentment. For more than five years, he and Gretchen had made a home in the suburbs outside the Twin Cities and lived the American middle-class dream. Billy was determined to have a stable family life as epitomized on television shows of the era. Gretchen even resembled Donna Reed, doyenne of TV domesticity.

The Martins' Richfield neighborhood had big, old maple trees and was close to the Twins' ballpark in Bloomington. There was a backyard for Billy Joe — Gretchen called him B.J. — and there was a garden where Billy grew vegetables. The Twins coaches, and some of the Richfield neighbors, had a yearly contest to see who could grow the largest tomatoes.

Billy contacted a friend of a friend who was in the tomato-growing business, making sure he won every year.

Nearly forty years later, remarried to a retired doctor and living outside Dallas, the former Gretchen Winkler Martin spoke very fondly of her years in Minnesota — as she almost always does of Billy.

"Billy was something of a homebody back then," Gretchen said of her husband, who with a steady diet and placid lifestyle had gained nearly fifteen pounds. "He played with B.J., he cooked, and he hung out with the neighbors. He liked being home. He was tired of eating in restaurants and staying in hotels."

The Twins finished second in 1966 to Baltimore, which was led by second-year starter Jim Palmer. Billy was still the team's passionate third-base coach. Now, he was also being mentioned as a future manager somewhere in the Major Leagues. But the 1966 season marked Billy's first behavioral misstep during his coaching or managing career, and it was the typically impulsive, flash-of-temper kind of mistake that would cost him in the future as well. Although, as was true of many of Billy's scuffles, he was not the only one at fault, and perhaps not even the instigator.

It all began when Howard Fox, the Twins' traveling secretary in charge of getting the team from one city to the other, invited the Yankees to piggyback on a Twins charter flight because available aircraft were scarce during an airline strike. What was going to be a crowded flight then became a delayed flight, too — by several hours. Players from both teams were drinking heavily during the delays, including Billy, who was reunited with Mickey Mantle and Whitey Ford.

Once they were airborne, the Yankees' part of the cabin, where Billy was standing, was far more raucous than the Twins' portion of the aircraft. Fox approached Billy and shouted, "Can you get your drunken buddies to shut up?"

That did not go over well. There was some shouting and cursing back and forth, but relative calm was eventually restored. Still, the Twins did not get to their hotel until nearly 2:00 a.m.

The traveling secretary's job is to call ahead to a hotel so that a team's guest keys are laid out on a large table in the lobby before the team arrives. The keys are put in envelopes with the name of each guest on the outside, then spread across the table. It speeds up the check-in process as players and coaches grab keys and go to bed. But on this trip from hell, the keys were not ready. Fox had to get them and hand them out individually. There is an unwritten rule in such cases and it is rarely breached. The manager always gets his key first, followed by the coaches, then the players, then the trainers, staff, and broadcasters, and then the writers.

Fox did not follow the established pecking order. Yes, Mele got his key first and then most of the coaches. Then the players and staff. But Fox kept Billy waiting.

When Billy protested, Fox threw his key at him. Some said he threw it in Billy's face.

"If you do that again," Billy told Fox, "I'm going to beat the living hell out of you."

Fox took off his glasses, put them on the hotel counter, and said, "All right, you loudmouthed bastard, you want me, then how about now?"

Billy leaped at Fox, who was about ten years his senior, and smashed him with a right hand. Fox went down and there was a pile of bodies on the hotel lobby floor breaking up the fight.

Fox, bleeding from a cut on his cheek, and Billy later shook hands and tried to put it behind them as a consequence of the aggravating travel circumstances. But Fox, a good friend of Griffith's, never forgot the episode. Neither did Griffith.

The 1966 season ended in dispiriting fashion, and when there was little improvement in 1967, Mele's job was in jeopardy. Billy was seen as the likely successor, but Griffith, still mindful of Billy's punch-out of Fox and what it predicted for the future, instead promoted the Twins' minor league manager from their top affiliate in Denver, Cal Ermer.

The Twins surged under Ermer but faltered badly on the final weekend of the 1967 season. When the Twins started the next season in fifth place, Griffith called Billy into his office. Billy expected to be offered Ermer's job.

Instead, the Twins wanted him to take over the Denver Bears, the Twins' top minor league team in the AAA Pacific Coast League. Denver's record at the time was 7-22.

Billy didn't like the idea. He took it as a demotion. Billy wondered if the Twins were trying to get him out of Minnesota so it would be easier to hand Ermer's job to someone else. The American League was also expanding by two teams in 1969, and Billy would be a candidate for those new managerial jobs, but he felt he would be out of sight and out of mind if he was in Denver.

Griffith encouraged Billy not to give him an answer yet, although he could read Billy's mood. He expected the answer to be no.

Billy drove home to Richfield and told Gretchen about the meeting with Griffith. She jumped out of her chair, hugged him, and immediately started talking about the move to Denver.

Billy told her he wasn't going to take the job.

"And I just started telling him over and over that this was his chance to show them he could lead a team as the number-one guy," Gretchen said. "I knew they thought he was just enough of a reckless character that maybe he couldn't run the whole show. And I kept saying, 'Billy, this is not a demotion, it's an opportunity to show what you can do.'

"But he was still worried about leaving the Major Leagues."

It was a Saturday and the Martins went to a dinner party that night.

"We got home at midnight but I was still talking until I was blue in the face," Gretchen said. "Finally, at 2:00 a.m., Billy said to me, 'Gretchen, I have to get some sleep tonight.'

"He went to bed and then to 9:00 a.m. Mass the next morning and then straight to the ballpark. I was too tired to get out of bed. I woke up not knowing if I had convinced him or not."

Billy took the job. Billy, Gretchen, and B.J. were in Denver within a week. Asked what kind of manager he was going to be, Billy told the *Denver Post,* "A good one. I'll use a little Stengel and a little Dressen, but most of all, a lot of Billy Martin."

Billy Ball now had a birthplace. It would be Denver, one month after Billy's fortieth birthday.

Just before he left Minnesota for Denver, Billy asked the Twins' farm director if the last-place Bears had any good hitters.

"Not this year," he was told.

How about pitchers?

"Not really."

Billy had the thought that he was being set up to fail. But he was determined to prove a point — that his managerial style would work and he could motivate a team of twenty-five players. For most of the last four years, he had generally kept his mouth shut working for other managers. Still, he had seen hundreds of things he would have done differently. Now it was his turn to prove his way was better.

The first day in Denver he got the Bears together and immediately started to enforce his rules, which included mandatory infield and outfield workouts before games and a zealous aggressiveness on the bases. The goal, Billy said, was to generate runs. He did not care about batting average or slugging percentage. He wanted more runs.

If that sounds familiar, it is one of the tenets of Money Ball, as popularized by the Oakland A's — and celebrated in a best-selling book and Hollywood movie of the same name. Some of Billy's methods would be considered anti–Money Ball, but there were many similarities, too.

Billy, for example, knew that walks by pitchers were deadly. When Billy got to Denver, the Denver Bears pitching staff led the league in walks. Billy announced that any pitcher with more than two walks in a game had to run laps around the field's warning track — four laps for every walk over two.

The pitchers were not the only ones warned by the new Denver manager. There was punishment for missing a sign — sprints after the game — and everyone had to take bunting instruction before every game until Billy was satisfied they could reliably bunt in a game.

He taught sliding drills. The infielders practiced pickoff plays before every game. A few were schooled in the hidden-ball trick. The outfielders weren't allowed to take batting practice until they had practiced relay throws.

This was Billy's plan, even if it was mid-season. He would show them a minor league version of the Yankee Way, mixed with Billy's pressuring offensive tactics. He preached doing the little things properly every time: squeeze plays, double steals, and stealing home. The little things, Billy said, add up to big wins. He implemented his entire program in ten days. There was only one problem.

"Everyone on the team hated him," said Graig Nettles, the Bears' twenty-three-year-old third baseman and best power hitter. "I couldn't stand him. You'd come into the dugout and he'd be yelling at you in front of everyone, just screaming: 'Why didn't you take the extra base? Didn't you notice that the right fielder has a weak arm? You went to college, why don't you use your brain out there?'

"I had never had a manager talk to me like that before."

George Mitterwald was a catcher and outfielder for the Bears. Born seventeen years after Billy in Berkeley, he had heard about Billy all his life but did not know him.

"He came in ranting about all these little details," said Mitterwald. "We had lost nine in a row when he got there. When we lost again the next night, he went crazy in the clubhouse. He was throwing things around. He just shattered a wooden chair that he threw against the wall. He said losing was not going to be tolerated, that it was a state of mind.

"I don't know that anyone believed him but we were afraid to lose after that. We knew he'd go nuts again."

The Bears rallied a bit, winning at least 40 percent of their games for the next two weeks. At this point, Billy started explaining the causes of the losses — a missed outfield cutoff cost one run, throwing to the wrong base cost another run, missing a bunt attempt cost another run.

Billy's managerial outline for success may not have been in writing, but he implemented it as if it had stages you could read from a PowerPoint presentation.

Billy stole opponents' signs and told his players about it, predicting an opponent's steal attempt before it happened. He'd say in the dugout, "Now after we pitch out and throw that runner out at second, watch the other manager, he'll look over here and make a face."

The whole bench would erupt laughing as things happened just as Billy said they would — right down to the frustrated manager glaring into the Bears' dugout.

Billy hoodwinked other teams into errors and missteps with his favorite trick plays, which impressed his players. With runners at first and third, Billy would have the runner at first base start to steal but trip and fall down just out of reach of the first baseman. The defense tended to chase the stranded runner and turn their backs on the runner at third, who, with the proper schooling on when to break for home, was rarely thrown out and scored. The runner from first might be out, but not before the Bears had stolen a run — and unnerved and embarrassed the opposition.

Soon, everyone was watching Billy, wondering what he would do next. And Billy would just keep pacing in the dugout, his hands in his back pockets and his chin jutting forward, yelling out to the field as he encouraged his charges to keep up the pressure.

The final step was breeding loyalty in his team by ardently defending his players in every dispute or close call. He drew a three-game suspension after his first ejection from a game in late June. Nettles was sure he had tagged a runner out at third base and jumped up to go nose-to-nose with the umpire over the safe call. Billy rushed toward third base, pushed Nettles out of the way to keep him from being ejected, then screamed and gestured at the umpire until he got himself thrown out.

The Bears then came from behind to win the game.

Billy was ejected eight times in the summer of 1968. He unveiled for the first time that odd bit of performance art that would become his calling card: kicking dirt on umpires.

"That kind of thing woke up the team," Nettles, who later played several seasons for Billy in Minnesota and New York, said. "You could see how much he cared. And as players, we thought, 'We've got to care that much.' Billy changed the team's attitude and united us, too."

It was part of the Billy Ball blueprint — the team, the unit, mattered more than any player. The team was in a warlike struggle, an army in uniform pitted against opposing armies in other uniforms. The Bears — "Billy's Bears," according to the Denver papers — started expecting to win and fighting not to lose.

"We saw that he could lead us to victory if we listened to him and did what he said," Nettles said. "He wasn't crazy at all. He had a plan. We started to believe that the mental part of the game and the strategy were as important as hitting, fielding, and pitching."

Attendance at the Bears' games doubled. Sensing that people came to see the unexpected, Billy had his two top sluggers and most slow-footed players, Nettles and Bob Oliver, steal home in the same game.

Taking a page from Stengel's book, Billy also went onto the field before games and entertained the fans. He had the public address system play rock-and-roll music and organized dance contests among fans he would pull from the grandstand. Billy was not above dancing himself. He posed for pictures and signed autographs. He used his Donald Duck voice on kids congregating at the field's railing.

The new energy enveloping the Bears was contagious, and Denver became a tough place for visiting teams to play. Everyone but the home team was on edge; that included the opposing players and the umpires, too.

Billy watched from the dugout with a little grin. Now this was exactly what he had in mind.

"There was a method to the madness," Mitterwald, who went on to become a coach for two of Billy's Major League teams, said decades later. "But our team in Denver was the first time. That team was playing terrible before he got there, and by the end of the year nobody could beat us."

There was a forty-five-year-old pitcher on the Bears in his eighteenth season in the minor leagues named Art Fowler. Billy ran into him at a Denver bar one of the first nights he was in town. The two men hit it off. Fowler did not have much of an arm, but he threw strikes and pitched with guile. He knew how to throw a spitball and he also threw a scuffed, marked-up baseball that dipped and darted. Billy started using Fowler like a second pitching coach.

The Bears won 26 of the final 35 games in 1968 to finish in fourth place. After Billy's arrival, the Bears were 66-50, a .569 winning percentage that equates to 92 wins in a 162-game season. As soon as the season ended, the two American League expansion franchises wanted to talk to Billy about their managerial jobs, but Billy said his loyalty was to the Twins.

Cal Griffith knew what he had to do, but he was an eccentric man by nature and highly unpredictable. Billy still worried him. Nonetheless, the 1968 Twins had been a ringing disappointment. Ermer was fired. On October 11, the Twins gave Billy a one-year contract worth $50,000. The move thrilled the Twin Cities area where Billy retained unquestioned popularity. As for his unruly side, Sid Hartman, an influential Minnesota columnist whom Billy had befriended and could count on as an ally, reported that Billy had mellowed.

"As an adult, he's learned to be calm and not lose his temper," Hartman wrote. "He can be down-right easy-going."

Griffith had a different take. Asked about hiring Billy, Griffith answered, "I feel like I'm sitting on a keg of dynamite."

19

TAKING OVER THE TWINS was nothing like taking over the Denver Bears. The core of Twins talent that won the pennant in 1965 and finished second in 1967 was still there. The team had underachieved the previous season, but there was an infusion of youth from Denver as Billy brought Nettles, Mitterwald, and infielder Rick Renick with him. The Twins still had Harmon Killebrew and Oliva, who were Hall of Fame–caliber talents. The pitching was strong with veteran starters Jim Kaat and Jim Perry and closer Ron Perranoski.

The key player to Billy was the twenty-three-year-old Rod Carew, whom Billy had helped win the Rookie of the Year award as a coach in 1967. Without Billy for most of 1968, Carew had slumped.

"He was my father and my brother," Carew said nearly twenty-five years after Billy's death. "He did not just coach you. He nurtured you — the whole you."

Carew came into baseball with a reputation for being hot-tempered and moody. Even in his prime as he was being elected to eighteen consecutive All-Star teams, he remained reserved and not easily approached by new teammates or reporters. As a young player, Carew would smash equipment and stalk off fields in frustration.

Billy went to him and said he had to tone down his act.

"I laughed at him and said, 'You've got some nerve telling me to tone it down — you of all people,'" Carew said in 2013. "And he said, 'You're right, I didn't always control myself but that doesn't mean I'm wrong about you. You're too good to throw your career away.'"

Carew's recollections of Billy are rich and multifaceted. He recalls every detail of 1969.

"People think he came in and started ordering everyone around," Carew said. "That's an incomplete picture. He had rules but he was also out there ninety minutes before every spring training practice working with me and other young players. I had some bad fielding habits and he'd stand behind me as I took ground balls.

"And I can still hear his voice behind me, 'Get your butt down, Rodney. That's it. Good, now soften your hands as you reach for the ball. That's it, Rodney. Do it again.' He would be out there in the hot sun for hours with me and other guys who wanted to get better. There was no end to his dedication to making baseball players."

Billy tailored his instruction in that first spring training to each player. He wanted the right-handed-hitting Killebrew to occasionally hit the ball to the opposite field, something he never did. And he wanted Killebrew to play third base, where he had not played regularly for years. But Billy had a reason — Killebrew at third got first baseman Rich Reese, a .322 hitter, into the lineup.

Billy wanted the left-handed Oliva, who normally hit the ball to all fields, to think about pulling the ball to right field more often so he could drive in more runs with men in scoring position. He wanted César Tovar, who played all over the infield and outfield, to steal whenever he felt like it. Carew also had a green light. Everyone else was to run only on orders from Billy.

Billy's first spring training as a Major League manager was unusually relaxed, more like a baseball laboratory where he taught basic principles — how to squeeze bunt and hit-and-run — even if he did not worry about other traditional spring training goals, like conditioning. Like Stengel, Billy did not have long workouts and he did not care what his players did off the field so long as they showed up on time and paid attention while on the field.

"He came to me and said, 'Your average dropped in 1968 because you hit the ball in the air too much,'" Carew said. "I don't know how he knew that when he was in Denver but he was right. He said, 'You're fast, let's learn to bunt and let's learn to keep the ball on the ground.' And he taught me how to do both."

Carew became one of the best bunters in the modern history of the game and a master of the one-hop single through the infield. Carew nearly hit .400 in 1977 and won seven AL batting titles (his first was in 1969).

And then there was Billy's pet project — attempting to make Carew the best stealer of home plate in the history of baseball.

"He came to me and said, 'We're going to drive the league crazy,'" Carew said. "And it's not a gimmick, it's a very effective way to get runs and demoralize the other team. During batting practice I would stand out at third base and he would be behind me teaching me how and when to break for home.

"There is a timing to it and it's based on the pitcher's windup. He showed me how to get a walking lead so I could more easily accelerate. You had to read the pitcher's windup because every pitcher gets to that point in their windup when they cannot change their motion. They can't speed up and they can't pitch out. Sometimes I would leave too soon and sometimes I would leave too late. Billy would be there, instructing me for hours. It's an art and I was amazed at how much he knew about it."

Carew was not the only one schooled in how to steal home, or steal in general. Everyone, including Killebrew, was expected to run. Killebrew stole second and third base in an exhibition game. Ted Williams, the Washington manager, was incensed when Billy had his team deftly execute squeeze bunts on consecutive pitches in a preseason game.

"When am I supposed to practice the squeeze? In May?" Billy asked afterward when Williams protested.

Like Casey Stengel, Billy had little reward and incentive programs for the team. Getting hit by a pitch in a game meant a player could leave early. Stealing second and third base in one sequence on the bases was worth $100. Mitterwald recalled that before one spring training game in southern Florida, Billy said he had a reward for the team if they did not make an error in the game and if they won by at least five runs.

"We hadn't made an error but in the ninth inning we were still only up four runs," Mitterwald said. "Billy didn't call it, but two guys got together and pulled off a double steal of second base and home so that we got the five-run lead.

"After the game, we got on the bus and we're all thinking, 'Hey, where's our reward?' It was like a three-hour ride back home. About thirty minutes into the trip, Billy had the team bus stop at a roadside bar and we all poured into it for about ninety minutes. Everyone was having a great time. Billy picked up the tab for the whole thing."

The Twins opened the season on the road and lost their first four games. But when they returned to Minnesota for the home opener, it was clear the locals still believed in Billy. The game drew the biggest crowd in the history of the franchise.

Carew electrified the crowd — if not all of baseball — when he stole home in the seventh inning to tie the game. The game-winning hit came on Killebrew's single to *right field, the opposite field.* The Twins kept winning, and Billy became more and more audacious.

In one game, with the bases loaded, they attempted a triple steal. The runner on third did not break until the catcher, a bit confused and not sure where to throw, heaved the ball toward third base. Everyone was safe. Billy tried another triple steal three games later. This time, the catcher threw wildly over the third baseman's head and two runs scored.

By the first week of May, the Twins were on an eight-game win streak and had taken over first place in the newly formed AL West. The 1969 season was the first after the American and National leagues had split into two divisions each.

"We were just a different kind of team — no one had seen such speed and aggressiveness," Carew said. "We confused the other teams. Billy saw things we didn't see. He looked at the game in three-inning sets. Set up certain things early, then look for the pitching matchups or baserunning matchups you want in the middle innings.

"The end of the game was about defense and a veteran pitcher who knew how to close out a game. We weren't just running all over the place; it was all very strategic."

The 1969 Twins pitching staff pitched 41 complete games — the staff of thirty-seven-year-old Baltimore manager Earl Weaver pitched 50 complete games, an average of almost one in three. Perranoski, whom Ermer had used only against left-handed batters, was Billy's full-time closer in Minnesota. He appeared in 75 games, won 9 of them, and saved another 31. Perranoski's season earned-run average was 2.11.

"He gave a lot of guys the confidence to succeed," Perranoski said. "I know he rejuvenated my career."

Carew said Billy had an especially close relationship with the Latin players.

"I often thought he got along better with us than the white guys," Carew said with a laugh decades later. "We sometimes were quiet and kept to ourselves. People called us moody, or worse, lazy. We were just young kids living away from home and not necessarily fitting in.

"Billy got to know us before he judged us and figured out what made us tick. At one point, I was really upset because my parents were divorcing. My mind wasn't on the game. I just wanted to go home. So in one game I hit a ground ball out and just turned from first base and ran right into the clubhouse. I was in there taking my uniform off when Billy walked in."

Said Carew, "I'm leaving."

Billy said, "Rodney, talk to me."

"I don't feel like talking."

Billy turned to the guard at the door to the clubhouse and ordered him not to let Carew out.

"Go get a cop if you have to but he better be here when this game ends," Billy said.

After the game, Carew told Billy about his parents.

"And Billy said to me, 'I understand, I come from a broken home, too. But you can't leave a game, you can't walk out. You have responsibilities to your baseball family, too. You want these guys to know you can be trusted to play hard and be there for them. If you want to arrange a quick trip home to see your parents we can do that at some point. But talk to me first.'

"I apologized and I did not go home. I played harder. That's what I loved about him."

Carew hit .332 in 1969 with 56 RBIs and he stole home 7 times (the record for one season is 8 steals of home, and Carew nearly tied it as he was called out in a controversial, close play late in the season). Leo Cárdenas hit .280 and drove in 70 runs. Tovar came off the bench to hit 11 home runs with 52 RBIs and a .288 batting average.

"That Twins team just terrorized the AL West," said Charlie Silvera, Billy's former Yankees roommate who became a Twins coach. "Billy had such balls as a manager. He would squeeze bunt with a five-run lead, he didn't care.

"Back then, before every game was on TV, the baseball adage was that you played conservative at home when your fans and executives were watching. Then on the road you could take risks or run a trick play because no one from your front office or hometown was watching. But Billy didn't care where we were, he did whatever he thought would work. He never considered whether he would be second-guessed. The most important thing was keeping the other team guessing. He never wanted there to be a pattern about his moves."

Billy also played all kinds of head games to get a mental edge on his opponent. In 1969, the young and promising Oakland A's were the Twins' closest rivals. When the A's came to Minnesota for the first time, Billy was irked when Oakland's twenty-three-year-old slugger Reggie Jackson slammed two home runs as the A's built a 7–0 lead.

When Reggie came to the plate late in the game, two pitches whizzed by his head. Jackson charged the Twins pitcher, Dick Woodson. The benches cleared.

"That's the kind of manager Billy Martin is," Reggie said after the game. "If someone is beating his club, he's going to put a little fear in that team's heart. I don't blame Woodson. He was following orders. I blame the manager."

Billy denied he was throwing at Jackson and said that as the two teams were being separated on the field, Jackson threatened him.

"He yelled at me that he was going to get me," said Billy, not looking overly worried. "I want somebody to write that so that if we ever get in a fight, he won't be able to sue me and say I started it."

Off the field, Billy's image continued to be reshaped. Joe Durso, a baseball writer at the *New York Times* from the 1960s to the 1980s, once told a story about how Billy and Gretchen would have all the New York writers over for dinner whenever the Yankees were visiting.

"I remember being struck by this domesticated Billy," Durso said. "We ate dinner and drank some wine, but not a lot. Billy showed off his garden. He lived on the edge of this rural area with rolling fields. After dinner, Billy would sit in a rocking chair in his living room and smoke a pipe as he talked about American history or current events.

"He was a country squire. There was a metamorphosis."

But not everything was so peaceable. Billy's life path usually diverged whenever a sense of consistency set in. Since he was a teen, he desperately pursued normalcy and tranquillity. And just as often, once it was achieved, some set of circumstances, some of them surely created by Billy, would fill his life with uncertainty and insecurity again.

Twenty years after his death, his son, Billy Martin Jr., wondered if his father didn't just get bored when everything was going right.

"He thrived under pressure but eventually it would get to him and he wanted some quiet," Billy Jr. said. "But that wouldn't last long. It was like he missed the tension. He'd do something to bring the pressure back into his life again."

Or, a deep-seated distrust of authority figures — an attitude bred into many West Berkeley Boys and passionately promoted inside the walls of

1632 7th Street — still welled inside the forty-one-year-old manager of the Twins, even if he did now smoke a pipe and placidly hold court in a living room near rolling midwestern fields.

Whatever it was, there were piecemeal episodes of disorder in 1969, little things that someone else might have avoided or smoothed over — especially with the team in first place. But that is not what usually happened in Billy's life.

There was, for example, the contretemps Billy created over the daily nap time of Twins owner Calvin Griffith. Griffith had requested that Billy meet with him two or three times a week before home games to talk about the team. Griffith said he would be available in the afternoon anytime except between 5:00 and 5:30 p.m. because that's when Griffith took his daily nap.

Early in the season, Billy visited with Griffith often, especially as the team struggled to find its footing. But he grew tired of the exercise. The team was winning, and Billy did not like explaining some of his moves and decisions. But Griffith was insistent.

Before a game in June, Billy came to Griffith's office and knocked on the door just after 5:00 p.m. Billy said it was the only time he could talk to the owner. Awakened, Griffith asked him to adjust his schedule and come back another day, but not between 5:00 and 5:30.

A few days later, Billy again knocked on Griffith's door just past 5:00 p.m. Griffith explained the timing of his daily nap once again. A week later, Billy was back, knocking at 5:15 p.m. Exasperated, Griffith at that point told Billy not to bother with the meetings any longer.

Billy's guile was not confined to triple steals and suicide squeeze bunts.

If the nap issue left Griffith vexed, then Billy's fight with Twins pitcher Dave Boswell terrified him. Boswell was a temperamental but gifted starting pitcher, a six-foot-three, 190-pound right-hander who by 1969 had already posted three double-digit-victory seasons for the Twins.

During a trip to Detroit in August, Boswell was inactive because of a shoulder injury, but Billy still required all the pitchers to run twenty laps from foul line to foul line before games. When Art Fowler, Billy's pitching coach, reminded Boswell of his running duties before a Thursday night game, Boswell swore at Fowler and refused to run.

After the game, which the Twins lost, Billy went to a bar called the Lindell A.C., owned by Jimmy Butsicaris, the best man at Billy's 1959 wedding to Gretchen. The Lindell A.C. was a big place not far from Tiger

Stadium and one of the first sports bars in America with the walls and tables lined with jerseys and autographed photographs. It was the Toots Shor's of Detroit.

On this night, Billy was drinking with Fowler and Bob Allison, one of his outfielders. While it might have been baseball tradition that managers did not drink with their players — or at least not for too long — Billy felt otherwise. He liked most of his players and he wanted to be with them. He would talk baseball and he would hear things from the players' perspective about the team. Boswell, whom Billy liked and always called "Bozzy," was at the bar, too, but across the wide room.

Billy asked Fowler how the pitchers' running had gone before the game, and Fowler told him about Boswell. Billy told Fowler that he would address it with Boswell before the next day's game. The group had a couple more drinks and Fowler went back to the team hotel. Once Fowler left, Boswell came over to Billy.

"Art told you about my not running, didn't he?" Boswell asked.

"That's his job," Billy answered.

"I'm going back to the hotel to kick his butt, the little squealer," Boswell said.

Said Billy, "Bozzy, you're not going to do anything like that."

"Yes, I am," said Boswell and he headed for the door.

Allison, who was as big as Boswell and one of his close friends, ran after Boswell and stopped him near an alley behind the bar. As usual, there are conflicting stories from this moment on. What is known is that everyone had been drinking.

"If you're going to be a tough guy," Allison apparently said, "why don't you hit me?"

And Boswell did, knocking Allison to the ground. Billy always maintained that when he got to the alley seconds later, Boswell was hitting Allison as he lay on the ground. Billy pushed Boswell away, grabbed a chain with a crucifix that hung around Boswell's neck, and used it to draw Boswell closer as he punched him repeatedly in the stomach.

When fighting a bigger opponent, Billy later explained, you have to get inside and close to him. Pulling on his chain kept Boswell close. Finally, according to Billy, he punched Boswell in the face, which sent Boswell bouncing off the alley wall. Reporters would later ask Billy what happened next.

"Well, when he came off the wall, I hit him again," Billy answered.

Boswell fell to the ground and Butsicaris intervened, saying, "Billy, he's out."

Years later, Billy wrote, "I looked at Boswell and I felt sick. He was bleeding badly, and I felt terrible because I really like the kid. I was saying to myself, 'How in the world did this happen? Nobody's going to believe it. How the hell do I get myself in these situations?'"

Billy ended up going to the hospital with Boswell. The fight made national news since it's not every day that a manager pummels one of his own players (although it was not altogether uncommon in the previous five decades in baseball). On the team, it was not a total surprise.

"Dave, at the time, was a problem," Carew said. "He drank a lot, and he was a problem. And he challenged Billy, and knowing Billy Martin, he's not going to back down from anyone. He put a whipping on Boswell."

But it did not look good. As Jim Kaat said, "Dave's face was all black and blue and it looked like he had been in it with Jake LaMotta or something."

Billy walked around for a few days with a badly swollen and cut right hand.

Griffith interviewed all the involved parties and ended up fining Boswell, who apologized to Billy in the owner's office.

"It was unfortunate," Billy said of the fight. "But sometimes those flare-ups happen."

Boswell would win 20 games for the 1969 Twins, the best season he had in the big leagues.

Griffith later said that he had considered firing Billy after the Boswell fight, just because he was scared for what else might happen. But like many team owners after him, Griffith decided he needed Billy. He had led the Twins to first place, and even if the ride had been like sitting on a keg of dynamite, Griffith wanted to see where the journey ended.

With Boswell winning eight games down the stretch, the Twins won the AL West by nine games over Oakland. When the division was clinched, the Twins celebrated with boxes of champagne that the frugal Griffith had saved since 1967 when the Twins fell short of the pennant on the final day of the regular season.

In his first year as a Major League manager, Billy had taken a team that was 79-83 the previous season and turned them into a 97-win juggernaut.

"This is the biggest thrill for me, more so than as a player," Billy said as the champagne flowed around him after the clinching victory. "To do it as a leader of a team, that means more to me. I remember celebrating like this as a player but this feels different. It's bigger, somehow."

For the first time since 1956, Billy would be back in baseball's post-season.

20

IN THE INAUGURAL AMERICAN League Championship Series, Billy's Twins would face the Baltimore Orioles, who had steamrolled the AL East on their way to 109 victories.

The skipper of the 1969 Orioles was Earl Weaver, a short, hot-tempered baseball lifer who had spent fourteen years as a minor league player and then eleven more seasons as a minor league manager. At roughly the same time Billy was taking over in Denver in 1968, Weaver first stepped foot in a Major League dugout when the Orioles suddenly named him their manager.

The Twins were a good team. The Orioles were viewed as nearly invincible. They were led by three future Hall of Famers (four, if you count Weaver): Frank Robinson, who was one of the best all-around players in the history of the game; Brooks Robinson, probably the best-fielding third baseman ever and a significant home run threat; and Jim Palmer, the high school prospect from Arizona whom Billy wanted the Twins to sign and who in 1969 compiled a 16-4 record with a 2.34 ERA.

But it did not take the nation's baseball writers long to zero in on the most absorbing story line of the Twins-Orioles series — it was the matchup of Battlin' Billy and the Earl of Baltimore. Both baited and argued with umpires, and both yelled at their players — and opposing players — with a red-faced fury. Even in 1969, they were considered old-school types, the kind of demanding leaders who wanted everyone in their dugout living and dying with every pitch because that's how they were. Players who did not hustle or who did not look pained by losses were benched. They were funny and engaging with the press, at least until crossed, and each was very familiar with a barroom when the game was over.

The 1969 ALCS was the first act of twenty years of memorable clashes between Billy and Weaver, who would become archrivals as well as the most respected and feared managers in the American League.

More than forty years later, when Earl Weaver was asked to recall the

1969 series, he answered, "I was frightened. Here we had won 109 games and we had to win three out of five against a Billy Martin team."

The opening game of the best-of-five series had both managers dueling throughout. The game at Baltimore's Memorial Stadium, a circular edifice where Johnny Unitas and the Baltimore Colts also played, saw the Orioles take an early 1–0 lead on Frank Robinson's home run. Baltimore led 2–1 in the seventh when Weaver chose to walk Killebrew, whose 49 regular-season home runs were the most in the Major Leagues. The strategy backfired when Tony Oliva followed Killebrew to the plate and lined a 1-2 pitch into the left-field seats for a 3-2 Twins lead.

Billy met Oliva at the top step of the dugout after the homer and hugged him so hard he knocked Oliva's batting helmet to the ground.

But in the ninth inning, it was Billy's turn to make a difficult decision. His 20-game winner, the right-handed starter Jim Perry, had given up just one hit since the fifth inning. But leading off the Baltimore ninth would be Boog Powell, a lefty pull hitter who had stroked 37 homers in the regular season. Billy's closer, Ron Perranoski, the league leader in saves, was warmed up in the bullpen.

But early in his managerial career, if one of his best starters was on the mound, Billy was not inclined to turn to his closer unless that starter was in trouble. Stengel's 1950s Yankees did not depend on a closer; they usually let the starters work until they were faltering. Billy would do the same.

But this time, Powell sent a long fly ball to the right-center-field bleachers to tie the game.

"I should have been in there pitching to Powell," Perranoski said in an interview forty-four years later. "I was getting out lefties all year."

Perranoski eventually became a close friend of Billy's.

"Billy's loyalty was one of his strengths but sometimes it got him in trouble," Perranoski said. "I think he didn't want to take Jim Perry out because Perry had pitched a hell of a game."

Perranoski was right. Loyalty mattered above all other things in Billy's view of the world, even when it hurt.

Perry gave up a single to Brooks Robinson after Powell's homer, which finally brought in Perranoski. He did not give up a hit in the inning, but a fielding error by Carew did allow Robinson to advance to third base with two outs. With a chance to win the game right then, Weaver sent up pinch hitter Merv Rettenmund to hit for his pitcher (there was no designated hitter in 1969).

Billy countered with one of his favorite trick plays, one taught to him by Stengel. Billy had Perranoski throw high and inside to Rettenmund. As Rettenmund threw himself to the ground to avoid the pitch, Twins catcher George Mitterwald caught the ball and quickly threw to third base. Robinson was picked off, out by five feet.

It was a set play, as Billy would explain later. "The base runner at third always freezes, it's a natural reaction when someone almost gets hit near the head like that," he said. "But our guys know it's a set play so the third baseman covers third on the pitch and the catcher comes up throwing. It gets the stunned runner every time — unless the pitcher is too chicken to throw the ball high and inside."

The game went to extra innings. The Twins loaded the bases in their half of the twelfth with one out but couldn't score. A Weaver pitchout thwarted a safety squeeze bunt attempt Billy called with Leo Cárdenas at the plate and the bases loaded.

In the Baltimore twelfth, the Orioles' light-hitting shortstop, Mark Belanger, reached on an infield single. A sacrifice bunt and a groundout advanced Belanger to third base with two outs.

Paul Blair, who had hit 21 home runs that year, was at the plate. This time Weaver sat back in the dugout and waited.

"On his own Paul decided to put down a drag bunt," Weaver said in December 2012, about a month before he died of an apparent heart attack. "I didn't know anything about it although Paul did signal to third-base coach Billy Hunter who then warned Belanger."

A great game of strategy and managing ended with a bold decision by a player. Who would have figured that?

Said Perranoski, "When he bunted that ball between the pitcher's mound and third base, I felt sick. I knew we couldn't get him and I watched Belanger run home."

Perranoski had not let a ball out of the infield in the inning but the game was lost, 4–3. He went out after the game with Art Fowler and Billy.

"We sat at a bar for about an hour," Perranoski said. "Nobody brought up the Boog Powell home run and whether I should have been in there. We just let it go.

"But I've always felt like that game turned the tide of the series. If we beat them in their park in the first game, we gain momentum and put the scare in them."

Instead, in Game 2, Baltimore's Dave McNally held the Twins to three hits as the Orioles won 1–0 in eleven innings.

The Twins flew back to Minnesota, trying to gain confidence from nearly defeating the powerful Orioles twice. And they could turn to Jim Kaat to pitch Game 3. Kaat had debuted in the Major Leagues ten years earlier, as a twenty-year-old. Though restricted by injuries in 1969, he was a seasoned vet who had already won 142 games in the big leagues.

To everyone's surprise, Billy informed the team that he was planning to instead start Bob Miller, a journeyman with a 53-62 career record. Miller had won some big games during the pennant drive, but Kaat still seemed the obvious choice. Griffith and others in the Twins' management begged Billy to reconsider.

Billy stood by his decision. The Orioles had seen Kaat for years, he reasoned, while Miller was a career National Leaguer with only eleven American League starts at that point. Miller would be unfamiliar, the surprise choice. To some, it seemed as if Billy was trying to channel his inner Stengel, who had made the ultimate unconventional starting pitcher choice when he sent Don Larsen to the mound in the 1956 World Series and was rewarded with a perfect game.

There were other factors. Billy never forgot even the most minor slight, and Kaat had sided with former Twins pitching coach Johnny Sain in 1965 when Sain and Martin were at odds as coaches under Sam Mele. Kaat was also chummy with former traveling secretary Howard Fox, who was now a vice president in the organization. That by itself might have been enough motivation for Billy to spurn Kaat and give the ball to Miller, who was devoted to Fowler, Billy's right-hand man.

Billy's loyalty and allegiance might have been his undoing again.

Miller did not fare well in Game 3, giving up five hits and three runs by the second inning. The Orioles won the game 11–2. Palmer pitched the complete-game victory. Billy's first postseason series as a manager — and his first match against Earl Weaver — ended in a sweep.

When the final game ended, the Twins fans who remained at Metropolitan Stadium rose to their feet and gave their team a long ovation. It was a thank-you sendoff. Home attendance had risen 35 percent. There was a buzz about Twins baseball again. The fans were eager to see what Billy would dream up next year.

But the mercurial Griffith stewed about the snub of Kaat. There was also the Boswell fight, the nap business, and the fight with Howard Fox years earlier.

Billy made Griffith uneasy, but he decided he might be able to hem in his excesses with some behavioral clauses in Billy's new contract. There was a meeting shortly after the playoff sweep. Billy surprised Griffith by asking for a raise and a two-year contract — had he not resurrected a seventh-place team?

Griffith asked for time.

Billy asked Griffith a series of questions:

"Did I do everything I said I was going to do?"

"Yes," Griffith said.

"Did I make them hustle?"

"Yes."

"Did they win?"

"Yes."

Billy left the room.

The next day, Griffith called a meeting of the Twins' brass, which was a disjointed collection that was supposed to include his brother, Sherry Robertson. But Robertson overslept and missed the meeting. Tom Mee, then a young public relations staffer, was the lone Billy supporter at the meeting. Fox, who had Griffith's ear, argued vehemently for Billy's ouster.

Griffith was not in a good mood that day. Billy had called the influential newspaper columnist Sid Hartman and told him off the record that the Twins were considering firing him (Billy talked a lot to his favorite writers off and on the record). Hartman wrote a column pleading with Griffith not to be so foolish. It was a power play that irked management.

Griffith knew that turning Billy away would outrage the fan base, although he may have underestimated the level of outrage. Griffith, whose family had run the hapless Washington Senators for decades, also might have been inured to public opinion.

Years later, his son, Clark, said the decision on Billy's fate was more complicated than it may have appeared. The Twins, Clark Griffith said, had received multiple complaints about Billy's drinking on the road. And Clark Griffith added that when Billy's fate hung in the balance, his uncle, Sherry Robertson, who was once Billy's close buddy, had not pushed his father to keep Billy.

In the end, Griffith's own words from before the 1969 season might have summed up the situation best. Having Billy as manager was like sitting on a keg of dynamite. It produced some majestic highs but it was volatile. Griffith, a man with reserved, Old World sensibilities, did not value volatility.

On October 13, one week after the inaugural ALCS ended, Griffith announced that Billy was not coming back as Twins manager. Billy heard he had been fired while driving back to Minnesota from Nebraska where he, Gretchen, and B.J. had spent a few days visiting Gretchen's parents.

"That was a very difficult time," Gretchen said. "Billy had made the young players believe they could win. He had brought all the Latin players into the fold. He had motivated and rejuvenated the veterans.

"Billy had changed the culture. He went to a hundred banquets and dinners for free. The fans were ecstatic. He put the Twins on the baseball map. Sure, some crazy things happened that season but it was also just Billy's first year.

"Billy didn't understand what he had done that was worth being fired. He felt certain that with one more good pitcher, the Twins might have won five or six divisions in a row."

Griffith told the *New York Times,* "The Twins are as much a part of me as of Billy Martin. I'm the one who has to sign the ballplayers. I should have a right to say what's what."

Twins fans hung Griffith in effigy in downtown Minneapolis. The team received hundreds of phone calls. Don Cassidy of the Twins' media relations staff said some fans "broke into tears" during the calls. The local Teamsters Union said it was organizing a boycott of Twins games in 1970. The Twins drew fans from Iowa and the Dakotas as well as Minnesota. State legislators from each of the three states petitioned Griffith to reconsider.

"Calvin Griffith has dealt a blow to his fans by failing to appreciate the importance to the organization of Billy's popularity," the *Minneapolis Tribune* columnist Dick Cullum wrote. "Martin is the people's choice, their only choice."

Rod Carew said the players were stunned.

"Who fires a guy who took a seventh-place team and turned it into a division winner?" Carew said. "Everyone was disappointed. We were obviously building a good thing. And then he was gone."

The disappointment in the area was not short-lived. In 2009, the fortieth anniversary of the 1969 Twins' division victory, the Minnesota newspaper columnist and radio host Patrick Reusse wrote about how in late 1969, you couldn't go anywhere in the Twin Cities without hearing the vow, "I'm never buying another ticket to a Twins game."

"The Martin effect was more than myth," Reusse continued. "In 1970, the Twins won 98 games and another division with Bill Rigney as manager as attendance fell 88,000."

By 1971, when the Twins were losers, attendance had dropped by more than 400,000 from the team record set in 1969, a drop of about 30 percent.

"And this is a fact," Reusse wrote in conclusion to his 2009 column. "A decade after Billy was fired, you still could run into a 40-year-old sipping a beer in a local bar, waving in disinterest at the Twins game on the corner TV and saying, 'I haven't been to a game since they fired Billy.'"

21

BILLY'S FRIEND CHARLIE SILVERA called 1970 "the loneliest year of Billy's life."

He had expected a managerial offer from some team but none came. His principal means of support was a job with Minneapolis radio station KDWB, where he hosted a radio show that was broadcast twice a week before Twins games. The show meant he had to carry a bulky microphone and tape recorder around before games — often on the road — interviewing players. He bunked with friends from the baseball network — Yogi Berra, Lee Walls, Bob Uecker — because the radio station would not pay for a hotel room.

He found the job demeaning and hated asking questions of the players.

Gretchen Martin said she and Billy spent more time together, drawing on each other.

"We tried to build a life outside of baseball," Gretchen said. "We bought a lake house and a boat. But Billy always had a baseball family and he needed that."

In July, Charlie Finley, the Oakland A's enigmatic owner, flirted with hiring Billy. It would have put Billy and Reggie Jackson in the same dugout seven years earlier than their union — if you can call it that — in New York. If Finley had hired Billy, it also might have changed the course of baseball history or Billy's baseball legacy since the A's were on the cusp of a run to multiple world championships. But in the end, Billy and Finley could not agree on various terms.

Later the same month, Jim Campbell, the Detroit Tigers' general manager, called Billy. Though he considered it a risk, Campbell thought Billy was perfect for his slumbering team. By the end of the summer, Billy agreed to a two-year contract worth $100,000 to manage the 1971 Tigers.

In the ALCS that fall, the Twins again played Baltimore, and the Orioles swept the Twins again. This time, Jim Kaat was the starter for the third game. He was knocked out of the game in the third inning and the Twins lost, 6–1.

The 1971 Detroit Tigers that Billy took over seemed much more than three years removed from the incandescent Tigers of 1968 who won the World Series in a stunning seven-game upset of the defending champion St. Louis Cardinals. Their pitching ace, the 30-game winner Denny McLain, was traded after a betting scandal. Fortunately, he fetched two starters: shortstop Eddie Brinkman and Aurelio Rodríguez, a defensive wizard at third base. The Tigers still had stars like Al Kaline and Norm Cash, but both were thirty-six years old. Most of the Tigers' other prominent starters, like Willie Horton, Bill Freehan, and Dick McAuliffe, were in their early thirties. The 1970 team had finished fourth with a 79-83 record.

Billy's 1969 Minnesota Twins had run and bunted their way to a title, stealing 115 bases as a team. The 1970 Tigers had stolen a total of 29 bases. The baseball world snickered when Billy was named Detroit manager, skeptical at what daring and dynamic Billy could do with the Tigers' slow-footed lineup that was now more sluggish than slugging. Many thought it was a poor match of managerial style and talent.

Billy had plenty of enemies in baseball, and some of them thought Billy had gotten lucky in 1969, catching lightning in a bottle in Minnesota. Those people looked at the decay on the Detroit roster and smirked: If Billy is such a managerial magician, let's see what he can do now.

Most of baseball had given up on the Tigers, and most of the country had given up on Detroit, which had been witness to some of the worst race riots of the late 1960s. The city's baseball team was seen as representative of the city itself — scarred and withering.

Billy, accustomed to being disregarded, told his new players not to worry about what they had heard about him and his managerial style. He was not a one-trick pony. He could adapt his tactics to the strengths of his roster. He only asked the players to believe in his ways and to be patient.

Of course, it was easier to take a team like the Twins, who had not tasted much success, and ask them to blindly follow. The veteran Tigers still felt the glow of the 1968 championship season as if it were yesterday. They were stars. But Campbell, the general manager, instead referred to his team as a lineup of "personalities." He did not mean it in a good way. In preseason meetings, Campbell told Billy to do whatever he had to do to break up the cliques on the team and to rattle the veterans out of their complacency.

Billy did not turn the 1971 Tigers into the 1969 Twins. In fact, they ended up stealing only six more bases than the 1970 Tigers.

But Billy said there was more to his system than just stealing bases. For one, there was the threat of a steal, or a double steal. He wanted the players to run even if they were not always successful.

Billy told the Tigers over and over that his system of winning baseball wasn't about speed as much as it was about aggressiveness. He wanted to always score the first run of a game, to put opponents on the defensive. He did not play for big innings early in games like many managers. He played to score first. If a game were a fight, a comparison Billy would readily make, then it mattered who got in the first punch.

He had other canons: He wanted his players to go from first to third on singles whenever possible. And he wanted hard slides into the third baseman.

"Let's see if their outfielders can make that throw and let's see if the third baseman will stand in and make the tag with the ball and the runner arriving at the same time," Billy said. "Slide over the bag — have the third baseman take the contact and the throw."

He wanted base runners faking a steal of home, hoping to draw a balk from the pitcher. It would steal a run and demoralize the pitcher. He wanted his players to knock down middle infielders trying to make double plays. He wanted to try more hit-and-run plays, teaching his players that they didn't have to hit the ball toward a particular hole in the defense — as many managers taught the play. Billy instead just wanted the batter to put the ball in play. Rodríguez later insisted he picked up at least a dozen hits doing just that.

Billy made it a standing rule that any player who got hit with a pitch with the bases loaded would get $150 in cash and the right to pick his next day off. And Billy made sure his players knew that he always had their backs. In the first ten days of the 1971 season, Billy got thrown out of two games defending his players who were upset with umpires' strike zones.

The Tigers had been surprised when Billy, whose feisty reputation always preceded him, was fairly docile during spring training. So they were astonished at the man in the same number 1 uniform who on the opening day of the season became a different person altogether — a jumpy, manic, and hyper dugout presence who was ready to go after everyone in the ballpark.

In the first inning of the first game, Billy started in on the Cleveland Indians' flamboyant first baseman, Ken Harrelson, who liked to wear a tight, tailored uniform, a Fu Manchu mustache, and multicolored wristbands. Off the field, Harrelson was the king of early 1970s style, known for his closet full of Nehru jackets.

"You clown, Harrelson," Billy yelled from the home dugout at Tiger Stadium, just feet from first base. "Where are your bell-bottoms? You think your clothes are going to hide the fact that you can't catch anything in the dirt anymore? Everybody knows you can't go to your right anymore. Everybody knows you can't hit a curve ball. You're washed up. You should get off the field. Go sit with your designer in some disco. That's where you belong."

The once-somnolent Tigers' dugout was sleepy no more.

"We were all looking around at each other," catcher Bill Freehan said. "This was a whole new ball game. Our manager was crazy. These games were a war — us against them. That was obvious five minutes into the season's first game."

Harrelson, as it happened, barely played in 1971 and then retired.

Billy's intensity was not directed only at the opposition. When Willie Horton, one of his stars and a crowd favorite as a Detroit native, did not run out a ground ball, Billy yanked him from the game and benched him for the next game, too. When Horton was reinserted into the lineup, he said he was injured and couldn't play.

Billy and Horton had a ten-minute screaming match in the manager's office afterward. They did not exit as pals. Billy wanted Horton suspended by the Tigers and told reporters so. Horton wanted to be traded. They feuded for a while, but Horton ended up back in the lineup and played well.

"Billy made me see some things for how they really were," Horton, who became a coach for Billy in the 1980s, said many years later. "He became a mentor."

Billy also chided the Tigers' left-handed-hitting fourth outfielder, Jim Northrup. Billy pleaded endlessly with Northrup to pull the ball more toward Tiger Stadium's short right-field porch. Northrup resisted but ended up hitting 16 homers and driving in 71 runs in '71. Northrup did not become Billy's chum; in fact, he was something of an arch-nemesis — almost every Billy team had one or five players who could be placed in that category. Northrup criticized Billy for decades, right until his death in 2011. But in 1971, he told the *Detroit Free Press* that Billy had "got all of us on one side — his side."

The team of "personalities" was developing a personality. And guess whose personality it resembled? He was pacing back and forth in the dugout with his hands jammed in his back pockets, his dark eyes darting around the ballpark.

The sculpting of the team psyche developed in pieces.

Earl Weaver's Baltimore Orioles were the defending World Series champions and had won the last two American League pennants. They were the prohibitive favorites in the AL East. Billy insisted they were overrated and over the hill. He made subtle jabs at Weaver, trying to get under the skin of the Orioles' leader. The message was unequivocal — the Tigers weren't playing for fourth place or second place. They were gunning for the Orioles.

When the Tigers lost their first regular-season game to Baltimore in April — a tight, one-run defeat — Billy came back to his team's clubhouse and saw his players surrounding the customary meal spread — a table in the center of the room piled high with a hot entrée like fried chicken, meat loaf, or pork chops, as well as cold cuts, condiments, and other food and drink.

In a scene that would be repeated in clubhouses from Oakland to New York from 1971 to 1988, Billy screamed, "Go ahead and stuff your faces, you fucking bunch of losers! We should have won that game. How can you eat?"

And then Billy charged across the room in a fury, grabbed the food table with both hands, and angrily flipped it over. Then he kicked at it once or twice.

"Stuff went flying everywhere," Horton said, remembering the scene decades later. "There was chicken in lockers, cole slaw in guys' shoes, beans on clothing, and food and drink all over the walls.

"Then Billy just stormed into his office and slammed the door. We kind of looked around — nobody had ever seen anything like that. But everybody knew that Billy really hated to lose and maybe we better start hating to lose, too."

There were other moments later viewed as motivational or as a case of team bonding. When Cleveland's hard-throwing Sam McDowell hit two Tigers in one game and threw inside to two more, Billy put reliever Bill

Denehy — known as "Wild Bill" — into the game. Billy told Denehy to use his natural wildness to its best effect. When Denehy hit the first batter, catcher Ray Fosse, in the back, Fosse charged the mound. In a flash, Billy sprinted from the dugout, the first one to get to the wrestling mob around Fosse and Denehy. The rest of the Tigers naturally followed. Both benches and bullpens emptied, and in the brawl that ensued, Denehy kicked Fosse in the head and cut him badly. Horton, a former amateur boxer, broke an Indians pitcher's nose with a one-punch knockout, and Gates Brown, who was a tough, 220-pound reserve outfielder who had once served time in jail for burglary, decked another Indians player and sent him to the disabled list with a concussion.

After the game, about fifteen Tigers were in a bar across the street from Tiger Stadium.

"Fans kept sending over drinks," said Charlie Silvera, one of Billy's coaches who was in the bar that night. "They'd raise their glasses and yell, 'To the slugging Tigers.' And you know what? The guys on the team loved it. The hitters loved that Denehy had protected them, and the pitchers loved that the hitters had run out to protect Denehy. It brought everyone closer."

Not everyone liked Billy's managerial style, or liked him. He yelled too much for many a player. Dick McAuliffe, the All-Star second baseman, was one who bristled at the hollering. But like most of his teammates, he listened to Billy. McAuliffe, who was not fleet of foot, won a big game in September by stealing third on his own with Kaline at the plate and one out in the ninth inning of a tied game at Tiger Stadium. Kaline then lofted a walk-off, game-ending sac fly that had the Detroit fans and press nearly in shock. The slow-footed Tigers won a game by taking an extra base in the ninth?

McAuliffe was asked afterward what made him head for third. "Billy taught us to watch the catchers when you're on second base. Sometimes they get lazy and they don't set up in their crouch with their weight on the balls of their feet as they normally do when a runner is on base. That's just what happened and I took off for third."

It was one of only four stolen bases McAuliffe had all season.

The 1971 Detroit Tigers did not catch the Orioles.

"The Orioles are a great ball club," Billy said at season's end. "They are better than I thought they were. But we'll give them a battle next year."

The Tigers had improved to 91-71, 12 more victories than in the previous year. Attendance had jumped 25 percent. Detroit baseball fans, some scared away from downtown Tiger Stadium by the race riots, were reconnecting with the Tigers and revisiting the Tiger Stadium neighborhood. There was optimism where there had been only uncertainty and despair. And few in baseball were now doubting what Billy the manager could do. The 1969 Twins were not a fluke. Billy could win with more than one style. And as the American League was finding out, he was just getting started.

"We can beat Baltimore," Billy said as he headed into the 1971–72 off-season. "And Baltimore knows it."

22

WHEN BILLY, GRETCHEN, AND their son, B.J., first came to Detroit after ten years in Minnesota, they were completely unprepared for the move. After several weeks, they had still not found a home and were instead living in a hotel downtown.

One day, Billy was speaking to a Detroit luncheon attended by about three hundred local businessmen, the kind of public relations work that he did at every managerial stop. At the end of the talk and after a question-and-answer period, Billy told the businessmen he had a question for them.

"We're living in a hotel and my wife can't chase our seven-year-old son all day in a hotel," Billy said. "Does someone in this city have a place for us to live?"

Soon the Martins had moved into a townhouse in a complex called Cranbrook Manor in the tony suburb of Bloomfield Hills. They were close to the Cranbrook Schools, one of the best prep schools in Michigan. The entire neighborhood had an aura of reserve and refinement.

"We had room to play, good schools, and the other ballplayers lived in the area, too," Billy Martin Jr. recalled. "I had a crush on Bill Freehan's daughter. We went to all the home games. We never, ever missed one."

John Fetzer, the Tigers' owner, was a pioneering radio and television executive who then acquired the soon-to-be-everywhere elevator music company Muzak. Fetzer was not much interested in running the club day to day.

"He was a silent owner," Gretchen said. "That wasn't something Billy had very often. Billy and Jim Campbell ran the club."

Before the 1972 season, Campbell had torn up Billy's original two-year contract that paid him $50,000 annually and extended it by a year with a $10,000-a-year raise. A sense of tranquillity enveloped Billy's life. Gretchen recalls the couple going to watch a new movie, *The Godfather*. President Nixon was visiting Communist China, the first U.S. president to do so. While Nixon was in Peking, his attorney general, John Mitchell, resigned to become the chairman of the president's 1972 reelection campaign. In about two months Mitchell would oversee the first of the Watergate burglaries.

The principal baseball news that year was the threat of a players' strike over pension dollars. But no one took it seriously. The former Twins broadcaster Bob Wolff, then doing New York Knicks games and national baseball broadcasts, recalled visiting the Tigers' spring training camp that year and meeting with a relaxed and confident Billy. Wolff had another reason to be at the Tigers' camp. His son, Rick, a recent Harvard graduate, had been a thirty-third-round draft pick of the Tigers. He was destined for the low minors, but he was nonetheless on some back field of Billy's camp.

"I remember I only had time to watch the first five innings of that day's exhibition game," Wolff said. "And I told Billy that. When the game started, my son was in the starting lineup with all the Tigers stars. That had not been the original lineup. I got to watch Rick steal a base and hear his name announced on the public address system.

"It was the thrill of a lifetime for a father. That's the kind of guy Billy was. He cared about people."

The players' strike movement did interrupt the season for about a week. The 1972 season would have each team playing anywhere from 154 to 156 games.

The Tigers' second game of the revised season brought them to Baltimore, and the tone of the nearly season-long competition between the teams was established from the first pitch. Earl Weaver immediately started getting on home plate umpire Dave Phillips because he thought he wasn't calling enough strikes for Orioles starter Jim Palmer. Unwilling to let his opponent get the advantage, Billy started yelling across the diamond at Weaver.

"Shut up, you little midget," Billy shouted.

"I will if you tell the guy behind the plate to do his job and call that pitch at the knees a strike," Weaver answered.

When Palmer's next pitch was called a strike, Billy howled at Phillips.

"Don't let him call the game for you," he yelled.

"Mind your own business, Billy," Weaver countered.

And that was only the first inning. By the fourth inning, Phillips had had his fill of the dugout repartee. He called both managers to home plate and insisted he would eject the next manager who said anything about balls and strikes.

Billy lasted until the sixth inning, then he was gone, thrown out by Phillips — Billy's first ejection in one hundred games with the Tigers. Weaver smiled and waved goodbye as Billy exited.

Afterward, Billy was heading to the Tigers' bus, walking across a darkened parking lot outside Baltimore's Memorial Stadium, when a fan accosted him. As late as the early 1980s, visiting teams sometimes had to wade through fans to get to a team bus. Security was often lax or nonexistent.

"You better win tomorrow," the approaching fan said to Billy.

"Take a hike," Billy answered.

"I'm not kidding around," the fan, Jack Sears, a twenty-five-year-old supermarket employee and former resident of Pontiac, Michigan, said.

"Go fuck yourself," Billy said, according to Detroit writers and players who were watching.

Sears replied with a "Fuck you" and a shove to the shoulder. Billy responded with a punch to the nose. The two scuffled a little until they were pulled apart. Billy boarded the team bus. Jack Sears, after giving his name to reporters, was never heard from again. /

The Tigers sprinted away from Baltimore in the next few weeks, taking a three-game lead in the AL East in mid-May. Back and forth throughout the summer the teams battled, joined by the Boston Red Sox and the New York Yankees, who were led by their sturdy twenty-five-year-old catcher, Thurman Munson. The Tigers were getting great pitching from Mickey Lolich but inconsistent hitting from the lineup. Billy tried various things to jump-start the offense. One game, he put all the starters' names in a hat and had Al Kaline pick out the lineup order. It had the lumbering Norm Cash leading off and the slight, banjo-hitting Brinkman at cleanup, but the Tigers won.

In another game, Billy used eighteen players, including six pinch hitters. The Tigers won again.

As the 1972 pennant races wound toward the fall, Major League Baseball itself was lurching on unsteady ground. At the same time, a subtle changing of the guard was going on. Economically, the game was suffering as attendance had dropped significantly. Crowds of seven thousand or five thousand were not uncommon at many ballparks. At first, it appeared to be a backlash against the players for their April strike, but there seemed to be more at play than that. In the early 1970s, baseball was paying for a cultural shift in America. As the country's oldest and most traditional team sport, baseball was an established institution, and anything linked to "the establishment" was unpopular in many quarters of America at the time. *Tradition* wasn't a word viewed with much regard either.

Baseball was also emerging from a second dead-ball era, a period from the mid-1960s to the early 1970s when batting averages drooped and strikeout ratios rose. The game looked tired, boring, and stuffy.

Then, along came Charlie Finley's Oakland A's. In 1972, as a marketing ploy, the A's began wearing solid green or solid gold jerseys with contrasting white pants. Their hats and helmets were often a radiant gold as well. Throughout the majors at the time, teams generally wore all white at home, with maybe pinstripes, and all-gray uniforms on the road. Baseball shoes were black. But not the A's. Their shoes were white and their uniforms all but glowed like neon.

At the same time, while many teams had rules against facial hair, the A's not only let their players grow mustaches and long sideburns, they encouraged it. Oakland owner Charlie Finley, in conjunction with a Mustache Day promotion, offered $500 to any player who grew a mustache by Father's Day. Nearly every player complied and collected the bonus.

The "Swinging A's," as they came to be known, also had the most-feared lineup and the best pitching staff in the American League. And when they came to Detroit in the late summer to face the AL East–leading Tigers, they took two of three games. Two of the A's stars, Reggie Jackson and Bert Campaneris, were also drilled by Tigers pitchers in the series. An accident? Not likely.

When the A's came back for another series in August, both benches emptied after some inside pitches from the Detroit rookie Bill Slayback. Various players squared off, and Horton remained undefeated, decking Oakland's Mike Epstein with one punch.

Both the A's-Tigers series drew an average of about forty thousand fans to timeworn Tiger Stadium, which had now become one of the rare American outposts where baseball was thriving. The blue-collar city of Detroit loved its hard-nosed, gritty manager and leader — the one kicking dirt on umpires and fighting for his team daily. To Detroit baseball fans, Billy was an antiestablishment guy in his own way. They loved his up-by-his-bootstraps background and Everyman appeal.

"Anywhere you went with Billy in Detroit back then, he would be cheered," said Ron Perranoski, the relief pitcher acquired by Detroit from Minnesota late in 1971.

As he had in Minnesota, Billy adapted to his environment — not that it was hard. Michigan has great fishing and hunting, and Billy spent many an off day or midday before a night game in the countryside throwing a line out on some lake as the guest of a Tigers business associate he had met — or even a random fan.

Detroit was a shot-and-beer town, and Billy and Art Fowler waded into the thick bar culture with unbridled merriment. It's where Billy first made friends with Bill Reedy, a local who knew Art Fowler and who would end up owning Reedy's Saloon, another Billy haunt near the stadium. These were homey saloons full of Teamsters, assembly-line workers, office staff, and tire manufacturers. It was one big convivial gathering, and if anyone got less than hospitable with the Tigers' manager, Reedy, a burly guy and a former amateur boxer, knew how to keep order.

By September, the Orioles surprisingly ran out of gas and dropped from the race. The Tigers were stumbling, too, and lost their AL East lead to the Boston Red Sox. Detroit nonetheless hung in there. It was a determined team, though maybe not quite as unified as Billy wanted. Northrup was slumping badly and blamed Billy for moving him around in the lineup. In mid-season 1972, Northrup simply stopped talking to Billy, who after a few attempts at breaking through the silent treatment gave up and refused to talk to Northrup. The two communicated through the coaches, if at all.

There were other whispers of discord that swept through the team, mostly on the road — Billy was drunk in the front of the plane or Billy almost got in a fight in the hotel lobby bar. The Tigers' front office heard the rumblings. There was added tension on this team because Billy essentially had only three regular starters (Rodríguez, Brinkman, and Kaline when he was healthy); everyone else was caught in a revolving platoon system that Billy felt was necessary to squeeze every last run out of a sputtering batting lineup. And some players in the Tigers' dugout were simply tired of Billy's incessant pressuring tactics, even if they kept their mouths shut — or kept their distance. The veteran core of the lineup continued to play hard, happy at least that Billy had them chasing a division title. In that sense, not much had changed in twenty years of baseball. Casey Stengel, who platooned his players, had once famously said that every manager has ten guys who love him, ten guys who hate him, and five who are undecided. The key for a manager, Stengel said, was keeping the five who are on the fence about you away from the ten who hate you.

By the last weekend of the 1972 regular season, the first-place Red Sox came to Detroit for the final three games of the season. Boston had a half-game lead over the Tigers. The division winner would be the team that won two of those three sold-out games in Detroit.

The Tigers quickly won the first two games, ending the drama. The Red Sox won the final game of the regular season, but the Tigers won the division with an 86-70 record, one-half game better than Boston's 85-70 record. The settlement of the April players' strike established that some teams would play fewer games than others, but it had been agreed upon in April that division winners would be determined by winning percentage. There were no makeup games. The Tigers would come to be known as the "half-game champs."

Billy had led two teams in three years to the American League Championship Series. Each team had been a reclamation project. It was the work of a budding baseball genius, which is exactly how most of the baseball community now viewed him.

On the eve of the ALCS against the AL West champion Athletics, even Reggie Jackson said, "I don't like Billy Martin because he plays tough baseball. But I'd probably love him if I played for him."

Billy had won in Minnesota with speed and young talent — some of them unheralded, discarded players from Spanish-speaking countries. The Twins were a middle-of-the-plains miracle. Three years later, in Detroit, a city reeling from racial strife, Billy had taken over an old team divided by cliques and the contempt that familiarity can breed. It was a team that was a mix of white and black players who lacked the spark of youth and the strength of unity. And yet, again, with his detractors chortling that he had walked into an untenable situation, Billy had produced a winner, upending a burgeoning dynasty in Baltimore.

Billy took satisfaction in those triumphs, but as he told his closest friends and family, he felt unsatisfied until he got back to the World Series and won it. He was happy to have given his players in Minnesota and in Detroit a glimpse of the promised land, but he had to do more than show it to them. He had to bring them there. He had to let them enjoy all its fruits.

Billy Martin the manager could not be fulfilled until he was what he was as a player — a World Series champion, a World Series hero. If Billy in the 1950s was chasing a childhood dream, then Billy in the 1970s was chasing the vision of himself he had fashioned as a young adult. That's when he was the best at his job, a perennial champion. He was baseball royalty, the game he loved giving back to him in innumerable ways. Billy the manager wanted nothing less. He had to reclaim his kingdom.

23

AS HIS TWINS WERE in 1969, Billy's 1972 Tigers were big underdogs in the ALCS. The A's had the better starting pitching and a more dependable bullpen, a more potent lineup, more youth, more athleticism, more speed, and a veteran, astute manager in Dick Williams. But few expected the Tigers to roll over. Detroit and Oakland had already come to blows on the field in consecutive seasons, donnybrooks that resulted in broken bones and stitches. In the baseball community, there was every expectation of more fireworks, a portent that proved prescient.

The sparring began before the first game of the series in Oakland. When the Tigers checked into their Oakland hotel, Billy discovered that he could not have his usual rooftop suite, which he always used to entertain his East Bay guests when the Tigers visited Oakland during the regular season. Aware of Billy's habits, and hoping to unnerve him, Charlie Finley had reserved the rooftop suite throughout the playoffs.

Privately, Billy fumed, but when reporters asked him about it, he laughed it off.

"You could probably fill a suite like that with all your friends from the area," a reporter remarked.

"Or my enemies," Billy quipped.

During the first game in Oakland on Saturday, October 7, Lolich, who won three games in the 1968 World Series, and the A's starter, Jim "Catfish" Hunter, kept the game at 1–1 through eight innings. Duke Sims led off the top of the ninth with a double. Cash was up next, but Williams had a deep bullpen and he went to it.

With Monday an off day in the series, Williams needed only three starters, so he relegated Vida Blue, the 1971 Cy Young Award winner who had sat out most of the 1972 season in a salary dispute, to relief duties. It was a wonderful ace to have up your sleeve. Not many teams have ever had a bullpen setup pitcher who months earlier was the youngest American League MVP in the twentieth century.

Billy didn't like the lefty-hitter Cash's chances against the left-handed

Blue, so he had Cash bunt. In the early 1970s, even cleanup hitters could bunt — at least on Billy's teams — and Cash put down a perfect sacrifice bunt toward third base. When the throw to first was misplayed, the Tigers had runners at first and second with no outs.

Horton was the next batter, but Williams took out Blue for the right-handed Rollie Fingers, a second ace up his sleeve. Billy countered with the lefty pinch hitter Gates Brown, but Fingers got Brown to pop out in foul territory. Northrup was up next, another lefty but normally a good bunter.

As Fingers went into his motion — a full wind-up — Sims sprinted toward home plate from third base. The suicide squeeze was on, but Northrup, who wheeled around to bunt late, fouled off the pitch. Billy always wondered if Northrup missed the bunt attempt intentionally, preferring to swing away. He also claimed that Northrup either missed or ignored the squeeze bunt signal since he had not given the third-base coach the return signal acknowledging the squeeze play. It may have been somehow apropos that a communication breakdown between a player and a manager who did not speak to each other got in the way of the potential winning run in a pivotal game.

With the element of surprise gone — Fingers went into the stretch on his next pitch — Billy could not try another squeeze bunt. Northrup smacked a hard ground ball to second base that became an inning-ending double play.

In the top of the eleventh inning, the Tigers took a 2–1 lead and Billy faced a familiar decision entering the bottom of the inning. Lolich had given up only seven hits and he had retired the last seven A's in order, but it was also the eleventh inning and Lolich had already pitched more than 2,600 Major League innings in his career. He had done enough in a tense playoff game. Then again, Lolich's postseason record at that juncture was 3-0 with a 1.46 ERA.

Billy did not have Vida Blue and Rollie Fingers in the bullpen. His closer was twenty-four-year old Chuck Seelbach, who had won the job by default when Perranoski's aging arm gave out during the summer and he was released. Seelbach had no playoff experience.

Trusting his heart, Billy chose to stick with his veteran. The Tigers ace promptly gave up back-to-back singles. The A's had runners on first and second base when Billy brought on Seelbach. Anticipating a bunt, Rodríguez played in from third base. Oakland catcher Gene Tenace did bunt, and Rodríguez pounced on it and threw to third base where Brinkman had run over from shortstop. The lead runner was out.

The Tigers seemed to have dodged the most dangerous bullet and had kept runners at first and second base with one out. But Oakland rookie Gonzalo Marquez slapped a slow ground ball through the right side of the infield for a single. The pinch runner from second base, Mike Hegan, scored easily. Kaline fielded the ball in right field, and with Tenace racing around second base, the ten-time Gold Glove winner — known for his strong and accurate arm — fired a strike to Rodríguez at third base.

The A's were giving Billy some of his own medicine, forcing the defense to make a play with Tenace sliding into the base just as the throw arrived. Kaline's throw was a one-hopper and on line, and Rodríguez, also a Gold Glove winner in his career, was in position. In the cloud of dust, the ball deflected off Tenace's hip and skipped by Rodríguez.

Tenace leaped to his feet and ran home with the winning run in a 3–2 Oakland victory./

Billy had managed four ALCS games, and three of them had now ended in one-run defeats. Not surprisingly, Billy focused on his team's missed opportunities.

"We should have won it in nine innings," Billy told reporters in his office after the game. "The screwed-up suicide squeeze beat us."

Game 2 was not close with Oakland jumping to a 5–0 lead after five innings. But as was expected, the combustible nature of the matchup eventually produced a notable flare-up.

In the first inning of the game, the speedy Campaneris had singled, stolen second and third base, and scored on a single. In the third inning, he had singled again. In the fifth inning, he had another single and eventually scored on a wild pitch.

The Cuban-born Campaneris, who would lead the AL in stolen bases six times and played with a fiery intensity, was Billy's kind of player. Indeed, in the 1980s, Billy would trade for him with the Yankees. But watching his team on its way to an 0-2 deficit in the series, Billy was fed up with Campaneris's unbridled assault on his Tigers defense. He had apparently anticipated as much, according to Tony Kubek, Billy's former Yankees teammate and now an NBC broadcaster working the game. The two had dinner the night before Game 2.

"Billy and I were sitting there and Billy said, 'We gotta stop Campaneris,'" Kubek said. "He went on, 'He's beating us with his feet. We gotta get him.'"

Campaneris led off the seventh inning, and the first pitch from Detroit rookie Lerrin LaGrow was a fastball down and in that struck Campaneris squarely on the left ankle. Campaneris fell backward but never released the bat in his right hand. When he rose to his feet, he flung the bat at LaGrow, the bat whirling through the air horizontally. The bat spun like a helicopter blade about five feet off the ground, and the six-foot-five LaGrow ducked low to avoid it.

Home plate umpire Nestor Chylak kept Campaneris from charging the mound, but now the Tigers were coming after Campaneris, led by Billy, who was restrained by three umpires as he tried to get at Campaneris.

Campaneris and LaGrow were ejected from the game. The rest of the game, a 5–0 Oakland victory, was uneventful. In his office, Billy said of Campaneris, "I don't know what that idiot was thinking. If there's ever another fight out there, I'm going out there and beat the shit out of him."

LaGrow said his pitch to Campaneris "just got away." Few were convinced it was unintentional.

Oakland owner Charlie Finley blamed the whole episode on Billy. Billy's response proved that he had been paying attention when Gretchen took him to see *The Godfather* in the spring.

"Tell Charlie that if something like this happens again," Billy said, "he may wake up some morning with his mule's head in his bed."

Campaneris was suspended for the rest of the series, but separately, the Tigers also lost their shortstop, Eddie Brinkman, who aggravated a pinched nerve running out a double. Brinkman, who had played 315 of the 318 games at shortstop under Billy in Detroit, was out of the series with a numb foot. Billy had used "Steady Eddie" so much he did not bother carrying a true backup shortstop. Now the Tigers would have to play McAuliffe, the second baseman who had not been a regular shortstop since 1966.

Still, an inspired Detroit team rebounded in Detroit to win the next two games. The Tigers had new momentum, spurred by the return to the lineup of All-Star Bill Freehan behind the plate. Freehan had sustained a hairline fracture of his right thumb on September 21 and had not played since. Declared healthy by doctors, he caught nineteen innings in Games 3 and 4, adding three hits and two RBIs including a home run.

Detroit baseball fans slept on the sidewalks outside Tiger Stadium in subfreezing temperatures to get tickets to the final game of the American League season, which was played on a raw, windy day. In interviews twenty-five years later for an ESPN documentary on Billy's life, two Tigers players, Northrup and Gates Brown, said Billy arrived late to the ballpark before the clinching game and appeared hung-over.

"I never could understand it," Brown said, "because I'm saying, you know, this is for everything."

Other players do not recall Billy's pregame condition. But they saw the tension in his eyes. The World Series was a game away.

When the game began, the Tigers scored a first-inning run on a Freehan groundout, but the A's tied it when Jackson stole home on a double steal, a play that concluded with a fierce home plate collision between Freehan and Jackson, who tore his hamstring on the play and was sidelined until 1973.

George Hendrick, who replaced Jackson in center field for the A's, led off the fourth inning with a routine grounder toward the hole at shortstop. McAuliffe, the emergency shortstop, threw the ball just a bit wide and low to first base, though Cash made the catch steps before Hendrick arrived. Umpire John Rice called Hendrick safe, saying that Cash had lifted his toe off the base while making the catch. In the modern era of endless television camera angles, umpires have been forced to be stricter about the first baseman's footwork. But in 1972, when "instant replay" was new and taken from one camera angle, it was not uncommon for first basemen to cheat by an inch or so around the base because it was seen as a harmless violation that was rarely called.

Rice's call sent Billy and other Tigers into a tizzy as they surrounded the umpire on the field, incredulous at the call and its timing.

It included this salty exchange from Frank Howard, the Tigers' six-foot-eight player-coach and a former first baseman.

"What's the matter with you, John, you see that play every day during the season," Howard howled.

"Are you calling me a liar?" Rice asked.

"No, sir," Howard answered. "But you are full of shit!"

After Howard was ejected, Hendrick did not stay at first base for long as he was quickly sacrificed to second base. Tigers starter Woodie Fryman got the next batter to strike out, but then Tenace lined a single to left field.

Duke Sims, the backup catcher and sometimes outfielder, had been Billy's choice in left field instead of Willie Horton as Billy tried to get another left-handed bat in the lineup against Oakland starter Blue Moon Odom. He had done the same thing earlier in the series. But on this play, Sims seemed to be slightly handcuffed by Tenace's hit, and he did not get his throw off quickly as Hendrick headed for home. Sims's throw was on line, and Freehan caught it and turned to tag Hendrick. It was a bang-bang play but the ball squirted out of Freehan's mitt. The A's were up 2–1.

The Tigers were confident they could get to Odom, but to start the sixth inning, Dick Williams summoned Blue from the bullpen. The Tigers barely threatened as Blue pitched four brilliant, scoreless innings.

Billy had lost another one-run playoff game and for the second time fallen short of the World Series in the postseason as a manager.

For years after the final game, Billy was second-guessed for playing Sims, who had hit .316 in the regular season, instead of Horton, who had hit .231. Horton said he would have thrown Hendrick out at home and prevented the second Oakland run. Horton was by far the more experienced outfielder. But Sims had already played 339 innings in the outfield in his Major League career, including 28 innings that year for the Tigers. It may have been a decision that backfired, but it was the same decision Billy had been making throughout the successful second half of the season.

Others pointed to whether Freehan might have been hampered defensively by his recently healed thumb injury since he dropped the ball trying to make the tag on the winning run. If Freehan looked impaired, there was no mention of it after he played nineteen innings at catcher during the previous two playoff games. In scores of newspaper accounts, he was instead lauded as the pivotal leader and driving force in the Tigers' rejuvenation in the series. With the designated hitter still one season away, it would have been difficult to keep Freehan off the field in the pivotal game.

The more permanent takeaway of the series was an appreciation for the compelling drama it provided. The league championship series was still new to baseball, but the matchup of the Tigers and Athletics made an expanded postseason seem like an idea that was long overdue. The Tigers were praised for getting as far as they did, only to be finally undone by an anemic offense that hit .198 in the series. The A's were celebrated and feted as a team on the rise, which proved true when they won the next three World Series.

In the losing locker room, Billy barred visitors and media until he addressed his team. Through the rickety clubhouse door of creaky old Tiger Stadium, reporters could hear Billy saying, "I'm proud of every one of you guys. Every one of you'se."

But on a personal level, Billy was crushed. Charlie Silvera, Billy's old Yankees roommate, sat with Billy in his office after all the reporters and players had left Tiger Stadium. They were drinking beer.

"We replayed and rehashed the key plays—the ump's call at first base, the two plays at the plate," Silvera recalled. "We did that maybe once or twice and then Billy said, 'Come on, we've got to go up and see Campbell in his office. We need to go talk to him, too.'"

The Tigers' executive suite was on the roof by the right-field line, and Billy and Silvera had to walk through the narrow concourse of the stadium beneath the seats to reach the elevator that would carry them to the offices. The fans had filed out and the concourse was empty but for a few maintenance men.

"We were walking in silence, neither of us talking, and then about halfway there, when there was nobody else around, Billy just stopped," Silvera said. "He said, 'Charlie, I really wanted this one.' And he started to cry.

"He put his head on my shoulder, kind of fell into my arms, and said, 'I wanted to win today so much.'"

24

THE MAGIC, UPLIFTING KARMA and providence that seemed to accompany the 1972 Tigers evaporated quickly in a new year. The harmony of effort soured long before the regular season, and the splintered factions grew farther apart.

For starters, Billy believed he had gotten almost all he could out of an aging roster in 1971 and 1972. He wanted Jim Campbell, the general manager, to trade many of the veterans to revamp the team. Campbell, who had drafted those stars, declined.

In spring training, Billy had another disciplinary run-in with Willie Horton and wanted him fined. When Campbell came up with a different solution, Billy quit as manager for roughly twenty-four hours.

When there was a reconciliation, the team's official position was that the dispute had never happened. Except that Tigers management never forgot it. And it was a first sign that Billy was starting to unravel the order and peace that had largely surrounded his life in Detroit.

In tandem, and perhaps not coincidentally, the 1973 Tigers weren't the same team they had been a year earlier. Lolich had a tired arm, and everyone but Horton and Northrup seemed to be having worse years.

There were positives, bred by Billy's unorthodox thinking. He promoted John Hiller, a reliever who had left the team after he had a heart attack in 1971 at the age of twenty-eight. Heart disease was not much understood at the time, and the Tigers had been unwilling to play Hiller, fearful that he might suffer another heart attack on the field.

Billy asked Hiller about his condition.

"He said I'm going to die of something eventually but it's fine if I pitch right now," Hiller said.

Billy asked Art Fowler his opinion.

"I agree, he's going to die of something eventually," Fowler said.

Billy made Hiller his closer in 1973, and he set a club record with 38 saves. He was one of the major reasons the Tigers stayed in the 1973 division race with the Yankees and the resurrected Orioles.

On a tip from Jimmy Butsicaris, Billy's old Lindell A.C. friend, Billy also visited Jackson State Prison in southern Michigan to see an inmate playing for the prison baseball team. Ron LeFlore was serving time for armed robbery, but Billy convinced the Jackson State warden to allow LeFlore to come to a tryout at Tiger Stadium in July of 1973. The Tigers then signed LeFlore to a contract and negotiated a limited and then full parole under certain conditions (Billy and the Tigers had to sign off as wards to LeFlore). By 1974, LeFlore was starting in center field at Tiger Stadium, the beginning of a nine-year career.

But if there were good vibes about the 1973 Tigers, and there were since they were in or near first place in the AL East as late as mid-August, there was also an undercurrent of simmering rancor. Billy and Campbell feuded constantly, with Billy criticizing the team's scouting department in the press, a public display of the team's dirty laundry that incensed Campbell and others in the Tigers organization. John Fetzer, the low-key owner who wanted his organization to have a defined and accepted chain of command, was disturbed by Billy's lack of professional protocol. In the past, Campbell would protect Billy, saying the end was worth the means. Increasingly exasperated, Campbell was no longer rushing to Billy's defense.

There were other hiccups along the way; Billy showed up uncommonly late for the occasional game, striding into the park about an hour before the first pitch. Without a batting order written out, the players did not know who was taking batting practice, or who was at what position for infield and outfield practice — something all teams did before every game in the 1970s. Players and team executives also noticed that Billy seemed more impatient than ever with umpires and with his coaches. In June, he missed a couple of games to fly home to West Berkeley to be with Jack Downey, who had suffered a heart attack. When he returned to the Tigers, players and coaches said Billy appeared gaunt and drained.

"Billy looked like he was getting kind of beat down," Silvera said. "The more he worried, the less he took care of himself. You could kind of see it slowly happening."

Billy lobbied strenuously for a couple of trades, only to be blocked by Campbell and the scouting department. Billy seethed anew. So it was something less than one, big happy Tigers family. But the team was winning. And in that case, almost everything else was overlooked.

Then, in late August, the Tigers started losing just as the Orioles roared through the end of the month by winning twelve of fifteen games. The Tigers fell 7.5 games out of first place.

At a game in Detroit against Cleveland on August 30, the Indians' noted spitball pitcher Gaylord Perry was beating the Tigers 3–0 after seven innings. Billy was livid with the umpires for not detecting Perry's illegal pitches. Truth be told, Billy was probably most incensed by the notion that someone besides him and Fowler was getting away with doctoring the baseball.

Billy's reaction was to have two of his pitchers start loading up the ball with Vaseline. As Fowler taught them, it was easy — put the Vaseline on the crotch part of your uniform and put your hand there before throwing a pitch. If the umpires came out to the mound to inspect the pitcher, it was presumed that no umpire, in front of an entire stadium of fans, would start pawing around in a player's crotch to investigate.

The Tigers still lost. After the game, to the astonishment of the Detroit writers, Billy announced, "My pitchers were deliberately throwing spitballs the last two innings on orders from me. I did it to prove a point that it can be done without the umpires doing anything about it. They're making a mockery of the game by not stopping Perry."

American League president Joe Cronin suspended Billy immediately. Three days later, Jim Campbell called Billy to his rooftop office and told him he was fired.

"Did I not make this team a winner?" Billy said, repeating himself from his Minnesota exit.

Campbell told Billy the same things he told reporters later: "From foul line to foul line, Billy did a good job. There were certain things that made me uncomfortable with him. You couldn't have somebody working for you who would destroy the rest of the organization. I don't know if Billy ever understood that there were different parts of the baseball team. There is more to it than just what goes on between the lines."

In some ways it was a sentiment that could have summed up Billy's managerial philosophy, meaning that there is so much more to winning at baseball than the obvious play between the lines. But the paradox was that it was an axiom Billy never agreed with or chose to live by. Billy's question would be: "Did I not get this team to win?" And often the response of his boss would be: "Yes, but at what cost outside the lines?"

It was the dual, and dueling, tenets at the core of a life strewn with conflict. And once again, and not for the last time, it put Billy at a crossroads.

When Billy called his wife, Gretchen, with the news of his firing, she was bewildered.

"I didn't see what Billy had done wrong," she said. "The city loved the Tigers."

The reaction of Detroit's baseball fans was similar to what transpired in Minnesota in 1969. They were enraged that the workingman's hero had been fired. They flooded the team's phone lines with complaints, filled the local radio airwaves with their anger and dismay, and protested outside Tiger Stadium, waving placards and vowing not to come back. Campbell became a recluse, locking himself in his office or apartment because fans cursed at him and yelled in his direction whenever he was in public.

Billy came home the day of the firing and talked with Gretchen about how the Tigers were going to honor the last year of his contract in 1974. To Billy, there was no rush to accept another job.

But a day later, Bob Short, a Minnesota politician for whom Billy had campaigned in 1970, called the Martin home in the Cranbrook Manor townhouses outside Detroit. Short was also the owner of the Washington Senators, and in 1972 he had moved that franchise to a town outside Dallas and renamed the team the Texas Rangers. The Rangers were in last place in the AL West and drawing crowds as small as two thousand people.

Short wanted Billy to come to Texas as his manager that day. Short said he would fire his current manager, Whitey Herzog, the future Hall of Famer. Billy said he wanted to rest. Short said he was offering a contract through 1975 worth $65,000 a year, plus the use of a new house and a new car.

Billy wanted to think about it. He was tired. He mentioned that another move would mean his son, B.J., would have to find another Catholic school to attend. A new school year had just started and his son liked his teachers and friends.

Short said he would find Billy another Catholic grade school in Texas. Billy was unmoved. He told Short to call him back in a couple of days.

When Short got Billy on the line again, he told him he had found the perfect Catholic school and it would be happy to accept B.J. Then Short offered Billy something new: control.

Billy would have the final authority over the twenty-five-man roster. He could call up whomever he wanted from the minors, oversee the farm system, and make all the trades.

Billy did not think long before accepting the job. It was September 8, six days after the Tigers fired him. Billy would be managing his third team in five years, and this time, he would be his own general manager. He was forty-five years old.

When Texas writers asked him what he could do with a team that had already lost 91 of its 140 games in 1973, Billy replied, "I've been fired twice. I'm a two-time loser. I know losing. But I also know winning. And I know how to get from one to the other."

25

WHEN BILLY'S WIFE, GRETCHEN, began relocating to the Dallas area during the winter of 1973–74, she went to a local bank to fill out an application for a checking account.

"I was asked for my husband's employer and I wrote, 'Texas Rangers,'" Gretchen said. "When the bank manager looked at my application, he said, 'Oh, your husband is in law enforcement.'

"I was so perplexed. I said, 'Oh, no, this is baseball.' And my goodness, then he looked so perplexed."

Bob Short had brought Major League Baseball to the Dallas–Fort Worth area, but few had noticed. One, the Rangers were such a lousy team. And two, Texas was football country. The average high school football game outdrew the average Rangers game, often by thousands of fans. College football was a religion, and the Dallas Cowboys, recent winners of their first Super Bowl, were surging behind new quarterback Roger Staubach.

In 1974, it is likely that the average Texan could name more Dallas Cowboys cheerleaders than Texas Rangers baseball players.

Billy was hired to change that. Maybe after a few months someone in Texas could at least name the manager of the Rangers.

But Billy knew that his name alone wouldn't get people to come to the Rangers' ballpark, Arlington Stadium, which was essentially an oversize minor league stadium between Dallas and Fort Worth. The stadium, surrounded by barren, sun-baked lowlands, was drab, squat, and lifeless. Its grounds were scorched by a Texas sun that made game-time temperatures, even in the evening, soar to 100 degrees. The Texas Rangers had the worst record in the Major Leagues, the worst attendance, and the worst attitude because no one, even the players, wanted to go out in the oppressive heat and in front of the empty stands.

Billy had to construct a winner fast, and he had to do it in a Texas sort of way.

"Texas was like another country," Gretchen said. "But Billy was ready to move to another country. Billy threw himself into the Texas culture."

Billy's first taste of Texas came during his annual winter visits to Mickey Mantle's Dallas-area home in the 1960s. It was an extension of their get-togethers as Yankees players when Mantle lived in Oklahoma. Billy enjoyed being around the ranchers and cattlemen Mantle befriended, a city boy drawn to the vast, open spaces and the frontier justice ethos.

"He used to say that the only other time in history that he would have liked to live was the Old West," his son, Billy, said. "He said he would have either been a gunfighter or a sheriff."

Long before he was hired as the Rangers' manager, Billy devoured the Western-themed books of Louis L'Amour and Zane Grey. Besides books on Civil War history, they were the only books he read.

As Gretchen said, "I could get him to any movie if I convinced him it was a Western."

The Wild West was still alive in 1970s Texas, and Billy's gunslinger's swagger fit in perfectly. He was also ripe for a middle-age crisis of sorts. Some men buy a red sports car at forty-five years old; Billy went out and bought himself a new Western wardrobe. He grew a mustache, like any good outlaw far away from his boyhood home.

"He loved the whole Texas wild and loose image," said Randy Galloway, a longtime Dallas-area newspaper columnist who in 1974 was a Rangers beat writer for the *Dallas Morning News*. "Almost from day one, he was wearing cowboy boots, a cowboy hat, and a big belt buckle."

The Dallas-area newspapers ran pictures of Billy holding a shotgun in front of the fieldstone fireplace of his home — a Texas longhorn above the mantel. In other pictures, he twirled a replica Colt .45 six-shooter while nine-year-old Billy Joe — in Texas, B.J. more often started to be called Billy Joe — had a hand on the shotgun.

Toby Harrah, the Rangers' shortstop, said Billy was known for walking into any bar in Texas and just talking up the locals like he was one of them.

"I don't know if all those Texans liked that," Harrah said, laughing. "He did play all those years for the hated New York Yankees. Billy probably got popped in the nose a few times. But that didn't stop him."

But you couldn't just put cowboy hats on the 1974 Rangers' roster and make it a success. Billy Martin the general manager made a good first trade, sending the twenty-two-year-old third baseman Bill Madlock to the Chicago Cubs for pitcher Ferguson Jenkins. Madlock went on to have a terrific career as a four-time batting champ. But the Rangers desperately needed an ace of the pitching staff, and Jenkins, who slipped to 14 wins in 1973, had won at least 20 games every year since 1967. He was on his way to the Hall of Fame and only thirty-one years old.

Combined with the dependable workhorse Jim Bibby and the third starter, Jackie Moore, whom Billy yanked out of the bullpen, the Rangers suddenly had a respectable top to the pitching rotation.

Next, Billy turned to his defensive lineup. He traded starting catcher Ken Suarez to Cleveland for Leo Cárdenas, who had played for Billy in Minnesota. The new catcher would be twenty-three-year-old Jim Sundberg, whom the Rangers had drafted out of the University of Iowa one year earlier.

Sundberg had played just one summer in the Class AA minors, but Billy had scouted him in an off-season instructional league game and declared him ready for the Major Leagues. It was the first of sixteen seasons in the big leagues for Sundberg, who became an All-Star three times and won six Gold Gloves.

"I don't think anyone other than Billy Martin would have had the guts to make that call," Sundberg, now a senior vice president with the Texas Rangers, said. "I don't know anyone else who would have shown that much confidence in a young player."

Billy was just getting started. From the Rangers' Class A team in the Western Carolina League, he promoted first baseman Mike Hargrove and gave him a starting job. Hargrove had hit .351 in his first minor league season. When a reporter in spring training quipped that Hargrove had never played above Class A ball, Billy had a waiting answer: "Did you know he had a slugging percentage of .542? I'll take anybody who can do that at any level."

When Billy elevated Lenny Randle from reserve status to starting third baseman, he talked about how Randle had been a minor league star "who just needs the chance to play." Billy raised eyebrows when he put designated hitter Alex Johnson in left field. The moody, sometimes incommunicative Johnson wasn't a stellar fielder, but Billy said it was important to get Johnson into the normal mix of games. Making him an everyday DH only isolated Johnson more and contributed to his brooding.

Buck Showalter, whom Billy mentored in the 1980s, has studied Billy's decision making for decades, and he is convinced that people underestimated how much deliberation went into Billy's choices throughout his career.

"Over the decades, a perception has developed that Billy did a bunch of wild, emotional things," Showalter, who has managed four Major League teams, said in 2013. "People think he just showed up for the games, tried some risky things, and got lucky. Listen, you don't get lucky over 162 games; that's the great thing about baseball. And if you look at his personnel moves in Texas, he obviously studied the entire minor league roster and other American League rosters.

"He had a detailed plan. It was not a bunch of seat-of-his-pants decisions. That's how he was. Billy was very prepared. Before a series, he wanted to know about every strength and weakness of the opponent. He wanted to know who was hurt or which player's confidence was fading. He wanted to know who the umpires were going to be for the series and what their tendencies were. He never wanted to be surprised by anything. He wanted to be prepared so he could take advantage of some opportunity."

For the first few months, everything was smooth sailing in Texas. Then, just before the season started, Billy's Texas gift horse burst from the barn and galloped out of town. Bob Short, whose financial footing was not as solid as Billy suspected, sold his controlling interest in the Rangers to a group headed by Fort Worth industrialist Bradford Corbett.

Corbett, a native New Yorker who started his business career in 1968 with a $300,000 loan from the government's Small Business Administration, had made a fortune selling plastic PVC pipe and copper tubing to the oil industry. He paid $9.6 million for the Rangers. Corbett, just thirty-six years old, announced that he was delighted to have Billy as manager but that he was firing the entire Rangers' front office and hiring new executives.

Billy's days as general manager with complete control over the twenty-five-man roster were over. The sale of the Rangers, announced two days before the season was to open, clearly rattled Billy, but he soon had other things to focus on. The two-time defending champion Oakland A's were coming to Texas as the opening-night opponents, and Billy had been playing up the series in the local media as a showdown of the top two contenders in the AL West.

Never mind that Texas had finished thirty-two games behind the A's the previous season and Las Vegas made the Rangers a 50-to-1 shot to win the division.

"In his first meeting with the players, Billy had told us that we were going to kick Oakland's ass," Randle said. "The A's at the time were beating everybody in both leagues."

Harrah, the team's shortstop, said Billy asked for the players' trust.

"He said, 'You might think I'm crazy sometimes but I know what I'm doing and if you stick with me I promise we'll win and it'll be fun,'" Harrah said. "What did we have to lose? We had already lost 105 games."

The Rangers won only one of the three season-opening games against the A's, but they were competitive contests with the spunky Rangers knocking the A's best pitchers around for thirty-four hits in the three games. Jenkins had pitched a one-hitter to win a 2–0 shutout. Most energizing, the series had drawn nearly fifty-two thousand fans to Arlington Stadium, the most for a three-game set since the team's inaugural games in Texas in 1972. With an average attendance like that, Arlington Stadium's thirty-five-thousand-seat bowl was almost half full.

Half full? Corbett and his investors' group were delirious.

By the end of the month, the Rangers had gone to Oakland and won a series that put them in first place.

"The days when the Rangers are patsies are over," Billy declared.

The Rangers won one of those games in Oakland on two squeeze bunts. Down by one run in the ninth inning of another game in Oakland, the Rangers had runners at first and second base.

"Billy called a double steal and it worked, putting runners at second and third," said Tom Grieve, an outfielder for Texas from 1972 to 1977. "Then Jeff Burroughs, who Billy just let swing away at anything, slapped a 3-0 pitch into right field to score both runs and we won.

"Any other manager would have probably played to tie the game. They would be afraid to try that double steal. Not Billy; he always played to win. In my career I played for Ted Williams, Joe Torre, and Ken Boyer, all of them pretty good baseball men. Billy was the best manager I played for by far. He made every single player better. There was a lot of pressure but I'll tell you what, it was a lot of fun, too. People don't talk enough about that. If you did things Billy's way, it was a ton of fun."

Losing was another story. Everyone who played for Billy had at least one story of how hard Billy took a loss. Billy always said he never wanted to be a good loser. He never was.

"I remember after one loss, I came into the clubhouse and on the way to my locker, I reached out and grabbed one potato chip from the meal spread," Grieve said. "As fate would have it, Billy was a few steps behind me and he went nuts, screaming, 'How can you eat? Goddamn it, you losing fuckers!'"

The players from Minnesota and Detroit could have predicted what happened next. Food was soon flying around the room.

"It sounds funny now, you know, all that for one potato chip," Grieve, now a broadcaster with the Rangers, said. "But the next day, Billy came to me and said, 'Hey, look, don't make anything of it because I don't. You just happened to be the one who touched the food but that message was for everyone.'

"And let me tell you, the guys didn't want to lose any game after that."

Some of Billy's methods were more subtle. Several of the young Rangers said Billy taught them lessons they used throughout their careers. Harrah, who played seventeen years in the majors, said Billy approached him in 1974 and wanted to know which AL pitcher gave him the most trouble.

"He said he wanted to know so he'd take me out of the lineup against that guy," Harrah said. "I told him I couldn't hit the Indians' Luis Tiant. So next time Tiant goes against us, I'm in the lineup. I said, 'Hey, skip, remember what I told you?' And Billy just smiled at me.

"Don't you know that I faced Tiant every time after that; I never came out for even an inning. And you know what? I started learning to hit him. I had to face him for another eight years and I got pretty good at it. That was Billy. Don't back down."

The Rangers performed just as Billy planned, with each of his off-season moves panning out: Jenkins was on his way to a 25-win season; Hargrove and Randle would both hit over .300; and Sundberg, although unnerved by the pressure Billy put on his catcher and his pitch calling, was one of the league's best defensive catchers.

The Rangers hung close to the A's until the All-Star break, then fell to fourth place. But they rallied in late July and chased after Oakland again. A Texas DJ recorded a song, "Billy's Turnaround Gang," and it played at Arlington Stadium between innings and on local radio airwaves. The flip side of the single was "I Want to Play Ball for Billy."

It was during 1974 that Billy's arguing with umpires became like performance art. There is no Wild West without outlaws and they're often beloved. Billy's confrontations with the umpires — the sheriffs of base-ball — came to be expected at Arlington Stadium, and the fans arrived ea-ger to cheer on their rabble-rousing manager. No baseball fans seemed to enjoy watching Billy go after the umpires — kicking dirt, throwing his hat, or flinging bats from the dugout — as much as the Texas fans did. Egged on, and adept at playing to the crowd, Billy took things to new levels.

He was thrown out of both games of one double-header. Twice, he was ejected before the game began.

"It was to fire up the crowd, and he also wanted the players to know he was fighting for them," Jim Evans, an American League umpire from 1971 to 1999, said. "Then maybe they would fight as hard as he was fighting. Crowds urged him on. He had a terrible temper, but that was just Billy. I never minded working his games. It was a challenge.

"Besides, off the field, he was such a charmer. We'd see him and he'd come over to the umpires and make jokes. He'd always want to buy ev-eryone a drink. On the field, things were different. Billy had essentially three kinds of arguments. He knew the rules pretty well, so one argument would be a rational discussion about the rules and you almost enjoy that.

"The second argument was all about trying to get the next call. Once I had two bang-bang plays at first base and I called his guys out both times. Billy charges on the field and says, 'I don't know if those two guys were out or safe but I better get the third call.'

"And the last argument was just crazy. He would snap from the los-ing or the pressure or whatever. He'd come out and not even be making sense. I'd try not to throw him out because that was almost too easy. I'd wait to see what kind of crazy thing he would do. But that didn't happen too often. He usually had a point when he came out there."

Evans noticed that Billy had other strategies when it came to umpires. In Texas, Billy would have Sundberg signal him in the dugout when a pitch close to the strike zone was called a ball.

"That would be Billy's cue to yell, 'Hey, come on, Jim, that's a strike,'" Evans said. "It wasn't a strike but since he knew it was close he wanted to put a seed of doubt in the umpire's head so maybe he could get the next one. It was all very calculated."

Evans has been retired nearly fifteen years and spends much of his time at umpiring camps and speaking engagements.

"The number-one person people ask me about is Billy Martin," Evans said. "He was unforgettable. A little off his rocker, but unforgettable."

In 1974, Billy did not have too many arguments with the Rangers' management and most of the rest of the season was without incident. Except for June 3 in Cleveland, when the downtrodden Indians decided to host a 10-cent-beer night. Patrons were served unlimited draft beer at 10 cents a cup. The game's attendance was 23,134, but Cleveland's Municipal Stadium sold more than 65,000 cups of beer. Predictably, by the later innings, fans were showering the players with debris and running onto the field. There were multiple streakers, and about six fans surrounded Burroughs in right field, stealing his cap and glove and pulling on his shirt. Led by Billy, the entire Rangers' dugout emptied to defend Burroughs. They threw some fans to the ground and wrestled with others as they retrieved Burroughs's equipment. After a few more chaotic minutes — newspaper reporters would call the scene a riot — the game was forfeited to the Rangers. Billy was thrilled by his team's show of corporeal unity.

The Rangers dogged the first-place A's through August and were within four games of Oakland by September 20. There were eleven games to play. Texas hung in until September 26, when the Rangers lost both games of a double-header as Oakland's Catfish Hunter was winning his twenty-fifth game in Minnesota. It was the last gasp for Billy's Turnaround Gang.

The Rangers finished with an 84-76 record, a 47 percent increase in the number of victories year to year. The second-place 1974 Rangers became the first team in baseball history to finish over .500 after losing 100 games in back-to-back seasons. Home attendance had more than doubled to 1.2 million. Billy was named the AL Manager of the Year. Burroughs was named the league's Most Valuable Player. Oakland won the World Series for a third successive time.

Billy spent the off-season on the winter dinner circuit, once again feted around the country as baseball's rising managerial star and dugout genius. Gretchen and Billy Joe were ensconced in Texas. Billy did not lack for companionship on his trips to the many baseball dinners. Girlfriends on the road had become part of his life, and the team's management looked the other way, if uncomfortably.

In spring training of 1975, many writers were picking the Rangers to usurp the three-time defending world champions. Billy, for once, held his tongue. He might have seen what others did not — that the Rangers had not improved their pitching, especially in the bullpen, which had been a weakness in 1974.

The 1975 Rangers got off to a slow start, recovered, then stumbled through May, finishing the month at .500 and in fourth place, five games behind Oakland. The dreamlike zest of the previous year was missing. Jenkins was mediocre and Bibby was hurt. Sundberg was batting under .200. There seemed to be a team-wide malaise. Only one starting pitcher would finish with a winning record, and no batter would drive in 100 runs.

"Billy was so intense and so focused on what he was doing to get things turned around," Hargrove said, "that there just wasn't a whole lot of energy left once it got turned around."

By the end of June, the Rangers were three games under .500 and twelve games behind Oakland. By the All-Star break, there were rumors that Billy's job was in jeopardy, and as usual, it was not just because the Rangers had slumped.

"We started to see the effect of his drinking," Grieve said. "He would come in late to the ballpark and look terrible. The players weren't mad at him. I think we felt bad it was happening. It was more sad than annoying.

"Almost forty years later, people ask, 'Why didn't someone say something to him? Why didn't someone talk to him about his drinking?' But that's not what people did forty years ago. We didn't think it was any of our business. No one would have dreamed of approaching him and talking about his drinking. But I admit I think about it now, even forty years later. It was sad because I loved playing for him."

Rangers road trips were getting wilder and wilder with the charter plane journeys resembling a flying saloon and casino. That did not exactly set the Rangers apart in baseball back then, but that kind of behavior always gets mentioned more often when the team is losing. And team owner Brad Corbett, wily and irrepressible in the George Steinbrenner mold of team owner, had encouraged several players to spy on Billy for him.

Corbett, who died in 2012, was told that Billy's girlfriend(s) were flying on the charters with the team, something that especially became an issue to the players when Billy's paramour bumped one of the coaches out of the first-class section into the back of the plane usually occupied by the writers, broadcasters, and staff. Protocol on a baseball team is unwritten, but some things are out of bounds and that was one example. Corbett heard all about it.

"The off-the-field stuff became a distraction," Grieve said. "It was discussed. It erodes the team a little."

Just after the All-Star break, Billy wanted to sign a journeyman catcher, Tom Egan, who had recently been released by the California Angels. The Rangers' general manager, Dan O'Brien, was against the move and Corbett concurred.

Billy told reporters, "He [Corbett] knows as much about baseball as I know about pipe. One year in baseball and he's already a genius."

Corbett called the minority owners and team executives and said he was considering firing Billy. He told Billy the same thing.

The next day, there was a clash unlike any other in Billy's lifelong succession of fisticuffs, scraps, and tussles.

As part of his adoption of the Texas lifestyle, Billy had become a big fan of country music. He attended concerts and befriended country music stars like Charley Pride and Mac Davis. During the seventh-inning stretch at Arlington Stadium, Billy wanted the public address system to play John Denver's "Thank God I'm a Country Boy." It had been the top-selling record in country music in 1974, and the Texas crowd loved it. But the Queens-born Corbett lobbied for the traditional baseball anthem, "Take Me Out to the Ball Game." The two men argued over which song to play throughout the 1975 season until finally Corbett insisted that "Take Me Out to the Ball Game" be played in the seventh-inning stretch at every home game. That was that.

The day after Corbett told Billy he might fire him, the Rangers were cruising to a 6–0 victory, a five-hitter by Jenkins. In roughly the sixth inning, Billy called the press box and asked to talk to the person who chooses the music played between innings on the public address system.

Umpire Ron Luciano was working the bases and wandered over to the Rangers' dugout for some water in the midst of another hot Texas night. He heard Billy screaming into the dugout phone.

"Billy was saying, 'I don't care what the owner says, play the God damned John Denver song,'" Luciano wrote in his autobiography. "I couldn't believe my ears. Billy's yelling, 'I better hear "Thank God I'm a Country Boy."' And he slams the phone down."

The public address system played "Thank God I'm a Country Boy." In the owner's suite, Corbett steamed. After the game, the Rangers announced that Billy had been dismissed as manager.

Corbett did not blame John Denver. He specifically said the decision was not based on the Rangers' losing record.

"The decision was made because of a lot of factors which had built up over the last month or so," said Corbett, who would end up having six managers in the next six seasons, including four in 1977.

Billy was disconsolate and red-eyed as he cleaned out his locker after the game.

"What I'm proud of is the fact that I brought Texas a winner," he said. "I brought them a million fans and I brought them some real Major League baseball."

Then Billy retreated to an equipment room where he wept as he shook hands with coaches, players, and reporters. "It was a pitiful sight, seeing Billy all broken up," Rangers trainer Bill Ziegler said.

A reporter asked the reigning American League Manager of the Year about his future.

"I have no idea," Billy said, pausing to wipe away tears. "I love this game; baseball is my life. I love the game. But at this very moment I feel like telling the game to shove it."

26

––––––––––

BILLY, GRETCHEN, AND BILLY JOE went on a fishing trip in western Colorado after he was fired. The phone at the family home in Texas was ringing unanswered. It was the Yankees.

Eventually, the Yankees started calling Gretchen's father in Nebraska with a message: Yankees general manager Gabe Paul wanted to talk face-to-face with Billy as soon as possible. He proposed meeting at the Denver airport.

George Steinbrenner was suspended by Baseball Commissioner Bowie Kuhn and prohibited from conducting Yankees business. Steinbrenner had pleaded guilty to making illegal campaign contributions to Richard Nixon's reelection campaign — and then encouraging his employees to lie about it. Gabe Paul was officially the senior Yankees official. But he was acting on orders from Steinbrenner.

But Billy wouldn't talk to the Yankees. He put Gretchen on the phone.

"You be my agent for now," he said.

"I got on the phone and told them that Billy was not in any hurry to get back to baseball," Gretchen said. "I knew Billy was upset. He had built three winning teams and got fired three times. He was the reigning Manager of the Year and yet he still got fired. He just wanted to fish right then and that's all.

"He didn't want to go to New York and I told the Yankees that. But the Yankees were insistent. Billy's heart ached, but I also knew in my heart what he actually wanted to do."

Seven years earlier, Gretchen had talked Billy into accepting the Twins' minor league manager's job in Denver, which proved to be a pivotal move in Billy's professional career. Without it, Billy might never have managed in the big leagues.

Now, as Gretchen and Billy sat in a fishing lodge high in the Colorado mountains, they faced another decision, one that Gretchen, if not Billy, knew was more complicated than the one seven years earlier. Now it was Gretchen's heart that ached.

"I said we should go to Denver and talk to the Yankees," she said.

So they made arrangements to meet Paul inside the Denver airport, then take a cab to an airport hotel.

"Our flight from western Colorado landed and we were standing in the airport waiting for the Yankees' flight from New York to land," Gretchen said, recalling the scene. "And all at once, this sad feeling came over me. I turned to Billy and I said, 'You know, if you go to New York, it's probably the end for us.'

"It just flooded over me and I was overwhelmed by the thought because I suddenly understood it all in that moment. And I was crying and Billy started to cry, too. He said, 'OK, well, then I won't go to New York.'

"And I said, 'Oh, yes, you are. This is your destiny. You were always a Yankee. It's what you've been working your whole life for. It's a self-fulfilling life moment.'"

Gretchen and Billy waited in the airport, clinging to each other and drying their tears so they could properly greet the Yankees executives.

"Our marriage wasn't over right then, but I could see down the road," Gretchen said. "It hit me in that moment that there was an end coming. I knew Billy would be captivated by all the excitement of New York and all the options there."

Gretchen had made a home for herself and her son in Texas. Billy was not committed to any one place or fully committed to his marriage.

"I knew where this was heading but I wouldn't stop it," Gretchen said. "I knew what had to happen. Billy had never said he wanted to be Yankees manager. But he never had to. We both knew he had to go."

Even if Gretchen would not go with him.

"They had started to have their problems before that — it was there, even I saw it," said Billy Martin Jr., who was eleven at the time. "It just wasn't outwardly acknowledged. I was about to start at a new school in Texas that I liked. My mom and I were going to stay in Texas and visit New York when we could."

The house the Rangers gave the Martins to live in was leased to the team, so Billy bought it to prevent any further upheaval to his family.

At the Denver airport hotel, the contract negotiations with the Yankees moved quickly. At one juncture, there was a squabble over a behavioral clause — "a good boy clause," as Billy's legal adviser, Eddie Sapir, called it. George Steinbrenner got on the phone and said, "Let's face it, Billy, this is the job you've always wanted. I'm giving it to you."

It was not the last time that George held a carrot in front of Billy and demanded that he take it.

On August 2, twelve days after he was fired by the Rangers, Billy was named Yankees manager. The New York newspapers had been predicting the move for days — news leaked by Steinbrenner. In a press conference in New York, Billy, his face flushed and his voice cracking, said the day was a dream come true. Eighteen years after George Weiss had banished Billy to Kansas City, then Detroit, Cleveland, Cincinnati, Milwaukee, Minnesota, Detroit again, and finally Texas, Billy was back. He had predicted as a child that he would play for the Yankees and he had. Now in middle age, three years short of fifty, he would be the Yankees manager.

Gaunt and weary as he exited Texas less than two weeks earlier, Billy now appeared revitalized. "This was the only job I ever wanted," he told reporters. "The only job, the Yankee job."

Then Billy thanked Casey Stengel for bringing him to the Yankees twenty-five years earlier. He was wearing his familiar jersey, number 1, and looked at home. It was as if any other uniform — there had been nine counting the Denver Bears — had been an ill-fitting substitute.

As it happened, the day Billy reunited with the Yankees was also the team's Old Timers' Day, and Billy, in a move that presaged Steinbrenner's love of showmanship, was to be introduced last during the on-field festivities, after DiMaggio, Mantle, and Ford. Public address announcer Bob Sheppard called his name, and Billy jogged out and waved his cap. The crowd stood and cheered. The 1975 Yankees had been lethargic. The anticipated dynamism of Billy Martin was appreciated and welcomed. The ovation continued, longer than it had been for the Yankees Hall of Famers. Billy was back; in his mind, the circle was complete.

He stood on the field and waved his cap repeatedly as he wiped away tears with his other hand.

At his home that day in Glendale, California, Casey Stengel was confined to his bed. In 1974, his wife, Edna, had sustained a stroke and was now living at a nearby nursing home. Casey, who had turned eighty-five three days earlier, had recently been diagnosed with leukemia. In pain and increasingly immobile, Casey had hired a housekeeper to help him, Mrs. June Bowlin.

Sportswriter Maury Allen interviewed Bowlin shortly after Billy was hired as Yankees manager. She said the television was on in Casey's bedroom when a newscast mentioned Billy Martin. Mrs. Bowlin got Casey's attention, pointing to the screen, which showed Billy on the field at Old Timers' Day.

"Casey, Casey," she said. "Billy is the new manager of the Yankees."

Mrs. Bowlin said Casey smiled. Then wept.

During the summer of 1975, Billy lived alone in a New York hotel, something he had not done in sixteen years. Billy was back in Manhattan, striding through the same streets he had once walked with Jackie Gleason and Lucille Ball, but everything around him was different. The vibrant, confident city of his Yankees playing days had vanished. New York's mid-century heyday had passed. In the mid-1970s, the Wall Street area was in decay, reflecting a faltering national economy. Times Square was no longer a place of panache and glitz as it had been in the 1950s or 1960s. It was now a repository of peep shows, strip clubs, and whorehouses. The Broadway show industry was in a decade of decline with many predicting its ultimate demise as television and film became more culturally relevant. Toots Shor's on West 51st Street had closed and was now a bank. Central Park, where Billy had walked from his suite at the St. Moritz, rarely saw a pedestrian after 3:00 p.m. now; people were too afraid of being mugged there.

Strikes had damaged the public schools and city services. Welfare rolls were expanding. The subway system was unsafe and undependable. The city's police force had been exposed as corrupt by former detective Frank Serpico. Cities like New York were failing all across America, and there was no apparent plan for reviving them. In 1975, when New York officials turned to the federal government for help with a fiscal crisis, President Gerald Ford announced he would veto any bailout.

The headline in the *New York Daily News* the next day — in huge bold type on page 1 of the tabloid — reverberated throughout the city: FORD TO CITY: DROP DEAD.

The city had seemed to lose its fight. The Yankees had not been in the World Series since 1964. The Mets, magical only a few years earlier, were like the 1975 Yankees, a third-place team. Three days after Billy was hired, the Mets fired their manager, Yogi Berra.

The football Giants had not been in the postseason since 1963. The New York Jets' last winning season was their 1969 Super Bowl team. They would be 3-11 in 1975. The New York Knicks were in the midst of three consecutive losing seasons.

Meanwhile, Yankee Stadium, once a majestic symbol of the city itself, had been shuttered so it could be modernized and renovated. That forced the Yankees to play the 1974 and 1975 seasons at Shea Stadium, squeezing in games whenever the Mets were on the road. Renting space from a fledgling baseball colleague was humiliating to the franchise of Ruth, Gehrig, DiMaggio, and Mantle. The Yankees were dressing in the Jets' locker room. And the ceiling there leaked.

"I had heard so much growing up about the Yankees and New York, and then I got there and it was like we were playing in some minor league place, like Toledo or something," said Lou Piniella, whom the Yankees traded for in 1974. "We all couldn't wait to get out of Shea."

The 1975 Yankees that Billy inherited were playing winning baseball, but they were still ten games behind first-place Boston, a team thick with young talent and power hitting.

The Yankees' lineup was a curious mix of holdovers from the ownership of the CBS Corporation, which had little baseball acumen, and the Steinbrenner regime, run astutely by Gabe Paul, a top baseball executive in Steinbrenner's native Ohio since 1951.

Paul had signed free agent Catfish Hunter and acquired Piniella, first baseman Chris Chambliss, and pitchers Rudy May and Dick Tidrow. Left over from the CBS days were Munson, an All-Star catcher; the third baseman, Graig Nettles, whom Billy had managed in Denver; Roy White, an underrated switch-hitting outfielder with power; starting pitchers Doc Medich and Pat Dobson; and Bobby Bonds, a productive but unpredictable and temperamental star whose eleven-year-old son, Barry, was a regular in the Yankees' clubhouse.

Billy spent 1975 assessing his roster. Catching the first-place Red Sox was highly unlikely; the goal would be preparing for 1976 when the Yankees would be back in the refurbished Yankee Stadium.

Billy wanted to build the team around Munson, already the team's on-the-field leader. He was happy to have veterans like Nettles, Chambliss, White, and Piniella. Hunter, everyone knew, was a Hall of Famer-to-be. The starter Rudy May was important as a left-handed presence, as was the reliever Sparky Lyle, whom the previous manager, Bill Virdon, had used sparingly. Billy told Lyle that he would be his bullpen closer, and in the mid-1970s that meant often pitching three innings in relief. Lyle was ready. He liked a lot of work.

Billy was calm in most Yankees settings in 1975, getting along with his players and the writers covering the team. One columnist noted that Billy started one pregame press conference by asking the questions himself. They were not baseball questions. Billy fell back on usual, favored topics.

"Which state was the first to secede from the Union at the beginning of the Civil War?" he asked (South Carolina was the answer).

But if Billy was playing with the press, he was educating his troops, getting them ready for the big battle coming in 1976.

Roy White recalled a game in August when he was the base runner at second base and Lou Piniella was at the plate.

"Thurman Munson was on first base and Billy put the bunt sign on," White said. "Lou fouls off the bunt attempt on the first pitch. I didn't even look at the third-base coach; I assumed the bunt was still on. But on the next pitch, Lou hits a single to right field and I went to third. I scored when the next batter hit a ground ball. I'm coming into the dugout and everyone is shaking my hand. I figured I did something good.

"Billy comes toward me and I extend my hand and he sternly says to me, 'You missed a sign and you cost us a run.' It turns out Billy had changed the bunt to a hit-and-run on the second pitch to Piniella. I had never heard of a hit-and-run with runners at first and second.

"Billy says to me, 'Thurman couldn't run on the hit-and-run because you didn't run. If you are both running on Piniella's single, then you score and Thurman gets to third. He scores on that groundout, not you. You cost us a run.'

"And I thought to myself, 'Uh-oh, I better start really paying attention. This isn't the same game I've been playing.' We all knew Billy could help us, but we didn't really realize how much concentration that would take."

One week later, Billy gave notice to the umpires that he was still watching everything. The uniform was different. His eye for the details of the rule book had not changed.

In a game against the California Angels, Billy protested that the bats used by Angels hitters had pine tar on the barrels more than eighteen inches from the handle end of the bat, which violated a league equipment rule. Home plate umpire George Maloney refused to take measurements of the bats. Billy argued, if without fervor. It wasn't worth getting thrown out of a game with the Yankees out of the pennant race, but as any fan of baseball history knows, he kept an eye on the opponents' bats and how much pine tar they used forevermore.

With Steinbrenner not allowed at the ballpark or the team offices, Billy was developing a good working relationship with Gabe Paul. The season ended with the Yankees at 83-77, twelve games out of first place. The team had been 30-26 under Billy. But heading into the off-season, Billy and Paul had agreed on a plan to completely remake the roster. The central goal was to give Billy some youth and quickness in the lineup. Billy was certain the Yankees would be a winner in 1976.

"I remember leaving the clubhouse after our last game in 1975," Piniella said. "I had an awful season at Shea Stadium and I was hurt. I hit .196. Billy was standing at the door and he says to me, 'Lou, don't worry about it. Go home and get healthy. We're going to win the pennant next year and you'll be a big part of it.'

"He told other guys that, too, and you know what? We believed him. And those who didn't believe him, it's like he knew who they were because by the time we got to spring training, they were off the team."

On September 29, the day after the 1975 regular season ended, Casey Stengel died. Billy went straight to Casey's home in Glendale, California, and on the night before Casey's funeral slept in his mentor's bed.

"Billy said he wanted to do it to connect with Casey one last time," said Charlie Silvera.

Billy, Silvera, and Yankees infielder Jerry Coleman were pallbearers at Casey's funeral, carrying the casket from the Church of the Recessional. The pastor reading one of Casey's eulogies quoted the Los Angeles sportswriter Jim Murray, who wrote upon Casey's death, "God is certainly getting an earful tonight."

Billy stayed another night at Casey's home before flying to the Bay Area to go hunting with Lew Figone. With Mrs. Bowlin's permission, Billy took with him some of Casey's old long-sleeved T-shirts that he had worn under his Yankees uniform. On occasion, Billy would wear them beneath his Yankees uniform and would show visitors the "37" stenciled underneath the collar of the shirt.

Over the next several weeks, Gabe Paul cleaned house when he traded Bonds to the Angels for center fielder Mickey Rivers and right-handed pitcher Ed Figueroa. On the same day, Paul sent Medich to Pittsburgh for pitchers Dock Ellis and Ken Brett and a twenty-one-year-old second baseman who had batted only .164 in 61 at-bats for the Pirates in 1975, Willie Randolph.

In the newspapers the next day, the news was all about the trading of Bonds, the powerful All-Star (who would never be an All-Star again).

The other focus was on the acquisition of Ellis, who had won 96 games in nine seasons for Pittsburgh but was considered a mercurial head case. Ellis would end up winning 17 games for the 1976 Yankees, but the key players in the trade, as Billy saw it, were Rivers and Randolph, whom he thought was a steal.

Rivers had driven the Angels crazy with his impulsive personality and because he ran up fearsome debts at the racetrack. He rubbed some team-mates the wrong way, jabbering constantly in an almost nonsensical language of his own. He was a fleet outfielder, though he had a weak arm. But he was also known as Mick the Quick, leading the American League the previous season in stolen bases (70) and triples (13). He had flair, he unnerved pitchers when he was on base, and he pressured opposing in-fielders because he chopped balls into the ground and could then beat the throw to first base. He was the leadoff hitter Billy was seeking.

Randolph, meanwhile, had almost as much speed as Rivers and more bat control. He had hit .339 in Class AAA in 1975 and had been a top pros-pect coming out of Brooklyn in 1972. But Billy and Paul loved Randolph's Brooklyn-bred toughness and determination — he never smiled on the field — and they appreciated his skill set: he could bunt, execute the hit-and-run, steal bases, hit line drives in the gap, and turn the double play as smoothly as any second baseman in baseball.

It was a gamble to turn the second baseman's job over to an unproven rookie, but Billy believed in taking chances on some rookies as Casey Stengel had with him.

Billy liked his remade roster. It had characters, as all Billy teams usually did, and it had character. But as he looked toward spring training he was also distracted.

His managerial career was a source of excited pride. His personal life was a mess.

In November, his daughter with Lois, Kelly Ann, had been arrested for trying to smuggle 450 grams of cocaine out of Barranquilla, Colombia, as she boarded a flight for Miami. It was a serious offense, and the Co-lombian authorities grew more interested in prosecuting Kelly Ann when they found out she was the offspring of a famous American personality. Kelly Ann, who had put the cocaine in plastic bags and strapped them to her legs, also would not identify who had given her the cocaine.

Kelly Ann was twenty-two, a secretary living near Berkeley, and she ran with a rough crowd. Though she initially claimed she had been duped

into carrying the drugs, she later confessed to her father that she was trying to make some extra money on a drug-running mission.

Billy was obsessed with trying to find back-channel ways to get Kelly
Ann cleared of the charges. The case lingered for many weeks as Billy tried
to call in every favor from his extended network of friends. Frank Sinatra
made some calls as did Bill Reedy, who worked for a politician with ties
to then President Ford. The Yankees used their resources and arranged
for a respected lawyer. Billy called then Secretary of State Henry Kissinger
because Kissinger was a renowned Yankees fan. Kissinger promised to
look into the matter. Colombian officials also extorted tens of thousands
of dollars from Billy.

The ordeal weighed on Billy. He blamed himself for not being more
a part of Kelly Ann's life. Through the years, Kelly Ann had visited her
father and lived one summer with Billy, Gretchen, and Billy Joe in Minnesota, but father and daughter were far from close.

In January, Kelly Ann was sentenced to three years in jail, but because
of the official lobbying of Billy's friends in high places, she avoided a
hardened Colombia jail. She was instead confined to a convent where she
was watched over by nuns. It was understood that she would likely serve
about two-thirds to one-half of her sentence.

As for his other child and the family left behind in Texas, Billy did return to live with Gretchen and Billy Joe for weeks at a time in the off-season. It was an uneasy standoff. Neither filed for divorce. Gretchen made
visits to New York and Billy made visits to Texas.

"It was tough; I was just trying to get through school and sports," Billy
Jr. said. "They wouldn't give up on it, but you could feel the sadness — for
everyone."

Billy was seen on the Manhattan bar circuit, and there was always the
occasional one-night stand for companionship. But he was a lonely figure.

"I remember Billy coming into our offices all the time that winter," said
Mickey Morabito, the Yankees' assistant public relations director who
would become a lifelong friend and confidant of Billy's. "It was strange to
see him hanging around the office like that in the off-season. Managers
don't usually do that. He had rejoined the Yankee family, but I think it was
the only family he had."

27

IN 1976, SPRING TRAINING camps did not open as baseball's owners and players sparred over the terms of a new era of free agency created by several court cases won by the players' union. Billy was disgusted. He believed the spring training period was essential to instilling his fundamentals. Besides, at this stage in his life, depriving him of a baseball team to lead left him in a personal purgatory.

Then, on March 1 came another blow. George Steinbrenner's suspension was supposed to extend to November. Instead, Baseball Commissioner Bowie Kuhn shortened Steinbrenner's suspension so he could reinstate him immediately.

Billy's life as Yankees manager would never be the same.

The labor discord was settled in mid-March with spring training cut to twenty days. Billy was not thrilled, but he was delighted that his players were soon filling the clubhouse.

He was less excited by the presence of Steinbrenner in that clubhouse as well.

Billy had never had an owner who treated the locker room as his place of business, too. Late in the 1975 season, Steinbrenner — a former assistant college football coach as a young man who himself had never played football — had taken to taping pep talks for his players on an audio cassette. Prohibited from going into the locker room himself because of his suspension, George ordered Gabe Paul to have the speeches played for the players before certain big games as a way to motivate them.

The cassette player would be placed on a stool in the middle of the clubhouse with the volume turned high.

The first speech was just two minutes long. The next one a week later was a little longer. When the third speech went on for more than three or four minutes, Billy emerged from his office, stalked toward the middle of the clubhouse, and kicked over the stool. Then he pushed the stop button on the cassette player.

The players roared their approval. Paul would later ask Billy if he was playing George's tapes to the players and Billy would say he was. In fact, after Billy kicked over the stool, players took turns stopping the Steinbrenner speeches, rushing to the cassette player and forcefully banging on the stop button.

But now Billy knew that Steinbrenner could deliver his speeches in person. And there would be no stop button to push.

So Billy negotiated a settlement. It was all right for George to be in the clubhouse for individual chats with players but no oratory.

That left the spring training fields for George to roam.

"George just loved to be seen and be involved, and truthfully, I think he thought he was helping," said Lou Piniella, an outfielder on the 1976 team and a future manager for Steinbrenner. "And at first, I think it just amused Billy. George would come strutting by and say something like, 'OK, Piniella, now let's whip that bat around.' Or, he would watch the infielders and shout, 'Step lively, boys.'

"And Billy would be standing there with his hands in his back pockets biting his lip. Then George would turn his back and walk to the next field and Billy would wait a minute and say, 'You heard the man, step lively, boys.' And everyone would start quietly laughing, turning away so no one could see."

Another time, one of the Yankees starters sprained an ankle and athletic trainer Gene Monahan had the player hustled into the dugout. Coaches gathered on the bench as Steinbrenner rushed over, peering into the scrum encircling the player. Monahan was pressing ice to the ankle, which was swelling nonetheless.

"Do something," Steinbrenner yelped. "Don't you have any colder ice?"

Steinbrenner was not just a noisy interloper the Yankees appeased. The players appreciated that he spent money on the roster. The Yankees' spring training home had been renovated with a more spacious locker room and additional fields. One of Steinbrenner's first acts was to upgrade the Yankees' travel arrangements. The team now had newer jets to fly them around the continent, and they stayed in the best hotels whatever the city.

Bill "Killer" Kane, the Yankees' traveling secretary who became a friend to both Steinbrenner and Billy — a difficult daily double — recalled that the upgrades were ordered by both men.

"George was obsessed with the Yankees always looking first-class," Kane said. "So we had to have the best planes, the best buses, the best bus drivers, the best-made uniforms. George spent his money; there was no limit for that kind of stuff.

"Billy, meanwhile, wanted to make sure the players' lives were easy and that they felt special. One of the first things he told me was that he wanted Chivas as the only Scotch served on the planes when we traveled. I told Billy that I didn't think we served Scotch at all and he said, 'That's not right; give the players the best. Let them have a drink to relax when together on the road. Let them have fun.'

"So we had Chivas on all our flights. And good food, too — shrimp cocktail, steak, you name it. It was Billy's idea that they should feel honored to play for the Yankees. And George thought the same thing."

Kane, from 1976 to the mid-1980s, was in a unique position to assess the thorny, benevolent, multifarious relationship between Billy and George Steinbrenner. Kane, who died in 2013, not only transported the team around America, he oversaw every detail for players, coaches, manager, owner, and the beat writers and broadcasters. Billy ran the team on the field and Pete Sheehy and clubhouse manager Nick Priore supervised everything inside the clubhouse; Kane, whom everyone called "Killer," controlled everything outside the clubhouse and the field.

Kane, who smoked unfiltered Lucky Strike cigarettes and closed many a hotel bar, was like a character from a Damon Runyon novel. But he was a real-life throwback, a funny Irishman with a twinkle in his eye and a thick Bronx accent who had been around the Yankees since 1961 when he was a statistician for legendary Yankees announcer Mel Allen. Killer, who picked up his nickname from an old comic book hero, had all-seeing eyes and was present, it seemed, for everything that mattered to the Yankees. As chief of provisions and accommodations, he knew every secret on the team. Who else got a player's — or the manager's — mistress a hotel room and a ticket to the game that night? Who else knew that the player's — or the manager's — wife had called Killer just before the same game asking for a hotel room and a ticket to that night's game so she could surprise her husband on their anniversary?

Who else stalled the wife on the ticket and then transferred the mistress to another hotel during the game? On the same day, who else would just as seamlessly arrange for another player to fly home during an off day in a long road trip so the player could spend some extra time with his wife during her difficult pregnancy? Nobody would even know the player was missing, except Killer. If George or Billy asked, Killer would lie and say he saw the player in the hotel lobby that morning. In truth, the player would be flying in the next day, landing just four hours before game time. And Killer would take a cab to the airport to personally pick up the player so that Killer and the player could arrive at the ballpark together, as if they had just come from the team hotel.

Killer knew everything about everybody. Who was cheap, who was afraid to fly, who got manicures on the road, who pretended to not drink but actually was getting drunk nightly in his hotel room, and who didn't bother to have state taxes withdrawn from his paycheck — a frequent Billy misstep.

Perhaps because he knew too much, Killer was the only Yankees employee to be fired more often by Steinbrenner than Billy. And he was rehired more often than Billy, too. Kane, who walked with a pronounced limp because of a childhood bout with polio, took confrontations with George to levels even Billy never tried. Killer and George, arguing over travel arrangements, once came to blows in a New Orleans hotel lobby during the exhibition season. Kane threw the first punch.

Nothing really came of the fight, and the next day the two went back to work together. Neither Killer nor George ever spoke to each other about their tussle. Other times George would fire Killer and banish him from the Yankees' offices, or Killer would quit during a dispute and go home. Like George Costanza in *Seinfeld,* Killer would simply come back to the office the next day as if nothing had happened.

Steinbrenner liked it this way. For all the words that have been written about Steinbrenner, he was not vindictive or mean-spirited. He could be a terrible boss, cruel and unyielding. Not many people truly enjoyed his company for long stretches of time because he was too opinionated and unrelenting.

But he also had a soft spot for authenticity. Guile disturbed him, but those who spoke their minds intrigued him. He was drawn to them. And so, he fired and rehired Killer Kane and then threw his arm around him and took him to dinner. He did the same with Billy.

"Billy and George had a lot of affection for each other," Kane said in 2012. "They were like two cousins who loved each other but couldn't stop fighting either. They rubbed each other the wrong way without even trying. But they both wanted the same thing. And in the end, George wanted the best for Billy and Billy wanted the best for George because that was best for the Yankees. And they both knew that.

"It's just when they disagreed, it was usually a loud disagreement."

Kane laughed heartily.

"I guess that's kind of an understatement," he said.

But in the spring of 1976, things were almost entirely peaceable at the dawn of what was later known as Billy I. George needed Billy to show him and his Yankees how to win. And he wanted a showman at the helm. George might have strutted around Fort Lauderdale, but once the regular season began, he generally kept his distance. He had brought Billy in to deliver the Yankees their first pennant since 1964. He got out of the way and watched Billy mold the 1976 Yankees in his image.

Before the opening game of the 1976 season in Milwaukee, Billy, with a black armband on his sleeve commemorating the death of Casey Stengel, assembled his team for a clubhouse speech.

"He didn't say much," Piniella said. "The first thing he said was, 'We're winning the division this year and then we're winning the pennant.'

"Then the next thing he said was, 'The only way that doesn't happen is if you don't believe in what I'm going to ask you to do. This is a good team and we're going to scare the shit out of the whole league if you buy into what I'm trying to do. Trust me, you do that, and we'll win.'

"And then he walked out the clubhouse door and headed for the dugout. I was standing next to Thurman and he turned to me and said, 'That SOB is going to win us a pennant. I believe him.'"

The Yankees lost the opening game of the 1976 season in Milwaukee when forty-two-year-old Hank Aaron, who was playing his last season, knocked in three runs with two hits in a 5–0 Brewers victory.

But the second game of the season sealed Billy's hold on his players. By the end of that game, they all believed in him. To them, he had performed a baseball miracle akin to Jesus Christ turning water into wine. He had literally turned nine innings that ended in defeat into a victory.

The game on Saturday, April 10, in Milwaukee was a cavalcade of runs and daring plays. Down 6–4 in the top of the ninth, the Yankees scored five runs, including one on a suicide squeeze bunt. But in the bottom of the ninth, the Yankees reliever, Dave Pagan, loaded the bases before facing the Brewers' third baseman, Don Money.

Money laced a long drive into the left-field seats for a game-winning grand slam. The home crowd was jumping up and down in the grand-stand, and the Milwaukee dugout spilled onto the field. The Yankees out-fielders had begun to dejectedly head off the field.

That's when Billy, his eyes narrowing, roared out from the dugout and ran toward the middle of the diamond. The twenty-six-year-old Pagan, who hailed from a tiny town in Saskatchewan but had certainly heard of Billy's temper, started running toward left field, fearing for his well-being. But Billy wasn't coming out to berate or beat up his young pitcher; he was heading for first-base umpire Jim McKean.

"You called time out just before the pitch," Billy was yelling.

McKean had no response. Billy started screaming, "I saw you raise your hand — you were calling time out."

After the game, McKean said that with the crowd cheering and Billy screeching, he couldn't make out exactly what was being said on the field.

Billy made it plain: McKean had raised his hand to call time out.

After conferring with the other umpires — and with the crowd watching uneasily — McKean conceded that Chambliss, with his back turned to the umpire, had asked for time out at first base. And McKean had indeed raised his arm just before the pitch.

No one, it appeared, had seen the gesture except Billy, who always claimed that he could see the entire field in one glance.

Money's grand slam was nullified. Money then flied out. The Yankees won the game, 9–7.

"I've got them now," Billy told Killer Kane after the game.

Two weeks later, against Kansas City, the Royals' Al Cowens appeared to score a late tying run. Billy signaled to third baseman Graig Nettles from the dugout, pointing at third base. When time was back in, Nettles appealed the play, suggesting that Cowens had missed third base. The umpires agreed. The Royals lost.

"We'll win this thing easy," Billy told Kane in the hotel bar that night.

And Kane nodded his head and smiled.

"Those guys on the '76 team would have tried to run across a pond if Billy told them to," Killer said. "They would have assumed somehow that they wouldn't sink if Billy told them so."

Day by day, Billy was challenging the rest of the American League to stop his refurbished, hard-charging Yankees. Rivers, Randolph, White, reserve Sandy Alomar, and even Piniella were running teams ragged, stealing bases with abandon. Billy was attempting stolen bases at a rate twice that of former Yankees managers Joe McCarthy and Ralph Houk and three times as often as Casey Stengel.

Moreover, the 1976 Yankees were feisty. Slides into bases were hard and tags were forceful. The pitchers weren't afraid to throw inside, and Munson scowled at everyone who approached home plate. Billy worked the umpires from the dugout ceaselessly.

"Billy just kept everyone on edge," trainer Gene Monahan said. "Right from the first inning, if he didn't like an umpire's call, he'd be on him. He'd yell, 'OK, pal, that's it, you're off the Christmas card list. You owe me one now. You don't get back on the Christmas card list until I get that call back.'

"And he'd turn and wink at the players on the bench. But that would get everyone paying attention. He would stand on the first step of the dugout with his hands in his back pockets and jut his jaw out there, almost like a challenge to the other team. Until that year, players usually sat back on the dugout bench. That season, I noticed half the team would be standing on the first step of the dugout with Billy."

The 1976 Yankees had veterans and young players, but most of all, they were a team in sync with their manager.

"Somebody would slide late at second base and knock me halfway into the outfield," Willie Randolph said. "And when we'd get into the dugout after the inning, Billy would make a show of coming over and asking me how I was. Then he'd say out loud, 'That was a bullshit play.'

"And he would walk slowly past the veteran guys like Munson, Piniella, Chambliss, and Nettles and he would just give them a look that said, 'You know what to do.' He didn't say anything, he just looked at them. And boy, the other team's middle infielders would be getting bowled over the next inning. That's just the way it went — you got my guy so I'm going to get your guy.

"But it got around the league. People knew Billy would punch back and maybe punch twice."

The Yankees were comfortably in first place by mid-May, but most of the American League still considered the Boston Red Sox the team to beat. Billy longed for a face-to-face confrontation.

The Red Sox had won the 1975 pennant and captivated the nation when their spunky team lost in seven games to Cincinnati's Big Red Machine in a thrilling World Series. The Red Sox had young stars and future Hall of Famers like Carlton Fisk and Jim Rice, and they had a still-formidable leader in Carl Yastrzemski, another Hall of Famer-to-be.

The Red Sox came to Yankee Stadium on May 20 trailing the Yankees by six games, but they still had the swagger of a champion. In the mid-1970s, players did not fraternize before games; in fact, oftentimes they genuinely did not like each other or resented one another's success. It was before the modern big-money era of baseball when the players, each flush with cash and the accouterments of prosperity, began treating each other as coworkers and comrades in a billion-dollar enterprise.

Munson resented that Fisk received more favorable media attention, something Munson attributed to Fisk's movie-star looks. Munson was squat and rough-hewn.

Fisk, a native New Englander, was raised to detest everything about the Yankees, most especially that they had won twenty world championships since the Red Sox' last World Series victory in 1918.

The game on May 20 was the first of four scheduled. In the sixth inning, Piniella slammed into Fisk at home plate as he tried to score on a single. Piniella was out, but Fisk didn't wait for the umpire's call to deliver his own verdict on the collision. The Red Sox catcher started punching Piniella. The benches emptied in a flash. Mickey Rivers and then Graig Nettles grabbed Boston starting pitcher Bill Lee from behind, with Nettles throwing the pitcher to the infield grass on his left shoulder. When Lee came at Nettles again, he got the worst of it again and later left the field with torn ligaments in his left shoulder.

Lee, who had won 17 games in each of the three previous seasons, wouldn't rejoin the Boston rotation until September. The teams split the four-game series, but Billy's team had made a statement.

"We had become like Billy — defiant, backing down from no one, willing to do anything to win," Randolph said. "There's no question we took on his personality."

The Yankees had a ten-game lead over the Red Sox by the Fourth of July and never looked back.

The 1976 Yankees became one of Billy's favorite teams, something he would say for the rest of his life. It was an eclectic group but balanced at the same time. Rivers, his teammates learned, was mysterious, comical, and prone to entertaining excesses. Rivers's finances were a constant source of disquiet and amusement. Killer Kane gave the players their entire allotment of meal money when any road trip began. Rivers would spend it the first day.

Once, he and his wife got into an argument in the players' parking lot outside Yankee Stadium, then jumped into separate cars and started crashing into each other, as if that would settle the dispute. Security guards had to intercede to put an end to the impromptu demolition derby taking place thirty yards from Yankee Stadium.

Reliever Sparky Lyle kept everyone loose with a series of one-liners for any situation. Catfish Hunter teased the sometimes truculent Munson and got him to relax. On the rare times when Steinbrenner was acting up and causing a stir in the clubhouse, it was Nettles who brought levity to the situation.

"George is Mr. Vesuvius with bullshit instead of lava," Nettles said.

Billy liked his cast of characters. They stuck up for one another, hung out together on the road. They drank together and Billy drank with them. Complaints were kept to a minimum. They did not seem to mind when he fell asleep on the couch in his office — sometimes nursing a hangover — and forgot to post the lineup card until an hour before the game.

When this had happened with past Billy teams, there was considerable consternation, especially over who would hit with whom during batting practice.

The 1976 Yankees went to Yogi Berra, a quasi–assistant manager who had joined Billy's staff. Berra had known Billy for nearly thirty years and turned out to be amazingly accurate at predicting that day's batting order. Berra would set the batting practice groups. There were few protests.

The resurgent Yankees were celebrated in the New York press, and the team would draw 2 million fans for the first time since 1950, Billy's rookie year.

The boost in attendance was in part due to what everyone was now calling the new Yankee Stadium. It had some features rare in ballparks at the time, like a 565-foot center-field scoreboard that played replays, escalators to whisk fans to their upper-deck seats, and air-conditioned dugouts. The home clubhouse was twice the size of the one where Babe Ruth and Lou Gehrig had dressed.

The Yankees felt like kings in their new palace. Major League Baseball, happy to have a vibrant team back in the nation's biggest city, was eager to fete the new ballpark, too. It brought the 1976 All-Star team to the new Yankee Stadium, and the league office used its influence to have Yankees home games featured often on the NBC and ABC television national broadcasts, which was important exposure in the pre–cable TV era.

New York City itself was still reeling with crime and rampant arson, especially in the Yankees' South Bronx neighborhood. But on the days and nights of Yankees games, the area might have been the safest place in New York. Swarming with police and prosperous fans from the New York suburbs, New Jersey, and Connecticut, Yankee Stadium became a place to be seen.

Manhattan's elite was not left out. From Billy Joel to Cheryl Tiegs to Dustin Hoffman to Gloria Vanderbilt, the bold-print set made regular appearances at Yankees games. In 1976, it was the surest way to get into the gossip pages of the city's tabloids. People did anything to be near the dynamic Yankees, and celebrated at the center of it all was number 1, Billy Martin.

Gretchen Martin recalls her visits to New York in the summer of 1976 when Billy Joe was out of school. Billy was staying at the Drake Hotel on Park Avenue and 56th Street, Frank Sinatra's usual choice of lodging in Manhattan.

"We couldn't walk down any street without people stopping Billy," Gretchen said. "It would take twenty-five minutes to walk four blocks to lunch.

"I thought he had been well known and well received in Detroit or Texas. New York was completely different. He was a hero to everyone and New Yorkers wanted to tell him so."

He was not a hero to everyone, and the attention had other consequences. Billy Martin's first file with the FBI was opened in 1960 when he received threatening mail as a player for the Cincinnati Reds. By 1976, the FBI had updated the file several times.

Billy received several disturbing letters, including one reprinted in his FBI file 9-61912. The letter, mailed from Brooklyn — perhaps no surprise there — was handwritten:

Dear Martin,

    How would your wife and kids get along after you're gone. Did you write out your will yet? Don't wait until it's too late. You better hurry up. You don't have long.

The letter was not signed. But later in the season, Billy moved to the harder-to-find Sheraton Hotel in Hasbrouck Heights, New Jersey. He had a top-floor suite.

But what he liked best about his New Jersey digs was that they were across the street from a dark little bar where no one bothered him after games. Billy's newest hangout was called the Bottom of the Barrel.

"That's not a joke; I used to call him there sometimes," Eddie Sapir said. "They'd answer the phone, 'Bottom of the Barrel,' and I'd start laughing. Only Billy. It's trendy to hang out in dive bars nowadays. Billy was forty years ahead of the trend."

With the Yankees' lead over second-place Baltimore at eleven games, on Saturday, September 11, Steinbrenner called a press conference ostensibly to announce that Yankees playoff tickets would sell for a Major League Baseball record of $24 per seat. Steinbrenner then surprised reporters with a second announcement: Billy had been signed to a three-year, $300,000 contract extension through 1979.

"A lot has been written in the past about Billy's difficulties with the front office," Steinbrenner told reporters. "But we have an outstanding working relationship and my respect for him as a leader of men has grown immeasurably.

"He could not have been more effective and outstanding in all respects."

Said Billy, "I want to thank George Steinbrenner with whom I've had a perfect relationship."

And yes, Billy said "whom."

On September 25, the Yankees won a day game in Detroit, and Steinbrenner held a party for the team at the Caucus Club downtown. While eating dinner, the Yankees were awaiting the results of a game in Baltimore. When the Orioles lost, the Yankees had clinched the division. They would eventually win 97 games, a 14-game improvement from 1975 that could have been larger except the 1976 team had its final 3 games rained out.

At the Caucus Club the night the division was clinched, Steinbrenner, in a scene that would be hard to imagine years later, started spraying the room with champagne. Piniella drank out of his own champagne bottle, talking about how each player had just earned $5,000 for a first-place finish. Munson was hugging Randolph. White and Chambliss clasped hands.

One key figure was not there.

Billy had come to the club at Steinbrenner's behest, but he had one drink and left before the Baltimore game ended.

"I'm not celebrating anything," he told reporters as he departed. "Whether we clinch tonight or tomorrow night or the next night, this will be my third division winner. So this is my third try. I won't be happy till I get into the World Series. The next series is everything."

28

THE JET CARRYING THE AL East champion Yankees back from Detroit landed at New York's LaGuardia Airport and was greeted by more than a thousand fans. One woman held aloft a sign: TODAY IS THE FIRST DAY OF THE SECOND YANKEES DYNASTY.

New York was in a celebratory mood, and the national media descended on the South Bronx to chronicle the ascendant Yankees and their magnetic manager. The number of reporters, broadcasters, and photographers who applied for media credentials to cover the 1976 ALCS was more than double the number who wanted to cover the National League Championship Series between the defending world champion Cincinnati Reds and the Philadelphia Phillies.

New York was the focus because the Yankees were a beguiling team with an intriguing leader, and best of all, they were making a comeback — a story within the story of New York itself.

But in the plains of middle America, the Yankees represented something else. The Yankees were another case of a big-city power broker trying to buy his way into the winner's circle. The Yankees had purchased Catfish Hunter and outmuscled the rest of the Major Leagues for other talent. The finances of baseball were changing, and the rest of America wondered if the Yankees were the moneyed blueprint of the future. Worse, in places other than New York, Steinbrenner was just beginning to hone his image as the ultimate wealthy, urban bully.

In Kansas City, where the 1976 ALCS would open, the Yankees were more than just the opponent for the AL West champion Royals; they were the enemy in a cultural war between traditional rural values and cosmopolitan flamboyance and privilege.

And if that wasn't enough to stoke the fires of a rivalry that would burn for nearly a decade, Billy had been feuding all year with two of the Royals' star players, pitcher Larry Gura and third baseman George Brett.

Billy had traded Gura from the Texas Rangers to the Yankees in 1974 and then dumped him again as Yankees manager early in the 1976 season.

Gura had asked for the trade from the Yankees, saying Billy mistreated him.

Billy fired back.

"I got rid of him because he wasn't as good as the other pitchers I already had," he said. "If I had him here now, I'd get rid of him again."

The hostilities with George Brett began when Billy traded Ken Brett, a pitcher and George's oldest brother, to the Chicago White Sox for Carlos May. George Brett told reporters that Billy lied to his brother, who had asked to be traded to Kansas City. It is one of baseball's oldest protocols that players say little about the trading of other players because sooner or later almost everyone gets traded and it never seems fair to someone. Billy, who knew all about being traded, seethed that Brett broke the unwritten code.

As fate would have it, Gura, Brett, and Billy factored prominently in the first game of the 1976 ALCS.

Gura started the game at Kansas City's new stadium, where the field was carpeted with artificial turf. The left-handed-hitting Mickey Rivers — Mick the Quick — immediately chopped a ground ball on the synthetic surface toward Brett at third base. The Yankees' dugout was on the third-base side at Royals Stadium. As Brett fielded the ball, Billy and his players jumped off the bench and roared.

"They were all calling him names and shouting to distract him," said Gura, who watched Brett fling the ball ten feet to the left of the Royals' mammoth first baseman, John Mayberry.

Then Billy and the rest of the Yankees' bench turned their attention to Gura.

"I wasn't the only one on him," Billy said after the game. "A lot of guys went after him. But we did it man-to-man, on the field. Not in the newspapers like they're doing it. Yeah, we were yelling at him and Brett. That's old-time baseball."

Gura walked Roy White, then gave up a single to Munson. With one out and the bases loaded, Chambliss hit a grounder to Brett that should have been an inning-ending double play. Brett touched third base and, with the Yankees in the dugout howling at him, skipped the relay to first base in the dirt well in front of Mayberry, who did not come up with the ball as two Yankees scored.

The Yankees never looked back, winning 4–1.

"I think Billy showed us right there that he knew how to take control of a postseason game," Piniella said. "There was a lot of pressure on everyone and it was like Billy said, 'Watch this, I'm going to turn the pressure up a notch.' And he did. It was all about who could take it."

The Kansas City fans responded in kind the next night, jeering at Billy as he brought the lineups to the umpires before the second game of the series. Nineteen years earlier, traded from the Yankees, he had played his first game for the then Kansas City Athletics. Billy looked at the rows of fans standing to shout at him, doffed his cap, and blew kisses at the grandstand.

But the aggressiveness of the home fans seemed to put a charge into the Royals as they blew past the Yankees to win the second game in a rout. The Yankees rebounded with a win at Yankee Stadium in the third game but, surprisingly, lost with Hunter on the mound in the fourth game, setting up the decisive game of the series on Thursday, October 14, 1976.

It was the most anticipated non–World Series game in New York since twenty-five years earlier, when Bobby Thomson's ninth-inning, three-run homer — the "Shot Heard 'Round the World" — won the 1951 National League playoff for the New York Giants over the Brooklyn Dodgers.

The fifth game of the 1976 ALCS was played on a cold night in New York with fans in overcoats and burly parkas. Broadcast by the ABC network, the telecast featured Howard Cosell, Keith Jackson, and a guest commentator, Reggie Jackson, who had been traded from Oakland to Baltimore in 1976. Jackson, as everyone in baseball knew, was going to be the game's most celebrated free agent not long after the final game of the 1976 World Series.

One of the principal story lines before the game was Billy's decision to start Ed Figueroa, who had been faltering late in the season and had been the losing pitcher in the second game of the series.

But Figueroa pitched well, and the Yankees led 6–3 in the eighth inning, in part thanks to another throwing error by Brett.

"I've got to give Billy Martin a lot of credit," Reggie said. "He picked Figueroa and stuck with him. He's a loyal guy. Everyone talks about the fiery, feisty Billy. He's shown me a lot of class."

Cosell gushed in consent.

"The best manager in baseball," Cosell said. "Some love him, some despise him. But he's the best. Maybe ever."

Baseball in 1976 was on the cusp of momentous change and was soon to be altered by the free-agency era. But as the Yankees and Royals clashed in the decisive game of the ALCS, baseball was still comfortable in the ways and habits of the 1950s and 1960s. Nine innings moved along quickly, and games almost always ended in about two and one-half hours, even during the playoffs. The players ran on and off the field with haste, as if worried the fans would get bored and leave. It was a legitimate concern — fourteen of the twenty-three Major League teams averaged fewer than fifteen thousand fans per game in 1976. Four averaged fewer than ten thousand fans a game.

In the stands, even the fans in the most expensive seats close to the field were dressed in common garb and looked like they had just spilled out of the subway, as many no doubt had. There were no personal seat licenses separating the fans by class back then, and the crowd clearly had an all-consuming commitment to the game. With few audio or visual distractions, fans cheered or groaned with every pitch, a back-and-forth reminiscent of the background cacophony heard during the radio transmissions of a 1930s heavyweight prizefight.

But in the eighth inning, Brett dramatically tied the game, 6–6, with a long three-run homer into right field. Yankee Stadium went uncharacteristically quiet but for the whoops and hollers in the Royals' dugout. Standing across the diamond with his hands in his back pockets, Billy suddenly looked pale, almost sickened. But noticeably, he nodded at Munson, who was standing at home plate. And Billy rubbed his nose, which was not an uncommon way for a manager to deliver a signal.

The next pitch to the next hitter, John Mayberry, sailed high and hard over Mayberry's head. After ducking, Mayberry glared at Billy, who yelled back, "What are you looking at? Get your fat ass back in the batter's box."

As Willie Randolph said, "Everyone had been kind of stunned by Brett's homer but that jerked us back. It was like, 'OK, the game isn't over. We've got to find a way to win it again.'"

In the top of the ninth, the Royals had runners at first and second with two out and the light-hitting Jim Wohlford at the plate. Brett was on deck. Wohlford hit a ground ball into the hole on the left of the infield, but Nettles snagged it and threw to Randolph at second base. It was a bang-bang play with the baseball and the base runner arriving at the same time. But Randolph caught the ball in stride and then quickly ran off the field before the call was made — something Billy, who had performed the same ploy in the minor leagues in the 1940s, had taught his second baseman. Umpire Joe Brinkman called the Royals base runner, Al Cowens, out. Replays of the sequence at second base later showed that Cowens had beaten the throw and catch. Brett should have come up with the bases loaded.

In the bottom of the ninth, the Royals pitcher was Mark Littell, a twenty-three-year-old reliever from Gideon, Missouri, a town that had a population that teetered above or below one thousand, depending on how many people the local box-making plant hired in any given year. Littell, whose nickname was "Country," was six foot three and 215 pounds, and he threw his fastball about 96 or 97 miles an hour. He was fearsome and intimidating on the mound and had a regular-season ERA of 2.08 in 60 games.

As the Yankees' half of the ninth began, the home fans were unusually restless. It was 11:37 p.m., late for a game back then when the beer taps were not turned off until the final out. The Bronx fans were throwing things onto the field at the Royals players, who were easy targets in their baby-blue uniforms.

The Yankees' first hitter of the inning was Chris Chambliss.

"I was shivering on the field," Chambliss recalled years later. "I was just so cold. I was determined to swing at the first pitch. I figured he was proud of his fastball and he'd probably throw."

At 11:40, Littell threw a high inside fastball and Chambliss swung early — jumping on it like a man who planned to swing all along. He lofted the ball on a line for the right-field wall, and when it crested that blue barrier, the Yankees had won their twenty-ninth American League pennant, but their first since 1964.

Chambliss, who batted .524 in the series, was approaching first base as the ball disappeared over the wall. He raised his arms, touched first, and looked toward second. By the time he got there, fans had flooded the infield, tripping him as he turned for third base. He got back up, pushing and blocking fans out of the way like a fullback trying to clear a path. Fighting through the crowd, sometimes with the help of police officers, Chambliss touched third base but gave up on the idea of touching home plate when he saw dozens of fans surrounding it. Some were lying on home plate. Chambliss charged for the dugout instead.

About a minute later, Nettles insisted Chambliss go back out and stomp on home plate. With a ten-man police escort, he did so.

The home run liberated a generation of Yankees fans whose parents had told them of Joe DiMaggio, Casey Stengel, and Mickey Mantle but who had been toddlers or grade-schoolers during the last pennants of the early 1960s. This was a new and unforgettable championship moment of their own that would take its place in Yankees history like no other because Chambliss's home run was preserved in color, captured on videotape from multiple camera angles.

Throughout the metropolitan New York area, Yankees fans celebrated, pouring out of bars and apartment complexes into the cold night. Outside Yankee Stadium, fans filled the streets.

"It's like New Year's Eve in Times Square," said Sanford D. Garelik, head of the city's transit police, who viewed the crowd from the elevated subway platform that ran over River Avenue.

Inside Yankee Stadium, the scene was almost as wild with Steinbrenner himself handing out bottles of champagne. Only a handful of players, and none of the everyday players, had won a pennant before. Billy stood in the middle of the clubhouse, the same place, if slightly rebuilt, where he had toasted several pennants as a player.

Interviewed for the television broadcast, Billy credited Steinbrenner, Paul, and the players for buying into his methods and tactics.

"It's a real credit to the Yankee Way," Billy said. "I just wish Casey were here to see it."

Walking through the narrow, concrete subterranean hallways of Yankee Stadium after the clinching victory, Billy turned to Doyle Alexander, a seldom-used starter who had not pitched in three weeks.

"You're starting tomorrow," Billy said.

"Me?" Alexander answered, surprised.

"You," Billy said.

Billy did not have many choices. All of the other starters except Ken Holtzman had pitched in the previous four days. There was some controversy that Holtzman was not the choice since he had a 4-1 record in the World Series while pitching for the Oakland A's, but Billy was unnerved by Holtzman's finish to the regular season when he lost three of four starts.

As usual with Billy's somewhat unconventional choices in the postseason, there was intrigue. But Billy believed Alexander's herky-jerky motion and change of speeds would confuse the Reds, a fastball-hitting team in a fastball-throwing league.

Alexander did not perplex the Reds very much at all, giving up nine hits and three runs in six innings. Holtzman probably could not have done worse. The Yankees hitters, meanwhile, looked tired and unfocused, losing 5–1.

"We had a little bit of a letdown," said catcher Thurman Munson. "Let's face it, we were flat, no question about it. If you'd won a championship series and partied to six in the morning and had to play 30 hours later, how would you feel?"

Some writers called attention to the Alexander decision, but there was a bigger story looming: the first night game in World Series history.

Game 2 was on a Sunday night, and both teams howled in protest when the weather forecast was for temperatures in the high thirties. They wanted the game moved to the afternoon.

But Baseball Commissioner Bowie Kuhn had sold the night game rights to NBC-TV for the then-astounding sum of $700,000. So everyone bundled up and played. It would be good for the television ratings.

"Sure it's good for ratings," Berra said before the game. "What are we playing for? The championship of Nielsen?"

Both teams looked stiff, and the game was tied 3–3 in the ninth inning when shortstop Fred Stanley threw away a ground ball and the Reds scored an unearned run off Catfish Hunter, who lost his first World Series game.

It did not get any better for the Yankees when the series returned to New York.

On another chilly night, Dock Ellis could not halt the surging Reds, who won again, 6–2. Billy had worn one of Casey Stengel's long-sleeved T-shirts beneath his uniform, hoping to change the Yankees' luck. Fifty-three years earlier, in the first World Series game in Yankee Stadium, Stengel had won the game for the visiting New York Giants with an inside-the-park home run. But Casey's undershirt held no magic for Billy's Yankees. Game 3 ended up being another desultory defeat for a drained team.

The Yankees and Reds were in the midst of rewriting baseball history, although they may not have known it.

Sunday night's Game 2 had been watched by 49 percent more households than had watched Game 2 of the 1975 World Series, which had been played on a Sunday afternoon. NBC-TV reported that it was going to stick with World Series night games for the immediate future.

The Yankees lost the fourth game of the series, becoming only the sec-

Billy (front row, second from right) joined a school basketball team sponsored by the local church. A parish priest sometimes donated food to Billy's struggling family. Years later, Billy reciprocated by giving the priest the car he won as MVP of the 1953 World Series. (*Lewis Figone*)

Berkeley Junior High School, where playground battles could be bloody and fisticuffs were a way of life. Billy is third from left, middle row. (*Lewis Figone*)

Billy's umpire baiting was well honed, and well known, at an early age. His high school yearbook had a cartoon noting as much, and also featured Billy's childhood buddy Rube de Alba. (*Lewis Figone*)

The 1948 Oakland Oaks were known as "Casey's Eight Old Men and The Kid." The Oaks' ballpark was just a few miles south of Billy's childhood home. (*Lewis Figone*)

Billy with the Oaks in 1949. (*National Baseball Hall of Fame Library, Cooperstown, NY*)

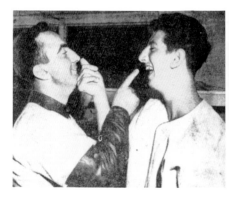

Billy with teammate Dario Lodigiani, joking that they'll win the Pacific Coast League title by a nose. As soon as he had the money, Billy had cosmetic surgery on his nose. (*Lewis Figone*)

Billy, with manager Casey Stengel, when he joined the Yankees. Billy eventually came to be known as "Casey's boy." (*National Baseball Hall of Fame Library, Cooperstown, NY*)

The Yankees' new double-play combination in 1950, Phil Rizzuto and Alfred Manuel "Billy" Martin. (*National Baseball Hall of Fame Library, Cooperstown, NY*)

In 1950 the New York press used the same words over and over to describe the new Yankees infielder. He was a sparkplug, an agitator, irrepressible, and, most often, Billy the Kid.
(*National Baseball Hall of Fame Library, Cooperstown, NY*)

Billy's method of turning the double play was controversial throughout his career.
(*National Baseball Hall of Fame Library, Cooperstown, NY*)

Billy's first marriage, to Berkeley's Lois Berndt, always seemed superseded by baseball. The wedding ceremony did not start until Billy finished an exhibition game.
(*Lewis Figone*)

Billy's lunging, game-saving catch of Jackie Robinson's windblown pop-up was the dramatic turning point of the 1952 World Series.
(*Corbis / Bettmann*)

World Series winners Hank Bauer, Yogi Berra, Billy, and Joe Collins. Billy was the 1953 Series MVP.
(*Billy Martin Jr. Collection*)

The Three Musketeers. Billy (center) with Mickey Mantle (left) and Whitey Ford, on their way to breaking another Yankees curfew. (*Billy Martin Jr. Collection*)

Billy is tagged out while attempting to steal home in Game 1 of the 1955 World Series against the Brooklyn Dodgers. Brooklyn and the Yankees met in the Fall Classic almost every year during baseball's Golden Age. (*National Baseball Hall of Fame Library, Cooperstown, NY*)

Billy and Mickey Mantle, whose pranks in the Yankees' clubhouse tested the patience of the team's veterans. Even the stoic Joe DiMaggio was not immune to their hijinks. "Billy and Mickey were like school kids when they were together," said teammate Bobby Richardson. (*Billy Martin Jr. Collection*)

In the 1950s, Billy (third from right) regularly rubbed shoulders with Hollywood's biggest stars. To Billy's left is singer-showman Jimmy Durante. Whitey Ford is third from left. (*Lewis Figone*)

Now a Cincinnati Red, Billy slugged Chicago pitcher Jim Brewer after a 1960 brushback pitch. The brawl kept Billy in court for years.

(*Corbis / Bettmann*)

Billy Jr. spent many hours with his father at the ballpark.
(*Billy Martin Jr. Collection*)

Billy and his second wife, Gretchen, with their son, Billy Jr., in the early 1970s. Billy relished his comfortable suburban existence for more than a decade, beginning in the mid-1960s.
(*Billy Martin Jr. Collection*)

Billy and his lifelong friend Lew Figone hunted frequently in Northern California. Figone became one of Billy's most trusted advisers.
(*Lewis Figone*)

In his first season
as a Major League
manager, Billy
revamped the
Minnesota Twins
and won the
inaugural AL West
Championship in
1969.
(*National Baseball
Hall of Fame Library,
Cooperstown, NY*)

In Detroit,
where Billy took
a downtrodden
Tigers team to
the playoffs.
(*Billy Martin Jr.
Collection*)

Billy and Reggie Jackson had a complicated relationship in 1977. They nearly came to blows in a Fenway Park dugout but months later horsed around in the outfield before a World Series game.
(*Associated Press*)

Gretchen with a Texas Rangers memento.
(*Billy Martin Jr. Collection*)

With Billy in the dugout, an umpire's night was rarely uneventful.
(*Jim Wilson / The New York Times / Redux*)

Billy's stunning Old Timers' Day return, days after he was forced to resign as manager. A boisterous standing ovation by the crowd went on for several minutes. Billy called it his best day in baseball.
(*National Baseball Hall of Fame Library, Cooperstown, NY*)

Billy and George Steinbrenner were all smiles during the 1978 news conference announcing his return. (General manager Al Rosen is in the background.) Billy would be dismissed and re-hired by Steinbrenner three more times.
(*D. Gorton / The New York Times / Redux*)

Something seen more often before games than after them: Billy in repose in his Yankee Stadium office. (*Jim Wilson/The New York Times/Redux*)

Billy leaving the Ohio funeral of Thurman Munson. (*Corbis/Brian Smith*)

Always the people's choice: a banner in a sold-out Oakland–Alameda County Coliseum welcomed Billy back in 1980. (*Ron Riesterer/Photoshelter*)

The fiftieth wedding anniversary party of Jenny and Jack Downey. Standing, left to right: Billy's older brother Frank, Billy, sisters Pat and Joan, and younger brother Jack Jr. (*Pat Irvine*)

Whatever uniform Billy wore, the men in blue were a frequent target of his ire. (*Ron Riesterer / Photoshelter*)

Billy and his mother walking on the field in Oakland in the early 1980s. Jenny threw out the first pitch. At the end of the decade, they died within weeks of each other. (*Pat Irvine*)

Billy's family gathered at Yankee Stadium in 1986 when Billy's number 1 was retired. Although Billy had been a fixture in New York since 1950, for many in his California-based family, it was their only trip to the city.
(*Pat Irvine*)

Billy brought his good friend Yogi Berra back to the Yankees as a quasi–assistant manager in 1977.
(*Billy Martin Jr. Collection*)

Billy with his longtime lawyer and confidant, Judge Eddie Sapir. The flamboyant, charismatic Louisiana judge got Billy out of some notably messy transgressions.
(*Courtesy of Judge Eddie Sapir*)

Billy in 1988, his last season in the dugout. The Yankees were twelve games over .500 when he was discharged as manager. (*Billy Martin Jr. Collection*)

Billy and Jill Martin at a Christmas party in the late 1980s. Together throughout the decade, they married in January 1988, roughly two years before Billy's fatal auto accident.
(*Courtesy of Jilluann Martin*)

Steinbrenner, Mantle, and President Richard Nixon beside Billy's casket.
(*Associated Press / Pat Carroll*)

Billy Jr., left, and Jill, whose hand is being held by President Nixon. Earlier, Nixon had taken a sobbing Billy Jr. by the arm and shown him the crowds outside the cathedral. "I want you to see all the people who loved your father," Nixon said. (*Associated Press / Susan Ragan*)

The crash scene of Billy's fatal accident in Fenton, New York. At dusk on a snowy Christmas Day, Billy's pickup truck roared through the intersection, took a left down the hill, and slid off the road, plummeting into a ditch. This picture was taken in 2013. The four-foot ditch was filled in by town workers in the 1990s. (*Bill Pennington*)

Billy's gravesite at Gate of Heaven Cemetery in Hawthorne, New York. Babe Ruth's grave is nearby. Visitors leave baseballs and Yankees memorabilia at both sites. (*Jack Pennington*)

ond Yankees team to be swept in the World Series. Billy wasn't around to see the bitter end. Arguing an umpire's call, he had been ejected from the game — a rare occurrence in the World Series.

"We just weren't mentally ready," Roy White said. "It all came on us so fast. They were the better team, but not 4–0 better. Somebody said the ALCS that year was our World Series and maybe that's right. We were gunning to get to the World Series; the Reds were gunning to win it."

Lou Piniella, a close witness to the last fifteen years of Billy's life, has always viewed the 1976 season as a pivotal, necessary step in the Yankees' evolution into a championship team. Piniella was Billy's kind of player. He smoked, drank, swore like a sailor, and played with a fury.

"On the field, he's always got a case of the red ass," Billy said of Piniella. "I like that about Lou."

But off the field Piniella was astute. He successfully made his own investments in the stock market and real estate. He was well read and a sage observer of people, someone who saw the little things. Piniella would notice when one reporter had started cinching his belt a notch tighter (or looser), or when one had stopped wearing a wedding ring.

To this day, Piniella believes Billy had a plan for the Yankees, even if it included losing the World Series.

"I'm not saying he wanted that," Piniella said. "But getting there and getting whupped was part of the learning curve. We needed that to get us hungry again. We needed to see the big stage before we could own it.

"The day after we were swept, I went to see Billy at that hotel in Hasbrouck Heights where he was living. We had a drink. Let me tell you, he was fine. He wasn't beaten. He knew what happened and he knew what we were going to do next.

"He looked me right in the eye and said, 'Lou, we're going to get a player or two and we'll win everything next year. You wait and see.'"

In the New York newspapers, Billy, who had been named Manager of the Year again, talked about how the Yankees had enough left-handed power hitters. He wanted a slugging right-handed-hitting outfielder. George Steinbrenner read the stories and understood everything his manager was saying except the right-handed-hitting part.

The Yankees' brass held a meeting at Yankee Stadium two days after the World Series. Everyone chimed in about what the team needed in 1977 — a shortstop, another starting pitcher, and another power hitter. There were several free-agent outfielders available. Billy, still adamant about getting a right-handed bat, lobbied for signing Joe Rudi, who had driven in 94 runs for Oakland in 1976.

Reggie Jackson's name came up. Several Yankees scouts were vociferous in their belief that Jackson would destroy the Yankees' team chemistry.

Billy left the meeting thinking that Reggie was not considered a priority.

Billy spent a week in Puerto Rico with Mantle and a few weeks hunting with Lew Figone. He returned to Texas, albeit briefly.

"My parents never officially separated," Billy Jr. said. "I've asked my mom, 'So when did you break it off?' She doesn't have an answer. I once asked my dad the same thing. He didn't know what to say. But it didn't happen in 1976.

"My dad came to some of my games that winter. He took me places. He was there. He wasn't missing. But I also remember he wasn't there for Christmas; that was kind of a red flag."

Home had become the Sheraton Hasbrouck Heights, a fourteen-story tower overlooking Route 17 in northern New Jersey, not far from that dark saloon, the Bottom of the Barrel. Another favorite haunt was four miles down Route 17, a 1930s-era hunting lodge that had been converted to a restaurant called Steve's Sizzling Steaks.

Billy would eat a steak and drink Scotch, bourbon, or vodka — he liked to change his liquor choice every few years. He would summon owner Steve Venturini, who would tell stories about how Babe Ruth made Steve's his favorite northern Jersey haunt in the mid-1930s, stories that involved huge quantities of steak and beer and trysts with the waitresses or women who had accompanied Ruth.

Billy had heard the stories before. He loved hearing them again anyway.

The routine was not always solitary.

Cousin Nick DeGennaro visited that winter.

"Billy did not lack for companionship when he wanted it," Nick said. "But he seemed to want to be alone a little more. Billy could be the life of the party but he didn't always want to be. There was maybe more of that during that winter after the World Series sweep than other winters."

There was an inherent pressure on Billy in the time between the 1976 and 1977 seasons and everyone knew it.

As columnist Dave Anderson wrote in the *New York Times*, "Billy Martin knows that many baseball people consider him a one-year manager. Billy knows that many baseball people will be surprised if turmoil does not develop on the Yankees next season. It's been the usual path in Minnesota, Detroit and Texas."

That winter, Billy also came to understand that Steinbrenner was going after Reggie Jackson at any cost. Billy did not try to talk him out of it. He told Steinbrenner that he could use a right fielder.

Steinbrenner courted Reggie with every inducement he could muster. He took him repeatedly to the 21 Club with the Yankees' general manager, Gabe Paul. George and Reggie had lunch with the New York mayor, Abe Beame.

Reggie had once made the comment, "If I played in New York, they'd name a candy bar after me."

With George's help, Reggie was already meeting with Standard Brands about producing a Reggie candy bar.

When Jackson signed a five-year, $2.96 million contract with the Yankees, Billy was not invited to the news conference.

"I kept reading about George taking Reggie to lunch at the 21 Club," Billy later wrote. "And I was sitting across the river in my hotel room the entire winter, and George hadn't taken me out to lunch even once. Reggie told a reporter, 'It's going to be great with the Yankees because George and I are going to get along real good.'

"I said to myself, 'You're going to find out that George isn't the manager of the team.'"

29

REGGIE NEVER CONTACTED BILLY after his introductory news conference. Billy did not reach out to Reggie. It might be customary for a manager to call a new player signed to his team, especially a player of such renown.

It would also be more than customary for that manager to have been invited to the splashy news conference announcing the acquisition of a celebrated new player. That would make it easy to welcome him.

But neither thing happened, a foreboding and awkward first step in the relationship between Billy and Reggie. Both said the right things when contacted by reporters. Reggie, who did not know that Billy had not been invited, praised Billy for getting the Yankees to the World Series. Billy did not bring up his preference for Joe Rudi or any of his reservations about how Reggie would affect the team chemistry.

"I'm happy to have another bat in the lineup," Billy told the *New York Post*. "Reggie will make us better. He's been a winner everywhere he went. And I like winners. We'll get along just fine."

Most of Billy's friends and allies now say that Billy was telling the truth when he said he did not have an issue with Reggie. Though perhaps not the whole truth.

"Billy had nothing personal with Reggie," Eddie Sapir, his adviser and legal consultant, said. "The problem was the people that Billy was loyal to on that Yankee team: Thurman Munson, Graig Nettles, and guys like that. Those were Billy's guys. And Billy knew they had a problem with Reggie, or probably would. They were blue-collar-type guys and Reggie had this big contract and you could see it all coming. It was going to be trouble."

Lou Piniella, a friend of Reggie's when they were Yankees teammates and a friend and managerial protégé of Billy's in the 1980s, agreed, although he saw both sides to the brewing acrimony.

"It was obviously going to be explosive," Piniella said. "And Billy was right, it did cause problems with Thurman and Graig. But at the same time, let's face it, Reggie was never Billy's kind of player. I think Billy did resent him a little. He didn't like most guys who called attention to themselves.

"And on the other side, Reggie had issues with anybody who didn't love him right away. He's a nice guy at heart but he wants to be noticed. He certainly didn't make it easy on Billy. And Billy wasn't going to make a big deal about Reggie out of respect for the other players who had already played hard for him and won a pennant."

Others saw Billy's dislike and resentment of Reggie from the start.

"He never wanted to give Reggie a chance," said Henry Hecht, the *New York Post* beat writer who had a complicated and eventually adversarial relationship with Billy. "That was always obvious to me."

Whatever the preconceptions, the rancor that Billy feared started before Reggie and Munson were ever in the same clubhouse together.

Before spring training started, Munson instigated a public snit with George Steinbrenner, claiming that Steinbrenner had promised him that he would always be the highest-paid Yankee other than Catfish Hunter. Now Reggie's salary exceeded Munson's. Steinbrenner appeased Munson with a few deferred payments, but the bad blood was already highlighted in the New York papers.

The atmosphere around the Yankees was tense not only because of the ramifications of the Reggie signing. Steinbrenner, embarrassed by Cincinnati's World Series sweep, was micromanaging every detail of the team's operations and began to exert the total control for which he would become famous in the next few years. Top executives were fleeing the Yankees' offices in droves, taking other baseball jobs to get away from Steinbrenner.

Three general managers had quit; so had the club's attorney, Joe Garagiola Jr. Two publicity directors had already resigned (there would be many more to follow), and so had a number of scouts and assistant general managers, such as Pat Gillick, who would go on to build winning teams in Toronto, Baltimore, Seattle, and Philadelphia.

Overall, more than twenty-five top Yankees' front-office workers left the team between 1975 and the beginning of the 1977 season.

They left despite knowing what everyone in baseball knew — that the Yankees were a team on the rise. They left because Steinbrenner was an intractable and unreasonable boss.

Decades later, it's easy to view Steinbrenner in a different light. By the time he died in 2010, Steinbrenner's image had been transformed into that of a benevolent, almost grandfatherly presence shepherding the Yankees family. He was the aging patriarch who doled out the big checks and smiled, even wept, as the Yankees raised championship trophies in the late 1990s and 2000s. Steinbrenner had been changed by his second suspension from baseball in 1990. When he was reinstated in 1993, he was chastened, at least compared to his earlier self. The edges had softened.

But in the 1970s and 1980s, Steinbrenner was tyrannical. He badgered everyone on the payroll and anyone else who was even remotely associated with the team. Reporters covering the team who wanted a season parking pass had to personally appear before him in his spring training office. If the reporter was new to the beat, George would subject the reporter to a grilling that might include all kinds of probing questions:

Who was the greatest president of the United States?
Should Truman have dropped the A-bomb on Japan?
Who was America's best author?
What's your favorite poem?

If George did not like a reporter's answers, he would start an argument that might end up with George standing, shouting, and calling the reporter names. Needless to say, that reporter would be sent away from George's office without a parking pass. Several days or a week later, George would call him back (George never grilled or argued with the very few female reporters who covered the team). In the second meeting, the reporter would then be grilled again on different topics, and though it might take thirty minutes, George would wait until he received answers that satisfied him. That made the reporter worthy of a parking pass (a privilege more or less assured by the press protocols of the day anyway).

Steinbrenner's demanding ways wore down everyone. At the team's spring training complex one year, he impulsively fired a teenage intern who had inadvertently left his aging Datsun compact car in the wrong spot in the team parking lot. George had a thing about his parking lot. In this case, the misplaced Datsun was making George's guest, Donald Trump, wait too long for his white Lincoln Continental.

With an unceremonious "You're fired," George discharged the young intern on the spot as Trump stood nearby. (Maybe that's where Trump got the idea for his catch phrase on *The Apprentice*, the TV show he starred in twenty-five years later.)

Anyway, with the intern no longer available to help, George soon realized there was no one left to move the cars. George jumped behind the wheels of the various cars and started moving them himself — gunning accelerators and jamming on the brakes until they squealed. Then George handed Trump his car keys with a theatric apology: "As you can see, I won't let this happen again."

No one escaped George's incessant meddling and browbeating. As Harvey Greene, one of many to work as George's press relations director, said, "When the team was on the road, you'd come back to your hotel late at night, and if your phone light was on, you knew that either there had been a death in the family or George was looking for you. After a while, you started to hope that there had been a death in the family."

If George was one continuous complication for Billy, and Reggie was a budding one, there were other changes to the 1977 team that required the manager's attention. Another new arrival was Don Gullett, a pitching star of the 1976 World Series for the Reds. He had signed a six-year, $6 million free-agent contract. That caused two other Yankees starters to hire Gullett's agent, hoping to get their salaries increased. Other Yankees were seeking raises, too. The reliever Sparky Lyle was holding out for a $150,000 pay increase. Mickey Rivers, upset that the Yankees asked him to draw more walks and drag bunt in 1977, announced that he wanted to be traded.

But for all the expected drama among Reggie, George, Thurman, and Billy, it was an uneventful spring training in 1977, and every Yankees starter or key contributor eventually signed a contract. Two days before the start of the season, the Yankees traded for Chicago shortstop Bucky Dent, maybe the last piece they needed.

The Yankees lost three of their first four games once the regular season started. As they headed to Milwaukee for their fifth game, Steinbrenner — not Billy — informed the team that he was calling for a voluntary workout during an off day. The players' union contract prohibited Steinbrenner from making the workout mandatory.

"It's not that I think we should be in a panic about being 1-3," Steinbrenner said. "But I think we should make sure everyone is in shape and focused."

At his locker, Munson had a response for Steinbrenner: "Did he really use the word 'panic'?"

Munson, Billy, Reggie, and almost all the players did not show up for the voluntary workout.

"I remember I went to the racetrack," Piniella said years later, adding with a laugh, "I saw most of the team and the coaches there."

The Yankees didn't play that well in Milwaukee, and the first tiff between Reggie and Billy occurred. Jackson told reporters after one game that his left elbow was sore and prevented him from throwing effectively from the outfield. Billy benched Reggie the next day.

"He just told the whole world his elbow was hurting," said Billy, who did not like his players to ever discuss injuries because it gave opposing teams too much information. "I'm not going to let Milwaukee run on us every time a ball is hit to Reggie in right field."

The next day Reggie and Billy had a two-and-a-half-hour meeting in the team's hotel. It was not the last meeting of its kind, to say the least. But this time, Billy emerged happier for it.

"He's the type of guy you have to explain things to," Billy said. "Like he didn't know I don't allow players to tell the press about injuries."

If things were smoothed over — a phrase Billy used repeatedly when speaking with Yankees beat writers in 1977 — somebody forgot to tell Reggie. At his locker that day, Reggie said he was "just glad to be here." He then brooded over answers to several follow-up questions.

Asked to describe his relationship with Billy, Reggie said, "I don't know what's between us."

It was the understatement of the season.

In truth, Reggie and Billy were more alike than either knew. There were striking parallels in their backgrounds, beginning with the most formative years of childhood. Both had been abandoned by a parent at an early age.

In Reggie's case, his mother, Clara, lined up the six children produced by an earlier marriage and her current marriage and abruptly left with half of them, leaving six-year-old Reggie and two of his much older siblings with his father.

As Reggie told many a reporter for years thereafter, he would not utter the word *mom* for decades.

"I couldn't do it," he said. "It disappeared from my vocabulary."

Reggie's father, Martinez Jackson, was a former professional baseball player. In a segregated America during the 1930s, Martinez Jackson was relegated to black barnstorming teams, principally the Newark Eagles of New Jersey, but he developed a deep understanding of the game and its nuances, which he later passed on to his son Reginald Martinez Jackson.

Like Billy, Reggie was raised by a strong, strict single parent, and he grew up poor, in Reggie's case in Wyncote, Pennsylvania, a northern suburb of Philadelphia.

Like Billy, Reggie was of mixed descent. Between his mother and father, he had African American, Spanish, Irish, and Native American blood. Like Billy's, Reggie's childhood neighborhood was an odd demographic mix — Reggie's was mostly white Jewish families but also Italian, Irish, and WASP-ish households.

Reggie went to high school in an adjacent, more affluent town, Cheltenham, where Reggie's old, worn clothes stood out. If there is some nefarious mystery about the employment background of Billy's mother, there were undoubtedly skeletons in the closet of Reggie's father, Martinez Jackson. He had been a runner for small-time crooks who had a gambling operation and perhaps helped with some bootlegging. By the time Reggie was in grade school, Martinez Jackson operated a dry cleaning and tailoring business — he and Reggie lived above the store — and in the basement Martinez had a corn liquor still that provided extra income (and eventually attracted attention from law authorities).

While Billy went to high school with mustard sandwiches, Reggie wrote in his autobiography, *Reggie,* that he never once had food to eat for breakfast. Reggie always had food for dinner, but he bummed food from friends for lunch. He recalled that there was never food in the refrigerator or cupboards.

There was discipline in the Jackson household. Reggie was required to speak properly and grammatically correctly. In school, English had been Martinez Jackson's favorite subject, and he stressed to his son at a young age that as a black man in twentieth-century America it was vital that he speak without using slang or dialect. Reggie addressed adults visiting the dry cleaning shop as "sir" and "ma'am."

Years later, Reggie used to laugh and joke that reporters liked to describe him as "articulate," knowing well that the term was rarely used to portray white players. It was code. No jive from Reggie. And years later, Reggie would say that his father had seen the future.

"He made sure I was marketable," Reggie said.

Reggie had only one pair of shoes per school year. He was allowed to buy two pairs of slacks a year and borrowed from relatives frequently. Athletics was Reggie's path to acceptance at Cheltenham High School, where he was a football and baseball star.

When Reggie was a junior in high school, police confiscated the corn liquor still in the basement and sent his father to prison for thirteen months. Reggie lived with his older brother Slug, who was usually working and not home. No family member attended Reggie's high school graduation, and no one saw him off in 1964 when he packed two suitcases and a gym bag and left for Arizona State, where he had earned a full football scholarship.

Reggie might have been a good college football player had he not been a *great* college baseball player. By 1966, he was drafted with the second overall pick by the Kansas City Athletics, soon to be the Oakland A's. The New York Mets had the first pick but were reluctant to take Reggie because their scouts reported that his college girlfriend was white (she was actually Mexican).

Reggie was sent to the A's minor league team in Birmingham, Alabama, where Reggie had trouble getting adequate lodging because he was African American. But within eighteen months, he was liberated from the indignities he faced in the minors and handed the starting right fielder's job with the A's. He was a shining star, but his teammates noticed that he was easily insulted, something that will surface quickly in the insular, biting culture of a Major League clubhouse.

"He was very insecure and sensitive," said teammate Gene Tenace.

Said another teammate, Rick Monday, of Reggie, "Likable but paranoid."

As if he could hear someone give him the finger.

But Reggie was a tremendous baseball player even at twenty-one years old, and within three years of his Major League debut, he was tangling with Billy's 1969 Minnesota Twins for a spot in the playoffs.

They were adversaries from first glance. They sparred in the press, calling each other names, then yelled at each other on the field. Reggie hit long home runs against Billy's teams and stood at home plate admiring the ball's flight before slowly circling the bases — a rare show of theater in the 1960s and early 1970s. Adding to the self-exaltation, Reggie would crow about those home runs to the press afterward. The next day, Billy's pitchers invariably threw at Reggie in the batter's box.

The confrontations continued until everyone wondered if there was a deeper source of the acrimony.

Most obviously and notably, Billy was white and Reggie was African American, and in a second autobiography, *Becoming Mr. October,* released in 2013, Reggie wrote he was told that Billy and some of his Yankees teammates made anti-Semitic references to the Jewish pitcher Ken Holtzman and that he felt sure that Billy and other players also told racial jokes.

Reggie did not write that he heard the jokes being told, and he did not describe the anti-Semitic references. Reggie wrote that these were things he had heard from others. In 2013 interviews, Reggie was very careful about how he phrased his accusations about Billy. The book was strident about Billy's biases, but when asked by multiple interviewers how he came to those opinions about Billy, Reggie said very little.

"When I looked back at it and from what I've heard and what I can surmise, these are things that I think were happening," he said.

Reggie had raised these issues before. In 2011, he had very briefly made similar comments to broadcaster Bob Costas in an interview, saying that he saw a racial bias in the way Billy treated another black player, Elliott Maddox.

Asked about the Costas interview two years later, Reggie clarified his accusations, although he continued to speak in generalities.

"It was the climate of the times, first of all," he said. "You had to know what it was like to be a prominent black man in the 1970s in New York City. It was in the air wherever you went. And it was in the air in Yankee Stadium.

"That was the sense I had. And it included Billy. I never figured out why he and I didn't get along but I'll tell you what, we sure didn't.

"I would almost want to say that I never had a relationship with him. I don't know what it was. Looking back, I think he never liked me. But at the time, I had no idea. I thought he would like me. He was from the Bay Area and I had played there. He was a scrappy guy and I always played hard-nosed baseball. Where was the problem?"

In *Becoming Mr. October,* Reggie also wrote that he was disappointed that all but one of the black players on the Yankees, Willie Randolph, sided with Billy. As a group, he wrote, the black players were unwelcoming to him.

Reggie's comments to Costas and his written words in *Becoming Mr. October* sparked a torrent of criticism from former teammates.

"Reggie is a friend," Rickey Henderson said in an interview weeks after *Becoming Mr. October* was released. "But that's the most wrong thing he has ever said."

Reggie's allegations are not, on their face, an outlandish suggestion, especially given the times, although the anti-Semitic portion of Reggie's accusation is hard to place, given the many close friends and business associates of Jewish heritage who surrounded Billy throughout his life. His widow, Jill, was part Jewish.

But there were certainly millions of white men born in 1928 in America who held racial biases the rest of their lives. It's not inconceivable that Billy told off-color or racist jokes sometime in his life, or tolerated them in his presence, although it is worth mentioning that there is no established historical evidence of it occurring. And there have been millions of words written about Billy in magazines, newspapers, and books from 1950 to the present. A couple of New York–based sportswriters from the 1970s, interviewed in retirement decades later, said they thought race was a factor in the Billy-Reggie feud and cast Billy as the bigot. Other writers disagreed.

During the 1977 season, beat writers repeatedly pressed black players on the Yankees on the subject of race. None would criticize Billy. Most were unsympathetic to Reggie's mostly latent cries of racism.

In Jonathan's Mahler's *Ladies and Gentlemen, the Bronx Is Burning,* a seminal account of the roiling 1977 summer in New York City, Mahler wrote that Chris Chambliss, the Yankees' black first baseman, was listening to Reggie complain in a hotel bar one night and finally confronted his teammate.

"Reggie, you know what you'd be if you were white?" Chambliss said. "Just another damn white boy. Be glad you're black and getting all the publicity you do, getting away with all the shit you do."

Mahler also noted that in the summer of 1977, while the Reggie-Billy strife was front-page news in the New York tabloids, the *Amsterdam News,* the city's only black newspaper, conspicuously sided with Billy. To the *Amsterdam News,* Reggie was not a "people's hero," à la Muhammad Ali, Joe Louis, or Ray Robinson.

Reggie's 2013 book revived the issue. When contacted about Reggie's book that year, Maddox, who played for Billy briefly in Texas and with the Yankees, said he agreed with Reggie. On the other side of the issue, multiple players rose to Billy's defense.

"It's not something I saw from Billy," said Randolph, whom Reggie described as his only black friend on the 1977 team. "Reggie went through a lot and I respect him so much, but I don't know about that."

"Billy? A racist?" Roy White said, repeating a question. White is African American. "There are plenty of words I would use for Billy. That isn't one."

Maybe Reggie saw something in Billy that he had seen before and attributed it to racism. But there is little proof of racial prejudice in Billy's life. There were plenty of people he didn't like, white, black, Latin, and Asian. He had plenty of enemies, too. He also had a host of African American players from Rod Carew to Henderson who viewed him as a benevolent father figure and essential to their maturation. More than five of his Latin-born players named one of their children Billy in their mentor's honor. On every one of his coaching staffs from 1976 to 1989, he had black assistant coaches.

He had major, public shouting matches and confrontations with players, executives, reporters, and umpires — as well as several celebrated barroom fistfights — in an adult life spent entirely illuminated by the media spotlight. There is no preponderance of trouble with men or women of color.

"You could call my dad a lot of things," his son, Billy, said, sitting in a Texas bar in 2013. "In a place like this you could see it all on the wrong night. He might drink too much, he might hit on somebody's girlfriend, and he might take offense at something someone said and want to punch him. He made lots of mistakes. But nobody ever called him a racist.

"Reggie needs to look in the mirror. My dad was a lot of things but racist wasn't one of them."

Racism can exhibit itself in multiple ways or be revealed in one instructive act or by one person who perceives an otherwise latent prejudice. Reggie Jackson, raised in an era when examples of discrimination were not hard to find, is convinced Billy was a racist.

His comments made prominent news in 2013, especially after Reggie appeared on CNN, HBO, and dozens of other media outlets promoting the book. But his revelations did not bring him allies.

Carew, whose daughter had Billy as a godfather, played with Reggie on the California Angels in the early 1980s. When Reggie's race comments were mentioned to him in 2013, Carew just shook his head ruefully.

"Reggie knows better," Carew said. "I don't know why he would say that. And it's interesting that no one rushed to agree with Reggie. I never met a manager in all my decades in baseball — then or since — who got along better with the guys of color than Billy. So that's just not something I ever saw and I was around the guy for twenty-five years and knew most of the players that played for him in those twenty-five years."

Carew's tone went from dismayed to amused. He laughed.

"We know the truth," Carew said, snickering. "There was just something between those two guys. Reggie and Billy didn't get along. We all have people like that — someone who you just can't seem to get on the same page with. I never talked to Reggie or Billy about it. But I never had to. It was there."

Mickey Morabito, the Yankees' public relations director from 1976 to 1980 whose job it was to spend every day with the team from February to November, summed up the relationship similarly.

"There were days when they loved each other and there were days they hated each other," Morabito said. "Something about Reggie irked Billy. Something about Billy irked Reggie."

"I don't know what's going on between us," Reggie said on April 9, 1977.

It was only the beginning.

By April 20, the Yankees had lost six of their last eight games, were five games under .500, and were in last place, which was so offensive to George Steinbrenner he called a meeting with Billy, the press, and the players before the next game.

Then the Yankees went out and lost again.

George's message to Billy and the press was that Billy had better get the ship righted, and soon. The writers eagerly wrote that Billy, reigning AL Manager of the Year, was on the hot seat 11 games into the season when the Yankees were 5 games out of first place with 151 to play.

Murray Chass, the Yankees beat writer for the *New York Times,* wrote a piece the next day in which he quoted an unnamed player who said, "George better stay off his back. One thing Billy has going for him is that he has more players on his side than the owner has."

Another player was more emphatic.

"The more we lose," he told Chass, "the more often Steinbrenner will fly in to our games. And the more he flies, the better the chance there will be of a plane crash."

The next day, Billy made up his batting order by having Reggie pick names out of a hat. The Yankees won 7–5 and went on to win the next five games in a row.

By mid-May, the Yankees were four games over .500 and neck-and-neck with Boston and Baltimore at the top of the AL East standings. That lowered the point size of the headlines in the New York tabloids, but things were still simmering beneath the surface. Everyone knew *Sport* magazine was coming out with a cover story on Reggie. The magazine had hinted the story contained inflammatory comments from Reggie about a teammate.

Billy stewed largely in silence. This was precisely what he had feared. He drove home to the Hasbrouck Heights Sheraton after games and drank at the Bottom of the Barrel and Steve's Sizzling Steaks. A fairly regular girlfriend, Patty Stark, whom Billy had met in Kansas City, occasionally visited. Gretchen and Billy Joe largely remained in Texas.

"He called often," said Gretchen. "He was tense. I'm not sure he was eating well. He would have good days and bad days. It always seemed like on Sunday mornings, after he went to church, he would be in a good mood.

"He almost always called on Sundays. For the rest of his life, we would hear from him on Sunday."

The June issue of *Sport* hit newsstands on Monday, May 23. In the article, titled "Reggie in No-Man's Land," the Yankees' new right fielder says he was brought to the Yankees because they lacked the right kind of leadership.

"I'm the straw that stirs the drink," the magazine quoted Reggie as saying. "Munson thinks he can be the straw that stirs the drink, but he can only stir it bad."

The article was filled with quotes from Reggie praising himself and predicting how he could help the imperfect Yankees.

The interview with the *Sport* magazine writer Robert Ward had taken place inside the Banana Boat Bar on the beach in Fort Lauderdale. According to the story, minutes into the interview, Billy, Mickey Mantle, and Whitey Ford walked into the bar and started playing backgammon in another section of the bar. Reggie bought the trio of ex-Yankees drinks. Of Billy, he said, "He's no dummy. He's smart. He knows I can help this team. Billy is a winner. We won't have any problems and I'll make it easier for him."

But Reggie added that he had to lead the team, not Munson, whom he called insecure and jealous.

The reaction in the Yankees' clubhouse when the article came out was predictable. Reggie might as well as have called Lou Gehrig a phony and Joe DiMaggio a choke.

Reggie claimed he was misquoted.

Munson had a response when he was told that Reggie insisted he was misquoted: "For three thousand fucking words?"

The *Sport* magazine piece was being read throughout the Yankees' clubhouse when Reggie arrived for the Yankees' home game with Boston on the night of May 23. Those players who had not read it were told about it by reporters, all of whom were writing stories before the game about Reggie's comments.

Billy dismissed questions about the story, refusing to say anything.

But by the time the Yankees headed out to batting practice, no one but Reggie's good friend, the backup catcher Fran Healy, was making any attempt to talk to Reggie. It was a blatant snub. The silent treatment continued throughout the pregame. Reggie was being ignored.

The Red Sox were leading 4–2 in the seventh inning that evening when Reggie hit a solo home run. As Reggie crossed home plate, Piniella, the on-deck hitter, was waiting with an outstretched hand to shake or slap. Reggie ran past Piniella without extending his hand or greeting Piniella.

As is customary, a gaggle of Yankees players and coaches, and Billy, waited near the top step of the dugout nearest to home plate to greet and congratulate Reggie.

But Reggie ran through foul territory toward the end of the dugout closest to right field and away from the crowd waiting for him. He descended the steps without acknowledging anyone and sat down in the corner of the dugout.

It was not a gesture that went unnoticed.

After the game, which the Yankees lost 4–3, reporters asked Reggie why he refused to shake hands. He said his right hand was sore and he didn't want to aggravate it.

Told of Reggie's excuse, Munson, who was not usually that forthcoming with reporters, said loudly, "He's a fucking liar."

Other Yankees were just as angry.

Years later, Reggie said it was just a reaction to the silent treatment he had gotten before the game.

"You guys are going to be that way? Okay, I'll deal with it," he wrote in *Becoming Mr. October*. "Let's just move on and be open about it. You don't like me. I don't like you. Why hide it?"

Reggie conceded he was sulking. Billy would not get drawn into the fray publicly.

"I didn't notice," he said about Reggie's dugout snubbing.

On most occasions, Billy was far more diplomatic than he will ever get credit for. His willingness to be diplomatic just had a limit. He did the tactful and judicious thing for a while until he felt pushed into standing up for himself.

Even after a tough loss, for example, 90 to 95 percent of the time he would politely answer questions from reporters — even those that bordered on second-guessing. If the question came from a reporter he knew at all, he would usually be candid or try to clarify his thinking. A stranger would get an answer but perhaps not an insightful answer.

But if the second-guessing persisted — two questions could easily be enough — and heaven help everyone in the room if it came from a reporter with whom he was unfamiliar, Billy's expression would grow suspicious. By the third question on the same topic or play in the game, you could see the tension in Billy's hands as he grasped a cup or the arms of his chair.

His willingness to be diplomatic would be running out. His tank of tact was near empty. Those who knew him or studied him knew to leave the room or change the subject. Those who did not know him — or in many cases wanted to provoke a scene — would keep pressing the matter.

And that's when Billy would erupt with an emotional, annoyed, and sometimes irrational outburst.

But that was far from his usual mien. In countless profiles of Billy over the years, people wrote that Billy lived by the credo instilled by his mother: Don't take shit from anybody. But Billy took a lot of shit from a lot of people. He just had a threshold. When the shit got too deep, Billy would snap.

But at the beginning of the first full-blown Reggie crisis, Billy stayed calm, at least in public.

The feud in the Yankees' clubhouse continued for weeks. Reggie made peace with a few players and even had dinner with Munson and Healy.

Resentment remained. For Reggie, the biggest issue was Billy's refusal to bat him fourth in the order, the cleanup spot he preferred. Reggie usually batted fifth instead. Having Reggie hitting cleanup was also what George Steinbrenner wanted, something the owner brought up to his manager almost daily. Reggie belonged in the cleanup spot; it was where he had been most productive throughout his career. It was the natural move, one backed up by years of statistical evidence. Reggie was a classic number-four hitter, and having him elsewhere was costing the Yankees runs.

But Billy was loyal to Chris Chambliss, the previous season's fourth hitter. And Billy was capable of not making the switch just out of spite. Billy was diplomatic but he was also almost maniacally obstinate. George would not get his way even if it meant hurting the Yankees' production — and distracting Reggie, too.

30

ON JUNE 16, THE rookie pitcher from Louisiana, Ron Guidry, shut out the Royals, pushing the Yankees into first place by a half-game in the AL East. Next up, a three-game weekend series in Boston against the second-place Red Sox.

In the first game of the series on Friday night, Boston hit six home runs to win in a rout. The Saturday afternoon game the next day was NBC's *Game of the Week,* a big deal when only two Major League games were broadcast nationally per week.

Four years before ESPN made its largely unnoticed debut as the world's first twenty-four-hour sports cable network — with a steady programming diet of Australian rules football games — the only way for American baseball fans to see games outside their local market was on Saturday afternoons (NBC) and Monday nights (ABC).

These games were major events of the sports culture, and because there was so little competition in the pre-cable era of the late 1970s, the TV ratings for the games were exceptionally high — much higher than most baseball playoff games now draw.

Every player knew when it was a nationally televised game and cared that it was, especially a player as transfixed with his national profile as Reggie Jackson.

Billy did not mind the attention either. He always knew when the national cameras were poised at the end of his dugout as well. He admitted as much.

As they did the night before, the Red Sox came out Saturday and immediately started slapping the Yankees around. By the bottom of the sixth inning, the Yankees were trailing 7–4 when Boston's Fred Lynn singled and Jim Rice floated a looping fly ball in front of Reggie in right field.

Reggie had no play on the fly ball, but he did not charge after the baseball as it lay in the grass. Rice, running hard from home plate, seized on Reggie's slow approach and easily raced to second base.

Billy came out to relieve Yankees starter Mike Torrez with Sparky Lyle. After Lyle reached the mound, Billy returned to the dugout, and that is when he sent Paul Blair to right field as a replacement for Reggie.

Lyle, no fan of Reggie's, was throwing his warm-up pitches but paused to watch.

"Wow, this ought to be good," he said to himself.

Reggie was stunned to see Blair running at him, and he pointed at his own chest as if to say, "You're here for me?"

"What's going on?" Reggie asked.

"You've got to ask Billy," Blair answered. "He told me I'm in for you."

Years later, Blair said he knew exactly what would happen next.

"I was happy to be out in the outfield so I didn't have to be near it," he said, laughing.

Reggie jogged in, and when he was a few feet from the dugout he turned his palms skyward, approaching Billy as if confused or puzzled.

"What did I do?" he asked.

Billy leaped from the dugout bench and snarled, "You showed me up by not hustling so I'm going to show your ass up."

Reggie: "What the fuck are you talking about?"

Billy: "You know what I'm talking about. You loafed after that ball. Anybody who doesn't hustle isn't going to play for me."

Reggie tugged off his glasses, not because he planned to fight, he later said, but because the glasses were fogging up in the heat.

"You're not a man," Reggie told Billy, to which Billy answered, "I ought to kick your ass."

"Who do you think you're talking to, old man?" Reggie yelled. "You showed me up on national TV."

A Yankees batboy had thrown a towel over the NBC camera at the edge of the dugout, but the center-field camera was able to capture everything in the tiny, low-ceilinged visitors' dugout constructed in 1912.

"They're gonna confront each other right there in the dugout," NBC's Joe Garagiola howled in the broadcast booth.

In the Yankees radio booth, Billy's old teammate Phil Rizzuto watched the quarrel escalating and saw something he had seen many times before.

"Oh, Billy's really hot now," Rizzuto said. "Watch out."

And indeed, Billy charged at Reggie. But Yogi Berra, who had known Billy since 1949 — and like Rizzuto knew when an explosion was about to occur — had already positioned himself between Reggie and Billy. Elston

Howard, another coach and former 1950s teammate of Billy's, made it his assignment to corral Reggie. Unnoticed in the drama, the two men had maneuvered like trained bar bouncers accustomed to defusing confrontations. Watching the two former Yankees catchers move tactically and in tandem without saying a word was Ron Guidry, the young pitcher who was sitting on the dugout bench.

As Guidry told author Harvey Araton, Berra and Howard both stood up as soon as Billy told Blair to get his glove.

"They had the smarts to know that this doesn't look good, something's going to happen here," Guidry told Araton. "Nobody else did, just them. Me, I'm just sitting there on my butt, never even thought about getting up."

Guidry actually had the thought that maybe it would be best if Billy and Reggie had the fight that many thought was inevitable right then — get it over with.

"At that moment, if you asked me, I would've said that we should have just let the sons of bitches go," Guidry said.

Howard, the first black Yankee, had been around Billy for parts of three decades now. The two were never close and less than friendly later in life, but Howard did not much like the way Reggie conducted himself either. With several current and former Yankees listening one night in 1977, Howard was asked where Reggie would have fit in on the great Yankees teams of the 1950s and early 1960s.

"Fifth outfielder," Howard said.

But now Howard knew that letting Billy and Reggie duke it out would be an epic embarrassment to the Yankees, and he and Berra had spent too much time behaving with class and dignity to allow a tiff over a fly ball tear the team's image apart.

Berra, fifty-two years old, was a bear of a man at the time, and he grabbed Billy by the belt and the crotch, which is an especially effective way to control someone.

"Yogi had hands like vises," Billy said later. "I wanted to get at Reggie in the worst way but Yogi had ahold of me."

Reggie, meanwhile, was not exactly straining to get at Billy, but he was close enough and agitated enough — until Howard moved him away.

With the two combatants at least momentarily neutralized, Torrez told Reggie in Spanish to go to the clubhouse and cool off, and another teammate, Jimmy Wynn, helped push Reggie to the ramp to the locker room.

"You've never liked me," Reggie screamed as he left.

It had been fewer than twelve furious seconds. Yet it left the dugout and a national audience spent.

In homes across America, there was a collective gasp and gulp. It was as if baseball fans nationwide had inched toward their television screens to take in every millisecond of the dugout drama, then leaned back in their easy chairs and let out a tension-relieving exhale.

What had just happened?

Billy was the best-known manager in baseball. Reggie was one of the four or five best-known players in the game. On a beautiful Saturday in Boston, they had nearly had a toe-to-toe fistfight, and it was framed in the confines of an undersize bench area.

Had there ever been a scene like it in a major American sport? The answer was probably yes, but it had never been broadcast on national television. You could feel the buzz created by the raw hostility of those few seconds wafting through the American sports community that summer afternoon.

And soon after, people wanted to take sides.

But not the Yankees.

Watching a videotape of the game, it's fascinating to see how quickly Billy and the rest of the Yankees try to pretend that nothing of consequence had occurred.

There was complete calm in the Yankees' dugout. Billy turned his attention to the field, mute and still but for a twitch in his eye. On the Yankees' bench, the players stared straight ahead. Lyle threw a pitch to Yastrzemski, who grounded out. Fisk flied out. No runs scored. Now the whole team was in the dugout.

A clubhouse boy ran over to Lou Piniella.

"The kid said Reggie wanted to see me in the clubhouse," Piniella said, retelling the story thirty-six years later. "All the players were sitting on the bench just going about their business. Nobody wanted any part of this.

"But I went into the clubhouse and found Reggie standing there in a T-shirt and his uniform pants."

Reggie told Piniella he had left his baseball spikes on so he would have good footing on the clubhouse carpet during the fistfight he planned to have with Billy when the game was over.

"I told Reggie to go get a beer, shower, and go back to the hotel," Piniella said. "You can't have a fight with the manager. That's no good for you, no good for Billy or for the ball club."

Reggie, who had doubled and singled earlier in the game, responded by saying that Billy had humiliated him on national TV.

Healy, Reggie's best friend on the team, arrived in the clubhouse as well.

Healy strongly advised Reggie to leave Fenway Park.

Finally convinced, Reggie dressed and was escorted to a little-used Fenway Park exit in center field. He emerged into the sunlight of Landsdowne Street and then walked — unnoticed — to the Boston Sheraton a few blocks away.

After the game, which the Yankees lost 10–4, Billy was irritated but certain he had done the right thing. The visiting manager's office, beneath the Fenway grandstand, was the same one where Casey Stengel had once expounded on the virtues of Billy's fight with Jimmy Piersall.

Now Billy sat behind that manager's desk, his back to a redbrick wall facing a throng of reporters from New York and Boston.

"You can't let any player think he's bigger than the team and his team-mates deserve maximum effort," Billy said. "When a player shows up the team, I show up the player."

The question-and-answer period was brief and had a rat-a-tat-tat tempo.

Reporter: "Did you think twice about pulling Reggie in a close game?"

Billy: "We won last year without him, didn't we?"

"Did you consider a more conventional means of discipline?"

"How do you fine a superstar, take away his Rolls-Royce?"

"Was the incident bad for baseball since the game was on national television?"

"What's television got to do with the game? Did that help us win? I don't care if it went out to the whole world."

The news conference ended and reporters scurried to find Reggie.

That task took several hours because Reggie remained sequestered at the Sheraton. Eventually, after fielding multiple requests, Reggie invited a handful of his favorite New York writers to his hotel suite, where he was drinking a bottle of white wine with Torrez. Reggie walked around the suite shirtless and holding a Bible. He had just received a call from the Reverend Jesse Jackson.

"It makes me cry the way they treat me on this team," Reggie said. "The Yankee pinstripes are Ruth and Gehrig and DiMaggio and Mantle. But I'm just a black man to them who doesn't fucking know how to be subservient. I'm a big black man with an IQ of 160 making $700,000 a year and they treat me like dirt. They've never had anyone on their team like me before."

Asked about George Steinbrenner, Reggie said, "I love that man, he treats me like I'm somebody. The rest of them treat me like dirt."

Billy, meanwhile, was easier to find than Reggie. About four blocks from the Sheraton on Boston's Newbury Street was Daisy Buchanan's, a bar populated by athletes, writers, tourists, and fans. Daisy's was Billy's kind of bar — below street level with a backroom where he could hunker down and drink.

And this evening, knowing that baseball fans everywhere — and that included George Steinbrenner — were talking about the scene inside the visitors' dugout at Fenway Park, Billy was pounding Scotch.

Moss Klein, the quiet, unassuming Yankees beat writer for the Newark *Star-Ledger* and a Billy favorite, found the Yankees manager at Daisy's and started taking notes. It wasn't much of an interview. Billy had only one message and he kept repeating it: "They're gonna say this was my fault."

Morabito shepherded Billy back to the hotel.

"He was really upset," Morabito said. "You know, Billy always felt he had to stand up for himself or for the Yankee Way. He thought he might lose the respect of the team if he didn't, but after it was over, he usually felt terrible. Not because he thought he was wrong but because he knew there would be trouble. For a guy who was in it a lot, he really didn't like trouble.

"There were a lot of nights like that in 1977 and 1978. He was Billy being Billy, but being Billy took a big toll on him. He'd be very upset and not know how to process all of it."

The photos of the dugout standoff were in all the newspapers Sunday morning, filling the front pages of the New York tabloids. Steinbrenner saw the photos and called Gabe Paul in Boston.

"This is how my team is perceived around the country?" he yelled into the phone. "We look like lunatics and screaming maniacs. Get Reggie and Billy together and fix this."

Gretchen Martin got a call in Texas Sunday morning.

"Billy said he was going to breakfast in Gabe Paul's room with Reggie," Gretchen said. "He promised me he would remain calm. He wanted to get it over with. But I was worried. I knew Billy didn't think Reggie was a good teammate."

The breakfast was, not surprisingly, a bizarre meeting. Paul tried to get both men to admit they had overreacted. Neither would, and the notion especially annoyed Billy, who expected Paul, as part of management, to support the manager. Reggie spoke to Paul as if Billy weren't in the room, accusing him of trying to embarrass him. Reggie insisted he did nothing wrong, that he had hustled after Rice's looping fly ball.

Billy, Reggie said, was just looking for an excuse to blame him for something.

Billy jumped up from the breakfast table.

"Get up, boy, I'm gonna kick the shit out of you," Billy yelled.

Reggie turned to Gabe Paul.

"You heard it, you heard him call me 'boy,'" Reggie said. "Gabe, you're Jewish, you understand the comment. How do you think I feel when he says that to me?"

Billy was unyielding.

"It's just an expression," he said. "We all called each other boy where I grew up."

Paul ordered Billy to sit down and soon realized his pacifying breakfast was going nowhere.

At Fenway Park later that day, Billy insisted the meeting had brought a resolution to the dispute.

"We went over everything and everything turned out fine," Billy said. "There is no problem. Yesterday is history."

Reggie played in the Yankees' 11–1 loss that followed and was 0-for-4, ending a fourteen-game hitting streak. It was an uneasy team that flew from Boston to Detroit Sunday night. The New York writers had been talking to Steinbrenner on the telephone, and soon there were stories in the papers quoting anonymous team sources — George routinely talked off the record — that put Billy's job in jeopardy.

Steinbrenner was flying to Detroit to meet his second-place team.

The next twenty-four hours played out like the 1960s Cuban Missile Crisis. The explosive device in this case was Steinbrenner, who arrived in Detroit convinced he should fire Billy for failing to get the best out of Reggie.

Enter Fran Healy, the backup catcher and Reggie confidant. By the time the Yankees left Detroit three days later, Healy was being called by a new nickname: "Kissinger."

On Monday, Healy met Reggie for lunch in the lobby of the team's hotel — the Pontchartrain, which had been Billy's temporary home when he was the Tigers' manager. Healy explained that the two had to work together to keep George from firing Billy. Healy's reasoning was twofold: one, it would probably not be the best thing for the team; and two, if Billy was fired, his legion of fans would mercilessly blame Reggie.

And so would most of the rest of the team. Reggie's life would go from complicated to untenable.

When Reggie agreed, Healy and Reggie went to see George in his hotel room. Reggie pleaded with George not to fire Billy because it would look as if Reggie were running the team.

George agreed to spare Billy but only if he and Reggie called some truce in their festering feud.

Billy knew his job was on the line, but instead of staying at the hotel, he allowed Rizzuto to persuade him to play golf in the morning. When Billy returned to the Pontchartrain, Healy was waiting for him. The backup catcher explained what had already transpired that day.

"Billy was pretty shaken," Healy said. "But he started to realize he had to do something right away, so he called George."

It was 5:00 p.m. and the Yankees were to play at Tiger Stadium at 8:15. Billy went to George's room where George laid down some new ground rules for his manager — principally, he wanted Billy to be civil to Reggie at all times.

As a first show of unity, Billy called Reggie and the two agreed to drive to Tiger Stadium together. At 6:00 p.m., with Billy at the wheel of a rental car, the manager and player who two days earlier had nearly slugged it out at Fenway Park drove to the ballpark. Imagine being a Detroit-area baseball fan driving home from work and pulling up to a stoplight and seeing Billy Martin driving Reggie Jackson to the ballpark.

Who would have believed that story?

Billy and Reggie arrived at Tiger Stadium uneventfully and walked into the clubhouse together.

With Steinbrenner seated in an upstairs suite for the game, Billy brought the lineup card to the umpires at home plate just before the first pitch. The Tiger Stadium fans, who like baseball fans everywhere were well aware of the Boston confrontation, rose to their feet, giving Billy a standing ovation. Billy waved his cap.

When Reggie took his place in right field, he was roundly booed. He, too, waved his cap.

During the game, the Yankees issued a statement: "There will not be a change in our organization . . . We don't feel there's a better manager than Billy Martin and we want the Yankees to have the best."

After the game, which the Yankees lost, Billy looked worn and drained. Asked about his golf game that morning, Billy said, "I couldn't concentrate at all. I must have shot 212."

Healy, in his last act of Detroit diplomacy, got Reggie and Munson to go to dinner with him that night after the game.

It did not settle much — Munson was still spitting mad — but the team's two best players were at least on speaking terms.

The Yankees lost their third consecutive game the next night. But Billy was at least smiling again.

"Yesterday, I felt like I had a 600-pound weight around my neck," he told reporters. "Today, it only feels like a 300-pound weight."

When the Yankees finally returned to New York, they swept a three-game series with the Red Sox. By July 2, they were back in first place.

With school out for the summer, Gretchen and Billy Joe had moved into the New Jersey hotel suite. Gretchen would not stay the entire summer. For the most part, Billy Joe remained with his father.

"It was uncomfortable," Gretchen Martin said. "I knew what was going on with Billy when I wasn't around. It was as I expected when he went to New York. I knew it was ending; it was coming apart."

Billy Joe went to all the home games with his father and often went on the road with the Yankees. It was an enjoyable time for him, running around in Yankee Stadium wearing a miniature replica of his father's number 1 jersey and spending days and nights with a father he had not seen regularly since Billy took the Yankees job in 1975.

A postgame routine developed, win or lose.

"After games, we would usually go to a restaurant with the coaches," Billy Joe said. "We'd get a big table but my dad would go off to the bar by himself. He would sit there kind of nursing his drink with this intense look and you could see the wheels turning in his head. He was replaying the game.

"You could almost see him going over situations — should I have hit for this guy? Did I take that pitcher out too late? Should we have bunted here? If it was a tough game, or a loss, then he might stay there for two drinks. But most times, just from his body language you could see when he was wrapping up his thoughts on the game. He had put it away.

"Then he would get up and come over to the table and say, 'Hey, pard, how was your day? What are you going to get for dinner?' Then he could rejoin the crowd. But he had to replay the game first. It was like a ritual."

Billy Joe, who was thirteen years old at the time, said his time at the ballpark was spent with the children of other players, and often with Reggie.

"Reggie went out of his way to be nice with me," Billy Joe said. "He played catch with me almost every day. He probably did it for obvious reasons but the fact is, he did it. And I think my dad appreciated that.

"They did have a relationship. They did clown around and talk to each other. They weren't always at odds. Those peaceful times just always seem to have had an expiration date."

There seemed to be a yin and yang element to everything about the 1977 season.

"Stressful but fun," Billy Joe said. "I did notice on some of the worst days my dad would not eat, or not much. And that worried me."

As a young teen, he was not privy to all things in his father's world. Years later, he was told about the different girlfriends Billy was juggling during the 1977 season.

"He hid all that from me then," Billy Joe said. "It was just the two of us. I never saw any women when I was there."

Billy Joe knew better later in life.

"There were things that were harder to deal with as I got older and wiser," Billy Joe said. "I knew better. But remember, he and my mom were together nearly twenty years. My dad never wanted to do anything to disrespect my mom. And certainly not in front of me."

While Billy and most of the rest of the Yankees were in New Jersey, Reggie, one of the few players to live east of the Hudson River, was leading a far different life in New York.

The East Side of Manhattan was not a bad place to be young, single, famous, and a millionaire. Reggie lived on Fifth Avenue, not far from the trendy restaurant/bars on Third Avenue, where he mingled with Ford Agency models. After a night game he would grab a quick meal at Oren and Aretsky's or McMullen's on 76th Street and Third Avenue. When he was done eating, with or without companionship, he would drive the roughly twenty blocks to Studio 54. He did not wait in the hours-long lines to gain entrance into what was perhaps New York's best-known party place in the twentieth century.

"I would park my Rolls-Royce at the curb just outside the Studio 54 doorway, flip my keys to the cop standing there, and walk in," Reggie said in 2013. "Never had a problem. It would be waiting for me when I came out."

But all was not always well. In both of his autobiographies, Reggie wrote that he sometimes felt like he was having a nervous breakdown in 1977. On some days he dreaded going to the ballpark.

"It was a great summer and it was a terrible summer," he said.

Near the halfway point of the season, the Royals swept the Yankees in Kansas City, and during that series Reggie made an error one night and then another in the next game. The second came when he butchered a ball in right field with Lyle on the mound. What should have been a double became an inside-the-park home run when Reggie dropped the ball at his feet three times.

After the inning, Lyle, in front of the rest of the team, told Reggie in the dugout to "get his head out of his ass."

Reggie said nothing to Lyle, although he told writers about it afterward, which further incensed Lyle. Billy stayed out of that dispute, too.

"I didn't hear anything," he said. "I know we didn't hit enough to win the game."

The season continued with its never-ending circuslike atmosphere. The combative 1977 Yankees were just part of the disorder in a deadly, dysfunctional New York that summer. The Son of Sam murders were terrorizing the city, several union workers' strikes had crippled municipal services, and a divisive mayoral election between Ed Koch and Mario Cuomo had imbued the political scene with a rancorous edge.

Billy, George, and Reggie, the Yankees' messy love/hate triangle, fit in perfectly.

On July 13, the Yankees lost 9–8 in Milwaukee and now trailed the Red Sox by 1.5 games. Reggie was still batting fifth or sixth, and he revived his complaints about batting cleanup. He was convinced he would hit better in the fourth spot and kept saying so in the newspapers.

The team stayed at the Pfister Hotel in Milwaukee, an Old World tower downtown near several German restaurants, which Billy liked to frequent after games. Piniella and Munson headed for the Pfister bar after the Yankees loss.

"Why is it so damn important to Reggie to bat fourth?" Munson asked Piniella.

"Who the hell knows?" Piniella said. "Who can figure that guy?"

"But it is, isn't it?"

"It sure as hell is."

As Piniella tells the story, the pair had a few more drinks. They knew Steinbrenner was on the trip with the team, and Munson suggested they go up to the owner's room and talk about the team. Piniella didn't want to go.

"Lou, George likes you," Munson said. "If you come with me, he'll listen. We can help the ball club. Everyone is pissed off. Let's go talk to George."

They had another drink. It was nearly midnight.

"Now, we were getting some courage," Piniella said years later, laughing. "So we got George's room number from Killer Kane and went up there. We knocked on the door and George came to the door in silk pajamas. He put on a bathrobe and he sat down and listened.

"We both wanted Reggie to bat fourth."

George had always requested that his hotel suite have a fully stocked bar — George enjoyed a drink back then, too; he just rarely did so in public. They made drinks and George went to a blackboard — another thing he always requested for his suite.

George was writing names on the blackboard: Rivers, Randolph, Piniella, Jackson . . .

The players said they would back the move if George stayed off Billy's back and if George talked to Reggie about keeping his mouth shut. He would get to bat fourth, but he had to end the public feud. Piniella and Munson volunteered to help George convince Billy of the wisdom of the move, too.

It was now almost 2:00 a.m., and the occupant of the suite next to George's had come back from his German dinner, which included a few post-meal brandies.

Billy heard familiar voices through the Pfister walls and was soon pounding his fist on the door to George's suite.

"I know you're in there plotting against me, goddamn it," Billy shouted.

George hustled Piniella and Munson into his bathroom.

"Be quiet, there might be trouble," George told the players.

Then he let Billy into the room.

"Take your job and shove it, George," Billy said.

"Billy, just calm down."

"Who's in here, George? Where are they?"

"I don't know what you're talking about, Billy."

But Billy stormed toward the bathroom and flung open the door.

"Two traitors," Billy screamed.

Piniella and Munson were two of Billy's favorites on the team.

"Come on, Billy, we're just trying to help," Munson said.

"I don't need any of your goddamn help," Billy said, before walking toward the suite's sitting area and sinking down into one of George's couches.

Piniella and Munson sat on either side of him. They started talking about the team and why Reggie should bat fourth. The conversation went on for more than an hour with Billy insisting he wouldn't be told what to do.

"What's wrong with at least trying Reggie at fourth?" Piniella asked. "We need to do something. We're the best team in baseball and we're not playing like it."

The group talked about the other provisos discussed — no more tampering from George (the first of dozens of times that would be promised) and getting Reggie to muzzle himself.

In a soft voice, Billy said he would bat Reggie fourth if that's what everybody wanted. The quartet shook hands and went to bed. The next day, George told the writers that he was stepping into the background and declared that Billy was the manager for the rest of the year no matter the team's record.

It sounded like big news, except virtually no one in New York read about it. On the night of July 13, while the Yankees were losing to Milwaukee, two lightning strikes at upstate New York generator substations caused a blockage of the electricity being transmitted to New York City. A series of missteps and bad luck, coupled with a stifling heat wave, taxed the city's electrical grid beyond capacity, and just after 9:30 p.m., the five boroughs of New York went dark.

A menacing mood enveloped New York in the blackout, especially in its poorest neighborhoods. Looting and vandalism were widespread, and thirty-five blocks in Brooklyn were soon on fire. Hundreds of cars were stolen from car dealers and stores gutted of their goods. More than 550 police officers would be injured, about 4,500 people arrested, and nearly 1,600 stores damaged.

By the time the electricity was restored the next night, even the Brooks Brothers store on Manhattan's posh Madison Avenue had been looted.

The Yankees heard the news in Milwaukee. Since few of them lived in New York, their families were safe (there was power in New Jersey). But the players were shaken nonetheless.

"I remember thinking, 'What else is going to happen during this season?'" said Roy White.

Despite the late-night, or early-morning, covenant in George's suite, Billy did not bat Reggie fourth the next day. Or the day after that. Or the week after that. Billy's obstinacy held sway. Reggie occasionally batted fourth, but only for one day, then he was back to fifth or sixth. In a bar in Seattle on August 7, Piniella and Munson cornered Billy and asked, "What about our deal?" The Yankees were five games behind Boston.

Three days later, on August 10, Reggie batted fourth. In his first at-bat as the new cleanup hitter, Reggie drove in a run off Vida Blue. The Yankees won at home, 6–3, the first of four successive victories. Reggie remained the cleanup hitter for the rest of the season.

At roughly the same time the game was ending on August 10, about ten miles due north of Yankee Stadium, police were waiting outside the apartment building at 35 Pine Street in Yonkers, New York. When a pudgy postal clerk named David Berkowitz got into his car, Detective John Falotico approached, wary of what Berkowitz had in a brown paper bag.

"You got me," Berkowitz said when Falotico pulled his gun and placed it at Berkowitz's temple.

"Who are you?"

"You know me."

"I don't; you tell me."

"I'm the Son of Sam."

Berkowitz's .44 caliber Charter Arms handgun was in the paper bag.

Later that night, as Berkowitz was in a Bronx station house confessing to the shooting of thirteen people, Reggie was holding court at his locker.

"I'm just more comfortable in that part of the batting order," Reggie said. "It lets me be me."

There was no arguing with the statistics that would follow.

Reggie would get hits in 7 of his next 14 at-bats, with 7 RBIs and 2 home runs. Reggie drove in 20 runs in the next 23 games, when the Yankees were victorious 19 times.

Billy approached Reggie after one of his better games that August — and after another Yankees victory — and said he wanted to reward Reggie with something, some gesture.

"Fly in some crabs from Baltimore for the postgame meal tomorrow," Reggie said.

Billy obliged, a feast the team devoured after the Yankees victory the next night.

Reggie hit over .300 the rest of the season, driving in nearly 45 runs.

It was still a close race, but the Yankees had the pitching advantage with a nice mix of seasoned pitchers like Catfish Hunter, who would finish with a 13-5 record and a 2.17 ERA, and the energy of youthful contributors like Guidry, who in his first full season with the team had a 16-7 record with a 2.82 ERA.

Overseeing the pitching staff was Fowler, Billy's former player with the minor league Denver Bears in 1968.

"Fowler was perfect for that team because he just made everyone laugh," Guidry said. "Art would come to the mound when you were in trouble and you'd be waiting for some advice on how he was going to solve the situation, and instead Art would just drawl, 'I don't know what's going on out here but you're making Billy awfully pissed off. So whatever you're doing I suggest you cut it out.'

"And then he'd walk away. But, you know, you would start laughing and relax and make some good pitches."

Guidry said Fowler, oft depicted as a boob who served as Billy's drinking aide-de-camp, was not the fool some thought he was.

"He had a lot of pitching knowledge; he just used it at odd times and it was very subtle," Guidry said. "He gave me the best pitching advice I ever got. He said you have to throw strikes because big-league hitters don't swing at balls. Just don't make it a strike they can hit.

"And if you think about it, that is the key to pitching. Throw the ball for a strike or what looks like a strike, but throw it in a way that they can't hit it."

Billy was notoriously hard on rookie pitchers and that included Guidry.

"Oh, he was brutal to me at first," Guidry said. "I'd walk someone and he'd be yelling from the dugout, 'You call yourself a pitcher? Pitcher, my ass. You're a candy ass. Throw the ball over the plate, you pussy.'

"I was pretty intimidated by him at first and I thought he hated me."

In fact, George Steinbrenner routinely wanted to trade Guidry. Billy stood up for his young, rail-thin left-hander. And Guidry said Billy's haranguing taught him how to win.

"All of us were much more afraid of letting him down than we were of our opponents," Guidry said. "And because of his intensity, I started to find the toughness in me to make good, daring pitches in tough situations. I got better and better and then at one point I knew it was my time to stand up to Billy."

With Guidry on the mound in 1977 and the Yankees clinging to a one-run, ninth-inning lead in an early-September game in Boston, Billy approached the mound with runners on first and second base. Lyle was warming up in the bullpen.

"As Billy got next to me I told him, 'The best thing for you to do is walk away,'" Guidry said. "I said, 'Get off my mound and go back in the dugout so I can finish this game.'

"He smiled, turned, and walked away. I got out of the jam. He never bothered me again. He knew his job was done. He was a master psychologist on top of all the other things that have been said about him."

Everything was coming together for the Yankees.

Leadoff hitter Mickey Rivers won the game with Cleveland on September 9 with a drag bunt — the very bunting tactic Billy had encouraged him to try back in spring training (when Rivers angrily refused).

Piniella recalled another Billy moment from the final weeks of the 1977 season. By late September, the Yankees had a 3.5-game lead on Boston and Baltimore with roughly 8 games remaining.

"We were playing in Baltimore and it was that time in the season when every win mattered," Piniella said. "So we were leading 5–2, and it starts raining in the top of the fifth. I'm in the on-deck circle and Billy calls me over and says, 'Lou, I want you to strike out. Swing and miss three pitches; I don't care where they are.'

"I thought he was crazy but I did what he said. So did Chambliss after me. Quickly, the inning was over. Then the Orioles went down in order in the bottom of the fifth. Between innings, it started to really rain, like a pouring rain — a deluge. We never played the sixth inning; the game ended up being called. We won, 5–2. I don't know how he knew it was going to start pouring rain and that we had to get the top of the fifth inning over with quickly, but that was his plan and it worked."

The Yankees finished the season with a 100-62 record, 2.5 games ahead of Boston and Baltimore, who each won 97 games but went home for the winter because there were no wild card teams in the 1970s.

It was the fourth time one of Billy's teams had won a division title. After the final game, fans were lining up outside the River Avenue gates at Yankee Stadium for $1.50 bleacher seats for the upcoming playoff series with Kansas City.

Inside the stadium, seated beneath a portrait photograph of Casey Stengel, Billy sat smoking a pipe. On a shelf behind his desk were two Civil War books. Billy turned philosophical.

"I might have been almost fired three or four times this year," he said. "But who cares? We're here now. But we're only one third of the way. Part two is with Kansas City and then part three is the World Series. When you're a Yankee, you're always looking at the big picture.

"The Yankees haven't won a World Series since 1962. That's too long."

Billy donned a beige cashmere sweater and light blue pants and drove over the George Washington Bridge to New Jersey.

"He had me meet him at the Bottom of the Barrel," Eddie Sapir said. "And we're sitting at the bar there for a while and he says to me, 'Judge, I have to get these guys a World Series championship. There aren't any excuses left. I've got to win one as Yankees manager or what's all this been worth? What's it mean?'

"And I said, 'Ah, come on, Billy, you've done so much.' But he wouldn't hear it. He said, 'If we don't win now, then what's all this worth? What have I been doing? I'll have failed.'"

31

GRUDGE MATCHES ARE RARE and often overstated. When it came to the Yankees and Royals of the late 1970s and early 1980s, there was no need to exaggerate. The hostility between the teams was outward and palpable.

In the second game of the 1977 American League Championship Series, Kansas City's Hal McRae executed a football-style rolling body block while breaking up a double play. In today's game, McRae's collision with second baseman Willie Randolph — the 190-pound McRae catapulted over the base at about waist high, knocking Randolph into the outfield grass — would have drawn a multigame suspension. In 1977, it was just one of many hard knocks in the series. McRae got up, dusted off his uniform, and jogged off the field. The teams played on.

McRae's takedown did seem to awaken the Yankees, who had lost the opening game of the series. They scored three runs in their half of the inning after Randolph was bulldozed and went on to win, 6–2, tying the best-of-five series as it switched from New York to Kansas City.

"Maybe I'm playing in the wrong era but there's more of that to come," said McRae, an outfielder and designated hitter.

Through tightly pursed lips, Billy had a message for McRae.

"You tell him that the Royals have a second baseman they like, too," Billy said. "His name is Frank White and he'll have to catch a double-play ball at second base one of these games."

Kansas City's Dennis Leonard pitched a complete-game four-hitter to dominate the Yankees in a 6–2 victory in Game 3 of the series. Baseball fans throughout the Midwest were thrilled by the prospect that the Yankees could be eliminated at Royals Stadium in Game 4.

"Everyone is rooting for us," said Royals manager Whitey Herzog, whom Billy had replaced as Texas manager four years earlier. "Nobody likes the Yankees."

Told of Herzog's comment, Billy said, "He ought to keep his mouth shut or somebody will shut it for him."

Herzog's response?

"I'm ready when he is," he said. "Let me know where."

In the first inning of the third game, Mickey Rivers doubled and Graig Nettles singled. With runners at first and third base, Munson hit a ground ball to Brett at third base. When Brett threw to second base trying to start a double play, Nettles crashed into White, the Royals' second baseman. Nettles did not so much as attempt to slide; he hit White shoulder to shoulder, throwing an elbow as both players somersaulted toward the outfield grass.

Nettles was out — an hour later he left the game because he felt dizzy from the collision — but Rivers scored on the play.

Gura was the Kansas City pitcher, and Billy had been goading him since the day before.

"I'm so anxious to face Gura I might send a bodyguard to his house tomorrow to make sure he gets to the ballpark safely," Billy told reporters. "I don't want him getting in an accident. I need him on the mound for Game 4."

During the game, as he had done the year before, Billy was mercilessly riding Gura. By the second inning, it was 4–0 Yankees.

"I don't know what Gura was doing out there," Herzog said afterward. "He was throwing all fastballs and sliders. He wins when he uses his change and curve."

Of course, Billy would howl every time Gura threw a breaking pitch.

"Candy ass! You're afraid to throw us a fastball!" Billy's high-pitched voice would bellow from the dugout. "We're going to wait for the goddamned fastball, Larry."

As much as the Yankees pounded on Gura, Yankees starter Ed Figueroa was also struggling. In the fourth inning, the Yankees were leading 5–4 when the Royals put runners on first and third base with two outs and Brett coming to the plate.

In a move that was so unorthodox it seemed absurd at the time, Billy brought his closer, Sparky Lyle, to the mound to face Brett. As Billy later explained, if the Royals took the lead, the Yankees might never have recovered and would have been eliminated from the series.

"Why save your closer for some other moment when that could be the do-or-die moment that decides a do-or-die game?" Billy reasoned.

Lyle got Brett to fly out to left field, then pitched five more scoreless innings, a rare achievement for a closer.

The Yankees victory set up another climactic Game 5. Except this time the final game was in Kansas City. And worse for Billy's team, the Royals were starting Paul Splittorff, a tall, cunning left-hander who bedeviled the Yankees' left-handed bats, especially Reggie, who was 1-for-14 in the series and did not have an RBI.

Throughout the night after Game 4 and on through the next day Billy consulted with his coaches about whether to play Reggie in right field or replace him with the right-handed-hitting Paul Blair. Reggie had also been having his problems in right field on Kansas City's hard, bouncy artificial turf field.

During the afternoon before the game, Billy went to see George Steinbrenner to inform him he might bench Reggie. George, who had given Reggie millions of dollars principally for his postseason prowess, was incredulous.

Billy and George took a walk through Kansas City's Crown Center Hotel lobby. They were going to get coffee. Billy explained that all of his coaches thought Reggie should sit, too. They had seen Reggie struggle mightily against Splittorff, who had been in the American League since 1970 and used his long arms and six-foot-three frame to flummox left-handed power hitters. He had also handily defeated the Yankees in Game 1 of the series. Reggie was 2-for-15 against Splittorff in 1977.

Billy and George happened to pass Catfish Hunter as they walked through the lobby.

"Hey, Cat," Billy said. "Can Reggie hit Splittorff?"

"Not with a fucking paddle," Hunter responded and kept walking.

George later gave his grudging consent, adding, "It's your call as the manager and you'll get the credit if we win. But if we lose, you get the blame."

Eddie Sapir said Billy and he then went to a Catholic church four blocks from the hotel.

"Billy went in and prayed," Sapir said. "He was very quiet. We were there for maybe twenty minutes. Just me and him in a pew in an empty church."

Once Billy got to the ballpark, he called Healy into his office. He wanted Healy to tell Reggie he wasn't starting.

"I'm not telling him, you're the manager, you tell him," Healy said.

"If I tell him, things might get ugly and that doesn't help the team," Billy said.

"Why don't you have one of the coaches tell him?" Healy asked.

"They won't do it," Billy said.

Healy said he was refusing as well. Billy implored his backup catcher, the quiet New Englander whom everyone now called "Kissinger."

"I know this is a rotten thing to have you do but you have the best chance of telling him and calming him down, too," Billy said. "If things go our way, I'm going to need Reggie later in the game. We need to keep him in a good frame of mind so he can help us win.

"And tell him that if he does this without making a scene and we win, I'll praise him to everyone and make it up to him during the World Series."

Healy reluctantly delivered the news. Reggie was predictably upset. He wanted to confront Billy, to ask him why he was humiliating him on national TV — again.

Healy kept Reggie at his locker. He also gave him all of Billy's message and convinced Reggie that it was in his best interest and the team's best interest to stay ready, that he might be needed later in the game. Healy made one other pivotal suggestion: Look like you're into the game and ready to play for the TV cameras during the game. Cheer for the team on the bench. In other words, don't sulk.

Reggie understood that concept.

Although, in *Becoming Mr. October,* Reggie wrote he only pretended to be cheering for the Yankees because "he was a broken man."

Regardless of Reggie's state of mind, he was witness to a good game. In the first inning, Brett tripled off Guidry to drive in McRae. Brett slid hard at third base at the end of the play, his momentum propelling him into Nettles, whom he also shoved with a forearm to the chest. Nettles responded by kicking Brett in the ribs as he lay on the ground. Brett jumped up and threw a right-hand punch that grazed the top of Nettles's head and knocked off his cap.

Nettles turned and jammed his right hand to Brett's face and slammed the Royals' third baseman back to the ground. The benches emptied, but no one seemed to want to get thrown out of the pennant-deciding game. It was mostly wrestling. Billy watched the tussle with a bemused grin. He stood apart and ended up with his left arm draped affectionately over the Royals' diminutive shortstop, Freddie Patek, as if they were at a barbecue watching the grill heat up.

In another sign of the times, no one was ejected. Splittorff and the Royals took a 3–1 lead into the eighth inning. When Randolph laced a leadoff single, Herzog replaced Splittorff with Doug Bird.

"We will always be grateful," Billy said, who accused Herzog of overmanaging the moment.

It opened the door for Reggie to pinch-hit, and he came to the plate with runners at first and third base after Piniella singled.

Reggie wrote that he was "kind of stuck between 'Should I give it my all? Or should I just say to Martin: Dude, you think I stink? Let me just stand there. Take three strikes and go back to the dugout.'"

But Reggie was no quitter. Like Billy, he had many layers to his motivations, but giving up rarely crossed his mind. And, besides, in Reggie's words, it would only make him as big a fool as Billy.

Reggie instead turned on a Bird fastball and smacked a crisp liner to center field that cut the Royals' lead in half. In the Yankees' ninth inning, Blair rewarded Billy's faith in him with a single, then Roy White drew a pinch-hit walk. Rivers's single tied the game.

With White at third base and one out, Randolph's deep fly ball to center field put the Yankees ahead. Another run scored on an error by Brett, his second of the game.

It was the final indignity for the Royals, who for a second year would fall short, undone by defensive lapses and a lack of clutch late-game pitching.

Lyle gave up a one-out single in the Royals' ninth, but Patek rapped a ground ball to Nettles, who relayed to Randolph, who stood in at second base to smoothly and calmly turn a game-ending double play in the Yankees' 5–3 victory.

Midwest baseball fans went silent. All that could be heard was thirty Yankees players and coaches celebrating on the Royals Stadium diamond. In the clubhouse afterward, Blair was still out of breath and gasping for air as he met with reporters.

"That was the most pressure I ever had on me because Billy gave me a chance and I didn't want to let him down," he said. "That took a lot of guts from Billy to start me and keep me in there. He probably gets fired if I make an out and we lose."

Champagne was flowing in the Yankees' clubhouse.

"My new suit," George Steinbrenner bayed as he was doused with a bottle of the bubbly.

Billy came by and poured more champagne on George.

"That's for almost firing me," he said.

"What do you mean almost?" George shot back.

Billy headed to his office where he immediately began praising Reggie.

"He really showed me some kind of class," Billy said. "A lot of other people would go off and sulk but he was just terrific about it. A real man."

Reggie entered Billy's office with a magnum of champagne in his hand.

"Want some?" Reggie asked.

"I will if you will," Billy said.

And Reggie sat beside Billy on a couch in the office. They toasted each other.

"I love you, big guy," Billy said. "You did great tonight."

Reggie smiled and put his arm around Billy as a flock of photographers snapped the picture, the flashbulbs of their cameras bathing the scene in a hypnotic, surreal off-and-on brilliance.

On the Yankees' charter flight back to Newark airport Sunday night from Kansas City, Billy sat in an aisle seat in the first row of first class — the manager's seat of honor on all flights and bus rides. He held a relatively new invention in his lap, a Sony Walkman, which was playing a country music tape.

George Steinbrenner was in the first row of coach, wearing another new suit.

Many players were asleep, their heads resting on their wives' shoulders. In some cases, it was vice versa with the wife exhausted from the series while the husband remained wired from the excitement of winning another pennant.

In the last row of coach, staring forward and sitting alone, was Reggie.

When the plane landed in Newark early Monday morning, some of the five thousand fans who came out to the airport broke through police barricades and charged toward the players and wives. The overwhelmed airport authorities had been expecting about three or four hundred people.

According to the *New York Times* story about the scene, George Steinbrenner was gleeful about the crowd reaction. The article recounted this interaction:

"Can you believe this?" Steinbrenner remarked.

A fan who overheard this said: "We believe it. But keep Billy, George."

This touched off a chant among the fans for Billy Martin.

"We want Billy, we want Billy," they shouted.

Billy emerged from the jet after the players and received the loudest ovation from the attending crowd.

"It was that way all year," Morabito, the team publicist, said. "Billy was always our most popular player. Except he wasn't a player."

The crowd pushed toward Billy on the tarmac, mobbing him as if he were one of the Beatles. A pocket from his pants was ripped off as was a gold chain around his neck. Police freed him from the crush, but a shoulder bag with papers and other personal effects was never recovered. Not one Yankee needed his own security detail to get to the team bus.

Outside Yankee Stadium, an overflow gathering started lining up for World Series tickets minutes after Patek grounded into his double play. It wasn't just another World Series, it was a Yankees-Dodgers World Series. From 1941 to 1963, the Yankees and Brooklyn Dodgers played eight times in the World Series. No two teams have ever met as often.

Billy had already called Dodgers manager Tommy Lasorda, his old rival from the 1950s and now one of his best friends. As historic as the upcoming series might be, there was none of the animosity that marked the Royals series.

The only apparent dynamic was that the Dodgers were this happy collective — "We all bleed Dodger blue," Lasorda said — while the Yankees were as close as the Hatfields and the McCoys. Piniella said he worried that the Dodgers might hug themselves to death.

The first game at Yankee Stadium, played two days after the ALCS finale, was tied 3–3 after nine innings. Billy turned to Sparky Lyle for the extra innings while Lasorda used four relievers. Keeping his word, Billy started Reggie but that did not mean he would play nine innings.

As he had for most of the second half of the season, Billy replaced Reggie with Blair, an eight-time Gold Glove winner, late in the game for defensive reasons. In the twelfth inning, Randolph led off with a double, and Munson was intentionally walked so the Dodgers right-hander Rick Rhoden could pitch to the right-handed Blair.

Blair, who had beaten Billy's Minnesota Twins in the playoffs with a clutch extra-inning bunt eight years earlier, slapped a ground single through the left side of the infield to score Randolph. The Yankees won, 4–3.

In the second game, Hunter took the mound, even though he had pitched rarely in the second half of the season because of a shoulder strain that would eventually bring a premature end to his career. The Dodgers teed off on Hunter's subpar pitching, swatting four home runs in a 6–1 rout.

The series was tied 1-1, the most common outcome after two World Series games. But there was nothing usual about the 1977 Yankees. Things had been calm around the team for nearly three days. That was way too long.

After the game, Reggie wasn't happy for two reasons: he thought Billy had unfairly asked Hunter to pitch when he was hurt, and he was convinced he would be benched in the third game of the series against the Dodgers' left-handed starter Tommy John.

"I'm not swinging well and you know what happens then," said Reggie, who had one hit in his six World Series at-bats.

When Reggie's remarks were relayed to Billy, he said, "I'm not taking Reggie out. Reggie's in there. Splittorff isn't pitching for them."

Back the writers went to Reggie with Billy's comments. The Splittorff reference incensed Reggie, who was packing his bag for Los Angeles, where the next three games would be played.

"I don't need to take that from nobody, especially from him," Reggie snarled. "I know what I can do. If he did, we might be a lot better off."

That was enough for one day for the New York writers. They had stories to write and a plane to catch themselves. They hustled to the press box knowing their stories would surely prompt a rejoinder from Billy.

That would be tomorrow's story.

And it was.

When the Yankees arrived at Dodger Stadium for their afternoon workout during an off day in the World Series, Billy had read the newspapers.

"Why do we have to have all this kind of talk — this shit — now when we're trying to win the World Series?" Billy asked, angrily flinging his Yankees cap on the visiting manager's desk.

The room was filled with reporters, an hour before the Yankees' 3:00 p.m. workout.

"I told Reggie after the Kansas City series that he would play every game in the World Series," Billy said. "Where's his memory. What happened to that 180 IQ?"

As for Reggie second-guessing him about starting the ailing Hunter, which most viewed as a strategic ploy to rest Guidry and the rest of an overworked pitching staff, Billy snickered.

"Reggie is having enough trouble playing right field," he said. "I don't think he has time to manage the team, too. He should leave that to me."

As Billy railed, Reggie was in a taxi to Dodger Stadium. The cabdriver, who was obviously not a big baseball fan, asked Reggie if he was a Dodger or a Yankee. When Reggie said he was a Yankee, the driver said, "I hope you win for Billy."

Reggie laughed and shook his head.

"Everywhere I go," he said.

Meanwhile, Munson was holding a press conference before the workout at Dodger Stadium. He was asked about yet another round of quarreling between Billy and Reggie.

"It's just an overheated argument," Munson said. "Reggie's been struggling and he'd like to be doing better. Billy just doesn't realize that Reggie is Mr. October."

It was the first time that anyone had called Reggie Mr. October.

Billy and Reggie coexisted on the field during the Yankees' workout without incident or much interaction. When the session was over and they retreated to the visitors' clubhouse, Billy was asked about Reggie again.

"I'm done with that," he said.

There was a ruckus in the clubhouse. Piniella was complaining that the tickets given to the Yankees families attending the three games in Los Angeles were lousy seats.

"Way up in the upper deck," Piniella was yelling loudly. "I bet we didn't do that to them. Total bullshit."

Billy heard Piniella's protest and stuck his head out of his office.

"Say something crazy, Lou," Billy said. "Take the heat off Reggie and me."

Then Billy went to shower and shave. He and Gretchen had a dinner date with Frank Sinatra.

Billy Joe Martin does not recall where his father and mother had dinner with Sinatra, who was accompanied by several friends including Lasorda. Gretchen does not remember either. What Billy Joe does recall is that he was not invited and that pleased him greatly. He would instead stay in the Yankees' Los Angeles hotel and hang out with the children of the players. They would have the run of the hotel, order room service meals, and play in the pool.

But first it was Billy Joe's job to escort his mother and father through the hotel lobby so they could find the limo that would take them to dinner.

"My dad said to me, 'Listen, pard, I need you to run interference in the lobby,'" Billy Joe said. "He told me to keep moving, that a teenager could be pushy in a crowd even if he couldn't."

Gretchen recalled those instructions, too. Sitting next to her son many years later, she said, "You failed."

The hotel lobby of the Los Angeles Hilton was packed with dignitaries, fans, families, Hollywood moguls, actors, actresses, directors, baseball executives, reporters, and others eager to catch a glimpse of the famed Yankees.

Into this atmosphere Billy and Gretchen emerged, trying to get from the guarded hotel elevators to the opposite side of the lobby where their limo awaited.

"I had my dad's arm and he had my mom's arm and I was trying to drag him through the crowd but it was impossible," Billy Joe said. "Every two steps, someone would stop him. My dad wouldn't refuse people. That was one of his things. He wouldn't brush people off or tell them, 'Not now.'"

Said Gretchen, "It took forty-five minutes to an hour for us to get through the lobby. When we finally got to the restaurant, Frank himself came out to meet us and said, 'What happened? We were so worried.'

"We were seated like the guests of honor, right next to Frank and his wife. It was a long table of about twenty people. Lasorda was in the middle telling old baseball stories. Tommy would start the story and Billy would finish it. We were there for hours with everyone eating, drinking, and laughing.

"I kept thinking that these two men were going to be managing against each other in the World Series in less than twenty-four hours. But boy, they were having a good time first."

Billy and Lasorda were like best friends, two baseball lifers from meager means.

"We knew we were two lucky SOBs but we also knew we had worked like dogs for everything we got," Lasorda said in a 2012 interview. Lasorda put in twenty-two seasons as a minor league player and manager before getting his chance to manage in the big leagues in 1976. "We could share that, and one other thing, if Billy Martin was your friend, he was the best friend you ever had."

Lasorda recalled an off-season visit to Minneapolis in the late 1960s when Billy was the Twins' third-base coach. Lasorda was the Dodgers' manager in Ogden, Utah, a rookie-league team.

"I called ahead and told him I was coming to Minnesota for a couple days," Lasorda said. "I was visiting some college player they wanted me to talk to. Billy met me up at the airport and we took a cab to my hotel. I asked him why he didn't drive his car and he said a cab was easier, which I thought was odd.

"But I check in and we go to my room and I unpack a little. We're talking and catching up. Then we went down and had a drink in the lobby and we're sitting there and I saw that Billy had this bracelet on his wrist, like the kind they give you when you're in the hospital.

"I said, 'Billy, what's that?' And he said, 'Oh, yeah, I'm in the hospital, I had hernia surgery the other day.'

"I was shocked. I said, 'Are you crazy?' And he said, 'Relax, I'll go back in a couple of hours. I wasn't going to let you come here and have you hang out by yourself.' I said I could have met him at the hospital and he said he didn't want to worry me.

"He just waved his hand at me and said, 'What fun would that have been?' But he did look kind of pale so I made him finish his drink and go back to the hospital early."

The morning after Billy, Lasorda, and Ol' Blue Eyes broke bread, there was another meeting of Billy, Reggie, and Gabe Paul, this time in Billy's Hilton hotel suite. More smoothing over. Paul hosted reporters in his room afterward, about six hours before the third game of the World Series.

"Another chapter in the tumultuous life of the 1977 Yankees," Paul said with a laugh. "And I don't mind the controversies. Controversial ballplayers are many times better ballplayers because they are not afraid of the consequences.

"Besides, so far, some of the unhappiest players on our team have played the best ball. We judge players by what they do on the field. If we want all nice boys, we'd go to church and collect them."

At Dodger Stadium several hours later, Reggie said, "Everything's resolved."

The game began with a moment of silence for Bing Crosby, who had died that afternoon when he collapsed of a heart attack on the eighteenth green of a golf course in Spain. The former Brooklyn Dodgers catcher

Roy Campanella, now in a wheelchair following a near-fatal 1958 auto accident, threw out the ceremonial first pitch.

Then Rivers lined his first hit of the series, which was followed by RBI singles by Munson, Reggie, and Piniella — the three players doing the most grumbling in the days before the game. Billy was first to greet Reggie on the top step of the dugout as he scored. The Yankees parlayed their 3–0 first-inning lead to a 5–3 victory.

The next day, Reggie doubled and hit a long home run, and Ron Guidry, the Yankees' lowest-paid player with a salary of $30,000, pitched a complete-game four-hitter. The 4–2 Yankees victory, preserved when Piniella climbed a fence and denied Ron Cey of a game-tying home run, gave the Yankees a 3–1 lead in the series.

How did the Yankees overcome three days, if not months, of turmoil to win so convincingly?

"You should probably give Billy Martin the Nobel Peace Prize for managing this damn, crazy team," Reggie said.

"I accept," Billy said when informed of Reggie's nomination. "With deep humility, I accept and thank you very much."

Asked what he would nominate Reggie for, Billy smiled, then said, "The good guy award."

The national television cameras were watching Reggie and Billy in the dugout on this day, just as they had been in Fenway Park four months earlier. This time the scene was nearly as stunning: the two embraced in a lengthy hug with each man whispering something in the other's ear.

"He told me, 'helluva job,' and I thanked him for letting me get one more at-bat," said Reggie, acknowledging that Billy had not replaced him for defensive purposes in the ninth inning.

Lasorda had a pep talk with his team before Game 5, telling them they were the best team in the world and he wouldn't trade them for any other team. The Dodgers then roughed up the Yankees' starter, Don Gullett, in a 10–4 victory that sent the series back to New York for a sixth game.

On the eve of the sixth game at Yankee Stadium, George Steinbrenner sat for a two-hour interview with the *New York Times.*

"Modern athletics is entertainment and we've proven that," George said.

He added, "Billy Martin could never have made it this far without me and I couldn't have made it this far without Billy."

Two stories below Steinbrenner's office, at the field level during the off day between the fifth and sixth games of the series, Billy welcomed a visitor: twenty-year-old Robert Violante of Brooklyn, a Yankees fan who had lost his left eye in the final Son of Sam gun attack. Billy and Violante talked and Billy gave Violante some autographed balls and pictures. He asked for Violante's Brooklyn address because he said he wanted to keep in touch.

Billy then returned to New Jersey, where he spent most of his time before the sixth game trying to avoid talk of a victory party in a ballroom at the Sheraton Hasbrouck Heights.

But a party was being planned, as much as Billy avoided all talk about it.

"I had to take my phone calls in the lobby about anything that wasn't directly related to the sixth game," Gretchen said. "The pressure at that point was enormous. The Yankees simply couldn't come home and lose the World Series. There was talk in the newspapers that Billy was going to be fired immediately if they lost the series.

"Billy heard it all. You could see in his eyes the pressure he was feeling."

The Yankees had not won a World Series in a generation. Billy, now forty-nine years old, had not won one in twenty-one years.

Around noon on the day of the sixth game of the series, Billy got a call from Gabe Paul, who wanted to see him in his office at 1:30. Billy feared it was another strategy session with George. Instead, the Yankees were extending his contract, giving him a bonus of $35,000, plus a new Lincoln Continental. They had also agreed to pay his $400-a-month rent at the Sheraton Hasbrouck Heights for as long as he was the Yankees manager.

The press was alerted immediately about the Yankees' gesture. Reggie was asked about it when he arrived at the ballpark.

"I saw Billy and congratulated him," Reggie said. "For the first time in a long time, he looked 49 instead of 99. I think it's great. And good timing."

Yankees fans knew of the new arrangement as well. When Billy brought out the Yankees' batting lineup to the umpires before the game, the stands overflowed with applause, which in many sections became a standing ovation. Standing next to him, Lasorda briefly clapped his hands as well.

The rest of the Dodgers were not in the mood to celebrate the Yankees and took a 2–0 lead in the first inning. Chambliss tied the game with a two-run homer after Reggie walked on four pitches. The Dodgers had regained the lead, 3–2, when Reggie came to the plate with a runner on in the fourth inning.

He laced the first pitch from Burt Hooton just over the railing in right field. Greeting him at the top step of the dugout after his homer was Billy. Billy patted Reggie on the cheek lovingly while vigorously shaking his hand. Piniella made it 5–3 Yankees with a sacrifice fly.

In the fifth inning, Reggie again hit the first pitch, this time from reliever Elías Sosa. It soared over the right-field wall, several seats deep in the grandstand. Another two-run homer and a 7–3 Yankees lead.

By the time Reggie came to the plate in the eighth inning — Billy said he never considered using Blair as a defensive replacement — the crowd of 56,407 was chanting, "Reg-gie, Reg-gie."

Throughout his career, Reggie loved to hit against knuckleball pitchers, and Lasorda had resorted to Charlie Hough, who would have a long career throwing mostly knuckleballs.

Reggie hit Hough's first delivery about 450 feet into the center-field bleachers, which were painted black because they were directly in the line of sight behind the pitcher's mound. The white ball bounded around in the black rows of wood as Reggie began circling the bases.

Babe Ruth had hit three home runs in one World Series game in 1926 and in 1928, but no one had hit three home runs on the first three pitches he had seen in one World Series game. Because he had hit a home run on the first pitch of his last at-bat of the fifth game, Reggie had hit four homers in his last four swings of the series — off four different pitchers.

The *New York Times* columnist Red Smith, who had covered Babe Ruth, wrote, "Not even that demigod smashed three in a row on three pitches, let alone four."

Reggie had five home runs in the series, another first.

As Reggie passed Steve Garvey at first base after the third homer, Garvey, only somewhat furtively, applauded inside his glove.

The celebration of the Yankees' 8–4 victory an inning later was replete with a surging crowd of thousands of fans who overwhelmed 350 police officers and tore up the Yankee Stadium field.

The teams quickly retreated to their clubhouses.

The television networks wanted interviews with Billy and Reggie, so they did one together with their arms around each other's shoulders. Each of them had a bottle of Taylor New York State champagne, from which they drank. Reggie laughed and patted Billy's chest.

"This man deserves the Congressional Medal of Honor, the Purple Heart, everything," he said.

Answered Billy, "This guy was sensational. One of the great World Series performances you'll ever see."

Billy was asked about whether he had imbued his team with a fighting spirit and Reggie nodded.

"Anybody fights you, skip," Reggie said, "he's got to fight both of us."

"And anybody who fights you," said Billy, grinning widely, "has got to fight the both of us."

They then went their separate ways, Billy to his office where he told reporters he was too drained to speak for too long.

"I'm going to have to calm down first — and that might take a while," he said. "I'm still uptight."

Billy summoned one of the front-office assistants to his office. He removed the Yankees number 1 jersey he was wearing and handed it over with a Brooklyn address.

"I want you to send this jersey to that Violante kid," said Billy, who wrote a note to go with the jersey that read, "My heart is with you."

Then Billy, the man who was often one of the last to leave the ballpark, scurried out the door, heading for an opulent party at a vast ballroom on the ground floor of the Sheraton Hasbrouck Heights.

Remaining in the clubhouse were a handful of Yankees, including Reggie and Munson. The two men hugged. Munson, who had been asking for a trade to Cleveland so he could be nearer to his family in Canton, Ohio, was heading to a party down the hall under the right-field stands.

Dave Anderson chronicled this remarkable exchange in the next day's *New York Times*:

"I'm going down to the party here in the ball park," Munson said. "Just white people but they'll let you in. Come on down."

Reggie laughed and said, "I'll be there. Wait for me."

But Reggie stood at his locker talking with reporters for 25 minutes and finally Munson returned.

"Hey, nigger, you're too slow, that party's over but I'll see you next year," Munson said.

"You'll be back," Reggie said.

"Not me, but you know who stuck up for you, nigger, you know who stuck up for you when you needed it."

"I know," Reggie said. "But you'll be here next year. We'll all be here."

Billy drove with Billy Joe and Gretchen to the New Jersey party. It was a mob scene with loud music, few players, and a diverse collection of fans and hangers-on who had been drinking since before the game started. The boozy crush of the packed room — Billy twice had a drink knocked from his hand — was overwhelming. Billy, usually the life of any party, was getting agitated.

"All the problems we had all year long had left me exhausted," Billy wrote years later. "The fighting to win the division title, fighting to win a pennant, fighting to win a World Series, the fight against an owner who doesn't respect you, all year long battling for players against him and he's telling the players just the opposite. It was all tearing me up and making me sick. It was a miracle I didn't have a stroke or a nervous breakdown."

There were other discomforting undercurrents to the party, specifically, the makeup of the guest list. Some of those pressing closest to Billy, who was the guest of honor, gave more than a hint of what Billy, his star bigger than ever, had become.

Gretchen Martin, standing in the Denver airport three years earlier, had foreseen the consequences of her husband taking the Yankees job. Now, somewhat unexpectedly given the utter triumph of the moment in her eighteen years as Billy's wife, Gretchen was coming face-to-face with her own premonition. In addition to the frenzy in the room, two or three women Billy had befriended during his years living in New Jersey — perhaps intimately befriended — were at the party and vying for at least some of Billy's attention on this night of great celebration.

Gretchen saw what was going on but did not tolerate it in this setting. Billy Joe was in the room, too.

Billy and Gretchen began quarreling, loudly and in front of other guests.

Billy had a drink in his hand and threw it to the ground, smashing the glass. He turned and stormed out of the party.

"They had a lot of fights but that was the final one that mattered," Billy Joe said. "That was it. That was *the* fight."

Years later, Gretchen, a baseball wife for decades, summarized her feelings in five words. What had she said to Billy?

"Play me or trade me."

Billy left the hotel ballroom for the Bottom of the Barrel.

"I sat there all by myself," he wrote of the moment. "I sat there and rested where no one could bother me."

32

THE YANKEES WERE FETED in a ticker-tape parade through lower Manhattan's Canyon of Heroes the day after their World Series victory. The team looked bushed, and not just because many of the players were hung-over.

"I am emotionally worn out from the season — not from playing the game but from all the questions about our internal problems," Piniella said in an impromptu news conference. "If things don't change from how they were this year, we'll be a good fourth-place club next year and that's it."

Nearby, Chambliss was asked if a championship would settle the Yankees. Wouldn't the 1978 Yankees be calmer, less rebellious?

"I really doubt that," he said.

There were issues throughout the roster. Munson wanted to be traded to Cleveland and kept saying so. Mickey Rivers said he wanted to go home to California (and he wanted another raise). Figueroa still felt snubbed about not getting the sixth-game start in the World Series. Mike Torrez, who had won two World Series games and the series clincher, was a free agent on his way to Boston. Nettles wanted a new contract.

"Give them a month off to enjoy their World Series win and they'll all feel differently," said Billy, who was in a noticeably better mood at the parade than he had been the night before.

The Yankees did take a month, or two, off after the parade. Billy went hunting in the Dakotas and Northern California. He made his familiar stops in Berkeley and Texas, although New Jersey remained the closest thing to home. Divorce proceedings between Billy and Gretchen had not yet begun, although each would contact lawyers within the year.

"They were upset about the divorce," Billy Joe said years later. "I thought they were both better off."

Billy was seen often in Manhattan that winter, a star of the dinner circuit and television talk shows. Madison Avenue was interested in using his face for advertisements, and he accepted almost every offer — and every check for it.

Generally speaking, he would not, however, pay income tax on those checks. He would just pocket them. His agent at the time, Doug Newton, who worked jointly with Eddie Sapir in a curious arrangement, worked hard to get Billy to understand the concept that state and federal taxes had to come out of every stream of income, but Billy never liked to consider the financial details of his life. So he kept cashing the checks without much thought.

This oversight, or recklessness, or deception, left him in debt to the Internal Revenue Service for most of the rest of his life. When he was paid only by a team, which took taxes out of his paycheck, there were no money problems. But after the 1977 championship, Billy's ancillary income ballooned.

"He was just terrible with money," said Sapir. "He'd never had any, and when he did get some, he just thought he should spread it around. I always said that when the Yankees were winning and Billy was managing, every maitre d', bartender, cabdriver, doorman, and cocktail waitress within twenty miles of Yankee Stadium went up an income bracket."

And so it was in the winter of 1977–78. Billy was also now moving in new circles. Like the Billy of the 1950s, he was rubbing elbows with the biggest TV personalities of the day. The cast members of *Saturday Night Live* — John Belushi, Dan Aykroyd, and Bill Murray — liked to drink with Billy. Who, after all, could show a couple of newcomers to New York a better time? They were a generation younger, but the Yankees were royalty again in Manhattan, and Billy loved the company of the young comedians, in part because they introduced him to twenty-something women.

It was during this winter that Billy first got involved with a relatively new product, Lite Beer from Miller. To convince Joe Six-Packs across the nation that they should be drinking a lesser caloric beer, Miller approached macho athletes as subjects in their humorous ads. Battlin' Billy Martin, fresh off a championship, fit the billing.

"Billy loved to perform," Sapir said.

Since the commercials also tended to feature an ensemble cast of athletes and comedians like Rodney Dangerfield, Billy not surprisingly became the ringleader — a quasi manager of the Lite Beer team.

Bob Giraldi, the maker of the commercials, considered Billy the straw boss of the group, a workingman's hero who bucked authority. He was also someone who could get men with credentials in line and lead them. Giraldi told author David Falkner in 1991:

> Here they are, these sports heroes, all banding together, drinking together, waking up together, having a great time, coming to the set in a bus . . . and Rodney only comes to the set in a limousine, he won't come to hang around. And Rodney, in the commercials, wonders why nobody likes him, you know? Billy would pick up on that and break his balls. I think Rodney was actually more petrified of Billy than he was of anybody. Billy was a genius, maybe that's why he was a good manager. But he was a genius at finding that vulnerability, that weakness of a person — that's what he obviously was able to do as a manager.

Giraldi left the commercials convinced that he wanted someday to make a movie of Billy's life.

Billy was the toast of the town again, and he did not need much encouragement when it came to the toasting that winter. Billy hired a driver, a tall, imposing former New York City cop named Carl P. "Tex" Gernand, who ferried him back and forth to New Jersey from his favorite Manhattan bars. He still visited Steve's Sizzling Steaks and the Bottom of the Barrel (though it would soon be unimaginatively renamed Jerry's Bar). But there were so many invitations to functions in the city, and Billy, shunned the winter before, was not sitting the party out.

Billy may have been onstage having a good time, but surreptitiously cracks were developing in the foundation of the championship platform upon which he was so happily cavorting.

In December, Gabe Paul announced he was going back to Cleveland to run the Indians. Paul decided that Steinbrenner's wrath was bad for his health.

Before he left, Paul talked Steinbrenner into signing the free agent reliever Rich "Goose" Gossage, who was twenty-six years old, instead of the thirty-one-year-old starter Mike Torrez.

It would prove to be a shrewd move for the Yankees in the long run, but heading into the 1978 season, it presented Billy with a significant headache. Sparky Lyle, the incumbent bullpen ace, did not want to share the closer's duties and neither did Gossage. And Billy, ever loyal, sided with

Lyle. He did not want Gossage, something the rest of the team, Gossage included, knew. Gossage, who ended up in the Baseball Hall of Fame, never forgave Billy for spurning him before he had thrown a pitch for the Yankees.

But Lyle was never again happy to be with the Yankees either. Gossage's arrival quickly ruined the happy, post–World Series buzz.

A crowded bullpen was not Billy's only problem. George had decided he should be more active in other ways. He wanted to restructure Billy's coaching staff, so he appointed Gene Michael, the former Yankees short-stop and then a valued Yankees scout, Billy's "administrative coach."

Billy immediately considered the tall and skinny Michael, who went by the nickname "Stick," George's in-house spy.

"Stick this," Billy said of the appointment.

Michael was just beginning his five-decade career in various roles for the Yankees and he was close to George.

"But I wasn't a spy," Michael said thirty-five years after his 1978 ap-pointment. "I know Billy hated me being there. But I was supposed to help implement some things and report to George on how they were go-ing. I know it wasn't a usual arrangement but I was not running back to George about things that were none of my business. I wasn't spying. I was trying to help Billy. Not that he believed me."

The Yankees' new president and general manager was Al Rosen, a Cleveland Indians third baseman in the mid-1950s and a sometime an-tagonist of Billy's. But Rosen approached his new job with a determina-tion to soothe the fractious relationship between the manager and owner, whom Rosen knew personally from his Cleveland roots.

Rosen, a former amateur boxer, was convinced he had the toughness to stand up to both Billy and George and to weather the storms of the tempestuous Yankees' state of affairs. Billy didn't mind Rosen's presence because George had promised Billy a new communication arrangement. Billy did not have to go through the general manager; he could talk di-rectly to George. It was just one of many misguided presumptions.

Reggie, for example, announced at the start of spring training that 1978 was going to be controversy free.

"This time, I won't get involved in all that stuff like I did last year," he said. "We're all over that."

He then said that playing for Billy had made him a better player.

"He makes you a more complete player because he demands that," Reggie said. "I've been working my butt off this spring to show him that I know I'm not too big to work on my defense and my bunting."

Reggie said he was not too big to work on his bunting. Store that thought.

Things were calm for a while. But a dose of bad karma descended on the Yankees' Fort Lauderdale camp. Dick Tidrow, expected to be a starter on a team short of starters, pulled a hamstring running out a bunt in an exhibition game. Don Gullett, perhaps the ace of the staff, developed a shoulder ache and stopped pitching (he would pitch only eight games that season and then retire). Randolph got hit in the face with an errant throw and sat out a month. His replacement, Fred Stanley, tore a thigh muscle on the same day. Andy Messersmith, another starter signed during the off-season, separated his shoulder and was declared unavailable for several months (he would end up pitching only six games and retiring in 1979).

The Yankees were losing most of their preseason games. Said Steinbrenner on March 18, "We're at the point where Billy better start buckling down on them or we won't repeat."

The first game of the regular season — the first game that counted — was still twenty days away.

Billy was ostensibly alone at spring training, which is to say that neither Gretchen nor Billy Joe spent much time there with him. That's not to say that Billy was lonely. He was soon to be fifty years old, and his tastes had not changed. He looked perhaps ten years younger than his age, and just as he did in the 1950s, he found plenty of women in their twenties who were still drawn to him.

Billy had reentered the realm reserved for the New York elite. He was a star in the biggest sports market in the world. The stable suburban family life Billy yearned for since childhood, and had lived in Minnesota, Detroit, and Texas, had disintegrated, never to be replicated. But Billy traveled in a new sphere now, and at a different, accelerated pace. A spotlight lit his path.

When he came to New York in 1950, he was identified in tabloid newspaper headlines as "Martin." Nearly three decades later, headline writers never used his last name; he was simply "Billy." It never led to any confusion. Alfred Manuel "Billy" Martin of Berkeley, California, was forevermore emblematic of New York and the Yankees. It was a representation so strong, Billy might as well have had the interlocking NY logo tattooed on his forehead.

The Yankees and Billy would be detached for years at a time but never separated. But first there was the matter of defending the Yankees' world title.

The Yankees' 1978 season started unevenly, but the mood remained calm in the clubhouse. For Billy, there was only one dustup, and it involved his old archrival Earl Weaver. Gossage had thrown a pitch over a Baltimore player's head in April, and Weaver had protested to the umpire who then warned Billy.

Billy did not mind being warned, but he was furious that the umpire, Joe Brinkman, appeared to issue the warning because it was Weaver's idea.

"I'm taking the lineup card out to home plate tomorrow afternoon and if that little midget of a manager says anything I'm decking him right there at home plate," Billy said.

Weaver always drove Billy crazy.

"That little shit never even played in the major leagues, what does he know about knockdown pitches?" Billy said. "Career minor leaguer. Go tell him to shut up."

Which the writers dutifully did. Responded Weaver, "I never played in the majors but I drove in 101 runs one season in the minors. I bet he never did that."

When the managers met at home plate the next day, Billy turned to Weaver and said, "Three-ninety-two."

"What's that?" Weaver said.

"That was my batting average in C ball in 1947," Billy said. "Did you ever hit .392? You want to talk about your 101 RBIs in the minors one year. I had 101 RBIs by July in 1947."

Weaver giggled.

"This is good," Weaver said. "And if we keep fighting, we'll have a big crowd in Baltimore when you come there next week. We need that."

Billy laughed and walked away.

But the month of May brought more uninspired play by the Yankees. On May 14, after Rivers lazily chased a fly ball that led to a crucial run in a defeat, Billy announced that he was going to bench Rivers for a while.

The mood around the team was foul. A benching of a star player puts everyone on edge. Making matters worse, the team was flying a commercial flight to Chicago after the game. More accustomed to convenient and sophisticated — and insulated — charter flights, the players weren't happy.

Then the flight was delayed, which gave the Yankees, Billy included, ninety extra minutes to drink in the airport bar (the drinking had started in the clubhouse). By the time the passengers boarded the flight, it was not a good combination in the cabin — semi-drunk, slightly ornery Yankees mixed in with midwestern men in business suits heading to Chicago.

Munson and Gossage, both well oiled from the bar, were in coach listening to country music on a portable tape deck that Munson held in his lap. The music was loud, and a man seated in front of Munson turned around and asked, "Would you mind lowering that a bit?"

As Moss Klein of the Newark *Star-Ledger* wrote later, Munson's retort was "Mind your own business, fuckface."

Word got back to Billy in first class that trouble was brewing back in coach with his players. He dispatched Elston Howard to talk to Munson about turning down the music.

"Who are you, the music coach?" Munson said to Howard when Billy's message was relayed.

Now Howard was mad at Billy and wanted him to reprimand Munson, which Billy tried to do. But Munson, usually one of Billy's best buddies, wasn't in the mood for peacemaking. A verbal row ensued, enough to get the rest of the passengers' attention. Rivers, playing cards in the back of the plane and annoyed in general, decided to take Munson's side of things and threw a deck of cards at Billy.

Coaches Dick Howser and Yogi Berra managed to keep the major combatants separated. The "regular" passengers on the flight had to scurry for their safety amid all the cursing, pushing, and shoving.

Two things happened in the wake of the incident:

One, after 1978, the Yankees never again flew commercial as Steinbrenner ordered Killer Kane to book only charter flights for his riotous Yankees.

And two, Steinbrenner once again started to believe that Billy did not have control of his team.

The off-the-record phone calls to reporters from George resumed, both to plant the seed that the owner was worried about his manager but also to gather information. Billy had his enemies among the writers, and some were willing to tell George their impressions of how the team was unraveling because Billy was not enforcing a code of discipline. The commercial flight experience was cited as proof.

In fact, Billy always had trouble telling his players what to do off the field. He did not believe in it, just as Casey Stengel had not believed in it. The players weren't supposed to embarrass the team — in other words, don't get caught — otherwise they could do pretty much what they wanted.

Not much had changed on the Yankees since the night at the Copacabana. But just like George Weiss in 1957, George Steinbrenner in 1978 did not like to think that his team was unfit to mingle with the general public. Fighting with each other was one thing; fighting with the rank and file was not acceptable and Billy was being put on notice again.

In that way, it was business as usual; conflict off the field irked management. But worse, the 1978 Yankees were losing. The combination of the two always brought trouble and typically substantial, deleterious change as well.

Billy was hurtling toward another career cataclysm, and as was usually the case, he did not see it coming.

On the occasion of his fiftieth birthday, not surprisingly, Billy was moved to think about his future. His musings on an older Billy Martin could not have been more at odds with the Billy Martin he came to be in the eleven years that followed. But those ruminations about his future depict a far more contemplative Billy than his familiar image suggests — which he also acknowledged.

On the day of his birthday, Billy sat down for a long interview with Murray Chass, the *New York Times*'s respected Yankees beat writer. Billy almost always gave Chass good quotes. Billy likely respected Chass's professionalism, though theirs was not a natural connection. Billy usually got along best with the writers who drank with him, something Chass generally did not do.

But in his birthday interview with Chass, Billy admitted that he had thought about a day when he would no longer manage. He wanted to be a team executive.

"Man would like to make his roots somewhere," Billy said. "I don't want to go around from club to club. I'm here where I started, I'd like to stay here as long as possible. Then someday, I'd hope they would say: 'You've done a good job. Come upstairs; there's a job for you.' I'm not anxious to be a general manager but I'd like to be something like assistant to the president where I'd help coordinate things."

Asked if he had the diplomacy for such a job, Billy answered, "I'm actually very patient. I only use my temper to get things done. It motivates me and it definitely motivates others around me. But I know what's going to happen 50 years from now. People will think I got mad every time somebody said hello to me."

In the story Chass wrote, he quoted Steinbrenner on Billy's evolution as a middle-aged man.

"People say he hasn't changed," George said. "But they're wrong. He's becoming a better man, a better organization man, a better business man and a better manager because of it."

Which was all well and good in May when Billy turned fifty, but by mid-June of 1978 the Yankees were seven games behind the Red Sox.

The Yankees had dropped in the standings largely because their starting rotation was in shambles. Messersmith couldn't pitch at all. Catfish Hunter's Hall of Fame career was running on fumes. Gullett had a seriously damaged arm. His last Major League game was only weeks away, on July 9, 1978, when he would face nine batters in the first inning in Milwaukee and get only two batters out. He never pitched again.

Tidrow was about to begin a long career as a setup reliever because he was faltering as a starter. Ed Figueroa had unspecific but debilitating arm pain that the Yankees' doctors could not diagnose. Munson's knees were keeping him out of the lineup, and second baseman Willie Randolph had been sidelined with a knee injury as well.

"So many injuries," Roy White said. "It wasn't Billy's fault. With everyone out, we couldn't jell."

To Steinbrenner, all that mattered was the losing.

"I'm not waiting until we're 10 or 12 games back to do something," he said. "We'll have to shake up the clubhouse somehow."

On June 20 Billy boarded a plane to Detroit, and while on board he assembled the writers.

"This talk about me getting fired is ruining my sleep," he said. "My son reads about it and it bothers him. My mother reads about it and it bothers her. There are managers all over baseball who have never won, let alone won two straight pennants and a World Series. They don't have to put up with this. But I do."

Multiple writers wrote how drained and gaunt Billy appeared. One suggested that he was 20 pounds below his 1950s playing weight of 175 pounds. Billy was indeed neglecting his body, eating less and drinking more with his mind fixed on whether he would be fired from the only job he ever wanted.

Munson met with Billy at a bar on the road in early July to try to raise his manager's spirits. But as the two men talked about what was happening with the team, and likely to happen, tears started to well in Billy's eyes.

Munson, fearful that others would see Billy crying, took him outside. The two walked around the block.

"That man doesn't know anything about what we do — what we go through," Billy said of Steinbrenner. "We're the real Yankees. What's he? Some rich guy."

Billy was sobbing.

"I'm a Yankee," he said. "I'm a Yankee."

Munson guided Billy toward another block. They would walk for fifteen minutes until Billy regained his composure. The next day, Munson became the anonymous source for a couple of newspaper stories. This unnamed, prominent Yankee implored Steinbrenner to get off Billy's back, saying that the team could still win if the stress level around the team was reduced.

Steinbrenner backed off and announced that Billy would be his manager for the rest of the season regardless of where the Yankees ended up in the standings. New York was still new to the meaninglessness of George's proclamations. When Billy appeared with the lineup card at home plate that night at Yankee Stadium, more than fifty-two thousand fans gave him a standing ovation. They believed their favorite Yankee was once again safe.

Then the Yankees fell 11.5 games behind the Red Sox.

By Monday, July 17, the Yankees were thirteen games out of first place. Before that day's game, Reggie met with Steinbrenner. Reggie, like many other Yankees, was not happy with the way the season was going. He was struggling against left-handed pitchers, his batting average had dipped 15 points from 1977, and he was on a pace to hit 10 fewer homers than he had hit in 1977. Plus, his fielding was a continuing source of concern, and he had been relegated to the designated hitter's role. Reggie liked playing the field.

He asked Steinbrenner to get him in right field more often. But Steinbrenner sided with Billy. He told Reggie that his fielding was lousy.

As Reggie tells the story, he and George started arguing about a variety of things. Rosen was also at the meeting, though he said little. George decided that the moment should be a tough-love pep talk for Reggie.

"You better get your head on straight, boy," George said at one point.

"Who the hell do you think you're talking to?" Reggie said.

"I'm talking to you."

"Well, let me tell you something. Don't you ever talk to me like that again as long as you live."

As he had in Gabe Paul's hotel suite a year earlier, Reggie turned to the Yankees' general manager.

"Al, you're Jewish, what do you make of that 'boy' remark?" he asked Rosen.

Rosen said Reggie was interpreting it incorrectly.

"I think you should both cool down," Rosen added.

But Steinbrenner was raving.

"Cool down, hell," the owner bellowed. "Reggie, you get the hell out of my office."

Reggie answered, "I don't feel like leaving. I kind of like it here. I'm staying."

So George stormed out of his office. And after several minutes, Reggie went down to the Yankees' clubhouse. He was the designated hitter, batting fourth, in the game against Kansas City that was starting in forty minutes.

Billy knew nothing of Reggie's meeting with George. He later said he noticed that Reggie was acting "pissed." He planned to ask Reggie about it after the game or the next day. It was nearly game time. He wasn't going to bother him now.

Nothing unusual happened until the tenth inning when Munson singled in a tied game. Reggie came to the plate. As Reggie stepped into the batter's box, Howser, the third-base coach, signaled for a bunt.

Reggie was incredulous. He was batting cleanup. Not inconsequentially, especially to Reggie, the game was also the Monday night nationally televised game.

Reggie turned to stare in the dugout at Billy, who did not flinch. Howser flashed the bunt signal again. When Reggie squared to bunt — way too early—the Royals' closer, Al Hrabosky, recognized what was going on and did what all pitchers of that era were taught to do in the situation. He threw at Reggie's head and Reggie had to get out of the way. There was no way to lay down a bunt on that pitch.

With the count now 1-0, Brett and Royals first baseman John Wathan each took a few steps toward home plate. This was part of Billy's ploy; if the bunt did not work, at least it got the corner infielders to play in. It was a one-pitch strategy, so Billy took the bunt sign off. But Reggie, angry at everything in the Yankees' world at the time, wasn't looking at Howser by this point. Instead, he made a halfhearted attempt at bunting the next pitch and fouled it off.

Lou Piniella was watching from the dugout.

"I looked at Billy and I thought he was going to explode," he said. "We all saw him take the bunt sign off. It was baseball mutiny."

Billy was yelling to no one in particular, "What the hell is he doing? Swing away, swing away."

Gene Michael felt as if he was witnessing a moment of déjà vu.

"I had not seen it before but it was like I had seen it in a dream or a premonition," Michael said. "I knew something like this would happen eventually. It was like destiny."

Billy and Reggie, on intersecting paths since 1969, were poised to clash again.

Howser called time out and jogged down to talk to Reggie. As Reggie wrote in *Becoming Mr. October,* "Billy Martin wanted a bunt; he was going to get a bunt. I was tired of all the crap . . . I suppose it was obvious that I was giving a half-assed effort at bunting. Dick came down, made sure I knew Billy wanted me to hit away. But I was past that now."

Howser told Reggie again that Billy wanted him to swing away. Said Reggie, "No, he told me to bunt. And no offense to you, but I'm going to bunt."

Answered Howser, "I hope you know what you're doing."

Reggie went back to home plate and fouled off another bunt attempt for strike two. Then he popped another bunt attempt into the air behind home plate where it was caught for an out. Reggie returned to the dugout, walking to the far end opposite where Billy stood. Reggie put his glasses on a ledge behind the bench. He later said that he was waiting for the fistfight he expected to have with Billy.

"I *hoped* I had done something to create a spark, to create a confrontation," Reggie wrote in his second autobiography. "I was *looking* for it this time!"

But Billy did not move from his post on the home plate side of the home dugout. He had been condemned in some quarters for initiating the tussle in the Fenway Park dugout.

This time, Billy did not try to have the national television cameras peering into the dugout covered with a towel. He seethed. But he kept it together. The inning went on. The Yankees did not score.

Billy called over Michael, a coach he could trust to keep his calm. He told Michael to go over and ask Reggie to go inside the clubhouse.

"Billy kind of spit out the words, but he didn't swear and he didn't call Reggie any names," Michael said. "You could see he wanted to explode but I think he was determined not to do anything where he could be at fault.

"I went over there wondering if Reggie was going to swing at me."

Michael approached Reggie in the silent Yankees' dugout.

"Billy wants you to go inside the clubhouse," he said.

"If he wants me to go inside," Reggie answered, "tell him to come here and tell me himself."

Reggie sat on the bench for an inning, then walked inside, passing Billy as he did. Neither man said anything. After the game, which the Yankees lost, Billy grabbed a clock radio on his desk and threw it against the wall. He slammed his office door and fired a cup of beer against the blue cinder-block walls. The beer spattered the picture of Casey Stengel behind Billy's desk chair.

Yogi Berra shooed reporters away. "No interviews right now," he said. "Later."

Billy called Rosen and then Steinbrenner, and the three agreed that Reggie would be suspended immediately. George issued a statement:

> The basic thing has to be the discipline of the ball club. There have to be a boss and a leader and Billy is the boss and the leader of this ball club. Everybody knows that Reggie is close to me. He's a good friend. But you've got to back the manager. If you don't, you get to the point where a player can disregard the manager and then you're done. You might as well hang it up.

Billy wanted Reggie suspended for the remainder of the season, but George settled on five games and $9,000. Informed of his suspension, Reggie was asked by the writers what he would do.

"I'm going to California on the first plane smoking tomorrow morning," he said.

If the grappling, snarling near-fight in the Fenway Park visitors' dugout was Billy-Reggie I, then Billy-Reggie II was more of a psychological, counterintuitive skirmish. Criticized for his excessive outbursts, Billy had kept his composure, at least publicly. It was Reggie, known as a cerebral player who always worried about his image, who had unraveled with a national television audience watching. He had deliberately hurt himself and his team.

In the aftermath, Reggie was vilified across the country and within his own team.

"It was basically an openly defiant act on Reggie's part to say, 'Look, I don't care what the manager says, I'm going to do what I want to do,'" Nettles said.

The Mets' manager at the time, Joe Torre, was incredulous at Reggie's behavior.

"Reggie out-and-out disobeyed him," Torre said. "Billy did the right thing."

Piniella recalled that no one supported Reggie in the locker room that week.

"We had all been asked to bunt," he said. "You can question whether it makes any sense strategically because maybe Reggie couldn't bunt. But you know, Billy tried the bunt once and it didn't work. No harm there. And then he took the bunt sign off. Billy was saying, 'OK, never mind. Go ahead and hit.'

"But Reggie snapped. Reggie thought Billy was trying to embarrass him. I don't know that I believe that because Billy liked to win more than anything else. But I know that's what Reggie thought."

Henry Hecht had his own theory.

"I thought that Billy was doing a *Gaslight* on Reggie," Hecht told ESPN during its 2000 documentary on Billy, referring to the 1944 movie with actors Charles Boyer and Ingrid Bergman. Boyer's psychological abuse was intended to drive Bergman insane.

Said Hecht, "Billy was Boyer, Reggie was Ingrid Bergman. Billy was trying, successfully, to drive Reggie crazy."

Reggie went to California; the Yankees went to Minnesota, where they swept the Twins in two games. Then it was on to Chicago. Billy's demeanor in Chicago was carefree and reporters noticed that he was relaxed.

"You could see his face just brighten," Michael said. "We all went out to dinner. He was feeling good. George had taken his side against Reggie; to Billy that was like a reprieve. It was probably the happiest he had been all season."

The Yankees had won four consecutive games. But everyone awaited Reggie's return and the fireworks that would likely ensue.

On the team bus the night before Reggie was scheduled to return, Nettles yelled to Billy that he was calling in sick the next day.

"Me, too," came a voice from the back of the bus.

"Me, too," said another eight to ten voices.

A day earlier, Chambliss had told reporters, "Reggie can't just come back and then things are rosy. His actions didn't just hurt the manager. They hurt the team."

Billy had addressed Reggie's return earlier with the press.

"I don't want any apologies," he said. "I just want him to go to his locker, get dressed, go out in the field and he'll be in the lineup."

Reggie entered the visitors' clubhouse at Chicago's Comiskey Park for the July 23 afternoon game and saw a gaggle of reporters waiting at his locker. He had taken a cab to the ballpark, eschewing the team bus, which transported Billy, his coaches, and nineteen other players to Comiskey.

Comiskey Park was built in 1910, and its visitors' clubhouse was tiny and cramped. Players were shoulder to shoulder and the coaches dressed in the same room. The manager had an office with no door. Everything Reggie said in a thirty-five-minute interview with about twenty-five reporters could be heard throughout the clubhouse and likely in the manager's office as well.

After some opening small talk, Reggie was asked repeatedly if he felt he had done anything to deserve his suspension. Reggie was adamant. He had no regrets.

"I would do it again," he said. "If I had known the consequences of all this, I would have swung away to avoid everything that's happened, but I still don't feel like I did anything wrong.

"In fact, I don't know why I was suspended."

This interchange with a reporter was caught on videotape and shown on New York television that evening:

REPORTER: "When you were away, when your mind dwelled on what had happened, what were the major thoughts that went through your head?"

REGGIE: "The magnitude of me. The magnitude of the instance. The magnitude of New York. It's uncomfortable. It's miserable."

Reggie was not in Billy's lineup that day after all. The Yankees won their fifth successive game and whittled Boston's lead to ten games, the closest the Yankees had been in more than two weeks.

Billy was happy about the victory but incensed that Reggie was feeling guiltless and still defying him. Then Billy went to the Bards Room, a famed lounge at Comiskey Park where White Sox owner and raconteur Bill Veeck would entertain managers, coaches, and writers after games. The Bards Room was named for the collection of politicians, business magnates, and journalists whom the founding owner of the White Sox, Charles Comiskey, used to gather each year and take on an all-expenses-paid hunting trip to Wisconsin in the 1920s. To be included in the group, an individual had to be interested in both baseball and Shakespearean verse and capable of twisting the two interests into nonsensical poetry that would be recited over blazing campfires in a cabin in the woods. It also involved much consumption of alcohol. The Bards Room commemorated those convivial, raucous gatherings and was an appropriately loud and genial place with a long, tall bar, a mammoth fireplace in the middle of the room, and wild-game heads mounted on the polished wood-paneled walls.

Billy loved the Bards Room and was good friends with Veeck. But on this day, Veeck took Billy aside and told him that in June George Steinbrenner had proposed switching managers. Veeck would send Bob Lemon, a former Cleveland Indians pitching star and idol of Steinbrenner's, to the Yankees and Billy would come to Chicago. Veeck said the deal had some legitimacy since American League president Lee MacPhail had been in on the talks.

Veeck ended up firing Lemon on June 29, but upon seeing Billy in his

Bards Room in mid-July, Veeck thought he would tell his friend about the conversation because the trade could no longer happen — if it was ever feasible contractually.

Billy was at first dumbfounded, then furious. From what Veeck told him, the talks with Steinbrenner were at about the same time that George had issued a statement insisting that Billy would remain the manager throughout the season. Billy felt betrayed. He had already downed one or two drinks with Veeck when Jack Lang, a reporter for the *New York Daily News,* sidled up to the bar.

Billy, as he often did with reporters after games, asked Lang what he wrote about.

"Reggie's pregame press conference," Lang said.

"What did it say — what did he say?" Billy asked.

"Read it yourself," Lang said.

Since reporters still typed stories on 8½ x 11 sheets of paper that were then transmitted via a faxlike machine to their distant offices, Lang's story was in his briefcase. He yanked out the typed pages and handed them to Billy.

As Billy read about how Reggie absolved himself of wrongdoing and as he read about the "magnitude of me," Billy sighed and said, "Yeech. That's awful."

Lang asked if that was a critique of his writing.

"It's a critique of everything he said," Billy said.

The Bards Room, with its hunting lodge motif stuffed within an old-time ballpark, almost always brought a smile to Billy's face. But not this day.

He ordered a Scotch and water to go in a paper cup. He held it in his hand as he left the Bards Room and boarded the team bus for Chicago's O'Hare airport. The Yankees had a flight to Kansas City to catch.

Sitting on the bus, the more Billy thought about George's duplicity and Reggie's audacity, the more agitated he got. As he rode the Kennedy Expressway to O'Hare's suburban locale and as he downed the Scotch in his paper cup, Billy ruminated, and the perfect storm was building in his overburdened mind. Reggie's insolence before the game infuriated him. Already, he missed the sense of relaxation he had felt in Reggie's absence during the previous week. A win streak had ended just as Reggie once again turned the attention to himself. Then Billy had been blindsided by Veeck, astonished to hear that just weeks before, George had wanted to jettison him. Nothing angered Billy more than disloyalty. He could be patient and practice caution, but not necessarily on an empty stomach after a few hours of drinking. It was a classic recipe for a Billy outburst. He did not plan to explode. He felt pushed to it.

As the team bus neared O'Hare airport, Billy leaned toward Murray Chass and told him he wanted to talk to him when they arrived. Once inside the terminal, Billy made Reggie the target of a rant, with a less-than-amiable challenge aimed at Steinbrenner, too.

"Here's what I'm saying, 'Shut up, Reggie Jackson,'" Billy told Chass. "We don't need none of your shit. We're winning without you. We've got a smooth running ship. We don't need you coming in and making all these comments. If he doesn't shut his mouth, he won't play and I don't care what George says. He can replace me right now if he doesn't like it."

Two other newsmen had joined the conversation.

"Is this off the record?" they asked.

"No, sir, it's all on the record," Billy said.

When the Yankees got to the gate for their flight, they learned that it would not take off for another hour.

The writers dashed to pay phones to update their stories with Billy's comments. Billy and most of the players headed for a bar near the gate. Reggie and Fran Healy, who had retired to become a Yankees broadcaster, went for milk shakes at a deli kiosk.

Billy had a few more drinks. About forty-five minutes later, as the team and the writers were heading toward the jetway, Billy turned toward Chass, who had been joined by Henry Hecht.

"Did you get all that in the paper?" Billy asked.

"Sure did, Billy," Chass replied.

Billy grinned.

As the three men walked to the gate, Billy referred to Reggie as "a born liar" for saying that he had no idea what his suspension was for.

"It's like a guy getting out of jail and saying he's innocent when everyone saw what he did," Billy continued.

Billy was walking. The reporters were taking notes.

"The two of them deserve each other," Billy said. "One's a born liar; the other's convicted."

Billy had not mentioned George by name, but he did not have to. Steinbrenner's guilty pleas to a felony charge and for making illegal presidential campaign contributions had been only four years earlier. The convictions were far from a joking matter to George Steinbrenner. He was deeply humiliated.

None of that was on Billy's mind at the time. Seconds after uttering the most famous words that ever came from his lips, Billy went to his seat in first class and smiled at his longtime friend Yogi Berra.

With fourteen words — "The two of them deserve each other. One's a born liar; the other's convicted" — Billy had delivered the most withering, lethal blow in the poisonous, volatile Billy-Reggie-George relationship, which was perhaps twentieth-century America's best-known love/hate sports triangle.

The triumvirate had always been unstable and erratic — Billy had challenged Reggie to a fight, Reggie had dared George to throw him out of his office — but walking toward a jetway in a Chicago airport, Billy had landed the first true knockout blow.

By all accounts, Billy at the moment felt relieved, even heroic. He had stood up to what he saw as the evil, corrupt forces in his life. He was noble and valiant, only seeking righteousness and rectitude.

But like all heroes in Greek or Shakespearean tragedies, the protagonist was flawed, and his cause, while honorable in his mind, was diminished by his methods. Because his strengths always also revealed his weaknesses, he might win a moral victory in the end, but the struggle was one that would defeat him.

As Billy settled contentedly in his seat, Chass and Hecht clambered onto the Yankees' flight to Kansas City. The duo dutifully wrote down the fourteen words that forever altered Billy's life (it was before reporters used portable tape recorders). They made sure they had the same two sentences, the same apostrophes in the same places, and all the grammar in sync. They looked at each other and knew they had the baseball story of the season, maybe of the decade. But for the next two hours or so, they had to wait with no way to communicate what they knew.

Billy sat at the front of the plane laughing and joking.

Before arriving at the team hotel, Chass and Hecht did have time to approach Reggie, read him the comments, and ask for his reaction.

Reggie raised an eyebrow as the words were read to him. He appeared surprised but unruffled.

"I don't have any comment," he said, then added, "It's just unfortunate."

Who was Gaslighting whom now?

Chass and Hecht finally charged into their hotel rooms and called Steinbrenner at his home in Tampa. Billy's comments were read to him.

The words left Steinbrenner, then an energetic, exuberant forty-seven-year-old shipbuilding titan, something he almost never was: speechless.

He stammered into the phone, asking that Billy's comments be repeated to him. He wondered if Billy was drinking.

Finally, George said, "I have no comment right now. I can't comment and I won't dignify it. I am stunned. I just don't know what to say."

After hanging up the phone, George called Rosen, yelling into the phone, "Did you hear what Billy said? He wins a few games and goes crazy."

Rosen arranged to be on the earliest flight from New York to Kansas City the next morning and started packing. Before he went to bed, just after 1:00 a.m. eastern time, he called his old teammate from the Indians, Bob Lemon, who was at home in Southern California. Rosen wanted to know if Lemon would be willing to manage the Yankees should Billy be fired. Lemon was flabbergasted; hadn't the Yankees won five straight?

Told what Billy had said, Lemon blurted, "Oh, Jesus."

33

"**WHAT HAVE I DONE?**" Billy said to Sapir, his devoted confidant.

"Did you say it?" Sapir asked.

"No," Billy replied. "Well, yes, but not like it has come out. But yes."

Sapir knew precisely what was in Billy's contract. There was a clause that prohibited Billy from criticizing George or Yankees management. There was also a clause that forbade Billy from embarrassing the team or being outwardly, publicly insubordinate.

Sapir did not have to think what to do. He told Billy to resign immediately, citing health reasons. It was early the next morning.

Said Billy, "Why would I do that?"

Answered Sapir, "Because you're going to get fired as fast as possible. But if you resign for health reasons, he'll have to pay you. If he fires you it's for just cause and you get nothing. If you resign for health reasons and say you're doing it in the best interests of the team, you haven't violated your contract."

Sapir knew the principles, and the principals, all too well. A lower-level judge in New Orleans and longtime member of the city council there, Judge Eddie Sapir had negotiated a lot of entertainment and sports contracts for New Orleans. He had dealt with many men of wealth and power, and like Steinbrenner, he enjoyed the dodge, parry, and concession of an artful compromise.

Sapir knew that Steinbrenner would be angry, but he also sensed that Steinbrenner would be afraid of the backlash that Billy's departure was going to spawn among Yankees fans. And Sapir believed that Steinbrenner had genuine affection and admiration for Billy.

"If Billy did not challenge George at that moment, I was sure the two would someday work together again," Sapir said. "So I told Billy, 'This is bad and you're going to have to leave that job. But make it your idea.'"

Billy wanted to hear none of it. This was his dream job, even if the incessant pressure was making him sick, even if he wondered if he was having a nervous breakdown. Again.

Billy's New York–based business agent, Doug Newton, who handled Billy's endorsements and other commercial enterprises, was soon on the phone as well. Billy told him he was considering resigning before Rosen arrived in Kansas City. It sounded like the best course of action.

Billy had few other people to turn to at the time. Gretchen and he were at odds over the ongoing details of their impending divorce.

Billy called his mother in Berkeley.

"Bill was crying into the phone," his sister Pat recalled.

Eventually, Billy summoned the Yankees' public relations director, Mickey Morabito, to his room at the Crown Center Hotel. The men were associates, colleagues, and friends, having closed many a bar together.

"He wasn't in any shape to do anything," Morabito said. "He was shaking and crying. But he had written out a resignation speech on six small pieces of Crown Center stationery. The writing was in pencil."

Morabito took Billy's handwritten resignation — six pages that Morabito kept and still has more than three decades later — and went to his room to get a portable typewriter he traveled with. Billy accompanied Morabito, sitting on his bed as the publicist typed up Billy's resignation speech so it would be easier to read. Then Morabito and Billy went to visit Rosen, who had just checked into the room next to Morabito's. Told of the decision to resign, Rosen did not try to talk Billy out of it.

"Keep in touch," Rosen said. When Billy left the room, Rosen called Steinbrenner in Tampa to tell him the news.

Billy took the elevator down toward the hotel's lobby. The Crown Center had an expansive atrium lobby with two-story escalators that led to a glass balcony that overlooked the lobby floor.

Morabito had been downstairs in the hotel earlier. He knew that a horde of newspaper reporters and local television camera crews had assembled in the lobby, hoping to catch a glimpse of Billy. To keep the lobby passable for hotel guests, hotel security had herded the media onto the balcony floor.

Billy emerged from the elevator onto the mezzanine wearing dark sunglasses with a light sweater draped over his shoulders. He held an unlit cigar in his left hand and his speech in his right hand. In front of an antiques shop along one wall, Billy stood and waited for the reporters and cameras to congregate around him. He announced he would not take questions, "because I am a Yankee and Yankees do not talk or throw rocks."

Then, Billy read from the paper in his hand: "I don't want to hurt this team's chances for the pennant. The team has a shot at the pennant and I hope they win it. I owe it to my health and my mental well-being to resign. At this time, I'm also sorry about these things that were written about George Steinbrenner. He does not deserve them, nor did I say them."

Billy paused to adjust the sunglasses with his left hand. The diamonds on his 1977 World Series championship ring sparkled in the TV camera floodlights.

"I want to thank," he said, his voice cracking, "the Yankee management, the press, the news media, my coaches and my players . . ."

Billy began to quiver and tremble.

"And most of all," he continued, pausing again for almost ten seconds before softly adding, "the fans."

Phil Rizzuto, Billy's 1950s Yankees roommate, was watching from a few feet away.

"It was a nightmare," said Rizzuto, who lurched forward and put his arm around Billy, leading him down a hotel corridor. "I had to get him out of there. I really thought he might have a heart attack or something. I know him, the Yankees, and this job are his whole life. I was worried he was going to throw himself off the balcony or something."

Billy, Rizzuto, and an old Kansas City–based friend, Bob Brown, guided Billy out of the hotel and the trio walked about ten blocks in downtown Kansas City in no particular direction.

"We were just trying to absorb what had just happened," Rizzuto said.

Then they returned to the Crown Center, entering through a side door near the kitchen. Billy had dozens of phone messages but he returned only two — to Mickey Mantle and Whitey Ford. Then Killer Kane helped Billy get a flight that night to Florida, where Mickey was playing golf.

"It was where Billy wanted to go," Kane said. "He didn't really have anywhere else to go."

At the ballpark that Monday evening, Rosen addressed the team. The players expressed a mix of shock and understanding.

"I think a lot of us really felt that it was best for Billy's health," Roy White said. "But almost everyone felt bad for him. He wasn't the reason we were losing."

Nettles was angry and felt Chass and Hecht had egged Billy on, taking advantage of his vulnerability.

"It was nasty and heartless," he said. "If you take the Yankee manager's job from Billy, you might as well stab him with a knife."

And tensions in the clubhouse had not diminished.

"There was certainly some resentment toward Reggie," Chambliss said. "He had set a lot of this in motion. But at the same time, pro athletes also instinctively turn toward the task at hand — let's win some games."

Ron Guidry, who was in his second year and would play for Billy four more times, considered the whole scene unfathomable.

"Here was the best manager in baseball and he's not with us anymore because of something he said," Guidry said. "I couldn't believe it. But you know, I learned, it was always the off-the-field stuff that got Billy, wasn't it?"

Reggie, who did not play that night, had little to say. Asked in the locker room for his feelings about Billy's resignation, Reggie replied, "Well, I really don't have any feelings. I'm just kinda, maybe the word is placid."

But the reaction back in New York was anything but placid. The Yankees' switchboard fielded hundreds of calls, most of them condemning Steinbrenner. Some callers threatened George's life, and many more said they would never attend another Yankees game.

The protests were real and perceptible. About twenty-five fans burned their Yankees tickets in the plaza outside the stadium, just below Steinbrenner's office, which attracted a crowd of another hundred people or so. New York police had to disperse the demonstration.

While no one defended Billy for his comments, analysis in the news media was decidedly pro-Billy and anti-Steinbrenner. Reggie was castigated for starting the whole affair with his intemperate bunting snit.

"Billy represented every regular fan who wanted to tell his boss to shove it or wanted to tell the overpaid ballplayers to shut up and play hard," wrote the *New York Daily News*'s Dick Young, the blue-collar tabloid columnist with the biggest following among everyday fans. "That's why people love him. He has been the genuine guy they could believe in. Sure, he has his problems but they loved him for that, too. It makes him human. And what happened? Billy got screwed by the bosses and bonus baby whiners anyway."

The outcry was relentless. Monday turned into Tuesday and it did not abate. Neither did the media reaction since Billy's apparent demise had a crossover appeal. Sports talk radio had not yet gained a foothold in New York, but there were plenty of general news talk radio broadcasts. They did hours of programming about Billy's cold-blooded exit.

The heartbreak of Billy's departure — and what fans were expressing was heartbreak — pushed local and national politics aside. Everyone wanted to talk about Billy.

Yankees fans and Billy Martin fans everywhere could not stand the despair.

On Wednesday, July 26, when the Yankees returned to Yankee Stadium two days after Billy resigned, the crowd of 31,631 started chanting, "We want Billy! We want Billy!"

That was twenty minutes before the start of the game with Cleveland. They chanted it almost nonstop as the players took the field and throughout the first inning. The chant enveloped the stadium periodically throughout the game.

Hundreds of fans showed up with signs expressing their support of Billy:

BILLY, NO. 1 FOREVER

BILLY MARTIN: OUR TRUE YANKEE

WE'LL NEVER FORGET YOU, BILLY

BILLY, ALWAYS NO. 1 IN OUR HEARTS

There were a number of signs critical of George and Reggie, but security confiscated those attacking Steinbrenner. Any other signs that were outwardly profane or otherwise deemed objectionable were also seized.

That was not true of signs condemning Reggie, and there were many:

REGGIE: ARE YOU HAPPY NOW?

YOU CUT THE HEART RIGHT OUT OF US, REGGIE

BILLY'S THE ONE WHO'S SANE. REGGIE IS THE ONE TO BLAME.

Now the fans were getting in on the Gaslighting theme.

Reggie sat out the game.

Years later, Steinbrenner admitted in interviews that he had underestimated the backlash Billy's exit would create.

"The fans loved Billy like family," George said in a 1992 interview. "It was personal to them. He was their manager. The older Yankees fans loved him from his playing days and the younger fans loved him for helping get the Yankees back to the World Series. Either way, they loved him."

George started second-guessing himself almost immediately. He was conflicted on several levels. There was the business side of the situation since Billy was a significant part of the Yankees brand in the late 1970s. As Morabito said, Billy was the best-known and best-liked personality on the team.

George was also feeling a level of personal guilt for his role in Billy's unreasonable behavior. Like Billy, who would feel remorse for an outburst or a fistfight, George would feel guilt about his relentlessness and meddlesome ways.

From a public relations standpoint, the Yankees and George were taking an interminable beating and not just from the writers and fans. Mantle and Ford had already said that they would likely never return to Yankee Stadium. Others from the 1950s Yankees were chiming in with similar reactions.

And if all that wasn't enough, deep down George had affection for Billy and worried for him personally.

"People always say George was bad for Billy," Sapir said. "But he never meant to be. In his heart, George wanted what was best for Billy. He just couldn't help himself sometimes. George and Billy were similar like that. They could each be their own worst enemy.

"But George would always say to me, 'I know Billy is the best manager for the Yankees, maybe the best manager anywhere. Yeah, he drinks too much, but goddamn it, he always wins and he puts people in the seats.'"

In the hours before the Yankee Stadium fans were holding aloft signs in praise of their Everyman hero and bemoaning the loss of their beloved number 1, Steinbrenner had already hatched a plan to appease and thrill them.

On Tuesday, the twenty-fifth, the day after Billy's resignation, George called Billy's agent, Doug Newton, in New York. He wanted Billy to fly to New York for a meeting.

Sapir also got a call.

"What Billy did was wrong and he's got to apologize and fix some things, but we've got to get him back," George said.

Sapir agreed, then asked, "How are you going to get that done?"

Replied George, "I've got a plan."

Did he ever.

Meanwhile, in Milwaukee, the Miller Brewing Company was stumped about what to do next. Two weeks earlier, it had filmed another one of its popular Miller Lite commercials with George and Billy. In the commercial, George and Billy are seated in a bar drinking Miller Lite, and the two start to argue about the merits of the beer. The argument, as scripted, ends with George firing Billy.

Everyone in the bar laughs.

The brewer had been very proud of the advertisement and informed the business press of its contents at the time of filming — provided the reporters not write about the commercial until just before it was scheduled to air in early August. Now what?

Bar patrons, even outside New York where Billy had a following, wouldn't be laughing at George's final line: "Billy, you're fired."

Miller issued a statement: "No air time is scheduled at this time."

When Newton contacted Billy in Florida about George's request, Billy was hesitant to leave. If George was going to offer him a front-office or scouting job, it could wait. Told that George wanted to talk about his eventual return as manager, maybe as soon as 1979, Billy flew to Newark airport and to escape notice stayed in a suburban hotel. The next day he met George in his suite in the Carlyle Hotel.

Steinbrenner spoke first.

"Billy, I woke up the day after you resigned and in my gut, I knew something wasn't right," George said. "It's not right having you not manage the Yankees."

Billy, of course, agreed.

George talked about how they were both strong-minded and opinionated. George said his weakness was that he liked to have a say in everything, and he believed that Billy's weakness was that he didn't like anyone butting into his business. It was, obviously, a bad combination.

"But if both of us could give a little," George said, "maybe we wouldn't have a problem."

It sounded so simple. It would prove to be almost impossible. It went against their natural instincts, dispositions, and impulsive tendencies. But on this day, as they would so often in the next eleven years, neither would follow the path they promised. But like any great coupling of famed and flawed personalities, in the moments of joyful harmony, anything and everything seemed possible.

George had a stipulation. He wanted Billy to promise to cut down on his drinking. George suggested something he would suggest for years afterward: he wanted Billy to drink only beer.

In *Number One,* Billy said that George conceded that he, too, was drinking too much. But Billy put George off on his suggestion.

"I take a drink and I'll get hot at times, but I'm not an alcoholic," he wrote.

George again insisted that Billy should acknowledge publicly that he had to drink less. If Billy agreed, he soon forgot about it.

George's plan included a bombshell. Saturday was Old Timers' Day at Yankee Stadium, which always assured a sellout in the South Bronx ballpark. He wanted to sneak Billy into the stadium and then introduce him to the crowd during the Old Timers' festivities as the once and future manager.

"The crowd will go wild; it'll be tremendous," said George, well aware that he would benefit from the reflected glow of Billy's triumphant, unforeseen return.

But George had one other issue. He had not told Rosen or Lemon about any of his plans. They did not even know that Billy was in New York, let alone in George's hotel suite. When Rosen was informed, he argued that Lemon deserved at least one full season. The notion that Billy would take over in 1980, not 1979, became the compromise. Lemon would become a front-office executive.

When this was relayed to Billy, he did not object. In the meantime, he said he would scout the Yankees' minor league players, do some advance Major League scouting, and assist Lemon however he needed it. Billy went back into hiding in New York and New Jersey, waiting for Saturday.

He told almost no one.

As the retired Yankees and current Yankees arrived for Old Timers' Day, the mood was light (the Yankees had won three of their last four games to cut Boston's lead to eight games). About two hours before the introductions of the former players would begin, Billy was dropped off at a little-used gate near left field. A trench coat was wrapped around his shoulders and his head was covered by a floppy hat. Once inside, he was spirited to an auxiliary locker room, one used for concert acts or boxers at the stadium. Pete Sheehy met him and handed over his number 1 uniform. After he changed, Billy was hastily taken to a boiler room under the stands where he would hide until it was his turn to emerge from the dugout.

One of the few people who saw Billy heading for the boiler room was Willie Randolph.

"I was shocked and I said, 'Billy, what are you doing here?'" Randolph said. "And he had this big grin and said, 'You'll see. But it's a secret. Don't tell anyone.'

"I remember walking back to the clubhouse thinking that this is a crazy place, man."

The clandestine operation worked. Most of the old-timers were on the field, including Mantle, Berra, and Ford, when Yankee Stadium public address announcer Bob Sheppard leaned toward his press-box-level microphone. Sheppard began by explaining that Bob Lemon was going to be promoted to the front office in 1980, "to be general manager," Sheppard said.

Examining the tape of the day, it is obvious that some of the old-timers on the field were puzzled by Sheppard's digression from the usual itinerary — and by the news about Lemon's status two seasons hence. The 1978 Yankees were sitting in the spacious dugout. They, too, were flummoxed.

Yankee Stadium in 1978 had a long, low-roofed, narrow tunnel that ran directly from the team's clubhouse to the home plate side of the Yankees' dugout. For those players sitting closest to the tunnel runway, at the top of the concrete steps there suddenly appeared a familiar visage. It was Billy in his home Yankees uniform.

Billy did not make eye contact and there was no time to say anything.

Sheppard went on, ". . . announcing at the same time, the manager of the Yankees in 1980, and hopefully for many years after that . . ."

Billy leaped out of the dugout, arriving on the field like an apparition.

"Number one!" Sheppard said as the center-field scoreboard flashed: BILLY MARTIN.

The crowd paused, flabbergasted. There was a brief millisecond of eerie quiet, then an eruption. It was not a typical sporting arena ovation. This was not applause springing from the anticipation of an at-bat or a long pass in a football game. It was so unforeseen, the cheering exploded like a thunderclap. After days of demoralizing hand-wringing about Billy's fate, there in uniform, trotting onto the field and holding his cap aloft, was Billy.

The television cameras caught people hugging in the stands. Others jumped up and down in place.

Billy shook hands with the old-timers' lineup in the middle of the diamond. The cheering went on for more than seven minutes. Every time the ovation began to fade out, Billy would doff his cap again to revive it — a move he had perfected over the years.

Sitting in the dugout, most players were grinning at the spectacle, though some looked astounded. A few shook their heads. One player appeared as if he might collapse on the spot.

"I felt like I was hit with a Jack Armstrong right hook," Reggie later told reporters. "It felt like an out-of-body experience. Was I really seeing what I was seeing?"

In *Becoming Mr. October,* Reggie called it the worst day of his baseball life. He asked George why he wasn't warned, at least told of the plan to ease the shock. Said Steinbrenner, "Well, I really didn't have to, Reggie."

Reggie also wrote that it would not have been a bad plan if Billy had gotten some help for his drinking in the year and a half before 1980.

At a brief news conference that followed the Old Timers' Day festivities, Billy apologized to George for the "liar" comments.

"I did say it, I don't know why I said it, I was angered at the time," said Billy, who did not apologize to Reggie or speak his name.

Steinbrenner stood at Billy's side during the news conference. With a public relations coup unrivaled in American sports at the time, George had become a hero that day, too. As George absolved his once and future manager for his transgression at Chicago's O'Hare airport six days earlier, he also knew that he was being forgiven all around Yankeeland.

"When he apologized to me it showed me that he was a man who realized that he had maybe made a small mistake," George said. "And it was small in the total picture."

Reporters were led to believe that Billy would announce his new drinking regimen: beer only. But when the subject was broached, Billy replied,

"I'm not overdrinking. I've never been an overdrinker in my whole life. I like my beer and I like my Scotch like everybody else does. But I've never overdone, I think I always control myself well."

"Have you promised Steinbrenner that you won't drink for this next year and a half?" Billy was asked.

"Well, no, I haven't," Billy answered. "I like Miller Lite and I drink it a lot."

The new Miller Lite beer commercial came out within days. George's final line, "You're fired," was redubbed in editing so that George says, "You're hired."

Billy's response in the original taping remained.

"Not again," he says with a rueful laugh.

34

THE YANKEES WON THE game that followed the Old Timers' Day ceremonies. In the locker room afterward, Nettles was asked for his reaction to a full day of twists and turns. He trotted out one of his favorite lines.

"Some kids want to play big-league baseball and other kids want to run away and join a circus," Nettles said. "I'm lucky; I get to do both here."

Most players shrugged their shoulders and moved on. As Lou Piniella said thirty-five years later with a hearty laugh, "Look, George always felt there was a time and place for Billy to manage the Yankees. That time and place just kept changing."

Randolph felt similarly.

"To us at the time, it was like, 'Well, that's good news, now we don't have to feel badly about Billy anymore. It's resolved,'" he said. "We'll see him later."

But 1980 seemed a long way off.

Billy left his news conference and watched the game in George's box. Using a Yankees office phone, he called many friends and family. Mantle and Ford took him out for a night of celebration in Manhattan. At about 4:00 a.m., the *New York Post* placed the trio at P. J. Clarke's, a foremost Manhattan saloon since the late 1800s that was, and is, a place of both élan and rank unsophistication. P. J. Clarke's, for example, was where Jackie Onassis took her children, John Jr. and Caroline, to lunch on Saturdays in the 1970s. They got the signature dish, a hamburger that the 1950s singer and Clarke's regular Nat King Cole dubbed the "Cadillac of burgers." Sinatra and Johnny Carson were regulars at the bar on Third Avenue and 55th Street, rubbing shoulders with office workers from the East Side neighborhood. The saloon was big enough to fit maybe seventy patrons but small enough that every imbiber was leaning on or wedged next to someone else. There was a long, deep dining room set back from the large picture window overlooking Third Avenue. George Steinbrenner frequented the small, cramped bar and noisy, more spacious dining room in the back, too. In the 2000s, Steinbrenner became a minority owner of the joint.

But on this night, Mantle, Ford, and Billy—and the *New York Post* reporters—knew that P. J. Clarke's had a private upstairs dining room where certain patrons could go after the bar closed at 4:00 a.m. And that's where the group, which included about ten young women according to the *Post*, went and remained until close to 6:00 a.m.

Billy finally exited into a waiting limousine.

"The rising sun cast an added glow on the golden blond tresses of his companion as they disappeared into the car," the *Post* wrote.

Billy remained in New York and New Jersey for several days thereafter. He was trying to extend one of the happiest days of his life.

"That afternoon at Old Timers' Day was really a shining moment for my father," his son, Billy Joe, said. "Maybe the shining moment."

In August of 1978 Billy was something even he had never dreamed of—he was a resurrected Yankee hero, something that had never happened before. He had endured a proverbial Yankee death and came back to wave his cap at a sold-out Yankee Stadium again. Other Yankees, like his mentor Casey Stengel, had returned late in life to doff their caps in ceremony and tribute, but for Billy this was no farewell tour. Billy had a Yankee future.

He recognized the reprieve. He never felt better.

For starters, in the love/hate Billy-George-Reggie triangle, Billy believed he had won again. In the end, George had taken his side. Yes, Billy had to step away for a while, but that would calm his nerves and settle his stomach. At the moment, he felt nothing could go wrong.

The 1978 season continued, although on August 9, the dynamic inside the team's clubhouse was altered significantly when each of the New York City newspapers ceased to publish because of an employees' strike. Some people think the newspaper strike, which lasted until November 5, saved the Yankees' 1978 season. There was no Internet, and with only a few New Jersey and wire service reporters working the locker room before and after games, the atmosphere in the Yankees' clubhouse was considerably lighter. The remaining reporters had jobs to do, too, but without the competitive intensity of the New York tabloids, whose desire to outdo one another ratcheted up the importance of every missed fly ball or budding clubhouse controversy, the locker room was a more placid place.

It also did not hurt that the Yankees were winning at a torrid pace. By August 15, the Red Sox' lead was down to seven games.

"Bob Lemon was very calm and that's what we needed," Piniella said. "You know, change for the sake of change works sometimes. And we did not have to come to the ballpark knowing there would be all these George, Reggie, and Billy questions.

"What we needed was some peace from that."

Said Roy White, "We also got healthy. Thurman's knees were good enough that he was behind the plate every game. We saw Boston struggling and feeling the pressure. They had a history of losing late leads back then. We became a baseball team chasing another baseball team and that's all there was to it for a change."

On September 7, the Yankees went to Fenway Park for a four-game series with the Red Sox' lead at just four games.

"You could see the tension in the Red Sox players' faces before the game," said Randolph, who had three hits and five RBIs in the first game, which was a 15–3 Yankees victory. "They were worried about choking away a fourteen-game lead and I didn't blame them for feeling that way."

The Yankees won the next game on a Friday night, 13–2, with Reggie and Piniella hitting home runs. On Saturday afternoon and before a national television audience, Guidry faced off against the Boston ace, Dennis Eckersley.

A scoreless game went into the top of the fourth when the Yankees began a two-out rally. The Boston defense collapsed. Yastrzemski made an error, Eckersley threw a wild pitch, and Fisk allowed a passed ball. Seven Yankees runs scored. Cruising along with that lead, Guidry went the rest of the way to improve his record to 21-2 with a shutout.

By Sunday, with the Red Sox all but defeated, the Yankees left a farewell calling card — a workmanlike 7–4 victory that gave them a share of the AL East title. The four-game series became known as "the Boston Massacre."

But as decisive as the Yankees' sweep was — they outscored the Red Sox 42–9 — the teams battled throughout September. Boston eventually played the role of the underdog and made their own dramatic comeback, winning on the final day of the regular season as the Yankees lost at home. Those results left a tie atop the AL East standings, forcing a one-game playoff at Fenway.

Billy did not attend the Fenway game. Like much of the rest of the sporting world, Billy watched on television as the game interrupted a sunny but crisp Monday afternoon in early October. Playing the game at night in prime time apparently never occurred to the television networks or baseball officials. Workers from New York to Boston stopped in offices or left for the local saloon to watch a tense game the Red Sox led 2–0 heading into the seventh.

Then Bucky Dent lofted a soft fly ball into the net above Fenway's Green Monster for a three-run home run. With Fenway Park silent and shocked, the next batter, Mickey Rivers, walked to home plate. Rivers had loaned his bat to Dent before the home run because he said it was "lucky" — perhaps Rivers's best gambling hunch. Now, Rivers worked a walk from the stunned ex-Yankees pitcher Mike Torrez. A few pitches later, Rivers stole second base.

Munson doubled to make the score 4–2. Reggie, who was the designated hitter and not playing right field, added a long home run into the center-field bleachers for a 5–2 lead, an insurance run the Yankees needed when Boston closed the deficit to 5–4 but could not finish a late rally against Rich Gossage. Carl Yastrzemski, the thirty-nine-year-old pride of New England, took the game's final swing, popping up to Nettles.

The Yankees were in their third successive American League Championship Series, and after vanquishing the Kansas City Royals yet again — this time in four games — they were once again playing for Major League Baseball's championship.

Billy watched the 1978 World Series in Texas with his son. "I remember rooting for the Dodgers against the Yankees in the first game of the '78 World Series," Billy Joe said. "And as soon as I did, my father said, 'Hey, pard, what are you doing?'

"And I said, 'I'm not rooting for the Yankees; they ran you out of there.' And he said, 'It doesn't matter; we never root against the Yankees. Besides, those are my guys out there.' So we rooted like hell for the Yankees."

The Yankees again won in six games; Reggie hit 2 home runs and drove in 8 runs. In the twelve games of the 1977 and 1978 World Series, Reggie had hit 7 homers and driven in 16 runs.

In early November, a Minnesota reporter caught up with Billy at the Chinese restaurant of Billy's longtime friend Howard Wong. Billy had befriended Wong in the 1960s because Wong's large and popular Bloomington restaurant was close to the Twins' ballpark and to his home. Though sixteen years older than Billy, Wong connected with Billy and shared his interest in hunting and fishing.

"Bob Lemon did a great job," Billy told the reporter. "I always knew that was a championship team."

Asked about his baseball future, Billy said that all he had planned was a hunting trip to the Dakotas with Wong. Then the two men were due in Reno, Nevada, where Billy was going to do another old Minnesota buddy a favor. It sounded rather uneventful, and the hunting trip was.

The Reno visit proved to be an errand that nearly turned Billy's grand and spectacular Old Timers' Day resurrection — one of the most entertaining moments in 1970s sports history — into a sardonic footnote. While the Reno trip was action packed, many of the details have never been fully reported and the established narrative of what happened is incomplete.

There is no disputing the basis for Billy's trip to Reno. Bill Musselman, a volatile, fiercely competitive basketball coach at the University of Minnesota in the early 1970s, became friends with Billy through Howard Wong. Musselman was a major personality in the Twin Cities after he led Minnesota to its first Big Ten basketball title in fifty-three years. But by the mid-1970s, Musselman had bounced around various pro coaching jobs. In late 1978, he was head coach of the Reno Bighorns of the Western Basketball Association. Musselman asked Billy to appear at the Bighorns' opening home game on November 10 to give the team a boost at the gate.

Billy agreed to come, pose for some courtside pictures, and sign autographs. Once there, he said a few words over the public address system to a crowd of about 3,500, waved to the stands, and left the basketball court.

Billy thought his job was done. Here is where versions of the oft-repeated narrative begin to diverge. It has always been written that Billy told Bighorns officials in advance that he would not do any media interviews during his trip. That may or may not be true, but there is no doubt that the team promoted Billy's appearance in advance of his arrival. Bighorns officials also arranged for an interview with the local paper to maximize the publicity for the team.

Ray Hagar, a twenty-five-year-old sportswriter for the *Reno Evening Gazette* and the *Nevada State Journal* who spent most of his time covering high school sports, drew the assignment to talk to Billy.

"The sports editor knew I followed the Yankees then because they were like America's team — the most famous group of athletes in the country,"

Hagar said in a 2014 interview. "I think the sports editor gave me the assignment as a reward."

Years later, Billy wrote that he went to a bar in the Bighorns' arena and Hagar showed up wearing a Yankees T-shirt. Billy said he thought Hagar was a fan. As Billy told New York reporters later, Hagar asked some general questions and Billy answered them. After several minutes, Billy said, Hagar's questions became more assertive and he started taking notes.

Realizing Hagar was a reporter, Billy got angry and reached for Hagar's notes, saying he never agreed to an interview. Billy said that Hagar brushed Billy away, and when Howard Wong reached for the notes as well, Hagar shoved Wong, who was then about sixty-five years old. Billy said he punched Hagar to defend Wong.

Since Hagar and his newspaper later filed civil suits and criminal complaints, Hagar did not say much afterward. He did have his picture taken with a cut lip, a swollen face, and an ugly shiner — a garish, hard-to-miss black eye.

The resolution of the court cases that came six months later — a madcap settlement straight out of a Barnum & Bailey circus — did little to clear up the actual details of the situation. It has not helped that Hagar refused to talk about what happened for the past thirty years.

But in a 2014 interview, Hagar, then a sixty-one-year-old political columnist in Reno, said he had come to terms with his Billy Martin moment and was willing to tell his side of the story. And he also revealed a previously unreported detail: there was a spark to the fight, a heretofore latent but incendiary flash point that emanated from Steinbrenner's office 2,700 miles from Reno.

"I did not show up in a T-shirt; I put on a nice shirt and a tie," he said, noting that he had a post-fight picture of himself in that attire. "I was an intimidated kid. The most famous person I had interviewed before that was the Douglas County High School coach. I had a clipboard with a list of questions and I approached Billy after he left the basketball court and introduced myself.

"He was wasted. Just shitfaced and he told me to go fuck myself."

Hagar said he went to a bank of pay phones — a 1970s reference if there ever was one — and called his office. He told them what happened and added that he was not sure he should even interview someone so drunk.

"My boss said, 'Sure, we'll interview the manager of the Yankees the next time he comes to Reno,'" Hagar said. "And then he added, 'Which will be, like, never.'

"He told me to go back and get the interview. And I said, 'Oh, shit.'"

By this time, Billy was in a bar by the arena entrance. Hagar returned to Billy's side and explained that there must have been some misunderstanding because he thought the interview was prearranged.

"And I told him that my boss was on me to get something from him," Hagar said. "And he said, 'OK, kid, I'll give you the interview.'

"So I'm going through my list of questions and he's answering them, talking about Yankee pride and how he will stress the Yankee Way when he comes back as manager in 1980. And he says the Yankees will keep winning because they have veteran, proven players.

"So I thought that was an opening to ask about Sparky Lyle."

Before leaving his newspaper office that day, Hagar had seen on the Associated Press sports ticker — the equivalent of the modern ESPN bottom-of-the-screen newswire — that Lyle had just been traded to the Texas Rangers along with catcher Mike Heath and three other minor league players for four Rangers, including a nineteen-year-old pitcher named Dave Righetti.

Lyle was one of Billy's favorites, the bullpen warhorse of Billy's 1977 championship team. Heath was also a personal pet. Billy saw Heath as the likely successor to Munson.

"I figured that Billy already knew about the Lyle trade so I asked him about it as he sat there," Hagar said. "And then I saw that he didn't know what I was talking about."

This part of the story has never been in the established narrative. But Hagar had written down all the trade details with the other players' names and he rattled them off. Billy was incredulous, then incensed, both at the trade of Lyle and Heath, and because he had been left completely out of the negotiations.

"You could tell he was really pissed," Hagar said. "He didn't want anything to do with me anymore. He was cursing and steaming mad. He was stewing over the trade and getting angrier. But I had other questions. My next one was whether he could get along with Reggie Jackson when he came back in 1980.

"And he just kind of lost it. He started into this broadside about how writers were always trying to twist what he said to get him in trouble. He started cursing out the New York writers by name. Then he said to me, 'I'm taking away this interview.' And he asked for my notes."

Billy reached for Hagar's clipboard, which the reporter put behind his back.

"I wasn't giving him my notes," Hagar said in 2014. "Can you imagine how embarrassing it would have been to go back to the office with no notes?"

But Billy wanted those notes and was trying to get at them.

"Billy was agitated, from the Lyle trade mostly I think, and finally with my hands still behind my back I said, 'I'm not giving you my notes,'" Hagar said.

It was like a line in the sand. There is a long historical record of how confrontations proceed when someone draws a line in the sand before Billy.

"I've had a lot of years to think about this," Hagar continued. "And I really think at that moment he thought I was being insolent. I was defying him. He just gave me this look.

"He paused and then hauled off and hit me in the face."

Hagar's knees buckled and his first thought was, "How did I screw up my first interview with a famous person?"

And what about the oft-repeated claim that he shoved Wong in the scuffle?

"That's a total fucking lie," Hagar said. "I was an awed, overwhelmed kid. I wasn't going to push anyone."

Various parties jumped between Billy and Hagar, although not completely.

"Things calmed down for a few seconds and then Billy popped me again," Hagar said. "This time, I went flying over a table like in some fight you'd see in a Western movie. I got up, found my notes, and walked out."

The fight has never been described as a two-rounder.

Hagar went to the hospital where he was treated for a cut lip, three chipped teeth, and a gash above his eye. He filed a criminal complaint of battery.

Billy spoke to several New York reporters the next day. He said he was set up. And he refused to talk about the Lyle trade.

"I didn't know him, never punched a reporter before," Billy said of Hagar. "Why would I want to fight him? I threw it because I felt he was going to punch me."

When the gruesome picture of Ray Hagar's face was printed in newspapers across the land on November 11 — Hagar said people sent him copies of the picture from Asian and European newspapers — not many people believed Billy was the victim in the fracas, or had been threatened.

One of the nonbelievers was George Steinbrenner. Billy's contract — he was still operating on the one that expired in 1979 — had a prominent "good boy" clause. Billy was not allowed to embarrass the Yankees with his personal conduct.

Steinbrenner told the New York press that the outcome of the Nevada civil and criminal proceedings against Billy could prevent him from ever managing the Yankees again.

Eddie Sapir called Steinbrenner for a clarification.

"George told me that Billy had to be found innocent of the criminal charges or have them dismissed and he said that Billy could not be found liable in the civil case either," Sapir said. "George said if Billy paid Hagar any settlement money in the civil suit that was the same as losing it. If Billy didn't win both cases, George would cut him loose.

"I called Billy and told him what George said. Billy said, 'Judge, I slugged this guy. I didn't mean to and I wish I didn't, but how are we going to get away with saying it never happened?'

"And I didn't know the answer to that but the more we talked, Billy kept saying, 'I told them in Reno that I didn't want to do any interviews. If only those fuckers had listened to me.'"

That's when Sapir decided the whole mess was the Bighorns' fault. That became the line of attack he took. Sapir threatened to sue the Bighorns' owners because they failed to keep a verbal agreement to shield Billy from the press. He also contacted Hagar's attorney, who was Hagar's neighbor and not terribly experienced, and asked what Hagar wanted.

"I was idealistic, and though people told me to go after a lot of money, I told my attorney that all I wanted was my medical bills paid and I wanted an apology from Billy," said Hagar, who had amassed about $7,500 in medical expenses, most of them for dental work.

Sapir went back to the Bighorns and said Billy would not sue the team if the Bighorns gave Hagar a check for $7,500. The team balked. Sapir kept up the pressure, explaining the grounds for the suit and revealing his ammunition. (Wong agreed to testify that Billy repeatedly told the team on arrival in Reno that he would not talk to any reporters and a Bighorns official assured Billy that he would be kept away from the press. Wong also said Billy was defending himself from a belligerent Hagar.)

As Sapir schemed, Hagar tried to get on with his life. The day after Billy punched him, Hagar went to his brother's wedding where he was the best man.

"The bride was furious because no one was paying attention to her," Hagar said. "Everyone wanted to talk to me about my fight with Billy Martin. It was awful.

"They took two sets of wedding pictures. One with me in it and my big black eye and one without me in it. You can guess which one they kept."

The settlement was on May 24, 1979. Billy, Sapir, and Wong flew to a news conference in Reno. All the details of the deal had been arranged ahead of time. Well, almost all the details. The Bighorns had caved and one of the owners cut an $8,000 check that would be publicly presented to Hagar. For that sum, Hagar would drop the criminal charges.

But there was still the matter of Billy apologizing to Hagar.

"We were flying to Reno and Billy was in a good mood," Sapir said. "This had been hanging over his head and he was happy it was going to be behind him. And I said, 'Skip, there's just one more thing. This Hagar guy wants you to apologize to him at the news conference.'

"And Billy got this look on his face and I thought, 'Uh-oh.' He said to me, 'Eddie, I didn't cause this fight. I'm sorry but I ain't getting up and apologizing.'"

At the news conference, which was well attended with photographers and television camera crews from all over Nevada and California, all the principals involved sat at a long table before the media. The Bighorns' chief owner, Bill Meyers, produced the $8,000 check. The civil suit and criminal charges were officially dismissed. Bill Musselman got to his feet and explained that the whole situation was an unfortunate misunder-standing.

Hagar, dressed in a suit, awaited the apology from Billy. Hagar had been told that Billy would speak at the news conference but Billy did not go to the microphone at the rostrum. Sapir did instead.

"I'm really glad we're all here and that this is all behind us now," said Sapir, dressed in an elegant suit with a showy, bright flowery tie. "I have talked to Ray and I have talked to Billy and I want you all to know how sorry they both are. They really both wish this never happened."

Sapir had no authority to speak for Hagar, but he was on a roll.

"So this is the end of this," the judge said, grinning. "They're both sorry, but as they say, love is never having to say you're sorry."

And with that, Sapir stepped away from the rostrum and encouraged Hagar and Billy to shake hands, which they did, as dozens of flashbulbs popped. Both men smiled.

"We left that room and got on a plane for Vegas to celebrate," Sapir said. "And we were having a drink on the plane and Billy says, 'Judge, that was just beautiful.'"

Later that afternoon, in a radio interview in New York, Steinbrenner announced that Billy would soon sign a new contract to manage the team in 1980.

Asked why the deal had been agreed to on that day, George answered, "I never said he wasn't going to manage in 1980."

35

THE OFF-SEASON OF 1978-79 might have started with a bang-bang in Reno, but otherwise, Billy kept a low profile. In mid-December, he did lend his name to an upscale Western apparel store on 69th Street near Madison Avenue in Manhattan. It was called Billy Martin's Western Wear.

The store, which sold expensive leather boots, belts, cowboy hats, shirts, and other Western-themed goods, would eventually move to the gilded Trump Plaza complex and was a busy and profitable midtown Manhattan enterprise for more than thirty years. It would ride the coattails of the *Urban Cowboy* craze.

But on the first day of operation, it was Billy who was center stage at a news conference, and he charmed both the sports and fashion press.

Asked what he knew about clothing trends, he answered, "I know that some people in New York long for the wide-open spaces of the range. They can't get there but they can feel some of that freedom with a nice pair of boots and a cowboy hat that expresses a kind of Wild West attitude. And, they just look nice. Even with a fancy suit."

When the topic turned to baseball, Billy handled questions about Reggie with aplomb, although he typically could not resist one dig at the Yankees right fielder.

When reporters noticed that the store had multiple photographs of Billy, Mickey Mantle, Whitey Ford, and Casey Stengel — but no pictures of Steinbrenner or Reggie — Billy answered with a grin, "Yeah, that's right. I want to get some pictures of George."

By early 1979, Billy was about twenty pounds heavier than he was when he resigned the previous season. He scouted other Major League teams for the Yankees and occasionally visited the organization's minor league system. That summer, the Yankees were about to begin a period of prudent amateur drafts. Among their 1979 picks was a line-drive-hitting first baseman/outfielder, Don Mattingly of Evansville, Indiana.

Billy occasionally had dinner with Bob Lemon. Lemon needed the companionship. Ten days after the Yankees' 1978 World Series victory, his son Jerry had been killed in a one-car automobile accident on an Arizona highway. Jerry Lemon was twenty-six years old and the youngest of the Lemon children.

Lemon was always an easygoing guy. He called everyone, from clubhouse boys to cleanup hitters, "Meat."

"Take a few pitches and work a walk, Meat," he would tell a batter in the on-deck circle.

"You got a question, Meat?" he would ask a reporter.

Lemon, a Hall of Fame pitcher, was once asked if he ever took a tough loss home with him.

"No," he said. "I left it in some bar along the way."

But in 1979, Lemon was haunted by the loss of his son. He had never been a disciplinarian. His managerial philosophy was to stay out of the way of talented players. But in 1979, an emotionally distracted Lemon was not fully paying attention either.

"We were a veteran team and veterans often don't want to do much in spring training anyway," said Piniella. "But that spring, we really kind of took advantage of the situation. We were sleepwalking through the spring, and poor Bob Lemon wasn't there mentally to give us a kick in the ass."

Not surprisingly, the Yankees quickly fell several games back in the standings at the start of the 1979 season. The team was lethargic and distracted.

Lyle had written a book with author Peter Golenbock, *The Bronx Zoo*, a salvo fired from the safety of the Texas Rangers' clubhouse. It was hard on Reggie and George Steinbrenner and the Yankees' crazed culture. The Yankees faced days and weeks of inquiries about the book, which became a bestseller.

Then on April 19, two heavyweights, the six-foot-three, 200-pound Rich Gossage and the six-foot-four and 215-pound backup catcher/designated hitter Cliff Johnson, got into a wrestling match in the shower after Gossage made a few verbal jabs at Johnson in the clubhouse after a game.

"That fight in the shower sounded like two semi tractor-trailers colliding," Piniella said.

In the tussle, Gossage fell against the shower wall and tore a ligament in the thumb of his pitching hand. He would be out for two months and never truly regain his form until the next season. If the 1979 Yankees had an irreplaceable player, it was Gossage.

Others were ailing, too. Munson's knees were so bad he was occasionally forced to play first base, making Heath's departure more noticeable. Reggie had a variety of leg issues. Everyone's production seemed condensed — Nettles, Chambliss, and Reggie all had lower-than-usual power numbers at the plate. The pitching staff was a mess.

"The 1979 team was tired," said Randolph, one of the few Yankees to have a stellar season. "Not just physically tired but maybe tired from all the stress of 1977 and 1978."

Billy was aware of the losing and the mounting frustration of George Steinbrenner, but he remained removed from it until May, when on a trip to New York Steinbrenner first talked to Billy about managing the Yankees earlier than expected.

While there might have been plenty of excuses for the Yankees' 1979 malaise, Steinbrenner was hearing none of it. The Yankees were the two-time defending World Series champions, and the Boss wanted another title. He called Billy and asked if he should fire Lemon and have an interim manager until Billy took over in 1980.

Billy convinced George to let him try to resuscitate the 1979 team — so long as it would not affect his tenure in 1980.

"Because the best way to build a winner is from spring training on," Billy said.

George said he understood that 1979 was not the litmus test for 1980. That would still be Billy's team. "No matter what happens," George said, using that phrase yet again.

On June 18, with the Yankees eight games out of first place — their record was 34-31 — George fired Lemon and brought Billy back.

Told a few days earlier that the move was imminent, Billy had called Lemon to warn him. Billy said he often felt sympathy for the managers he was replacing, especially when they were friends like Lemon. But there is a saying in baseball: Managers are hired to be fired. Billy knew the adage well. Collectively, the fraternity of managers rarely held a grudge. Each of them had replaced someone at some point, and it almost certainly had not happened after their predecessor retired.

The exiting manager felt bad and might be peeved. The new manager saw fresh opportunity, even if he knew the time would likely come when the shoe was on the other foot.

In 1979, Lemon said, "It's OK. Maybe you can get the boys playing again, Billy."

Lemon stayed on as a Yankees consultant. Al Rosen cried when he had to fire Lemon. Within a month, Rosen had resigned from the Yankees and never came back.

Stepping into this vortex of gloom, Billy was excited to have his number 1 jersey back on even if he sensed the enormity of the challenge facing him.

"It's going to take a total turnaround but we've got the championship players for that," Billy said on June 18 as he arrived at LaGuardia Airport on a flight from Chicago where he had been playing in a charity golf tournament.

At the airport, he was greeted by a mob of about two hundred Yankees fans and reporters who had been tipped off about his arrival.

"Thanks for the nice welcome," Billy said. Asked about what the 1979 Yankees needed, Billy said that "Reggie is the key guy to getting this turned around."

At Yankee Stadium the next evening, a crowd of just more than thirty-five thousand stood and cheered as Billy brought out the Yankees' lineup card before the game. Throughout New York, a dull, hot summer got a little livelier. As the New York Knicks' general manager, Eddie Donovan, told a reporter that day, "Billy is New York."

Billy tried to infuse his team with some of his emblematic fire and tenacity by managing the team from the third-base coach's box in his first game back. It did not matter; the Yankees lost to the Toronto Blue Jays, 5–4.

The next day, the Yankees won the opening game of a double-header but lost the nightcap, and in that game they lost another starting pitcher when Jim Beattie took a line drive off his pitching hand.

In the next game, Billy was up to his old tricks in a 3–1 victory. He put an infield shift on Toronto's left-handed power hitter John Mayberry at a critical juncture of the game — an unusual defensive strategy in 1979 — and got a groundout to the extra infielder who was playing in short right field.

At the start of the ninth inning, Billy left the left-handed reliever Jim Kaat, his former player on the 1969 Twins, in the game to warm up. The Blue Jays sent up a right-handed pinch hitter to lead off the inning. Billy countered with right-handed reliever Ron Davis.

"That's the matchup I wanted," Billy said after Davis induced three fly-ball outs to end the game.

It was the first of four successive victories. But that was all the magic that was left in the Yankees' 1979 season. The next day, Steinbrenner made public Reggie Jackson's demands to be traded. Reggie did not want to play for Billy. Steinbrenner said the team tried to deal Reggie but could not receive fair compensation.

Reggie continued to ask to be traded, and he was sitting out with a leg injury as well. Steinbrenner kept urging his best slugger to give Billy a second chance in what would later be called Billy II.

"I keep telling Reggie that he should try Billy again," Steinbrenner told reporters. "The first time I ate broccoli, I didn't like it. The second time I didn't like it. Now it's one of my favorite vegetables.

"I know Reggie is distraught but he should come out of it."

Which, amazingly, is apparently what happened. Reggie called Billy and the two talked. Reggie showed up to play the next day. The Yankees lost anyway.

"Billy has been great; I'm just not in playing shape," Reggie said.

Reggie did hit three home runs in his next four games, but the Yankees struggled nonetheless. In every way large and small — call it karma, the law of averages, old age, whatever — it was not the Yankees' year. It was evident in every meaningful or insignificant step along the way. In Seattle, they lost 16–1, and Billy was ejected from the game by umpire Nick Bremigan for arguing a call at first base. Billy immediately started kicking the dirt near first base on Bremigan's shoes.

But the game was being played in the Seattle Kingdome where the artificial surface had only small cutouts of dirt near the bases. Bremigan simply moved onto the artificial surface portion of the infield where there was no dirt.

Billy was flummoxed. No ump had ever escaped in that way.

Two nights later, Nolan Ryan one-hit the Yankees. Two days after that, the Yankees lost on a walk-off two-run homer.

But what was a dreary, cheerless season would then turn tragic.

Munson, the first Yankees captain since Lou Gehrig, was raised in Canton, Ohio, and despite ten years as a Yankee, he never permanently moved his family from the town where he grew up. To make it easier to fly home to his wife and three small children in Ohio, Munson had trained for his pilot's license. The Yankees' spring training complex was adjacent to the Fort Lauderdale executive airport, and it was easy for Munson to log hundreds of hours in the cockpit. By 1978, he had acquired his flying license and often spirited Piniella on jaunts to the Bahamas and elsewhere.

Most off days, whether the Yankees were at home or on the road, Munson flew his Beechcraft Baron, a turboprop plane, to Canton, catching up with his family and trying to ensure some normalcy in his household. Munson also flew Piniella and Reggie Jackson, whom Munson had accepted and now considered a friend, back to the New York area after a game in Baltimore one evening.

"He was totally in control of that plane," Piniella said. "I remember he buzzed his house and avoided a thunderstorm with a new flight plan. He was a good pilot in the Beechcraft."

But later in June 1979, Munson decided to buy a Cessna Citation, a sleek, powerful, twin-engine jet that cost him $1.4 million. It would cut the flying time to Canton, but it worried his friends, family, and teammates because of its higher speeds and because the pilot had to acquire multiple advanced skills — and be able to perform them without hesitation. It was the difference between being able to drive a sports car on an interstate and a stock car on a racecourse.

Munson showed off his new jet to Piniella and Bobby Murcer, a good friend from the early 1970s Yankees who rejoined the team in a mid-season trade.

"I know that Bobby Murcer and I both told Thurman that he didn't need that big, scary jet," Piniella said. "It looked like a rocket ship. You couldn't tell Thurman some things. He was going to have that jet."

More influential voices in Munson's sphere thought he should get rid of the Cessna, in which Munson had logged only thirty-three hours of flight time. His wife, Diana, was pretty sure she had convinced him to sell it as soon as the season ended.

On August 1, the Yankees finished a series in Chicago, and the team returned on a charter flight to New York. August 2 was a day off, so Munson did not go to New York with his teammates. Instead, he flew the Cessna to Canton. He had been certified as a jet pilot about two weeks earlier.

Munson noted some minor problems with the Cessna on the way home but rose early to have breakfast with his children. He then visited with his in-laws and some friends and headed to the Akron-Canton Regional Airport for lunch. He was not planning to fly that day, but when he saw a flight instructor, David Hall, and another friend and pilot, Jerry Anderson, he offered to show them his new jet and practice some touch-and-go landings.

The first four touch-and-go landings were uneventful. A fifth, on a different runway because of aircraft traffic, was more challenging. According to air traffic safety reports filed months later, Munson was distracted by a minor complication, did not follow the proper prelanding checklist, and failed to maintain the proper altitude. The jet clipped some treetops, lost a wing, and headed for the ground. Munson kept the jet level to the ground so that it landed with the nose up. The jet's fuselage remained mostly intact as it burrowed through some brush on the ground. Then it struck a large tree stump in a violent high-speed collision, spun, and came to rest near a road six hundred feet short of the runway.

All three occupants were conscious, but Munson's legs were trapped in the wreckage of the fuselage after the collision with the tree stump.

Munson yelled, "Are you guys all right?"

Fire began to engulf the jet's cockpit as Hall and Anderson tried to wrestle Munson free. The duo could not move the Yankees catcher. Twisted steel held him in place. The main doors to the jet were also jammed.

"We just couldn't get Thurman out of there," Anderson later told the *New York Daily News*. "We tried, but we just couldn't budge him. Smoke and flames shot in and it was so intense we didn't have any choice but to get out of there."

With Munson now unconscious, Hall and Anderson burst through an emergency exit and threw themselves to the ground. They would sustain multiple burns, be hospitalized, but survive. Firefighters were on the scene minutes later, but Munson, thirty-two years old, was pronounced dead from the effects of the blaze that consumed what remained of the Cessna. It was 4:02 p.m.

Expecting her husband to come home and barbecue the family dinner that evening, Diana Munson was surprised to hear the doorbell ring at the sprawling brick colonial she and Thurman had built not long before on a sweeping property with a rural view. Her three children, none older than nine, yelped, "Daddy's home."

It was instead officials from the airport who told Diana about the accident. "Thurman is gone," one said. Diana fell to her knees on the front lawn.

"After a while, I got back up and went inside to tell the kids that God wanted more good people in heaven," Diana said in an interview thirty-five years later.

George Steinbrenner got the news first and began calling the players, coaches, and manager individually. A calm Thursday in the New York sports world suddenly became a day forever remembered for the most jarring tragedy in the history of the city's best-known sports franchise.

Baseball Commissioner Bowie Kuhn called Munson's death "an almost indescribable loss."

Billy issued a statement: "For those who never knew him and didn't like him, I feel sorry for them. He was a great man, for his family, friends and all the people who knew and loved him, my deepest sympathy. We not only lost a great competitor but a leader and a husband and devoted family man. I love him."

Billy Joe, fourteen years old, was in New Jersey at his father's suite at the Sheraton Hasbrouck Heights.

"Thurman was my dad's favorite and he was just crying and a mess," Billy Joe said. "Dad was alternately crying and angry that it happened and he said he needed to go out to dinner. And I said, 'Dad, you can't go out. You'll drink and someone will say something, and even if they mean well, who knows how you'll react.'

"He agreed with me. I ordered a steak from room service and put some videos in the TV. We stayed home. We watched two John Wayne movies with him crying from time to time. He nibbled at his steak. Before dinner, I made him a Chivas and soda and set it down right in front of him. He never touched it. He was in a lot of pain, just breaking up every once in a while. We just sat there."

There was a ceremony at Yankee Stadium the next night, with home plate left empty for a moment of silence as the Yankees took the field to start the game. The Yankees lost, 1–0. They lost the next night as well. Munson's funeral was to be held Monday, and Steinbrenner chartered a jet to take the team to Canton that morning. They had a nationally televised game back in the Bronx that evening.

The funeral was held at the Canton Civic Center to contain the large crowd wanting to attend, and the eulogies left the assembly weeping. At the gravesite, Billy sobbed loudly. During another moment of silence before that night's game, Reggie Jackson convulsed in tears as he stood in right field. Murcer, the main speaker for the Yankees at the funeral, won the game by driving in all five runs in a 5–4 Yankees victory.

Munson's corner locker in the Yankees' locker room, near the trainer's room so he could easily escape the press, was left largely as it would have been had he been playing that night—his catcher's equipment hanging on hooks, his Yankees cap on a shelf, and his number 15 uniform on a hanger. A miserable Yankees season had become a nightmare.

"It started with Bob Lemon's son before the season," Roy White said many years later. "But after Thurman's death, that really destroyed everything. People were numb."

The Yankees, who would still win 89 games (in only 160 games played), stumbled to nowhere. In current times, the Yankees would have easily qualified for a wild card berth. But in 1979, they were just another non-playoff team.

Nonetheless, it is interesting to note that the 1979 Yankees were 34-31 for Lemon (a .523 winning percentage) and had a 55-41 record under Billy (a .573 winning percentage). Only four American and National League teams had a better winning percentage in 1979. And the Yankees lost their captain and on-field leader just past mid-season.

The demise of the Yankees did not generate the attention it once would have. In the fall of 1979, the New York tabloids had moved on. Americans had more pressing things on their minds. The United States embassy in Iran had been seized by a mob incited by the Ayatollah Khomeini. Hostages had been taken. A pivotal presidential election between Jimmy Carter and Ronald Reagan was weeks away.

The two-time defending champion Yankees became something they rarely were in New York during the 1970s: small headline news on the less-observed inside pages of the newspapers.

All the New York sports teams were in the doldrums again. The 1979 New York Mets, under Joe Torre, lost 99 games. The 1979 New York Giants lost 10 NFL games, completing the entire decade without making the playoffs. Only two other NFL teams never made the playoffs in the 1970s—one of them was the New York Jets.

The Knicks would not make the postseason in the coming 1979–80 season. The Rangers would lose in the second round of the Stanley Cup playoffs. The New Jersey Nets were a last-place team. The New York Islanders were the lone bright spot, on their way to winning their first Stanley Cup in the spring of 1980.

In this lull, Billy appeared to be rebuilding his life in divergent and not necessarily restful ways. His divorce from Gretchen was final, and he had girlfriends in multiple cities, a rotation that troubled his family back in California — not that his wives had been popular either.

Then, attending a game at Yankee Stadium in 1979, his daughter, Kelly Ann, came upon two young women seated nearby, which meant they had been given the tickets from a Yankees player, coach, or manager. Throughout the game, based on what she overheard, Kelly Ann deduced that at least one of the women had been spending time with Billy. She thought the woman was young, perhaps still a teenager.

Another of Billy's Berkeley relatives, Lucille Sabatini, told Billy biographer David Falkner that she also met a young woman at a 1979 Yankees home game. Her name was Heather. She was dating Billy, and Sabatini thought Heather was about sixteen years old.

Falkner, and other Billy biographers after him, wrote that Billy was dating a sixteen-year-old. Those accounts usually added that Steinbrenner was distressed that Billy might be arrested for having sexual relations with a minor.

Public records of the woman in question, Heather Elise Ervolino, seem to indicate that she turned twenty years old in August 1979. Others in Billy's circle are convinced Heather was younger, but they do not know how much younger and have no proof of her age. Heather, meanwhile, is elusive about her age — she declined to give her date of birth in a 2014 exchange — but in court proceedings and sworn affidavits filed in the 1980s, she listed the year of her birth as 1959.

What is known is that Heather was raised and lived in a scruffy South Bronx housing project with an extended family that included her grandmother.

"Heather was a nice young girl who never asked for much," said Eddie Sapir. "If she had food to eat and clothes — and she did not need anything fancy — then she was happy. She came from very little but she was a lady. Very well mannered.

"And she was fascinated by Billy. She wanted to make him happy."

Heather met Billy in 1978 or 1979. No one, including Heather, seems to be quite sure which of those two years it was. They met outside Yankee Stadium when she stood by a railing with her younger brother trying to get players' autographs. She was young, and looked even younger, but she had everything Billy liked in a woman: she was curvaceous, buxom, and sexy.

Heather would become Billy's third wife in November 1982. Late in 1979, she was at his side more often than not.

But Heather was far from worldly. She did not have her driver's license. She had received only a rudimentary education navigating the rough-and-tumble school system in the South Bronx. She came from little money. And she was devoted to her family.

Seeing some of his own family struggles in Heather's upbringing, Billy wanted to help all the Ervolinos. Soon Billy was treating Heather's younger brother like a nephew or stepson. Heather's mother and grand-mother came to Yankees games and occasionally on road trips. Billy never purposely excluded the family, so long as he also had enough time to be alone with Heather.

Billy was happy to be done with the 1979 season. It had been a miserable year. But it was not done with him yet.

In late October, after a weeklong hunting trip with his Minnesota buddy and restaurateur Howard Wong, Billy and Wong returned to Minneapolis. Billy planned to catch a late flight to Dallas to do some more hunting with Mickey Mantle. But the flight from South Dakota was late and Billy missed his Dallas flight. He got a new one the next morning. Billy searched for a hotel, but his usual choices in the Minneapolis area were full. Wong suggested the Hotel de France not far from Wong's restaurant.

Wong drove Billy to the Hotel de France and double-parked his car at the entrance. Billy checked in, put his bags in his hotel room, and the two men went to a bar in the hotel restaurant, the Café Colette, for a nightcap, which in Billy's case usually meant at least two or three drinks.

As often happened, some of the bar patrons recognized Billy. Two traveling salesmen seated next to Billy and Wong struck up a conversation. One of the men, Joseph W. Cooper of Lincolnshire, Illinois, did most of the talking to Billy.

Billy was usually happy to talk to people in a bar, but he did not like being lectured about baseball. Cooper had helped finish a bottle of wine at dinner and had a few after-dinner drinks when he approached Billy, who probably had as much to drink. For whatever reason, Cooper decided to share some of his baseball opinions with Billy, and the subject was a poor choice given his audience.

Cooper wanted to discuss the recently named 1979 Managers of the Year, an award Billy had won twice. Cooper said he thought the winners, Dick Williams in Montreal and Baltimore's Earl Weaver, deserved the award.

Cooper might as well have kicked Billy in the groin and jabbed a thumb in his eye. Because Steinbrenner was always threatening to replace Billy with Williams, Billy hated him.

Weaver and Billy were friendly but they were also archenemies. Billy thought Weaver got away with manic on-field histrionics that were no different from his own, and yet, Weaver still had the unqualified respect of baseball writers and administrators while Billy was called out of control and a troublemaker.

Late on a long day after a crappy season, Billy did not want to hear about what great seasons Dick Williams and Earl Weaver had.

"Dick Williams is an asshole," Billy said to Cooper. "They both are and so are you for saying that."

Cooper let the remark pass. The bar was busy with conventioneers and Billy was signing autographs.

"What do you do for a living?" Billy asked Cooper.

"I'm a salesman."

"What do you sell?"

"Marshmallows."

As Cooper told the story to the *New York Times* a week later, "He and Mr. Wong thought that was a big joke, as everybody does. They had a big laugh."

Billy had another drink and chatted up some other people at the bar. Cooper remained in his seat alongside Billy.

Here the versions of the story differ — as usual — although the one Billy related and the one Cooper told remained fairly consistent over time. Wong told a wild tale to reporters afterward that had Billy hardly even present other than being introduced to Cooper. That is not a credible version.

In Billy's telling of the next several minutes, Cooper was rude to him and kept bringing up the Yankees' failed season. Cooper wanted to know what Billy was going to do to fix the mess the team was in. Cooper never mentioned those comments in his account.

One thing is certain: Billy at some point decided he had had enough of the marshmallow salesman. That was not unusual. Billy's anger toward an antagonist — or a perceived antagonist — could intensify the longer that person hung around.

"Tell you what, Joe," Billy finally said, laying five $100 bills on the bar. "I bet you $500 to your penny that I can knock you on your ass."

Cooper, who was about three inches taller and forty pounds heavier than Billy, did not respond right away. But Billy did not take away the $500 and did not stop reminding Cooper about it. In Billy's side of the story, he eventually picked up his money and left the bar. Cooper followed him and shoved him from behind, and when Billy turned to confront him, Cooper swung and missed. Billy then punched Cooper in the lip, and the marshmallow salesman collapsed with a thud to the marble floor of the hotel.

Billy went to his room. A hotel security guy found Cooper on the floor and helped him get to a hospital where fifteen stitches closed the gash in his face.

That's not what happened, Cooper said. In his version, it was his own ego that got the best of him.

"Time comes when pride comes into focus," Cooper said. "I put a penny on Billy's $500 and said, 'Let's go.'"

The two men left the bar.

"Between the bar and the lobby is probably about 30 feet, and there's an archway in between," Cooper said. "He was ahead of me and I was behind. As we walked through the archway into the lobby, he abruptly turned and hit me in the mouth."

Cooper gave that account a week after the fight. A married father of two, he wanted to forget about the incident, as he suspected Billy did. Both men checked out of the Hotel de France the next day.

But the hotel security guard, who did not witness the fight — there were no witnesses other than the combatants — did call the local police about the injured traveling salesman. Billy's name naturally came up since he had been seen with Cooper for at least thirty minutes in the bar. Then someone in the Bloomington police alerted local newspaper reporters, who wrote about the incident two days after the event.

The first stories said only that a hotel guest who had been seen with Billy ended up lying on the lobby floor with a split lip. It did not take much of an imagination to run with the possibilities. Especially the likely possibilities. Eventually a police report surfaced, and in it Cooper said Billy hit him.

Billy denied it. His first response, delivered in a statement, was to say that Cooper slipped and fell and cut his lip. Or so Billy thought. He was on his way to his room. He wasn't paying attention to Cooper.

An alarmed Steinbrenner did not believe Billy and said he was launching an investigation. Steinbrenner was also being pressured by Commissioner Bowie Kuhn, who announced that he might instigate his own investigation into Billy's increasingly tumultuous off-the-field conduct.

George called Eddie Sapir in New Orleans.

"The first thing he says is, 'Who the hell is Howard Wong?'" Sapir said. "'And why is he always around for these fights?'"

It was a good question. Wong was a friend, and often in bars with Billy, but apparently not young enough or burly enough to prevent a fistfight when one was brewing.

Sapir suppressed a laugh and gave Steinbrenner a similar explanation. But the Yankees' owner grew serious.

"Somebody is lying," he told Sapir.

As Sapir listened, George continued: "Eddie, that guy in Minnesota fell and hit a marble floor. The manager of the New York Yankees probably put him there. The guy could have hit his head and been killed. What would we do then? I can't keep going through this."

Sapir thought for a minute.

"But I didn't have a comeback for that; I couldn't refute any of it," Sapir said in 2013. "The fact was, Billy was in trouble again. And, you know, we couldn't turn that one around."

Steinbrenner never released the findings of his investigation. He did not have to. Five days after Billy popped the marshmallow salesman who said too much about Dick Williams and Earl Weaver, Billy was fired as Yankees manager.

When he got around to answering reporters' queries, Joe Cooper asked, "Why would someone in his position jeopardize his career for something as foolish as this?"

In Reno, Nevada, the man at the cynosure of a similar ruckus the year before felt a measure of relief.

"The marshmallow salesman got me off the hook," Hagar said.

Billy saw little humor or irony in the situation.

As he always did when he was fired, he called his mother in Berkeley. She suggested he fly to California to see his family. It had been a long time since he had been in the old neighborhood. Billy went home and visited with his old chums and saw his granddaughter, Evie, Kelly Ann's child.

He was despondent, his sisters and cousins recall. His longtime friend Lew Figone took him hunting in Northern California. He hung out with some of his old Oakland Oaks buddies. In interviews many years later, each described Billy as being in a similar state of mind.

Billy had a lingering resentment toward Steinbrenner. To Billy's way of thinking, he had followed all of the owner's directives in 1979. He had gotten along with Reggie Jackson, and he managed the team through an arduous, heartbreaking season without an off-the-field incident or major disagreement with his bosses. There had been no dustups with the press, no problems whatsoever.

He had been professional in every way. Hadn't George promised that he would be back in 1980? Hadn't he said that would happen, "no matter what"?

Sure, he had slugged a loudmouth in a bar far away from the team in the off-season. To Billy's way of thinking, it was a random, unrelated act. Joe Cooper deserved it for being rude. Was that a firing offense?

Not to Billy it wasn't. He felt betrayed.

"I think the worst thing was that he thought that maybe this was the end of his time as a Yankee," his cousin Nick DeGennaro said. "He didn't know if he'd ever be back."

Billy stayed in the Bay Area for another week. Then another subject came up while Billy was there.

The last-place Oakland A's, who lost 108 games in 1979 and averaged slightly more than 3,700 fans at home games, were likely going to be looking for a new manager. Billy could come home and manage in the American League.

Billy laughed off the notion. Thirty years before, at twenty-one years old, he had left Oakland for New York, a trip that became more like a passage into another life altogether.

After all these years and all the seismic changes experienced since, who would attempt a return trip?

36

IN FEBRUARY 1980, COMMISSIONER Bowie Kuhn publicly vowed to buy out the Oakland A's mercurial owner Charlie O. Finley so that Major League Baseball could take over the hapless and financially strapped team and move it to New Orleans.

But Finley would not cooperate with Kuhn or sell the A's. There would be at least one more season in Oakland — not that anyone in the Bay Area was lobbying hard for that outcome. With the San Francisco Giants suffering through recent lousy seasons as well — the Giants would soon average just 7,800 fans per game — baseball was on life support in the Bay Area.

Finley needed a savior, someone desperate enough to try to revive a broken-down team with an uncertain future. He needed someone who feared being away from a baseball dugout so much that even the oppressed, left-for-dead Oakland A's looked appealing since the alternative was not managing at all.

Finley, who had fired the preceding year's manager, Jim Marshall, called Billy and soon had a new manager. Billy's annual salary on a two-year contract was $125,000, and Steinbrenner also gave Billy a lump sum of $150,000 to terminate his Yankees contract. Billy's coaches were Art Fowler; Clete Boyer, the former Yankees third baseman; Lee Walls, his old teammate and drinking buddy in Cincinnati; and George Mitterwald, who played for Billy in Denver and Minnesota and coached for him in Texas.

"I could have probably waited for a better job to open up with a good club that got off to a bad start," Billy said shortly after he donned the A's brassy green-and-gold uniform for the first time. "One of those jobs will open in May or June this year, but if I sat around, it would have been awful. I already had a tough year last year. I couldn't wait."

He was coming home, and most everyone around him was certain that would be good for his equilibrium.

"The most relaxed and happy I saw him since he turned forty-five was when he came back to manage the A's," his sister Pat said, recalling 1980. "He knew what he could do. That was his kind of project."

Said Augie Galan, his former mentor at James Kenney Park who was still living in Berkeley in 1980, "Some people around here said, 'Poor Billy, it's nice that he's come back. But he's stuck with a dog of a team.' And I said to those people, 'Just wait. You'll see.'"

The 1979 Oakland A's had the worst record in baseball, but the roster was not without talent. There were four durable starting pitchers under the age of twenty-eight. There was no bullpen to speak of, but Billy had a plan for that. The infield play was sketchy, but Billy thought the A's were underutilizing an infielder on their roster who had been a Yankees farmhand, Mario Guerrero. Billy made him the starting shortstop. And he elevated Mickey Klutts, one of his favorites from the Yankees, who had been buried on the A's bench. He had solid hitters at the corners with first baseman Dave Revering and third baseman Wayne Gross.

But the real stars of the team were the three young outfielders. In left field, Rickey Henderson, raised in Oakland, was in the second year of a Hall of Fame career. Under Billy's tutelage, Henderson became the best leadoff hitter and base stealer in the history of Major League Baseball. He was also a stellar outfielder.

Center fielder Dwayne Murphy was a fleet defensive player who could hit for average, steal a base, hit-and-run, and, like Henderson, had a high on-base percentage. The two were tough outs, took a lot of pitches, and unnerved opposing pitchers. The final piece to the trio was right fielder Tony Armas, a prototypical right fielder who hit for power, had a strong arm, and was a clutch hitter with men in scoring position.

So how did the A's lose so many games?

"We didn't know how to win," said Rickey Henderson. "All we knew was how to lose."

There was more to it than that. The 1979 A's had stolen 104 bases and had an on-base percentage of .302, which was the worst in the American League. In fact, the '79 Oakland A's were last in seven other categories: batting average, slugging percentage, total bases, hits, runs, doubles, and at-bats. They were second to last in home runs.

The pitching staff was last in hits and walks yielded and second to last in earned-run average.

Billy had his work cut out for him. There was a reason sportswriters had begun to call the team "the Triple-A's" or "the Oakland Pathetics."

But from the first day of spring training, Billy put in place a premeditated plan that was a little of his work in Denver, Minnesota, and the South Bronx. There were also some new strategies tailored to the 1980s, things that also suited the kinds of skills on the A's roster. Billy was beginning his thirtieth season around Major League Baseball (with one season, 1970, out of the game). He was ready to utilize everything he had learned from his many and varied experiences.

But mostly he was going to teach the fledgling A's the value of rattling an opponent, so that the opposing infielders, pitchers, and catchers were unsettled and unsure what the A's might try next. He wanted to show them the possibilities and how they led to runs. And just as "Money Ball" rediscovered two decades later albeit in a different way, it was all about producing runs — any way you could.

It came to be called Billy Ball, and it may have been his best work as a manager given the lack of resources available to him and how little the community cared about the team initially.

It began, as it always did for Billy's teams, in spring training. The first drills were about sliding with everyone in rubber pants. The next drills were about how to take a lead off first base, then second base, then third — especially third base. Billy told the A's they were going to steal home at least seven or eight times in 1980.

They laughed. The twenty-eight Major League teams combined probably didn't steal home eight times in 1979.

"You're crazy, Billy," Henderson said, giggling.

Answered the new manager, "Rick, you'll steal home at least four times. And you're going to break Ty Cobb's American League record for stolen bases in a season."

Henderson, a peculiar, inscrutable man whose crude language skills hid an astute knowledge of baseball, knew the record.

"That's 96 bases, skip," he said.

Said Billy, "We don't stop until you've got at least 100."

Then Billy explained how to execute a double steal, and a triple steal.

A triple steal? Trust me, Billy said, it confuses and demoralizes the other team.

The tutoring was nonstop at the A's spring training complex in Scottsdale, Arizona. The pitchers were retaught how to throw an inside brushback pitch, how to safely throw at a batter's head on a suicide squeeze bunt attempt, and how to cover first base on a ground ball.

"I don't care how else you already learned it," Billy said. "Now you're going to learn it the right way."

The infielders learned bunt coverage and how to pull off the hidden-ball trick and were instructed to let throws from the outfield bounce on the infield dirt when there wasn't a play on a base runner. Why let the ball bounce?

Because it might scar and dent the baseball, and Art Fowler was teaching his pitchers how to throw a scuff ball that broke down in the strike zone. Fowler also instructed his young charges in how to throw a spitball if they wanted to try it. The method went like this:

The pitcher vigorously rubbed the inside of his pant leg — right leg for right-hander, left leg for left-hander — with a bar of soap before the game. As the pitcher warmed up and began to sweat, a slimy but largely unnoticeable goo began to ooze through the pant leg, which the pitcher could easily access on the mound for the spitball. If an umpire suspected something, he would check a pitcher's glove, cap, jersey, and sleeves for illegal substances, but he would not pat down the pitcher's legs, especially the inside part of the leg.

So that the pitchers could learn all these tricks out of the media's view, Billy had a mound and plate set up near his trailer, behind a fence that obscured what was going on. When reporters asked him about it, Billy said it was a conditioning area.

A brainwashing center might have been more accurate.

Overall, the A's pitchers were getting an education in pitching from Fowler and Billy in multiple ways. The chief message was this: Walk more than two batters in an outing and you're going to be doing a lot of running as punishment.

The A's had led the AL with 654 walks in 1979. In 1980, they had 133 fewer walks. In fact, the pitching staff went from ranking at the back of the pack to ranking first in the league in several important categories, like earned-run average, earned runs yielded, and hits given up.

Billy also made it his personal project to raise the spirits of the twenty-four-year-old starter Matt Keough, who had a nasty array of pitches but also lost 15 straight starts in 1979. He finished with a 2-17 record and a 5.04 ERA.

"He just needs a manager who believes in him," Billy said. "He's a mixed-up kid who needs a father figure."

The 1980 A's, like many previously unsuccessful teams that absorbed and believed everything Billy said in spring training, started the season fast, winning seven of their first ten games and nine of the next fifteen games.

By late April, the A's had already stolen home twice — *and did it in the same inning.* On May 3, they entertained the Detroit Tigers at home in Oakland. On the mound for the Tigers was their ace, Jack Morris, an intimidating, fierce right-hander who had won 17 games the season before.

When the A's first base runner, the burly 220-pound Gross, reached third base, he broke for home as Morris began his wind-up on the first pitch to the next batter. As a right-hander, Morris saw Gross lumbering toward home — how could he miss him in that garish A's uniform? — but the startled Morris rushed his throw home and threw so high that catcher Lance Parrish had to leap to catch it. Gross slid in safely.

In the next inning, with the bases loaded and two outs — surely not a stealing situation — Billy called a triple steal with the fleet Dwayne Murphy at third base.

This time Morris threw so high the ball went to the backstop. Murphy scored standing up, and his teammate Mitchell Page, running from second, scored as well.

Morris was so enraged, after he got the final out of the inning, he flung the baseball into center field where it bounded to the wall. Parrish did Morris one better, going into the dugout and destroying the water cooler with a bat, which caused a minor delay in the game when the Tigers' dugout flooded and players were forced onto the field to escape the cascade of water.

Billy smiled under his black mustache, the one that would have been at home on either a riverboat gambler or a gunslinger. The A's won the game, 5–3, and kept their hold on first place in the AL West. The word spread in the East Bay. Attendance at A's games soon averaged more than twelve thousand fans, quadruple what the team was drawing in 1979.

People came to see what Billy would try next. With a runner on first base, he would call a hit-and-run but have the batter bunt instead of swing away. Why?

Because he would have the batter bunt toward the third baseman, and he had instructed the base runner not to stop at second base. A surprised shortstop would usually be too late trying to outrace the runner to third base for a throw.

"I can't tell you how many times that worked," Henderson said. "And the other team starts grousing and complaining. They're half angry and half embarrassed. And we're smiling. I tell you, it was fun. We felt like Billy knew something nobody else did."

Billy also taught Henderson to score from second base on a routine infield ground ball.

"It's about getting a good jump and watching to see if there's an opening for it," Henderson said, explaining the ploy. "Is the first baseman watching me? Can I surprise him by not stopping at third? Did the guy fielding the ball just lightly toss the ball over to first? That could give me extra time to score. I scored several runs that way.

"It took some guts to try it. But that wasn't a problem. Billy never flinched. 'Keep the pressure on,' he'd say in the dugout."

Billy's family was delighted to be able to watch him at work whenever they wanted. And they attended regularly. The team photographer, Mike Zagaris, recalls standing near the A's dugout before a game when a tiny old woman in the stands leaned over the railing and started screaming at him.

"Hey, photographer! Yeah, you, come over here," the woman said.

Zagaris walked over.

"Where's Billy?" she asked.

"I'm not sure, ma'am, probably in the clubhouse."

"Well, tell that little cocksucker to come out here," the woman said. "His mother is here to see him."

His sisters Pat and Joanie remember going to the games and seeing the excitement that Billy Ball was generating.

"That was Bill at his best," Pat Irvine said. "He had everything. He had it all."

Heather Ervolino was a semipermanent visitor. Her relationship with Billy had evolved far beyond the dating stage. She was his regular girlfriend, and Billy and Heather talked about her moving to live with him in California.

But Heather, at least twenty-nine years Billy's junior, worried about her mother, younger brother, and grandmother who would be left behind in the Bronx.

Without hesitation, Billy suggested that the entire family should come to the West Coast with Heather when the time came to do that.

In the summer of 1980, Billy also saw his daughter more regularly. Billy

Joe came to visit. Off the field, Billy occasionally went to the showy bars of Oakland's Jack London Square on the waterfront, but he usually didn't stay long, choosing to do his drinking in less boisterous, peaceable joints where the bartenders and most of the clientele knew him well. He favored the same places over and over, most of them in the town of Danville in San Ramon Valley not far from the apartment he kept. His regular stop was the Danville Hotel, an old stagecoach stop that in 1980 was mostly just a bar. No one bothered him there.

On the road, it was another story.

The two prominent fights with Ray Hagar and Joe Cooper, who in every story was now simply called "the marshmallow salesman," had permanently altered Billy's reputation and legacy. Before those two bar incidents, he had been known as Battlin' Billy, and he was noted for his fights on the field. Yes, there had been other bar fights, but they were more obscure and years removed when the media coverage was less obtrusive.

Most significantly, he had not been the manager of the world champion Yankees when they occurred. A Twins manager punches out one of his players in a Detroit bar and it's a one- or two-day story. But when the Yankees manager almost fights his best-known player on national television in the visitors' dugout at Fenway Park, then knocks out two other guys between seasons, those are stories with legs. That got the public's attention forever.

Billy was suddenly as renowned for his fists in drunken brawls as he was for his managerial career. He was likely more famous for the former than for the latter. He had always likened himself to a desperado from the Wild West; now he was living that life.

In bars, he was a marked man. Every guy with a few beers in his belly who thought he was a pretty good barroom brawler wanted to test himself against the most famous saloon slugger in America.

Even outside of bars, everywhere he went, people seemed to make a remark about his temper and inclination to start duking it out.

"When I checked into our hotel the other day, a guy held up his hands and said, 'Don't hit me now,'" Billy told Dave Anderson of the *New York Times* in 1980. "I get that all the time now. Like I'm going around slugging people. But some guys are hoping I will. One night in New Jersey, four different guys in four different bars tried to goad me. I finally had to go home. It must have been a full moon."

It would be this way for most of the rest of his life.

"I lived it a thousand times in a thousand places," said his son, Billy Joe. "Even when we'd be sitting at a table eating dinner some guy would almost always come over. It starts sort of harmless. Most guys come up and say, 'Hey, Mr. Martin, can I buy you a beer?' And my dad would say, 'That's OK, pard, I've got one and we're eating. But thank you.'

"But the guy wouldn't stop. 'Come on, let me buy you a Miller Lite.' And my dad would say, 'That's OK, thanks. Why don't you go back to the bar while we eat?' And then the guy would say, 'Why? Are you going to punch me now?'

"And it would escalate. The guy would say, 'Did you get fired today?' Or, 'Why don't you take a swing at me? Come on, you don't look so tough.'"

Billy's appearance was definitely part of the problem. Only five foot nine or five foot ten as he aged, Billy was a wispy 160 pounds.

"I watched hundreds of big bruising guys come up to my dad in a bar and say they were going to kick his little ass," Billy Joe said. "Big, scary guys. And my dad wouldn't back down. But he did try to talk them out of fighting. It just didn't always work. Frankly, that's why he hung around with some big guys like Lee Walls, who coached for him for several years. It was Lee's job to get those guys away from Dad.

"When I was in my twenties, it was sometimes my job. But I'm telling you, it never stopped. And if there was no one there to defuse it, and if some guy kept at it, sometimes my father would deck him. He didn't start fights but he was very good at ending them. People just never heard about those fights."

Billy's friend Lew Figone, who was a fearsome, brawny guy as a younger man, recalled a day around 1980 when he was meeting Billy at a bar in Northern California. From there Billy and Figone were to drive to Figone's hunt club.

"Billy used to wear this cowboy hat with a feather in it and in this bar before I got there, there were three guys at the other end of the bar who recognized him and started making fun of his hat," Figone said. "Billy apparently didn't say anything and these other guys kept drinking and getting more bold. Pretty soon they're challenging Billy to go outside and fight. It was the usual stuff: 'I'm no marshmallow salesman, Billy; why don't you try beating me up.'

"Billy just kept smiling at them. When I walked in, he stood up and announced to the three guys, 'OK, now we can go fight.' And he said to me, 'Let's go, these guys have been giving me shit for thirty minutes.'"

Everyone got up to walk toward the parking lot. Figone asked one of the other guys for his phone number.

"Why do you want that?" the guy said.

"Because I'm going to have to call your house," Figone said.

"Why?" the guy asked.

Answered Figone, "Because you're going to be unconscious in the parking lot and someone will have to come pick you up."

The guys who had been hassling Billy decided to just go home.

"But Billy had to put up with these guys and their beer muscles all the time," Figone said.

This kind of pugilistic celebrity did not attach itself to other managers and athletes, even if they got in a public brawl. The Dodgers' Tommy Lasorda traded punches with a former coach, Jim Lefebvre, in the greenroom of a Los Angeles television station before the two were scheduled to go on an interview show in 1980. Lasorda was bloodied and left the station without going on camera. Newspaper stories were written about the episode. It was big news in Los Angeles for a day or two. Then it was soon forgotten.

Earl Weaver was no stranger to gin joints, and he had a few late-night tussles with unnamed patrons that made minor news. Those fisticuffs had no longevity in the public consciousness. Lasorda and Weaver are in the Baseball Hall of Fame.

"I always thought Billy got a bad rap for all that bar-fighting stuff," Weaver said a few months before he died in 2013. "It's true that he didn't control, or manage, himself as well in those situations as he maybe should have. He would snap. Public figures aren't allowed to snap. It would have been nice if he could have found a way to avoid all that. But people didn't make it easy on him either."

When Weaver's comments were related to Lasorda, he had another opinion.

"Maybe Billy was just better at punching people than the rest of us," Lasorda said. "Maybe that's why everyone knew about it when it happened. He was laying guys out."

Steve Vucinich, the A's clubhouse manager then and now, became Billy's driver and quasi-official team companion whenever Billy made public appearances, which he did frequently when promoting the A's in the East Bay community in 1980–81.

"Billy was great with the crowds, people loved him," Vucinich said. "He was great with kids and did his Donald Duck voice, which they loved. Women were drawn to him. He could charm anyone and it was a lot of fun being around him, I'll tell you that. After a public appearance, we'd go off to some bar and it didn't matter the neighborhood because he was good with ethnic or diverse gatherings, too. He was especially good with regular workers, tradesmen, dockworkers, just all those kinds of guys. He was authentic and they sensed that.

"But on some of those nights, as it got later, there would just be one guy who didn't like him. Billy would get up to go to the bathroom and I'd hear some guy say, 'That Billy Martin is an asshole.' And I knew there could be trouble.

"I remember one night, the guy sitting next to him just kept flicking his cigarette ashes on Billy's arm and hand. Billy kept asking him to stop, but the guy just stared at him and kept flicking the ashes on him. We got up and left.

"Another night, at the Oakland Hyatt bar — a nice place — a guy hauled off and sucker-punched Billy without warning. Billy didn't hit him back. We left. But that's what could happen. Not every night but it happened."

Early in the 1980 season, on the road fans found a novel way to remind Billy of his new place in the American culture. They pelted him with marshmallows. It was a cheap, and almost harmless, way to taunt him. Would stadium officials throw someone out of the ballpark for flinging a marshmallow? And how would they do that if dozens of people were doing it?

In Minnesota during a 20–11 loss, hundreds of people were throwing marshmallows at Billy.

Billy did not help his cause when he filmed a Miller Lite beer commercial that featured Jim Shoulders, the rodeo cowboy. Shoulders talked about how real cowboys liked Miller Lite because it had fewer calories and kept them light on their feet.

Standing next to a crowded bar, Shoulders says, "You don't want to be filled up when you're out there punching doggies."

He taps the turned back of a seemingly anonymous patron in Western garb and asks, "Ain't that right, cowboy?"

Billy spins around on his barstool and says, "I didn't punch that dog-gie."

So maybe Billy was more at peace with his image than those around him were.

As Vucinich said, "I think Billy knew what Billy Martin had become. Some of it he didn't like. But he liked being famous. He liked having the money and flying first class. We'd be driving across the Bay Bridge and people would recognize him and pull alongside the car to take pictures.

"He liked that. He had once been a nobody in the East Bay. Now they're snapping his picture on the Bay Bridge. He'd wind down the window and give them a big smile."

Billy's 1980 A's were no longer in first place on June 13 when the Yankees made their first visit to Oakland. Dick Howser, Billy's former third-base coach, was the visiting manager. On the first pitch of the game, Billy had starter Brian Kingman throw a brushback pitch under the chin of the Yankees' leadoff hitter, Willie Randolph.

Reggie was backed off the plate twice. But the Yankees won anyway. A week later, the A's made their first trip to New York and Billy was greeted with a long ovation from the Yankee Stadium fans. They still loved him. A couple of days later, he wore his number 1 Yankees jersey at the Old Timers' Day game. Before he was introduced to the Yankee Stadium crowd, wire service photographers caught Billy sitting alongside Reggie, the two laughing and talking.

In the Yankees' clubhouse afterward, Howser said he was just happy to get through an Old Timers' Day without Billy being announced as the future manager of the Yankees.

The Yankees and Reggie were having spectacular years, with the Yankees well on their way to claiming the AL East with a 103-win season. The A's would rally late to win 83 games and finish second to the high-flying Kansas City Royals, who won 97 games. Again, there were no wild card teams.

Billy was named Manager of the Year for a third time for improving Oakland's record by 29 victories.

The 1979 A's had won 33.3 percent of their games. With roughly the same roster and no additional financial backing — the A's were the only team in Major League Baseball not to sign a single free agent — the 1980 A's won 51.2 percent of their games.

Henderson stole exactly 100 bases, including home 4 times. He had a

.420 on-base percentage. Matt Keough, the hard-luck starter in 1979, had a 16-13 record with an impressive 2.92 ERA. The A's stole home 8 times, just as Billy said they would. The A's scored 109 more runs in 1980 than in 1979 and had 136 more hits, including 24 more home runs. In the field, they made 44 fewer errors.

Perhaps the most important stats were off the field. The A's drew about 500,000 more fans. That made it easier for Finley to sell the club for $12.7 million to the owners of Levi Strauss, the Bay Area apparel company. A year earlier, the estimated value of the team was about $5 million.

The chief executive of the A's new ownership group, Roy Eisenhardt, quickly gave Billy a new five-year contract. It named Billy as manager and director of player development, which put him in charge of all baseball personnel decisions in the Oakland system. The A's would not have a general manager. Billy was running the entire baseball side of the franchise.

The deal also gave Billy the use of a sprawling mansion in tony Blackhawk, an exclusive master planned development east of Danville and Oakland. Billy quickly made plans to move Heather Ervolino and her family to the Blackhawk mansion.

"Billy was set," said Morabito, the publicity director and Billy's good friend who had left the Yankees to take a similar job with the A's in 1980. "He had it all."

That fall, the Yankees were swept by the Royals in three close games during the AL Championship Series. Shortly thereafter, George let Howser go. Gene Michael was named the new manager.

"Billy and I were sitting in a bar in Oakland after Dick Howser got fired," Morabito recalled. "And Billy said, 'Do you believe what George did?' I said, 'Of course I do. Let's just be happy we're here and not there. This is good. This is as good as it gets.'

"And he kind of looked at me funny. And I said, 'What? You're not thinking of ever going back there, right?' And he took a sip of his drink and slowly said, 'No. No way. Not right now.'"

37

BILLY'S NEW LIFE AS a field manager and general manager began with baseball's winter meetings in Dallas. Joe DiMaggio was there to receive an award and greeted Billy in the vast lobby of the Anatole Hotel. The two were going to dinner.

"Hey, Dago," DiMaggio said as Billy walked up. Some things do not change.

The sixty-six-year-old silver-haired DiMaggio sized up Billy and asked, "Are you growing taller or am I growing shorter?"

"Don't worry, it's my cowboy boots," Billy replied.

Unexpectedly, an elderly man appeared at Billy's side, grabbing him by the arm as if to capture his attention. The man, whom Billy had never seen before, gently began pulling Billy in another direction for a private conversation.

"Hey, easy, pard," Billy calmly said.

"I just need to talk to you for a minute," the man said.

Billy smiled at DiMaggio, turned to the man, and asked, "You're not a marshmallow salesman, are you?"

Billy was in good humor heading into 1981. He believed he was sitting on a young, maturing A's team that was ready to explode.

"He told me one night that we were going to destroy the division," Clete Boyer said.

A's pitcher Mike Norris, a castoff before Billy arrived who had become the ace of the staff, said many years later that the 1981 team fed off Billy's cheery, joyful demeanor heading into the season. Matt Keough said Billy had created a giddy, happy family.

"And Billy encouraged us to hang out and enjoy the togetherness," Keough said.

In spring training in Arizona, party central was the Pink Pony bar. It was the social hub of the Cactus League, which back then was not much more than a handful of Western-based teams. The Pink Pony might as well have been Toots Shor's West.

Zagaris, the team photographer, had a background as a photographer for British rock stars. He was friends with the Who and the Rolling Stones. He thought he had seen it all on their tours of the world.

"I'd been around a lot of crazy shit, but Billy, his coaches, and some of the players, they kept up to that level," Zagaris said. "I didn't see drugs. It was all alcohol based. But some of these older guys were serious, professional drinkers. Some mornings at the batting cage in spring training with the coaches standing there, it didn't smell like alcohol. It smelled like someone had dumped a quart of Jim Beam on home plate.

"The players didn't stay out as late, but they'd come by to catch part of the fun. It probably wasn't good for anyone's health, but Billy forged a close-knit bunch of guys."

When the regular season began, the A's won their first eleven games, eight of them on the road. At the second home game of the year, it was two years to the day since the A's drew 653 fans to a game. Now the A's had a crowd in excess of 50,000.

By the third week of the season, Oakland had a 17-1 record. At the end of April, the A's were 18-3. *Time* magazine put Billy on the cover under the headline IT'S INCREDIBLE!

The five-man starting rotation of Norris, Keough, Kingman, Steve McCatty, and Rick Langford was plowing through the American League, overwhelming batting lineups. The starting five's cumulative ERA was 1.42. Because there was little help in the bullpen, the starters usually finished what they started.

Years later, there was concern that the young arms on the staff were being ruined by overuse. At the time, it did not come up.

"That's because it really wasn't Billy's idea," said McCatty, now the pitching coach for the Washington Nationals. "It became a badge of honor among the five of us. One of the things Billy and Art had taught us was how to get batters out the third time around the batting order. Your fastball velocity is down at that point, they've seen your other pitches. Can you get those batters out again?

"It took guile and guts and once we learned to do it, we wanted to keep doing it. We hung our pride on that as a group. Billy tried to get us out of games; we just didn't want to come out. And Billy was loyal. He was the kind of guy who stuck with you. He liked to see that mettle."

A few years later, when the same five pitchers struggled and had significant injury issues, the strategy to let the starters pitch so many innings would not look so prudent.

But in 1981, the A's were pressing the accelerator to the floor. The A's were a streaking comet, challenging some of the best starts in the history of the Major Leagues. And that turned out to be important in a season that was being played with a discernible undercurrent of labor unrest.

At issue was free agency and how it would be carried out in the future. With the owners taking a hard line, the players' union voted to strike in June. Most expected the season to be interrupted with a new agreement and contract coming along about a month after the players' strike began. (Previous work stoppages since 1972 had not lasted much longer than five weeks.)

The prevailing belief was that the 1981 regular season would be split in half. The division winners of the two halves — if two different teams won each half — would play in a postseason divisional series with the winners advancing to the league championship series.

With the likely interruption of the season coming in June, every team was trying to make sure it was in first place when the strike occurred since it assured a postseason berth.

The A's were in better position than anyone. At home, they passed the million mark in attendance for the first time in several years and did so in early June. Billy was enjoying life, although he did twice wear a bulletproof vest — once at a game in Oakland and once in Chicago — when a man called and threatened to shoot him.

Police told Billy to stay off the field. He did not listen, even going out for several minutes to argue with an umpire in Chicago. And Billy, in general, was not getting along with the umpires any better than he had in the past.

In May, Billy was suspended for a week for bumping umpire Terry Cooney. The umpires' union said they were considering suing Billy for assault. It was not the first, or the last, time that was considered. Billy also had an ugly exchange with another ump in 1981, kicking and throwing dirt at him.

Now fifty-three years old and well into middle age, Billy was not mellowing when it came to the arbiters of the rules. It was a battle he never stopped fighting.

"Probably the meanest, most unfair man of all on the field," umpire Durwood Merrill said of Billy in 1981.

When the players' strike did indeed interrupt the 1981 season on June 12, the A's were in first place with a 37-23 record and became the first-half winner of the AL West. They could relax for the so-called second half of the season.

It took about six weeks for labor peace to be achieved. Billy used the time to try and sort out a personal life that had grown increasingly complicated and byzantine, even for him.

Heather Ervolino, her brother, mother, and grandmother were living in the Blackhawk house leased to Billy (with an option to buy). Heather, demure and never demanding of Billy, had been in Billy's sphere for several years. That didn't stop Billy from courting other women.

In July 1980, while the A's were playing in Anaheim, he spotted Jill Guiver, a twenty-five-year-old freelance photographer working near the visitors' dugout. Jill was not hard to notice. Pretty and shapely with long blonde hair, Jill had a sultry appeal along with what people once called a "nice figure" because it was impolite to say that she easily filled out a tight blouse.

Other ballplayers had noticed Jill, who was occasionally a stringer for the Associated Press. Billy got her to go out on a date with him.

"I agreed to go but I knew I wasn't going alone because the thought made me nervous," Jill said, sitting at her summer horse farm in Massachusetts during one of multiple interviews in 2013. "I called my girlfriend Jodi and told her she was coming with me. We met Billy at the Stox Restaurant by Disneyland. We waited and waited and waited and he didn't show up at first. So we were like, 'Oh, this is great,' and we headed for the door. And that's when Billy walked in with George Mitterwald, who was a coach for him in those days. So off we went, back into the bar.

"And we just hit it off immediately. Right from the start, we had the best time together. After that, whenever we could be, we were pretty much inseparable. Although obviously, he was in Oakland and I was in Southern California so it took some maneuvering.

"I now know a lot more about what was going on, of course. But at that time, all I knew was that we had a good time. We laughed. He was romantic and sent flowers and presents. He was the best dancer I ever knew, and when he would twirl me across the dance floor, it was breathtaking.

"He made me feel like I was the most special person in the world."

But Jill was not like any other woman who had ever taken a serious, years-long twirl in Billy's life. For starters, she came from a family well versed in the ways of big-time sports, and she was acquainted with wealth. Her father, Russell Guiver, ran a mortgage company and was a real estate developer. Russell's brother, Harold Guiver, became a sports agent representing many NFL players. After a few years, he was named a vice president of the Los Angeles Rams. Through her father and uncle, Jill grew accustomed to attending every major sporting event in Southern California — she recalled, for example, briefly meeting Billy at the 1977 World Series through Frank Sinatra, who was acquainted with her family.

"I was very familiar with all of that stuff," she said.

Jill was athletic, competing in the horse show circuit from a young age. The breeding and training of horses has remained a lifelong vocation and avocation.

After graduating from high school, Jill attended some community colleges but was soon drawn to photography. In the late 1970s, she got part-time jobs as a photographer, landing a gig as a stringer for the *Los Angeles Times* and other news outlets. She also completed her training and apprenticeship to be a flight attendant for Golden West Airlines. In July 1980, a friend of a friend asked her to work the game in Anaheim where she met Billy.

Soon, she was hopscotching the continent to be with Billy, although exclusively on the road. She knew that Billy was in another relationship in Oakland. She says she did not know how serious that relationship was.

"He told me there was this young girl and she had a family from the Bronx that he was helping out and so there was this girl he was seeing and that it was going to end," Jill said. "It's not a great excuse but that's what he told me."

For the rest of 1980 and into 1981, Billy saw Jill at A's away games and during well-timed off-season visits to Southern California. Billy saw Heather when he was at home with the A's.

Billy's double life was well known to the A's community.

"He had two steady girlfriends basically," said Sapir. "He helped support them in two homes — Heather in Blackhawk, Jill in Newport Beach in Southern California."

Sandy Alderson, the current general manager of the New York Mets who has had a long career as a respected baseball administrator, started his time in baseball as the A's general counsel in 1981. Alderson, who had graduated from Harvard Law School five years earlier, recalled how Billy felt he had higher moral standards than some of his players who would have one-night stands with random women while traveling. Billy proudly explained to Alderson that he kept to one woman on the road. And one at home.

Billy did have to jump through elaborate hoops to maintain his dual lives. In the off-season, he sometimes told Heather he was flying to two cities — say, Denver and Kansas City — for speaking appearances when he was actually spending the week in California with Jill. Returning to the Oakland airport after his trip south, he would tip skycaps $20 or $30 so they would give him Denver and Kansas City baggage tags, which he would place on his luggage after he removed the airline tags from Southern California.

Then he would head back to the Blackhawk house. Once in a while, someone might tell Heather that they saw Billy with another woman, a sexy blonde. If Heather asked Billy about it, he would say that the woman was friends with Eddie Sapir or dating the bachelor Mickey Morabito, since one or the other usually traveled with Billy.

"The whole thing was kind of dangerous and crazy," Sapir said. "And I told him that at some point, but you could only advise Billy so much on his personal life. You couldn't tell him what to do.

"He lived day to day, and in his mind, he wasn't doing anything wrong. Both of his girlfriends were happy. So was he."

Jill, who gave rare, brief interviews in 1990 and then did not speak to any reporter, biographer, or baseball historian about Billy for the next twenty-three years, agreed to speak at length for this book. Asked if she was indeed happy in 1980–81 even though she knew Billy had another relationship, she nodded her head in agreement.

"Granted, I didn't know the whole story, especially what was to come," she said. "I'm not proud of that time. But he was who I was in love with. So if he said he was going to make it good, that's all that mattered to me. And he did make it good.

"We had a great thing. I can't explain it to other people. I can't condone everything he did but in my particular circumstances, it worked out to be the correct thing to do."

Billy's family did not like either woman. Heather rarely, if ever, set foot in the old West Berkeley neighborhood. Jill was not welcome there.

The writers covering the A's saw more of Jill than of Heather and often blamed her for his disposition day to day.

"He fought with her," Kit Stier, the most veteran A's beat writer, said of Jill. "He'd come into the ballpark on the road and he'd be in a bad mood and all the guys would go, 'Jill's here.'"

Said another writer, Bruce Jenkins, "You'd see Jill in the hotel bars with him and in public and Heather was sort of this mysterious figure."

Heather Ervolino, whom others in Billy's circle described as someone who always tried to avoid the spotlight, has virtually never talked to reporters about her life with Billy. She refused to assist or engage with previous Billy biographers and has spurned interview requests since she and Billy separated in the mid-1980s. Heather was cooperative at various times during the research of this book and helped verify facts in the chronology of her time with Billy—important assistance since many of the details of their relationship are shrouded by misinformation.

Remarried for several years now, with children she raised in the East Bay, Heather said she did not want to revisit in detail the soap opera–like conditions of her existence in the early 1980s. Of her time with Billy in that period, Heather preferred to recall what drew her to Billy in the first place.

"He had a great heart," she said. "People always associate Billy with his temper, but he had a great heart as well."

Her memories of Billy are, interestingly, of his loyalty and passion.

"Billy was very loyal to his true friends and would do anything for them," she said. "And baseball was always his greatest love and passion."

Of the other many convoluted or irregular details of her life with Billy, Heather, who has stayed in touch with many of Billy's friends, called them "something from a long, long time ago."

Billy's son, Billy Joe, spent ample time with Heather from 1980 to 1984.

"I was prepared not to like her because this was a woman who came into my father's life after my mother," he said in 2014. "But I became a big fan of Heather's. She was good for my father and I know she loved him very much."

But since Billy Joe and Heather were not far apart in age, it led to some unusual moments.

"I remember going to the mall with her friends and flirting with all of them," he said. "I remember that Heather and I could tell people that we were brother and sister and they would believe us. We could tell them we were boyfriend and girlfriend and people would believe us.

"The only thing they wouldn't believe is if I told them that Heather was my stepmother."

Billy Joe called Heather "a pleaser."

"She wanted to make people happy, especially in my father's sphere," he continued. "If she found out what kind of food you liked, she would have it in the kitchen the next time you came over to the Blackhawk house. She was very mothering.

"But she was also very shy by nature. My father had lots of dinners and things to go to and Heather did not want to go to those. It didn't fit her personality."

She would stay home.

"And the whole deal with Heather and Jill? Well, that was just crazy. I don't know what to say. My father was a connoisseur of women."

If Billy's off-the-field life was a bit nontraditional, when the 1981 season resumed in early August, everything in his professional life was business as usual. The A's continued to play well. They did not keep the pace they had in the first half, but none of the four first-half "winners" in Major League Baseball were also "winners" in the second half of the strike-shortened season.

Billy did not take some of the losing well. After one defeat, his A's were treated to the always-memorable scene of one enraged, 160-pound manager flipping over a long table of party platters and assorted food and refreshments.

"He did it with a lot of power, man — guys were wiping mayo and mustard off their gloves, shoes, and uniforms for the next two days," said Zagaris, the team photographer. "But he got their attention."

In the inaugural American League Divisional Series, the Yankees squeaked past the Milwaukee Brewers in five games while the A's authoritatively swept the Kansas City Royals. Heading into the AL Championship Series, another best-of-five series that began in New York, the A's looked like the team to beat. Steinbrenner was worried and jealous. He had already dumped Gene Michael as manager, on September 6, and replaced him with Bob Lemon. Secretly, George told one and all that the A's stunning success made him question his decision to part with Billy over the marshmallow salesman fight.

The Yankees still had the edge in depth and experience, two things the A's lacked. But the focus, to no one's surprise, was the obvious story line: Billy's upstart A's against Steinbrenner and the owner's post-Billy, retooled Yankees.

"If Billy and all the ex-Yankees beat him," Oakland's Jim Spencer, one of the ex-Yankees, said of Steinbrenner, "I think George would be especially humiliated."

But the pressure on Billy was evident, too. He had willed and nurtured his young team to this moment, and he was expected to somehow steel them through the intensity of the playoff environment — or steal a victory or two. But playoff baseball is a different game from the one played in the regular season. With no long-term strategy concerns, managers try to maximize every situation with pitching matchups, and the games tend to be close affairs where a team's pitching diversity matters more than ever.

With sturdy starting pitchers, the A's felt confident. But in a playoff series, a team's bullpen is almost always tested as well. Complete games by a starting pitcher are rare. Since 1970, fewer than a handful of teams have advanced to the World Series — or won a World Series — without a stud in the bullpen or a versatile relief corps to complement the starters.

Billy was putting all his faith in his young, homegrown starters because the penny-poor A's had a ragtag band of castoffs in the bullpen. In their bullpen, the Yankees still had the Hall of Famer-to-be, Gossage.

"We're young but we're also the future of this league — and maybe the future starts now," Billy said on the eve of the first game.

Maybe, but first someone had to rid Mike Norris of some typical youthful jitters as he made a start before a packed Yankee Stadium crowd and national television audience. Unfortunately for the A's, there was no time for nervousness. The veteran Yankees pounced first.

In the bottom of the first, Norris walked two batters. A single loaded the bases with two outs.

Pitching to Graig Nettles, Norris quickly got two strikes. Knowing that the left-handed-hitting Nettles liked to slap two-strike pitches the other way — lofting them over the shortstop's head — Billy moved Henderson in two steps in left field. Norris's delivery was on the outside half of the plate, and Nettles went to left field with it, but he did not flick his bat at it; he ripped a hard line drive.

Henderson raced back, but the ball just eluded his grasp and rolled into Yankee Stadium's cavernous left-center field, often called Death Valley. Nettles's double emptied the bases and the Yankees had a 3–0 lead.

Norris and reliever Tom Underwood did not give up another run, but the A's batters scored just once against Yankees starter Tommy John and the Yankees' fearsome bullpen. The Yankees won 3–1.

It was up to McCatty, who led the AL with a 2.33 ERA, to get the A's even in the second game. But McCatty, a dominant, tough-nosed pitcher in 1980–81, was winless in five career starts against the Yankees. In the second game, he did not survive five innings against the Yankees' bats.

It was Billy's worst nightmare as he had to go to his inexperienced and undertalented bullpen early. McCatty left and four A's relievers proceeded to give up thirteen hits, including five straight after McCatty exited. The Yankees' newest star and the league's highest-paid free agent, Dave Winfield, had a stellar game offensively and defensively in a 13–3 Yankees rout.

The series returned to Oakland, where a sellout crowd greeted the A's. Before the game started, the circular stadium was in full throat, performing a new ballpark phenomenon: the Wave. Fans had also brought drums to bang and horns to blare. It was a carnival atmosphere, and when Billy took the lineup cards to home plate, he got a standing ovation. He waved his cap and his arms, encouraging more of the intimidating noise and tumult.

The A's got the steady starting pitching they needed from Matt Keough, Billy's pet project. Then, Oakland's first inning started promisingly with Henderson singling and stealing second. Dwayne Murphy, the second half of the A's one-two punch at the top of the lineup, was at the plate. But after Murphy's second swing at a pitch from Yankees starter Dave Righetti, Murphy collapsed to one knee, writhing in pain. He had strained a rib cage oblique muscle. Within an hour Murphy would be in an Oakland hospital getting his injury treated.

The A's did not score in the first inning and a tense, scoreless game ensued. Righetti, the AL Rookie of the Year, was matching Keough pitch for pitch.

In the bottom of the fifth, Henderson swung and missed a pitch to strike out. He went back to the dugout grasping his right wrist in pain. A strain, or worse, was suspected. Henderson left the game to ice his wrist.

Three batters later, in the top of the sixth inning, Willie Randolph, Billy's earliest protégé with the Yankees, lashed a solo home run to left field.

Keough kept the Yankees in check until the ninth inning, when Nettles contributed his second three-run double. The Yankees swept the series with a 4–0 victory.

The raucous, rowdy Oakland–Alameda County Stadium crowd went silent, the air deflating from an inspiring two-year run that had ended quickly and ingloriously. The Yankees were heading for their fourth World Series in six seasons. Nettles, who had also made three spectacular plays in the field, was named the Most Valuable Player of the series. At a Yankees party in Oakland after the game, Nettles got into an argument with Reggie, whom he never liked. Nettles punched Reggie in the head, knocking him to the ground.

Among the Yankees, it was said that Reggie was the only thing Nettles dropped that October.

As the unexpected and thorough sweep was being digested afterward, both teams were gracious; Piniella visited the A's locker room to hug Billy.

"That man taught us how to win and I wanted him to know that," Piniella said.

Keough approached Billy in the losing clubhouse and apologized.

"I'm sorry," he said.

"Nah," Billy said. "You did good."

"Not good enough."

Later, at his locker, Keough said he was most upset for his manager.

"That guy got us here; that guy made it happen," he said. "I know how much this meant to him. So it hurts not being able to help him. I know he's very disappointed."

It would be more accurate to say that Billy was anguished. It was his third defeat in five appearances as a manager in the AL Championship Series.

Reporters found him afterward, alone in his office.

"No excuses," he said in a low, barely audible voice as he sat behind his desk and in front of a broad wall adorned with photos of Casey Stengel and other mementos of his career. "They beat us. We battled. They just did better."

He looked around the room, then answered a few more questions, lamenting the injuries to Murphy and Henderson and crediting the Yankees. Finally he said, "I've got nothing else to say. That's what happened. They beat us."

Billy got up and started to unbutton his game jersey. Then he jerked the jersey from his shoulders and in one swift, fierce, angry motion hurled it into a corner. He sank back into his swiveling office chair, his back still turned as he slouched forward and stared at the floor between his feet.

Billy Martin, a World Series hero in baseball's Golden Era and a world champion manager just four years earlier, would never appear in another postseason baseball game.

38

THE A'S LOSS IN the American League Championship Series did not diminish Billy's star in the Bay Area or the rest of the nation. He was, in fact, hotter than ever. Billy Ball was an incorporated trademark with most of the profits divided between the A's and Billy, although the team got the lion's share. But Billy did a host of television commercials in the Bay Area. And he went to New York to act in two more Miller Lite beer commercials. His fame had not waned in the least.

While he had multiple endorsements, he also squandered the chance at a potential big one. The national department store chain Sears wanted to introduce a line of Billy Martin casual wear. It would be a lucrative deal. The top executives at Sears wanted to meet Billy beforehand, and they invited him to their headquarters, sending a private jet to whisk Billy and Sapir to Chicago for an evening dinner and a get-acquainted session.

The Sears folks perhaps should not have stocked the jet with Scotch. Billy showed up drunk. The Sears officials canceled the deal.

But there was more money rolling in from other sources, most of it from a long procession of public appearances and autograph-signing opportunities. The checks did not go through the proper tax channels. The IRS was already onto him. Billy never claimed he did not get the checks. He was not charged with fraud, just forgetfulness, a fault that cost him dearly (plus interest).

In late 1981, the IRS informed Billy that he owed the federal government about $200,000 in back taxes.

Billy, who never grasped the concept of saving his money, estimated that he had about $85,000 in his bank account. He was still supporting his two principal households: the Ervolinos in Blackhawk and Jill Guiver in Southern California. He also was giving his mother a monthly stipend. He paid for other expenses in his extended family and network of friends.

Moreover, Billy's bank account dwindled significantly just about every time he walked out the door.

"He thought nothing of tipping 100 percent on a bill," his son, Billy Joe, said. "He'd give money to people on the street. He'd go buy a cone at an ice cream stand, then on the spur of the moment decide to buy ice cream for everyone in line — like, maybe twenty people.

"I was still just a teenager but even I thought, 'Does he have to support the whole state of California?'"

Oakland's management continued to give Billy their unqualified support.

Spring training opened, but some of the joie de vivre seemed to be missing. Billy was distracted by his money issues, his secret dual life continued to be more than a little stressful, and there was new, strong competition in the AL West because the California Angels had signed the winter's biggest free agent, Reggie Jackson.

In the World Series the previous fall, the Yankees, after winning the first two games, lost the next four games to the Dodgers. Reggie made a crucial error in the outfield that led to a decisive run in the pivotal fourth game when a line drive bounced off his forehead. It would be the last World Series appearance of Jackson's career. The Yankees never tried to sign him after the season ended. Steinbrenner had decided to remake the team in the image of the 1981 Oakland A's.

"He's going for speed," Billy said that spring with a snicker. "Except he plays in a ballpark built for left-handed power hitters. You can't just copy somebody and expect the same results."

The Yankees would end up having their first losing season since 1973.

At the A's spring training complex, Billy seem distracted. He sequestered himself for hours in a trailer he had situated behind the left-field fence. He insisted he was watching everything through the windows of the trailer, but his players felt a sense of abandonment.

Billy's languor about his own team was not easy to explain. Years later, Clete Boyer said he felt Billy was mostly preoccupied with his money woes, but he also said that Billy had health issues.

"His stomach was bothering him and I know he stopped drinking for about two months because of that," Boyer said. "No trips to the Pink Pony. He was losing weight and that kind of worried him, too."

In the late 1970s, Billy had suggested publicly that there was a spot on his liver, something that was never substantiated. (When he died, doctors said he was in near-perfect health for a sixty-one-year-old.)

Boyer summed up the early months of 1982 this way: "Billy just wasn't completely himself that spring."

Boyer added that he also thought Billy might have been missing the challenge of the previous seasons when the young A's were so inexperienced and overlooked.

"He had already schooled these guys," Boyer said. "I just think he thought they would pick up where they left off in 1981."

But that did not happen, largely because the starting rotation was falling apart. The five-man rotation, called "The Five Aces" on a *Sports Illustrated* cover in 1981, was ailing and ineffective. Of the five, only McCatty had a winning record in 1982, and he was 6-3.

Baseball historians have looked back and unequivocally come to an assessment: Billy and Art Fowler burned out an entire staff.

It is the most prevalent theory about what happened in 1982 and the years beyond. And there is telling evidence to support the theory, like failed careers and sore arms. The statistical backing is damning. No one could win an argument at a modern baseball analytics conference trying to defend Billy's handling of the Oakland pitchers. Billy certainly worried about winning in the present and not the future. Everything about his managerial style was about seizing an advantage now, not one or two years down the road. He had already been fired five times, so overtly or subconsciously he had to be worried about chasing as many wins as he could while he could.

At the same time, each of the five pitchers from the 1980–81 Oakland A's will steadfastly, even vehemently, refuse to say they were overworked or that the 1980–81 seasons led to their downfall. They will point out that many pitchers from their era pitched more innings than they did. Dozens of pitchers from the 1980s, including future Hall of Famers Steve Carlton, Jim Palmer, Bert Blyleven, Gaylord Perry, Nolan Ryan, Catfish Hunter, and Phil Niekro, pitched more than 320 innings in one season. The A's starters averaged 251 innings in 1980.

As McCatty has pointed out, the top three starters for the Baltimore Orioles in 1970 — Palmer, Dave McNally, and Mike Cuellar — averaged 299 innings pitched that year. The Orioles were World Series champions, the only world championship that Earl Weaver won. As a group, Palmer, McNally, and Cuellar threw more than 250 innings in a season nineteen different times.

The five 1980 A's starters pitched an average of 18.6 complete games. The 1970 Orioles starters, all of whom had long careers, averaged 18 complete games.

Is anyone disparaging Earl Weaver's Hall of Fame credentials because he appears to have overworked pitchers throughout a seventeen-year managerial career?

As Gene Michael said in 2013, "All the managers back then pitched their pitchers too often and for too many innings. They didn't know better. No one did. Billy wasn't any worse. He wasn't any better."

Said McCatty, still immersed in the overworked pitcher debate as a current pitching coach for the Washington Nationals:

The problems the 1980s Oakland pitchers developed had more to do with bad luck and poor medical science. Norris hurt his arm in 1982 after we got in a fight on the field. He lost some feeling in his right hand a couple of minutes after it happened. It was a nerve problem that started right then.

Keough slipped on a wet mound in Baltimore — we shouldn't even have been playing that day. He came off the field and said, "Something happened to my shoulder." But instead of getting it checked out, he kept pitching. Billy didn't make him ignore it. Matt just did it. Today, he would have gotten an MRI that day and shut it down.

Langford one day felt something pop, just like that. I had a problem with my arm that took eight years to diagnose. Nowadays, it wouldn't take that long. I had some hidden cartilage damage and a bone spur under a bicep. I tried to pitch through it.

All that happened in one season, 1982. You can't ruin all five of our arms that fast. That's some weird, bad luck.

None of the five regained their old form. After 1982, Norris battled drug addiction. Langford had elbow surgery.

"I'd been throwing a baseball since I was six years old," Langford said in 2012. "I threw 195 innings in 1981, which isn't that many. I don't think that caused it. It was part of a long process since I was a kid. Part of building it up is breaking it down."

Keough lasted the longest, but he won a total of 20 games in seven seasons after 1982.

"I don't buy that Billy broke all our arms," Keough said. "We didn't do any conditioning or weight training. The medical advice was sketchy. It was a lack of knowledge that hurt us."

Kingman descended the fastest. He was out of baseball by 1984. He comes the closest to suggesting that Billy's tactics cost him in the end.

Kingman told the *Los Angeles Times* in 1990, "I never thought all the work hurt our arms, but history says maybe it did."

But McCatty is defiant.

In the same *Los Angeles Times* article, McCatty said, "It was our own macho trip. We did it to ourselves."

In modern times, with pitch counts and a new world of exercise science, the manager — and the strength and conditioning coach, a position that did not exist in 1980–81 — would not let five outstanding starting pitchers throw that many innings. Especially since the team would likely have had about $80 million in salaries wrapped up in those arms.

But the early 1980s were a different era, borrowing much more from the middle of the twentieth century than the early part of the twenty-first century. In 1982, while Billy's starters imploded, forty-one other pitchers in the Major Leagues threw 220 innings or more.

By way of reference, in 2013, five Major League pitchers threw more than 220 innings.

But the 1982 Oakland A's, missing their Five Aces, went down fast. They were a .500 team for the first two months of the season, then started to slide. By the end of June, they had a 33-45 record and were 13.5 games behind the streaking Angels. It was a death march for the A's from there.

One highlight was the play of Rickey Henderson, who was on his way to becoming the most dangerous, complete player in the game. Henderson may have been the best overall player in baseball in the mid-1980s. He was an unmatched combination of power, speed, and cunning, a player with a tiny strike zone he knew well, and he had the ability to intimidate a whole team just with his presence on the bases.

He had the perfect manager to maximize his talents.

Said Dwayne Murphy, "Billy saw all the things Rickey was capable of doing, maybe even before Rickey really knew it."

Rickey, like Billy, had grown up poor in the East Bay. From the beginning Billy shepherded his young charge, taking him to dinner, buying him clothes, and arranging for the use of a new car.

"A star like you shouldn't drive a broken-down heap," Billy told Henderson when he flipped him the keys to a gleaming red Ford Mustang. Billy had convinced a local car dealer to lease the car to the team.

Said Henderson's mother, Bobbie, "I think with Rickey, there was a trust factor there. Billy saw that Rickey's career was going to take off and he knew what to teach him to get there. So Rickey could see what Billy was doing and they sort of had that bond. I don't think there's a day that goes by that Rickey doesn't think of Billy."

Henderson is an odd man. He tended to call other players by nicknames although his teammates were occasionally convinced he did this only because he never learned their names. John Olerud, a first baseman who wore a batting helmet in the field because of a brain aneurysm he suffered in college, played with Henderson as a New York Met in 1999. Olerud went to the Seattle Mariners the next season and in mid-2000, Henderson also signed with the Mariners.

Approaching Olerud in the field during batting practice one day, Henderson asked Olerud if he always wore a helmet in the field. Olerud explained that he did.

"We had a guy on the Mets last year who did that, too," Henderson said.

"Yeah, Rickey," replied Olerud. "That was me."

Henderson had two stints with the A's, and during his second tour with the team he earned a $1 million bonus at the end of the season. Months later, the A's accountants were flummoxed as to why their books were off by $1 million. They discerned that Henderson had not cashed his bonus check.

When the team asked him about it, he said he had instead framed the check and put it on a wall in his condominium.

In 1982, Henderson set the record for stolen bases in one season with 130. There were not too many other highlights for the A's that year.

Late in the season, Billy asked for a loan from the team's owners for his IRS debt, and they refused. A day later, the A's lost a close game at home.

Billy came into his office with Boyer and Fowler and locked the door. The three men then proceeded to destroy the office, tearing light fixtures off the wall and breaking up the furniture by slamming it against the walls. The players heard the commotion. No one dared to investigate.

The noise abated, and after a few minutes, Billy, Boyer, and Fowler emerged. Left behind in the office were a pile of broken glass, a desk in pieces, and smashed chairs and tables. There were multiple punctures in the walls. The screen of the television set was kicked in, and the refrigerator looked as if it had been thumped multiple times with a baseball bat. There were no longer pictures hung on the walls.

"It looked like a bomb had gone off in the office," said Jackie Moore, an A's assistant coach.

Billy went to have a drink in the trainer's room.

"The A's called me to come get him," said Lew Figone, whom Oakland's management had begun to value as a consigliere to their increasingly irrational field general. "Billy had just had it with all that was going on around him. But what has never been reported is that he also had a fight on the phone that day with that woman — Jill."

Like many of Billy's friends — although not all — Figone detested Jill. Sitting in a bar with Billy, he would sometimes leave whenever she arrived.

"Lew was a good guy to have around and a terrific influence on Billy," said Vucinich. "He was there for Billy that day he trashed the office. He and Billy left and we started cleaning up."

The destruction took place after reporters had exited the clubhouse, so the goal was to rebuild the office by game time the next day. That way, in theory, no one would know what happened. (It got out anyway.) But first, Vucinich called construction contractors of all kinds — drywallers, furniture makers, appliance outlets — and had the office put back together.

"That was some night, finding a new TV, a new refrigerator, a new desk, new wall outlets — heck, new walls," Vucinich said, laughing about it thirty years later. "But we got it done."

As impressive as the rebuild was, Sandy Alderson and the A's ownership began to believe that Billy was becoming seriously unhinged. They called Sapir the next day.

"The A's management at the time was a bunch of preppy guys — Cal-Berkeley guys and Ivy Leaguers," Sapir said. "They felt embarrassed by Billy. First of all, they didn't like the two girlfriends. They couldn't live with that. They didn't like some of the extreme behavior. They said to me, 'We won't find a better manager and the losing this year isn't his fault but we have to consider a change. We just don't feel good about all this.'"

Vucinich recalled something Roy Eisenhardt, the club's chief executive, said at the time.

"Roy said, 'I don't worry about Billy from the first inning to the ninth inning, I worry about him from the end of the ninth inning to the first inning the next day,'" Vucinich said. "After Billy was cut loose, people said he lost the team, but that's not true.

"The team never stopped believing in him. He lost the support of management. He worried them. Obviously, he drank too much after games. I never saw Billy drink before a game or during a game. I never saw it affect his performance. But there was a lot of booze after games back then. It was a sign of the times. But management had lost its tolerance."

Billy, who was among the sports world's worst losers, had helped push Oakland's management to the decision. As his son, Billy Joe, said, "He was not a person that was happy going through the motions. That was hell for him. And you look at his career, he manufactured some of his own firings almost.

"You could make the case that he had everything he wanted in Oakland. He had color back in his face. He even had a little gut. He was comfortable. That's the problem. He didn't want comfortable."

The A's did not make a switch immediately. The season concluded with a 68-94 record for the A's — the lowest winning percentage by far of any team that Billy guided for a full season. About three weeks later, on October 20, Oakland let Billy go with three years remaining on his contract.

Billy was allowed to remain in the Blackhawk house, although he was supposed to buy it at the original asking price (he did not, once again showing his lack of financial acumen because the house would have been a fabulous real estate investment).

Billy, meanwhile, was not too worried about what he would do next. George Steinbrenner had already floated the notion that Billy should come back to the Yankees. George had reached an all-time high, or low, for him in 1982 when he had three managers: Lemon, Michael, and the former Dodgers pitcher and frequent Yankees adviser Clyde King. The Yankees had finished in fifth place.

But Billy did not run into George's arms. Gabe Paul, then the Cleveland Indians' general manager, was interested in Billy, too. Billy stalled.

In November he went with Jill and Sapir to shoot another television commercial in Manhattan. At a nightclub party during the visit, a *New*

York Daily News photographer spotted Billy and took a picture of him standing close to Jill.

The next day, with Billy still perceived as the likely next Yankees manager, the photograph took up half a page in the *Daily News*. Billy was certain that Heather would hear about the photo from one of her many cousins, aunts, and uncles who still lived in the Bronx. He was furious.

With the photo on newsstands across the city, Billy and Sapir ended up in a Blarney Stone bar, a chain of unsophisticated but popular Irish pubs that seemed to be in every Manhattan neighborhood in the 1970s and 1980s.

"Billy was all upset about the picture in the paper," Sapir said. "He kept talking about how Heather was going to see the picture and how much it would bother her. After a couple drinks he asked me if I could get a justice of the peace or someone for a wedding in New Orleans.

"And I said, 'Yeah, I could do that.' And he asked, 'Could you set up all the licenses and get a hotel for a day?' And I said, 'Sure.'

"He didn't say much else. Then he got up to go to the bathroom. It took him a little while but when he came back he said, 'I just proposed to Heather.'"

Sapir was astonished. Billy then added that Heather wanted Sapir to call her.

"I called Heather and she said, 'Eddie, is he serious?'" Sapir recalled. "And I said, 'Well, Heather, you know he loves you and he asked me to set up a wedding in New Orleans. He wants me to get all the licenses, a hotel suite, and all of that, so, yes, he's serious.'

"I went back to my seat and Billy said he wanted to get married that month. I started thinking of New Orleans hotels to call."

But first Billy and his lawyer, the New Orleans judge, left the Blarney Stone to meet Jill across town for dinner.

The wedding was on November 30 at the Maison Dupuy Hotel in the French Quarter. The guest list was limited. Billy instructed the Sapirs and others not to say much about it.

Sapir, who rarely interfered in Billy's personal life, felt relieved.

"Because I figured that it would be the end of Jill and the two-girlfriend situation," Sapir said. "I thought Jill would go away. But obviously, Jill didn't go away."

Billy continued to see both women, although he hid the marriage from Jill and almost everyone else.

On January 11, the Yankees announced that Billy would be the Yankees manager for a third time. He had a long-term contract. In fact, he would remain in the Yankees' employ for the rest of his life.

His son called him when he heard the news from New York.

"Dad, please, not again," Billy Joe said. "Not the Yankees. Not again. Why?"

Answered Billy, "That's what I am, pard. I'm a Yankee."

39

THE 1983 MEDIA GUIDE published by the Yankees, an essential reference tool distributed to thousands of newspaper reporters, broadcasters, and other journalists in an age before the Internet, had a cartoonlike caricature of Billy as he pointed a finger and screamed face-to-face at an umpire. It was a strange thing for a team to be promoting, and it would prove to be prescient, although perhaps not in the winsome way the Yankees intended.

Billy, and his owner, would have problems with umpires all season. The 1983 media guide was notable for another reason. It included a detailed, pages-long biography of Billy with a glaring omission. The bio chronicled Billy's playing and managerial careers and the four Manager of the Year awards he had won. While the other similar bios of players and coaches in the media guide mentioned the player's or the coach's marital status — and usually included a spouse's name — in Billy's 1983 bio there was no mention of Heather. It made no mention that Billy was married at all.

Billy's wife was seen at his side from time to time in New York, although she remained primarily in Blackhawk. Jill, meanwhile, was spotted everywhere. Also omnipresent was Billy's chauffeur, Tex Gernand, the imposing ex–New York City cop who almost looked like a larger version of Billy himself with a thin black mustache. Gernand also wore a lot of Western wear like his boss.

Gernand, a former officer with the 109th Precinct in Flushing, Queens, served as Billy's unofficial bodyguard on many occasions, and he was very proud of the fact that Billy never got in a fight or was harmed in any way when he was on duty.

In 1983, Billy had a stately, long Town Car with the license plate YAN-KEE1 and he told Gernand to always park it next to Steinbrenner's plain Oldsmobile in the VIP parking lot just outside Yankee Stadium.

"I want him to see that big car and the YANKEE1 license plate every time he comes out after a game," Billy said to Gernand. "Let him know who the real top Yankee is."

"What if George says something to me about the fact that we're always right next to him?" Gernand asked.

"Say that you only take orders from me and then tell him to go fuck himself," Billy said with a roaring laugh.

It was 1948 again in the Oakland Oaks parking lot, except instead of parking his ragtag car next to the veterans' trophy cars he was trying to torment his multimillionaire owner with a luxurious Town Car and a license plate.

But Steinbrenner was, in fact, delighted that Billy had a driver. Like many in Billy's sphere, he had long feared for Billy's safety — and the safety of others — when Billy drove after he drank.

Gernand could soon be found throughout the eastern United States driving for Billy. A considerate, wise man behind the gruff exterior, he also began to feel like a guardian to his boss in more ways than one. Tex Gernand, for example, expressed his concern to Sapir about Billy's two-woman lifestyle.

Gernand did not understand the relationship with Heather, whom he saw irregularly whenever she stayed at the Carlyle Hotel suite Billy was renting. Tex usually spent more time with Jill, and the whole situation vexed him.

"She seemed like a young girl, someone still growing up," Gernand said of Heather. "I didn't understand the whole setup."

Tex wasn't the only one to feel the need to say something.

"I said to Billy, 'Look, you are a big-time public figure and it's not going to end well if this gets out,'" Sapir said. "I suggested that if Jill was going to stick around that we had to give her a job and a title. We had started a Billy Martin public relations firm run out of my office in New Orleans. I suggested that we hire Jill as Billy's official photographer. Then we have an explanation for her presence and all the travel."

Jill described 1983 as a year of awakening for her.

"I had never lived on the East Coast and I had never seen so many things but Billy showed me the world," she said. "Billy wanted everyone around him to be having a good time. And he wanted to share his world.

"He taught me to cook. I have the recipes to this day — Italian food, chicken Florentine, a lovely lamb he stewed all day. He had a temper and he could be very jealous, which was not always nice, but that usually passed very quickly. We were having a blast most of the time."

The 1983 home season opened with a record 55,579 fans welcoming Billy back to the old Bronx ballpark, a crowd recruited in part by a thorough marketing campaign by the Yankees that included billboards and television commercials that featured a new team slogan, BILLY IS BACK.

By the third inning of the home opener, the crowd was howling as Billy got into a snit with an umpire at second base. It was not a good omen. The Yankees lost.

By early May, Billy had been suspended three games for kicking dirt on umpire Drew Coble. Steinbrenner was suspended for a week for his nonstop haranguing of the umpires in the newspapers.

The 1983 Yankees were not a powerhouse team, and they stumbled at the start of the season, losing sixteen of their first thirty games. George, who had vowed to reporters in spring training not to interfere in the managing of the team until at least the All-Star break, broke that promise in early May while the Yankees were in Texas.

Steinbrenner personally addressed the team, admonishing the players for their sub-.500 start. He also had a private, closed-door meeting with Billy and his coaches during which he ridiculed relief pitcher George Frazier, according to coaches who later spoke off the record to reporters about the meeting. For his part, Billy also went into the clubhouse afterward and told the players to ignore what George had said, eliciting a round of chuckles.

Billy's old adversary, Henry Hecht of the *New York Post*, wrote about the players and coaches' meeting, giving the details of both, including the derision directed at Frazier. The day Hecht's story ran, reporters were in Billy's office when Steinbrenner called. Billy was heard saying that he hadn't read the article.

Then he said, "Henry? OK, I'll take care of it."

The next day, about two hours before a game, Billy was in his office telling reporters that Hecht's story was false on several accounts when he was informed that Hecht was in the clubhouse. Billy hurried out of his office.

"Hey, can I have your attention for a second," he announced to the players. "We had a private meeting in Texas, a clubhouse meeting, and nothing leaves the clubhouse and I don't think anything did. At least I haven't read anything written that was accurate. But we have a writer right here who has me knocking Frazier, George knocking Frazier, and me knocking George. And he wasn't even in Texas."

Billy continued, pointing at Hecht, who was about ten feet away: "I don't ever say don't talk to the writers, but don't talk to Henry Hecht — that's him, right there. If you do talk to him, you're making a mistake. He doesn't care if he hurts you or gets you fired. He's using you. He is the worst fucking scrounge we've ever had around this club."

In a stunned and silent clubhouse, Hecht looked at Billy and said, "You can imagine what I think of you."

"I've read what you think of me," Billy said.

"You're paranoid," Hecht added.

"I'm not paranoid," Billy said. "I don't have to be paranoid to see that you're a little prick."

Billy went into his office, telling Hecht that he wouldn't deny him his ability to make a living before adding, "But stay away from me or I'll dump you in the whirlpool."

When Billy was asked afterward if Steinbrenner put him up to his rant against Hecht, Billy said, "George called me and told me to handle the article."

There was plenty of coverage of Billy's diatribe in the New York papers. Then it died out quickly, although not in the mind of Hecht.

"It was just another sign of how disturbed and unbalanced he had become," Hecht said many years later.

Still, the brouhaha went away, although some players were aghast at what they had witnessed. It was just the first of many bizarre moments during 1983.

On the field, the Yankees had their own problems. They were a winning team that would stay in the AL East race until mid-September, but Steinbrenner was still experimenting with the concept of building a team around speed and hitters who slashed the ball into the outfield gaps — hitters like Ken Griffey, center fielder Jerry Mumphrey, and the new shortstop, Roy Smalley. There was also a new catcher, Butch Wynegar, whom Billy terrorized for his handling of an uneven pitching staff.

The team had All-Stars in Randolph; the superb Dave Winfield, who loved playing for Billy; and the designated hitter, Don Baylor. Guidry would win 21 games and Righetti contributed 14 victories as did an underrated lefty, Shane Rawley. But the rest of the rotation was largely ineffective.

The team's play was erratic and the players were aging. Still, the Yankees were neck-and-neck with the Orioles, Tigers, and Toronto Blue Jays for the division lead throughout most of the summer.

But hours before a June home game there was another firestorm, and it began with a researcher for the *New York Times* named Deborah Henschel, who was in the Yankees' clubhouse handing out ballots to the players for a poll about the All-Star Game. All the facts of the scene that played out next are unclear, although it is indisputable that Billy ended up loudly escorting Henschel from the clubhouse. He later said he did not know she was a representative of the *New York Times*.

Art Fowler had also been fired that day, which did not improve Billy's mood.

Billy said he thought Henschel was dressed provocatively — something about a skirt with a slit in it — and he thought she was a girlfriend of a player. Henschel said Billy angrily cursed at her.

Eventually, the Yankees made sure Henschel could complete her assignment in the visitors' locker room.

The episode made the newspapers and the American League launched an investigation, interviewing Henschel and Yankees employees, all of whom said they had not seen anything. The investigation absolved Billy of wrongdoing.

The Yankees were only three games back in the AL East standings, but the controversies — none that had anything to do with baseball — kept piling up. On a trip to Milwaukee County Stadium, the Yankees were playing a game on a sunny Sunday afternoon. Billy was sitting on a towel on a concrete wall at the edge of the dugout. Reporters could not help but notice a striking, fetching blonde in short shorts lounging in the front-row box next to where Billy sat.

Throughout the game, Billy appeared to be conversing with the blonde, who had kicked off her sandals and placed her long, tanned legs on a railing by the field's boundary. It was Jill. At some point, the press box watched as Jill started passing handwritten notes to Billy by writing them on a small piece of paper and then placing them between her toes. In the dugout, Billy was plucking the notes from Jill's toes.

At first, the reporters decided not to write about the scene. But as often happened, press box pacts dissolved in the heat of a competitive newspaper environment. Bill Madden of the *New York Daily News* wrote about the young woman passing notes to Billy.

The next day in the visitors' clubhouse, Billy was told what Madden wrote.

"He did *what?*" Billy yelped. "How the hell could he do that? Doesn't he know I'm married! I'm married!"

Players were often seen with paramours or girlfriends on the road, known as "imports" — but that was never written about. A nighttime rendezvous away from the ballpark didn't seem like anyone's business. Now some woman was passing the Yankees manager notes with her toes next to the dugout in broad daylight. It became big news.

Steinbrenner was not pleased, although he didn't know quite what to do. He flew to Cleveland to meet the team on their next stop. So did Sapir. The three had lunch, and Billy and George yelled at each other throughout much of the meal.

When the lunch ended, George actually said he felt better.

"At least we got some things off our chest," George said. And that was the end of it. The woman in the short shorts had become a mirage.

Sapir, in fact, issued a memorable statement. As Madden and the Newark *Star-Ledger's* venerable reporter Moss Klein wrote in their 1990 book, *Damned Yankees,* Sapir announced to gathered reporters in the team hotel, "Reports of the girl are unfounded."

It was unclear if Heather, still in the Bay Area, knew of the Milwaukee situation. If only that had been the end of the madness during the 1983 season. In some ways, it was just beginning.

On July 24, the Yankees, who were just 1.5 games out of first place, played the Kansas City Royals. They took a 4–3 lead into the ninth inning when Gossage came into the game to face George Brett with two outs and a runner at first base.

Brett lashed a long home run into the right-field seats for a 5–4 Royals lead. Billy, with Nettles's help, had noticed in a game three weeks earlier that Brett had pine tar, the sticky substance batters use to improve their grip on a bat, far up the barrel of the bat.

The rule at the time was that the pine tar could not extend more than eighteen inches past the knob of the bat. It was a silly rule — pine tar had no impact on the flight of a batted ball — but it was in the rule book because the pine tar stained the baseball — and possibly gave pitchers something to use for an illegal pitch afterward. Obscure as it was, the rule was still called from time to time. It was called on the Yankees' Thurman

Munson in 1979, which had brought a screaming-mad Billy from the dugout. It might be a ticky-tacky rule, but it had been enforced before.

Billy had waited to say anything about Brett's bat, delaying a protest until Brett produced a big hit. With Brett celebrating his go-ahead home run in the visitors' dugout, the time was right. Billy calmly strode out to home plate umpire Tim McClelland to question the legality of Brett's bat.

"The pine tar is beyond the eighteen-inch mark," Billy said.

McClelland took the bat from the Kansas City batboy who was still holding it. The umpire knew that the front part of home plate was eighteen inches in width.

Waiting in the dugout, Brett was pacing, vowing revenge if Billy's protest nullified the home run.

"If they call me out, you're going to see four dead umpires," Brett said.

McClelland measured the bat against home plate and saw that the pine tar extended beyond eighteen inches. He pointed at Brett in the dugout and held up his fist, making the signal for an out. The bat was illegal under rule 1.10 (c), and that made Brett out under rule 6.06. The game was over. The Yankees were declared 4–3 winners.

Billy smiled and walked back to the dugout with his hands in his back pockets, another victory stolen from the jaws of defeat.

In one of the most-replayed video scenes in baseball history, Brett stormed from the dugout in a crazed fury trying to get at McClelland. Another umpire grabbed Brett by the neck. Various players and the Kansas City manager, Dick Howser, were being ejected.

The league immediately said it would review the matter at a later date. A precious few games in the history of American sports have been replayed after the game officials have made a determination of a rule and left the playing field — even when it was later established that the officials were wrong — but in this case, American League president Lee MacPhail decided to replay the end of the game in August. MacPhail, fed up with the constant berating of his umpires by Billy and Steinbrenner, conceded that the umpires had executed the pine tar ruling justly. But in MacPhail's judgment, the umpire's decision was "not in the spirit of the rule."

MacPhail ordered the game replayed from the moment after Brett's homer.

Eleven days after what forevermore became known as "the Pine Tar Game," the Yankees were playing in Toronto's aging Exhibition Stadium, which was perched at the edge of Lake Ontario. Because of its proximity to the lake and because fans leave behind lots of discarded food scraps, the stadium was routinely overrun with large white seagulls. They would stand on the field and occasionally disrupt play or get hit by a ground ball in the outfield.

In the middle of the fifth inning, Dave Winfield was warming up in center field, having a catch with the left fielder. When it came time to throw the baseball off the field to resume play, Winfield turned and faced a ball boy standing in foul territory. A seagull was standing between the two, about a hundred feet from Winfield.

Winfield, who had one of the strongest arms in baseball, threw a hard, low throw to the ball boy that took one hop and struck the seagull in the head.

"Pow!" said Jeff Torborg, a coach who had a perfect view from the Yankees' bullpen. "Right in the head. The bird went *pffft*."

Another ball boy ran onto the field with a towel and removed the dead gull. Winfield stood in center field with his cap held over his heart. It wasn't clear whether he was clearly aggrieved or trying to be funny. But the Canadian fans were incensed. They began chanting obscenities about Winfield and throwing debris onto the field.

When the game ended, Winfield was met in the dugout by police, who charged him with cruelty to an animal. The seagull was also a protected species in Canada. Winfield was taken to a station house where he had to post a $500 bond.

The Yankees were trying to fly home, and the chartered aircraft had to wait forty minutes for Winfield.

With a grin, Billy said, "They obviously haven't been watching him throw all year. That's the first time he's hit the cut-off man all year."

With the Yankees and the American League lobbying the Toronto authorities, the charges were dropped two days later. Winfield said he was exonerated.

Fourteen days after that incident, on August 18, the Pine Tar Game resumed at Yankee Stadium. Once everyone was on the field, Billy told the umpiring crew chief, Dave Phillips, he wanted to appeal whether Brett had touched all the bases after his blast into the stands on July 24. And since it was a different umpiring crew overseeing the resumed game from the one that had overseen the original game, how could they verify that Brett had touched each base?

Good question. But someone had tipped off the league office to Billy's thinking. The league had gotten all four umpires from the original game to sign an affidavit affirming that Brett had touched each of the bases. In front of Billy, Phillips pulled a piece of paper from his back pocket.

"I've got here an affidavit," Phillips said.

"An affi-what?" Billy yelped.

"You'll see, Billy," Phillips said.

Billy read the paper on the Yankee Stadium diamond. His shoulders drooped. It had been twenty-five days since the Brett home run and the pine tar dispute. The game's outcome, up in the air for weeks and an ongoing distraction, had come to haunt the Yankees. When Brett was originally called out on July 24, the Yankees were, however briefly, only one game out of the division lead and in a virtual tie for second place. Since then, they had won just twelve of twenty-five games, and when the Royals' Dan Quisenberry set down the Yankees in order to earn the save in the resumed Pine Tar Game, the Yankees had fallen to fifth place, 3.5 games back.

The life had been drained from the season. The Pine Tar Game seemed to have some symbolism with the old mojo of the swaggering, late-1970s Yankees briefly resurrected as Billy plied his magic. It had been another electric moment in old Yankee Stadium.

Then someone pulled the plug. Victory had been snatched from the jaws of defeat, then handed back to the original victors. The magic was gone.

On September 12, the Yankees were only five games behind Baltimore and had a double-header with the Orioles in the Bronx. The Yankees lost both games. The stars of the games were former Yankees minor leaguers, catcher Rick Dempsey and bullpen closer Tippy Martinez. Both were traded by the Yankees in mid-1976 for veteran pitching to shore up the Yankees' pennant drive. By 1983, none of the players acquired in that trade were still on the Yankees' roster. The Yankees were aging as their younger American League rivals were maturing.

"The 1983 team was kind of a transition team," Ron Guidry said. "We had good players but the mix was off. There was kind of a disconnect. And there were more players on that roster who had problems with Billy than in the previous years.

"And frankly, Billy was having more problems off the field than before. He had a lot going on."

The Yankees finished 91-71, which in most modern-day baseball circles would be cause for at least modest celebration. But 20 games over .500 did not get you much in the 1983 AL East. If there had been a wild card play-off format, the Yankees once again would have made the playoffs — more than 80 percent of the teams Billy managed in his career to the end of a season would have been playoff teams if the wild card format had been in place for those seasons.

But 1983 was viewed by Yankees fans as a failed, subpar season, even though the 1983 Yankees had a better record than nine of the next ten Yankees teams (and the one that had a better record, in 1985, was also a Billy-managed team).

The roster was about to get a total makeover with more than a dozen players jettisoned.

On December 16, citing a need for change, Steinbrenner replaced Billy as manager with Yogi Berra. Steinbrenner made it a point to say that Billy was not fired.

"I don't like to talk about firing managers," George said. "I'm shifting people in everyone's interest: Billy's, Yogi's, mine."

It was the eleventh managerial change in George's eleven years as Yankees owner. Billy had four years remaining on a $2 million contract. Billy was promptly named an adviser for trades and personnel, although he was allowed to pursue other managerial jobs if he chose to (something he did not do).

Billy's legion of fans were saddened by his exit, but there was not the wailing and riotous tumult of Billy's first departure in 1978, nor was there the noticeable if more measured backlash when he left after the marsh-mallow salesman fight in 1979.

The 1983 season had ended with a whimper. It was hard for fans to get too riled up about anything.

Billy receded into the background, awaiting his longest layoff from the dugout since 1970.

Around Christmastime, there were reports that Billy was hospitalized in Minnesota at the Mayo Clinic. One news report stated that Billy could have cancer.

On January 11, back for a checkup at the Mayo Clinic, Billy met with a local wire service reporter.

"I do not have cancer," Billy said, adding in an unsolicited comment that he had not sipped a drop of hard liquor in six months.

He had lost about fifteen pounds because of surgery to remove bleeding hemorrhoids. He had indeed, according to his friends, stopped drinking altogether except for the occasional beer or wine. He said he was disheartened about losing the Yankees managerial job, but not despondent.

"I'm not going to lie," Billy said. "I love managing, it's like living and breathing for me."

But he said he was ready to take a step back.

"I'm very content with the way George has handled everything in a true Yankee manner," he said. "I hope in the near future I can be of assistance to him and to the Yankees in any way."

Billy then used a simile, saying that he was going to spend some time in repose — like a man sitting in a rocking chair on a front porch.

"I haven't done anything like that for quite a while," he said. "I'm going to see what that feels like."

40

————

BILLY MAY NOT HAVE settled into a rocking chair somewhere, but he did stay out of sight. There would be only one day in 1984, and one episode, when Billy made any kind of news. But the incident, and the coverage of it, did not help convey an image of someone peaceably sitting on a front porch.

More to the point, it contributed to the pattern of worrisome behavior, a trend that stained his public image and continued to taint his public persona. It began in mid-April, when Jill Guiver flew home from Seattle, where the Yankees had played a series. She had been with Billy, who was scouting the team for Steinbrenner. On the plane she saw the wife of a Yankees player, whose name Jill chooses not to reveal.

The player's wife had not seen Jill in Seattle, and spotting her on the flight, she approached and asked, "So what are you doing now that Billy's married?"

"I was so mortified and embarrassed," Jill said in 2013 at her Massachusetts horse farm. She insisted that she had not known of Billy's marriage to Heather until that moment.

Jill continued, "Being in love, you're hurt. I thought, 'What have I been doing with my life?' Certain things started to click, like some things that had happened over the last year. Now they all made sense. It's like these tumblers click in your head. But I hadn't put it all together before. I mean, he had hid it from almost everyone. The Yankee players didn't know. Lots of people didn't know."

Others in Billy's community of friends, many of whom despised Jill, find it hard to believe that Jill didn't know of the marriage. Maybe she did not know of it right after the wedding, they say, but she learned of it certainly within a year. They say it is revisionist history.

"She knew what was going on," said Lew Figone.

Eddie Sapir: "Of course she did. Jill was very smart and shrewd."

Billy's good friend Mickey Morabito, however, was not so sure.

"That whole time was hard to figure out," he said. "I don't know what to think. I don't know who knew what."

But Jill's memory is clear.

"I called Billy and told him what I now knew — and I was going fairly berserk," she said. "Then I went and stayed with friends because I didn't want to be seen. Billy was calling my house in Newport Beach nonstop. Remember, there were no cell phones then and Billy didn't know where I was.

"But eventually I came back to Newport Beach and he was waiting for me there at the doorstep. He was very passionate and certainly very truthful when it all came out. But I was so angry."

Jill said she took what clothes and belongings Billy had left at the Newport Beach home and threw them on the front lawn.

"As any woman would have and should have," she said. "And we started having a terrible, screaming argument. We made a terrible racket and the police came and arrested him.

"The story that people later wrote said that we were fighting over a horse of mine that I wanted a new trailer for. But that's false. It was not a fight over a horse. It was because I found out he was married."

The Associated Press filed a story about the incident, quoting a Newport Beach police investigator who said Billy was arrested for public drunkenness and disorderly conduct. Billy spent four hours in a jail cell and was released on $100 bond at about 4:00 a.m. In the AP story, the investigator said Jill and Billy argued over a horse.

The New York Times published the Associated Press story with the headline MARTIN JAILED AS DRUNK.

In the city's tabloid newspapers, it was not back-page news — Billy was the ex-manager — but there were conspicuous stories. The charges were dropped soon afterward, and the incident was Billy's doing, as were most of his public transgressions. But the effect and consequences this time seemed to be more lasting. The "drunk" headlines, when added to his other high-profile, recent barroom episodes, were all part of the ongoing denigration of his reputation in the 1980s.

The Hagar fight, the Miller Lite commercials, the suspensions for arguing with umpires, the Pine Tar Game fiasco, the marshmallow salesman, the outburst against a New York Times researcher, and the tirade against the New York Post's Henry Hecht were all adding up. Now, he was drunk and disorderly in California. The headlines this time had a more acerbic tone. The media had a field day with Billy, and many of those reporters and commentators soured on him for good.

Many members of the media were now from a younger generation, and they came to their jobs with different attitudes and sensibilities from the writers raised in the 1950s. The previous generation of scribes was brought up in another era when mischievous Rat Pack–like stars were celebrated for their alcohol-fueled roguishness. These writers had also known and esteemed Billy as a prominent player and leader on the country's best-known athletic team. He was Casey's boy who had been a miracle-working manager in Minnesota, Detroit, and Texas. Those writers had perhaps been charmed by Billy in face-to-face meetings in less threatening settings and found him flawed but engaging.

Their stories usually reflected at least an arm's-length appreciation of Billy, and their opinions of him often seemed mixed with an empathy for a complicated if imperfect soul.

The next generation of writers tended to look at Billy with more scorn. He was the guy who disrespected umpires, was frequently suspended, and had a penchant for being where alcohol and fistfights occurred — so much so it was a source of parody on TV. For many of them, it was not a picture that they found intriguing or amusing. Billy still charmed many columnists and announcers. He had friends in high places — national broadcasters like Howard Cosell, Joe Garagiola, Curt Gowdy, and Bob Uecker were vocal Billy supporters.

But the tenor of the criticism of Billy, especially in the nation's newspapers, unmistakably changed in the mid-1980s. Billy remained popular with fans, but for the rest of his life he regularly encountered a sector of the media whose opinions had primarily been shaped by the police blotter notices of Billy's conduct. They knew what they thought of him before they met him — if they ever met him. Who could blame them for their viewpoint given the mounting misbehavior, but it was evident in their writing that Billy was someone to distrust or avoid. This segment of the media did not see him as endearingly imperfect and oddly productive. They were either wary of Billy or repulsed by him.

On the most palpable level, the Newport Beach incident added up to nothing except that it became another discredit easily resurrected — one that fit a developing caricature.

In the timeline of Billy's life, however, the confrontation in Newport Beach became a turning point. Soon after, Billy and Jill reconciled.

"It was a terrible time we went through," Jill said. "And people, of course, have asked me why I didn't leave him then.

"But when you think about it, he was all I had. He was who I was in love with. He promised me that he would make it good — that we would be together. He was going to leave Heather.

"He said he would be with me and take care of me for the rest of my life. And he did."

In the New York baseball community, Billy remained an afterthought. There were bigger issues, like the Yankees' awful record in 1984. Detroit was running away with the AL East and on their way to a World Series victory. Steinbrenner strangely withdrew from the public eye. He told associates the season was lost. The Yankees finished in third place. On the final day of the 1984 season, eight Yankees expressed their displeasure with how they were being used or being treated by Berra. That's when Steinbrenner came out of hiding. He wasn't happy either.

"I don't know where to rate Yogi as a manager," Steinbrenner told the beat writers. "In spring training, I didn't feel we were ready but my baseball people assured me we'd be ready when the gong rang. They were wrong. I'm not letting that happen again."

Most telling, and Steinbrenner mentioned it to reporters, the Yankees' home attendance dropped by nearly 450,000 fans from 1983 to 1984.

Billy's life away from the field was going through yet another transition. He was distancing himself from Heather. He went home to Blackhawk after the regular season and spent time in the Bay Area. Morabito recalls going to lunch with Billy and Heather at Joe DiMaggio's restaurant on San Francisco's Fisherman's Wharf. But it was one of the last times Morabito saw Heather and Billy together.

According to news reports about the divorce proceedings filed about a year later, there was no final act that spurred the separation. Depending on whose side of the story you want to believe, the trigger was the Newport Beach episode or it was something more complex, a falling-out that evolved over months if not years. But it is indisputable that there was no decisive moment that signaled the end of Billy's marriage with Heather. It ended in a series of lawyers' offices.

It was not a competition, but to Billy's friends and family, Jill had won in the love triangle. She would remain at his side for the next five years, omnipresent and in command of many aspects of Billy's life. They did not marry until January 1988, but long before that Jill had taken control of Billy's finances, hatched a new marketing plan for him, and, for a little while, gotten him to stop drinking completely. As Billy and Jill grew closer, several of Billy's best and oldest pals — Eddie Sapir and Lew Figone among them — felt pushed away and stepped into the shadows of his life. Some but not all severed their ties with Billy, feeling that Billy, or Jill, wanted the relationship to end.

"Yeah, I know, I became that woman who took the great guy away from everyone," Jill said in 2013. "All those people hate me for that. In any new relationship, in the newness, both parties spend more intense time together and other people feel left out or feel eliminated. Isn't that common in a new relationship?

"So it happened with us. That's how it works. But Billy had a lot of people in his life and he was used to doing a lot of different things, not all of them good for him."

Jill did not approve of all the outings and junkets and the time spent with his buddies drinking. She was not fond of the hunting trips.

"I didn't like the killing of animals," she said. "So, yes, my presence probably kept him from some trips and outings. But all I cared about was the time I had with him. He was a wild and crazy guy, but we had a blast. He was a busy guy and he wanted me to be with him. So, yes, we were together a lot and some people went the other way."

At baseball's winter meetings that December, Billy convinced the Yankees' brain trust to trade for Rickey Henderson. The Yankees sent Oakland several young pitchers, including José Rijo, who ended up winning 116 Major League games. But now the Yankees had the game's best leadoff hitter, which made for a fearsome top of the lineup. Batting behind Henderson would be Randolph, Mattingly, Winfield, and Baylor. A young power-hitting third baseman and a Billy protégé, Mike Pagliarulo, would hit next.

Said Steinbrenner, looking ahead to 1985, "With that lineup, we've got a team that should never be out of it. We're now the favorites in the AL East. I could manage that team and not screw it up."

Anyone paying attention knew the quote was a missile fired across Berra's bow.

Spring training in 1985 was calm. The Yankees had acquired Yogi's son,

Dale, to be a utility infielder and perhaps platoon at third base with Pagliarulo. If there was a frequent story line out of Fort Lauderdale that spring, it was the unusual father-son combo now in Yankees pinstripes.

The Yankees had a host of new players besides Dale Berra and Henderson. There was the talkative and excitable pitcher Eddie Lee Whitson, who was signed as a free agent. Raised in the mountains of eastern Tennessee, he was not much prepared for the pressure or the culture shock of being a Yankee. He was so confused by the bridges and tunnels of the New York metropolitan area that teammates or a coach had to drive him from his house in New Jersey to Yankee Stadium. When he tried to drive himself, he ended up in Staten Island.

Joining Whitson was catcher Ron Hassey and a diverse team built around the powerhouse at the top of the batting order. But Henderson, Mattingly, and Winfield were all injured in spring training. The Yankees were not winning often in the exhibition games, and Steinbrenner felt the laid-back Berra was once again not enforcing enough discipline. Rumors began to circulate that another managerial term for Billy was forthcoming.

Billy was resting and, as it happened, getting tanned on assignment for the team in Arizona and California.

Still, Steinbrenner insisted that Berra would be the Yankees manager for the entire season — no matter what.

"Even if we get off to a bad start," George said.

He had said the same thing three years earlier, then fired Bob Lemon fourteen games into the 1982 season.

The Yankees did not start the 1985 season well. First of all, Henderson was on the disabled list, still nursing an ankle he sprained three weeks earlier. The Yankees lost their first three games in Boston, getting outscored 29–11. Leaving Boston, Steinbrenner said, "Our pitching stinks."

Then the Yankees went to Ohio, George's home state, and were routed in an exhibition against the franchise's AAA minor league affiliate from Columbus.

Steinbrenner was not pleased and blamed Yogi for letting his players take the minor leaguers lightly.

"I've been a coach," George said. "You do that and it carries over. I'd like to see more discipline from them, but the owner can't force the manager to do something he doesn't want to."

That wasn't a shot across the bow. George was getting Yogi Berra in his range finder just three regular season games and one exhibition into the season.

The Yankees won their next four games but were lurching along with a 6-7 record. Then they lost three straight games in Chicago.

It was April 29, and the Yankees were 6-10 and in last place, 4.5 games behind the first-place Detroit Tigers, who had run away with the division with an early spurt the year before.

In the middle of the Yankees' third and final game in Chicago, Steinbrenner called Billy. George asked Billy if he would take over for Berra. Billy happily agreed. He was already under contract but received a raise and a bonus. Billy flew to Texas, the Yankees' next stop after Chicago.

The task of informing Berra of his dismissal was given to Clyde King, the Yankees' general manager at the time. King entered Berra's office after the game while Steinbrenner issued a statement that read: "This action has been taken by the Yankees, and we feel that it is in the best interests of the club. I would rather fire 25 players than to fire Yogi, but we all know that would be impossible."

Berra did not open the door to his office after King left. In the clubhouse, Steinbrenner's statement was distributed to the players. Baylor read it, turned, and kicked a garbage can across the room. Few players had much to say other than to express their sympathy for Berra.

Henderson said he was looking forward to seeing Billy again.

After about thirty minutes, Berra's office door opened and his son, Dale, emerged with tears in his eyes. Yogi greeted reporters with a smile.

"I'm not in a very good mood," he said. "But this is still a very good ball club, and they're getting a good manager in Billy Martin. I don't think my players laid down on me."

Berra eventually walked around the clubhouse talking to the players. He encouraged them to play for Billy.

"He's a good man," Berra said. "It's not his fault that Steinbrenner is the Yankees' owner."

Yogi and Billy remained friends, although their paths crossed less often since Yogi refused to return to Yankee Stadium for any occasion for more than fifteen years.

Billy greeted the 1985 Yankees at the Texas ballpark the following afternoon. Baylor explained to his new manager that his trash-can-kicking outburst in Chicago — which had received much play in the newspapers — was "because Yogi got fired, not because you were hired."

Nonetheless, Billy did something he had never done before. He announced that he had a new coach, Willie Horton, Billy's former slugger from the 1970s Detroit Tigers. Horton, a bull of a man with an imposing glare who had been a Golden Gloves boxing champion, was named the Yankees' "tranquillity coach."

Billy also made several batting order changes and informed the players of various new team rules, which included a prohibition against playing golf on the road. Jackets and ties were made mandatory for flights. Infielders had to report early during the next few games for additional drills on trick plays and how to handle certain baserunning situations. Billy also called a workout on an upcoming off day to go over pickoffs, rundowns, and special circumstances, like suicide squeeze bunts.

Billy then donned his road-gray Yankees uniform and went to the visitors' dugout to pose for a picture. Facing the field with one leg up on a dugout step, Billy smiled and looked over his left shoulder, the familiar number 1 on his jersey in full view.

The photo would become the cover of *Sports Illustrated* the following week under the headline BILLY'S BACK.

Meeting with reporters afterward, Billy was definitely tanned and he appeared rested. He said he was relieved.

"I had to accept that I was let go after the '83 season but deep down it hurt and I really missed it," he said. "Thank God, I'm back. As I told somebody today, how long can you keep watering your garden?"

Playing as if shell-shocked, the Yankees lost their fourth successive game that evening. The besieged Yankees lost the next night, too. They were six games out of first place and had the worst record in Major League Baseball.

41

<hr>

THE 1985 SEASON HAD brought a shift of power in the American League. The team to beat was the Toronto Blue Jays, a nascent squad with few weaknesses. The Blue Jays had the exuberance and fearlessness of youth and a versatile lineup that had grown up together through Toronto's stocked farm system. The Blue Jays were what the Yankees became in the late 1990s with a core of players whose skills complemented each other. Toronto's top three hitters, outfielders George Bell, Lloyd Mosley, and Jesse Barfield, were each just twenty-five years old in 1985 but had already been in the Major Leagues for four years. The Blue Jays' slick-fielding shortstop, Tony Fernandez, was twenty-three. The starting rotation had four quality pitchers, and three of them were in their twenties.

The Blue Jays' manager was the future Hall of Famer Bobby Cox, a Yankees infielder in the early 1970s. The Toronto general manager was the quiet and astute Pat Gillick, a one-time rising star in the Yankees' front office who was part of the mass exodus from New York about six months after Steinbrenner took control of the team.

The Blue Jays were poised to go on a long, successful run in the American League, a winning streak that would last into the early 1990s when they won consecutive World Series.

But the 1985 Yankees were an imposing team, too. The patchwork pitching staff was yet to jell, and a few injuries needed to heal, but what the team was waiting for was someone to jump-start Henderson, who remained the game's most dynamic player even if he was yet to display any of that vitality for the Yankees.

The Yankees also had a promising if unproven left side of the infield in shortstop Bobby Meacham and Pagliarulo, the third baseman. Both lacked experience and desperately needed a mentor who would stand by them. Meacham and Pagliarulo had talent — Meacham had been the eighth overall selection of the 1981 amateur draft — but they did not have the support of the Yankees' upper management, which was constantly trying to trade them for veteran, established players.

And Meacham and Pagliarulo knew it, which eroded their confidence.

As a scout who was part of those talks in 1984, Billy had advocated for both players and voted against trading them, especially Pagliarulo, who Billy insisted would become a feared left-handed power hitter.

Pagliarulo, who would end up hitting 94 home runs for the Yankees from 1985 to 1988, was Billy's kind of player — a product of a tough, blue-collar neighborhood just north of Boston. Along with his best buddy on the team, Don Mattingly, Pagliarulo, known as "Pags," loved to take hours of extra batting practice before games. Pagliarulo and Mattingly would beg a coach to come to the park early to throw extra batting practice before a night game.

"How early?" the coach would ask.

"About one."

"One o'clock? But the game isn't until 7:30."

"OK, then 1:30," Pags would say.

Meacham was a switch-hitting, laid-back Californian who played with a smooth efficiency. He had good range at shortstop, and the Yankees thought he could become a bottom-of-the-order slashing hitter who would hit about .260 — something that happened only during two seasons for Meacham. But Meacham was fast on the bases and he was a good bunter. That made him Billy's kind of player, too.

One or two days after Billy took over for Berra, he called Meacham and Pagliarulo into his office and told them they were his permanent left side of the infield. He was calling off the trade talk.

Most of the rest of the Yankees — veterans like Winfield, Baylor, Randolph, Griffey, Mattingly, and catcher Ron Hassey — did not need Billy's private encouragement. But they apparently needed a jolt of passion and aggression from the manager in the dugout.

Led by Henderson, Meacham, Randolph, and Winfield — four players who had each stolen 25 bases or more in one season — the Yankees began to make the running game a part of their arsenal.

"Home runs are fine when they come but I want singles and walks — it's on-base percentage that matters," he said, echoing some of the Money Ball tenets to come forward years later. "Then we put pressure on the defense and see what happens."

In Billy's third game as the 1985 manager, the Yankees won 5–2 with five singles, five walks, and four stolen bases. A run scored when Henderson induced a balk from the opposing pitcher with a bluffed steal of home plate. Meacham was thrown out trying to steal home. Most of the Yankees thought he was safe.

"We surprised the umpire and he didn't know what to call," Mattingly said of the call at home plate. "I know we surprised the pitcher."

It would be the first of five consecutive Yankees victories.

But when the Yankees returned to Yankee Stadium for the first time since Berra's firing, Billy did not get his usual rousing welcome from the home fans. The comeback act was getting old, even for someone as popular as Billy. There was an overwhelming sympathy for how Berra had been ingloriously ditched so early in the season. Also, the indifferent performance of the Yankees since 1982 and the circuslike atmosphere Steinbrenner had created with seven managerial changes since 1980 had bred a burgeoning disgust with the team's owner and his bombastic ways. The backlash against Steinbrenner's Yankees was substantial, and there was now an alternative in town, too.

The 1985 New York Mets were an ascending, trendy other choice with a brash, energetic, stylish team. The Yankees were fighting for the back page of the tabloids even with Billy's return. An announced attendance of just 20,603 greeted Billy on his first game back at Yankee Stadium on May 3. In fact, the actual crowd was several thousand fans fewer.

Billy was cheered as he brought the lineup card out before the game, but there was also a first for this kind of occasion: random booing. The ovation lasted only long enough for Billy to wave his cap once. In the past, the cheers had been sustained enough to ensure at least three or four waves of the cap. When Billy walked back to the dugout, the response was muted.

Billy was back in the Bronx, but it was no longer 1978.

The 1985 Yankees would do their best to bring the crowds back. In mid-May they won seven straight, improving their record under Billy to 12-5. They were now only 2.5 games behind first-place Toronto.

The mood around the Yankees quickly changed. There was loud music playing in the Yankees' clubhouse after most games. On Billy's fifty-seventh birthday, the Yankees won when Pagliarulo laid down a perfect suicide squeeze bunt to score Randolph from third base.

"We all know how to play aggressively," Randolph said afterward. "Billy just gives you the green light to go do that. His confidence in those situations is contagious and we feed off of it."

A couple of days later, Billy brought in the twenty-three-year-old reliever Brian Fisher to face Reggie Jackson with two runners on base in a tight game. Billy had called up Fisher from the Yankees' minor leagues on his first day back as manager, and he had become Billy's bullpen project, a setup man for closer Dave Righetti. Now Billy was testing the young right-hander's 94-mile-an-hour fastball against the lefty-swinging Jackson. Fisher induced a tapper back to the mound that became a double play.

"Within a few weeks after he got there in 1985, I knew Billy was going to be a better manager than he was in 1983," said Gene Michael, who was the third-base coach in 1985. "He was a little distracted in '83, but in '85 a lot of that off-the-field stuff was behind him. He looked better and was eating better.

"He was sharp during games and doing all his usual things — stealing the team's signs, talking to the players a lot during the game. He watched the interaction of the opposing catcher and opposing manager and instinctively understood everything they were trying to do. Having been a middle infielder, he could watch their body language and know what they were planning. He was always one or two innings ahead of his opposing manager and that guy knew that, which got the opposing manager to start second-guessing himself. Billy had that edge. He hadn't completely turned back the clock to 1977, but it was the old Billy in a lot of ways."

Michael had been fired by Steinbrenner twice at this point and vowed never to manage for George again. Michael meant it and Billy knew it. That was like a badge of honor to Billy, so he welcomed Michael into his inner circle, which now also included Piniella, who had retired and was the hitting coach. The former player Bobby Murcer was a Yankees broadcaster, and Murcer was included in the group close to Billy (Art Fowler was not a coach in 1985).

The foursome spent a lot of time together, some of it on the golf course before games when they would pair off in teams and wager a couple of hundred dollars in best-ball matches.

There was a rule against players golfing, but it did not apply to coaches, managers, or broadcasters.

"The golfing was actually a strategy I dreamed up to get Billy out of the bars earlier," Michael said. "You know, if nothing was planned for the next day, Billy might be more likely to stay up late drinking. But if we had a golf date the next morning, Billy would turn in early because Billy loved to compete at anything and he hated losing. If he was hung-over, he wouldn't play well and he knew it.

"I think that really worked in 1985. We played a lot of golf because Billy could make a call and get on any golf course in the country. And Billy laughed a lot on the golf course. It relaxed him. That might have been when he had the most fun during the season. Baseball games were tense to him and he had trouble unwinding after games, too. But on the golf course, he was a funny guy. Although he would cheat a little to win. We used to kid him that his cheating at golf was the real Billy Ball."

The Yankees' longtime trainer Gene Monahan also felt that Billy had changed in 1985. He thought Billy had reestablished some measure of control over his life.

"Billy was a tough guy but he had a soft, compassionate side, and that year I think he was willing to show the players more of that other side of him," Monahan said. "He was getting a little older. I think one of his best attributes was that he was very sentimental. He had a lot of empathy for people and he read people very well right from the start. Billy knew how to manage a game but he knew how to manage personalities, too.

"With the '85 team, he had guys like Winfield and Randolph who didn't need much from him. Billy would say, 'You play hard every day and I'll have your back.' And he would do that. If Mr. Steinbrenner or an umpire went against one of those guys, he would fight to the death to protect them.

"But there were younger guys, like Pags, Meacham, or the rookie out-fielder Dan Pasqua, who needed Billy and he was there for them. He would alternatively ride their ass and coddle them to get the most out of them. He was always very good around young people; he had an instinct about what to say. He'd have these half-hour conversations in a hotel lobby with a young player.

"He was the same way with a teenager or college kid he had just met. Here was this tough bastard and he'd be talking at length about their lives and their dreams. If it was a younger kid, he'd be sure to go to the kid's parents and say, 'That's a great kid you got there.'" Ron Guidry said the 1985 team was also more pragmatic than Billy's previous Yankees teams in 1983 and 1979.

"We were tired of losing," Guidry said. "By 1985, it was more businesslike. We were like, 'OK, Billy, we don't care about the drama and all the other off-the-field stuff, just help us win. You do your job during the games and we'll do ours.'"

Guidry said the feuds of the past, with Reggie, with the writers, or with George, were long gone in their minds. The players didn't care so much about Billy's drinking or what was going on between games.

"Some guys grumbled about him but every team has guys grumbling," Guidry said. "Every team has guys who don't play as much as they want to and they don't like the manager. Billy lost some guys that way or because of something he said or did.

"But to the core of the team, the starting players, it was about whether he could help us get wins. We had gotten to the point where that's all that mattered."

If Billy did come into the clubhouse looking wan and unsteady from a late night of boozing, which happened sporadically in the beginning of the season and a little more often toward the end of the season, Monahan had a ready remedy. He used it to perk up players, too, several of whom were also heavy drinkers.

Monahan periodically gave Billy a vitamin B^{12} shot in those circumstances. He also mixed up a concoction that he said was a recipe passed down from the 1920s when Yankees trainers had to work on a hung-over Babe Ruth almost daily.

"We'd mix seltzer with some extra-strength Bufferin and add a little peppermint," Monahan, now retired, said. "We'd put some coloring in it to make it look more appealing and some fruit for the nutrition. We'd shake it to make it foam and bubble and then quietly take it over to Billy or a player and say, 'OK, this worked for the Babe all those years ago and only our team knows about it. It's been passed down through the decades.'

"And you know, I do think it worked most of the time. More often than not, Billy would come to me in about twenty minutes and say, 'You know, Geno, I feel pretty good.'"

Gene Michael's golf strategy inhibited some of the late-night carousing, and there was another frequent presence at Billy's side after games that curbed his drinking. Jill was at many home games as well as on the road. Jill did not like to sit at a bar for two hours and she got Billy to turn in earlier because of it.

"Jill was good for him," Morabito said. "Obviously, you'll get different opinions about that from his other friends. But I remember going to a bar one time when the Yankees were in Oakland and he ordered a club soda. I turned and said, 'What's this?'

"And he said, 'Jill has convinced me to not drink a couple days a week and this is one of them.' And he was fine with that."

For the most part, the 1985 season unfolded without controversy or incident for Billy. There were the usual squabbles with umpires, but off the field Billy made no extracurricular news.

By August, the team was winning 59 percent of the time, which was a higher rate than all but three teams in Major League Baseball, including the Mets, which pleased Steinbrenner. The attendance numbers were climbing.

A typical Yankees game started like this in the 1985 season: Henderson would rap a single or draw a walk. He would steal second, after which Randolph would bunt him to third base. Mattingly would either get a run-scoring hit or hit an RBI sacrifice fly. Winfield would come up and perhaps drive in Mattingly with an extra-base hit. And if Winfield failed, Don Baylor usually did not.

"We went into the second inning of so many games that year ahead 1–0 or 2–0," Piniella said. "It seemed like all we needed was five minutes to get a lead. It wears on the opposition to be behind all the time."

Winfield said the players also believed that their manager would win some games for them.

"He had the other teams all jumpy and nervous and you don't play well when you're like that," Winfield said many years later. "You could see the pitcher, catcher, and the other manager were saying to themselves, 'What's Billy going to do now?'

"We would be in the dugout laughing. Rickey Henderson had a saying, 'We've Billy-blitzed another team.'"

There were some Yankees hiccups but the 1985 team was resilient.

Guidry was on his way to 22 victories and the ageless Phil Niekro would win 16 games. Mattingly was flirting with his second successive batting title but instead would settle for winning the AL Most Valuable Player award with a .324 average, 35 homers, and 145 runs batted in, the most RBIs for a Yankee since Joe DiMaggio in 1948. Winfield would drive in 114 runs. Henderson would steal 80 bases, score 146 runs, and hit 24 homers while driving in 72 runs. Pagliarulo hit 19 homers and Randolph and Meacham combined to turn 207 double plays.

On September 12, when the Yankees defeated the Blue Jays in the first of four games at Yankee Stadium, they trailed Toronto by only 1.5 games.

The Mets were in first place in the National League East, the first time the Mets and the Yankees were in serious contention for the postseason at the same time. In New York, there was talk of the first Subway Series since 1956.

Pitching the next game for the Yankees would be Niekro, who would be seeking his 300th career victory. The forty-six-year-old Niekro had won each of his five previous decisions.

A big crowd was expected at Yankee Stadium to watch both the AL East pennant race and Niekro's achievement. Everything was looking up for Billy's team. Nothing would have predicted what happened next. The Yankees had no idea how turbulent the next week and a half would be. In the more than 110-year history of the franchise, no ten-day period compares for on- and the off-the-field dramatics and histrionics.

On Friday, the thirteenth day of September 1985, in front of 53,303 fans, Niekro did not win his 300th game although he pitched a complete game in a 3–2 loss.

The next day, before another crowd in excess of fifty-two thousand, the Yankees lost 7–4 and Winfield was 0-for-4 with four groundouts that stranded two base runners.

Late in that game, Steinbrenner suddenly appeared at the back of the Yankee Stadium press box. The owner made these appearances only when he wanted to make a proclamation for print. Steinbrenner had a sheet in his hand on Yankees stationery that contained the batting statistics of several Yankees during the three recent games with Toronto. He read them aloud: Griffey was 0-for-8, Baylor 0-for-7, and Winfield 3-for-11 with only 2 runs batted in.

"Where is Reggie Jackson?" George said in a loud voice as if he were trying to shout to the dugout two levels below. "We need a Mr. October or a Mr. September. Winfield is Mr. May. My big guys are not coming through. The guys who are supposed to carry the team are not carrying the team."

What became known as Steinbrenner's "Mr. May speech" was big news, and it brought shock waves to the Yankees' clubhouse where Winfield had many allies, including Billy. Winfield was one of the team's spiritual leaders, a freakish athletic talent who had been taken in the Major League Baseball draft as well as the NFL and NBA drafts.

The six-foot-six Winfield always played hard and was a respected teammate who deflected attention from his locker. Other players made fun of his parsimonious ways — he collected the free soaps, shampoos, and mouthwash from hotels and took them home in his suitcase on every road trip for years — but he was also admired for a fearsome, attacking style of play. He terrorized opposing infielders when he roared around the bases, and he routinely gave up his body, saving a pitcher's mistake with a diving catch or a full-speed crash into an outfield barrier. As the number-four hitter, Winfield protected Mattingly, the team's other foremost leader, in the batting order, ensuring that Mattingly got good pitches to swing at since walking Mattingly meant facing the hard-swinging future Hall of Famer Winfield.

So in the midst of a two-game losing streak — and a pennant race — no one on the Yankees wanted to hear about Winfield being singled out for not being more like Reggie Jackson because of a few ill-timed ground-outs.

When George's words were repeated to Billy in his office after the game, he slammed his hat on his desk and walked out of the room without comment.

Winfield, who had driven in his 101st run in the game, declined to address Steinbrenner's remarks after the game. Mattingly was not as circumspect.

"He may think he's helping, but as usual, he's only making things worse," Mattingly said of Steinbrenner. "Nobody in their right mind would criticize Dave Winfield. We need to band together in a tough stretch and the man upstairs is picking us apart."

When the game was played that Sunday, Whitson started for the Yankees and did not survive the third inning, leaving the mound with Toronto on its way to an 8–5 rout. Whitson, whose relationship with Yankees fans had been toxic since he lost six of his first seven decisions to start the season, was booed mercilessly as he left the field. Yankees fans reached for whatever they could throw at Whitson. A torrent of rolled-up paper, beer cups, popcorn, and Cracker Jack boxes rained down on him.

The Yankees lost again. More than 214,000 fans had come to Yankee Stadium for the four-game series, a Major League record for 1985. But the Yankees were now 4.5 games behind the Blue Jays.

"I'm not going to get on 'em today," Steinbrenner said afterward. "If they're not embarrassed, they should take the uniform off and walk away from the pay window."

The Yankees were more shocked than embarrassed. Years later, it is easy to see that the Blue Jays were a team on the rise. At the time, in front of a packed Yankee Stadium day after day, the Yankees believed they could impose their will on the youngsters from Toronto. They were wrong.

But Billy's team left the stadium quickly on that Sunday. The next day they had to play an odd afternoon makeup game with lowly Cleveland at Yankee Stadium. Then the Yankees would fly to Detroit for three games followed by three games in Baltimore.

The aura of doom enveloping the Yankees did not lift the next afternoon. For eight innings things appeared routine. The Yankees went into the top of the ninth with a 5–3 lead over the Indians, who started the day forty games out of first place. Fisher was in the game to get the final three outs to preserve the victory. Righetti was warming up in the bullpen as insurance against an unlikely occurrence in 1985, a Cleveland rally.

The first three batters facing Fisher singled, loading the bases. Billy walked to the mound, presumably to replace the right-handed Fisher with the left-handed Righetti since the next hitter, Brett Butler, was left-handed. But Fisher had not given up more than two hits in his last fifteen appearances — and had a victory and seven saves. Righetti had been hit hard in his last appearance. Billy left Fisher in. It did not prove to be the right move.

Fisher got Butler to ground out (one run scored) but the next batter, Julio Franco, a right-hander, tripled to put Cleveland ahead, 6–5.

Now everyone expected Billy to go to the more experienced Righetti. But Billy's logic was that the Yankees were now losing and he wasn't going to use two young bullpen arms in pursuit of a comeback victory. He wanted to save Righetti for the tough road trip coming up.

In this case, trying to preserve an arm got Billy in trouble when Andre Thornton hit the next Fisher pitch into the stands for a two-run homer. At this point, Billy wasn't backing down. Fisher remained in the game even as Cleveland rapped another single, stole a base, and scored a final run in a 9–5 victory. The twenty-three-year-old Fisher had given up six hits and six runs. The Yankees were now five games back.

After the game, Billy was being grilled for leaving the young Fisher on the mound to take a relentless beating. Billy did not take the second-guessing well. To him, he had rolled the dice with Fisher, which did not work, but he had saved Righetti for another day.

In a voice that kept rising and gaining volume, Billy confronted reporters: "Hasn't Fisher done a good job against right-handers and left-handers? Come on, he's been sensational. I'm not gonna burn up two pitchers in one losing ball game. I'm not gonna do that to please you guys or the fans. Fisher's only mistake was when he shook off the catcher and threw the slider to Thornton."

The Yankees hustled for the bus that would take them to Newark airport for a flight to Detroit.

"Maybe we just need to get out of here for a while," said Joe Cowley, the good-humored starting pitcher who had handed the baseball and a lead to Fisher. "A change of scenery might do us good."

The next night in hitter-friendly Tiger Stadium, Guidry, going for his twentieth win, gave up five home runs in a 9–1 rout. The following evening about seventy members of the Niekro family drove up from Ohio in hopes of seeing forty-six-year-old Phil capture victory number 300. The game was tied 2–2 in the sixth inning when the Yankees seemed on the verge of getting to Detroit pitcher Mickey Mahler, a journeyman left-handed reliever. The Yankees had runners at third and first base with two outs. The left-handed-hitting Mike Pagliarulo was due up next.

Pagliarulo was not usually pinch-hit for against lefties. But Mahler had yielded only one hit since coming on in the first inning for Detroit's starter, Juan Berenguer, who gave up both Yankees runs. Mahler also had a history with Pagliarulo.

"He was very tough on me," Pagliarulo said.

Before he could get to home plate, Pagliarulo was called over to the Yankees' dugout. Billy could have chosen to substitute right-handed infielder Andre Robertson, who hit .328 in 125 at-bats in 1985. Billy Sample, who hit .288 that year, was another possibility.

There was a third option. Pagliarulo had been a switch hitter in high school and college. He still hit right-handed in the Yankees' intrasquad games and during informal workouts.

In fact, a week earlier, the Yankees had played a simulated game to get extra work for one of their pitchers, Marty Bystrom, who was coming off the disabled list. In it, Pagliarulo batted right-handed and had four hits including a double off the left-field wall.

Billy left that day convinced that Pags should try to return to switch

hitting once the season ended when he had a winter to work on it. Piniella, the hitting coach, was impressed with Pagliarulo's right-handed
stroke, too.

But the off-season plan got an accelerated start at that moment inside
Tiger Stadium. Billy told Pagliarulo to go to the plate right-handed. Piniella agreed with the strategy.

Pagliarulo did what he was told but his heart wasn't in it. As he dug
into the dirt of the right-handed batter's box, Detroit catcher Bob Melvin
asked, "What the hell are you doing?"

Said Pags, "What's it look like I'm doing? I'm trying to get a hit."

Years later, Pagliarulo's perspective had not changed much.

"I hadn't hit right-handed in a real game since I was in the minors in
1981," he said. "But I would do anything Billy told me. In general, Billy
didn't like to take me out of games because he felt our team defense was
much better with me at third base.

"I honestly didn't want to bat rightie because I didn't feel I was prepared but I didn't want to get taken out of the game either."

In the press box and among most of the players in the Yankees' dugout,
the consensus was that Billy had asked the impossible. Pagliarulo looked
overmatched and struck out. The Yankees lost, 5–2, but the Pagliarulo
move was a prominent tabloid story back in New York.

Had Billy lost his mind? The Yankees had lost six successive games and
now the players were batting from the wrong side of the plate?

One New York columnist compared Billy to Captain Queeg from *The
Caine Mutiny.*

Said Piniella, "It certainly backfired but you know it was a tied game.
That's not why we lost. But Billy drew attention to himself with those
chances. That's why other managers never try them. If it goes wrong,
you get hammered. It was certainly unorthodox in the middle of a Major
League game."

The Yankees lost the next night as well, 10–3, then packed up and
boarded their charter flight to Baltimore. On the flight, Billy appeared
especially drained, withdrawn, and disheartened, not an uncommon reaction for a manager in the midst of a seven-game losing streak. Billy
sat apart from his coaches, who knew enough to leave him alone. Only
traveling secretary Bill Kane remained seated near Billy. Kane was always
welcome.

A baseball team on a chartered jet in the 1980s reserved the first-class section for the manager, coaches, trainers, and traveling secretary. The next few rows were set aside for the writers and broadcasters. The rest of the cabin was for the players. In general, coaches, writers, broadcasters, and other non-players did not go back to the players' area, even to use a restroom. It became the players' sanctuary, a place where they could do whatever they wanted — and the jet usually became something of a flying casino with the liquor cart left in the aisle and card games breaking out everywhere. Flight attendants usually ventured to the back of the cabin sparingly, and at their risk.

Everyone else mostly stayed in the front of the jet. After takeoff, the cockpit door would often be open and the pilots never minded if they had visitors sit with them as they flew.

On the flight from Detroit to Baltimore, nearly all the coaches and trainers cleared out of first class and crowded into the little area reserved for the media at the front of the jet. Piniella played cards with the writers. The broadcasters were either asleep or in the cockpit.

It was a short but tense flight with Billy quietly talking to Kane. The pilots, usually excited to see Billy onboard and eager to talk to him, took one look at his dispirited countenance in the first row of first class and walked past him silently. The pall of defeat was profound. It felt as if the Yankees would never win another game.

Two buses greeted the team on the airport tarmac for the short drive to the Cross Keys Inn, a low-slung hotel plunked in the midst of a suburban commercial park.

The Yankees players, coaches, and media grabbed their room keys. Billy got in the back of an elevator that quickly filled up. No one said a word as the floor buttons were pushed and the elevator began to ascend in an awkward hush. Then, from the back, Billy said, "For Christ sake, nobody's died. Let's just play the next series."

The elevator stopped at the third floor and Billy got off.

"See you tomorrow," someone said.

Billy turned with a smile and replied, "I hope so."

42

THE NEXT SERIES DID indeed start the next day. But things did not calm down. Volatile Eddie Lee Whitson was scheduled to start that night's game. But Billy considered Whitson — with some justification — undependable under pressure. Billy announced that Whitson was being scratched from his start.

Billy had a reason for the switch. "Whatchamacallit," as Billy tactlessly referred to Whitson that evening, had a tender arm. When approached by reporters, Whitson was stunned to discover that his arm was bothering him. He said he was healthy.

This turn of events did not sit well with either Billy or the high-strung Whitson. The two had had a touchy relationship to that point although there had been no outlandish disagreements. But privately, Whitson despised the way Billy wanted to call every pitch and routinely made every outing seem a do-or-die affair. Billy, meanwhile, distrusted Whitson after his horrible start to the season and wondered if Whitson had the stomach for the pressure of playing New York, which was an imperative attribute to Billy. Still, the two had coexisted under an uneasy, unspoken truce, and Billy kept Whitson in the rotation. Whitson responded by winning most of his decisions from June to late August.

But beginning with a start on August 31, Whitson's pitching statistics had been alarming. In four starts, he had given up 31 hits and 19 runs in 19.2 innings pitched. His ERA in that period was 7.32.

With the Yankees in a death spiral, Billy was sure that Whitson was not the best choice to end the losing streak.

Instead, he gave the baseball to spot starter Rich Bordi for the first game in Baltimore. In the visitors' clubhouse at Memorial Stadium, Whitson stomped around the room. His teammates ignored him.

Whitson was an odd fit on the 1985 Yankees. He was liked but he had few friends. His interests were hunting and fishing and he kept a pile of outdoor sports magazines in his locker. If he had ever talked at length with Billy about deer or quail hunting, they might have become friends. There is no evidence the two ever had that conversation or shared a beer.

But even the Yankees who did know Whitson never grew close to him. Few of the players in 1985 were outdoorsmen or had been raised in the country. Whitson's was the only locker with a tape player regularly belting out country music. He was the rare voice with a southern drawl. The African American players were largely from urban areas. Most of the other Yankees — Pagliarulo, Mattingly, Hassey, Pasqua, Righetti, Wynegar, Dale Berra — were also from northern or West Coast cities or their close suburbs. The only truly rural compatriot of Whitson's was the Louisianan Guidry, but Guidry was not gregarious. Guidry kept to himself and was usually either in the gym staying fit or working on his hobby, which was playing the drums (he had a kit under the stands at Yankee Stadium). On the road, Guidry tended to dine in his room, the king of room service.

The rest of the 1985 pitching staff was a rough-and-tumble group, almost a cult within the team. They were like fraternity brothers, and their favorite form of amusement was insulting each other with biting humor. Whitson, his teammates said, was thin-skinned and shied from the banter. He ended up isolated from the only group that would have him.

The Yankees fans, meanwhile, berated Whitson ceaselessly.

"Eddie couldn't even go on the field during batting practice before a game at Yankee Stadium," said his 1985 teammate and fellow pitcher Dennis Rasmussen. "If he did, people threw stuff at him. He developed a hatred of New York and eventually of Billy.

"The funny thing is that he and Billy were of the same mold, I think. They both liked to tip a few at the bar, and when they were drinking you knew you better not say the wrong thing to them because he'd want to fight everybody. It just wasn't hard to get him riled up. That wasn't the best personality to have on that 1985 team when everything that happened seemed just absolutely and totally crazy."

Bordi, pitching for Whitson, did not end the losing streak. During the game, a key run scored when Billy mistakenly scratched his nose, which was the signal for a pitchout. Billy didn't mean to call a pitchout; his nose was just itchy. The details of the gaffe did not get out to the press at the time, but the players knew of it. It seemed to fit a trend. The despair continued to build.

After the game, Billy was nearly speechless, mumbling barely audible answers.

"We just need a spark," he said.

Losers of eight straight, the Yankees retired to their hotel, the Cross Keys Inn. Most went to bed. It was after midnight and there was a day game the next afternoon. At the Cross Keys, they did not have many choices at that hour anyway.

In the 1980s, most baseball teams stayed in large, luxury hotels in downtown areas where there was likely a plethora of restaurant and bar choices within walking distance. This kind of location scattered the post-game drinking, which is often a good idea. Cliques form on teams, so better to let different groups unwind in their own orbit. And, while Billy liked to drink with his players, an urban environment also made it easier for the players to *not* drink with Billy — as some of his players preferred.

But Cross Keys Inn was seven miles from downtown Baltimore. It was surrounded by parking lots and shrubbery and office buildings shuttered at night. Killer Kane, the Yankees' traveling secretary, had vacationed at the property during the winter of 1984–85 when he was touring Baltimore with his family. Kane thought it would be a nice change of pace to bring the team to a leafy environment.

But on the Friday night after the game, Billy and several players — Righetti, Henderson, and Pagliarulo among them — congregated in the small bar just off the lobby of the Cross Keys. The players swilled beer and cocktails at a table along with some writers. Billy, as was often the case, was at the bar, which was parallel to a wall with a mirror facing back to the lounge and tables. A two-man band was playing in a corner.

As was also usually the case, Billy struck up a conversation with strangers at the bar. Near him were two young couples. Billy quickly learned that one of the couples had gotten married that day. He bought the newlyweds a bottle of champagne.

Later, he danced one song with the bride. The newlyweds eventually thanked Billy, got autographs, and retired to their room. No one, obviously, expected to see them again that night.

But within minutes, the groom, still in his tuxedo and weaving somewhat unsteadily, reappeared at Billy's side at the bar.

"Hey, Billy, we've got to talk," he said loudly. "You told my wife she has a potbelly."

Everyone in the bar heard him. While it was hard to believe that Billy had ever heard such an accusation before, especially from a bridegroom, Billy nevertheless seemed unmoved.

"I did not say she had a potbelly," Billy said flatly and without emotion. He pointed at the woman from the other couple at the bar and added, "I said this woman had a fat ass."

Now there were two men upset at Billy. Some minor shoving ensued. Henderson and a couple of coaches intervened to separate the potential combatants. There was some yelling, but the bridegroom and the other couple departed and nothing else became of the tussle. The whole thing lasted about twenty-five seconds.

The scuffle with the bridegroom — which was hard to imagine — and the equally unfathomable "potbelly" and "fat ass" quotes would be all but forgotten. In the history of the team, they are lost in the recounting of more momentous events.

The Yankees finally snapped their losing streak Saturday afternoon when Cowley and Fisher combined for a five-hitter in a 5–2 victory (maybe Cowley and Fisher did need a change of scenery). The Yankees trailed the Blue Jays by 6.5 games. Whitson had still not pitched and he was not happy about it. Several reporters who approached his locker before the game heard all about how he had already instructed his agent to get him out of New York as soon as the season ended.

At about 6:00 p.m. Whitson perched at the bar, his hand wrapped around a bottle of Budweiser. A reporter asked if he had heard about the little fracas with the bridegroom.

"Oh, yeah," Whitson said with a smile. "I'm having a beer now, then getting out of here before the real festivities start."

Like most of the Yankees' traveling party that night, Whitson was leaving the hotel by cab to eat dinner downtown. The Cross Keys cleared out. But by 11:00 p.m. various parties returned to the hotel, and by 11:45 the bar was packed again. Billy had also gone to dinner downtown, stopping at the same crab restaurant he always visited, but as midnight approached, he was at the Cross Keys Inn bar, too, talking with announcer Frank Messer as well as Dale Berra and his wife, Leigh. Billy's tranquillity coach, Willie Horton, was asleep. Horton did not go to bars because he did not drink. Another coach, Doug Holmquist, who had become Billy's unofficial barroom bodyguard in 1985, was in Toronto scouting the Blue Jays in advance of what the Yankees hoped would be the final weekend three-game showdown in Toronto.

The lounge of the bar — an area Billy could see easily by looking at the mirror above him — was busy. In it, seated at a booth, was Eddie Lee Whitson, who, like Billy, had been drinking most of the night.

Sitting next to Whitson, only a few feet away, was Albert Millus, an attorney from Binghamton, New York, who came down to watch the Yankees games in Baltimore. Millus did not know any of the Yankees, although he would later befriend Billy briefly when Billy moved to the Binghamton area in 1988. (Millus was by then the town attorney for Fenton.)

"Whitson was agitated and talking loudly about Billy Martin; he was upset with him," Millus said in an interview years later. "A woman, I think Dale Berra's wife, came over to Whitson and was trying to calm him, I think. But Whitson kept saying things like, 'That man won't pitch me' or 'That SOB won't play me.'"

In a sworn affidavit he provided to Eddie Sapir several days later, Millus described what happened next:

> At this point I deduced that Mr. Whitson was a ballplayer . . . I turned to look at him. When Mr. Whitson saw me looking at him, he focused his attention on me, and loudly demanded to know why I was eavesdropping on his conversation. I do not remember the words he used, but I believe it was something like, "Who do you think you are to stick your nose into my business?" I told him in words or substance that I did not know who he was, and had no interest in his business.

Several Yankees had been privately worried that Whitson was going to snap soon and fight someone before the season ended, and they feared it would not be a small-time scrap. In addition to being tall and barrel-chested (six foot three and 200 pounds), Whitson had also taken martial arts training.

As Whitson and Millus were having their contentious exchange, someone, perhaps Leigh Berra, told Billy that Whitson was arguing with a stranger in the lounge a few feet away. Billy later said he looked at the mirror and saw Whitson face-to-face with Millus. Billy jumped up and moved in Whitson's direction.

At some point, Millus scolded Whitson. "I told him in words or substance that he was misbehaving," Millus said in the affidavit.

Whitson responded by grabbing Millus by the throat.

"I looked up and saw Billy Martin between us," said Millus, who added in his statement that he did not think that Billy or Whitson was drunk.

But, with most of the bar patrons now watching, Billy said to Whitson, "Eddie, you're drunk, you don't need this."

Those were not the words Whitson wanted to hear, and Billy was probably the last person on Earth that he wanted to hear them from. Whitson's eyes were wild and his face contorted as he started yelling at Billy to get away.

"What's the matter with you — you're crazy," Billy said. "I'm trying to help you. What's wrong with you?"

The two were squaring off. Dale Berra and a few coaches were sprinting toward the confrontation. Whitson could be heard calling Billy a "motherfucker," and according to several witnesses, he then swung at Billy.

Billy had come over as a peacemaker, but in an instant that was no longer his intent. Billy and Whitson were furiously wrestling in a dark bar at about 12:20 a.m. Punches were thrown, and according to Billy, Whitson kicked at him several times, with Billy blocking one of the blows with his forearm. The two men tumbled to the floor after about twenty seconds and then they were separated by various Yankees personnel.

Whitson was now yelling at Billy for starting the fight.

If the details of the first punch remain murky, the rest of this four-round brawl is not in dispute. All but a couple of the beat writers watched it blow by blow and took notes.

When Billy and Whitson were initially separated, Billy appeared to compose himself quickly.

He kept saying, "What's wrong with that guy? Can't he hold his liquor?"

Whitson, however, was not composed. He was enraged and kept screaming insults at Billy. A yelling Whitson was pushed and half-dragged out of the bar. Billy followed after him.

In the lobby, Whitson was being held from behind with his arms pinned to his sides, but he was still able to lunge at Billy. Billy met that aggression with a charge of his own, but Whitson was quicker. Though his arms were being held, Whitson powerfully swung his leg and kicked Billy squarely in the groin.

The kick seemed to lift Billy off the ground, and everyone watching seemed to either gasp or wince. The crowd parted for a second, waiting most likely for Billy to drop to the floor. Billy was doubled over in pain.

But then he stood up straight and took a deep breath, like something a character in an action movie would do. It was as if he suddenly found new strength. And then, in a firm, defiant voice he said to Whitson, "Now I'm going to have to kill you."

Billy stormed at Whitson. But cooler heads interceded and summarily pushed Whitson out of the lobby toward the entranceway to the hotel, which included a circular driveway. Two or three Yankees players and coaches, including Gene Michael, tried to corral and appease Whitson outside while another one or two Yankees employees desperately scurried around the hotel lobby in an effort to keep Billy from going outside. No one had his hands on Billy; it was more like a game of tag or dodge ball with multiple people darting around trying to block Billy's path. Billy was making evasive countermoves, like a football running back hoping to evade a linebacker.

Near the sliding-glass door entrance, at one point the catcher Ron Hassey played cat-and-mouse with Billy. With his back to the door, Hassey tried to stay in Billy's way, periodically stepping on the sensor that opened the door. As the doors opened and shut, Billy would back away and try to get around Hassey some other way.

Finally, Billy faked left and went right, which got Hassey to step on the door sensor but also left him out of position.

Once outside, Billy threw himself at the group enveloping Whitson. It became like a four-man scrum, almost like a group hug except Billy and Whitson were snarling at each other and trying to throw punches.

Eventually, some legs in the group got tangled and the whole mass of men fell over with Billy on the bottom of the pile. Billy hit the ground with a thud, the back of his head loudly smacking the pavement.

That confrontation brought more bodies out into the hotel entranceway, and this time Whitson was pushed in the direction of the hotel parking garage, a multilevel structure maybe two hundred feet from the hotel, though attached to it.

Whitson yelled at Billy, "You've tried to bury me here; you're trying to ruin me."

Billy, looking dazed, was guided back into the hotel lobby. Lou Piniella and Killer Kane had arrived. They had gone to dinner in Baltimore's Little Italy and come back to the hotel just behind police cars making their way to the Cross Keys Inn.

"My first thought was that I hoped Billy wasn't involved in a fight," said

Piniella, who came into the lobby to see Billy being attended to by trainer Gene Monahan. Billy's arm had swelled precipitously.

Piniella, Kane, and Monahan talked Billy into going to his room, and the four men got on an elevator to head to Billy's third-floor room. Reporters dashed up the stairs after them.

Unbeknownst to those escorting Billy, the group shepherding Whitson had circled around to the parking garage's basement elevator. They were taking Whitson to his third-floor room.

When Billy's elevator doors opened on the third floor, so did Whitson's just a few feet away. Billy and Whitson were suddenly face-to-face and charged at each other for a fourth time. It had been about twenty-five minutes since the first punch or kick.

This last confrontation was the most benign — mostly shouting and incriminations.

"You're gutless," Whitson yelled as multiple people separated him from Billy.

"You're the gutless one, they told me you were in trouble," Billy said. "I was just trying to help, Eddie."

Billy was ultimately led down a hallway to the right while Whitson went to his room down a different hallway.

Kane went with Whitson, who dabbed at a cut lip and a few abrasions on his arms. Kane arranged for Whitson to be driven to New York early the next morning. Then Kane called Steinbrenner to give him the news.

Kane described the opening tussle, then the part where Billy was kicked in the crotch.

"George was saying, 'Wait, they fought again, and what happened then?'" Kane explained years later with a laugh. "And I said, 'Wait, George, there's more.' And he goes, 'More? Whattaya mean more?'"

The whole story left Steinbrenner's head spinning.

Piniella and Monahan went with Billy to his room.

"I was checking out the arm and you could feel the bones moving and cracking," Monahan said. "I told Billy I was pretty sure it was broken."

Monahan also thought it was likely that Billy cracked a couple of ribs. There were a few lacerations on his face and back, too.

"Just wrap my arm up, I'm fine," Billy told Monahan.

Piniella recalled that he was worried for Billy.

"He looked terrible; he was really beat up," Piniella said. "But, you know, Billy is one tough guy. He said to me, 'Do me a favor and go knock on Whitson's room. Tell him I'll meet him in the parking lot in five minutes.'

"I looked at him and said, 'That Scotch is lying to you, Billy. Why don't you do me a favor and stay here.'"

Piniella and Monahan went to see Whitson, who was mostly unharmed physically. They were happy to hear that Kane had arranged for Whitson to go home.

As Piniella and Monahan were meeting with Whitson, Billy emerged from his room with a drink in his left hand. Across the hall, writers had gathered.

His speech was uneven, his gait unsteady.

"Go to the parking lot in five minutes," Billy said defiantly. "You'll see a guy get his ass kicked."

Billy then retreated to his room and closed the door.

"After about an hour of friendly arguing, Billy agreed to go to the emergency room," Monahan said. "They put his arm in a hard cast. Broken ulna."

Billy returned to his room at about 4:00 a.m.

The next morning, most of the players, who had turned in before the scuffle, awoke to the news of the fight.

"I remember going to get breakfast and Dennis Rasmussen said to me, 'Did you hear about Billy?'" Mattingly said. "And I thought, 'Oh, no.' Then Dennis said, 'He had a big fight in the bar with Eddie Lee.' And as much as you get used to anything around the Yankees, I was pretty surprised this time. And I immediately knew the clubhouse was going to be a zoo when I got there."

The clubhouse was swarming with reporters and television camera crews. Billy arrived early for him, about two hours before the game. With his arm in a sling, he walked through the locker room toward his office. A Baltimore television reporter came alongside, stuck a microphone in his face, and asked, "What happened to your arm, Mr. Martin?"

Billy did not stop walking and deadpanned, "I hurt it bowling."

In his office, he answered questions from the assembled media for about five minutes, but he refused to discuss the fight.

"Whatever happened, it's over," he said. "We've got a division to win. All I'm focused on is winning today and every day after that."

Then Billy had the team's press chief, Joe Safety, escort everyone out of the room except the eight traveling writers from the New York–area newspapers. Billy's countenance changed. He smiled and was at ease.

He then talked about the fight like he was recounting a minor fray at Kenney Park back in West Berkeley. He did not seem angry. He was almost bemused.

"It figures that when I go over to try and stop a fight, I get in an even bigger one," Billy said. "I was trying to break it up. That's always how you get hurt."

Knowing that several of the writers had witnessed the fight, he replayed sections of it, as if it had been something out of a game, and he asked, "Did you see when he kicked me?"

Billy did not mention Whitson by name nor did he criticize him. He only seemed upset that Whitson had used his legs in the brawl.

"I can't fight feet," he said.

It became like a scene from any other day in Billy's office. He was funny, irreverent, politically incorrect. Asked if Whitson could still pitch for him, Billy answered, "I've always said I would play Adolf Hitler and Benito Mussolini if they could help me win. I don't have to like them. If he can help us win the pennant, I'll pitch him. And I'll yank him from the mound, too, if he has to be yanked. But I'll watch his feet."

Everyone in the room laughed, Billy included.

Then Billy dressed for the game, pulling a long-sleeved undershirt over his cast. He remained in the dugout, sending a coach out to talk to starter Ron Guidry on occasion. When Rickey Henderson hit a third-inning home run, he met Henderson on the top step of the dugout and extended his left hand in congratulations.

The Yankees prevailed for Guidry's twentieth win of the season and Billy was all smiles afterward. He deflected questions about the fight, as did most of the Yankees.

"It's over; these things happen on teams," Billy said. "I've had it happen before. You move on."

Said one reporter, "But you've never had a fight where you ended up with the broken arm."

Billy glared. It appeared as if he wanted to say something biting or spiteful. But he did not.

"Hey," he said. "We've won two in a row."

43

THE MONDAY AFTER THE three tumultuous days in Baltimore was an off day in the schedule for the Yankees. Alone at the Carlyle Hotel, Billy went for a walk and kept walking.

His destination he later claimed was an accident, but Billy walked about sixteen blocks south on Madison Avenue to 10 East 60th Street and stood outside the Copacabana nightclub. He had not been there in twenty-eight years. His last visit had made considerable news.

Billy walked into the Copa and was given a little tour. Shown the featured showroom of the nightclub, where Billy and his teammates had been seated at a large banquette table on his birthday in 1957, Billy looked around the room wistfully.

"Yeah, I remember this room," he said.

He then went upstairs to the bar.

"I was just walking by," Billy said when someone at the club tipped off a *New York Post* reporter about his visit. "I thought I'd just stop in and have a beer. I just wanted to see what it looked like.

"You know, long time ago."

If Billy saw the symbolism of his nostalgic choice of bars less than two days after another barroom fracas had left his right arm in a cast and his future with the Yankees once again in doubt, he did not say so.

"I was thirsty and curious," Billy said, which could have summed up a lot of his saloon stops.

The same day, Steinbrenner announced he was launching an investigation into the Cross Keys Inn fight. Eddie Sapir knew that he had to start getting testimony from witnesses who could prove that Billy did not start the fight. There were plenty of people willing to do that, including the young attorney from upstate New York, Dale Berra, and Gene Michael.

Sapir forwarded all that information to George, who eventually became convinced that Billy might not have meant to fight Whitson. Within a day, George announced that neither Billy nor Whitson would be suspended or punished in any way. What upset Steinbrenner most was that so many players had obviously been in the hotel bar well after midnight, the supposed curfew.

It was a classic reaction by George. He knew Billy might get in fights; that was a given. But if Billy wasn't enforcing the discipline George wanted, well, that could be a firing offense.

As in past years, what did not come up was whether Billy needed to do anything about his drinking. The players certainly did not think it was their place.

"Back then, it was not a thought that crossed anyone's mind," Winfield said. "Having a manager who drank too much was not exactly unheard of, if you know what I mean."

Roy White was working in the Yankees' front office that season. He had been with the team since Billy's first managerial gig in 1975.

"I never heard anyone talk to Billy about his drinking or late-night habits," White said. "I didn't have that kind of authority. I guess others did. He lost jobs but I don't know that anyone felt the need to address why."

In an ESPN documentary made after Billy's death, Steinbrenner was asked if he had ever regretted not trying to counsel Billy about his drinking.

"I did feel that I had failed to a certain extent to turn him around," Steinbrenner said. "But I couldn't be with him every minute. I couldn't convince him, I just couldn't convince him."

It was the story of Billy's career. From the 1950s to the 1980s, few people in baseball were going to intervene about his drinking. It was the same way everywhere in baseball. On the New York Mets, two of the team's biggest stars, Dwight Gooden and Darryl Strawberry, were about to throw away much of their outsize promise because of alcohol and illicit drug use. Most of the Mets in the mid-1980s drank heavily and caroused late into the night. From Keith Hernandez to David Cone, the Mets were proud of their wild ways and did nothing to disguise it.

This attitude cost many their careers. For others, it ruined marriages and family life. For a few, a lifestyle cultivated in the white-hot spotlight of baseball stardom — cocaine was a burgeoning problem in the game in the 1980s — became a fatal dependency. At the time, baseball, and baseball fans, looked the other way.

Suffice it to say, late in the 1985 baseball season, Billy's risky drinking habits were not a hot topic of conversation. There was still a pennant race to follow with less than two weeks left to the season.

Then the Yankees lost a few more games to fall seven games behind Toronto. The 1985 Yankees were understandably given up for dead.

Whitson rejoined the team, and Billy told him that he would make his next scheduled start the following week.

Whitson, who watched games in the bullpen for the rest of the year, addressed reporters briefly outside the locker room.

"I'm here for one reason — to help the Yankees win the pennant," he said in an even, somber voice.

Whitson has never addressed the Cross Keys Inn fight since. Contacted at his home in southern Ohio in 2012, he said he would talk about baseball in general.

"But I won't talk about that man," he said when asked about Billy. He later said he refuses to so much as speak Billy's name.

The 1985 season resumed, amazingly, almost as if nothing had happened.

"I think we were so hardened to every other crazy thing by then that we really could put it away and try to focus on the baseball," Mattingly said when he looked back at 1985. "We really could. And, you know what, it worked. That's the thing."

With virtually no one paying attention — the Yankee Stadium crowds had dwindled to about ten thousand — the Yankees won five successive games.

The Yankees then won five of their next eight games while Toronto lost five of eight. The Yankees had improbably climbed back into the AL East race and were three games behind the Blue Jays with the season-ending, three-game weekend series beginning in Toronto the next night.

Whitson would be the starting pitcher of the first game.

On the Yankees' charter flight to Toronto that night, spirits were high — and being consumed generously. Billy and all the coaches broke the normal protocols and spent most of the flight standing and drinking together in the back of the plane with the players. The music was loud and the setting was convivial, more like a party than a voyage. There were no card games, just a team laughing and joking and excited that it somehow had something to play for after an eight-game September losing streak.

The Yankees' jet did not land in Toronto until around 2:00 a.m. The team buses rolled down the wide Gardiner Expressway heading for downtown and passed close by Toronto's Exhibition Stadium, where some of the lights were still on. Pointing through the bus windows, Billy rose in his seat and yelled in the bus, "Let's beat those bastards three times and get on with it. Fuck them!"

There were cheers and there was laughter.

The mood the next night was much the same. The Yankees took a 2–0 lead and Whitson pitched four effective innings before he gave up two runs in the fifth. But Toronto seized the advantage and held a narrow 4–3 lead into the ninth inning. Toronto manager Bobby Cox brought in his best reliever, Tom Henke, who had a blazing 94-mile-an-hour fastball and whose nickname was "the Terminator." Henke got the first two Yankees batters out easily in the ninth.

Wynegar walked to the plate before a standing, raucous sold-out home crowd eager to celebrate Toronto's first division title.

"All I was thinking was don't make the last out," Wynegar said. "I didn't want to be running off the field trying to get through their celebration."

The New York writers had already filed their "Yankees lose the division" stories and were standing in the back row of the press box near the exit so they could get quickly to the locker room.

Wynegar, a switch hitter, turned on a Henke fastball on the inner half of the plate and drilled a game-tying homer over the right-field fence. The Yankees won in extra innings.

Now the Blue Jays' lead was just two with two games remaining in the season.

"I can't believe it," Mattingly said. "It's the team that won't die."

Billy bought everyone in the Yankees' hotel bar in Toronto a round when he arrived there after the game. An hour later, he did it again. Several players were there. But everyone, including Billy, turned in just after midnight. It was not an accident. In the clubhouse after the game Billy had reminded his players that the owner would probably have spies planted at the hotel.

The next day was windy and raw, not good conditions for Joe Cowley, the Yankees starter who relied on a big, sweeping curve ball. Toronto lit up Cowley for three early home runs. Billy used five pitchers and eleven position players trying to find something to ignite his team. But the Yankees had only five base runners. This time, there was no miracle comeback.

"I'm glad we made it close," Righetti said. "That shows something."
Billy was having none of it.

"Second place in the standings leaves you with nothing," he said.

After 1994, second place often left teams in the postseason as a wild card team and several of those teams have won the World Series. The 1985 Yankees would finish with a 97-64 record, the fourth-best record in baseball and six games better than the AL West–winning Kansas City Royals, who would win the 1985 World Series.

Following their 6-10 start to the season, the Yankees were 91-54 under Billy, a .628 winning percentage that was higher than that of any team in baseball that season. For the rest of the twentieth century, only one team would have a higher winning percentage.

Nearly thirty years later, Mattingly still thinks the 1985 Yankees are underappreciated.

"Our team scared other teams," he said. "I remember we beat Kansas City something like eleven of twelve games that year. We just abused them. And they won the World Series."

But the 1985 Yankees were heading home.

"It just leaves me empty," Billy said. "You don't know what to do next."

There was the business of the final day of the season in Toronto. Niekro was once again going for his 300th victory, and he would mercifully get it. Leading 8–0 in the ninth inning, Niekro looked out at the Yankees' bullpen and started laughing.

"Billy had gotten every pitcher off the bench to pretend to be warming up in case I couldn't finish," Niekro said. "I think some of the catchers and backup infielders were warming up too."

When the game ended, the Yankees scattered as a cheerful bunch. Their manager may have had his arm in a cast from a fight with one of his pitchers. Their original manager may have been callously ditched after sixteen games. The owner was often criticizing the best players, and there was that ten-day period in September that was complete chaos, but the 1985 team nonetheless felt it was going places. Yankees fans rarely remember the 1985 team for how good it was, but the players on the team felt things were looking up.

"Look, it was an insane season," Mattingly said decades later. "But we won 97 games. I mean, 97 games is an impressive number no matter what else happened. We felt like we needed another starting pitcher or two but we were on our way up. There was a lot of optimism."

Billy felt the same way. In fact, he apparently felt too confident about where the team was heading. Before the final game of a season, it is customary for the manager to speak at length with reporters to give a summation of the season. Billy delivered a traditional end-of-the-year soliloquy and more. He shocked his pregame audience by demanding a raise.

"Earl Weaver is making $500,000," said Billy, who was making about $265,000. "Sparky Anderson just got three more years and the guy in Cleveland, Pat Corrales, finished last and got a new contract. It doesn't make any sense. I'm not putting any pressure on anybody, but it's up to George.

"Managing the Yankees is special, but I have to take into consideration my responsibility to my family. I have to have more money. I have to put that first for the first time in my life and put the Yankees second."

Putting the Yankees second was not a customary thought, nor a rational one, when pleading for a raise. But Weaver's salary filled Billy with envy and stoked his jealous nature, a feature of Billy's personality that rarely needed stoking anyway.

"Something about Earl drove Billy nuts," said Piniella, who had played for both men. "All you had to do was mention Earl and you could see the veins on Billy's neck start to bulge."

The 1985 Orioles barely had a .500 record under Weaver, and they finished fourteen games behind Billy's Yankees, an outcome that Billy just happened to mention a couple of times.

As it turns out, Billy was also once again struggling with money woes. During the season, the IRS had put a lien on his salary for payment of back taxes. He also knew, even if he had not yet acknowledged it, that he was facing another possibly costly divorce.

But Billy's salary demands were horribly ill timed, which was fitting in a sardonic sort of way. If nothing else, late in life Billy always seemed to lack good timing. In October 1985, Billy's status with Steinbrenner was already considered tenuous. It was well known that George wanted Piniella to manage the club in the near future. Like Billy, the Yankees' owner also did not think much about second-place finishes. It had now been four years since the Yankees had won the division, the longest drought since Steinbrenner had bought the team eleven years earlier. And there had been plenty of turmoil in Billy's wake in 1985. As Billy was making a public, undiplomatic petition for a raise, he was still at least a month from getting the cast off an arm broken in a barroom brawl, and he had to be careful when standing up from a sitting position because his cracked ribs were still healing.

Incredibly, Billy had led the Yankees to a 97-win season, but given everything that happened, he was not bargaining from a position of power. Not surprisingly, Steinbrenner had little reaction to Billy's demands.

But after all these years, some saw consistency in Billy's actions. As his son, Billy Joe, said of his father, "Sometimes it was as if he almost manufactured excuses to get out of a situation."

After the final game, Billy left the Toronto ballpark heading for Southern California where he was to meet Jill. He stopped for a beer at the airport bar. Four stools down was Ed Whitson, waiting for a flight to Tennessee. There was a conciliatory conversation. They bought each other drinks.

Billy twisted in the wind in mid- to late October as rumors swirled that Piniella was going to replace him.

"That was a tough time for Billy," said Killer Kane, who kept in touch with Billy. "With the cast, he couldn't play golf. He couldn't hunt. He couldn't fish. He sat at home. He told me he took walks."

Kane laughed.

"He told me he was sick of taking walks," Kane added. "It's driving him crazy, just him and Jill."

There was one other significant development — Billy did not make any attempt to go back to Blackhawk. He had essentially stopped communicating with Heather. When Heather filed for divorce about three months later, the court papers said she did so because her husband did not come home after the 1985 season. Heather was living in the Blackhawk house with her mother, grandmother, and brother.

At the Yankees' small compound in Tampa, there were meetings about what to do with the existing manager. There were new voices in the room, including Hank Steinbrenner, George's eldest son, who was in his late twenties. A new consensus was developing in the Yankees' meetings about Billy. Everyone agreed he had done a spectacular job with the 1985 team on the field. But there was also the business image of the Yankees, which was being increasingly threatened by the fresh-faced, more dynamic crosstown Mets.

There was a feeling among the Yankees' brain trust that the better marketing and public relations choice for manager was Lou Piniella, a younger, good-looking, and popular player from the Yankees' glory years of the late 1970s. Piniella, like Billy, was a fiery, emotional player and a bad loser who promised to bring the same feet-to-the-fire intensity into the dugout. He might counteract the youthful, increasingly trendy Mets.

It was time to turn a new leaf. It might help reshape the Yankees' image in the late stages of the twentieth century.

On October 27, the Yankees announced in a statement that Piniella would be the Yankees manager in 1986. Billy would remain on the payroll as an assistant to the principal owner. His role was not defined.

There was no real effort made to explain why Billy was relieved of his duties. The details did not seem highly important at the time. In New York, Billy being dismissed as Yankees manager was starting to be accepted as a formality. The newspapers were now labeling Billy's managerial terms with the Yankees with roman numerals, and so this was just another chapter. Billy IV had ended. The page turned.

"I think we were all surprised," Mattingly said. "I mean, 97 wins and you're fired? But at the same time, we weren't surprised. It was getting pretty hard to be surprised by anything."

George did something privately that went unreported. He gave Billy a big raise and tore up a loan of about $150,000 he had given Billy two years earlier. The Chicago White Sox needed a manager. George made sure Billy was being paid almost twice what the White Sox were likely to offer. With the IRS on his back, Billy could not afford to manage elsewhere.

He may not have wanted to go somewhere else anyway. Many in his circle of friends and acquaintances believed he did not want to start over in another town. He was fifty-seven years old and getting more set in his ways.

"By then, Billy didn't really want to manage except in New York," said Ron Guidry, who in 1985 had known Billy for nearly a decade. "Those other places were jobs. But managing the Yankees was a love to him. So, yeah, he had to leave. But that was his fault. Billy's biggest enemy was his mouth and everybody knew that."

Morabito wondered if his friend sensed that he was teetering out of control.

"He was kind of beat up physically and mentally," Morabito said. "He hated getting fired but he almost needed to hit the reset button. He stepped back. He was very resilient in that way. He wouldn't stay down for long."

He would take the punch, retreat a bit, and wait to charge again.

For 1986, Steinbrenner's new job for Billy was as a television broadcaster. Billy would appear in a pregame show and occasionally during games. With his old double-play partner, Phil Rizzuto, guiding him, Billy could be funny and charming on the air. But overall, his work was pedestrian. Billy and Rizzuto had amusing repartee about baseball in general and about the "old" Yankees, even if it was the 1970s Yankees. But worried about second-guessing Piniella, Billy was overly careful about commenting on the 1986 Yankees. Before the camera, Billy was a milquetoast, almost unrecognizable.

But to some people, the television appearances were an accomplishment because he did not go on television inebriated, as some had feared. The telecast producers had made it clear to Billy that he was not allowed to have any alcohol of any kind before games or during games since he was going on TV afterward.

John Moore, a young TV producer just beginning a decades-long career directing Yankees broadcasts, was assigned to shepherd Billy. In 2014, Moore said he did not recall any time that Billy appeared under the influence while working. During games, he tended to watch the Yankees on television at the press box level. He would not watch the game itself from the press box.

"Then I might start thinking like you guys," he told the writers with a snicker.

Billy also did not work at more than about a third of the games. That left him plenty of time for bringing in extra money on the side with public appearances. And Billy was actively working at recruiting such income. Or, more accurately, Jill was trying to be sure it happened.

In early 1986, Billy had asked Jill to marry him — at some indefinite date. It had been a spontaneous decision by Billy, and later, when he informed his family and friends, many of them were aghast. For one thing, Billy and Heather were separated but the divorce papers had not yet been filed. And second, a host of Billy's closest pals did not like being around Jill.

"I wasn't shocked like some people," Morabito said. "They were just so attracted to each other in a way you couldn't describe. They had a lot of passion for each other and Billy clearly loved her. But they fought like crazy, too. The fact is, they couldn't live with each other but they couldn't live without each other.

"Billy would say, 'She can be such a bitch.' But then he would always go back to her. It happened every time."

Whatever the tenor of the relationship, Jill was now in a position to wield her influence. The daughter of a prosperous businessman, Jill began by surveying Billy's financial misfortune and decided that she could clean up the mess. One way to start was to maximize Billy's name, fame, and appeal. Jill started a public relations effort to get Billy to more outings, and not just the usual rounds of golf or dinner speeches. She had Billy speaking at schools, doing work for the Salvation Army, and helping out at kids' summer camps. She wanted Billy to elevate his scope of influence. She had him reading the poem "Billy the Kid" as part of a symphony orchestra performance.

Jill also accompanied Billy so that she could take possession of the checks for the appearances — and pay the taxes. On his own, Billy might do anything.

Bobby Richardson, Billy's teammate in the 1950s, tells the story of Billy's appearance at Coastal Carolina University, where Richardson was the baseball coach and athletic director in 1986. Richardson had asked Billy to come down to the university's major fundraising event, which was a one-day golf tournament followed by a luncheon and auction the next day. Billy agreed to come without charging a fee so long as Richardson paid for his expenses. Jill did not make the trip.

"Billy came and played golf with all our big donors," Richardson said. "He charmed all the bigwigs. I got him a suite by the ocean and I'm not sure he ever checked into it. He might have been out all night. But the next day he was back and hobnobbed with everyone. He talked to people, spoke at the luncheon, and was so charismatic.

"Then we had the auction and he outbid everyone for everything. He paid in cash, and when the event was over, he gave all the stuff back to the university and told us to auction it off again at our next fundraiser. That was Billy, always so giving."

The number of people who wanted the newly available Billy to help with causes was limitless. It included several umpires, who tended to have foundations or charitable groups for which they helped raise money with dinners.

"Umpires loved having Billy come to their events — he was the best draw for them," Morabito said. "And Billy never turned them down. Here they were supposed to be his mortal enemy. But I remember Billy would do Larry Barnett's dinner all the time."

Barnett was an umpire for thirty-one seasons.

While Billy was on the dinner circuit, the 1986 Yankees got off to a fast start, taking over first place by winning twelve of their first eighteen games. The White Sox lost twelve of their first eighteen, reigniting the rumors that Billy was going to replace Chicago manager Tony La Russa.

"Nobody likes to hear about their own firing, but I couldn't blame them if the replacement was Billy," said La Russa when he was asked to recall 1986. "Billy was the most brilliant manager I knew. No one worked a game better."

At baseball's winter meetings in 1979, through some mutual acquaintances, a dinner and several get-togethers had been arranged between Billy and La Russa.

"He just gave me a schooling and it ran the gamut," La Russa said in 2013. "Every manager has his own way, usually molded by others. But Billy's way was like no one else. It was a magnificent combination of learned baseball knowledge and intuitive logic mixed with incredible guts.

"Lots of managers think of things to do but they don't have the guts to try it. Risk didn't worry Billy. His genius is really not properly understood."

The White Sox were not the only team interested in Billy. The Seattle Mariners were in the hunt, too. But a deal with either team was never struck. La Russa's Hall of Fame managerial career continued.

In May, Heather filed for divorce and shortly after that sued Billy for $500,000, saying that Billy was trying to evict her, her mother, brother, and seventy-five-year-old grandmother from the Blackhawk house. In the court papers, Heather gives her birthday as being in 1959. She states that she began living with Billy in 1980.

"No one is throwing anyone out of the house," Billy told the *New York Daily News*. "Once again, I'm being made out to look like the bad guy."

The 1986 Yankees continued to win. Piniella indeed proved to be a fierce, passionate manager.

"He was a carbon copy of Billy — that's what he was," Michael said. "He did everything Billy did, every little thing, big thing, and technical thing. Some managers would send a base runner at first base on a 3-2 pitch to stay out of a double play. But Billy always said it made no sense if a left-handed pitcher was on the mound. He said the runner never got a good jump on the pitch because of the leftie on the mound and then he usually got thrown out at second base. You would run into a double play if the batter struck out. And, if the batter did hit a ground ball, the runner wouldn't get a good enough jump to stay out of a double play anyway. It just made no sense.

"But Billy was probably the only guy who thought that way. As soon as Lou took over, no Yankee base runner ran on a 3-2 pitch against a left-hander.

"And Lou handled the umpires the same as Billy. He'd run out there and put on a show. He argued and kicked dirt and threw bases. He did it because he had a temper, but just like Billy, he did it to get the players riled up, too. Lou the manager was Billy the manager."

But things started to go sour for Piniella's Yankees in June when they lost ten consecutive times at home. By the Fourth of July — Steinbrenner's birthday — the surging Boston Red Sox had an eight-game lead on the Yankees. The Yankees would not seriously challenge the Red Sox for the rest of the year.

For Billy, the highlight of the season was Billy Martin Day on Sunday, August 10. As usual, Steinbrenner felt bad about the relative exile in which he had placed Billy, so in a grand pregame ceremony, he retired Billy's number 1 jersey and showered him with gifts.

It was the only time Billy's mother and his sisters came to Yankee Stadium. They came for the weekend and enjoyed the festivities, but behind the scenes, there was considerable arguing going on with Jill about who got to do what and when. The quarreling went on unabated for days. During the ceremony, Billy's mother, in a wheelchair after falling and breaking her hip, was brought onto the field. So were his sisters and brothers. Billy, wearing a light beige suit with a boutonniere affixed to his lapel, beamed as various speeches were made in his honor. The crowd gave him long ovations multiple times, and most of the current Yankees stood on the top step of the dugout during the ceremony. Billy also received a bevy of gifts, including a boat and a car.

The highlight of the celebration was the retiring of Billy's number and a plaque in Yankee Stadium's Monument Park alongside those for Billy's friends Mickey Mantle and Joe DiMaggio. It was Billy's lifelong dream come true to be immortalized at Yankee Stadium.

Presented with a framed replica of his number 1 jersey, Billy made a short but emotional speech, thanking many coaches, players, family, and mentors. He was eloquent in thanking the fans, saying that they accepted him when he showed up as a brash kid in 1950.

"The fans always lifted me up no matter the circumstances," Billy said. "If I ran faster and hit the ball farther, it was because you gave me the strength. I know you were always rooting me on. I wanted to make you proud and I hope I did."

He closed with a sentence that has become part of his legacy: "I may not have been the best Yankee to put on the pinstripes, but I am the proudest."

Talking with a couple of writers afterward, Billy said he marked the occasion by sending flowers to Casey Stengel's grave in Glendale, California.

"I actually wanted to end the speech with a thank you to Casey," Billy said. "But I couldn't get anything else out. I started crying after I said I was the proudest Yankee. I had to stop."

Billy's enshrinement alongside other Yankees greats was not greeted by all as heartwarming news. Several columnists scorned Steinbrenner for recognizing a manager known for kicking dirt on umpires and slugging people in saloons. Others defended Billy. Howard Cosell had a nationally syndicated column at the time. He wrote:

> Why is it when Billy fights with an umpire it is further proof of his "instability and unsportsmanlike conduct," when the same behavior by Tommy Lasorda and Earl Weaver is somehow portrayed as amusing or even charming?
>
> The fact is that no one plays Weaver Ball or Lasorda Ball but they do play Billy Ball. That phrase alone sums up a whole style, an era if you will, of baseball that has contributed as much to baseball history and tradition as home run records or a perfect game. That's why Billy is out there at Yankee Stadium with Ruth.
>
> Like all of us, Billy is not without flaws. But perfection, idolatry and canonization are not the point — although there are those who would insist that they are. George Steinbrenner was not conferring sainthood, but recognizing the contributions of a talented man in the field of baseball. He was right to do so.

The 1986 season moved on, and Billy moved on with it. The Yankees rallied in September and finished with a 90-win season, only 5.5 games back of Boston. On the Yankees' final television broadcast of the season, Billy sat between Rizzuto and announcer Bill White. White pointedly wanted to know if Billy was going to manage next year.

"We'll see," Billy, looking tanned and rested, said.

"Do you want to manage?" White asked.

"I believe I will again — yes," Billy said.

In the winter of 1986–87, there was ample consternation over Piniella's future and whether Billy V was about to begin. But Steinbrenner stuck with Piniella for another season.

Billy had a quiet off-season. His divorce from Heather was finalized. In time, Heather and her family would depart the Blackhawk house. She quickly remarried and started a family. She continues to live in the Bay Area and regularly attends Oakland A's games.

Contacted in 2014, Heather said of Billy, "He was a very loyal person who had a lot of compassion. That's what I will remember."

By 1987, most of Billy's friends agree that his drinking had been reined in noticeably.

"His drinking was under control most of the time," Jill said. "He developed some healthier habits. There were days and weeks when he did not drink at all. Other times, he would drink much more than he should but it was not constant."

Jill's campaign to raise the quality of Billy's appearances seemed to be working. Billy went on David Letterman's show with George Steinbrenner in the spring of 1987. They traded jokes and barbs. With Letterman's urging, Billy told the hunting-with-Mickey story when he mistakenly shoots two of the Texas farmer's cows. The audience roared with laughter.

Dressed in a gray suit with well-coiffed, stylishly longer hair framing a tanned face, Billy appeared at ease. Gone were the hollow features of a man worn out by managing. Later in the same month, Billy sat for an extensive magazine interview. In it, he was asked if he had ever seen a psychiatrist. Billy said he had not.

"All a psychiatrist knows is what you tell him," he said. "You know what direction you're going in. And you know what direction you want to go in. So what can a psychiatrist tell you that you don't already know?"

Billy said he was mentally strong because he knew how to release any tension in his life.

"Having a temper is a release," Billy said. "That's right. Didn't Jesus get angry and whip the moneychangers?"

Told that Jesus did not use a whip but overturned the tables in the temple when he was angry, Billy replied, "What's the difference, he got his anger out."

The 1987 Yankees were very similar to the 1986 and 1985 teams from the Bronx: a good team but not good enough in the toughest division in baseball in the era before wild card teams. Several players did not like Piniella's intense managerial style and complained behind his back. Piniella was also accused of mismanaging the pitching staff and overusing the relievers. He raged after tough losses, shattering water coolers with bats in the dugout and lashing out with angry outbursts in the clubhouse. Those displays of temper were said to be distracting to the team and contributing to its inconsistency.

It had a familiar ring.

Billy stayed conspicuously distant from the '87 team. As he had the previous year, he never stayed in the team hotel on the road. Throughout 1987 there was talk of Piniella being fired and Billy returning to manage, but Piniella survived. Before the last game of the season, Piniella had dinner with several writers, and when the meal was over he lit up a cigarette and ordered a snifter of cognac. Leaning back in his chair, Piniella talked about how he knew Steinbrenner would fire him.

"George doesn't think I did a bad job," Piniella said. "He just can't stand not being in the playoffs. And he keeps saying Billy is tanned and rested. I think we all know what that means."

Piniella, who has a loud, contagious laugh, cackled.

"And you know what the funniest part is?" he asked. "Son of a bitch if Billy isn't tanned and rested."

On October 19, during the World Series, Steinbrenner announced that Billy was returning as manager and Piniella was promoted to general manager.

There were no words from Billy, Steinbrenner, or Piniella in the announcement, which was made by the Yankees' public relations chief, Harvey Greene. For several days, the Yankees said nothing. There was finally a news conference in Gallaghers Steakhouse restaurant in Manhattan. George posed for pictures with one arm around Piniella and the other arm around Billy. Everyone smiled.

Billy and Lou agreed they had to remake the team.

"We've got a lot of big plans during this off-season," Piniella said.

"You bet," Billy added.

44

BILLY'S OFF-SEASON DID INCLUDE some big plans. His wedding to
Jill was by far his biggest, most extravagant, and boisterous. It was January 25, 1988, at the Blackhawk Country Club not far from the house in
Blackhawk, which Billy and Jill had made their home after the divorce
from Heather was finalized.

An elaborate video of the wedding day begins with Billy and Jill getting
ready for the ceremony, dressing in separate bedrooms but together in the
house. Mickey Mantle, the best man, flits in and out of the video, telling
jokes in his syrupy drawl. He always has a glass in his hand with some
kind of brown liquor. With each appearance in the video, Mantle appears
less and less sure on his feet.

Just before Billy and Jill leave the house for their wedding, the camera pans on a fancy, ornate door with raised panels. The door is not a
part of the house and rests against a wall. It is a wedding present, and its
most prominent feature is a pronounced blemish — one of the panels has
a large hole, a gouge that has splintered the wood.

As Billy explains, a friend who owned the Manhattan hotel where the
door originated had sent it to the wedding couple.

"I'm mild-mannered Billy Martin," Billy says to the camera.

He then explains that he and Jill were having a big fight and she kicked
in the door. Billy laughs.

The wedding was lavish. Jill arrived in a white Rolls-Royce and walked
through a corridor of male attendants dressed in Yankees pinstripes.
There were a multitude of bridesmaids in flowing dresses. Billy and Mantle wore light gray striped tuxedos. Hundreds attended the wedding.

The night before the wedding, some of Billy's friends were still trying
to talk him out of marrying Jill.

"Aw, come on," Billy said. "She's all right."

After the ceremony, Mantle decided to make his best man's toast with
the newlyweds still at the altar.

Perhaps Mickey knew he would not make it to the reception. He passed out soon after and had to be brought back to the Blackhawk house.

Weaving noticeably, Mickey said, "I'm Mickey and I've been Billy's friend since 1950. This is the fourth one of these I've been to. It's getting to be an everyday deal."

Billy grinned but made a pained face at his friend. Mickey had been Billy's friend during every marriage, but he had, in fact, not been to any of Billy's previous weddings.

"Well, everyone knows that Billy is number one on your scorecard," Mickey continued. "And I know he's number one in everybody's hearts. I wish the both of you the best and I hope I don't ever have to go to another one of these Billy weddings."

Billy and Jill walked down the aisle to applause, passing a variety of baseball personalities, including the White Sox manager, Tony La Russa.

At the reception, the dance floor was busy. At one point, Billy's mother, Jenny, serenaded Billy with one song, "My Man."

In the video, Billy seems to be holding Jill's hand or dancing with her throughout the reception, at one point cheek to cheek. Toward the video's conclusion, Billy is singing along to "New York" as he dances. The camera zooms in on Billy as he intones the words: "If I can make it there, I'll make it anywhere."

On the eve of the Yankees' 1988 spring training camp, Don Mattingly, one of the most soft-spoken Yankees, guaranteed that the 1988 team would win the American League East. The Yankees had signed Jack Clark, who had driven in 106 runs and had a league-leading .459 on-base percentage in the National League the previous season. They had traded for or signed three new starting pitchers, including left-hander John Candelaria, who had already won 151 Major League games.

"We'll definitely win it," Mattingly said. "It's a good time for Billy to come back."

Spring training was a tranquil place, especially since the Yankees won twenty-one of thirty exhibition games. One of the new coaches working under Billy was thirty-one-year-old Buck Showalter, who had already won two championships as a Yankees minor league manager.

Billy had met Showalter while he was touring the team's minor league system in 1987, and he took a liking to the plucky, precocious Showalter, who had been a career Yankees minor leaguer as a player. Steinbrenner also had plans for Showalter and told Billy to take him under his wing.

Showalter, an All-American in college and a future two-time American League Manager of the Year, got an education in Billy Ball in February and March of 1988.

"After talking with Billy for a couple of weeks, I felt like I had never seen a baseball game before," Showalter said in 2013. "It opened my eyes to everything I wasn't seeing from the dugout."

The lessons came at Showalter in a steady stream.

"I remember he had me walk around the spring training complex with him, which was an experience in itself," Showalter said. "We came out of the dugout for practice, and the crowd of five or six thousand watching started buzzing. They got real quiet, then they all started cheering. Winfield, Mattingly, Henderson — all those guys were already on the field. But the fans didn't cheer until Billy came out.

"Then he showed me a thousand things like how to read the pitcher's front foot and arm angle so a runner can know when to break for second base on a steal. There's a point when you know it's safe. He talked about how he stole signs. It was watching the other manager and the catcher but the opposing batter too.

"Every team has the batter give a return signal to the third-base coach that acknowledges that a bunt or a hit-and-run is on. If you watch, you can pick up the return signal — the batter taps his cleats or touches the brim of his cap. The key is to watch closely early in the game when they're not doing any of those things, then notice the differences later in the game when more of those kinds of plays are going on.

"He instructed the infielders in all these intricacies — how you should make tags with a V motion, not a U motion, because a V is quicker. How you should never reach for a throw and never catch it in front of the base. Instead, let it come to you; a thrown ball travels faster to the base than your hands can. He was a stickler for how to perform a rundown, and his big thing was not to catch and chase the runner with the ball in a rundown. The runner has got to go back to some base; let him come to you. Be patient and don't panic.

"He taught me to have my eyes darting everywhere, looking for something to use later in a game. Take a ball that one of your guys hits into the right-center-field gap. Billy said don't watch the ball; you know it's going to be a double or a triple. Watch to see if the pitcher is backing up third.

Is the left fielder moving? Are the relay guys in the proper order? How are the outfielders' and infielders' arms? You have a checklist of things to look for that might tell you something that you can use later.

"He had a saying: Preparation always shows itself in the spontaneity of the moment. Watch what the opposition is doing. Billy said you'll learn something. You might not use it in that game but some future game you will."

But Billy's tutoring of Showalter was only beginning. In March, the Yankees made a weeklong trip to the west coast of Florida, hundreds of miles from Fort Lauderdale — and a respite from the peaceful condo where Billy was living with Jill during spring training. This was not a family trip. This was for the boys only.

"I was the left-handed coach pitching batting practice so they took me with them," Showalter said.

Showalter saw that the road version of Billy Ball was another level of education.

During the first game of the trip in Sarasota, Showalter did something that put him permanently in Billy's good graces. The Yankees were tied with the White Sox in a game that went into the tenth inning. The Yankees' Bobby Meacham was at first base when Chicago brought in a young reliever and former Yankees farmhand, Ken Patterson.

"Billy starts screaming in the dugout, 'Does anybody know this guy?'" Showalter said. "He meant Patterson. I'm sitting there and I just want to keep my mouth shut and stay with the big-league team. I'm thirty-one years old and I don't want to piss off any of the veteran coaches. I just want to keep getting the $65 a day in big-league meal money, which was huge to me at the time.

"But I had coached Patterson the previous year and I started to think that if Billy finds out I had him last year and didn't say anything he'll be livid."

So Showalter mentioned that he knew Patterson from the previous year. Billy raced over to ask what Patterson's move to first base was like.

Said Showalter, "I told Billy that Patterson actually has a phobia about throwing to first base. He can't do it. It's like the yips in golf. He will step off and fake, but he won't throw it. He does it again and again. As soon as it came out of my mouth, I thought, 'What have you done?'"

Billy turned and ran to the top step of the dugout and yelled to first-base coach Mike Ferraro, "Make the pitcher throw over."

Meacham took a four-foot lead, then a six-foot lead. Patterson only faked to first base.

Billy yelled, "Take a bigger lead."

Meacham moved eight feet off the base.

"Bigger," Billy yelled.

Meacham was twelve feet off the base and Patterson was still only stepping off and faking a throw.

"You could have rolled the ball to first base and picked Meacham off first base," Showalter said. "Billy is loving this now because he knows he's showing up the other manager. Finally, Patterson throws it but it's ten feet over the head of the first baseman and Meacham goes from first to third base. Somebody hit a sac fly and we won."

Billy hugged Showalter, who retreated to the locker room and showered. He was getting ready to pocket most of his meal money after a quick trip to McDonald's. Instead, third-base coach Clete Boyer walked over.

"Clete says to me, 'You think you did pretty good today, don't you, kid? Well, you screwed up,'" Showalter said. "Then he flipped me the keys to the car and told me Billy wants me to be part of that night's dinner with the coaches. I was the designated driver. We were to leave at 7:00 p.m."

Then Boyer gave Showalter some other instructions.

"He told me to go to the deli across from the team hotel at 6:30," Showalter said. "He said that I should order a club sandwich and I should eat it right then."

Said Showalter, "But we're going to dinner at 7:00?"

Answered Boyer, "Just do what I tell you."

Showalter did as he was told, then drove the coaches to dinner and watched as round after round of drinks were ordered. No one ordered any food until almost 10:00 p.m.

"The Scotch was flowing like crazy," Showalter said. "I had never seen anything like it. I was dumping my drinks in the potted plants to stay upright. At maybe 10:00 p.m., we got appetizers. I don't know if we ever got dinner, and if we did it wasn't until 11:00. Thank God for that club sandwich."

There was a lot of baseball talk at the dinner table — for a while at least.

"Billy was holding court, moving the salt and pepper shakers around on the table to explain a trick play or something," Showalter said. "He talked about how to attack another team — always attack, he said, don't let them relax. And he talked about how to identify smart players because he said to me, 'Buck, dumb players will get you fired.' He never stopped teaching and you could learn a lot before the fourth or fifth drink. But after that, things deteriorated. You saw the other side of things, which was a lot less fascinating and darker.

"I remember we eventually left the restaurant and went to a bar and then I was driving everyone home at 3:00 a.m. Art Fowler made me stop at a 7-Eleven to get ice cream and a six-pack of beer. But the next day, and I don't know how, those guys were as fresh as a daisy. I was half their age and I remember telling my wife that I wasn't going to survive the trip."

Billy's Yankees sprinted into the regular season, winning nine of their first ten games. A fast start was always Billy's goal, and those who had played for him before expected the intensity of the first two weeks.

"Some of the new guys to the team, like Jack Clark and Candelaria, were shocked at how different Billy was once the regular season started," Mattingly said. "They were telling me in spring training how relaxed and easygoing Billy was. And I told them to just wait.

"Once the regular season started, they came to me and said, 'Man, every game is intense. He never sits down in the dugout. He's pacing and yelling even when we're leading 8–0 in the ninth inning.' And that was true. That was Billy."

With the Yankees' brilliant start, they had a stranglehold on first place that lasted for months. They were a potent offensive club, with Henderson playing hard for Billy as he always did and Randolph slashing singles and drawing walks. The steady Mattingly anchored a formidable middle of the order that also featured Clark and Winfield. The pitching staff was a little aged, but in the opening parts of the season, it got more than enough outs to buttress an explosive, productive batting order.

There were bumps in the road. Billy's issues with umpires continued, and he had some temperamental players, too, which led Billy to have more on-field arguments.

Candelaria was ejected from two of his first six starts. Billy was thrown out of two other games. His old nemesis, Durwood Merrill, tossed him one of those times. Billy accused the umpires of targeting the Yankees.

"They can't stand all the winning we're doing," Billy said.

Trouble was brewing.

On May 6, the Yankees and their gleaming 20-8 record went to Texas for a three-game series with the lowly sixth-place Rangers. Texas was leading 7–1, but the Yankees began the ninth inning by loading the bases with no outs. Mattingly was called out on strikes and did something he almost never did — he turned on home plate umpire Tim Welke and disputed the third strike call.

Welke immediately expelled Mattingly, who was so incensed, he got in a chest-to-chest beef with Welke. Spit was flying and the normally placid Mattingly was getting more riled with each passing second. Cincinnati manager Pete Rose had just been suspended thirty games for shoving an umpire, a penalty the umpires thought was inadequate. In general, umpires were feeling defensive in 1988. There seemed to be a lot of abuse directed at them and they did not think the commissioner's office had their back.

When Billy ran onto the field after Welke and Mattingly, he was mostly trying to keep one of his most valuable players from doing something untoward and debilitating to the team. But Welke wasn't happy to see the Yankees manager either and quickly threw Billy out of the game, too. Billy was enraged and later said he had barely opened his mouth before Welke tossed him. Billy reached into his full arsenal of umpire mistreatment tactics, throwing his hat and kicking dirt on the umpire with a flourish.

Billy was even more upset when his Yankees rallied for five runs but fell short, leaving two runners as the game ended with a 7–6 defeat.

After the game, Billy retired to the bar at the team hotel, the Arlington Hilton, where he had planned to meet Mickey Mantle and Mantle's son, Danny. Coach Mike Ferraro joined Billy and the Mantles at the bar and the crew had a few drinks. But the hotel bar was packed with Yankees fans trying to spot a player, or even better, the manager.

"Isn't there somewhere quiet we can go drink?" Billy asked Mantle, who said he knew just the place.

The four men took a cab one mile down the road to Lace, Arlington's only topless club. Set back from Majesty Drive and surrounded by parking spaces, Lace was a large, windowless building with stucco exterior walls and pay phones positioned outside. Inside, it featured hundreds of strobe lights that illuminated a smoky haze, with a throbbing music beat and a squad of dancers gyrating on the long rectangular bar. It was filled with local men, many of them in cowboy hats and boots. Some had come to Lace from the Yankees-Rangers game.

"You SOB, this is the quiet place you talked about?" Billy asked a laughing Mantle.

Billy, the Mantles, and Ferraro headed inside and began drinking.

Three guys in cowboy hats across the bar who had apparently been at that night's game recognized Billy and playfully tossed some insults at the Yankees manager about his ejection.

"People in Lace saw and heard that, and later they thought those guys were the problem, but my dad told me that it was all in fun and that the guys had sent drinks over and weren't any problem," said Billy Joe Martin, who still kicks himself for not being at Lace that night.

Billy Joe wished he had been there because he considered himself something of a lucky charm to his father when it came to bars.

"He never got in any trouble when I was around," Billy Joe said. "I had seen guys drop out of the clouds to taunt him so many times I had a sixth sense about it and could defuse it. I'd say, 'Dude, that's my father, leave us alone.' Or something stronger. Or more profane."

What happened inside Lace is something of a mystery despite multiple investigations later. Billy Joe faults a Lace bouncer, who felt insulted by Billy during an exchange at the bar, for instigating things. Eddie Sapir conducted an inquiry, and his report fingered two motorcycle gang–like individuals who targeted Billy, perhaps because Billy had said something to one of their girlfriends. The police said there were two assailants but they never identified them.

What is certain is that Ferraro escorted the Mantles home, which may have been Billy's idea. But Billy was not supposed to be left alone. Over the years, it is hard to think of a late-night episode when he was alone. Except inside Lace.

The other certainty is that at some time just after 1:30 a.m., Billy went to the men's room. Standing at a urinal next to another Lace patron at an adjacent urinal, Billy said something he often said in this setting: "Mine's bigger."

"You had to know him, he was that guy who would break the tension at the urinal," Billy Joe said. "He thought that was funny.

"Anyway, he told me that the guy next to him zipped up and left. And without any warning, two guys came into the men's room and whacked him on the head with some kind of blackjack or hard object.

"My dad said he was knocked to the ground and remembers being punched and kicked and thrown out a side or back door to the place. He said to me, 'I've never been jumped like that before. I was still standing there peeing. I had my deal still out.'"

The police, Sapir, and the doctors who attended to Billy agree that someone hit him in the head with a blunt instrument. Everyone agrees that Billy was pushed out a back door where he was shoved into the raised stucco exterior of the building and the side of his head was dragged along the rough, serrated wall. The stucco outside Lace was a pattern of jagged, pointed pieces of concrete, and they tore into Billy's left ear. The ear was all but sheared off, and it bled profusely onto Billy's shirt.

Billy ended up in a taxi. His plan, he later said, was to sneak into the hotel unseen since the hotel bar had long since closed and most everyone had gone to bed. Billy would go directly to trainer Gene Monahan's room, where he figured Monahan could stitch him up or get him the help he needed.

Unbeknownst to Billy, at about the time he was losing his second straight barroom fracas, there had been a minor, smoky electrical blaze near the hotel's sauna. A fire alarm had sounded, and while fire department officials arrived to quickly extinguish the small flame, every guest in the Hilton had been herded out the entrance to the hotel with the fire alarm. A few hundred people, including the players, coaches, and reporters, were standing on a lawn and a grand circular drive in front of the hotel. So was George Steinbrenner, who had made the trip with the team. George had wrapped himself in a silk robe.

That's when an Arlington taxi pulled up. From the back seat of the vehicle emerged Billy, his shirt covered in blood. He was using a light jacket to hold his torn, battered ear to the side of his head. It was an almost incomprehensible sight.

Billy looked around and admitted he had one thought: "You've got to be kidding me."

Steinbrenner, his robe straining against his legs as he ran, rushed over to Billy, who was brought into the hotel manager's office off the lobby. Monahan and another trainer, Steve Donahue, dashed in behind him. Guests were soon told they could return to their rooms, but the reporters remained to see what had happened. Steinbrenner was giving orders to various personnel and waving his arms.

Soon Billy was taken to Arlington Hospital.

"Billy was saying he was jumped and that he didn't know exactly what happened," said Monahan, who accompanied Billy to the hospital but until 2013 had never described the events as he saw them. "He was mostly upset that it might affect the season. He said to me, 'Geno, we don't need this. We're in first place.' And he kept saying, 'You know, I can't go any-where anymore.'"

At the hospital, doctors prepared to use about fifty stitches to mend Billy's ear. Billy, who was ten days from his sixtieth birthday, had a swollen eye, a gash on his cheek, and big, ugly bruises on his right shoulder and left knee as well as a lumpy contusion on the back of his skull.

"We're in the emergency room and the doctor starts working on Billy's ear," Monahan said. "A nurse is there filling out a form for Billy. She's asking him all the usual questions — name, age, address, medications taken. And she says, 'Are you allergic to anything?'

"And Billy says, 'Yeah, people. P-E-O-P-L-E.' The doctor started laughing so hard he had to stop doing the stitches in his ear."

Word got back to Jill in Manhattan. In the middle of the night, she tried calling Gene Monahan at the Arlington Hilton. She instead was connected to the room of New Jersey sportswriter Kevin Manahan.

"Gene, this is Jill, how is Billy?" Manahan heard a voice say.

Manahan tried to explain who he was.

"But Gene, how is he?" Jill persisted.

"I don't know," Manahan answered and hung up.

Steinbrenner visited Billy in Arlington Hospital and was driven to and from the hospital by an old high school classmate of Billy Joe Martin's.

"My high school buddy told me that when George came out of the hospital he was as white as a sheet," Billy Joe said. "He was terrified of the condition Billy was in. My friend told me George looked really shaken, nervous, and sweating."

Billy arrived at the ballpark the next day looking far worse than he did after the Whitson fight. This time there were no wise-guy cracks about hurting himself bowling.

"I just feel embarrassed because I got caught off guard; I didn't think I'd get hit in the head in the toilet," Billy said. "I'm like a western cowboy who's noted for something. People want to go after me. I never got a punch in."

The Arlington police said Billy had done nothing to provoke the fight and Steinbrenner's reaction was succinct: "Billy was the victim. Case closed."

The players were somewhere between aghast and awestruck that Billy was in the dugout.

"The way he looked and the way he was moving, I couldn't believe he got himself to the ballpark at all," said Mattingly.

Added Randolph, "He was really messed up this time. There was blood caked in his ear and along the stitches. It was kind of scary."

During the game, the Yankees' television broadcast channel, which had a cozy relationship with Yankees management since the team approved the selection of announcers, was asked not to show any close-ups of Billy in the dugout. The program directors obliged.

Reporters flocked to Lace trying to get some insight from the club's employees — there was little — and from the scene (Billy's blood was still on the stucco wall).

The Yankees lost the next two games in Texas. Before the last game in Arlington, Billy had breakfast with the *Post*'s Michael Kay, who had worked to gain Billy's trust.

"I'm not gonna fight anymore," Billy told Kay. "I'm gonna walk away. I never did go looking for fights but it's past that now. Things happen whether I want them to or not. I'm not afraid of getting killed in a fight someday but that's what scares my wife. I'm gonna have to stop."

Lace, as far as anyone knows, was Billy's last fight.

Billy and the Yankees flew home from Texas the night of May 8. Tex Gernand picked Billy up from the airport. He, too, was shocked by Billy's appearance.

"Billy was a tough guy who could take a lot," Gernand said. "But boy, when I saw him after Lace I knew he had really gotten the worst of it. He just laid down across the seat in the back of the car."

With an off day in the schedule, Gernand drove Billy and Jill to upstate New York. The day in the country was restful. They were also looking at farms to buy near the city of Binghamton, where they had made some friends after Billy spoke at a function there. There were horse farms in the area, and Jill, the former equestrian champion, was drawn to the area.

When the Yankees resumed play at Yankee Stadium, the New York columnists, none of whom had been in Texas, got a look at Billy and they were close to horrified. The injuries were bad, and the fact that it happened in a strip club, to many, made it worse. Billy's image, in decline for the past few years, now had a hint of immorality.

But Jill thought that missed the point, and she went on the offensive. In a quote that made headlines, Jill said of the Lace incident, "I don't care where my husband gets his appetite. I know where he comes to dinner."

Decades later, she remained as defiant.

"What worried me was the fight, not the location of it," she said. "You're telling me that no else's husband went to a topless bar? The real problem was that I didn't want him in fights. He was getting older. The people coming after him were getting younger."

Steinbrenner was of the same mind, but in what was a bad sign for Billy, the Yankees' owner also seemed to be less tolerant or willing to forget the episode than he had been initially.

"He's a 60-year-old man and when I saw him his ear was hanging," George said. "He shouldn't have been there. He has to use better judgment."

Steinbrenner was talking about hiring a full-time bodyguard for his manager until Jill came up with an alternative. She announced to reporters that she was going to accompany her husband on all road trips for the remainder of the season.

The Yankees won five of their next six games and regained a solid lead in the AL East. But there were bad tidings everywhere. On May 28, Lou Piniella resigned as general manager, saying he would remain with the team as a scout. Piniella had been Billy's buffer, his protector against Steinbrenner. But Piniella was fed up with a role that was maddening.

Piniella's replacement, Bob Quinn, was a former Cleveland scouting director who had never been a general manager and knew nothing of the crossfire between Billy and Steinbrenner. Whereas Piniella would visit Billy in the Yankee Stadium manager's office, light a cigarette, and talk with Billy for twenty minutes about George's crazy schemes or suggestions and how to handle them, Quinn had no experience in that realm.

The day after Piniella resigned, the Yankees took their 32-15 record—the second best in baseball and good enough for a 2.5-game lead in their division—to Seattle. Then it was off to Oakland, where they were to play a Memorial Day afternoon game.

It was a bright Monday afternoon and there was a crowd of more than forty-four thousand. A midday rain had kept the field damp, but the nationally televised game began on time. To lead off the third inning, Oakland shortstop Walt Weiss hit a soft, looping line drive toward Yankees second baseman Bobby Meacham, who was playing for an injured Willie Randolph. Meacham, replays showed, caught the ball on the fly. He made a backhand grab with his glove just above the ground.

But second-base umpire Rick Reed, standing behind Meacham, was screened from the play. He could not see the ball and Meacham's glove and ruled that the ball had bounced just before Meacham snagged it. He made the safe sign, which meant it was not an out. Meacham could have easily gotten Weiss with a throw to first base, but knowing that he had caught the ball and not seeing Reed's safe signal, he turned and fired the ball to shortstop Rafael Santana. He was beginning the ritual of an out with no runners on — he was throwing it around the horn.

Weiss ran to first, safe on what was ruled a single.

Meacham, pitcher Richard Dotson, and Santana argued with Reed, who stood by his opinion that from what he could see the ball was trapped. Billy jogged onto the field, and as he did he turned to first-base umpire Dale Scott, who had a good view of the play.

"The second-base umpire couldn't see it," Billy said to Scott. "You had the best view. You've got to help him with the call. Talk to him and get it right."

Billy then took his case to Reed, who was unmoved. He appealed to home plate umpire Rich Garcia, the crew chief. Garcia said Billy could ask Scott his opinion.

The Hall of Fame second baseman Joe Morgan was the color analyst on the broadcast. Said Morgan, "They're going to make a mistake if they don't reverse this. One of those umpires should get it right. Meacham caught it."

Scott did not get involved in the call, which sent Billy over the edge. Being screened from a play and missing a call was one thing, but for another umpire to let an error be perpetuated was worse than being wrong. Billy yelled something at Scott, who threw up his arm and ejected Billy from the game.

Billy tried to kick dirt on Scott, but the infield was too wet and no dirt could be scraped forward by his cleats. The infield was almost muddy. Frustrated by the conditions, Billy reached down with both hands and tried scooping the infield dirt to fling at Scott's legs. This may have worked a few miles away at West Berkeley's Kenney Park, but the hard clay of a big-league ballpark's infield is not easily displaced. Billy grasped what dirt and clay he could and shoveled it at Scott's legs.

There wasn't much in Billy's hands as he flung it, but that was not the point. It looked bad. Many a columnist would note that Billy looked like a brat in a child's sandbox, irate and ill mannered.

Said Morgan on the telecast, "This is unfortunate because Billy is right.

If Randolph had been there, he probably would have thrown to first base anyway and this never happens."

Billy was calm a few seconds later, and he left the field with Garcia, talking to the umpire almost placidly. Years later, Garcia talked about how up-and-down and incongruous an infield squabble with Billy would be for an umpire.

"He would blow up and then be composed in a matter of seconds," Garcia said. "He could be wild-eyed furious and then completely reasonable in one ten-second period. And Billy always wore a religious cross in between the interlocking NY on his hat. So all the while he's yelling at you, you're looking at that cross on his hat.

"It was a unique experience for an umpire."

After the game, which Oakland won, 3–2, when Jose Canseco — whom Billy had drafted as the A's general manager in 1982 — hit a home run, Billy said that Scott at first said he did not see the play well enough to make a call. But after conferring with the other umpires, Scott, Billy said, changed his mind and said that the ball had bounced.

"I don't mind errors or being screened from a call, but I can't tolerate untruths — he changed his story," Billy said.

The *New York Times* contacted several sports psychologists, asking them to assess Billy's behavior in Oakland.

"Kicking dirt and throwing dirt are obvious simple displacements from kicking the person and hitting the person," said Dr. Stanley Cheren, a Boston psychiatrist who works with athletes. "Dirt adds another quality — filth — ultimately meaning contempt. It's an expression of contempt."

The Scott situation was an embarrassment, but Billy expected only a fine. Earlier in the year, he had paid $300 for kicking dirt on Tim Welke in Texas. But two days after the Scott dispute, Billy was at his desk in the visiting manager's office in Oakland when the phone rang.

The Yankees had won the previous day; he had visited his mother and hung out in the Danville Hotel the night before. He was in a good mood and he answered the phone with a wink at reporters.

"Hello, Copacabana," he said, a quip he frequently made, proving that the 1950s were never too far from his mind.

It was American League president Dr. Bobby Brown, Billy's 1950s teammate.

"Yes, Bobby," Billy said, then listened for a while.

The grin on Billy's face vanished.

"OK, thanks for calling, Bobby," Billy said, and hung up.

He had been suspended for three games and fined $1,000.

"There is no excuse sufficient enough to warrant dirt being kicked and thrown on an umpire," Brown said in a statement. "I have warned Billy that this type of action must cease, and if repeated it could result in harsher penalties."

It got worse. The umpires were infuriated that the suspension was only three games. Richie Phillips, lawyer for the umpires' union, issued a resolution condemning Billy after a conference call with the seven umpiring crew chiefs. Phillips said that Billy could no longer leave the dugout during games.

"For Martin to stay in the game, he's going to have to behave like an altar boy," Phillips said. "He's going to have to fold his hands, shut his mouth and that's it. Otherwise, he's going to be ejected, ejected, ejected, ejected. Every time for the next couple of weeks that he comes out of the dugout, he'll be ejected. Then we'll review the situation."

By mid-June, with the Yankees still in first place, Billy and the umpires had reached an uneasy truce. Billy was allowed on the field. But it was understood that he had a short leash. The bitterness of the umpires toward Billy troubled Steinbrenner, and he did not see a resolution.

"They're not letting him do his job and I don't know how that's going to work," he said.

On Monday, June 20, the Yankees headed to Detroit with a 40-25 record, the third best in baseball. The lead over Detroit was still half a game. Billy had recovered from his Lace injuries. Before the first game in Detroit, he was told that catcher Don Slaught, who had been on the disabled list with a groin injury, had been activated by Quinn. That was against Billy's wishes because he believed that Slaught was not yet healed.

Quinn disagreed. Billy called George, who backed Quinn. Then, Slaught tried running before the game and told Billy he could not play. Billy again called Quinn, who declined to activate another player.

Billy ripped Quinn and Steinbrenner to reporters for making him play the Detroit games with only twenty-four able-bodied players when the Tigers had twenty-five on their roster.

That didn't go over too well back in New York.

In the game that night, Winfield missed a game-winning home run by two inches, his long fly ball hitting near the top of the outfield wall in left field. The drive instead became a game-tying double. In the tenth inning, Billy brought on reliever Cecilio Guante, a right-hander who had been paired with Righetti as a closer. Guante had earned his keep for Billy with stellar late-inning relief. But Guante had also logged a lot of innings and been on the disabled list. In the tenth inning at Tiger Stadium, Tom Brookens took Guante deep, knocking a solo homer over the right-field fence to win the game, 2–1.

It was a nationally televised game, and the Yankees had fallen out of first place for the first time since early May. The next night, with Slaught still unused on the bench, the Yankees took a 6–1 lead into the ninth inning. When middle reliever Neil Allen gave up a single and a walk to lead off the ninth, this time Billy called on Righetti to close the game.

Righetti liked to pitch often, but he had not been in a game in six days. He quickly gave up a hit to load the bases, but then got two outs. Next, Righetti walked in two runs. Billy summoned Guante.

"You know those moments when you just feel like something is not right?" Boyer said years later. "That was one of those moments. Sitting in that dugout you just have this sick, uneasy feeling. In that series, there was just something eerie, something not right."

Standing at first base, Mattingly thought about breaking the tension by going over to the mound to say something to Dominican-born Guante.

"But he didn't speak a lot of English," Mattingly said. "So I just got ready to play. I was reminding myself that we just needed one out."

Detroit shortstop Alan Trammell was a six-time All-Star who was having one of his best seasons. He was thirty years old and in the prime of a twenty-year career. Trammell hit 185 home runs as a Tiger, but few of them were more stunning and majestic than the grand slam he launched at Tiger Stadium on June 21, 1988, when the home team scored six runs in the ninth inning to defeat the Yankees, 7–6.

Billy entered the clubhouse after the game and toppled the postgame food table, sending it somersaulting end over end. He went into his office, slammed the door, and did not come out until well after reporters had left the clubhouse. Several players hid out in the trainer's room, which was off-limits to reporters. The tiny seventy-six-year-old visitors' clubhouse in Tiger Stadium was funereal.

The next night, the Yankees lost on a tenth-inning single. They had lost three successive one-run games on the Tigers' last at-bat.

Arriving in Detroit, the Yankees were beginning their seventh consecutive week in first place. Now they were 2.5 games back, albeit with about fifteen weeks left to play in the regular season.

But there was bad news all around. Henderson and Clark were hurt. Al Leiter, the prized rookie starter, had been put on the twenty-one-day disabled list with a finger blister. The bullpen was in shambles, unsteady and inefficient, with Billy being accused of mishandling that sector of the pitching staff. Steinbrenner was firing shots at Billy from afar again, complaining to reporters that a running and conditioning program he had ordered the Yankees pitchers to perform every other day during the season had been largely ignored.

Billy did not yet know about George's comments — they would be in the next day's newspapers — but leaving Detroit he tried to offer perspective and lift his team.

"This leaves you a little numb but we just need to go home and get a couple of wins," he said in his office. "Every team has down periods. That's why we built the big lead early to survive this. We don't have to panic.

"This is June; it isn't September. It doesn't mean anything."

Billy was packing a small bag for the trip home. A suit, dress shirt, and tie were draped on a hanger behind his desk. Outside, clubhouse workers were nosily filling trunks with bats, equipment, and clothes. A cargo truck had backed down the narrow aisle beneath the Tiger Stadium grandstand so the Yankees' gear could be more easily hauled out of the clubhouse. From there, it would be taken to the airport so it could be placed in the hold of the Yankees' charter jet.

The Yankees' head clubhouse man, Nick Priore, came into Billy's office. He needed Billy's uniform to pack on the truck.

Billy peeled off his Yankees jersey and pants and handed them to Priore. The change of clothes was going quickly, and as reporters were leaving the room, Billy had started to button his dress shirt.

"Tomorrow is another day," he said.

45

LOU PINIELLA WAS DRIVING south on the New York State Thruway from Albany, New York, where he was visiting the Yankees' Class AA team. It was a sunny Thursday morning, one of the first days of summer. Piniella was planning a barbecue at his house in northern New Jersey. Then he would watch that night's Yankees game against Cleveland on television.

Cell phones were still a few years in the future, but there were beepers, and Piniella got a message to call George Steinbrenner and Gene Michael. He stopped at a rest area. He called George first.

"George said he was moving Billy to an adviser again and he wanted me to take over managing the club," Piniella said. "My first reaction was no, because I didn't want to become someone who he hired and fired all the time. I had seen what it did to Billy."

Piniella only said that he would think about it. But Steinbrenner said he needed an answer by early afternoon, if not sooner.

Piniella then dialed Michael, who was acting as a special scout and adviser to the Yankees.

"You've got to take the job," Michael told his friend.

"Why? You're the one who says that you'll never manage for George again, why should I?" Piniella answered.

"Because he's hiring Dallas Green if you don't," Michael replied. "Is that what you want? Look, Billy is gone, there's nothing we can do about that. But this is a good team — a first-place team. They should win the division. If you come back, I'll coach for you."

Green had managed the Philadelphia Phillies to a 1980 World Series victory, but he was a loud, domineering presence and definitely a Yankees outsider. He was a career National Leaguer who would probably try to drastically remake the roster. And he would surely clash with Steinbrenner. Their partnership would likely be a calamity.

The best alternative seemed to be Piniella trying to manage for Steinbrenner again. Piniella called Steinbrenner back and accepted the job, although on the remainder of the drive home he twice pulled over to the side of the road and considered calling Steinbrenner back to renege on the deal. Piniella also was upset for Billy and thought George might be acting rashly.

"I just knew that Billy had to be devastated," Piniella said. "It was always like a small death for him when he was separated from the Yankee job. Nothing else made him feel totally alive."

Piniella went to his house in Allendale, New Jersey, but his wife was not at home. He left her a note because he had to get to Yankee Stadium for the pregame news conference announcing the fifteenth managerial change in Steinbrenner's fifteen-year tenure.

The note left for Anita Piniella on the kitchen counter briefly summarized Piniella's day: "Accepted Yankee manager job, left for stadium, see you tonight."

Many years later, Piniella said he should have started the note: "Lost my mind . . . accepted Yankee manager's job . . ."

Billy learned he was reassigned—fired in practical terms—by Steinbrenner for the fifth time via a phone call from Eddie Sapir, whom Steinbrenner had called. The conversation was brief. It was the ninth time Billy had lost a big-league managerial job.

"He did not see that one coming," Jill said of Billy. "He never saw it coming at all. Billy was really shocked. George did things with spontaneity. He was a generous guy but an impatient one."

At Yankee Stadium, the players seemed almost oblivious. Another season with more than one manager. Ho-hum.

Among Yankees fans, there was angst for Billy. The team, after all, had a 40-28 record, which was the fourth best in Major League Baseball. Billy's legion of fans took to the airwaves of something new in New York—sports talk radio—and lamented their loss.

But the drumbeat of Billy's 1980s transgressions, underscored by the beating he took at Lace and his ongoing issues with umpires, had irreparably altered the conversation about the most beloved Yankees manager in the team's history to that point. His critics said he needed to seek treatment for alcoholism, and his supporters mostly worried for him.

Now he was gone again. Yankees fans hoped Piniella could turn the team around from its recent slump—or at least keep up the pace that had kept the Yankees close to a division title.

Neither would happen. The Yankees would not have a winning record again until 1993, when Billy's protégé, Showalter, took over the club.

Jill said Billy did indeed take his firing hard. He blamed Steinbrenner, but unlike Yogi Berra, he could never completely turn his back on him. Berra stayed away for years; Billy remained drawn to Steinbrenner's Yankees like a gnat to the light. He could not do without them.

Privately, Billy would rail against what he saw as the unfairness of it all. He hated that George controlled him like a puppet, and he found the firings demeaning. But ultimately, he justified them as the conditions of life around the modern Yankees. His Yankees.

And there was something else: he needed George to keep paying him. He needed the money. He also needed to stay in George's good graces so he could come back and manage again. There was always going to be another time to manage the Yankees.

About a week after his firing, Billy and Jill escaped to upstate New York where some new acquaintances had been kind enough to offer guest quarters on their property. It would also give Jill and Billy more time to look for land and a home that could possibly be converted into a horse farm.

"Billy when he was fired would usually stay away from people for a while, just become kind of a homebody and not go out for a period of time," Jill said. "We had places where he could go and fish. We were finding the place outside Binghamton and then rebuilding it. We had things to occupy our time."

Billy came back to New York to meet with Steinbrenner at the Carlyle Hotel in early July. They talked for ninety minutes. Eddie Sapir attended the meeting, too.

Sapir recalled that Steinbrenner was remorseful (his Yankees had fallen farther from first place since Billy left). The Yankees' owner gave Billy another raise.

"Billy was pretty down, but I remember leaving that meeting at the Carlyle and we were walking down Madison Avenue and a guy working on a scaffold looked down and called to Billy," Sapir said. "The guy yelled, 'Hey, Billy, we still love ya.' Whenever Billy was down, all he had to do was walk around Manhattan because the people there never stopped rooting for him. He was one of them forever."

While visits to New York City might have been restorative to his psyche, he retreated to upstate New York for refuge in the middle of the

1988 baseball season. Billy and Jill had found their sanctuary, or at least a version of it, in the Binghamton area.

Binghamton is a city of forty-seven thousand about 180 miles northwest of Yankee Stadium. Situated at the confluence of two major rivers, the Susquehanna and the Chenango, it was a transportation crossroads during the railroad era and is home to a large state university. Binghamton in 1988 was a blue-collar city with ties to its heyday as a manufacturing center.

The city, which sits in a bowl-like setting, is surrounded by rolling hills. It was on one of these steep hills, about thirteen miles east and north of Binghamton, that Billy and Jill bought their farm on Potter Hill Road. They paid a little more than $340,000 for about 150 acres, getting a mortgage from a local bank. The farm was on a bluff with sweeping westward views. It had a three-story, five-thousand-square-foot farmhouse that was all but gutted and remodeled in the next year. A barn was constructed near the main house, which was set back about six hundred feet from the road. It had the feel of an estate, with an ornamental stone entryway at the foot of the driveway that included an electronically controlled black iron gate with an intercom connected to the house.

The farmhouse had broad display windows and a large deck that looked out on a ten-acre pond that was rife with bass and trout. There was a large garden on one side of the house and apple trees a short walk away.

"Billy was not a farmer at heart, he was a city kid," Jill said. "But the trips to Texas and Oklahoma and all those fishing and hunting outings had changed him over time. I remember being surprised when we first looked at that farm. We were walking down the driveway and Billy just stopped and said, 'I want this.'"

The farm was rough around the edges with many dense, wooded sections, but it also had a vast network of trails and open fields. The land had potential for multiple uses.

Driving around on a golf cart he had brought to the property, Billy made friends with his new neighbors quickly, learning everyone's name, occupation, and interests. He otherwise kept to himself, but he was available when someone needed an extra hand on a small project. He also donated to the local firehouse — a fire truck still has a plaque noting that it was the benefit of a donation by Billy. He went to the local Catholic church for Mass, made friends with the priests and parishioners, and donated to the local Catholic Youth Organization, which sponsored area youth sports.

"He was always so friendly; he fit in so well," said Betty Jenks, who lived next door to Billy. "He was just one of us. He didn't put on airs. The arguing or aggressive person they talk about on television and in the newspapers is different than the person I knew."

It took months for the farmhouse renovations to be completed, and Billy and Jill lived in a nearby Comfort Inn while the biggest work was being done. Eventually, they moved in even as more work was being done, most of it to complete an extravagant, sumptuous, and profligate master bedroom suite that had a fireplace, hot tub, sauna, and, among other things, a twenty-four-karat-gold-plated urinal affixed to a bathroom wall. When Billy got up late at night to relieve himself, he was apparently notoriously inaccurate.

So a normal toilet would not do. The man used to bars and saloons made less of a mess with a urinal. The gold plating apparently added some dignity to an unusual household bathroom fixture.

Jill hired a local housewife, Mary Lynch, to help her around the house. For Lynch, who was in her twenties, it was the start of a three-year relationship. Lynch became a combination housecleaner, caretaker, valet, and aide-de-camp of Fenton's most famous residents.

Jill, Lynch said, was detail oriented and a taskmaster — critical of the contractors and others she was doing business with in Billy's sphere.

"Billy would spend the day tooling around on his tractor, and they had bought all these sheep, a ram, geese, and ducks," Lynch said. "Billy wanted to be a farmer. He wanted to try that life. But Jill would spend her day in the house in an office just off the kitchen. She would be watching the stock market tables and on the telephone talking to people.

"She was smart; she was always reading manuals and architectural magazines. She was studying things. And if someone crossed her, she could cuss up a storm. But she could turn it on and off. She'd be on the phone in the office just reaming someone out — screaming into the phone. And then she would come out to the kitchen and be as sweet as could be. In a calm, pleasant voice she would say, 'Hi, Mary, how are you?'"

Lynch saw how the roles in the household had developed. Jill had to take some control. Billy was carefree but highly irresponsible, too.

"The UPS driver was coming to the house every day because Jill was ordering things for the house — or getting Victoria's Secret lingerie delivered," Lynch said. "And Jill or I would have to make sure we got to the driver before Billy did because Billy might tip him fifty bucks.

"Billy could be like a big kid. He loved to cook spaghetti sauce from scratch. But he'd leave it on the stove and walk down to the pond to fish. The burner on the stove would get hotter and hotter until the sauce would just explode out of the pan. I swear I was always up cleaning spaghetti sauce off the kitchen ceiling. He also loved Häagen-Dazs strawberry ice cream, which he would eat out of the container while watching TV. But he'd fall asleep watching TV while eating the ice cream and the whole container would melt into the living room couch. I'd have to clean that up, too."

From Fenton, Billy kept in touch with his extended family in California and in Texas. But it was not an easy period for those friends and family now at an arm's distance from Billy. They were upset and confused why he had invested in land in upstate New York. The family wanted him back in California, where he had periodically promised to return for good. According to Eddie Sapir and Billy's children, Jill had made it difficult to get in touch with Billy. Calls to the Fenton house went unreturned. Letters and other missives went unanswered. Billy was hardly seen in California after 1987.

Kelly Ann told a story from that time period. She said Billy's granddaughter hardly knew her famous grandfather.

"When people ask Evie what her grandfather does, she used to say that he kicks dirt on people," Kelly Ann said. "Now she just says, 'He gets fired.'"

Back home in Northern California, where the Blackhawk house had been returned to the Oakland A's, there was not much else to say.

"That woman, that mean-spirited witch," Pat Irvine said of Jill. "She cut him off from all of us."

Billy Joe had graduated from Texas Tech — something he says his father did not know until a year later. He was in the early stages of what would become a successful career as an agent for baseball players.

"But I didn't see him for quite a while there," said Billy Joe, who as an adult started to ask people to call him simply Billy Martin. "I had gotten used to those periods when he disappeared. I learned more about what was going on with him through Bill Reedy."

There were a few still on the inside. Reedy, who had become Billy's best friend, remained in the loop. With Jill taking over Billy's finances and public relations bookings, Sapir said he had largely been pushed out.

"To make it easier on him, I wrote him a letter saying that I was getting more involved in politics in New Orleans," Sapir said. "I made it sound like I was going to be busier and stepping aside.

"But I also told him I'd be there for whatever he needed. I wrote that I loved him because he used to tell me all the time that he loved me. And I also wrote that I know what Jill wants. She wants to run things. And if that's the way things were going to be, I was fine with it."

The Yankees' season had ended badly with the Yankees 45-48 under Piniella. They had finished in fifth place. An inconsistent, erratic pitching staff, the downfall of the team in Billy's last days, had only gotten worse as the year progressed. The content, united team that charged to the front of the division in the season's first three months limped to the finish bickering and resentful. At least six players wanted to be traded. One of those who did not return, Jack Clark, always blamed Billy's firing for the team's demise.

"We all knew our roles when Billy was there," Clark said. "And I still will always feel, if he would have been there — and I'll feel this for the rest of my career and the rest of my life — that no matter what happened on or off the field, there was no way we wouldn't have gone to the World Series and won."

In a 1994 interview, Steinbrenner, who by then had turned the baseball operations of the team over to Michael and Showalter and rarely intervened, addressed Billy's firing in 1988.

"That was my biggest mistake with the Yankees," he said. "We really weren't that far out. I probably should have backed off and let things calm down. But it was hard. There was a lot going on. But, yes, I have reflected on that move. Letting Billy go then was a mistake."

Piniella was discharged as Yankees manager on October 7 and replaced by Dallas Green.

Billy was still lying low on Potter Hill Road. He did attend baseball winter meetings that December in Atlanta. Jill was with him. In the hotel lobby, where all the business gets done, Jill was showing off pictures of the farm.

The photograph that drew the most reaction was one taken of Billy in overalls looking elfin as he rode an enormous John Deere tractor.

"I'm really a poor farmer, and maybe not that good at it, but I like it," Billy said in an ESPN interview. "I'm Port Crane, New York's, best-known farmer. I like that very much."

Asked if he still thought of himself as the best manager in baseball, Billy replied with a smile, "No, I'm the best manager out of baseball."

46

IF BILLY WAS GOING to be a farmer, he needed a pickup truck. A friend brought him down to Corey's Northgate Ford on Upper Front Street, a family-owned, prominent Binghamton dealership since the mid-1960s. The Coreys knew Billy. Everyone on Upper Front Street did.

The street, which parallels Interstate 81, was a major thoroughfare of bars, restaurants, car dealerships, banks, and hotels. It was not far from the Comfort Inn where Billy and Jill had briefly lived. Nearby, there was another restaurant with a small bar where Billy had spent some time, Morey's.

Billy was a familiar sight along Front Street. The locals liked how he would sometimes appear at a bar in dusty overalls, then sit and talk about hunting, harvesting, the day's news, or baseball. The locals said they felt as if he was one of them.

Billy would not usually be on Front Street late at night, although that did happen. More commonly, he would be there in the twilight of afternoon or in the evening, after making a trip to Home Depot, the gas station, the lumberyard, or the supermarket. Billy would stop in for a few pops on the way home two or three times a week.

"It was part of his routine," said Earl Wagstaff, the owner of the Fireside Inn. "I think he needed to get out of the house sometimes. Who doesn't, right? But he would be unrecognized for a while — jeans, boots, maybe a floppy hat. He was one of the nicest guys I've had in my bar."

A favorite Billy haunt was the Bull's Head.

"Billy was the one of the guys in the Bull's Head," another Bull's Head regular, Johnny Franklin, said. "We might have been surprised to see him the first couple of times, but after that it was never like, 'Oh, there's Billy Martin, the famous Yankee.' It was just like, 'There's Billy.'"

Franklin also added that on at least two occasions, other Bull's Head patrons drove Billy home. Corey Ford had given Billy an F-Series blue-and-white pickup truck in exchange for two television commercials promoting the dealership. Once, as Billy climbed into the truck and drove himself home, some of his friends from the Front Street bars followed him to make sure he got back to Potter Hill Road safely.

Davey Springer, who worked at a deli on Front Street, said of Billy, "I never saw him have a cross word with anyone."

In the good weather months of 1989, Billy spent many days sitting alongside his ten-acre pond fishing. After a few trips to Home Depot, he had built wooden stairs between the house and the pond. The house was on a bluff about fifty feet above the pond, and the stairs were anchored into the soil of the hillside. It was a two-week project, but the stairs were sturdy and proved to be durable, still in use twenty-five years later.

Fishing by the pond was relaxing but it had its limits.

As Billy told his friend Bill Reedy, "Jill is always saying, 'Why don't you go down and wet your line.' And that's fine but how many days in a row can I do that?"

Billy did escape upstate New York frequently, flying to appearances, dinners, and charity golf outings. He stopped at Yankee Stadium sporadically but tried to keep his distance from the disaster that the Dallas Green regime was becoming.

As expected, Green had remade the Yankees in the image of a National League team, spurning Willie Randolph to sign former Dodgers second baseman Steve Sax. He acquired other National Leaguers and tried many National League tactics. Years before interleague play, the mingling of the two styles of play did not work. Plus the team was aging — Mattingly and Winfield were both injured.

By the Fourth of July, Steinbrenner's fifty-ninth birthday, the Yankees were 1 game under .500 and 6.5 games out of first place. Green was rumored to be on his way out. Steinbrenner was leaning toward the 1978 playoff game hero, Bucky Dent, who had been managing in the Yankees' minor leagues.

Steinbrenner kept in touch with Billy. He knew the phone number to the farmhouse. Mary Lynch, who was not a baseball fan, recalls fielding some of the calls.

"The phone was ringing all the time and I hung up on Steinbrenner several times," Lynch said. "He'd start yelling at me and saying, 'You need to go get him now.'

"And I'd say, 'Listen, you need to understand that Billy is a private person and he likes his privacy.' And I'd hang up. Billy would come in a little while later and I'd say, 'Some guy, George Steinburner or something, called.'

"Billy loved that I did that but he always called him back."

As a daily presence in the household, Lynch became intimate with many details of Billy and Jill's life in 1989. She ran errands for them, driving Billy's pickup truck to fetch Drano or mousetraps. She mailed their packages and made the check deposits at the bank, which averaged about $35,000 a month.

"Even with the urinal in the bedroom upstairs, Billy still wasn't that accurate in the middle of the night," Lynch said. "He had a hard time hitting it. I was potty training my young boys at the time and they weren't too accurate either. I had tried a trick with them so I tried it with Billy. I put Cheerios in the toilet and urinal and I left him a note, 'Please aim to sink the Cheerios.'

"That definitely helped."

While others close to Billy and Jill witnessed frequent screaming arguments that ended with golf clubs thrown on the front stoop or a hotel door kicked in, Lynch said Billy and Jill never quarreled in front of her during her years with them.

But Mike Klepfer, a former New York state trooper who later started a Binghamton-area trucking company and befriended Billy, said he saw or heard serious, vicious disputes in which Billy and Jill threw heavy objects at each other or charged at one another. Klepfer, who died in 2012, told biographers David Falkner and Peter Golenbock that one of these fierce confrontations ended up with Jill heading to a doctor for a neck brace.

"Looking back, being a little wiser as an older woman and not a young kid, I did see things that mean a little more to me now," Lynch said in 2013. "I'd come in for the morning and there would be broken glass everywhere like he or she had been throwing things. She'd say, 'We had a slight accident.' So looking back, there must have been some real big fights.

"And every once in a while, he would leave for New York in kind of a huff and not come back for two days."

Lynch also insisted that Jill knew how to keep her husband happy.

"She pampered him, she would draw his bath for him," Lynch said. "She was definitely out to keep him happy. She kept up her appearance; that was extremely important to her, with the long blonde hair and clothes

470 ○ BILL PENNINGTON

that played up her figure. I mean, she was a looker, no doubt about it, and he liked hanging out with her in public. He loved showing her off.

"They had a healthy sex life. She had a dresser full of matching Victoria's Secret outfits."

Asked to assess the tenor and volatility of her marriage to Billy, Jill, who has since remarried, smiled.

"Our marriage was not any more tumultuous than any other marriage," she said. "We had our fights. We disagreed. We got mad. He might storm away or I might storm away. What couple does not have those moments?

"So, yes, that happened. And the alcohol could enhance whatever emotion was going on there. But he could also calm down very quickly. That was an extraordinary gift of his. So I don't think it was out of the ordinary; we lived a pretty normal life."

Jill was troubled by Billy's drinking in 1989, and she said that Billy knew he had to do something about his alcohol dependence, too.

"Billy had a drinking problem, there's no question about that," Jill said. "At times it was under control and there were times when it wasn't. As we've learned over the many years now and been educated, I think it's clear that there are different levels of alcoholism. Twenty or thirty years ago, we didn't know as much and didn't handle it the same.

"Billy would go weeks or months without drinking. He didn't drink every day. He didn't usually overdrink when he did drink. Other times he was a very well-functioning alcoholic."

Jill sighed.

"In the last year of his life, I did confront him and he got it back under control," she said. "I do think eventually that he would have stopped altogether. He knew his drinking was something he had to confront. It had to be addressed. New opportunities were coming up in his life. He was making appearances, speaking to more groups and different groups, and I think he saw the rest of the world out there and wanted to keep being part of it. And that probably meant change.

"I think he would have gone to get help. He was a brave guy and he was starting to realize that he had a problem. I think that's the first step, right? But it was hard for Billy because it was a different era. It was wrapped up in his persona. Back then, society wasn't as accepting of people who admitted to a problem. It wasn't as easy to reach out for help in those days. It's a different world now and it's so easy to look back and judge. But it wasn't the same. Which is a shame. But it's something I believe he would have addressed at some point."

She continued, "If he had stopped drinking, he'd probably still be alive right now."

By August of 1989, Steinbrenner fired Dallas Green, who had a 56-65 record as Yankees manager. Dent took over. Billy remained far away, ensconced in Fenton, sitting on the back deck of his farmhouse and gazing across the rolling hills of central New York.

But he was restless.

He called trainer Gene Monahan to talk about baseball and what was going on with the team.

"It wasn't anything specific," Monahan said. "He just needed a little connection to the game. There was obviously a hole in his life. Sinatra didn't stop singing until he no longer had the health to continue. Billy was still vibrant and eager to stay with it."

Billy was also still an adviser to the Yankees. Buck Showalter recalls receiving calls from Billy on multiple occasions.

"He would just want to talk baseball," said Showalter, who had become a coach in the South Bronx. "When Billy called, I would tell him what I was doing, and because he watched most of the games, he would help me with suggestions and his observations, which were incredible.

"It was like learning from the master because nobody had an eye for a game like him — nobody. But I also had to ignore some of his other advice. I would give him a taste of some of the internal Yankees' politics and he would give me his opinion of what to do. His advice was usually not the most tactful approach. He had no diplomacy.

"I would say, 'Billy, I'm not trying to win every battle; I'm trying to win the war.' And his answer would be, 'Let's win every battle and every war.'"

Showalter snickered.

"That's Billy in a nutshell, right?" he said. "He refused to lose at anything, even if it was going to cost him in the end."

Late in 1989, Billy reconnected with his childhood friend Lew Figone, too. Figone had gotten caught up in the vicissitudes of Billy's life thousands of miles away from his West Berkeley roots. He was pushed out of the inner circle. But Billy reached out late in 1989, and Figone listened and wanted to help. He told Billy he would give Billy whatever he needed. To Figone, Billy sounded confused and depressed.

Sitting in his office twenty-three years later, Figone had a succinct assessment of Billy's problems — in 1989 and throughout most of his life. To Figone, who had known Billy since he was a toddler, every setback or difficulty was rooted in his pursuit of the wrong women — or women in general.

"Billy's downfall was not drinking," Figone said. "It was women."

Told of Figone's assessment, Morabito, also one of Billy's oldest friends, amended it.

"It was a combination," he said. "The drinking led to the women."

The 1989 Yankees got no better under Dent, whom the players treated as an interim leader. The 1989 Yankees finished in fifth place with a 74-87 record, the worst record for the team in twenty-two years.

At the season's end, Steinbrenner told reporters that Dent would return as Yankees manager, but privately he was thinking otherwise. He felt he had to give Dent a chance to manage a team from the beginning of the year, but he had little faith in Dent's ability to make the Yankees champions again. Steinbrenner was hatching another plan.

Separately and unaware of George's plans, Billy had written George a personal letter from the Fenton farm imploring Steinbrenner to give him a more active role with the Yankees. Billy wanted a job with genuine input. He wasn't asking to manage the team, but he was all but begging George to let him get closer to the field again.

Steinbrenner was delighted to get the letter. He loved that Billy wanted to be involved in the governance of the team again. And the Yankees' owner planned to put him in uniform during spring training and then keep him very close to the team, even if Billy would watch games from the owner's box.

It was part of a grander scheme. Billy would be the manager-in-waiting should Dent falter — as almost everyone expected because the pitching-poor 1990 Yankees once again looked overmatched. But George kept his thoughts to himself in the early fall of 1989.

So Billy did not know of George's scheming when he attended a New Jersey baseball card show in late November. Speaking to a New Jersey reporter, Billy was asked how he was doing outside of baseball.

Billy explained, with some enthusiasm, about his life on the farm. But he grew melancholy as the interview went on. At one point he offered a striking appraisal of his life situation: "Now I know why people who retire die soon after."

47

DURING ONE OF THE last days of November, George summoned Billy
to Yankee Stadium. He said he wanted to discuss the roster, which the two
men did. They were alone in Steinbrenner's office overlooking the Yankee
Stadium diamond. Steinbrenner's office in the 1980s was equipped with a
large desk behind which the owner almost always sat. Another prominent
feature of the spacious room was an oversize brown leather lounge chair
shaped like a baseball mitt.

George typically would insist that visitors sit in the mitt/chair, perhaps
because it would swallow up a person and make the visitor feel small.
Looking down from his tall, straight-back chair and leaning on his impe-
rious, massive desk, George would do what came naturally to him: dominate the conversation.

But when Billy came to George's office late in 1989, after thirty minutes
of talking about personnel, the two men did something Yankees' front-
office workers had never before seen — they left the office and went down
to the empty field.

According to multiple Yankees employees at the stadium that day,
George and Billy donned coats against the fall chill and took the elevator to the lowest level. It was a short walk to the Yankee Stadium diamond. Because the infield was covered with a tarp, the team owner and
the team's five-time manager walked along the warning track encircling
the grass field.

They remained on the field for about twenty minutes, then exited
through the home dugout and up through the dark tunnel that led to the
clubhouse. They did not enter the dressing quarters. Instead, George and
Billy took a right and walked through the narrow, serpentine passageway
underneath the first-base stands, which eventually wound to a flight of
spare, timeworn stairs leading to the principal stadium exit and entrance.
Every Yankee since the stadium opened in 1923 — Babe Ruth, Lou Gehrig,
Joe DiMaggio, Mickey Mantle — used this bunkerlike walkway with the
blue-painted cinder-block walls.

On this day, George and Billy lingered at the bottom of the stairs talking in low tones. Then the duo climbed the stairs. At the landing, Billy and George shook hands. Billy exited onto the plaza outside the stadium, heading to his car in the team parking lot for the drive up the New York State Thruway to Fenton.

With a wave, George turned and headed for the elevator that would return him to his mezzanine-level office.

No one heard George and Billy speaking on the field or in the hallway during that late-November day. But several Yankees executives, security guards, and clerical workers noticed the uncommon, furtive meeting on the field.

And within a few days the phone rang at Clete Boyer's home in Atlanta.

"Don't get yourself another job — stay put," Billy told Boyer, who had been fired as one of Billy's coaches the previous year and remained out of baseball. "I'm going to be managing the Yankees next year and I'll need you as a coach."

In early December 1989, Boyer called Buck Showalter.

"Billy wants you on his staff next year," Boyer said.

"The Yankees have a manager and it isn't Billy," Showalter told Boyer.

"Yeah, but George feels like Dent isn't going to cut it and he told Billy to be ready to take over," Boyer said. "He's going to have Billy at spring training so he can watch the team up close. Then when Bucky Dent messes up, Billy just jumps in."

The phone at the home of Willie Horton also rang. The message was the same.

"Don't take another job in baseball for next season," Horton said Billy told him. "I'm going to need you."

Billy told Horton he might be back in uniform by May.

Lee Walls, another former Billy coach and bar buddy, got the call, too.

"Billy said to sit tight and I'll call you as soon as they need me," Walls said in 1990.

A few days later — it was now almost mid-December — Billy telephoned his favorite New York–area sportswriter, Michael Kay, who was then a reporter for the *New York Daily News*. Kay said Billy told him, "I'm coming back, kid. Once Bucky fucks this up, I'm in. I already got the word from George. And I've got my coaches all lined up. You can't write it now but when it's about to happen, I'll give it to you first."

Kay kept the story to himself, although he did check with some other Billy associates who confirmed that Billy had been calling his former coaches with the news. Kay couldn't, and wouldn't, break Billy's confidence by writing the story. But he definitely was going to be on his toes if Steinbrenner adopted a pessimistic tone about Dent.

There was little doubt Steinbrenner was sincere about bringing Billy back. It was a secret but not all that well kept. Many years later, George would occasionally deny that Billy VI was coming, but in 1989 he had told others in the organization that Billy once again riding to the rescue was indeed Plan B for the 1990 Yankees season. During interviews in 2012 and 2013, after Steinbrenner died, those Yankees executives confirmed it. Billy was coming back again.

There was another factor that might have played into Steinbrenner's decision. A group of Denver-based investors were backing a team that would become the Colorado Rockies, a new National League franchise. Their first season was three years away, but they were looking for a manager/general manager to build the team from the ground up. They had called Billy two weeks before George called the Fenton farmhouse in late November.

"The Colorado people were going to let Billy run the whole show," Jill Martin said. "There was a lot of interest there."

The Japanese professional baseball leagues had called as well.

Billy was revitalized by the attention. It was like old times. Though sixty-one years old, he once again felt he had something that baseball people valued. In the Binghamton bars, at Morey's, the Bull's Head, and the Fireside Inn, a buoyant Billy began dropping little hints that something big might be on the horizon for him.

At nearly the same time, Billy received some bad news, even if it was not totally unexpected. His eighty-eight-year-old mother, Jenny, who had been in declining health, was now hospitalized. Billy's sisters had called and made it plain that while Jenny was not in immediate danger, Billy should come visit before Christmas to be safe. Jenny might rally and recover, which had happened before. But she might not.

Billy had an appearance to make in Terre Haute, Indiana, on December 9. He planned to fly there and then continue on to California. He had to be back by December 15, when Jill had planned a lavish, black-tie Christmas party at the Fenton house.

In Terre Haute on Saturday, December 9, Billy spoke at a sports function benefiting Indiana State University, where Larry Bird had been a bas-ketball star. The appearance went well, and afterward Billy went to the sports bar in Larry Bird's Boston Connection Hotel where he was staying. As he was seated at the bar, and minding his own business, a gunshot sud-denly rang out behind him.

The bullet hissed by his head, missing him by inches. It slammed into the ceiling above the bar. A female patron, who had been seated at a table near the bar, had a two-shot Derringer pistol in her purse that discharged when the purse was inadvertently knocked to the floor.

"Mr. Martin was a little shaken," Terre Haute police chief Ray Watts said afterward. "It just missed his head."

When Billy went back to his hotel room about an hour later, there was a message from Jill.

His mother was doing much worse. Billy had better hurry to Berkeley. He arrived the next day, rushed to the hospital, and found his mother in-firm and frail and all but motionless under the white sheets of the hospital bed. They conversed and held hands. Billy told Jenny that he loved her and she said the same, adding that he looked handsome.

Jenny dozed off, and after about fifteen minutes Billy left the room. An hour later, Juvan "Jenny" Salvini Downey was gone.

Billy was overcome with grief, inconsolably so at times. He had seen his mother little in the past six months, and that absence weighed on his mind and filled him with guilt. He had felt prepared for her death, but the certainty of it had been a greater emotional blow than he had planned. Losing a parent is wrenching for any son or daughter, but as Billy kept telling everyone he saw in the old neighborhood, as the lone biological parent in his life, Jenny had been a guiding force. When Billy doubted himself as a youngster, as he often did, Jenny emboldened him.

"Take shit from nobody" might not have been the motto for his life, but it was a useful thought in many tight situations. It came from Jenny.

Jenny had been the sole connection to a singular heritage that made Billy different from his brothers and sisters. To be sure, Jack Downey had been a meaningful, pivotal father figure, and his siblings had helped shaped his life as well. But he derived much of his purpose, resolve, and personality from his mother. Billy, as he told one and all, felt something within himself die with Jenny. He was alone.

"He was really in rough shape," his boyhood pal Ruben de Alba said. "He kept saying, 'I'll never be the same.'"

Jill flew from New York to California and joined Billy.

"His mental status was in the gutter," she said. "I had never seen him so low and devastated."

Billy's family had a big reception at Spenger's, the sprawling fish house by the docks where in the 1930s the workers used to leave crabs out by the back door for the local children to "steal." Everyone from the old neighborhood was there.

"I was sitting at a table with my brother Nick and Billy came over crying," said cousin Mario DeGennaro. "He smelled of alcohol but I understood — his mother had just died. But he was also all pissed off. There had been some argument with his sisters or brother, something about money or who was going to get Jenny's house."

There was indeed bad blood on the eve of the funeral, and some of it involved the house and money spent on it. Billy and his sisters remained at odds until a truce was called.

"I felt sorry for Billy in the middle of all this," Mario said. "I got up to hug him and I was shocked at how bony and small he felt. Hugging him through his suit jacket, he felt frail and thin. Billy was always a wiry, strong guy. I don't know what it was about that hug, but to me he felt so fragile.

"When he walked away I turned to my brother and said, 'What happened to Billy?'"

There were a variety of reunions going on during Billy's few days in Berkeley. One was with Billy Joe, who had flown to the wake and funeral from Texas. Billy Joe, who had graduated from Texas Tech that year, had remained in touch with Bill Reedy, who told Billy Joe to bring his college diploma with him to California.

The night before the funeral in Berkeley, Reedy, Billy, Sapir, and Billy Joe got together for a quiet drink away from everyone else.

"I pulled out my diploma and I showed my dad," Billy Joe said. "He just broke down and cried. Then he started pacing around and he said, 'Things are going to change.'"

Billy also spent considerable time with Kelly Ann. He frequently said how much he missed California and wished he had spent more time there.

And Billy went down to San Pablo Avenue to visit some of his old drinking haunts and met up with what was left of the West Berkeley Boys. Everyone was older and not in fighting shape.

"I remember somebody told Billy that most of us hadn't been in a fight for forty years, but Billy had more than carried on the West Berkeley Boys tradition for us," said Jack Setzer, Billy's teenage friend. "He got a big kick out of that. I remember that at some point we sang the school song. We were a bunch of sixty-year-old guys singing an old song in the old neighborhood."

Billy then drove north on San Pablo Avenue to catch up with Figone, visiting him at the office of his prosperous company. Figone said Billy told him he was going to leave Jill, sell the New York farm, and "come back home."

"He told me he might need $100,000 to rebuild his life in California," Figone said in 2012. "I told him I'd give him the money."

Billy told Reedy of his moving plans, too. Reedy did not believe his friend. He had heard it before. He was resigned to the notion that Billy would never leave Jill.

Billy had another topic he wanted to discuss with Reedy. He desperately wanted Reedy to come to Fenton for the Christmas holiday.

"I don't want to be alone up there," Billy said. "You've got to come hang out with me, pard."

Reedy knew that Billy had an aversion to Christmas. It went back to Billy's childhood when he received few gifts in a poor household. Billy never warmed to Christmas, even when he had the money to enjoy it. Reedy knew of Billy's mindset and he felt sorry for his grieving friend, but he wasn't sure what his wife's reaction would be to the trip. Then Billy suggested that the visit to Fenton could include a trip to Manhattan where the couples could attend Christmas Eve High Mass at St. Patrick's Cathedral. It would be a spectacular sight with all the holiday flowers and decorations. This convinced Reedy, who knew his wife had never seen St. Patrick's Cathedral. He would come to upstate New York for Christmas.

Jenny was buried with a traditional Italian funeral and a solemn prayer service. The gathering included some of Billy's former Oakland Oaks teammates and former players, and the ex-Oakland A's pitcher Mike Norris. Heather Ervolino attended.

Billy and Jill returned to New York, and the Christmas party at the restored Fenton farmhouse was a huge success. About sixty couples dressed in formal dresses and tuxedos arrived, most of them linked to the Binghamton fine arts community. Billy then made a quick side trip to Tampa. Steinbrenner had asked Billy to appear before two thousand underprivileged children at the Tampa Performing Arts Center. Billy read the children "'Twas the Night Before Christmas."

George dressed up as Santa Claus. When Billy saw the portly Steinbrenner in costume, he said, "You don't really need that pillow under your belt, George."

After Billy returned to New York, Steinbrenner told associates that Billy appeared relaxed.

"His color was good and he was calm," Steinbrenner said in a 1990 interview. "I remember thinking that being married and living on that farm was good for him."

The Reedys arrived in Fenton on December 23. The same day, Billy and Reedy made a trip to Lowe's, the home improvement store on Front Street. From Lowe's, it was a short trip to the nearby bars. They drank for a few hours, then drove one exit east on Route 88 until they began their ascent to Potter Hill Road. Billy cooked dinner and started a blaze in the fireplace. Both women retired early, especially Jill, who felt as if she might be getting a cold.

Billy and Reedy sat up a few extra hours watching a Western movie and drinking. But it was not an especially late night. Everyone was anticipating the trip to Manhattan the next day.

Jill, however, awoke the next day seriously ill from what she felt was a powerful case of the flu. She had a high fever and was bedridden and much too sick to travel to New York. Billy was certainly not going to leave her alone on Christmas Eve. The trip to St. Patrick's Cathedral was called off.

Disappointed but accepting, the Reedys did some last-minute Christmas shopping. Billy called around to friends he had made in the area to invite about a dozen people over to the house for a small Christmas Eve party and feast.

When the crowd left, Reedy and Billy sat up late watching television again.

On Christmas morning, Jill was still sick but improving. Billy made everyone a hearty breakfast of eggs, bacon, and pork chops. There was some more puttering around the farm to do — feeding the chickens, sheep, and other animals, including the ducks down by the pond, which had an aerator so it did not freeze.

Like some of the other farmers in the neighborhood, Billy had begun to raise his own quail. He did so in a brooder, which was like a miniature chicken coop. It was out by the barn, but on cold nights in central New York — and this night the temperature was expected to be in the low twenties — the brooder was warmed by a kerosene heater.

About 1:30 p.m., Billy came back to the main house and announced that he had to go to Binghamton to get kerosene for the quail brooder. Which may or may not have been true.

Whenever they were together, Billy and Reedy always seemed to need to go to town for something. It didn't matter whether they were in Reedy's hometown of Detroit or in Texas, Manhattan, or Oakland. They usually had to go get something, the errand always took at least a couple of hours, and they came back with alcohol on their breath.

Billy grabbed the keys to the Ford, and the two men buttoned their coats and headed out the door. Through a second-floor window, Jill watched the pickup truck roll down the gravel driveway and disappear through the stone entranceway with the iron gates. Billy was at the wheel, and he made a right turn to continue down the steep grade of Potter Hill Road. There was a storm in the weather forecast that was expected to bring either gusty snow showers or freezing rain.

In anticipation, some of Billy's neighbors — preparing for work on Tuesday, December 26 — had already spread sand and rock salt on their driveways.

48

IT WAS TEN MILES from Billy's home to the Front Street highway exit in Binghamton. Billy's usual stop, the Working Man's gas station, was out of kerosene. Billy instead went to the Sunoco down the road, made his purchase, and loaded the kerosene into the bed of the truck. Then Billy and Reedy pointed the truck south on Front Street, looking for somewhere to get a drink.

Not surprisingly, most of his usual stops were closed for Christmas. As the truck approached Morey's, the lettering on display outside the restaurant read: HAPPY HOLIDAYS! SIRLOIN DINNER FROM 1 TO 6 PM.

Reedy, who gave multiple interviews about the day in 2009, said Billy pointed at the sign.

"They have a bar and if they're serving dinner, they're serving drinks," Billy said. "We can get a few pops there."

Billy pulled the pickup into Morey's parking lot. They sat side by side at the bar and each ordered a screwdriver. After one drink, Reedy switched to Budweiser. Billy continued to gulp mixed drinks with Stolichnaya Russian vodka.

The bartender was Robert Dunlop, who worked at Morey's only part-time. His real job was at Johnny Antonelli's Firestone tire store just up the road. Antonelli, a former pitcher for the New York Giants in the 1950s, was an acquaintance of Billy's since they had played in the same city for many years. After Antonelli retired from baseball in 1962, he returned to his native Rochester, about 130 miles from Binghamton, and opened a chain of tire stores throughout upstate New York.

But on this day Dunlop was working the Christmas afternoon shift, and he later said that he served Reedy about five beers across the nearly three hours that the two men were at Morey's. Billy had several mixed drinks. Dunlop did not know how many, but enough that the barkeep was concerned about whether Billy would be driving home.

There were not a lot of employees in Morey's that afternoon. Lisa

Tierno was the waitress along with the owners, Morris and Dorothy Conroe, who opened the restaurant in 1966.

In the course of the three hours, only four other people came to drink at the bar. A bartender from another Front Street restaurant stopped for one drink, waved goodbye to his friend Billy, and left. A local golf pro had a couple of drinks, chatting about golf with Billy and Reedy. A car salesman made conversation with Billy and Reedy for about thirty minutes before he departed. A man who had tried to go hunting but was frustrated by the snow on the ground sat at the opposite end of the bar from Billy and Reedy. He had a puppy in his lap. He talked with Billy about hunting in the area and then paid his bill and exited as well.

Billy and Reedy were alone in the bar for about ninety minutes. Reedy said Billy did most of the talking.

"He was still hurting about his mother, but he wasn't completely down because he was also looking forward to the next year," Reedy said. "He then was talking about how he couldn't wait for spring training to start. He held his glass up and toasted: 'Two months to Fort Lauderdale, pard.'"

The sun was setting when Billy and Reedy finally pushed back from the bar to head home. A light snow in a swirling wind had begun to fall about an hour earlier.

"Who's driving?" Dunlop asked.

Reedy held up his hand with the keys to the Ford pickup and shook them. Dunlop was relieved. Reedy, he thought, seemed sober enough to drive. Billy did not.

For years afterward, there has been uncertainty about who actually drove home that evening because at the crash scene Reedy admitted he was driving, then recanted his story about five hours later. Reedy said that initially he was covering for his friend, knowing that a drunk driving conviction would be devastating to Billy's image and upcoming managerial prospects. Besides, Reedy felt he could pass a Breathalyzer test. (Police officials would disagree.)

Later, facing possible vehicular manslaughter charges, Reedy changed his story and insisted he was now telling the truth.

There were two court cases in subsequent years that were meant to unequivocally establish whether Reedy was driving. Testimony went on for weeks, reams of forensic evidence was presented, and lawyers for and against Reedy argued before judges and juries. At stake was not only

Reedy's criminal culpability in the accident, but later, a large monetary award to Jill Martin in a wrongful death civil claim against Reedy's insurance company, the Ford Leasing Company, and the town of Fenton for improperly maintaining the road.

Unfortunately, the investigation into the accident was bungled, and some pertinent evidence was never gathered. Presaging the O. J. Simpson murder trial, which happened about five years later, there was even a mysterious glove left at the scene that could have been pivotal but never factored into the case. In the end, there is room for debate on both sides.

But after a lengthy trial with lawyers sparring for and against Reedy, a jury of eight men and women found that Reedy was the driver — and that he was impaired with a blood alcohol level of .10, which was the minimum necessary for a drunken driving arrest at the time in New York State. He was fined $350 and his license was suspended. Other charges were not pursued.

That verdict was crucial to finding Reedy liable for the crash in the succeeding civil case. Again, forensic evidence could be construed to put Billy in the passenger seat or the driver's seat — it depended on your interpretation (or motivations). But the fact is that a second court found that Billy was a passenger.

Billy was known to be stubborn about not yielding his keys — "I saw him bowlegged shitfaced drunk and refuse to give me the keys," said Eddie Sapir — but other friends, family, and associates said there were cases when Billy did let others drive.

And he had already been driven home from Front Street bars at least twice. One regular Front Street bar patron said in 1990 that he had run into Reedy during one of his court cases that year and that Reedy had admitted that he was driving. Billy had fallen asleep for parts of the drive home, Reedy said.

Many of those closest to Billy — Sapir, Mickey Mantle, Billy Joe Martin — believed that Reedy was the passenger. They came to that opinion principally because of their faith in Bill Reedy's reliability, character, and integrity. Reedy was well liked by most everyone who knew him, a round-faced man who put everyone at ease.

"If Bill Reedy said he wasn't driving, then I believe him," Billy Joe said.

But those are the rare voices that put the steering wheel in Billy's hands that evening. Overwhelmingly, the bulk of the evidence, most notably

the position of the bodies after the crash — Reedy closest to the steering wheel, Billy against the passenger-side door — seems to indicate that
Reedy was the driver.

It is by far the more likely conclusion — and why a jury thought so, too.
It is a conclusion supported by Reedy's admission at the scene, which he
made repeatedly over several hours to emergency workers, police, and
doctors at the hospital. It is supported by most of the testimony. And it
is supported by the most convincing and indisputable proof of the evening: Reedy had the keys in his hand as he left Morey's. He could not
have gained possession of those keys unless Billy handed them to him or
agreed that he should take them.

The path of the truck after exiting Morey's parking lot also suggests the
driver was not overly familiar with the route. Because one known truth
is that Billy's Ford pickup truck missed the first exit off the highway that
would have brought the two men home on the most direct and safest
route. But, instead of leaving the highway at exit 3, which would have led
the pickup truck up Ballyhack Road and to the foot of Potter Hill Road,
the pickup sped through the blowing snow to exit 4.

There was a pivotal difference in the routes. From exit 3, the usual
route, the truck would have climbed the precipitous grade of Potter Hill
Road, and because of that mile-long, uphill path, the truck would have
had to slow to almost a stop before making a left turn into the driveway
of the farmhouse. From exit 4, the truck was forced to follow a path that
eventually brought the truck to the opposite end of Potter Hill Road — arriving at the peak of a treacherous rise. That required the truck to make a
sharp, downhill, ninety-degree left turn and, after about a hundred feet, a
quick right turn into the driveway.

Exit 4 off Interstate 88 first led Billy's pickup truck to Pleasant Hill
Road, which then feeds into Hunt Hill Road. Unlit and barely two lanes,
Hunt Hill Road travels northward and uphill for almost its entire length.
Its four miles traverse dips and hollows as Hunt Hill Road passes hundreds of acres of farmland, rows of massive pine trees, wide-open fields,
and the occasional horse farm. Running parallel to the road is a drainage
ditch — five feet deep in some sections. At various points along the road,
the drop from the paved road to the grassy ditch is guarded by guardrails.

Finally, at the top of Hunt Hill Road, the treeline recedes to reveal a
striking vista to the west. At roughly 5:45 p.m. on December 25, 1989, the

view was obscured by night and the landscape had become both dark and forbidding with snow gusting across the glazed road. The left turn onto Potter Hill Road was tricky even in good weather. The pavement at that section of the road slants dramatically to the right, pulling any moving object away from a left-hand turn. The slope of the road is by design; it helps water run into the drainage ditch.

As Billy's neighbor Betty Jenks said, "We've had a lot of people's cars in that ditch by the corner. We call the police and they come fish 'em out."

There had been periodic calls for the town to fill the ditch at the bend of Potter Hill Road with gravel, soil, or some other material. But the ditch remained as it had been for decades.

As police reconstructed the accident later from skid marks and tire tracks, the truck was moving about thirty miles an hour, which was generally thought to be too fast for the icy, slick conditions. As the truck slid sideways and failed to negotiate the turn, the passenger side of the vehicle plunged into the ditch. But the truck apparently did not slow down, perhaps because Reedy tried to get back onto the road by turning the steering wheel to the left and stepping on the accelerator.

But instead of climbing the steep embankment, the truck lurched violently forward for about fifty feet, then slammed into the immovable concrete culvert and a four-foot-thick metal drainage pipe that spanned the ditch and formed the beginning of the farmhouse driveway.

The hood of the pickup truck buckled on impact. The windshield was smashed and propelled toward the front bumper by the blunt force of Billy's head striking it. The engine, now partially exposed, stopped but remained warm, the falling snow melting on contact with it. Billy had recoiled from the impact with the windshield and was slumped against the passenger-side door, motionless and silent. His neck was awkwardly tilted forward. Reedy was lying on top of him, his hip broken and his legs wedged under the misshapen dashboard. Neither man had been wearing a seat belt. Grabbing the steering wheel with his left hand, Reedy pulled himself partially off his friend.

"Billy, you OK?" Reedy called out. "Billy!"

There was no response.

"Billy," Reedy said, "if you can get up, I can push you out the window."

There was silence. Shortly thereafter, Peter Piech, a neighbor, drove past and saw the wreck. When he approached the truck, Reedy asked him to pull him up so that he was no longer leaning on Billy. Opening the driver's-side door, Piech grabbed the heavyset Reedy by the lapels of his jacket and yanked him toward him.

When the members of the Port Crane Volunteer Fire Department arrived minutes later — a neighbor had heard the crash and called — Chief John Eldred said he thought Billy looked dead. Reedy was pinned in the truck, but another fireman said he thought he felt a pulse for Billy.

Through the passenger-side door, Eldred grabbed Billy in a bear hug and pulled him out of the truck before passing him to another firefighter, who passed Billy to another fireman who laid Billy on a long, straight board on the ground. It was not exactly the safest way to extricate a passenger suspected of a head or neck injury.

An ambulance was minutes from the scene when another Port Crane fireman pushed the intercom button next to the iron gates at the foot of the driveway.

"The intercom was set up so that my phone would ring," Jill said.

She was upstairs in the master suite and had been in and out of bed all day, still recovering from the flu. There was a turkey in the oven. Something was wrong with the heating system and the house was colder than normal. Jill was under the covers of her bed. Carol Reedy was in the guest bedroom down the hall.

"It was a bitter cold day outside and it was kind of cold inside the house," Jill said. "It was dark and nasty outside. It had all the elements."

Until an interview for this book, Jill has never publicly talked in extensive detail about the accident and the immediate aftermath. Seated in a gazebo at her horse farm in the summer of 2013, when asked about the accident and her memories of it, she answered with a five-minute monologue. Rarely pausing, she explained the scene, her words tumbling forward from one recollection to the next in chronological order. Her tone was mournful but detached, perhaps a byproduct of the nearly twenty-five years that had passed.

"I was reading in our bedroom upstairs, a mystery book," she said. "There had been an accident in the book and someone in the book had to go get help and that's when my phone rang. I've always thought that was so odd, just a premonition.

"On the phone, someone said to me that there was an accident out front by the driveway and that I needed to come out right away. I threw on a pair of sweats and drove our other Ford vehicle down the driveway and it was just flashing lights and people scurrying around. It was dark and hard to see. This big burly guy, a fire department guy, said I couldn't go down where the accident was."

Jill could see the smashed front end of Billy's pickup truck. She screamed and cursed at the fireman, pushing past him as she ran through the iron gates.

"I saw Billy lying there and I knelt down in the snow next to him and tried to communicate with him," Jill said. "I held his head in my hands. His eyes were kind of in the back of his head. He wasn't responding but I told him I loved him and that we had so much more to live for. I wanted him to hold on. I said, 'Billy, stay here, don't go. There's a world out there for us to live. You have everything to live for.'"

Billy was limp and lifeless. Carol Reedy, who had hustled down the driveway, thought he looked like he was asleep. The wind was whipping as she ran to the truck where she saw her husband under a blanket still trapped by the dashboard.

The situation was harrowing with emergency workers trying to revive Billy, eager to get a response of any kind.

"But that wasn't happening," Jill said. "It was looking pretty bleak."

The snow was falling more heavily.

"We were obviously losing Billy," Jill said. "The ambulance was getting ready to take Billy to the hospital. But suddenly, they got a pulse so he was still alive."

Soon, Jill was in the back of the ambulance with Billy heading for the Wilson Memorial Hospital in nearby Johnson City, New York.

"They had to pull over a couple times to get his heart started again," Jill said. "There was a lot going on in the back of the ambulance. They were doing a lot of different things and looked worried. When we arrived at the hospital, they told me to wait in the ambulance and to not come in right away. And I told them I wasn't going to wait in the ambulance.

"Someone directed me into a private room, where I waited and I waited and I waited. At one point, I picked up the phone to use it. The line that I got, it was someone from the press asking point-blank questions of someone. And they weren't saying anything. I hung up and waited some more."

Reedy was pulled from the truck and driven to the emergency room as well. Doctors were concerned about nerve and vascular damage in his broken hip and prepared to transfer him to a trauma center in Syracuse, about seventy miles to the north. Local reporters had arrived in the emergency room waiting area pleading for information. Doctors were dashing in and out of the area, looking both harried and uneasy.

No one as famous had ever been seriously injured in the Binghamton region. The mayor was alerted and began to drive to the hospital. The police chief, the fire chief, and several Catholic priests were contacted, startled on an otherwise sleepy Christmas night by the news that Billy Martin was lying unconscious in Wilson Memorial Hospital.

Jill remained alone in a noiseless room. She paced.

Then, a doctor, whose name Jill never ascertained, entered the room. Jill spoke first:

"Are you coming in here to tell me my husband has died?"

The doctor replied, "Yes, I am."

Jill said she was then asked if she wanted to talk to the reporters who were waiting in the lobby. She declined. She instead asked to see Billy and was led to a bay of the emergency room. She went alongside the gurney and reached for Billy's hand.

"I had a few minutes with Billy and I talked to him," she said. "I felt the blood and the warmth rush away from his hand. I stayed for another few minutes, just talking. I told him I loved him and I told him that I would take care of everything and that I wouldn't let him down."

Jill returned to the private room where she had been waiting minutes earlier. On the way, she asked how she could get an outside phone line to make some calls. Then she called, in order, Billy Joe, Kelly Ann, and George Steinbrenner.

In the waiting room, Michael Doll, a hospital spokesman, told reporters that Billy had been pronounced dead of head and neck injuries and severe internal injuries at 6:56 p.m. Dr. Patrick Ruddy, the county coroner, added that Billy had "basically died of a broken neck." Billy also had a compressed spinal column.

Within minutes, the Associated Press and United Press International filed dispatches labeled URGENT, a designation reserved for major breaking news. The headline was YANKEES MANAGER BILLY MARTIN DIES IN AUTO ACCIDENT, which was a revealing slip-up because Billy was not the Yankees manager at the time.

The news filtered into newsrooms across the country. The timing meant that many evening television newscasts were interrupted with a bulletin: "Billy Martin dead at sixty-one." Around the nation, it was the most common way people learned of the accident. Since Billy was still the best-known baseball manager in America, it was weighty, substantial news. It was delivered by a dinnertime news program as a holiday was winding down.

"I was at home and having fun because Christmas is also my birthday," said Rickey Henderson. "There were people over and we were laughing and having a good time. But then the TV said Billy was dead. I ran over and I listened. The room went quiet and I fell to my knees. I couldn't believe that he could be gone. How could that happen?

"I got up and sat in a chair but I didn't eat or drink anything for probably a day. I just sat there crying or staring at the TV. Everyone went away and just left me sitting there."

Jill reached Kelly Ann's home but she was not there. Jill instead told the news to Kelly Ann's mother and Billy's first wife, Lois. The news spread in California, where there was haunting disbelief. Less than two weeks earlier, Billy had been shoulder to shoulder with his family and friends burying Jenny Downey. Some expected to see him again in a few days.

Jill left a voice mail at Billy Joe's house, but he was at his mother Gretchen's house on Christmas night. Then a friend of Gretchen's called with the news, having been alerted to it on her television.

"I started crying hysterically," Gretchen said. "And I remember saying, 'I'll never talk to him again.' I was so overcome I think it traumatized my son to the point where he did not shed a tear.

"It stunned him until he was in shock. He just said, 'I have to get to New York right now.' But the grief—our grief, his grief—was all-consuming."

Billy Joe went to his home where friends began to arrive.

"I may have been stoic at my mom's but when I got home I was a mess," Billy Joe said.

In Tampa, Steinbrenner talked with Jill and promised to take care of all the funeral and burial arrangements. Then he started calling various Yankees.

In a 1990 interview, Steinbrenner said he was at a loss for several moments.

"It wasn't just my sorrow; I didn't know who to call first," George said. "Billy meant so much to so many people. And how many people do I call? I couldn't figure out what to do. Billy touched so many people. Where do I start? There were so many calls to make."

One of those he called was Ron Guidry.

"I told Mr. Steinbrenner that it was an end of an era," Guidry said. "We'd move on but not quite the same. The Yankees would be different; baseball would be different. And part of that was because of what Billy had taught us all. He had that much impact."

Trainer Gene Monahan heard from Steinbrenner.

"I remembered the number of times Billy told me he loved me," Monahan said. "I remembered his compassion. And I thought, 'He really was like an old Wild West gunfighter to the end.' Those guys always leave us one night without warning. It figured that Billy would go like that — just *poof* and he's gone."

Willie Randolph answered the phone when Steinbrenner called. But he did not stay on the line long.

"I was too upset to talk to anyone," Randolph, renowned for his stolid countenance, said. "I put my wife on the phone. I couldn't control my emotions."

When reporters called the reliably accessible Randolph shortly thereafter, his wife took the calls and explained that her husband could not come to the phone. Try again tomorrow, she said.

Lou Piniella, who was skiing in Vermont, got the call, too.

"There was a snowstorm the next day, so going to New York right then wasn't possible," Piniella said. "We went to the local Catholic church and paid the priest to say a Mass for Billy. And my whole family sat there remembering Billy."

Don Mattingly heard the news at his sister's house in Indiana.

"I started telling people about how alive Billy became just before the first pitch of every game," Mattingly said. "That was his moment — pacing up and down in the dugout with his hands in his back pockets. It put a charge in everyone on the team. That was him at his best.

"But I also thought about the demons that went with him after the game. I thought about the alcohol and all the dangers that go with it. He was so brilliant, but there was a piece of him that was so tragic."

Earl Weaver was home when he got the news.

"I felt like part of me had died, too," Weaver said. "It hit me like that. It hit me harder than I thought it would. And I felt bad for baseball."

Bobby Richardson, who had played alongside Billy with the Yankees and become his successor at second base, received a call from a local reporter.

"I flashed back to the 1950s and how Billy willed those Yankees teams to victory," Richardson said. "I remembered the things people didn't know about Billy — like how many times we took a cab on a Sunday morning to church.

"And I realized that now Billy was with Casey again."

For some of Billy's friends, the unusual circumstances of his death only added to the shock and dismay. Battlin' Billy Martin died on a country road?

"It added kind of a heartbreaking element," said Steve Vucinich, the Oakland A's clubhouse manager and Billy's longtime confidant. "It made it feel so avoidable."

"An auto accident?" Rizzuto said, incredulously. "No, none of us saw that coming."

But others found meaning in the setting of the accident.

"Maybe it was finally a place for him to be at peace," said Rod Carew, who saw Billy as a father figure and became the star of the first team Billy managed in 1969. "It was his own quiet time.

"Instead of it being in a big city with noise, bright lights, and hoopla, it was somewhere serene and away from all that. I found comfort in that. I like that he left us in a peaceful place."

Jill returned to the house on Potter Hill Road on Christmas night, where housekeeper Mary Lynch was waiting for her.

"I made a stiff drink and started planning to leave for New York," she said. "George said he would have the funeral there and I was relieved he was taking care of that. He was wonderful.

"People were calling from around the country, from around the world in fact. They were getting ready to fly to New York from wherever they were. I left a few hours later. I didn't even remember to pack clothes."

Lynch stayed behind for a while to tidy up. The table had been set for dinner, so she put all the dishes, utensils, and glassware back in the cabinets. She removed the Christmas turkey from the oven. She put water at the base of the twenty-foot Christmas tree. She fed the animals in the barn and checked the quail brooder, which was still warm.

Then, before locking the doors and returning home, she took pictures of the farmhouse's first-floor walls, which were lined with memorabilia from Billy's career.

"Jill wanted me to do that to remember what it looked like that night," Lynch said. "But I took extra pictures because that was the stuff that Billy wanted to remember about his life.

"I figured if that's what he wanted to remember then maybe it was a good way for me to remember him."

There were pictures of Billy and Casey Stengel in the Yankees' dugout and a photograph of the 1953 world champion Yankees alongside a photo of the World Series–winning 1977 Yankees. There was a shot of Billy sitting with his mother in her kitchen at 1632 7th Street in West Berkeley. Billy had his arm around Jenny. They were singing.

There were pictures of teams from each of his managerial stops — Minnesota, Detroit, Texas, New York, and Oakland. There were pictures of Billy in an army uniform, Billy as a minor leaguer in Arizona, and Billy pouring champagne over the head of George Steinbrenner. There were pictures of his children and pictures of Billy hunting with Mickey Mantle and fishing with Whitey Ford. There were pictures of Billy at dinner with Joe DiMaggio, Marilyn Monroe, and Frank Sinatra.

There were pictures of Billy at spring training, Billy arguing with an umpire, and Billy doffing his cap for the crowd during his stunning resurrection in 1978 at Old Timers' Day.

There was an ink portrait of Billy that had become the 1981 cover of *Time* magazine and framed copies of the half-dozen times Billy graced the cover of *Sports Illustrated* — from April 1956 when he was identified as SPARKPLUG OF THE YANKEES, to May 1985 when the headline proclaimed, BILLY'S BACK.

Lynch took pictures until she ran out of film in her camera. Then she turned out the last light, closed the door, and drove toward the front gate, her tires crunching in the new snow. When she reached the end of the driveway, she saw broken glass and crumpled pieces of chrome. A sheriff sat in his cruiser at the crest of Potter Hill Road.

The multicolored Christmas lights in the evergreen trees bobbed in a gusty wind.

49

THE DAY AFTER BILLY'S death, Dr. Bobby Brown, Billy's former Yankees teammate, went to his mailbox and saw a letter with a return address he did not recognize: Potter Hill Road, Fenton, New York.

Inside, there was a Christmas card from Billy.

Brown was an established star when Billy arrived in the Yankees' clubhouse in 1950. He had watched Billy develop into a persevering player and inspiration to five championship teams, and he had witnessed Billy's managerial ascent in five American cities. Somewhat unhappily, when Brown was the American League president, he was frequently forced to spar with Billy. Brown disciplined him, fined him, and suspended him multiple times.

But on this day, December 26, 1989, he was holding a Christmas card from Billy's upstate New York home.

"Billy included a handwritten note," Brown said. "Billy was like that. He would write you something."

The newspaper on Brown's doorstep that day had a series of articles about the startling death of Billy Martin. Brown looked at the card in his hand.

"He wrote that he hoped we could get together for dinner after the holiday."

It was signed, "Your teammate, Billy."

In another part of the city that morning, Jill was having a late breakfast with Mickey Morabito, who had been visiting his mother on Staten Island for the holidays until he heard the news about Billy.

"Jill was pretty shaken up but she was composed, and she had to be because a lot was going on already," Morabito said.

The IRS that day had attached a lien on Billy's estate for unpaid back taxes in the amount of $86,137. Billy's family in Berkeley was furious that the funeral and burial were taking place in New York, and even more irritated that they had not been consulted about that decision. And while

Billy's body had already been sent to New York City, there was some controversy about that, too — and Jill was in the middle of the dispute.

The county coroner had initially not requested an autopsy of Billy's body. Bill Reedy had said he was the driver. The coroner considered Billy a victim of the accident as opposed to part of its cause, so he saw no reason to further examine Billy.

But now Reedy had changed his story. In light of Reedy's retraction, an autopsy on Billy's body might help prove who the driver was. A full autopsy would never be performed. Over the next couple of years, there were all kinds of theories as to how and why that came to be. There were reports that Jill had told doctors at the hospital that she was Jewish and that her religion forbade an autopsy. Other people have said that Steinbrenner interceded and used his influence with state authorities to get Billy's body whisked that night to the Frank E. Campbell Funeral Home on Madison Avenue in Manhattan.

At the heart of the matter, at no time did the upstate authorities ever seem eager to keep Billy's body. In 2013, Jill said she never brought up her religion.

"My father was of a Jewish heritage but my mother wasn't Jewish and we never practiced Judaism," she said. "It's just heritage. I don't know how Billy got to Campbell's funeral home. I just know that he did."

Before the funeral, however, a compromise was made and Billy's body was subjected to what was called a "visual autopsy" conducted by a noted New York City medical examiner and pathologist, Dr. Michael Baden. Baden agreed with the cause of death determined by the Binghamton-area coroner and concluded that Billy was the passenger, adding that Billy would have lived if he had worn a seat belt.

That was the behind-the-scenes drama. In the New York media, Billy's death remained a major story and dominated the headlines and newscasts throughout the final week of 1989. There were three well-attended and highly publicized wakes for Billy at the Campbell Funeral Home. Two were mostly private, with Howard Cosell as the principal speaker at the first one. Reporters did attend the wakes, quoting many of the attending celebrities.

"I think I still don't believe it," Mickey Mantle said during the second wake. "I keep thinking Billy will pop up and say, 'How ya' doing, pard?' Like this is all a big joke."

On Thursday, December 28, the public was invited to view Billy's body inside the funeral home. The line of fans who showed up stretched down Madison Avenue for two blocks. Police estimated the daylong crowd at about 2,500 people.

The Campbell Funeral Home had been hosting the wakes of prominent New Yorkers since 1898, and its rooms had seen overflowing crowds that arrived in tribute to everyone from Jimmy Cagney to Ed Sullivan to John Lennon. The throng that turned out for Billy was as big as any the funeral home had seen.

Billy was laid out in a chapel within the building, his Yankees jersey and Yankees cap nearby. He wore a dark blue suit, pink shirt, and multicolored tie. The casket was enveloped in flowers, including one arrangement in the shape of a number 1.

Bob Pecario came from his home in Berkeley Heights, New Jersey.

"Like a lot of people, I was a fan of Billy's all my life," he said. "He stood up for the little guy. He was one of us. That's why we're all here."

The waiting crowd was old and young, white, black, and Latino. There were laborers and white-collar workers who stepped away from nearby office buildings.

Yankees fan William Brady drove down from Niagara Falls.

"I had to come down and see him today," Brady said. "He meant too much to me. I had to be here."

Mike Moran took a train from his home in Secaucus, New Jersey.

"I'm not naive and I know Billy had his faults," Moran said. "But there was more to him than that. He was a good guy caught in some tough spots. I think everyone knew that and understood his passion. We loved his passion. We forgave him the rest."

Although a Mets fan, Ramon Fontanez parked his cab a couple of blocks from the funeral home so he could pay his respects. Fontanez did so, he said, because he respected Billy's accomplishments and because he thought Billy made New York a better place.

Tony Inniss, a forty-year-old from Round Lake, New York, was first in line for the viewing, wearing a wool ski cap as he stood on the Madison Avenue sidewalk at 7:00 a.m. Temperatures were in the twenties. The doors did not open until 10:00 a.m.

"I'm here because Billy was a true Yankee and a man that I loved," Inniss told the *New York Post*. "He was brash but a real person with a soft spot. And for a lot of us he was the true embodiment of the New York Yankees."

In line about ten persons behind Inniss, Kevin Dumont, a Yankees fan from Staten Island, had arrived at 8:00 a.m.

"I was home when one of my friends called me on Christmas to say it was too bad about Billy Martin and I thought he was joking," Dumont said. "When I found out it was true, I went into my room and just started crying so hard I couldn't catch my breath. I didn't stop crying for about two hours."

Dumont said that he met Billy once outside Yankee Stadium when he and two friends had called out to Billy as he made his way to his car.

"He came over and after we got an autograph he said he wanted to buy us a drink," Dumont said. "He gave us $20 and told us to go have a beer for him. And we did. For $20, we had two or three beers."

The morning after the public viewing of Billy's body, Cardinal John O'Connor officiated at a funeral Mass at St. Patrick's Cathedral. It was Friday, December 29, and the cathedral's seats were full with rows of people standing five deep in the back and beside the pews. Alcoves, side altars, and vestibules at the cathedral's supplementary entrances were jammed. Officials from the Archdiocese of New York estimated that 3,000 people were inside the cathedral, which has a listed capacity of 2,400.

Morabito, Randolph, Mantle, Ford, Art Fowler, and Steinbrenner were pallbearers. Scores of other past and present Yankees were in attendance, as were executives and players from several other teams and dozens of New York dignitaries.

Jill sat in a front pew with Billy Joe, Kelly Ann, Mantle, Steinbrenner, and former president Richard M. Nixon, who in the 1980s lived in New Jersey and was a frequent visitor to Yankee Stadium.

"I looked around and in the crowd I saw all kinds of people I knew," Morabito said. "There were about five umpires at the funeral. It felt like half of Major League Baseball was there. Three of Billy's wives were there. Lois was the only one who couldn't make it, but then Kelly Ann was there for her."

Ron Perranoski, Billy's bullpen closer with the Minnesota Twins and Detroit Tigers, flew up from Florida.

"After he died I was so upset I was pacing around my house," Perranoski said. "My wife said, 'You should go to the funeral; you'll feel better.'

"I'm glad I came but I don't know that I feel better. I'm so sad."

The service lasted seventy minutes. Rev. Edwin Broderick opened his eulogy with a line that drew laughter from the crowd.

"At first blush, this cathedral is undoubtedly the last place you'd expect to find Billy," Broderick said.

When the quip was later repeated to Billy's sisters, who did not attend the funeral in protest over its location, they were incensed.

"Bill always went to church," Pat Irvine said. "That wasn't the right thing to say."

But inside the cathedral, it seemed to break the ice.

"Billy gave us thrills and spills, ups and downs, but his was an interesting show with exciting and different endings," Broderick said. "Despite all his bravado and bravura, Billy was a warm, sentimental, kind person, generous with his time and money."

Broderick continued: "Billy always wore his St. Christopher's medal and carried a rumpled prayer card to St. Jude in his pocket. We pray that his is a safe slide into home plate. It seems a coincidence that Billy went home to God on Christmas Day."

The crowd, many of whom were wearing Yankees jackets and other apparel of the team, burst into applause when Broderick concluded, "Billy is with all the other Yankee greats now. They are together in an eternal World Series."

Billy's casket, draped in a white cloth, was carried out of the church with his family walking a few steps behind.

"As we got close to the door, I was convulsing in sobs," Billy Joe said. "I felt a little weak and unsteady. At that moment, I felt someone grab my arm. It was Richard Nixon. He said to me, 'I want you to see all the people that loved your father.'

"And he led me outside so I could look at the sea of people in the streets. It was a mass of thousands. President Nixon said, 'Those are all the people your father touched.'" Police had set up barricades along Fifth Avenue and 50th Street. A crowd of about five thousand stood behind the barriers ten deep. St. Patrick's Cathedral, built in the 1870s of stone and marble, takes up a city block. Billy's mourners had enveloped the entire cathedral block. More people were waiting on other side streets and north of the cathedral.

"I had never seen a New York crowd like that for anything other than a major parade," said Randolph, who grew up in Brooklyn. "The last time I saw a crowd like that was our ticker-tape parade after the 1977 champion-ship."

Billy Joe stood with Richard Nixon on the steps of the cathedral.

"I'll never forget that sight," he said twenty-five years later. "It was a sorrowful day but it is a wonderful memory."

The crowd, most wearing scarves with their collars pulled up to their ears, waited despite the bitter cold. Reporters conducting interviews outside the cathedral found people who had come from as far away as California, Texas, and Minnesota. It was a reverent gathering, quiet and solemn, as Billy's casket descended the steps leading to a long black hearse.

Rudy Stallone of Long Island, who was standing across from the cathedral on Fifth Avenue, had his son, Paul, on his shoulders.

"He's three years old so he might not remember this," Stallone said. "But I want to tell him one day that he was here. My father is a Yankees fan and a Billy fan. I'm a Yankees fan and a Billy fan. Hopefully, one day my son will be a Yankees fan and a Billy fan."

Jill recalled that she and other family members got into a limousine behind the hearse. The radio was on.

"That Clint Black song, 'I'm Leaving Here a Better Man,' came on the radio which seemed like fate," she said. "We just jacked it up to all levels. It was so appropriate.

"I remember that all along the streets, there were so many people on the curb. It went on like that for block after block."

The motorcade rolled past Yankee Stadium where the marquee outside the huge ballpark read: BILLY MARTIN, ALWAYS NUMBER ONE.

The Gate of Heaven Cemetery in Hawthorne, New York, about twenty-five miles northeast of New York City, was built by the trustees of St. Patrick's Cathedral in 1917. Its 260 acres are home to the gravesites of many famous New Yorkers, but none better known than Babe Ruth.

The day after Billy died, the Yankees called the cemetery. The cemetery said it had a plot available about thirty yards from Ruth's final resting place.

It was a flat spot not far from the cemetery access road with a tree nearby that offered ample shade. Billy's funeral procession stopped just below the area. The walk to the gravesite was short. Huddled against the cold and wind, Billy's closest friends and family, his pallbearers, and many of his former players gathered for a brief graveside service. The congregation was led in two quiet prayers.

"Everyone was kind of leaning on each other," Jill recalled. "We were bracing against the cold and the sorrow."

The service lasted no more than ten minutes. The Gate of Heaven workers on duty — gravediggers, landscapers, office workers, and clerics — stopped what they were doing and assembled near the gravesite, watching from a respectful distance. There were final goodbyes beside Billy's casket, and then the funeral procession began its return trip to Manhattan. From there, the mourners scattered; many of the ballplayers attended a private reception at Mickey Mantle's restaurant across from Central Park. Jill remained with her family, who had arrived en masse from California. A day later, she returned to Fenton, where she spent a somber New Year's Eve at the farmhouse.

Soon, it was a new year and a new decade, the last of the century. The page had turned. The festive ceremonies on opening day of the Yankees' 1990 season were interrupted for a moment of silence in Billy's honor. The players also wore a black armband on their uniforms to commemorate Billy.

On June 6, Bucky Dent was fired.

By then, a handsome gray headstone commissioned by George Steinbrenner had appeared next to Billy's grave.

At its base, the tombstone has one long, horizontal rectangular piece bisected by a vertical piece of granite about five feet in height. The center of the vertical stone is inscribed with large block letters:

MARTIN

Below that, in smaller writing, it reads:

ALFRED MANUEL
"BILLY"
MAY 16, 1928 — DECEMBER 25, 1989

Both ends of the horizontal piece of the headstone are decorated with carved cutouts of the number 1. There is a sculpture of St. Jude at the left end of the stone. On the right, there is a quotation:

> I may not have been the greatest Yankee to put on
> the uniform but I was the proudest.

Andrew Nagle, the associate director of the trustees of St. Patrick's Cathedral, oversees the Gate of Heaven Cemetery. A lifelong Yankees fan who grew up in the South Bronx, Nagle said a steady stream of fans make their way to Billy's grave every year and have done so nonstop since 1989.

"His grave gets the same attention year after year," Nagle said. "It has never slowed. Sometimes, it's a sixty-five-year-old guy showing the grave to his thirty-five-year-old son, and sometimes it's a bunch of out-of-town Yankees fans who come here before they go to a game at Yankee Stadium. But they always drive up here. The attention never stops.

"And everyone wants to take a picture next to the 'proudest Yankee' quote. I'm told Billy said that when they retired his number at Yankee Stadium. People just love that quote."

Frequently, visitors leave things at the grave, little tributes to celebrate their memories of Billy.

"It might be an old Billy Martin baseball card or a picture of Billy," Nagle said. "Or a baseball bat, a poster, or anything with a Yankees logo. People want to leave some acknowledgment of what he meant to them. Most of all, they leave baseballs."

The most popular inscription on the baseballs left behind is "Billy Ball."

One day in 2013, workers passing Billy's grave found another baseball. There was a small piece of paper beneath it. In the uneven, shaky penmanship of a child, it read:

Hi Mr. Martin, my team has a tournament this weekend — wish us luck.
My Dad says you are his favorite Yankee ever.

The tokens left behind do not surprise Nagle.

"We don't let go of the people that touched us," Nagle said. "We see that all the time in a cemetery. It's why people come to a grave. It's the same with Billy Martin.

"People won't let him go. They won't forget him."

THROUGH THE 2014 BASEBALL season, there were twenty-two managers in the Baseball Hall of Fame. Billy Martin is not one of them. As a manager, Billy has a higher winning percentage than thirteen of the Hall of Fame managers, including Tony La Russa, Tommy Lasorda, Casey Stengel, Sparky Anderson, Whitey Herzog, Dick Williams, and Joe Torre.

Three other Hall of Fame managers — Bobby Cox, Walter Alston, and Miller Huggins — had winning percentages that were no more than .005 higher than Billy's career winning percentage of .553.

But, clearly, induction into the Hall of Fame is predicated on more than winning percentage, as it should be. The number of championships won is a factor, and Billy won one World Series.

Four other managers in the Hall of Fame — Herzog, Cox, Earl Weaver, and Leo Durocher — also won only a single World Series. Another Hall of Fame manager, Al Lopez, never won the World Series at all.

As a thirty-year member of the Baseball Writers' Association of America, which is the principal voting group that determines who is inducted into the Hall of Fame, I have been a party to the debates about Hall of Fame worthiness for decades. There are infrequent times when the voting verdict is incontrovertible. There are usually a myriad of contributing considerations and side issues to weigh. In Billy's case, there is at least one that might be significant when assessing his record.

Unlike Lasorda, La Russa, Torre, Anderson, Cox, and Herzog, Billy never managed in the era of wild card playoff teams. In Billy's sixteen years as a manager, five of his teams went to the playoffs. If the modern wild card format had been in effect when Billy was managing, six more of his teams would have qualified for the postseason, which would have given him six more chances to win another World Series.

These statistics could make a case for Billy's induction into the Hall of Fame, and two of the recent managerial inductees — La Russa and Cox — are steadfast in their support of Billy's candidacy. But statistics ignore the obvious reason Billy is not in baseball's most august and honored fraternity. As much as Billy is known for winning teams, as much as he is with-out peer for his almost magical ability to resurrect dormant teams, Billy is probably best known for getting in drunken barroom brawls, warring with his bosses, and kicking dirt on umpires. And, especially late in life, Billy had a serious drinking problem.

Those are not the usual Hall of Fame credentials.

Even if many of the managers now in the Hall of Fame drank heav-ily, got in off-the-field fistfights, and mercilessly kicked dirt on umpires, those transgressions did not stick to those managers the way Billy's mis-steps stuck to him.

There is no one to blame for that. More so than his contemporaries, Billy treated his life as an open book. He hid nothing. He let his excesses or his most indecorous habits be known.

He knew nothing of public relations and did not care to learn about it. And for most of his life, in pivotal times, he had a problem controlling his temper.

For a public figure, it is not the best combination.

Alcoholism is an insidious disease, and it clearly brought turmoil to Billy's later life. It took a terrible toll on him physically, cost him jobs, brought stress to his personal affairs — not to mention to those around him. In the end, it likely contributed to his Christmas Day demise.

More than a quarter-century later, it is easy to surmise that Billy's drinking problem would be treated very differently now. Ours is a culture in which public figures freely and unashamedly admit to needing help for a drinking habit that has spiraled out of control. Friends and families often intervene to ease the transition to a nondrinking life. Professional counseling is available in virtually every town in America, and there is no stigma to asking for help.

Little of that was readily available to Billy in his times. Moreover, he was immersed in a very different culture — both society-wide and in baseball — one that largely looked the other way when it came to drink-ing in excess.

"It was as if alcoholism did not exist back then — certainly not in base-ball," said Marty Appel, the Yankees' public relations chief and broadcast executive in the 1970s and 1980s who spent countless hours at Billy's side. "Baseball almost encouraged drinking, with the long hours after games and all the travel on the road. It was like the manly thing to do.

"I never once heard anyone say a word about how Billy might need help with his drinking. No one ever said anything to his face either. If Billy was tipsy — and he wouldn't be the only one when that happened — people just smiled and winked."

Which leads to a fascinating thought: What if Billy Martin had been born in 1948 instead of 1928?

His might have been an entirely different story. There is no guarantee that he would have addressed his drinking problem, but it seems far more likely that he would have been comfortable seeking help, which is an essential, elemental first step. Perhaps, then, he would still be here to tell us his story.

But that is not what happened. The baseball genius who developed before a captivated, charmed national audience was indeed flawed on many levels. People loved him anyway. People may have loved him more because of his imperfections. They made him seem familiar, which is to say, one of us.

Then and now, acknowledging that Billy had faults should not obscure the complete picture of an engaging, dynamic, memorable life full of accomplishment. Sadly, losses and devastating personal failures were part of Billy's story. Happily, they were far from the whole story.

And what a story it was.

ACKNOWLEDGMENTS

NO BOOK HAPPENS BY accident. It takes a few breaks and a lot of help from others.

To that end, in the roughly thirty months I was working on this book, people often asked me how I came up with the idea. I told them I always had the idea, I just didn't know it.

In 2011, at lunch with Houghton Mifflin Harcourt editor Susan Canavan, with whom I had worked on a previous book, I somehow started telling Billy Martin stories. It was a habit whenever someone asked about the most fascinating people I had covered.

"Billy Martin would make a great book," Susan said.

So the first thank-you goes to Susan, and it is a big one. Susan also shepherded the manuscript through the many months and was a wise eye during revisions and amendments. Susan always remained the book's biggest ally.

My agent, Scott Waxman, knew how to keep things moving, too, and was always there with his counsel and expertise.

Within weeks of beginning this project I reached out to Billy Martin's family and closest friends. Part of me expected them to be weary of explaining a complicated personality like Billy Martin — especially after all these years. Instead, Billy's family was welcoming and forever helpful, most notably Billy's only son, Billy Martin Jr., who was the go-to guy who opened countless doors for me.

Gretchen Creswell, Billy's wife of nearly twenty years, was also immensely accommodating and gracious and as a witness to decades of Billy's life was an invaluable resource. In fact, I was in touch with each of Billy's four wives, which was an illuminating experience and something that, to my knowledge, no other journalist or biographer has done for an article or a book.

Those interviews included several with Billy's widow, Jilluann Martin-Valliere, who has not spoken to reporters for roughly a quarter-century. My thanks to Jill for trusting me with her recollections of life with Billy, for her plainspoken willingness to elucidate her perspective, and for her memories of the final stages of Billy's life.

Other members of Billy's family and his friends from childhood were amazingly perspicacious, especially his sister Pat Irvine, cousins Mario and Nick DeGennaro, and Billy's lifelong friend Lew Figone. Many of the West Berkeley Boys are alive and well, too, and while they might not be marching up and down the East Bay hills to annoy the Goats any longer, they are still great company and raconteurs.

The same goes for Billy's many 1950s teammates and the players who played under him from Minnesota to Detroit to Texas to New York to Oakland and back to New York.

Not long after I began this project, I headed to the Baseball Hall of Fame in Cooperstown. The Hall of Fame's president, Jeff Idelson, gave me a big boost early in my research, handing over many contact numbers and doling out some interview advice. The Hall of Fame library and its voluminous files were a significant asset. Thanks to John Horne for his help with the photo archives. I hope the greater baseball community knows what a priceless resource and treasure the Baseball Hall of Fame is.

At the same time, I can't imagine writing a historical baseball book without websites like baseball-reference.com and retrosheet.org. The latter is almost like sorcerer's magic when it comes to uncovering the smallest details of games from half a century ago.

I also want to thank my buddies on the baseball beat from the mid- to late 1980s and beyond — Michael Kay, Bob Klapisch, Moss Klein, Bill Madden, Michael Martinez, the late, great Mike McAlary, Marty Noble, Tom Pedulla, Claire Smith, and Tom Verducci.

If we did not realize we were living through historic times, it was only because we were too busy having fun.

I am indebted to the many journalists who so scrupulously documented Billy's career and life day after day. This went on from the 1940s to the 1980s. Somewhere in the middle of that span, Murray Chass must have written nearly a thousand articles about Billy (and I read them all). The same is true for Phil Pepe, Steve Jacobsen, Dave Anderson, and, years earlier, Milton Richman, Leonard Koppett, and John Drebinger, who somehow covered 203 consecutive World Series games from 1929 to 1963.

At the *New York Times,* Tom Jolly, Jason Stallman, and Jay Schrieber have helped guide my career in abundant ways and made me be a better reporter and writer. At Houghton Mifflin Harcourt, I benefited from the ever-thorough copy editor Barbara Wood, publicist Laura Gianino, the intrepid Chesalon Piccione, and executive manuscript editor Larry Cooper.

The Yankees' Jason Zillo paved the way for multiple interviews as did John Blake with the Texas Rangers. Thanks to Mickey Morabito for being a key eyewitness to much of Billy's life and for having such a terrific memory. The same is true for Morabito's predecessor, Marty Appel, and Morabito's successors, Harvey Greene and Lou D'Ermilio.

I am forever thankful to hundreds of baseball people who happily shared their stories, and special thanks go to Bobby Richardson, Lou Piniella, Willie Randolph, Ron Guidry, Gene Michael, Gene Monahan, and Buck Showalter.

I am grateful to Rhoda and Bob Lerman, who happened to buy Billy's final home in upstate New York. When I knocked on their door unannounced in August 2013, they took me in and rounded up the neighbors for five entertaining, informative hours.

As she did for my previous books, my wife, Joyce, threw herself into the research of the manuscript without being asked. I now assume that I have the greatest library of Billy Martin material on the planet — thousands of newspaper clippings dating from 1942, plus books, magazines, photos, videotapes, DVDs, blog posts, memorabilia, FBI files, correspondence, and cartoons. The files created are now stored in a big, dull cabinet, but their vibrant, real-time words and brilliant images breathed life into every page of the book. Joyce's work was a contribution beyond any other in this project.

My children, Anne D., Elise, and Jack, were also drawn into the venture on numerous occasions, whether it was reading random old baseball books and summarizing key chapters, transcribing interview tapes, or finding obscure videos of long-ago games and Billy Martin television appearances. I'm sure they thought it would never end. I appreciate their everlasting willingness to help.

As everyone in baseball knows, you can't win without teammates. I've been fortunate to have some of the best on my side.

NOTES ON RESEARCH AND SOURCES

I BEGAN THE RESEARCH for this book roughly thirty years before I ever wrote a word of it. I first met Billy Martin in 1980 as a young reporter just out of college, but a few years earlier I had been a Boston college student in the stands at Fenway Park watching with the rest of the baseball world as Billy and Reggie Jackson almost duked it out in the visitors' dugout.

I had never seen that before. It is the kind of thing that sticks in the mind of a developing writer. As a traveling beat writer in the 1980s covering the Yankees for the *Bergen Record* and a syndicate of other smaller New Jersey newspapers, I got to know Billy well and also spent countless hours with those who played for him and against him. I also knew Billy's contemporaries in the managerial ranks, heard the umpires complain about him and laugh with him. It was part of my job to have close, professional relationships with many in his inner circle, like his coaches, his confidants, and his ex-teammates from the 1950s Yankees. I also developed a rapport with George Steinbrenner and was a part of hundreds of interviews with the Yankees' owner, including several one-on-one conversations at breakfast, lunch, or during meetings in his office. Billy Martin was often a central figure in those Steinbrenner talks, including three interviews about Billy after his death.

I relate these years-long associations to explain that much of the reporting for the book I did personally — if subconsciously — in the 1980s and in subsequent years as a reporter for the *New York Times*. I did not know for certain that I was going to write a book about Billy at the time, but it was a recurring thought in the back of my mind. Besides, as a New York baseball writer, it was my job to chronicle Billy's life.

And so, I was frequently witness to many of the scenes, games, and postgame settings described in these pages from 1980 to 1989.

As just one of many examples, I was there at the Cross Keys Inn for Billy's four-round fight with pitcher Ed Whitson. My hotel room, in fact, was across the hall from Billy's that night as he emerged with a swollen, broken arm. In the research for this book, I still gathered the recollections of many others from that memorable night and so many others, but inevitably — and fortuitously — the reporting of those turbulent days and nights was greatly informed by being there.

As an aside, or perhaps a badge of honor, Billy also wanted to beat me up one night in a Cleveland bar in 1986. It was a misunderstanding — as many of Billy's fights were — but I'll never forget that he had a firm grip on my hand as he tried to escort me outside "to settle our differences." The sagacious, all-seeing Yankees traveling secretary, Killer Kane, talked Billy out of his simmering rage. The next day, Billy apologized — in his own way.

"I don't remember what made me so mad at you," he said.

"So, instead, kid," he continued, "I'm going to forget about it."

In 2011, as the prospect of this book became a reality, I began roughly three years of interviewing to flesh out the details, facts, stories, highs, lows, and specifics of the entirety of Billy's life. I went back to the dozens of players and coaches whom I knew and approached others I did not know to reconstruct my memories and theirs. With the perspective of twenty-five or thirty years, many of the stories came alive with new insight. People often spoke more frankly than they might have before. Time seems to afford almost everyone a new level of perspicacity.

I was also fortunate that there is a long, vibrant assembly of Billy's family and friends, teammates, coaches, associates, adversaries, and players from his birth in 1928 to his death who are available, accessible, and eager to talk about a memorable figure in their lives. I contacted about 225 people whose lives intersected with Billy's in some way — players, baseball executives, managers, coaches, fans, clubhouse workers, trainers, umpires, bartenders, chauffeurs, waitresses, writers, broadcasters, agents, filmmakers, advertising executives, counselors, teachers, subway workers, restaurateurs, hotel managers, and certainly a few others in walks of life I cannot now recall. Billy got around.

For factual veracity, I was lucky that New York City had more than ten daily newspapers in the 1950s, and the New York Public Library has meticulously kept most of them on file. That was a bountiful source of material on Billy's playing days with the Yankees. Countless stories — roughly ten to fifteen a day from the busy and famed New York sportswriters of the era — bolstered the narrative immensely. The same is true for the well-organized online archives of the *New York Times* and the files of the Baseball Hall of Fame library. The Baseball Hall of Fame also has a thick Billy Martin file with stories, photos, cartoons, and some of Billy's personal papers, including personal anecdotes handwritten in Billy's neat penmanship. The archives of the *Berkeley Gazette* and *Oakland Tribune* were also helpful, as was Billy's pivotal autobiography, *Number One,* written in 1980 with Peter Golenbock at a critical and emotional juncture in Billy's life.

The following is a list of people who granted interviews, or multiple interviews, for this book. The list excludes a handful of club officials or ex-teammates who received anonymity because they were describing scenes they did not feel authorized, or comfortable, speaking about on the record because they were still employed by the Yankees or another Major League team.

INTERVIEW SUBJECTS
Sandy Alderson, Maury Allen, Joe Altobelli, Dave Anderson, Sparky Anderson, Marty Appel, Jesse Barfield, Larry Barnett, Allen Barra, Hank Bauer, Don Baylor, Lois Berndt, Carmen Berra, Dale Berra, Yogi Berra, Paul Blair, Johnny Blanchard, Clete Boyer, Ralph Branca, George Brett, Bobby Brown, Gates Brown, Jay Buhner, Bert Campaneris, Rod Carew, Howard Cassady, Bill Castell, Rick Cerone, Rick Cerrone, Bob Cerv, Chris Chambliss, Jack Clark, Jerry Coleman, Mark Connor, Don Cooper, Bobby Cox, Gretchen Creswell, Ron Davis, Ruben de Alba, Mario DeGennaro, Nick DeGennaro, Rick Dempsey, Bucky Dent, Lou D'Ermilio, Mel Duezabou, Joe Durso, Heather Ervolino, Gerald Eskenazi, Jim Evans, Dan Ewald, Lew Figone, Ron Fimrite, Rollie Fingers, Whitey Ford, Art Fowler, Johnny Franklin, Bill Freehan, Jim Fregosi, Augie Galan, Randy Galloway, Rich Garcia, Bob Geren, Tex Gernand, Frank Gifford, Rich Gossage, Dallas Green, Jerry Green, Harvey Greene, Tom Grieve, Cecilio Guante, Ron Guidry, Bill Guilfoile, Ray Hagar, Mike Hargrove, Toby Harrah, Sid Hartman, Ron Hassey, Mike Heath, Rickey Henderson, Joan Holland, Doug Holmquist, Willie Horton, Frank Howard, Roy Howell, Jeff Idelson, Pat Irvine, Jerry Izenberg, Reggie Jackson, Steve Jacobsen, Ferguson Jenkins, Betty Jenks, Tommy John, Al Kaline, Bill Kane, Michael Kay, Matt Keough, Harmon Killebrew, Clyde King, Ron Kittle, Moss Klein, Tony Kubek, Lerrin LaGrow, Jack Lang, Don Larsen, Tony La Russa, Tommy Lasorda, Cookie Lavagetto, Ron LeFlore, Eddie Leish-

man, Al Leiter, Bob Lerman, Rhoda Lerman, Mickey Lolich, Sparky Lyle, Mary Lynch, Fred Lynn, Elliott Maddox, Kevin Manahan, Mickey Mantle, Charlie Manuel, Bruce Markusen, Billy Martin Jr., Jill Martin-Valliere, Don Mattingly, Dick McAuliffe, Steve McCatty, Gil McDougald, Tom McEwen, Bobby Meacham, Sam Mele, Doug Melvin, Matt Merola, Stump Merrill, Frank Messer, Gene Michael, George Mitterwald, Gene Monahan, Bill Monbouquette, Jackie Moore, John Moore, Mickey Morabito, Diana Munson, Bobby Murcer, Kay Murcer, Dwayne Murphy, Andrew Nagle, Graig Nettles, Phil Niekro, Ken Nigro, Howard Noble, Mike Norris, Jim Northrup, Tony Oliva, Mike Pagliarulo, Jim Palmer, Dan Pasqua, Tom Pedulla, Phil Pepe, Ron Perranoski, Gaylord Perry, Jimmy Piersall, Lou Piniella, Boog Powell, Nick Priori, Ed Randall, Lenny Randle, Willie Randolph, Dennis Rasmussen, Bill Reedy, Rick Rhoden, Bobby Richardson, Arthur Richman, Dave Righetti, Bill Rigney, Cal Ripken, Mickey Rivers, Phil Rizzuto, Spencer Ross, Billy Sample, Rafael Santana, Eddie Sapir, Dale Scott, Jack Setzer, Buck Showalter, Charlie Silvera, Lou Skizas, Bill Skowron, Don Slaught, Roy Smalley, Duke Snider, Jim Spencer, Davey Springer, George Steinbrenner, Hank Steinbrenner, Tim Stoddard, Pat Summerall, Jim Sundberg, Bob Tewksbury, Syd Thrift, Dick Tidrow, Wayne Tolleson, Joe Torre, Mike Torrez, Bob Uecker, Steve Vucinich, Earl Wagstaff, Lee Walls, Earl Weaver, Bill White, Roy White, Ed Whitson, Stan Williams, Dave Winfield, Bob Wolff, Dick Young, Bill Zagaris, Don Zimmer.

BIBLIOGRAPHY

BOOKS

Allen, Maury. *Damn Yankee: The Billy Martin Story.* New York: Times Books, 1980.

Anderson, Dave. *The New York Times Story of the Yankees: 382 Articles, Profiles and Essays from 1903 to Present.* New York: Black Dog & Leventhal Publishers, 2012.

Appel, Martin. *Pinstripe Empire: The New York Yankees from Before the Babe to After the Boss.* New York: Bloomsbury, 2012.

Appel, Marty. *Now Pitching for the Yankees: Spinning the News for Mickey, Billy, and George.* Toronto: Sport Classic Books, 2001.

Araton, Harvey. *Driving Mr. Yogi: Yogi Berra, Ron Guidry, and Baseball's Greatest Gift.* Boston: Houghton Mifflin Harcourt, 2012.

Archibald, Joe. *The Billy Martin Story.* New York: J. Messner, 1959.

Baylor, Don, and Claire Smith. *Don Baylor: Nothing but the Truth, a Baseball Life.* New York: St. Martin's Press, 1989.

Coffey, Frank. *The Wit and Wisdom of George Steinbrenner.* New York: Signet, 1993.

Cramer, Richard Ben. *Joe DiMaggio: The Hero's Life.* New York: Simon & Schuster, 2000.

Creamer, Robert W. *Stengel: His Life and Times.* New York: Simon & Schuster, 1984.

Daley, Arthur. *Sports of the Times: The Arthur Daley Years.* New York: Quadrangle/New York Times Books, 1975.

DeMarco, Michael. *Dugout Days: Untold Tales and Leadership Lessons From the Extraordinary Career of Billy Martin.* New York: AMACOM, 2001.

Duren, Ryne, and Tom Sabellico. *I Can See Clearly Now: Ryne Duren Talks from the Heart About Life, Baseball, and Alcohol.* Chula Vista, CA: Aventine Press, 2003.

Falkner, David. *The Last Yankee: The Turbulent Life of Billy Martin.* New York: Simon & Schuster, 2009.

Ford, Whitey, and Mickey Mantle. *Whitey and Mickey: A Joint Autobiography of the Yankee Years.* New York: Viking Press, 1977.

Golenbock, Peter. *Wild, High and Tight: The Life and Death of Billy Martin.* New York: St. Martin's Press, 1994.

Halberstam, David. *The Fifties.* New York: Villard Books, 1993.

Jackson, Reggie, and Kevin Baker. *Becoming Mr. October.* New York: Doubleday, 2013.

Jackson, Reggie, and Mike Lupica. *Reggie: The Autobiography.* New York: Villard Books, 1984.

James, Bill. *The Bill James Baseball Abstract, 1985.* New York: Ballantine Books, 1985.

Klapisch, Bob. *High and Tight: The Rise and Fall of Dwight Gooden and Darryl Strawberry.* New York: Villard Books, 1996.

Leavy, Jane. *The Last Boy: Mickey Mantle and the End of America's Childhood.* New York: Harper Perennial, 2011.

Luciano, Ron, and David Fisher. *The Umpire Strikes Back.* Toronto: Bantam, 1983.

Madden, Bill, and Moss Klein. *Damned Yankees: A No-Holds-Barred Account of Life with "Boss" Steinbrenner.* New York: Warner Books, 1990.

Mahler, Jonathan. *Ladies and Gentlemen, the Bronx Is Burning: 1977, Baseball, Politics, and the Battle for the Soul of a City.* New York: Farrar, Straus and Giroux, 2005.

Mann, Arthur. *The Jackie Robinson Story.* New York: Grosset & Dunlap, 1956.

Mantle, Merlyn. *A Hero All His Life.* New York: HarperCollins Publishers, 1996.

Mantle, Mickey. *The Quality of Courage.* Garden City, NY: Doubleday, 1964.

Mantle, Mickey, and Phil Pepe. *My Favorite Summer, 1956.* New York: Doubleday, 1991.

Markusen, Bruce. *Baseball's Last Dynasty: Charlie Finley's Oakland A's.* Indianapolis, IN: Masters Press, 1998.

Martin, Billy, and Peter Golenbock. *Number 1.* New York: Delacorte Press, 1980.

Martin, Billy, and Phil Pepe. *Billyball.* Garden City, NY: Doubleday, 1987.

Masters, Todd. *The 1972 Detroit Tigers: Billy Martin and the Half-Game Champs.* Jefferson, NC: McFarland, 2010.

McMillan, Ken, and Ed Randall with Bruce Markusen. *Amazing Tales From the New York Yankees Dugout.* New York: Sports Publishing, 2012.

Montville, Leigh. *Ted Williams: The Biography of an American Hero.* New York: Broadway Books, 2005.

Murcer, Bobby, and Glen Waggoner. *Yankee for Life: My 40-Year Journey in Pinstripes.* New York: Harper, 2008.

Negron, Ray, and Sally Cook. *Yankee Miracles: Life with the Boss and the Bronx Bombers.* New York: Liveright Publishing, 2012.

Pepe, Phil. *The Ballad of Billy and George: The Tempestuous Baseball Marriage of Billy Martin and George Steinbrenner.* Guilford, CT: Lyons Press, 2008.

Piniella, Lou, and Maury Allen. *Sweet Lou.* New York: Putnam's, 1986.

Podell-Raber, Mickey, and Charles Pignone. *The Copa: Jules Podell and the Hottest Club North of Havana.* New York: HarperCollins, 2007.

Prato, Greg. *Just Out of Reach: The 1980s New York Yankees.* Published by Greg Prato, 2014.

Randolph, Willie. *The Yankee Way: Playing, Coaching, and My Life in Baseball.* New York: HarperCollins, 2014.

Ritter, Lawrence S. *East Side, West Side: Tales of New York Sporting Life, 1910–1960.* New York: Total Sports, 1998.

Schoor, Gene. *Billy Martin.* Garden City, NY: Doubleday, 1980.

Shropshire, Mike. *Seasons in Hell: With Billy Martin, Whitey Herzog, and "the Worst Baseball Teams in History," the 1973–1975 Texas Rangers.* New York: D. I. Fine, 1996.

Smith, Red. *Strawberries in the Wintertime: The Sporting World of Red Smith.* New York: Quadrangle/New York Times Books, 1974.

Stout, Glenn, and Richard A. Johnson. *Yankees Century: 100 Years of New York Yankees Baseball.* Boston: Houghton Mifflin, 2002.

Thorn, John. *Glory Days: New York Baseball 1947–1957.* New York: HarperCollins, 2008.

Vancil, Mark, and Alfred Santasiere. *Yankee Stadium: The Official Retrospective.* New York: Pocket Books, 2008.

Winfield, Dave, and Thomas Trebitsch Parker. *Winfield: A Player's Life.* New York: W. W. Norton, 1988.

Wolff, Bob. *Bob Wolff's Complete Guide to Sportscasting: How to Make It in Sportscasting With or Without Talent.* New York: Skyhorse, 2013.

MAJOR ARTICLES

This list excludes hundreds of daily game and news accounts of on- and off-the-field items from 1948 to 1989.

Allen, Maury. "Billy Cries at Night." *True* magazine, September 10, 1972.

———. "Billy Martin: Momma's Boy." *Sport* magazine, June 27, 1981.

———. "Billy Martin's Dilemma." *True* magazine, July 10, 1969.

Anderson, Dave. "Lonesome Billy Assesses Reggie." *The New York Times,* December 14, 1978.

———. "The Yankees' Two Managers." *The New York Times,* July 2, 1979.

Bondy, Filip. "Billy's Final Hours." *New York Daily News,* May 13, 1990.

Chass, Murray. "Emotion Rules the Way Martin Lives and Works." *The New York Times,* July 3, 1983.

———. "Mourners Pack Cathedral for Martin's Funeral." *The New York Times,* December 30, 1989.

Cohn, Lowell. "The Exploitation of Billy Martin." *New York Post,* October 23, 1985.

Cosell, Howard. "Billy Deserved His Day." *New York Daily News,* August 3, 1986.

DiIonno, Mark. "Mantle Mourns His Pal." *New York Post,* December 29, 1989.

Durso, Joseph. "How Martin Is Winning the West." *The New York Times,* May 2, 1981.

———. "Martin Inquiry Opened." *The New York Times,* June 20, 1983.

Fimrite, Ron. "Berkeley Billy Comes Home Again." *Sports Illustrated,* March 10, 1980.

———. "Whatever Happened to the Class of 1981?" *Sports Illustrated,* September 10, 1984.

Flanagan, Barbara. "The New Martin . . . He Cooks and Reads Shakespeare." *Minneapolis Star,* October 16, 1965.

Flannery, Michael T. "Affairs of the Heart." *Moorad Sports Law Journal,* Vol. 10, 2003.

Furlong, William Barry. "The Yankee Revolution." *The New York Times Magazine,* October 10, 1978.

Galloway, Randy. "Off-Field Clash Cost Martin His Rangers Job." *The Sporting News,* August 9, 1975.

Ginnetti, Toni. "Umpires on Umpiring." *Chicago Sun-Times,* April 20, 1986.

Haraway, Frank. "Twins Hail Martin for 'Fantastic' Job as Bears' Skipper." *The Denver Post,* September 14, 1968.

Harris, Elliott. "Fiery Billy Martin a Hot Item." *Chicago Tribune,* September 18, 1985.

Hawkins, Jim. "Off-Field Remarks Set Up Martin's Exit From Detroit." *Detroit News,* September 22, 1973.

Jenkins, William. "Priest Talks About Little Billy Martin." *Oakland Tribune,* October 27, 1953.

Jones, Jeremiah. "Billy's Non-Violent World." *New York Daily News Sunday Magazine,* July 23, 1976.

Katz, Michael. "Ron LeFlore: A Man for This Season." *Inside Sports,* April 17, 1980.

Kay, Michael. "An Intimate Look at Billy." *New York Post,* February 25, 1988.

Kornheiser, Tony. "That Damn Yankee." *The New York Times,* April 9, 1978.

Madden, Bill. "Billy Will Be Billy — at Any Price." *New York Daily News,* October 7, 1985.

Mari, Al. "Billy's Battlefield." Gannett News Service, October 6, 1976.

Markusen, Bruce. "The Original Billy Ball." *Cooperstown Confidential,* September 14, 2012.

Martin, Billy. "I've Never Started a Fight in My Life." *The Sporting News,* April 26, 1961.

Martinez, Michael. "The Martin Affair: Questions Emerge." *The New York Times,* May 9, 1988.

Nichols, Max. "Matchless Billy Built Fire Under Twins." *The Sporting News,* October 9, 1965.

———. "New Tutor Martin to Jab Slow Twins with Sharp Needle." *The Sporting News,* February 6, 1965.

Pepe, Phil. "Billy Survived Firing Squad on 5 Occasions." *New York Daily News,* October 13, 1977.

———. "Yanks Give Billy a Second Chance — in 1980." *New York Daily News,* August 12, 1978.

Pitoniak, Scott. "Remembering a Gentler Billy Martin." *Rochester Democrat and Chronicle,* July 29, 1990.

Reusse, Patrick. "For One Summer, Martin Was All the Rage." *Minneapolis Star-Tribune,* July 15, 2009.

Smith, Red. "Billy Hatfield and Earl McCoy." *The New York Times,* April 19, 1978.

———. "It Hurts Says Billy Martin." *The New York Times,* June 30, 1978.

———. "Notes on the Bronx Zoo." *The New York Times,* April 4, 1979.

Stump, Al. "He's Never Out of Trouble." *Saturday Evening Post,* June 1956.

Van Vliet, Jim. "When the Aces Were Wild: The A's of 10 Years Ago." McClatchy News Service, July 29, 1990.

Ward, Robert. "Reggie Jackson in No-Man's Land." *Sport* magazine, May 1977.

Wulf, Steve. "Strangers in the Limelight." *Sports Illustrated,* May 26, 1980.

Young, Dick. "Billy May Have Finally Slugged the Wrong Guy." *New York Daily News,* November 28, 1979.

———. "If That Midget Says a Word, I'll Deck Him," *New York Daily News,* April 15, 1978.

NEWSPAPERS/WIRE SERVICES

Arizona Republic

Associated Press

Baltimore Sun

Bergen Record

Berkeley Gazette

Boston American

Boston Globe

Boston Herald

Chicago Tribune

Cleveland Plain Dealer

Dallas Morning News

Denver Post

Detroit Free Press

Detroit News

Fort Worth Star-Telegram

Hartford Courant

Kansas City Star

Los Angeles Times

Minnesota Star Tribune

Newark *Star-Ledger*

Newsday

New York Daily News

New York Post

New York Times

Oakland Tribune

Orange County Register

Philadelphia Inquirer

Reuters

San Francisco Chronicle

Seattle Times

St. Louis Post-Dispatch

Tampa Tribune

United Press International

MAGAZINES

Esquire

Inside Sports

Life

Parade

People

Saturday Evening Post

Sport

Sporting News

Sports Illustrated

Time

True

VIDEO/BROADCASTS

DVD, "Billy Martin: The Man. The Myth. The Manager." Rhi Entertainment, September 2007.

ESPN interview with Roy Firestone, December 11, 1988.

ESPN Sports Century Billy Martin documentary, 2000, Parts 1 and 2.

The Arthur Murray Party, television show video, June 28, 1953.

Late Night with David Letterman, May 15, 1986.

Saturday Night Live, May 26, 1986, Billy Martin host.

The Tonight Show with Johnny Carson, August 21, 1977.

WPIX Billy Martin Memorial, 1990.

YES Network Yankeeography episodes: Billy Martin, Mickey Mantle, Willie Randolph, Chris Chambliss, George Steinbrenner, Lou Piniella, Joe DiMaggio, Yogi Berra, Whitey Ford, Reggie Jackson, Casey Stengel.

YES Network videotapes of American League Championship Series in 1969, 1972, 1976, 1977, 1981; World Series 1977.

INDEX